D0944985

ILLINOIS

A DESCRIPTIVE AND
HISTORICAL GUIDE

FEDERAL WORKS AGENCY

WORK PROJECTS ADMINISTRATION

F. C. HARRINGTON, Commissioner

FLORENCE KERR, Assistant Commissioner

HENRY G. ALSBERG, Director of the Federal Writers' Project

ILLINOIS

A DESCRIPTIVE AND HISTORICAL

GUIDE

Compiled and Written by the
Federal Writers' Project of the Work Projects
Administration for the State of Illinois

AMERICAN GUIDE SERIES

ILLUSTRATED

Sponsored by

HENRY HORNER, Governor

A. C. McCLURG & CO. 1939

CHICAGO

Republished 1976
Scholarly Press, Inc., 22929 Industrial Drive East
St. Clair Shores, Michigan 48080

Library of Congress Cataloging in Publication Data

Federal Writer's Project. Illinois.
  Illinois.

    Original ed. issued in series: American guide series.
    Bibliography: p.
    1. Illinois--Description and travel--Guide-books.
2. Illinois--History. I. Title. II. Series:
American guide series.
F539.3.F4 1972   917.73'04   72-145010
ISBN 0-403-01292-9

FOREWORD

EACH OF THE MAJOR VOLUMES in the American Guide Series is a portrait of a State, in which history and tradition are blended with present-day effort and achievement. Collectively these books afford a clearer and more complete picture of American life than has ever before been attempted. Each individual State guide makes a rich contribution to a more profound appreciation of the State by its own citizens, as well as to the knowledge and understanding of the State by others.

A portrait of Illinois, at once historical and contemporary, on the scale called for in the American Guide Series, would have been a wholly impossible task without the generous co-operation of the people of the State. Literally thousands of persons have helped in the making of this book. Business men, teachers and clergymen, newspaper editors, local historians, farmers—men and women representing every phase of Illinois life—have given freely of their time and effort, in personal interviews and special investigation, to make the Illinois Guide as complete as limitations of space would permit, and as accurate as possible. I have no doubt that in spite of the help of these many friends and of our own earnest endeavor, some mistakes occur among the many thousands of statements of fact in this volume. I shall welcome corrections, which will be embodied in subsequent editions.

As official sponsor, author of the essay on Abraham Lincoln, and generous friend of the whole enterprise, Governor Henry Horner has made a contribution of paramount importance to this book of Illinois. I wish to express my sincere gratitude to him, and also to Lieutenant Governor John Stelle, for courtesies extended during his services as Acting Governor of the State. To Paul M. Angle, Secretary, Illinois State Historical Society, and A. L. Sloan of the staff of the *Chicago Evening American,* who have read the entire manuscript, I am deeply grateful.

Though it is impossible to mention here all of those who have shared in building the Illinois Guide, I wish to express on behalf of the editorial staff of the Federal Writers' Project our very real sense of obligation to each of these persons. We are especially appreciative, also of the gracious and effective aid given by librarians and their staffs throughout the State, and of the valuable help of the following special consultants and technical advisers: Josephine Boylan, local historian, East St. Louis, Illinois; Fay-Cooper Cole, Professor of Anthropology, University of Chicago; John Drury, Chicago *Daily News;* Ernest E. East, Peoria *Journal-Transcript;* Dr. Philip Fox, Director, Museum of Science and Industry; A. T. Griffith, Harbormaster of the Port of Peoria; H. B. Harte, Public Relations Counsel, Field Museum of Natural History; Jacob L. Hasbrouck, Bloomington *Daily Pantagraph;* Very Reverend Monseigneur Reynold Hillenbrand, S.T.D., Rector of St. Mary of the Lake Seminary; Effie M. Lansden, Librarian, Cairo, Illinois; William Morgenstern, Director of Press Relations, University of Chicago; Bessie Louise Pierce, Professor of History, University of Chicago; Earl Reed, Chicago architect; Daniel Catton Rich, Director of Fine Arts, Art Institute of Chicago; Carl Sandburg, poet and historian; Thomas Tallmadge, architect and author of *Story of Architecture in America;* Barney Thompson, Rockford *Register-Republic;* L. O. Trigg, Eldorado *Journal;* George B. Utley, Librarian, Newberry Library; Ray Williams, Secretary, Chamber of Commerce, Cairo, Illinois. To Edgar Lee Masters we extend particular thanks for his generosity in granting permission to quote freely from his works and for helpful suggestions.

Charles E. Miner, WPA Administrator for Illinois, and Mrs. Mary Gillette Moon, State Director of Professional and Service Division, have given unusual and invaluable assistance in this work. Their interest and co-operation have been unfailing. Toward each of them I feel a strong sense of personal appreciation.

Finally, it is the deepest pleasure to record here my grateful recognition of the loyal interest of the whole staff of the Federal Writers' Project for Illinois, nearly all of whom—typists, mapmakers, and research workers as well as writers and editors—have shared in some way in the making of this book; and of the especially devoted effort of the six editors—James Phelan, Parker Van de Mark, Jacob Scher, James Baxter, Nathan Morris, and James Gilman—who have given the text its final form.

John T. Frederick,
State Director,
Federal Writers' Project for Illinois.

CONTENTS

PART III

ILLINOIS: Tours

ILLUSTRATIONS

MAPS

GENERAL INFORMATION

Steam Passenger Railroads: Alton R.R.; Atchison, Topeka & Santa
Fe Ry.; Baltimore & Ohio R.R.; Chesapeake and Ohio Ry.; Chicago
and Eastern Illinois Ry.; Chicago & Illinois Midland Ry. Co.; Chicago and North Western Ry.; Chicago & Western Indiana R.R.;
Chicago, Burlington & Quincy R.R.; Chicago Great Western R.R.;
Chicago, Indianapolis & Louisville Ry.; Chicago, Milwaukee, St.
Paul and Pacific R.R.; Chicago, Rock Island & Pacific Ry. Co.;
Chicago, Springfield & St. Louis Ry. Co.; Cleveland, Cincinnati,
Chicago & St. Louis Ry.; Erie R.R.; Grand Trunk Western R.R.;
Illinois Central R.R.; Louisville & Nashville R.R. Co.; Michigan
Central R.R.; Minneapolis & St. Louis R.R. Co.; Minneapolis, St.
Paul & Sault Ste. Marie Ry.; Missouri-Illinois R.R.; Missouri
Pacific R.R.; Mobile and Ohio R.R.; New York Central System;
New York, Chicago and St. Louis R.R.; Pennsylvania Railroad;
Peoria & Eastern Ry.; Pere Marquette Ry.; Rock Island Southern
Ry.; St. Louis Southwestern Ry. Lines; Southern Railway System;
Toledo, Peoria & Western R.R.; Wabash Ry.

Electric Railroads: Chicago, Aurora, and Elgin R.R.; Chicago, North
Shore and Milwaukee R.R.; Chicago South Shore and South Bend
R.R.; Illinois Terminal Railroad Co.

Bus Lines: All American Bus Lines, Inc.; Bluebird System; Chicago
and North Western Stages; De Luxe Motor Stages; Greyhound
Lines; Indian Trail Stages; Interstate Transit Lines; National
Trailways System (Burlington Trailways, Lincoln Trailways, Safeway Trailways and Santa Fe Trailways); Sioux Ltd. Lines; Southern Limited, Inc.; Union Pacific Stages; and Yankee Coach Lines.
(*See cities and towns for local and branch lines.*)

Air Lines: American Airlines, Inc. (Chicago to Detroit, Buffalo, New
York, Washington, D. C., Fort Worth and Los Angeles), Chicago
only Illinois stop, (Chicago to St. Louis) stops at Springfield;
Braniff Airways, Inc. (Chicago to Kansas City, Dallas and Fort
Worth), Chicago only Illinois stop; Chicago & Southern Air Lines,
Inc. (Chicago to New Orleans) stops at Springfield; Eastern Air
Lines (Chicago to Jacksonville, Miami, New Orleans and Houston),
Chicago only Illinois stop; Northwest Airlines (Chicago to Minneapolis, St. Paul and Seattle), Chicago only Illinois stop; Transcontinental & Western Air, Inc. (Chicago to Dayton, Pittsburgh,
New York, Boston, San Diego, Los Angeles, and San Francisco),
Chicago only Illinois stop; United Airlines Transport Corp. (Chicago to Cleveland, New York, and Boston), Chicago only Illinois
stop, (Chicago to Moline, Omaha, Denver, Salt Lake City, Los

Angeles, and San Francisco) stops at Moline. (Schedules subject to frequent changes. Special stops may be arranged when conditions warrant. See local agent.)

Waterways: Illinois River from Joliet with barge service to Peoria and way points connecting with the Mississippi River at Grafton, Ill. near Alton; the Illinois-Mississippi Canal, starting at the Illinois River at Hennepin, near La Salle, connecting with the Mississippi near Moline.

Highways: Twenty Federal highways, three of them transcontinental; one of them international; all of them with transcontinental or international connections. State highway patrol. (*See State map for routes.*)

Motor Vehicle Laws (digest): Maximum speed, 45 m.p.h., business districts, 20 m.p.h., residence districts, 25 m.p.h., suburban districts, 35 m.p.h.; do not exceed 10 m.p.h. in overtaking and passing a school bus (when clearly marked) which has stopped on a highway to receive or discharge children. No special license required for non-residents; minimum age for drivers, 15 years. Hand signals must be used. Windshields must be equipped with wipers. One spotlight permitted. Personal injury must be reported to a civil authority. *Prohibited:* driving while under the influence of intoxicating liquor or narcotic drugs, reckless driving, passing on curve or crest of grade, passing street cars on left in cities and towns, driving through a safety zone, coasting in neutral, parking on highways, parking within 15 feet of a fire hydrant, following fire apparatus closer than 500 feet, driving a motor vehicle when there are more than three persons in the front seat.

Accommodations: Ample accommodations in hotels and private homes both in urban centers and rural districts. Tourist camps usually subject to sanitary and hygienic rules and regulations, located in many sections; overnight camping grounds in many of the State parks.

Fish and Game Laws (digest): Game fish defined as black, white or yellow bass, crappie, sunfish, bluegill, perch, pickerel, wall-eyed pike, trout. *Open Seasons:* (dates inclusive): The State is divided into three latitudinal zones known as the northern, central and southern. Black, white or yellow bass, northern and central zones, June 16-Feb. 28; southern zone, June 1-Feb. 28. Rock bass, crappie, sunfish, bluegill, Jan. 1-Dec. 31. Pickerel, wall-eyed pike, May 1-Sept. 28. Trout (except lake), Apr. 15-Aug. 31; lake trout, Jan. 1-Dec. 31. *Licenses:* resident, 75¢; non-resident, $3. Not required of persons under 21 years of age. Issued by county, city and village clerk; expiration date, Jan. 31 of each year. *Limits:* Black bass, not less than 10 in. and white or yellow bass, not less than 8 in., daily limit, any one species or in the aggregate, 10, possession limit, 20.

Rock bass, not less than 6 in., crappie, not less than 8 in., sunfish and bluegill, not less than 5 in., daily limit, one species, 15, in the aggregate, 25, possession limit, one species, 30, in the aggregate, 50. Perch, any size, no limits. Pickerel, not less than 16 in., wall-eyed pike, not less than 12 in., daily limit, any one species or in the aggregate, 10, possession limit, 20. Trout, not less than 7 in., daily limit, 8, possession limit, 16; lake trout, no limits. *Prohibited:* taking of game fish except by hook and line attached to rod or held in hand while angling; unlawful to operate in the taking of any fish, a snare, spear, gig, grain, firearms of any kind or artificial light except when used strictly for illumination purposes.

Open Season for Hunting (dates inclusive): Deer, prairie chicken, closed. Dove, duck, brant, goose, rail, snipe (Wilson and Jack), governed by Federal regulations. Dove, Sept. 1-Sept. 30. Bob White quail, Nov. 10-Dec. 9. Cock pheasant, Nov. 10-Nov. 15. Rabbit, Nov. 10-Dec. 31. Squirrel, northern zone, Sept. 1-Nov. 30, central zone, Aug. 15-Nov. 30, southern zone, Aug. 1-Nov. 30. Raccoon, mink, skunk, opossum, northern zone, Nov. 15-Jan. 31, central and southern zones, Nov. 15-Jan. 15. Fox, northern and central zones, Jan. 1- Dec. 31, southern zone, Nov. 15-Jan. 15. Muskrat may only be taken with traps; northern zone, Nov. 15-Jan. 31, central and southern zones, Dec. 1-Jan. 31. *Licenses:* Resident, $1.50; nonresident, $15. Issued by county, city and village clerk; not available to aliens or persons under 16 years of age without written consent of parents or guardian. One shipping permit (fee $1), showing name of consignor and consignee, number of permit and hunting license, issued during period of license; six separate shipments waterfowl allowed on each permit; game and shipments open to inspection. *Limits:* Bob White quail, daily limit, 12, possession limit, 24. Cock pheasant, daily limit, 2, possession limit, 6. Rabbit, daily limit, 10, possession limit, 20. Squirrel, daily limit, 8, possession limit, 16. Fur-bearing animals, no limit. *Prohibited:* All feeding or baiting; shooting over live decoys. Only a shotgun, not larger than 10 guage or holding more than three shells, may be used in shooting migratory game birds.

Liquor Regulations: Sale of liquor and restrictions vested in local authorities, subject to Federal regulations. Sale of liquor prohibited in some cities, towns and communities by local option.

Miscellaneous Laws: Picking wild flowers in State parks and similar areas, destroying shrubbery or trees, prohibited. Camp fires, where permitted, must be thoroughly extinguished before leaving.

Poisonous Snakes and Plants: Many species of snakes are found in Illinois, but only four are of the poisonous variety: the swamp rattlesnake throughout the State except in the Ohio River valley, the timber rattler in the southern and western portion, the copperhead in the southern third, and the cottonmouth moccasin in the extreme southern end of the State. Poison ivy, a climbing shrub with three broadly ovate, notched leaflets is common in most sections, occasionally found climbing around trees or growing in shrubs. Poison sumac, an upright shrub 6 to 18 feet high, is common, especially in the swamps of Lake County. *First-aid for Poisonous Snakes and Plants:* Snake bite: if possible apply a tourniquet between the wound and the heart. Suck the wound immediately, spitting out the saliva. Do not give alcohol; it will do more harm than good. If a stimulant is needed, give hot black coffee. Poison ivy, poison sumac, etc.: scrub the skin with suds of strong soap; rinse with warm water, then scrub with alcohol or gasoline until all oil caused by the poison is dissolved. Vaseline or cocoa butter may then be rubbed on the skin to relieve itching.

Information service for tourists: No State maintained service; information generally available through local chambers of commerce, motor club branches, and at hotels. Department stores and newspaper offices in larger cities maintain public service and information bureaus.

RECREATION

Illinois' peculiar internal structure, with half of her people centered in one great metropolitan area, affects the pattern of her recreation as well as that of her commercial and industrial activity. The clustering of population in the northeast portion of the State dictates a more thorough development of nearby facilities than of those "downstate" where there is not the pressure of large masses of people seeking a place to play and relax.

Fortunately a sound basis for this development existed. The whole shoreline of Lake Michigan in Illinois lies close to Chicago. The extensive dunes region just over the State line in Indiana, and a smaller dunes area north of Waukegan have been developed as recreational centers. Inland from the lake, near the Wisconsin line, stretches the Chain-O'-Lakes region, the only considerable group of natural lakes in the State. Until recently this area has been developed by private endeavor, but the newly projected Chain-O'-Lakes State Park, when completed, will comprise 3,200 acres, by far the largest of the State parks.

Near at hand are the Cook County Forest Preserves, 44 units with a total area of 33,000 acres roughly bordering the city on the west. Within them lie more than 150 miles of hiking trails, 40 miles of bridle paths, and special facilities ranging from ski and toboggan slides to swimming pools. Only a few minutes out of the city, they are extensively used by picnickers, hiking and nature-study clubs, and those merely seeking a brief respite from the roar and clamor of the metropolis.

Chicago, of course, is the State's most concentrated recreational center; while city-dwellers seek the country-side on their vacations, many "downstaters" flock to the metropolis, attracted by its museums, theaters, and beaches. Internally, Chicago's chief recreational attraction is Lake Michigan, and a maximum extent of the shore line has been developed for the people's pleasure. Public beaches, ranging from tiny street-end beaches to those that stretch for almost a mile, dot the lake-front throughout its twenty-odd miles. All of them are patrolled and many have public bathhouses. In summer the eastern horizon is specked with the countless white sails of catboats and yachts; three major harbors—Belmont on the north, Grant Park opposite the Loop, and Jackson Park on the south—accommodate innumerable small craft and make sailing and speed-boating a major Chicago pastime. Lake steamers provide excursions that range from moonlight cruises and one-day trips to Michigan and Milwaukee, to long cruises of a week or more through the other Great Lakes.

Also of major importance is the Chicago park system, comprising 215 parks and playgrounds under the control of the Chicago Park Board. Four of the larger parks, Lincoln, Grant, Burnham, and Jackson, stretch in a green-belt along the lake-front. Their public recreational facilities, which include beaches, bridle paths, tennis courts, and golf courses, are supplemented by the privately endowed Field Museum, Shedd Aquarium, Adler Planetarium, Art Institute of Chicago, Museum of Science and Industry, Chicago Historical Society Museum, and Chicago Natural History Museum. The Chicago Zoological Gardens, better known as the Brookfield Zoo, on the west side, attracts thousands of sightseers annually, not only because of its widely advertised giant panda, Mei-Mei, but also for its excellence and completeness. These are the show-places most frequently seen by visitors to Chicago, but the remainder of the park system, permeating the whole of the city, has been extensively developed for neighborhood use. Field houses, gymnasiums, swimming pools, and tennis courts are scattered throughout the city's various sections; classes and competition in sports ranging from archery to wrestling and in such diverse hobbies as model airplane building and photography are conducted under municipal leaders.

Commercial recreation in Chicago is of such varied extent that not even a cataloguing is possible (*see Chicago; General Information*). An important innovation of recent years is the chartering of special recreation trains at excursion rates: snow and ski trains in the winter and bicycle trains in the summer. The Chicago Recreation Committee, a municipal organization, functions to co-ordinate the various public and semi-public recreational agencies. Its annual publication, *Leisure*

Time Directory, lists the city's recreational facilities both geographically and by categories.

Outside of the Chicago area, the major factor in recreation is the State Park System. Twenty-two areas, chosen for both scenic beauty and historical interest, are maintained throughout the State. These range in size from the seven acres of Campbell's Island State Park, near Rock Island, to the Pere Marquette State Park, 1,670 acres in Jersey County, largest of the completed units. Among the more important and most widely used are Starved Rock, in La Salle County, Mississippi Palisades State Park, in Carroll County, Giant City State Park, in Jackson County, New Salem State Park, in Sangamon County, and Cahokia Mounds State Park, in Madison County. The newer parks, notably Giant City, have been extensively improved by the Civilian Conservation Corps, which has cleared underbrush, marked trails, built shelters and lodges, and improved roads.

Although the pageant of steamboats has dwindled and almost vanished, excursion boats are still to be found on the Mississippi and Ohio, and occasionally on the Illinois. Built especially for excursions, they have a huge main deck that is given over entirely to a dance floor. Although most of them operate out of St. Louis, almost every major river town on the Mississippi and the Ohio is visited by them several times each summer. At very rare intervals a show-boat will dock for a week's run.

A State of few lakes, Illinois has utilized well those that she has, and has created others. Lakes Springfield, Bloomington, and Decatur, all artificial, are widely used as recreation centers.

Because of Illinois' agricultural importance, her annual State Fair at Springfield is a major event and draws thousands of city-dwellers as well as farmers. Throughout the major agricultural counties, similar fairs are annually given, on a smaller scale.

In addition to those areas already mentioned, two general sections of the State are widely used by vacationists and week-enders. The Illinois Ozarks, stretching across the extreme southern portion of the State, are visited by many; several hundred miles removed from Chicago, they have not been extensively developed and accommodations are limited, but many look upon this as an attraction rather than a shortcoming. For years a small town publisher, L. O. Trigg of Eldorado, has conducted a tour through the Ozark hills in a caravan of trucks each summer. The unglaciated region of Jo Daviess County, in the northwest corner of the State, has the similar attraction of a hilly terrain, as well as being historically important because of the century-old lead mines scattered throughout.

Part I
ILLINOIS:
The General Background

THE ILLINOISAN

His Background

HE WHO WOULD DESCRIBE a typical Illinoisan may well find, after carefully combing the State, that his only valid generalization is that an Illinoisan is one who resides in Illinois. The Illinoisan is first and foremost a heterogeneous character, and symbols fit him with little grace. The only concept that has achieved considerable circulation—that of a rural fellow, a bit coarse but possessed of shrewdness and humor—is at best an anachronism. Such a concept probably stemmed from Lincoln, as portrayed by eastern cartoonists. For want of an apter figure it has persisted here and there, although rather than describing an average resident, it represents a type difficult to find anywhere in the State today.

But the rural symbol is certainly not without basis. Illinois ranks fourth in total farm income among the forty-eight States. Among the lasting impressions of the traveler on his first visit to Illinois is that of miles of corn-rows springing from the rich black soil, of the little roads that depart every mile or so from the highway and follow a long hedgerow back to a tree-shaded farmstead. Only when one examines the make-up of the total population does it become evident that such a symbol is an over-simplification. Fifth in the United States in its percentage of farmers, Illinois nevertheless has three times as many industrial as agricultural workers. And if a hundred Illinoisans were picked out at random, 44 of them would be residents of Chicago.

That the residents of the Prairie State are three-quarters urban is only the broadest aspect of their variety in make-up. Elsewhere the roots of heterogeneity run deep into the history of the State.

Only in the earliest days of this region did the population follow a discernible pattern. In the early decades of the eighteenth century the French, bound together by their race and common purpose of subduing the wilderness, achieved the rough outlines of a unified society. "Under the utmost difficulties," wrote a Jesuit from the American Bottom, "we are striving to bring order to this wilderness."

3

The few French settlements scattered about Illinois followed many of the patterns of the Old World. The church was the center of social as well as religious activity, and the priest ranked in importance with the civil authorities. A portion of the land was designated for common fields, and agricultural workers went out to their narrow strips of soil each day, and returned to the village each night. But the British conquered the French without setting up a substitute for their Gallic orderliness. The period of chaos that followed was ended with American conquest, but by that time the frontier reached Illinois, and settlers began pouring in. Today the remnants of the French period are no more than the fourth echo of an echo, surviving in little more than the names of a few old towns.

From all along the Middle Atlantic seaboard settlers came, from Kentucky and Tennessee, and from the South; most nearly to a dominant group were the Southerners. But it is significant that Nathaniel Pope, who guided the bill to admit the State into the Union through Congress, was opposed to slavery, despite his Kentucky origin. Pleading that the extension "would afford additional security to the perpetuity of the Union," Pope had the upper border of the State moved fifty-one miles north and thereby gained unsettled land and a port-of-entry for anti-slavery New Englanders. That this port was to grow into the metropolis of Chicago, furthering the heterogeneity of the State, Pope could not know.

The opening of the Erie Canal in 1825 abetted his plan. As New Englanders came to Illinois via the canal and the Great Lakes, Illinois began to take on much the same political complexion as a cross-section of the country as a whole. Princeton, Galesburg, Rockford, and dozens of other northern Illinois cities were settled by New Englanders, while at the other extremity the influence of the South was everywhere prominent, in accent and vernacular, as well as in architecture. "Where New England emigrants do not venture," wrote a Northern Illinoisan, "improvements, social, agricultural, mechanic, or scientific, rarely flourish, and seldom intrude." The Southerner, in turn, excoriated "Yankee kinks in politics"—and tradition of heterogeneity became more firmly established.

With the opening of the railroad era in the fifties, and the first faint rumblings of industrialization, there entered a new element. In 1856 one-fourteenth of all the immigrants landing at New York came to Illinois. By 1860 their total had passed 300,000, with Irish and

Germans predominating, and almost half of Chicago was foreign born. As Chicago boomed, many of the foreign born remained in the city, easily finding jobs in the countless new industrial plants. But others, particularly the Swedes, Germans, and other races of an agricultural bent, filtered out into the State and eventually settled in many of the smaller towns. Ernest Elmo Calkins, in *They Broke The Prairie*, tells of how the Swedes, followed by other nationalities, came to Galesburg, and how the stiff New England traditions of that town gradually underwent the infiltration of a new and vital force. In its broader aspects, it is a case history of the last great contribution to the variety of Illinois.

Today the population of the State is almost equally split between native white stock of native parentage and those who were foreign born or who had foreign or mixed parentage. Assimilation, however, has been a major factor for at least forty years; since 1900 the number of foreign born has remained constant while that of foreign and mixed parentage has steadily increased. That this assimilation has been cultural as well is evidenced in the State's low percentage of illiteracy—2.4 per cent against 4.3 per cent for the country as a whole.

Clearly the infusions into Illinois from its very beginning have rendered a symbol for its residents improbable. Yet, since a land can mold its people into a pattern, it is pertinent to examine briefly the profile of the State.

Both agriculture and industry are of fundamental importance. Geographically the State belongs neither to the North, South, East, nor West, but at a peculiar focal point of all four. The visual evidence of this is frequently missed by through-State motorists because a large portion of transcontinental traffic traverses only the Corn Belt. Even there the fusion of the industrial East and the agricultural West occasionally occurs where farmers' fields extend almost into the shadows of mine tipples and industrial plants. In latitude the agricultural economy shifts from Northern dairying through Midwestern corn-raising to Southern fruit-farming and cotton-growing. And at the lower tip of the State the heat of the South seeps up the Mississippi, ripening the crops a month earlier than elsewhere and slowing down the pace of human activity.

What is an Illinoisan? In the voices of the people there is no clue, neither in the stridency of Chicago's street urchin nor in the Southern accent, tinged with a faint twang, of the lower Illinoisan. It is not

wholly without meaning to say that the Illinoisan is simply a resident
of Illinois, and that his heterogeneity is in itself the final key to his
nature. Historically his State has been one where paradox blossoms
continually, where both Lincoln and the suppressors of Lovejoy were
nurtured; where the Utopias of the Janssonists and the Icarians rose
in counterpoint to the lusty individualism of old Chicago; the home
of both William Jennings Bryan and Robert Ingersoll, of John Peter
Altgeld and Samuel Insull. Across this State have eddied almost all
the major currents from both without and within the country. Criss-
crossed by railroads from all corners of the country, a steel-maker as
well as a wheat-stacker, Illinois in its entirety functions as a working
model of the Nation as a whole. Therein the heterogeneity of the
State takes on meaning and becomes in itself a symbol burdened with
deep significance.

THE LAND ITSELF

SEEN FROM THE AIR, the land of Illinois reveals graphically the agricultural importance of the State. Carved by intensive cultivation into an intricate mosaic of squares and rectangles, the level prairie resembles nothing so much as a vast stretch of modernistic linoleum. In the grainfields no land is wasted; pasture adjoins field, farm fits snugly against farm, and between them is nothing but the straight line of a fence or hedgerow of osage orange.

Lying between the Great Lakes and the Mississippi, Illinois enjoys a drainage system extraordinarily complete and extensive. Water from 23 of the 48 States crosses its surface and flows along its boundaries, eastward through Lake Michigan to the Atlantic Ocean and southward in the Mississippi to the Gulf. Although its topography presents no striking contrasts of surface contour, the State is separated into seven gentle but distinct basins, bearing the names of Lake Michigan, the Illinois, the Rock, the Kaskaskia, the Big Muddy, the Wabash, and the Ohio Rivers. The arteries and branches of these six great rivers serve 87.2 per cent of the 56,665 square miles of the State's surface. The largest, the Illinois, runs from northeast to southwest and drains an area 250 miles long and 100 miles wide, comprising 43 per cent of the State.

The conception of Illinois as an unrelieved table-top admits pleasant and unexpected contradictions. A portion of the hilly Wisconsin driftless area projects into the northwest corner; there, at Charles Mound, is the highest spot in the State, 1,241 feet above sea level. An extension of the Ozark Range, with several hills exceeding a thousand feet in altitude, crosses southern Illinois. The Mississippi and its tributaries, especially the Illinois, have carved long ranges of bluffs, the more rugged portions of which have been enclosed in State parks.

Elsewhere is prairie, but its original extent and appearance have been greatly altered. The earliest settlers found almost half the State in forest, with the prairie running in great fingers between the creeks and other waterways, its surface lush with waist-high grasses and liberally bedecked with wild flowers. Here occurred the transition from the wooded lands of the East to the treeless plains of the West.

7

Since this was the pioneer's first encounter with the prairie, Illinois came to be known as the Prairie State, although westward lay lands more worthy of the title than the semi-wooded surface of Illinois.

The pioneers admired the grasslands, but clung to the wooded waterways. At the time of early settlement the fertility of the prairie was not known nor was it available until the invention of plows capable of breaking the tough sod. The waterways furnished timber for fuel and building, a convenient water supply, and protection for the settlers' jerry-built cabins from prairie fires and windstorms. Fires invariably swept the grasslands in the late summer, when the Indians burned off the prairie to drive out game. When the settlers at last began to venture cautiously out from the groves, they took the precaution to surround their homesteads with several plowed furrows as a fire check.

The fame of the great stretches of treeless grasslands spread eastward, even to England, and magazines carried articles of description, speculating upon their origin (which is still unexplained) and the possibilities of their cultivation. Dickens, while visiting St. Louis in 1842, especially requested that he be shown the "paroarer," as he noted it was pronounced locally. A rumbling, ancient coach took him out to Looking Glass Prairie, near Belleville, and he returned to write:

. . . . there lay, stretched out before my view, a vast expanse of level ground; unbroken, save by one thin line of trees, which scarcely amounted to a scratch upon the great blank . . . . a tranquil sea or lake without water, if such a simile be admissible . . . . and solitude and silence reigning paramount around . . . . I felt little of that sense of freedom and exhilaration which a Scottish heath inspires, or even our English downs awakens. It was lonely and wild, but oppressive in its barren monotony.

Lumbering activities and the pioneer's early preference for the woodland reduced the forests from their original extent, 42 per cent, to little more than 5 per cent. What is now commonly thought of as prairie is often the increment gained from the clearing of woodlands. Given over now almost wholly to farms, the prairies are constantly in flux as the landscape alters with the agricultural season. April transforms the Illinois country into a vast patchwork quilt of fresh color. Spring planting brings forth teams and tractors that comb and dress the land with geometric nicety. By summer the contours of the prairie are soft and round with ripening crops. July ushers in three months of intense industry. Crops are gathered, threshing machines build mounds of chaff, trucks and trains loaded with grain begin to move toward the cities. When autumn comes, the prairies, gashed by plows and stripped of their harvest, have a worn, desolate aspect that is heightened by the somber browns and yellows of the season. The prairies are dull throughout winter save for intermittent snowfalls, and then, in late March, the land stirs, splotches of green appear, and farmers turn again to the soil.

The level aspect of Illinois topography has its explanation in the State's glacial history. As late as 25,000 years ago—a tick of the clock in geological time—there was still to be found in Illinois the last of the great ice sheets that had crept down from the North and with a leveling action comparable to that of a road-scraper, effaced hills and valleys carved by centuries of erosion. Ninety per cent of the State's surface was covered by ice; the only unglaciated areas are Jo Daviess County in the extreme northwest, Calhoun County in the west-central section, and the seven southernmost counties. In these areas the rugged terrain, sharply dissected by valleys, indicates the probable appearance of the whole of Illinois before the ice age. Elsewhere, save for sporadic outcrops, the uneven relief lies beneath a mantle of drift averaging 75 feet in depth.

The four ice-sheets that invaded the United States are definitely known to have reached Illinois. The next to last of these covered so great a portion of the State that it has been named the Illinoisan by geologists. Occurring approximately 150,000 years ago, it pushed south to the northern edge of the Ozark Range, and there, halted by increased melting and the barricade of hills, piled up rock debris 20 feet deep on the hillsides. This was the greatest southern penetration of any of the North American glaciers.

The Wisconsin Glacier, which moved into Illinois 50,000 years ago and receded 25,000 years later, covered only the northeast quarter of the State, but because of its geological lateness its effects are more obvious to the layman. The great central portion of the State which was covered by the older Illinoisan sheet, but not overlaid by the Wisconsin, is much more nearly even in relief and mature in drainage. The terminal moraines—ridges of drift piled up where the glacial front stopped—are low and inconspicuous. Those of the last glacier, however, are among the largest known to geologists. Sharply defined and extensive in length, they comprise the chief topographical relief of the northeast portion of the State. The major ones are named for cities that have been built upon them; the Shelbyville, Bloomington, Marseilles, and Valparaiso moraines are four of the most important.

Marked with the characteristics of recent glaciation, the land bordering Lake Michigan near the Wisconsin State line is poorly drained, with many lakes and marshes formed by the melting Wisconsin glacier. Thus was created the lake region of Illinois, major recreational area for the metropolis of Chicago. At the time of recession, the waters of the glacier were impounded between the Valparaiso moraine and the receding edge of ice, forming Lake Chicago, ancestor of Lake Michigan. The site of Chicago lay deep beneath the surface of this ancient lake, and deposition from its waters accounts for the table-top flatness of the city today. In successive stages the water receded north and east.

Glaciation and climate largely explain the agricultural distinction of the Illinois country. The average growing season varies from 160 days in the north to 211 days at Cairo, in the south. The drift laid down by the ice had been gathered from so great a variety of bedrock that an ample percentage of essential minerals was assured. Lying at the southernmost reach of the ice-sheets, Illinois was not strewn with the boulders and heavy débris that pock-mark the land further north. Much of the State is veneered with a layer of loess, the finer particles of drift that were sorted out by the wind and spread across the land. Enriched by prairie grasses during thousands of years, it possesses an even texture which, with the regular terrain, fits Illinois admirably for mechanical cultivation.

Buried beneath the glacial drift, the rock strata of Illinois effect little influence upon the topography, but their minerals yield to the State an income placing it tenth in the country in mineral output. All of the substructure that has been explored by geologists is sedimentary in nature, with the exception of a deep-lying mass of red granite encountered at 3,700 feet near Amboy, in the northern part of the State. At an unknown depth, the entire State is underlain with igneous rock, mother-rock of all formations, but vast processes of sedimentation have buried it beyond reach.

Of the five geological eras, the third, the Paleozoic, was by far the most important both geologically and economically. Beginning some 600 million years ago, it was characterized by repeated submergences and uplifts. What is now Illinois was then covered by a series of shallow seas. In great cycles, the seas advanced, covered the land for millions of years, and then retreated to expose the surface again to weathering and erosion. The strata laid down during each submergence differ sharply from each other, the degree depending upon the depth of the sea and the nature of the land at its shoreline.

The oldest period of the Paleozoic Era was the Cambrian, during which thick layers of sandstone and dolomite were deposited over the entire State. This, like the igneous rock, does not outcrop in Illinois, but slants upward from the south to come to the surface in Wisconsin. Rainfall in the latter area, seeping through surface soil to the sandstone layers, follows these to northern Illinois, where it serves as a reservoir for the wells of many municipalities.

The second period of the Paleozoic Era was the Ordovician, which saw a series of submergences of long duration. Its first deposits, the Prairie du Chien group, included a limestone which was the basis of Utica's natural cement industry, important in the last century but now abandoned. Another of the early Ordovician deposits is a layer of St. Peter sandstone, which outcrops in Ottawa and nearby in a remarkably pure form that has achieved national industrial importance as a source of silica sand, used in glass-making and a hundred other processes. St. Peter sandstone also forms the picturesque bluffs that comprise Starved Rock State Park. Platteville limestone, likewise an Ordovician deposit, is used in the manufacture of Portland cement. Late in the period a layer of Galena dolomite was laid down. It bears the lead which gave Galena its name and its early mining boom. Related to this formation is the Kimmswick limestone, source of petroleum in the southwestern field at Dupo.

The third period, the Silurian, laid down several strata of dolomite and limestone. The latter is quarried extensively near Chicago and Joliet for road material, aggregate, and soil replenishment. The following period, the Devonian, is likewise chiefly important for its limestone. Among the Mississippian deposits are the sediments that store the southeastern oil pool, long a steadily producing field and lately (1939) the scene of a spectacular boom of revived activity.

Near the end of the Paleozoic Era occurred the Pennsylvanian period, when Illinois' great coal measures were deposited. The coal strata, but a small portion of the Pennsylvanian deposits, far outstrip all other geological periods in the wealth they have yielded. The land at this time was low and marshy, a few feet above sea level. A favorable climate encouraged the growth of giant trees and ferns that subsequent eons compressed into the coal veins that underlie two-thirds of the State. Despite a half-century of extensive mining operations, not more than 2 per cent, it is estimated, of Illinois' coal reserve has been tapped.

Following the close of the Pennsylvanian period, the greater portion of Illinois remained above sea level. Great land movements that raised the Appalachians in the east, folded the land of Southern Illinois into the present Ozark range. The work of the seas was done, and now rain and wind attacked the surface to erode and crease it with great valleys and ridges. But then, following a vast climatic change, snow began to fall in the northern region, year after year, deeper in the winter than the brief summer sun could melt.

So began the glacial period, the *deus ex machina* in the making of Illinois. Even as the curtain descended upon the State's geological drama, the ice sheets appeared, effaced the ruggedness, and retreated— so recently that Indian legends make awed mention of the Ice God that once came down from the North.

BEFORE THE WHITE MAN

WHEN THE FIRST WHITE MEN came to Illinois, they found large mounds of earth rising up out of the prairies, usually near navigable rivers. Because these mounds contained burials, pottery, stone implements, and the ruins of buildings, and were sometimes shaped like birds and beasts, various legends arose about the people who built them. One story had it that they were a lost tribe of Israel. Another described them as a people related to the Mayas and the Aztecs. A third told of an ancient race, of much vision and beauty, with large cities and widespread commerce and trade, that flourished in the Mississippi Basin about the time of Christ. For many years the mound builders captured the imagination of story-tellers.

Today, however, these myths have been exploded, and the mystery of the mounds has been solved, at least in part, by archeological expeditions. Archeologists have been able to show clearly that the mound builders were simply Indians who built mounds.

These mounds were not all of one period, nor were they all built for the same purpose. Some, like the effigy mounds in the northwestern part of the State, were of a ceremonial nature; many were built primarily for burial purposes; others were sites for buildings. Those of the latter type seem to show influences which came from the Lower Mississippi, and possibly from the higher cultures of Mexico and South America. With the great tribal unrest among the Indians during the sixteenth and seventeenth centuries, largely due to the incursions of the Iroquois from the East, a great shifting of tribes occurred, so that by the time the first explorers came to Illinois, there were few mound-building Indians left in the region.

More than 10,000 mounds are scattered throughout the State. Because Illinois was situated at the confluence of the great highways of primitive travel—the Mississippi, Missouri, Ohio, and Illinois Rivers —various mound-building cultures shuttled back and forth across the State. Here are found obsidian from Yellowstone, Catlinite from Minnesota, copper from Michigan and Minnesota, mica from the Alleghenies, and shells from the Gulf of Mexico. And in the mounds of other States are found the kind of flint mined only in the ancient quarry in Union County, Illinois.

Archeologists have found two major culture patterns in the State, of which the Woodland is the older and more basic. One phase of this culture is represented by the effigy mounds in northwestern Illinois; this came down from Wisconsin. Another is the Hopewell phase which probably had its origin farther east. The other major pattern is known as the Mississippi culture, and is divided into Upper, Middle, and Lower phases; it runs up along the Mississippi, the Illinois, and other rivers, as far north as Astalan, Wisconsin.

Woodland pottery is crude and unevenly colored; textiles and shell work are absent; and only its stone work is definitely well-fashioned. Houses of the period were circular and temporary. The mounds themselves are round, are generally smaller than those of the Mississippi culture, and were not used as substructures. The dead were usually buried in the mounds in flexed positions; a few of the remains found had been cremated. In the Hopewell phase of this culture—so-called because it probably came to Illinois from the vicinity of the famous Hopewell mounds in Ohio—copper and mica ornaments occur. One of its chief characteristics is the frequent use of log tombs, over which the mounds were built.

In the more recent Mississippi culture, the pottery work is well-fired from carefully prepared clays; it is evenly colored and of many forms. Shell work is highly developed. Finely woven textiles are frequent. The dwellings were square or rectangular, of a permanent or semi-permanent nature, and the mounds were often used as substructures for these houses. In the cemeteries near the mounds the dead were buried in extended positions, together with projectile points, pottery, charms, and amulets.

One of the richest archeological areas in the Middle West is at the junction of the Spoon and the Illinois Rivers in Fulton County. Expeditions from the University of Chicago under Professor Fay-Cooper Cole found as many as three cultural manifestations of the two basic patterns existing in the same mounds. In the eight hundred mounds in Fulton County, six different cultural manifestations have been discovered, with the Middle Mississippi and the Hopewell phases often existing side by side, although different in time. Thus, though the religious practices and beliefs among the mound builders apparently differed, they continued to use the same spots for their burials.

In the same area, near Lewistown, on a high bluff overlooking the two rivers, is the Dickson Mound Builders Tomb. Here a museum has been erected over a mound of the Middle Mississippi phase containing more than two hundred skeletons, the largest and most interesting display of its kind in the country. The remains, together with their accompanying artifacts, are exposed in their original positions. With the skeletons are pottery vessels, mussel-shell spoons, L-shaped pipes, bone needles, beads, and fish hooks, flint arrowheads, stone adze blades, and effigy forms. The mound itself, originally crescent-shaped, with the points toward the east, measured 550 feet along its outer curve, and was 35 feet high. A reproduction of one of these burials, contributed by Mr. Don Dickson, explorer of the mound and owner of the museum, is exhibited at the Field Museum of Natural History, Chicago.

Fifteen miles southwest of Joliet is the Fisher Group, explored by George Langford, a local engineer. Three successive occupancies were revealed here: under the original surface, buried in the limestone gravel below the base of the mounds, were skeletons, with medium and long skulls, interred in a flexed position, and unaccompanied by relics; this complete absence of pottery, and the difference of physical type, probably indicate an extremely ancient culture. In the middle levels of the mounds were found burials of a short-headed people; with them were many pottery vessels, and artifacts of stone, bone, and shell. The upper levels held mixed types and mixed artifacts. In one of the smaller mounds of this group occurred skeletons of a short-headed people, extended on their backs with their heads to the west; in these graves were iron, brass, and silver utensils and trinkets, of white man's manufacture, indicating that some of the mound builders lived here down to historic times.

In the American Bottom, near East St. Louis, are the mounds of the world-famous Cahokia Group (*see Tour 19A*), known throughout the archeological world. Here the mounds of the Middle Mississippi phase were used as substructures for ceremonial buildings. The pottery is highly developed and sometimes, in form and design, indicates southern connections. Near the center of the area, which contains eighty-five smaller mounds, stands the largest earthwork in the world, the Cahokia or Monks' Mound. A truncated pyramid, rectangular in form, with a broad terrace or apron extending from the south side, it covers sixteen acres. Its greatest height is 100 feet; the east-west width is 710 feet, and the north-south length, including the terrace, 1,080 feet. The general similarity of mounds of this type to those found in Mexico has often been noted. The herculean labor involved in their construction denotes either the existence of slavery or an almost fanatical religious belief. Though there is much evidence that a large community, equal in size to a modern small city, existed in the vicinity of these mounds, no cemetery, strangely enough, has been found.

Also belonging to the Middle Mississippi phase are the four Kincaid Mounds near Metropolis, in Massac County. The largest, a truncated pyramid, rises 32 feet above ground, and covers 2 acres at its base. The nearby village site comprises more than 100 acres. The whole area has been made available to the University of Chicago for archeological research.

Effigy mounds, belonging to the Woodland culture, occur in the northwestern part of the State. They possibly represent totems or clan symbols; usually no burials are found in them. Near Galena is a mound shaped like a serpent, which strikingly resembles the famous Serpent Mound of Ohio. At the junction of Smallpox Creek with the Mississippi is the effigy of a bird with outspread wings. Also belonging to the Woodland culture are seventeen conical mounds on the bluffs overlooking East Dubuque and the Mississippi River, the largest of which is 70 feet in diameter and 12 feet high.

Thousands of small mounds, usually called bluff mounds, line the Illinois River. In culture they are of two types, for here again the Woodland and the Middle Mississippi, separated by considerable lapses of time, are found in the same area. Among other larger mounds of the State are the Montezuma Mounds near Pearl and the Beardstown Mounds in Cass County.

Of the historic Indians, the Illinois Confederacy was first in importance and one of the oldest. It was of Algonquian linguistic stock, and consisted of six tribes—the Cahokia, Kaskaskia, Michigamea, Moingwena, Peoria, and Tamoroa. Once the Illinois Confederacy occupied most of the Illinois country, but the early Jesuits found that there had been vast movements of all the tribes of the region due to wars with the Iroquois. Closely related to them, if not at one time actually a part of the Confederacy, were the Miami, who dwelt for a time in the region south of Chicago.

The Indians in the Confederacy called themselves Iliniwek (superior men), and indeed were physically well-built, especially the men. They were friendly and talkative, but most of the early explorers reported them rather shiftless and treacherous. In war they were excellent archers; they also used a war club and a kind of lance with dexterity; but their proud title of "superior men" was not earned in war, for they were often defeated by the Iroquois and the northern lake tribes, sometimes by smaller numbers than their own.

Father Allouez first met a party of Illinois at La Pointe, Wisconsin, in 1667, when they came to trade at that post. Three years later he found a number of them at the Mascouten village on the upper Fox River, from which point they were setting out to join their tribes then living on the west side of the Mississippi. It was also on the Iowa side of the river that Father Marquette first encountered the Kaskaskia tribe which proved so friendly; on his return he met the same band at its ancestral village of seventy-four cabins on the Illinois River near Peoria. The estimates of the number of the Illinois vary. Father Hennepin estimated that they numbered 6,500 in 1680; Father Sebastian Rasles gave an estimate of 9,000 in 1692. The Kaskaskia village on the Illinois near Lake Peoria was an important gathering place for all the tribes. When La Salle visited the town in 1680, it had 460 lodges, each housing several families. He reported that the annual assemblies of the tribes were attended by 6,000 to 8,000.

The lodges of this town topped the banks of the Illinois for more than a mile. Corn, beans, and pumpkins matted the adjacent meadows, and maize, planted in the spring, was given special attention by the squaws. When the maize crop was gathered, it was usually stored in pits, often under the houses. Pumpkins were sliced into discs and dried. When the work of harvesting was over, the tribes began to file westward for the serious task of obtaining enough meat to last through the winter and early spring. The men stalked and killed the game; the women dried the meat and carried it back to the village. The Indians' diet was further supplemented by wild fowl, nuts, roots, berries, and fish, which they speared in the lakes and streams.

The usual totems of the Illinois tribes were the crane, beaver, white hind, and tortoise, although the Kaskaskia sometimes used the feather of an arrow, or two arrows fitted like a St. Andrew's cross. Each village had several leaders, each of whom controlled from thirty to fifty young men. A reed mat with the feathers of various birds wrapped in it was carried on the warpath by the leader. The *De Gannes Memoir,* the most accurate description of the Illinois, probably written by the Sieur Deliette, nephew of Tonti, notes that though women and children captives were spared as slaves, the male captives were tortured by fire, their bodies cut open, and their hearts eaten raw. Mothers then hastened to dip the feet of their male children in the blood of the thoracic cavity.

The Illinois, according to one account, did not immediately bury their dead; bodies were wrapped in skins, and attached by the foot and head to a tree. After the flesh had rotted away, the bones were gathered up and buried in rude sepulchres. The *De Gannes Memoir*, however, declares that the Illinois buried their dead in shallow trenches lined with planks. Both kinds of graves have been found in Illinois. Grave gifts for the deceased, to accompany him on his journey to the "land beyond the milky way," consisted of an earthen pot, his bow and arrows, a handful of corn and tobacco, and often a calumet pipe.

The *De Gannes Memoir* further states that men frequently had several wives. As all persons in the village addressed one another in terms of kinship, the sisters, aunts, and nieces of a man's wife were *nirimoua,* and they in turn called him by the same name; if a brave were a successful hunter, he could marry all the women thus related to him. When a man died, his wife was prohibited from marrying for a year; the penalty for breaking this tribal law was death, after which the offender's scalp was raised over the lodge of her husband's family. Many shamans, or medicine men, lived among the tribes, and attempted to cure illnesses by chants and ceremonies which they professed to have learned through visions; once a year they held a colorful dance at which they gave a preview of their nostrums and powers. In their leisure time, the warriors played a brutal form of lacrosse, or gambled at a game of matching odd and even with sticks. So earnestly did the players engage in the latter that they often gambled away their female relatives.

According to the *De Gannes Memoir* and the reports of Father Hennepin, the Illinois built their cabins like long arbors, and covered them with a double mat of reeds, which the women gathered from the rivers and wove into rectangles sometimes 60 feet long. Each house had four or five fires and accommodated eight to ten families. Some of the villages were enclosed within palisades; others were set in the open with a good view of the surrounding country.

About 1680 the Iroquois descended upon the Illinois tribes, wiped out the principal villages, and pursued some of the conquered bands down the Illinois River to the Mississippi. There they attacked the

Tamoroa, and took 700 of their women and children prisoners. In 1682 La Salle built Fort St. Louis at Starved Rock and gathered about it 3,000 warriors of the various Algonquian tribes in a confederation against the Iroquois; 1,200 of these were Illinois. Twenty years later, we find the Illinois dispersed again; Peoria, Cahokia, and Kaskaskia were centers for the tribes of those names; the Tamoroa were associated now with the Kaskaskia, and the Michigamea lived near Fort de Chartres on the Mississippi. In 1729 Illinois warriors helped the French subdue the Natchez, and later fought in the Chickasaw War. Though they became involved in the Conspiracy of Pontiac at the conclusion of the French and Indian War in 1763, they had by then taken over many vices of the white man and had lost much of their vigor. When Pontiac was killed by a Peoria Indian near Cahokia in 1769, his tribes—the Chippewa, Ottawa, and Potawatomi—descended from the north and east upon the Illinois and almost annihilated them. A widespread but unauthenticated legend relates that a band of fugitives took refuge on Starved Rock, where they were besieged by the Potawatomi. Their provisions failed; the cords of buckets they dropped to the river for water were cut by the enemy; finally, decimated by thirst and hunger, they were attacked and killed.

In 1778 the Kaskaskia numbered 310 and lived in a small village three miles north of Kaskaskia. The Peoria and Michigamea lived a few miles farther up the river and together numbered 170. By this time all had become worthless and demoralized through the use of liquor. In 1800 there were only 150 Illinois surviving. In 1833 they sold their holdings in Illinois and moved west of the Mississippi; by 1855 the consolidated Peoria, Kaskaskia, Wea, and Piankashaw, living on an Indian reservation in Oklahoma, numbered 149, with much admixture of white blood.

In the seventeenth century, enemies other than the Iroquois came to make war on the Illinois and settle on their land. The Sauk and Fox moved down from Wisconsin to the northwestern part of the State and claimed all the territory between the Mississippi and the Rock Rivers. Originally they had lived along the St. Lawrence; subsequently, harassed by the Iroquois, they moved to Wisconsin. Father Allouez set up a mission among them at Green Bay in 1669. After defeating the Mascoutens near the mouth of the Iowa River, they formed an alliance with the Potawatomi and forced the Illinois to move southward. Their defeat during the Black Hawk War in 1832, when they resisted the encroachments of the white men, caused their ultimate removal from the State.

By the time the French explorers came, the Winnebago sometimes drifted down from Wisconsin into northern Illinois, the Kickapoo had moved into the area at the foot of Lake Michigan, and the Mascouten, friendly to the Illinois, lived in the great grassy plains east of the Mississippi. Along the Wabash dwelt the Piankashaw, and around the southern and western shores of Lake Michigan stretched the hunting grounds of the Potawatomi, a particularly warlike tribe, who, in the Conspiracy of Pontiac, annihilated the garrison at St. Joseph, and in 1812 committed the Fort Dearborn massacre. Associated with the Potawatomi were the Chippewa and Ottawa, among the most energetic and powerful tribes of the Northwest; they lived on both sides of the Wabash. At one time the Shawnee dwelt in the southeastern part of the State.

The mythology of the Potawatomi shows rare beauty and imagination. According to Schoolcraft, they believed in two spirits, Kitchemonedo, the good spirit, and Matchemonedo, the evil spirit. Kitchemonedo made the world and all things in it. He peopled it with beings who looked like men, but were perverse, ungrateful, and wicked, and never raised their eyes from the ground to thank him for anything. At last the Great Spirit plunged the world into a huge lake and drowned them. He then withdrew the world from the water and made a single man, very handsome, but also sad and lonesome. Then, to allay his loneliness, Kitchemonedo took pity on the man and sent him a sister. One night the young man had a dream. When he awoke, he said to his sister, "Five young men will come to your lodge door tonight to visit you. You must not talk to the first four. But with the fifth you may speak and laugh." She acted accordingly; the first to call was Usama (tobacco); being repulsed, he fell down and died. The second was Waupako (pumpkin); the third, Eshkossimin (melon); the fourth, Kokees (bean); all met the same fate. But when Tamin (maize) presented himself, she received him kindly. They were immediately married, and from this union the Indians sprang. Tamin buried the four unsuccessful suitors, and from their graves grew tobacco, melons, pumpkins, and beans.

As white civilization advanced westward, the Indians found their forests despoiled and their rivers polluted. Corrupted first with liquor and disease, then used as pawns in colonial politics, they were herded to reservations in the West, there to await extinction. In 1832, the year the Sauk and Foxes were driven from Illinois after the Black Hawk War, the Winnebago ceded to the United States all of their territory lying southeast of the Wisconsin and Fox Rivers. In 1833, at a grand council of chiefs in Chicago, the Potawatomi, Ottawa, and Chippewa also ceded their holdings, and prepared to move across the Mississippi to Indian reservations, together with the Illinois.

THE LAND AND THE PEOPLE

French and British (1673-1818)

THE FIRST EXISTING RECORDS of white men in Illinois were made by Father Jacques Marquette. On May 17, 1673, he and Louis Jolliet, with five *voyageurs,* left Mackinac, paddled over parts of Lakes Huron and Michigan into Green Bay, thence up the Fox River, crossed at the portage, and went down the Wisconsin. On June 17 they entered the Mississippi. On the west side of the river, in what is now Iowa, they encountered and exchanged friendly greetings with the Kaskaskia tribe of Illinois Indians. The adventurers passed the mouth of the Missouri, saw the famous Piasa or Thunder Bird painted on the cliffs near the present city of Alton, and reached the mouths of the Ohio and Arkansas Rivers. There, having determined that the Mississippi flowed not into some western ocean, but into the Gulf of Mexico, and fearing Spaniards and hostile Indians, the Marquette party turned back late in July 1673.

They returned by way of the Illinois River, which Marquette described in his *Journal:* "We have seen nothing like this river for the fertility of the land, its prairies, woods, wild cattle, stag, deer, ducks, parrots, and even beaver." And Jolliet later reported that the valley was "the most beautiful and most suitable for settlement."

Near Starved Rock they encountered the same tribe of Kaskaskia, now returned to their ancestral village site (about nine miles below the town of Ottawa), and their friendliness so won Father Marquette that he promised to return and set up a mission among them. From the Desplaines River they took the ancient portage trail to the Chicago River, thence to Lake Michigan, and up to Green Bay. Here Marquette, ill from the hardships of the voyage, was left behind, and Jolliet went on alone to Montreal where, almost in sight of the town, his canoe overturned and his carefully kept *Journal* was lost. Nevertheless he gave enthusiastic verbal descriptions of the new country, of its fertility, and ease of cultivation; he spoke of its marvelous transportation facilities, and showed how, with a canal built through "but half a league of prairie," a boat could sail from Lake Erie down the Mississippi to the Gulf of Mexico.

On October 25, 1674, with two *voyageurs* as companions, Father Marquette set out from Green Bay to keep his promise to the Kaskaskia. The voyage proved a hard one, and not until December 4 did the party reach the mouth of the Chicago River. Because of the severe cold and the recurrence of his old illness, Marquette stopped "two leagues" above the mouth of the river for the winter. With the spring his strength returned, and in Easter week, 1675, he established the first mission in the Illinois country at the Great Village of the Illinois, calling it the Mission of the Immaculate Conception of the Blessed Virgin. But then, weakened again by illness, he decided to return to St. Ignace (Mackinac). He was canoed up the eastern shore of Lake Michigan by his two faithful companions; finally, when he was unable to go farther, they landed near the river named for him in the present State of Michigan. There, on May 18, 1675, he died.

Robert René Cavelier, Sieur de La Salle, the French explorer, came later to the Illinois country. In 1679, after the sinking of his *Griffon* on Lake Erie, he erected a fort at the mouth of the St. Joseph River, ascended that river, portaged to the Kankakee, and canoed up the Illinois River to Lake Peoria, where he made friends with the Peoria tribe of the Illinois. About two miles below the lake, on the south side of the river, he built Fort Crèvecoeur in January 1680. In his absence the men mutinied and plundered the fort, and raiding Iroquois burned the Peoria village. Upon his return to the Illinois Country in 1682, La Salle, with Tonti, built Fort St. Louis at Starved Rock as a key to the vast empire of forts and commerce he had conceived. But his enemies at court prevailed, and he was soon recalled. Returning to France, he received permission from the king to establish a colony at the mouth of the Mississippi; on March 20, 1687, on a branch of the Trinity River, he was shot from ambush.

Tonti, La Salle's lieutenant, obtained in 1690 the privileges previously granted La Salle. In 1691-92 he moved Fort St. Louis from Starved Rock to Pimitoui, on Peoria Lake. For ten years he devoted himself to bringing in settlers, missionaries, and trade supplies. When he died in 1704, a chain of forts stretched from Montreal to Mobile. Tonti had at last succeeded where his chief, La Salle, had failed.

The Mission of the Holy Family was established at Cahokia (*see Tour 8*) in 1699 by priests of the Seminary of Foreign Missions. In 1703 the Jesuits moved the Mission of the Immaculate Conception to the Indian village of Kaskaskia, sixty miles below Cahokia, a short

distance from the mouth of the Kaskaskia River. These two towns on
the American Bottom, Cahokia and Kaskaskia, soon became the centers of French life in the Illinois country. In 1720, after the collapse
of the Mississippi Bubble, the commandant of the Illinois country
completed Fort de Chartres, 17 miles north of Kaskaskia. The name
Illinois was first officially used when the seventh civil and military
district of the French province of Louisiana was so designated.

Meanwhile British colonists were advancing on French territory.
New York fur traders reached the Great Lakes by way of the Mohawk
Valley; Carolina frontiersmen pushed around the southern end of the
Appalachians into the lower Mississippi Valley; the English continued
their Hudson Bay fur trade. Land speculation grew among the English
colonists.

In 1747 the Ohio Land Company was organized, and in 1749 was
granted 200,000 acres of land near the forks of the Ohio on condition
that the territory be fortified and a hundred families settled on the
land within seven years. Thus began the struggle which, at the end of
the French and Indian War, found England in possession of all French
territory on the North American continent.

The English occupation of the Illinois country did not begin at
once. Pontiac, chief of the Ottawa, rose against the British in 1763,
and captured all but three of the newly acquired forts in the Lakes
Region. He was not defeated until the following year, and it was not
until October 10, 1765, that the French flag was lowered and the
British raised at Fort de Chartres. Here, on December 6, 1768, was
held the first court under English jurisdiction in the Illinois country.

By this time the British colonists were moving into the land beyond
the Alleghenies. Speculators in Virginia, Connecticut, and New York
were organizing colonies, and colonial firms engaged in extensive
trading operations. But few if any American settlers were attracted
to Illinois, and the British showed no capacity for dealing with the
French inhabitants. Chaos prevailed, and the population diminished.

Thus there was widespread sympathy in Illinois for the Colonial
cause in the American Revolution. In 1776-77 powder purchased from
the French and Spaniards was run up the Mississippi and Ohio Rivers
from New Orleans to Wheeling, West Virginia. As the war progressed, the strategic position of the Illinois country as a link with
Spanish and French allies, and as a base for attack on the British at
Detroit, became apparent.

The task of winning this country was undertaken by George Rogers Clark in 1778. Authorized by the Governor of Virginia, he floated down the Ohio River with a band of 175 men. From Fort Massac he set out overland for Kaskaskia. On July 4, 1778, while Rocheblave, the expatriate Frenchman in command for the British, was penning another of his whining letters to England, Clark entered the village, and was greeted warmly by the inhabitants. Father Gibault, at Clark's request, traveled to Vincennes, won the allegiance of the people there, and persuaded them to sign the Oath of Vincennes. Hearing of Clark's successes, the Virginia Assembly decreed on December 9, 1778, that Illinois was to be a county of Virginia. But six days later Vincennes was lost to the British under the command of Governor Hamilton of Detroit.

Seeing the entire territory threatened, Clark set out for Vincennes with 170 men. It was February; the rivers and bottom-lands were flooded; for miles the men waded in water up to their waists on one of the most courageous marches in American history. At Vincennes Clark succeeded in detaching the townspeople from the garrison, and on February 25, 1779, Hamilton capitulated. Later that year Clark planned a campaign against the British at Detroit, but it was not carried out. The next year, when the British attacked the Illinois towns, Clark came to the aid of Cahokia and helped beat them off. As the war drew to a close, military operations ceased except for periodic Indian raids at the instigation of the British.

To organize the vast territory which Clark's conquest had secured for the United States, the Ordinance of 1787 was passed. It created the Northwest Territory as a Federal territory to consist of the present States of Illinois, Indiana, Michigan, Ohio, and Wisconsin; slavery here was prohibited, except as a punishment for crime; a territorial government with limited suffrage was set up; provision was made that any area with sixty thousand persons could organize as a State and apply for admission to the Union.

Despite the Treaty of Paris in 1783, trouble with the British and their Indian allies continued. In 1794 American forces defeated the Indians at the Battle of Fallen Timbers, and by the Treaty of Greenville of the next year the Indians ceded small tracts of land at every important post and portage throughout the territory, including the site of the future Fort Dearborn, one at Peoria, and another at the mouth of the Illinois River. The United States then adopted an Indian policy which by 1809 had obtained from the Indians practically all of Ohio, eastern Michigan, southern Indiana, and most of western and southern Illinois.

Against this growing threat of the white man rose Tecumseh, and his brother, the Shawnee Prophet. They organized the Indians of the Northwest Territory, ordered white men barred from Indian villages, and forbade the selling of any more land to them. The Battle of Tippecanoe in November 1811, though a victory for the whites, had deterred Tecumseh little, and the Indians in the conspiracy remained active throughout the War of 1812, aiding the British in gaining possession of most of the Northwest Territory. Detroit was captured; the garrison and inhabitants of Fort Dearborn were massacred by the Indians a few miles from the fort as they attempted to flee on August 15, 1812. The end of the war brought the Northwest Territory back to the American republic, but the problem of the Indians continued down to the Black Hawk War of 1832.

Illinois remained part of the Northwest Territory until 1800. In that year, by an Act of Congress approved May 7 but not effective until July 4, 1801, it became part of Indiana Territory. In 1809, by an Act approved February 3, the Territory of Illinois was created, which included within its bounds the present State of Wisconsin. Illinois became a territory of the second class on May 21, 1812; during all of this territorial period Illinois was governed by Ninian Edwards. Finally, on December 3, 1818, shorn of the Wisconsin Territory, it was admitted as a State of the Union, although its population was only 40,258, far short of the 60,000 stipulated by the Ordinance of 1787.

A State constitution was ratified without being submitted to the people, and Shadrach Bond, elected without opposition, became the first State governor of Illinois. The first capital was Kaskaskia; two years later Vandalia succeeded it. Through the efforts of Nathaniel Pope, territorial delegate from Illinois, the northern boundary of the State, fixed by the Ordinance of 1787 at an east-west line placed at the tip of Lake Michigan, was moved 51 miles north, to a line along the longitude 42° 30', and as a result Illinois obtained a shoreline on the Great Lakes. The reason given was that "additional security for the perpetuation of the union" would be afforded if Illinois were identified with the northern States. Today this added territory contains 55 per cent of the population of the State.

"The Prairie's Dreaming Sod" (1818-1848)

Through the gateway at Shawneetown, down the main highway of the Ohio River, settlers converged upon the young State from many directions—from North Carolina, Tennessee, Virginia, Kentucky, Maryland, Pennsylvania, New York, and the New England States. In flatboats and keelboats loaded with horses, cattle, and furniture, they came. Some, too poor to pay for this kind of transportation, struck out across country and braved the wilderness.

"The eye sometimes surveys the green prairie without discovering on the illimitable plain a tree or bush, or any other object, save the wilderness of flowers and grass," wrote an English traveler who crossed the State in the twenties. "On other occasions the view is enlivened by groves dispersed like islands on the plain, or by a solitary tree rising above the wilderness."

Because of a widespread belief in the superior fertility of woodland, because of the toughness of the prairie sod and the pioneer's constant need for timber, the first settlers built their cabins along the river bottoms and in the groves. But as population increased and desirable sites became scarce, hardy adventurers pushed out into the prairies, and thus discovered the almost limitless richness of the great treeless regions.

Despite hardships, they kept coming, first the advance guard of lone-wolf trappers and hunters, then the poor squatters, followed by farmers with stock and capital, and finally young men of education seeking their fortunes in land and trade. Socialistic and religious colonies organized elsewhere and migrated here: Birkbeck's English colony at Albion (1818), the Quakers on the Fox River (1835), Swiss wine-grape growers along the Ohio, Bishop Chase and his Jubilee College at Robin's Nest (1839), later the Swedish Janssonists at Bishop Hill (1846), and the Mormons (1839) and Icarians (1850) at Nauvoo.

In *Illinois As It Is*, Fred Gerhard wrote in a chapter entitled "Hints To Immigrants": "A pair of good horses, a wagon, a cow, a couple of pigs, several domestic fowl, two ploughs (one for breaking the prairie, and the other for tillage), together with a few other tools and implements, are all that is necessary for a beginning. A log house can soon be erected."

The frontier towns were busy centers of trade; the produce of the land and the forest—furs, skins, honey, corn, whiskey, venison, beef, pork—could be bartered for goods and shipped down to New Orleans in flatboats. In these towns all elements rubbed elbows, "the young college graduate and the lone-wolf trapper, the fine lady and the squatter's wife."

But the great curse of the expanding frontier fell on these towns and farms: they lacked capital. The produce of the West poured down the Mississippi—only to accumulate on the wharves at New Orleans. The small sums of money that dribbled through to the West went directly back East to pay debts. The Federal banking system, inadequate in its credit mechanisms, and the State banks, unstable and uncontrolled, made merchants and farmers distrustful of all banking systems. The State banks at Edwardsville and Shawneetown failed in the early twenties, but in the late thirties a much more serious confusion occurred, in both Federal and State banking systems. Soon all bank notes were so suspect that barter of tangibles was quite commonly preferred to any kind of paper money. But there was only a small market for produce, and debt-ridden farmers, unable to dispose of their goods and too numerous to be dispossessed, filled the State.

Not far behind the first settlers came the frontier church. A Methodist circuit-rider, the Reverend Joseph Lillard, stopped at New Design in 1793. The first Baptist church was founded there three years later; the denomination was strengthened by the coming of John Mason Peck and his establishment, the Rock Spring Seminary, in 1827. The Methodists, with their circuit-riding preachers, began to arrive in 1801; they taught simplicity in dress and living, and sowed the beginnings of the anti-slavery movement in the State. In 1796 came the Presbyterians with the Reverend John Evans at their head; insisting on a learned clergy, they quickly established their denominational colleges. Despite its early missionary work and the adherence of the French settlers, the Catholic church grew more slowly; not until 1844 was the separate diocese of Chicago established.

The question of public education was debated bitterly. The largest part of the population had been drawn from the South, which had developed no public school systems. Those from the North thought that education was a function of the church. Finally, in 1825, a law allowing localities to levy school taxes was passed, only to be repealed soon afterwards; it was not until 1845, as the result of a campaign waged by the workers and farmers of the State, that a free education law was again passed, and even then years elapsed before many communities took advantage of it.

The population of the State grew from 55,211 in 1820 to 157,445 in 1830. With this growth came a tremendous shift in the distribution of population. Opened in 1825, the Erie Canal brought swarms of immigrants by way of the Great Lakes, repeating the process of settlement that had been occurring through the Ohio River Valley for half a century. Fort Dearborn, rebuilt in 1816, was the nucleus of a settlement incorporated as the town of Chicago in 1833, and as a city in 1837.

A feverish campaign for internal improvements spread in the thirties; by the end of the decade the movement had brought the State to the verge of bankruptcy under a staggering debt of $14,000,000. In 1837 a flood of measures had been passed by the legislature, providing for the building of railroads, canals, and turnpikes, and the improvement of rivers and harbors. A canal charter had been granted in 1825; in 1827 Congress had given 224,322 acres to the State. The Illinois and Michigan Canal was begun in 1836. The Wabash, Illinois, Kaskaskia and Rock Rivers were to be deepened and improved. A great Illinois Central Railroad from the western terminus of the canal at La Salle to the mouth of the Ohio River at Cairo was proposed, with two east-west lines, "the Southern Cross" from Alton to Mount Carmel, and "the Northern Cross" through Springfield and Quincy.

At the same time the question of removing the State capital from Vandalia arose; Alton, Jacksonville, Peoria, Springfield, and others, wished to succeed it. They also wanted the benefits of the internal improvements. Consequently, in the session of 1837, the Sangamon County delegates, called the "Long Nine," because all its members— including Abraham Lincoln—were exceptionally tall men, arranged a trade. They voted internal improvements for these towns in return for votes for Springfield as the capital.

The hysteria of the internal improvement scheme was broken by the panic of 1837. For the enormous debt with which the State was burdened, it was able to show only one short railroad line, the Northern Cross from Springfield to Meredosia; built at a cost of $1,850,000, the road was sold at auction some years later for $21,000. The Illinois and Michigan Canal, begun in 1836, was not completed until 1848.

A tragic episode in the history of the State, the Black Hawk War of 1832, saw the passing of the Indian from Illinois forever. The Sauk and Fox once claimed all the land west of the Fox and the Illinois, and east of the Mississippi Rivers. In 1804, while five of their chiefs were in St. Louis arranging for the release of one of their tribesmen charged with murder, they were plied with drink. In return for an annuity of a thousand dollars a year, and the right to live and hunt in the area so long as it belonged to the Federal government, they deeded the land away. In 1816, 1822, and 1825, the agreement was renewed, although how well the Indian chiefs understood the terms of these treaties will always remain a mystery. The tribes continued to live at their great villages, the Sauk on the north side of Rock River near the present city of Rock Island, and the Fox three miles away on the Mississippi. Miners heading for the newly discovered lead mines at Galena saw their fertile lands, and by 1825 white settlers began to move in upon them. Realizing the inevitability of a conflict, Keokuk, the peace-time chief of the tribes, decided to move across the Mississippi into what is now Iowa.

But Black Hawk, a war chief less friendly to the settlers, persuaded by British and Indian friends that one thousand dollars a year was manifestly inadequate payment for this vast region, decided to remain on the land. The majority of the tribe left for Iowa, but friction soon developed between those who remained and the settlers; Black Hawk ordered the whites to stop plowing up the burial grounds of his ancestors and planting in the cornfields of the tribes. Governor Reynolds proclaimed Illinois in a "state of actual invasion" by the Indians and called for volunteers. When the volunteer army approached the Indian village on June 25, 1831, Black Hawk ordered the village abandoned, and under cover of night the Indians moved across the Mississippi into Iowa without a struggle.

In the spring of 1832, Black Hawk and four hundred braves, together with their women and children, crossed the Mississippi, apparently intending to go to the Winnebago in Wisconsin, and raise a corn crop with them. Their mission was misunderstood, and troops again took the field. Under Major Isaiah Stillman, they came upon the Indians encamped. Black Hawk sent three braves with white flags to explain that no hostilities were intended. In the excitement accompanying the negotiations, shooting began; three Indian tribesmen, including one of the truce-bearers, were killed. In the ensuing Battle of Stillman's Run, the white men were ingloriously routed.

Guerrilla warfare began, with the Indians proving elusive in the forests. In July, his forces weakened by hunger, Black Hawk decided to surrender. He wanted to return his people to Iowa, but again his offer of truce went unheeded. Most of the warriors were killed at the Battle of Bad Axe, August 2, 1832, where the white men turned savage and committed indescribable acts of cruelty, even scalping the Indians. As women and children of the tribes tried to cross the Mississippi on rafts, a gunboat opened fire, killing or drowning most of them. Those who escaped the Battle of Bad Axe and managed to cross to the west side of the river were set upon by the Sioux, the traditional enemies of the Sauk and Fox. These events, together with the great peace pow-wow held in Chicago in 1833, in which the Potawatomi and their allies ceded all their land in Illinois and moved west of the Mississippi, removed the last of the Indians from the State.

A decade later came the Mormon wars. Driven from Missouri, the Mormons moved across the Mississippi to the town of Nauvoo in 1839. They received many concessions from the State legislature, and built a community that exceeded Chicago and Galena in population and industry. Then dissension developed; men who were excommunicated, turned on the colony with exposés, charging that the interests in the community of Joseph Smith, the leader, were financial and political rather than spiritual. Trouble with neighbors grew. In 1844 warrants were issued against Joseph Smith and his brother Hyrum for rioting and treason. They were arrested and incarcerated in the jail at Carthage. While the prisoners were awaiting trial, the jail was broken into by a mob on June 27, and the Smith brothers were murdered. Then began the acts of violence which, for two years, amounted almost to civil war, with Governor Ford marching and countermarching the militia across the State in an effort to preserve peace. The problem was finally solved after it had flared into open battle; the Mormons, yielding to superior force, left the State and migrated to Utah.

A new constitution was adopted in 1848. The population of the State increased from 157,445 in 1830 to 851,470 in 1850. The constitution of 1818 was obviously inadequate, and many reforms were needed. The new constitution provided for popular election of all State officials and popular referendum on questions of policy. As a compromise between the township system brought from the North, and that of counties from the South, the new constitution provided for both forms of local organization.

A House Divided (1848-1870)

Illinois now entered the transition stage during which Chicago developed from a mud-rutted town of 29,963 in 1850 to a city of 296,977 in 1870, probably the swiftest growth of a metropolis in history. The State boasted ten incorporated cities in 1850: Chicago, Alton, Springfield, Beardstown, Pekin, Quincy, Peoria, Bloomington, Galena, and Rock Island. Their difficulties were many: houses were scarce, rents high, the streets so bad they became quagmires in rainy weather; according to a contemporary newspaper, the gutters were filled with "manure, discarded clothing, and all kinds of trash, threatening the public health with their noxious fluvia." One of the issues of the day was the hog nuisance; the streets, squares, and parks were public hog-pens. "Urbana had a record of more hogs in the community than people, and the porker had an equal right with the citizens to the streets." Nor were there public utilities until the middle fifties, when the more progressive communities began to install water systems and gas for street lighting.

Twenty years after the rush to the lead mines at Galena in the late 1820's, at which time a group of tent-cities containing more than 10,000 people had sprung up, the gold rush to California swept through Illinois. In 1849 more than 15,000 men and boys left the State for the western fields. The exodus subsided in 1850 as a result of discouraging letters and editorial warnings, but in 1852, with new stories of gold discoveries, the rush was revived. With the opening of the fertile lands of Kansas and Nebraska to settlement in 1854, still another migration took place. In the gold rush to Pike's Peak in 1859, additional thousands left the State. The whole of the fifties was characterized by this draining of Illinoisans to the West.

In their place came new families from the East and South. In 1849 there appeared in the Boston *Post* a poem which began:

Westward the ☆ of Empire Moves:
Come leave the fields of childhood,
Worn out by long employ,
And travel west and settle
In the State of Illinois.

The Yankees settled in the northern area, the Southerners in the "Egypt" delta and the southern region. The sharp division of Illinois into "upstate" and "downstate," reflected in habits, politics, and culture, persisted for years.

In even greater numbers immigrants arrived from Europe. French Icarians under Cabet set up a communistic colony at Nauvoo, the old Mormon city, in 1849. Portugese came to Springfield and Jacksonville; Scandinavians to Chicago, Rockford, Galesburg, Victoria, Andover, and Moline. The Bishop Hill colony was settled by Swedish Janssonists in 1846. But by far the most numerous were the Germans, fleeing their country after the defeat of their Revolution in 1848, and the Irish, driven out by potato famines and British oppression. By 1860 there were 130,804 Germans in Illinois, living chiefly in Chicago, Belleville, Galena, Quincy, Alton, Peoria, and Peru, perpetuating their rich culture in music societies, literary clubs, and *Turnvereine*. Many of the Irish were brought to Illinois to work on the canals and the railroads under the infamous system of contract labor; herded like cattle from Boston, New York, and Philadelphia to further Illinois internal improvements, they found, not the promised land of newspaper advertisements, but bad housing, improper diet, and unsanitary conditions, which took a large toll in illness and death.

Nowhere in the United States did the railroad fever of the fifties rage more than in Illinois. Farms were mortgaged, counties and municipalities subscribed to stock, Eastern capitalists poured millions into the enterprises. Many of the politicians in the State, from Governor French and Senator Douglas to township officials, speculated in land and railroad stock, and became wealthy. Charges and countercharges of corruption were hurled; the *Illinois State Register* declared in 1853 that the railroad bills "were prepared in New York and first canvassed by Wall Street men before they were sent to Springfield to secure legislative endorsement." Senator Douglas persuaded Congress to grant 2,707,200 acres of land, scattered over 47 counties, for the long-awaited Illinois Central Railroad, and in 1851 articles of incorporation were granted by the legislature to a group of Eastern financiers, headed by Robert Rantoul of Massachusetts, on condition that the State be paid 7 per cent of the gross receipts annually. In September 1856 the railroad was completed. Seven other roads were constructed in this period, and one, the Galena and Chicago, was able to pay dividends of 20 per cent after the first year of operation.

The railroads had a revolutionary effect on the life of the State. Most of the early settlements had been near rivers. Now the rich fertile prairie lands of the vast interior were opened to farming and mining, to become soon one of the greatest corn-producing and coal-mining areas in the world. The coming of the railroads brought a wave of prosperity; by 1860 farm values had risen 50 per cent over those of 1850; farm and city, raw materials and markets, were brought together. Towns sprang miraculously out of the prairies. Communities off the railroads faded away.

In the struggle that split the Union and led to the Civil War, Illinois furnished the two opposing national leaders, Stephen A. Douglas and Abraham Lincoln. The State itself was soon as divided as the Nation. As early as 1796 and again in 1802, memorials from the Illinois country had been addressed to Congress asking for repeal of the prohibition against slavery in the Ordinance of 1787. In 1824 a movement to amend the State constitution to allow the introduction of slavery was defeated. The kidnapping of free Negro residents in the State was countenanced for two generations, and the "black laws" of 1819 were still in effect. In 1837 the State legislature, excited by the spread of Garrison's abolitionism, passed a resolution excluding abolition papers from the State and making the circulation of abolition petitions to Congress illegal. In the same year, November 8, the valiant abolitionist newspaper editor of the Alton *Observer,* Elijah P. Lovejoy, while defending his fourth press from destruction by Alton mobs, was shot dead. Lovejoy's fight was continued by such men as Benjamin Lundy and his *Genius of Universal Emancipation* at Hennepin. Anti-slavery societies grew. In 1840 the Liberty Party was formed in Illinois, and by 1846 it had gained a majority in 13 northern counties.

Yet in 1853 an act drawn by John A. Logan providing that free Negroes who entered the State could be sold into servitude was passed by the legislature. This bill aroused the anger of Democrats and Whigs alike. Even so, the Democrats might have maintained their power in the State if Douglas had not in 1854 sponsored the Kansas-Nebraska bill enabling settlers in the new territories to choose between free soil and slavery, with an amendment thereto repealing the Missouri Compromise of 1820 which had prohibited slavery forever in the Louisiana purchase above the line of 36° 30'. From the opposition to this bill, in the form of a coalition of disapproving Democrats, Whigs, and Free Soilers, came the germ of the Republican Party in Illinois. After a mass meeting in Rockford on March 18, 1854, and another at Ottawa on August 1, a State Republican convention was held in Springfield on October 4 and 5. In the elections of 1854 the State was almost equally divided; the northern or Yankee half voted solidly anti-Nebraska, while the southern or downstate half voted with the solid South. Looking now toward the national elections, the Republican Party of Illinois was organized at a convention in Bloomington, May 29, 1856, with some leaders in the Democratic Party of the State taking active parts. The first Republican governor, William H. Bissell, was elected that year.

The Dred Scott decision hastened the coming of the Civil War. When the United States Supreme Court in 1857, held that the Missouri Compromise was unconstitutional, and that Congress had no power to pass a law forbidding a master from carrying slaves into the territories, it posed a serious question. Could slavery be excluded from the territories by any means? Douglas contended that it could, because the people could withhold the protective local legislation essential to its existence. Yet even this doctrine had its faults, for soon he found himself at odds with President Buchanan and the slavery Democrats over popular sovereignty as manifested in the case of Kansas, then seeking admission to the Union. At the same time Douglas was losing ground. The senatorial contest in 1858 between Lincoln and Douglas was fought on the issue of free soil or popular sovereignty.

On the evening of his nomination for the senatorship by the Republican convention, at Springfield, Lincoln declared: "A house divided against itself cannot stand. I believe this government cannot endure permanently, half slave and half free." Forecasting another decision like that in the Dred Scott case, but applying to the States as well as territories, he said, "Such a decision is all that slavery now lacks of being alike lawful in all the states." The famous Lincoln-Douglas debates at Ottawa, Freeport, Jonesboro, Charlestown, Galesburg, Quincy, and Alton carried on the controversy. In the last debate, at Alton, on October 15, 1858, Lincoln summed up his position in memorable words: "That is the issue . . . It is the eternal struggle between two principles—right and wrong—throughout the world . . . . The one is the common right of humanity, the other is the divine right of kings. It is the same principle in whatever shape it develops itself. It is the same spirit that says, 'You toil and work and earn bread, and I'll eat it.' " Douglas won the election in 1858; Lincoln won the presidency two years later.

With Lincoln in the White House and war declared, southern Illinois was spotted with sympathy for the Confederacy. At meetings such as that held at Marion in Williamson County, there was wild talk of setting up "Egypt" as a separate State aligned with the South. Douglas rushed back to Illinois from Washington to bring his followers to the support of the Government. But his strength sapped by years of political battles, he died on June 3, 1861, striving valiantly to turn back the flood he had helped to unloose. Discontent with Lincoln was soon manifest, and in the fall of 1861 at the elections to the constitutional convention, the Democrats outnumbered the Republicans more than two to one. The Emancipation Proclamation and the arbitrary arrests for disloyal utterances during the war were responsible for the existence of a strong party of protest. But on the whole loyalty to the Union was strong in all parts of the State. In four years Illinois contributed more than a quarter of a million men to the Union forces, and her soldiers died bravely on many battlefields. In 1864 Lincoln received a 30,736 majority vote in Illinois; and at his untimely death his most savage critics in the State paused to pay homage to him; the Chicago *Times,* suppressed once for disloyalty during the Civil War, declared that the public had come to "realize something of the magnitude of the concerns involved in his lease of existence."

The war over, Illinois began to take stock: it had contributed heavily in money and men; 5,857 had been killed in action; 3,051 had died of wounds, and 19,934 of disease. Now, with its railroads and fertile farm lands, its factories and mines, its people from all over the world, the State settled down to the problem of construction. The Civil War had released the forces of industrialism and swung the balance away from agriculture throughout the Nation with the emancipation of slave labor, the beginnings of mechanization of farm work, and the gradual closing of the frontier.

Patrons of Husbandry and Knights of Labor (1870-1893)

The Constitution of 1848, designed for a rural State, had made no adequate provisions for this new industrialism, creating such problems as police and fire protection in congested areas, sanitation, metropolitan city governments, and a flexible judicial system. A constitutional convention had been called in the midst of the Civil War, but the proposed new constitution had been rejected by the people. Newspapers continued to denounce the evils under the old constitution. The right of the legislature to pass private laws, said the *Illinois State Register*, was "a practice which invited corruption on the part of the members of the State legislature and instilled in the minds of the people a suspicion that state laws and bribery were intimately associated, if not inseparable." In 1870 another convention, almost equally divided between the Democratic downstate and the Republican north, submitted after long sessions a constitution which was ratified. It granted the franchise to Negroes, but not to women; one delegate remarked during the debate that the adherents of women suffrage were "long haired men and short-haired women." It also provided that the Illinois and Michigan canal was never to be leased or sold without referendum, established a system of cumulative voting, (*see Government and Education*) for the State representatives, created enlarged courts in Cook County and necessary legal powers to govern metropolitan Chicago, and increased the responsibility of the State for the support of educational institutions.

The new industrialism brought a raw transition period in the life of the State. Newspapers cried out against the lawlessness that prevailed. It was said that in Cairo a man a week was killed, while Chicago was a haven for gamblers, "bunko ropers," confidence men, and murderers. Springfield, declared the *Illinois State Register,* was infested with "an unwholesome debris of bullies, strumpets, vagrants, and sneak-thieves." But by far the greatest calamity of the decade was the Chicago Fire of October 8-9, 1871 *(see Chicago),* as a result of which 250 people lost their lives, thousands were left homeless and destitute, and the financial loss was estimated at 200 million dollars. With the aid of other States and even foreign nations, the city was quickly rebuilt, but the terror and suffering were not soon forgotten.

Discontent was growing among the farmers. They objected strenuously to excessive charges by middlemen, exorbitant freight rates, and the high price of manufactured goods. Illinois was still a farm State, with six-sevenths of its 35 million acres under cultivation as late as 1880. The invention and manufacture of farm implements had made considerable progress *(see Agriculture),* and yet in 1873 the secretary of the Illinois State Farmers' Association described the typical home of the Illinois farmer as "a bare black wretched abode, fit for nothing but the squalid and pigs."

The farmers organized. The Order of Patrons of Husbandry,

founded in 1868, was the forerunner of the Grange movement in Illinois. The original purpose of the Patrons—the purchasing of machinery for members at a discount—broadened in the early seventies when hundreds of new granges organized, with a peak of 761 in 1873 and 704 in 1874.

With the Grange movement came political pressure that forced the passage of the railroad acts of 1871, which stipulated that charges for long hauls were never to be less than for short hauls, that storage fees were to be uniform, and that no road was to charge a greater mileage rate on one section of its line than on any other. The second State railroad commission in the country was created, but the railroads refused to recognize the rates set. Farmers boarded the trains and offered the "legal fares," with results such as these reported in the *Prairie Farmer* of February 15, 1873: "The railroads of the state, in some cases, carry passengers free who will only pay the legal fare. In other cases such passengers are ejected by force. At Rantoul, the other day, a whole carload of legal fare passengers were switched off on a side track and left, while the engine and the balance of the train went on." In some instances hired thugs were employed by the railroads. When the railroad act was held unconstitutional by the State Supreme Court in 1873, the indignation of the farmers soon forced the passage of another act. The farmers were now a powerful political factor; to win an election, a politician had to entitle himself the "farmers' candidate"; they carried the judicial elections of 1873, and in 1874 elected a State superintendent of public instruction.

The Chicago *Tribune,* an enemy of the movement, aptly summed up the issues in the Greenback fight of 1876: "The creditor East, having unloaded his sixty-cent dollar on the West, can hardly object to being paid in the same kind of currency, worth now, however, ninety-five cents on the dollar." But Republicanism won both the 1876 and the 1880 elections after bitter campaigns, and the Greenback movement merged with the growing labor movement that developed rapidly after the great railroad strikes of 1877. The National Labor Union had been organized in 1866 and the Knights of Labor in 1869. The Workingmen's Party of Illinois, with a platform advocating the prevention of monopolies, abolition of child labor, compulsory education of children under 14, public ownership of the means of transportation and communication, State management of banks, and a number of wage regulations was formed. Its program was branded by the Chicago

Tribune as "socialistic heresies too far from our institutions to gain a foothold among us." Social forces were at work that broke the hold of John A. Logan and his Republican political machine in 1892, the only time the Republicans in the State were defeated from the Civil War to 1912.

In thriving young cities diversified industries were springing up—machine shops, foundries, coal mines, steel plants, and stockyards. The number of wage earners in manufacturing grew from 11,559 in 1850, to 82,979 in 1870, and 312,198 in 1890. With this industrial growth came poverty and unemployment, disease and slums; people began to talk about "trusts and combinations." Men and women who had deserted farms and towns for factories and cities were buffeted and beaten. To their aid came the labor organizations. Membership in the Knights of Labor grew rapidly; strikes became more numerous. Employers answered the growing protest of labor with the lock-out, the legal and political machinery, Pinkerton operatives, and strongarm men. In 1880 the *Illinois State Register* characterized workers locked out at the Chicago Stockyards as "traitors, not only to their wives and children, but to society and government. They are entitled to the severest penalty of the violated law, supplemented, if need be, by copious showers of shot and shell."

The Knights of Labor met in Chicago in June 1884, and passed resolutions calling for the eight-hour day, the incorporation of labor unions, the prohibition of work by children under 14, an employers' liability act, and a mechanic's lien law. Sympathy with the labor program became so great that in the next two years politicians became "friends of labor," as in the preceding decade of agrarian revolt they had been "friends of the farmer."

The fight for the eight-hour day continued unabated; the Knights of Labor formed a hundred new lodges throughout the State each week early in 1886. Even the press began to favor the eight-hour day, saying it was theoretically sound, so long as labor asked only for eight hours' pay, but warned against allowing the movement to "degenerate to a demand for the 8-hour day with 10-hour pay." The fight would probably have been successful but for the unfortunate Haymarket bomb of May 4, 1886, and the subsequent hysteria. Every manifestation of sympathy with labor thereafter branded one as an anarchist, and strike after strike collapsed in June and July.

Despite the reaction, general restlessness continued. Farmers, harassed by the discriminatory protective tariff and the vexing currency problems, joined with the Illinois State Labor Association at Decatur in April 1888 to form the Illinois Labor Party, which disintegrated rapidly through lack of harmony. The Democratic nominee for governor, John M. Palmer, took a stand for labor, denouncing the Pinkerton corps of private detectives who, he said, had been hired by the industrialists to break the strikes of the preceding year. He was repudiated by the conservative voters and members of his own party.

But the road was paved for the farmer-labor-Democratic coalition, which in 1892 elected Judge John P. Altgeld to the governorship. Altgeld personified the whole spirit of the revolt of the farmers and workers in the seventies and eighties. His enemies called him an anarchist, but the *Illinois State Register,* in answering the attack on Altgeld by the *Journal* in 1892, asked why it was strange "for a candidate for governor to notice the workingman, much less shake his soiled hands; it tries to cast ridicule on Judge Altgeld for visiting railroad shops and mines to meet and become acquainted with intelligent and worthy toilers . . . it is not the custom of the fine haired Republican office-holders to do so."

After the election Altgeld cleaned house. He appointed Florence Kelley, who had been associated with Jane Addams at Hull House, as factory inspector; he inaugurated the indeterminate sentence and the parole system, built hospitals for the insane at Bartonville and Peoria, improved the State school system, gave liberal grants to the University of Illinois, pardoned the three anarchists who had survived the Haymarket trial in a message that condemned the proceedings as unfair and illegal, and objected to the sending of Federal troops into the State by President Cleveland during the 1894 Pullman strike. Although he was not re-elected, and his acts brought him financial as well as political ruin, he had won for himself a lasting place in the history of the State; he is remembered as an uncompromising lover of justice and humanity, and as one of its greatest Governors. In Altgeld the hopes of farmers and workers were resurrected temporarily after two decades of crushing defeat.

In a far different sphere the World's Columbian Exposition of 1893, "the World's Fair," gave Illinois a chance to exhibit its development. Of it Henry B. Fuller wrote, "for the first time cosmopolitanism visited the western world, for the first time woman publicly came into her own, for the first time on a grand scale, art was made vitally manifest to the American consciousness." Congresses on social reform, women's progress, science and philosophy, literature, education, and commerce, were held. Said Theodore Dreiser:

All at once and out of nothing, in this dingy city of six or seven hundred thousand which but a few years before had been a wilderness of wet grass and mud flats, and by this lake which but a hundred years before was a lone silent waste, had now been reared this vast and harmonious collection of perfectly constructed and showy buildings, containing in their delightful interiors, the artistic, mechanical and scientific achievements of the world.

While the Exposition was making cultural history, the University of Chicago was progressing through the efforts of President William Rainey Harper, formerly professor of Hebrew at Yale, aided by the gifts of John D. Rockefeller. With "metropolitan" dailies in Springfield, Peoria, Bloomington, Cairo, and Chicago; with baseball teams that toured the world; with an Art Institute housed in a "Palladian Palace" built in 1892; with the University of Chicago, the State university at Urbana, Northwestern University in Evanston, and many normal schools and colleges; Illinois by 1893 had accepted the culture and had become an opulent symbol of industrialism.

The Modern State (1893-1933)

The Fair of 1893 opened its doors in the worst depression of the nineteenth century. During the first eight months of the year, 24 local banks failed; pig-iron production fell from 949,450 tons in 1892 to 405,261 in 1893; business failures increased 50 per cent; only 62 miles of railroad were laid in that year. Mills, factories, furnaces, and mines throughout the State closed down; unemployed workers crowded the streets of the cities begging food or work, while laborers from the farms and mines fled in desperation to the cities. Suffering continued until 1898.

With recovery Illinois achieved third place among the manufacturing States of the Nation. By 1914 Chicago was the greatest slaughtering and packing center in the country, first in production of farm implements, second only to New York City in printing, and its steel furnaces had the largest capacity in the United States.

By the turn of the century Illinois was able to record a phenomenal growth in population. In 1810, an outpost in the wilderness with only

12,282 inhabitants, it had grown to 2,539,891 in 1870, and by 1900 to
4,821,550. In 1910, 62 per cent of the State was urban, with Chicago
housing one-half of the population.

Important changes were also taking place in the character of the
population. At the end of the great wave of European immigration
in 1910, Germans ranked first among the foreign-born population in the
State, with 26 per cent (319,182) ; Austrians and Hungarians next,
with 16 per cent ; Russians and Scandinavians, about 12 per cent each ;
Irish 8 per cent, and Italians 6 per cent. Because of the exhaustion of
cheap lands by the time these people arrived, and the greater immediate opportunities in the manufacturing centers, they settled largely
in the cities and towns in the northern part of the State. Half the
population of the cities of Chicago, Joliet, and Rockford was foreign-
born. Negroes also began to settle here, mostly in towns of the southern
counties ; in 1870 they numbered 28,762 ; by 1910 there were 109,049 ;
in that year Negroes comprised 37 per cent of the population of Cairo.

Notwithstanding the repeated victories of the Republican Party in
State elections, Populist sentiment, born in the 1880's, remained strong
in Illinois. In 1896, at the Democratic national convention in Chicago,
William Jennings Bryan delivered his famous "Cross of Gold" speech,
which was warmly received by the workers and farmers of the State ;
but in 1896 elections Bryan and Governor Altgeld were defeated by
the Republicans. A Democratic governor was not again elected until
1912, when the Bull Moose campaign split the Republican Party, permitting the Democrats to take the major offices of the State.

Dissatisfied with Populism as an ineffective political movement,
some workingmen turned to more radical politics. In 1901 the Socialist
Party of the United States was organized in Chicago by Eugene Victor
Debs, Seymour Stedman, and other well-known radicals. The party
grew ; by 1915 there were 44 Socialists holding political offices in the
State : one mayor, 18 aldermen, 2 State legislators, 5 school officials,
and 18 others. In 1916 William Cunnea, law partner of Clarence
Darrow, ran on the Socialist ticket and was almost elected State's
Attorney, losing on a recount. Another radical organization was the
Industrial Workers of the World ; organized in 1905, with Chicago as
its center, its doctrine of "One Big Union" spread throughout the
West. Chicago, too, was to see the demise of the I. W. W. in the
famous trial of a hundred leading members before Judge Kenesaw
Mountain Landis on charges arising out of their opposition to the war.

THE BRADY PHOTOGRAPH OF LINCOLN

PROGRESSIVE DEMOCRACY—PROSPECT OF A SMASH UP.

POLITICAL CARTOON

POLITICAL RALLY AT LINCOLN'S HOME

GRANT'S HOME, GALENA

LINCOLN-BERRY STORE, NEW SALEM

OLD STATE HOUSE, VANDALIA

STATE CAPITOL, SPRINGFIELD

METAMORA COURT HOUSE

WATER TOWER, CHICAGO

CHICAGO FIRE

QUINCY, OLD PRINT

FORT ARMSTRONG

BLACKHAWK

And it was at Chicago in 1919 that the Communist Party was organized by the left wing of the Socialist Party, which split on the question of support of the Russian Revolution.

In the first twenty years of the new century Illinois was one of the most progressive States in the Union in the field of social legislation. After the passage of the first mining law in 1872, it continued to provide for the safe operation of mines by enacting supplementary legislation in 1899, 1910, and 1913. Child labor legislation was adopted in 1891; a law fixing the maximum hours of labor for women was passed as early as 1893; the first workmen's compensation acts of 1911 were improved in 1913 and 1917. Many other measures were adopted; governmental reforms were undertaken, among which were the establishment of civil service, and the act of 1910 providing direct primaries in the State elections. After the 1907 local option law was adopted, dry areas spread throughout the State, until Illinois became at least technically "dry" by the Volstead Act. An attempt to redraft the antiquated Constitution of 1870 was made by a constitutional convention, which assembled in 1920 and labored for two years, only to have its draft repudiated by the voters in 1922.

Illinois played its part in the World War. By June 1917, less than three months after the declaration of war, 351,153 Illinois men were in uniform. Illinois was one of the three States to furnish an entire National Guard Division. Officially designated the 33rd, it was popularly called the "Prairie Division," and saw action at St. Mihiel, Verdun, Chateau Thierry, and Meuse-Argonne. At the conclusion of the war the 33rd came home to be cheered and welcomed. Parades were reviewed by the Governor upon the arrival of each contingent. But missing in the demobilization were more than five thousand men from the farms, offices, and factories of the State.

After the war Illinois, along with the rest of the Nation, enjoyed a boom, an extraordinary period of construction and speculation. Politics, prohibition, crime, and the high cost of living filled the headlines of the newspapers. Governor Len Small launched an extensive program of building hard roads throughout the State. His political ally was the colorful William Hale Thompson, serving his second term as mayor of Chicago, who called himself "Big Bill the Builder." There followed the reform administration of Mayor Dever in 1923, but in the next election in 1927 Thompson was returned for a third term.

In 1931 Anton Cermak was elected mayor of Chicago. Then came the Democratic landslide of 1932, which turned the Republicans of the State out of office. Henry Horner, judge of the probate court of Cook County for five years, was elected Governer. Mayor Cermak was fatally wounded on February 15, 1933, when an assassin made an attempt on the life of President Franklin Roosevelt in Florida. Democratic policies again triumphed in 1934 when 22 additional Democrats were elected to the State House of Representatives.

During the twenties Illinois ranked as the third State in the Union in population, manufacturing, and wealth. It continued to lead the country in meat packing and slaughtering. Because of the State's strategic position between the iron mines of the Upper Lakes region and the large coal mines in its southern counties, foundry and machinery products ranked second in Illinois manufacture. Chicago remained an important center for printing, the making of men's clothing, farm implements, and electrical machinery. Railroad coaches were manufactured at Pullman and Chicago Heights. Important national centers for agricultural implements were Moline, Rock Island, and Canton.

By 1928 about 65 per cent of the children of school age were enrolled in public schools, requiring an annual expenditure of 143 million dollars. In addition, more than a thousand private schools were scattered over the State. Enrollment at the State university began to average fourteen thousand a year. Northwestern University and the University of Chicago recorded similar gains. Catholic parochial schools and universities, notably Loyola and De Paul in Chicago, also grew in importance. Greater care for the health of school children was provided with the introduction of regular medical and dental examinations.

As the cities expanded in the twenties with their skyscrapers, automobiles, electrical goods, chain stores, department stores, radios, and movies, there was another decline in agriculture in the State. From 251,872 farms in 1910, the number fell to 214,497 in 1930, and acreage fell from 32,523,000 to 30,695,000 in the same period. By 1935 the former had risen slightly to 231,312, and the latter to 31,661,000. Although the ox, the flail, the cradle, and the scythe were replaced by the combine, the four-plow cultivator, and the tractor, prices of farm goods continued to fall, and more and more people left the farms for the cities. This protracted agricultural recession of the twenties was regarded by economists as responsible, at least in part, for the devastating financial depression that began in 1929.

Under conditions strikingly similar to those of 1893, the Century of Progress Exposition opened in 1933. The times were critical: unemployed descended upon the State capital to demand relief; the coal fields were torn by a factional war between rival labor organizations; court dockets were clogged with foreclosure proceedings and evictions. To add to the suffering of the farmers came great droughts to parch their fields. The collapse of the Insull utilities empire and the widespread closing of banks impoverished thousands.

Despite all this, the fair opened with a note of hope and optimism. The exposition contained 84 miles of scientific, cultural, industrial, and commercial exhibits, seen by 39 million people, who came from all over the world. Its massive architecture of futuristic design was made brilliant at night by a dazzling revelation in new electric lighting.

Where visitors to the Columbian Exposition had marvelled that a Midwestern State could produce such evidences of culture, the urbanity of the Century of Progress was accepted without comment. In less than a century Illinois had been assimilated into the national economy, and what frontiers she faced at the end of the second fair were the frontiers of the Nation as a whole.

MAN OF ILLINOIS

By Henry Horner, Governor of Illinois

RARELY IS THE FAME of a great man inseparably linked with his place of residence. George Washington, for example, lives in the Nation's memory as the successful leader of the American Revolution, or as the first president of our new-born country, and only secondarily as a Virginian. Alexander Hamilton is known as the financial genius of the new Nation, and probably there are but few who know him as a New Yorker. Franklin is world-famous as philosopher, and scientist and statesman; not as the great Pennsylvanian.

But Lincoln is always the Illinoisan. He was born in Kentucky; he attained his majority as a resident of Indiana; and the national capital saw the final flowering of his genius. Nevertheless, in his own time, he was Abraham Lincoln of Illinois, and so I believe he would have liked to be known as long as the American people revere his name.

Perhaps this is so because Lincoln grew with his State. In the spring of 1830, when his family left Indiana to settle in Macon County, Illinois was young. Only twelve years had passed since it had been admitted to the Union. Population was sparse. In 1830 the Federal census-takers had found only 157,445 inhabitants, and almost all of these lived in the lower two-thirds of the State. Macon County, where the Lincolns settled, had only 1,100 residents, while Decatur, the county seat, was no more than an infant village.

The prevalence of frontier conditions enabled Lincoln to identify. himself with the pioneer stage of the State's development. On the bank of the Sangamon River, ten miles west of Decatur, he split rails and helped his father build the rough cabin which housed the family during the ensuing winter—the terrible winter of the "deep snow." And in the spring, when he struck out for himself, while his father turned back to find more congenial surroundings in Coles County, in eastern Illinois, it was not to leap into the relatively sophisticated life of an established town, but to become, for six years, part and parcel of a frontier village.

New Salem, in what is now Menard County, where Lincoln lived from 1831 until 1837, was typical of a stage in the growth not only of Illinois, but of most of the Middle West as well. It was small; never in its brief existence did it contain three hundred inhabitants. Its log houses and cabins were types of the structures in which new settlers everywhere housed their families. The settlers themselves were a cross-section of the population of the State—native Americans, mainly from the South, but with a considerable sprinkling of Easterners and Yankees. One man was as good as another, and natural ability was certain to be rewarded. No one was rich and no one was destitute, and all had firm faith in the future. The State of Illinois has reverently restored this little village to its picturesqueness of a century ago, as a memorial to Abraham Lincoln.

In this community young Lincoln, then twenty-two years old, settled in the summer of 1831, and here he remained for six years. A variety of occupations enabled him to keep body and soul together. First he clerked in a general store. When that failed, the Black Hawk War, in which the settlers expelled the last of the Indians from Illinois, offered a temporary occupation. Lincoln enlisted and served throughout the campaign, part of the time as captain of a company of mounted volunteers. The war over, he formed a partnership and set up as a frontier merchant himself—a venture which ended in failure and left him burdened with debt for many years. Appointment as the village postmaster contributed something to his support, but his main reliance, during the remainder of his years at New Salem, was upon odd jobs and the fees he received as a deputy county surveyor.

Meanwhile Lincoln was doing what he could to perfect his education. In boyhood he had attended schools for short intervals, which in all totaled no more than a year. He recognized his educational deficiencies, and at New Salem set out to make up for them. First he undertook the study of grammar, recognizing that without knowledge of the structure of language, clarity of expression was impossible. Then, in order to qualify for work as a surveyor, he studied mathematics and surveying. Finally, under the encouragement of John T. Stuart of Springfield, with whom he had served in the Black Hawk War, he began the study of law. Stuart, himself a lawyer, lent him books and guided his reading, with such success that by the time of his removal to Springfield, Lincoln had secured his license and was ready to take up practice.

At New Salem, also, Lincoln began his political career. In 1832 he announced that he was a candidate for election to the legislature. He was defeated, but the voters of his own precinct paid him a remarkable tribute when they cast 277 of their 300 votes for him. Two years later he ran again, this time successfully. In 1836 he was again a candidate, and again he was elected. By this time, moreover, he was one of the leaders of the legislature (which was then meeting at Vandalia), in spite of the fact that his was the minority party. When, in the session of 1836-37, Sangamon County's delegation, the "Long Nine," undertook to have Springfield designated as the State capital, Lincoln was both strategist and field general. That campaign called for all his resourcefulness of political skill, but it ended successfully on February 28, 1837, when the General Assembly voted that in 1839 the seat of government was to be established at Springfield.

In the spring of 1837 Lincoln left New Salem for Springfield. The first weeks were lonely ones for a young man whose entire life had been spent in much simpler surroundings, but he soon found a place in the town's lively social life, and was a welcome visitor in its many hospitable homes. Here he frequently met Mary Todd, whose home was in Lexington, Kentucky, and who was visiting her sister in Springfield. Friendship grew into a stronger attachment which, after a broken engagement and many searchings of heart, culminated in marriage on November 4, 1842. The young couple first lived in a boarding house, the Globe Tavern, but in 1844 Lincoln purchased, from the minister who had officiated at his marriage, the home in which the family lived throughout the remainder of their residence in Springfield. That residence is now the property of the State and to it come countless visitors annually.

As soon as Lincoln settled in Springfield, his friend Stuart took him into law partnership. Their association lasted until 1841, when Lincoln became the junior partner of Stephen T. Logan, one of the greatest lawyers Illinois has ever produced. That partnership continued until 1844, when Lincoln formed his own firm, with William H. Herndon as his junior partner, an association which continued until Lincoln's departure for Washington in 1861, and lasted nominally until his death.

Beginning modestly, Lincoln rose steadily in his profession until he became one of the leading lawyers of the State. In the twenty-four years of his practice he tried nearly 200 cases before the State Supreme Court. In the Federal and State trial courts his practice was large, as was his office practice. In spite of his success, however, and in spite of the fact that he was frequently engaged in cases of great importance, his earnings from his profession were not large. It is doubtful if his income averaged more than $3,000 a year, and that only in the latter years of his practice.

Throughout his career at the bar, Lincoln was absent from home, traveling the circuit, for nearly six months out of every year. For judicial purposes the State was divided into districts composed of many counties each. In each district one judge presided, and held court in each county in rotation. Members of the bar followed the judge from county seat to county seat, and trusted to their reputations and good luck to bring them enough in fees to cover their expenses and leave them something besides.

Lincoln's name is inseparably associated with the eighth judicial circuit, organized in 1839. Originally it contained eight counties in central Illinois, but as population increased, and new counties were organized, the number increased to fifteen in 1845. Thereafter, as growth continued and longer terms became necessary, county after county was cut off until at the end of Lincoln's practice, only five remained.

Nevertheless, throughout most of his years at the bar, the eighth circuit covered an immense area. Most of the lawyers practised only in their own and adjacent counties, but Lincoln, who delighted in circuit traveling as a way of life, usually visited them all. As a result, he not only came to know thousands of his fellow citizens, and their problems and troubles, but he himself became a familiar figure over a large part of the State. And thus was furthered his identification with all Illinois.

Politics made the bond between Lincoln and his State even stronger. In Springfield he continued the political activity he had begun in New Salem. In 1838 and 1840 he was re-elected to the legislature, and at the same time he was an active member of the group of Springfield Whigs who gave the party such leadership as it received.

After four terms in the General Assembly, Lincoln set election to the National House of Representatives as his goal. His chance came in 1846. His term in Congress, however, was a disappointment. Not only did he fail to attain the distinction he cherished, but because of his opposition to the Mexican War, which most of his constituents favored, he became temporarily unpopular. When, after the presidential election of 1848, his own services were not rewarded with appointment to the office he desired—Commissioner of the General Land Office—he resolved to devote himself exclusively to the law.

This resolution he kept until 1854, when the passage of the Kansas-Nebraska Bill thoroughly aroused him. Henceforward he threw all his energies into the fight against what he considered to be the growing menace of slavery. In 1856, when the Republican Party was organized in Illinois, he became its acknowledged leader in the State. Two years later there was unanimous agreement that he was the only candidate who could challenge Stephen A. Douglas' re-election to the United States Senate with any prospect of success.

For a quarter of a century, Lincoln and Douglas had been rivals. As they faced the voters in 1858, however, the odds appeared to be with Douglas. Successful achievement—on the State supreme court, in the National House of Representatives, and in the United States Senate, where he was a match for such statesmen as Clay, Webster, and Calhoun—had characterized his career. Twice, in 1852 and 1856, he had been a formidable contender for the Democratic presidential nomination. His sponsorship of the Nebraska Bill, his skill in debate and political maneuver, and the magnetism of his personality, had made him an attractive and admired figure to the masses.

In comparison, Lincoln considered himself a failure. From Congress, whence Douglas had vaulted into the Senate, Lincoln had relapsed into the routine practice of his profession. But thoughtful observers knew that Lincoln possessed the makings of greatness. Since 1854 he had grown steadily. His speeches—and he was making many of them—were marked by depth and seriousness and tolerance to a degree which set them apart from those which he had made as a younger politician. He was a ready debater, and even Douglas knew that he would be a difficult opponent.

In appearance, two men could hardly have been more dissimilar. Douglas was almost abnormally short and heavy, but his large head, wavy hair, and natural dignity made him an impressive figure. Lincoln, on the other hand, towered to six feet four inches. He was gaunt and awkward, but marked by a loftiness of character which shone through and beautified his homely features.

The contest—the great debates—which began in the summer of 1858, still stands as the most memorable and momentous of its kind in the history of the Nation. Ostensibly, the prize was election to the United States Senate, a matter with which only the General Assembly of Illinois was concerned; but actually what was sought was a popular verdict on the policy regarding slavery which Douglas asserted and of which he was the leading exponent. Formal debates were scheduled for seven cities in Illinois—Ottawa, Freeport, Jonesboro, Charleston, Galesburg, Quincy and Alton—but each candidate planned to speak in practically every fair-sized town and city in the State. The campaign lasted from August until November of 1858. Everywhere great crowds turned out to hear the speakers, with the result that by election day almost every voter in the State was thoroughly familiar with the issues involved.

The result was a victory for Douglas, though not a decisive one. Voters, of course, could express their convictions only by their votes for candidates for the State legislature, and enough pro-Douglas men won places in that body to insure the latter's re-election. However, the popular vote, which the existing apportionment made ineffective, favored Lincoln by a small majority. Moreover, the contest gave Lincoln a reputation he could have obtained in almost no other way. Heretofore he had hardly been known outside his own State; now he was famed as the man who had given battle to Douglas on Douglas' own ground, and had not been vanquished.

Invitations to speak poured in to Lincoln from all over the North. Some he accepted, appearing in 1859 in Ohio, Indiana, Wisconsin, Iowa and Kansas. Early in 1860 he spoke from the platform of the Cooper Institute at New York City, and made an excellent impression upon a metropolitan and politically important audience. A trip through New England followed, and again this man from the West more than measured up to the expectations of those who came to hear him.

When the Republican National Convention met in Chicago in May 1860, Lincoln was at least somewhat of a national figure. Nevertheless, in the minds of contemporaries, he was not an important candidate for the nomination. That distinction was reserved for men who had been on the national stage much longer than he—Seward, Chase, Bates, and McLean. But as the delegates gathered, and as the merits of each contender were weighed in the hotel lobbies and barrooms, distrust and antagonisms developed. It was murmured that Seward and Chase were too radical, McLean was an old fogy, Bates had been a "Know-Nothing" and was anathema to the then all-important German vote. Lincoln's friends, headed by David Davis of Bloomington, for many years the presiding judge of the eighth circuit, saw their chance and grasped it. Lincoln had not been long enough in public life to have aroused strong enmities, his speeches were conservative enough to appeal to those who feared that the party might go too far in its anti-slavery policy, he was a typical Westerner with a colorful past, and most important of all, it was believed that he—and he alone—could carry the four doubtful states of Pennsylvania, New Jersey, Indiana, and Illinois, which all agreed must go Republican if that party were to be victorious in the election. On the third ballot, Abraham Lincoln of Illinois was nominated. Five months later he was elected.

For four years Lincoln guided the destinies of a war-torn Nation. Victory, which finally came, would have assured anyone in his position a place in history, but Lincoln achieved it in such a way that immortal fame is his reward.

In achieving victory, he freed the slaves. In the beginning, the primary issue of the Civil War was union or disunion. Moreover, Lincoln himself, in deference to the South, sought first only to prevent the spread of slavery. He felt confident that by staying its spread the institution of human bondage would die of itself by reason of its own basic wrong. It is true, also, that the Proclamation of Emancipation applied only to regions in rebellion, and left slavery in the border states for the time untouched. But with all these qualifications, Lincoln remains the Emancipator. The Proclamation of Emancipation changed the character of the war and charted its result unerringly. The thirteenth amendment to the Constitution, which finally abolished the ownership of one man by another, was its inevitable consequence.

In achieving victory, moreover, Lincoln expressed the democratic ideal so clearly, so convincingly, that the ideal has never ceased to be the guiding light of American progress. To Lincoln, the preservation of the Union was essential, yet there was to him even more at stake. The importance of the Union, to him, lay also in the fact that it was the world's prime example of democratic government. Time after time he stressed this conviction. "And this issue embraces more than the fate of these United States," he said in his first message to Congress. "It presents to the whole family of man the question whether a constitutional republic or democracy—a government of the people by the same people—can or cannot maintain its territorial integrity against its own foes." At Gettysburg he said the same thing, though in more memorable words, and on many another occasion he emphasized his belief that the fate of the Union and the fate of democracy were inextricably bound together.

But it was not merely the depth and force of Lincoln's conviction that gave permanence to his words; it was the genius with which he spoke and wrote that made what he said a part of the living heritage of our people. Statesmen before him had spoken time after time of self-government, but not until Lincoln asserted that from the example of the thousands who had died at Gettysburg the living must renew their determination "that government of the people, by the people, for the people, shall not perish from the earth" was the tremendous importance of democracy indelibly borne home. The eloquent skill, moreover, with which he uttered his world-famous Gettysburg address on that bleak November day of 1863 at the scene of that decisive battle, characterized his pronouncements, so that his words alone assure him a place among the great figures and prophets of mankind.

And finally, in achieving victory, Lincoln set an example of human nobility which has never been surpassed. Wielding power such as few rulers have possessed, he retained his capacity for simple and intimate human relationships. He had full confidence in his own abilities, yet that confidence never led to arrogance. Before a God whose purposes were not always revealed, even to Presidents, he remained humble. The mass-slaughter of war left intact his inborn tenderness, and he refused to hate the enemy whom he was forced to defeat. And, when victory came, it aroused in him neither exultation nor vengeance, but led him only to think of widows and parentless children, and to place charity and forgiveness foremost among the virtues.

Thus Lincoln became a part of the spiritual endowment of the Nation. But he did not cease to belong to Illinois. Thirty years of intimate and vital association had made his identity with his State too close for severance. Lincoln and Illinois had met in youth and grown together; the people of the prairies had taken this young backwoodsman to their hearts and made him one of them, and he repaid them with trust and affection and an implicit recognition of their common destiny. His body, cherished symbol of all that is best in American life, rests fittingly in the deep dark loam of Illinois. There at Springfield, in an appropriate setting, is the shrine to which lovers of freedom from all parts of our Nation, and from every country of the globe, come to pay homage to the undying memory of matchless Abraham Lincoln of Illinois.

THE HUB OF THE CONTINENT
Transportation, Commerce and Industry

WHEN ILLINOIS was admitted to the Union in 1818, the only settled part was that south of a line across the State from St. Louis to Terre Haute; and even here there were large areas of wilderness. Kaskaskia on the Mississippi and Shawneetown on the Ohio were the two most promising centers of population. The former lies today at the bottom of the river, while the latter, after braving periodic inundations, has moved itself bodily three miles inland to the bluffs. Fort Dearborn on Lake Michigan, with a few score soldiers and a half dozen civilians, promised to remain forever a mere outpost. A scientific expedition sent there by the United States Government in 1823 reported that the climate was inhospitable, the soil sterile, and the scenery monotonous and uninviting.

Yet today Illinois is truly "the hub of the continent." Into Chicago, the world's largest railroad terminal, run 33 major interstate trunk lines, "as though," says the hero of a Dreiser novel, "it were the end of the world." In total railroad mileage the State is second only to Texas, and supplementing the rails are 13,000 miles of concrete highways. Passenger buses and interstate freight trucks have followed the railroads in making Chicago the center of their operations. Scattered over the State are 64 Federal-licensed airports, with transcontinental lines radiating in all directions; one line flies 38 passenger planes simultaneously over its Chicago-New York and Chicago-California routes.

In industry Illinois ranks third among the States. Situated in the heart of the corn belt, it leads the Nation in the production of agricultural implements and corn refinery products. Chicago leads the world in the slaughter and packing of meats; the city has been aptly characterized by Carl Sandburg, "Hog Butcher for the World, Tool Maker, Stacker of Wheat, Player with Railroads, and the Nation's Freight Handler." With iron ore secured from the Lake Superior mines and easily transported in lake boats, and coal and limestone mined in the State, Illinois stands high in the manufacture of iron and steel products. Bituminous coal fields underlie 35,000 square miles in 54 of its counties.

Thus the cities and towns which line the rivers and rise out of the prairies of Illinois are busy centers of manufacture and trade. The largest industrial area, of course, includes Chicago and its suburbs— Chicago Heights, Blue Island, Maywood, Harvey, and Cicero, together with Gary and Hammond in Indiana. Another cluster of industrial cities includes East St. Louis, Collinsville, Wood River, and Granite City. A third consists of Rock Island, Moline, Silvis, and East Moline, with Davenport, Iowa; other larger cities are Rockford, Joliet, Decatur, and Peoria.

This amazing development of industrial Illinois in less than one hundred years resulted from its great natural resources and its strategic geographical position in the center of the continent. It is bordered east and west by the two largest inland waterways in North America— the Great Lakes, and the Mississippi River system. At its southern boundary is another great navigable river, the Ohio. Possessed of these important arteries of traffic, the State early took an important role in the economic development of the Nation.

The first white man known to have traveled between the Illinois River and Lake Michigan recognized the strategic importance of this portage. After his trip through the Illinois country in 1673, Jolliet reported that these two main waterways could be connected by a canal dug through only "half a league of prairie."

Jolliet was also first to see the wealth abounding in the rivers and prairies of Illinois. He told his friends in Canada that a "settler would not spend there ten years cutting down and burning trees; on the very day of his arrival he could put his plough to the ground. He would easily find in the country his food and clothing."

A few years later came La Salle; in 1680 he built Fort Crèvecoeur on Lake Peoria as the key fort in a chain he planned to erect from Canada to the Gulf of Mexico to protect the fur trade and settlement in a far-flung empire. After La Salle's death, his lieutenant, Tonti, continued the work, and by the beginning of the eighteenth century *voyageurs* and *coureurs de bois* were passing back and forth along all the rivers of the Mississippi drainage.

In 1696 fur trading in the Illinois country was prohibited by the French monarch at the request of the Jesuits at court, who complained that the traders nullified all the good work of the priests by bringing firearms, firewater, disease, and indolence to the Indians. As a result of this edict, such an extensive illicit fur trade developed that in 1714 the prohibition was lifted.

In the early eighteenth century the centers of French life in the Illinois country were three towns along the Mississippi—Kaskaskia, Cahokia, and Fort de Chartres—for the river was the only practicable means of travel. Most Illinois products were conveyed downstream to New Orleans; but furs, because they spoiled easily in the heat, continued to go to the Great Lakes' posts, Mackinac and Detroit. From the south came most of the merchandise offered for sale, but the cost of transportation was so high that the goods usually sold for 100 per cent more than in France.

In the beginning three types of river craft—canoes, *pirogues,* and *bateaux*—serviced these French towns, plying the waters between the American Bottom and New Orleans, but gradually the canoe and the *pirogue* were discarded: the first because it was so fragile; the other, which was made from a hollowed log, because it capsized so easily. In 1732 two large *bateaux*—sturdy, flat-bottomed, pointed boats—were launched on the Mississippi. The following year an even larger *bateau,* 43 feet long with a 9-foot beam, was constructed and equipped with a covering to protect merchandise from the weather. A boat of this size could make the downstream trip to New Orleans in 13 days; the return in 70 days.

But early travel was not confined exclusively to water. Buffalo trails and blazed Indian paths crossed the woods and prairies. Connecting the Illinois and Chicago Rivers was the ancient Portage Trail, known to Indian tribes across the continent, over which Marquette and Jolliet had traveled on their homeward voyage. The two great trails through the Illinois country were the St. Louis Trace and the Great Sauk Trail. The former, known also as the Vincennes Trail, ran from the Falls of the Ohio opposite the present city of Louisville, crossed the Wabash at Vincennes, Indiana, and then ran straight west across miles of unbroken Illinois wilderness to Cahokia; today the Baltimore & Ohio Railroad follows its route. The Great Sauk Trail began at the Indian villages of the Sauk and Fox tribes near Rock Island, ran east to Lake Michigan, then swerved around the lake into Canada. After the founding of Detroit another trail connected that city and Kaskaskia. The present Green Bay Road north of Chicago, an early Indian path, was also used extensively. In the early eighteenth century the French began to build roads between the towns in the American

Bottom and from Cahokia to Peoria, and from Peoria to both Galena and Detroit.

In 1717 John Law's "Mississippi Bubble" brought sudden commercial expansion to the Illinois country *(see Tour 8)*. Colonists were brought in from France, Italy, Switzerland, and Germany, many against their will. Money poured into Law's Company of the West for the exploitation of the territory until the bubble burst three years later and Law fled France penniless. Although the new country lacked the gold and silk advertised by the company, its prairies were so fertile and its countryside so beautiful that most of the immigrants remained.

The Company of the West undertook the first mining operations. Pierre Charles le Sueur had received mining concessions from the crown as early as 1698, but had never exercised them. In 1719 Philippe François Renault, a former Paris banker who had been appointed director-general of mines for the company, began to mine lead along the banks of the Mississippi. To aid in this work, he brought the first Negro slaves to the Illinois country. After the failure of the Company of the West in 1723 his mining concessions at Pimitoui (Peoria) on the Illinois River, at Fort de Chartres, and at the village of St. Philippe on the Mississippi, were renewed. Two years later he complained that though he was taking 1,500 pounds of lead a day out of his mines, had built a furnace, and was supplying all the needs of the whole Illinois country, he was receiving no adequate protection from the Indians, but he continued to mine until 1744, when he sold his holdings to the French government and returned to France.

At the conclusion of the French and Indian War (1756-63), when the Illinois country passed into the hands of the British, speculators and businessmen came from the East. The outstanding trading venture was undertaken by the Philadelphia firm of Baynton, Wharton and Morgan Company. In one year this firm had $150,000 invested in Illinois. It maintained a force of carpenters at Pittsburgh to build boats, and had 300 boatmen on the Ohio River to carry goods to the Illinois country. Among the goods transported in 1766 the following were listed: dry-goods and clothing—particularly shoes, household utensils, musical instruments, guns and munitions, brooches and earrings; for the Indians it brought medals, tomahawks, silver arm and wrist bands, vermilion, and wampum. The chief product of the new region was fur. Despite the efforts of American firms, the fur trade continued to be exploited by Canadians until after the War of 1812.

Then John Jacob Astor and his American Fur Company, sponsored by
the United States Government, opened two stations in the Illinois
territory, one in the Sauk-Fox-Winnebago area, the other on the Illinois River. In 1816 the company took $23,000 of peltry from the
Illinois River valley. The fur trade finally came to an end with the
northward advance of settlements after the admission of Illinois to the
Union in 1818.

In 1812 a land office was opened at Shawneetown, and in 1816
another at Edwardsville; by 1818 the best lands in these two southern
districts had been taken up. Illinois was emerging from the wilderness.
Towns were springing up. In 1814 the first newspaper was published
at Kaskaskia, the *Illinois Herald*. The second was the *Illinois Immigrant*, at Shawneetown in 1818.

Towns began to boast of primitive manufactories. Newspapers of
the day contained numerous advertisements of grist mills, distilleries,
and sawmills. A carding machine was set up at Cahokia in 1817. All
the towns offered special inducements to mechanics, and newspaper
notices revealed the presence of coopers, tanners, watchmakers, and
milliners.

The most important function of the towns was to distribute store
goods. Alluring lists of articles "just in" were advertised and offered
"cheaply for cash, for produce, or on terms." The two largest wholesale centers were Edwardsville and Shawneetown. These were typical
advertisements:

Philo Carpenter. Will constantly keep on hand a general assortment
of drugs, medicines, oils, paints, Dye stuffs &C&C—also Dry Gro-
ceries, Glass, Nails, &C.

W. Kimball—Dry Goods, hardware, cutlery, etc. will be sold at the
lowest prices for Cash or Country Produce.

With transportation overland costing $10 per ton for each twenty
miles, river flatboats and keelboats were generally used for shipping in
the 1820's. Sometimes the farmer floated his own produce down the
river, sold it, and worked his way back. More often he entrusted his
shipment to river-boatmen—a hard-drinking, lawless fraternity who
terrorized the villages along the river.

The first steamboat on the western waters, the *New Orleans,* appeared at Shawneetown in 1811 en route from Pittsburgh to the Gulf.
The initial steamer trip up the river from New Orleans to the Falls of

the Ohio occurred six years later. By 1820 there were 70 steamboats on the Mississippi and Ohio; by 1830, more than 200. The flatboat continued in use for some time, however; Abraham Lincoln piloted one from the Sangamon River to New Orleans as late as 1831.

New Orleans, rather than Pittsburgh, was the trading center for Illinois. Downstream freightage between Pittsburgh and Shawneetown was $20 a ton in 1817; upstream freightage between these points was $70 a ton. As the same ton could be sent from Shawneetown to New Orleans for $20, the Southern port got the business.

Notwithstanding critical financial conditions in the 1820's, resulting from the farmers' inability to sell their produce, immigrants continued to come. Wagon trails developed in the southern part of the State, used chiefly by poorer travelers who could not afford river passage. They ferried across the Ohio, and continued on such overland routes as the St. Louis Trace, or the roads from Shawneetown and Lusk's Ferry (Golconda), on the Ohio, to Kaskaskia. In 1819 a stage ran to St. Louis from Kaskaskia, and later another line from Shawneetown. Two-day stage service between Springfield and St. Louis, once every two weeks, was inaugurated in 1822.

In the northern part of the State, trails first opened by traders or soldiers became roads for the new settlers. One of these, Hubbard's Trace, blazed by a hardy fur-trader from Vermont in 1822-24, led from Danville to Fort Dearborn; part of it later became Chicago's State Street. In the 1830's the Old Chicago Trail was opened, the first direct wagon road from Bloomington to Chicago. The rush to the lead and zinc mines at Galena gave birth to Kellogg's Trail from Peoria.

Two factors hastened the colonization of the northern part of the State and gave the first impetus to the phenomenal rise of Chicago: the opening of the Erie Canal in 1825, and the removal of the Indians after the Black Hawk War of 1832.

The canal enabled Chicago to surpass Shawneetown on the Ohio as the port of entry into the young State. In 1832 a land boom throughout the northern part of Illinois increased Chicago's population from 150 to 2,000 within the year. "Every day you see steamboats and vessels put in here from the lake crowded with families who come to settle in Chicago. Every day new houses may be seen going up on all sides," wrote Father St. Cyr to Bishop Rosati in 1833, the year Chicago was incorporated as a town. Seventy-five buildings were erected in the spring of 1834, and that year immigrants came in such numbers that they had to sleep on floors because of inadequate accommodations. Provisions were scarce; flour sold for $20 a barrel; between 1835 and 1836 the price of lots jumped from $9,000 to $25,000. In 1835, 255 sailing ships arrived at Chicago; in 1836, 40 steamboats and 383 sailing ships docked. By 1837, the year of its incorporation as a city, Chicago had a population of 8,000, with 120 stores, 20 of which were wholesale concerns. Chicago soon became a wheat center; in 1841 it paid a dollar a bushel while the Peoria market was paying only 40¢. Lines of 30, 40, even 80 wagons came as far as 250 miles loaded with wheat for the new metropolis; their loads completely overtaxed the capacities of the 150 vessels which docked at Chicago in 1841.

In the remainder of Illinois the flow of the rivers into the Mississippi determined the flow of commerce, the Illinois River particularly becoming an important commercial tributary to the larger stream. In 1828 steamers ventured as far as Naples; in 1829, to Pekin; in 1830, to Peoria. One hundred and eighty-six steamers arrived at Naples in 1831, 32 at Beardstown, 17 at Peoria. In 1837 the Peoria *Register* announced that seven packets offered regular service between Peoria and St. Louis, and one between Peoria and Pittsburgh. But the difficulties of river navigation and the shortness of the season were to prove overwhelming handicaps to steamboat traffic in the ensuing competition with the railroads. In his *Life on the Mississippi,* Mark Twain later wrote:

Steamboating was born about 1812; at the end of thirty years it had grown to mighty proportions; and in less than thirty more it was dead! . . . It killed the old-fashioned keel-boating, by reducing the freight trip to New Orleans to less than a week. The railroads have killed the steamboat traffic by doing in two or three days what the steamboats consumed a week in doing; and the towing fleets have killed the through-freight traffic by dragging six or seven steamer-loads of stuff down the river at a time, at an expense so trivial that steamboat competition was out of the question.

The movement for internal improvements culminated in the bills passed by the State legislature in February 1837; rivers and harbors were to be deepened and widened; a railroad with 1,341 miles of track was to be built from Galena in the north, down the center of the State, to Cairo, with two intersecting lines—the Northern Cross and the

Southern Cross. The long-awaited canal connecting the Illinois River and the Great Lakes was to be realized. Land values mounted.

But over-speculation, aggravated by the Nation-wide panic of 1837, impeded the movement. The State awoke to find that, for the $14,000,000 debt it had assumed, it had only 24 miles of railroad—the Jacksonville and Meredosia section of the Northern Cross, later extended to Springfield—and only a small section of the Illinois and Michigan Canal. Not until 1848 was the Canal completed to become an avenue for the transportation of much-needed Michigan lumber to the treeless prairies along the Illinois River, and opened an artery into Chicago which diverted to the north much of the trade that had formerly gone to St. Louis.

The State-owned Northern Cross, the first railroad pulled by a steam locomotive west of the Allegheny Mountains and north of the Ohio River, made its initial run late in the fall of 1838, using thin strips of iron mounted on wood for its rails. As the engine required great quantities of water, male passengers were often recruited for water-carrying expeditions from the nearest source of supply, and they were also expected to help the crew load wood into the tender at the numerous refueling points. Traveling on this road was not only slow but dangerous. The inadequate rails made accidents frequent; now and again they became unspiked at the ends and curled up into "snake heads," which pierced the floor boards of the cars. Another cause of serious accidents was the theft of rails; iron was scarce in the prairie country, and farmers quickly conceived many uses for them, chiefly as sled runners. Occasionally engines in need of repairs had to be hauled home ignominiously by struggling teams of horses, while the passengers settled themselves for a long wait. The expense and trouble of operating the Northern Cross proved so great that the State finally leased the property to private concerns. Subsequently two locomotives were sold to a man who conceived the idea of running them as trackless steam wagons across the open prairies. His scheme was fairly successful for a time, but he was soon forced to abandon it because this mode of transportation did not appeal to travelers.

Generally, throughout the 1840's, the stagecoach ruled the Illinois roads. A short-lived craze for planked roads reached the State from Russia through Canada. Although these roads were more sturdily and evenly built than in Russia, where they "shook the soul out of your body," the expense of construction and maintenance proved so high that few brought profit to the companies which laid them. By 1850 the plank roads were being dismantled, and the railroad boom once more gripped Illinois.

Congress granted Illinois over 2,500,000 acres of land in 1850 for the construction of a central railroad. Robert Rantoul and a group of Eastern capitalists organized the Illinois Central Railroad Company, and in six years the road was completed. Rails were brought from England by way of New Orleans, the Erie Canal, and the Great Lakes; Irish, Scotch, German, and Scandinavian laborers, hurriedly brought to the scene from New York, plunged into the work. Almost 100,000 men wrestled with the construction of the 366 miles of track between Chicago and Cairo, which made the Illinois Central the longest road in America at that time.

The same decade also saw the chartering and building of other railroads: the Wabash, taking over the ill-fated Springfield and Meredosia line; the Chicago and North Western; the Chicago and Alton; the Chicago, Burlington & Quincy; the Chicago, Rock Island & Pacific and a number of interstate lines like the Baltimore & Ohio, the Michigan Central, and the Cleveland, Cincinnati, Chicago & St. Louis, known as the Big Four.

Railroad companies, especially the Illinois Central, platted and developed towns along their rights-of-way. Some communities passed by the roads uprooted themselves and removed themselves to the line. Occasionally an old town, suspicious of modern ways, unwisely opposed the advent of railroads. The French village of Bourbonnais, for instance, fought the approach of the Illinois Central, with the result that the tracks were rerouted to nearby Kankakee; today Bourbonnais, decimated in population and trade, is a mere hamlet.

In 1858 George M. Pullman, a cabinet-maker, began to convert old railroad passenger cars to the uses of long-distance travel for the Chicago and Alton line. When his sleeping-cars proved successful, he founded the Pullman Palace Car Company in 1867, and in 1880 built the town of Pullman for his employees; it has since become part of Chicago. The refrigeration of beef in railroad cars was perfected in Chicago in 1857; nine years later fruits were likewise transported. The first steel rails made in this country were rolled in May 1865, at the Chicago Rolling Mills. In 1873 the Joliet Iron and Steel Company began to produce Bessemer steel. In 1874, 1,398 miles of steel rails were laid in the State.

The shift from agriculture to manufacturing in Illinois at the end of the Civil War may be seen in the following table:

YEAR	MANUFACTURING	AGRICULTURE
1870	$205,620,672	$210,860,585
1880	414,864,673	213,980,137
1890	908,640,280	184,759,013

This development, the result of a pronounced westward thrust of industry, brought important manufacturing enterprises to the State. In 1865 the National Watch Company was organized in Chicago by several former employees of the Waltham Company; that same year they erected a factory at Elgin on land donated to them. Later this concern became the Elgin Watch Company. At first they made only the works for watches, putting them in tin cases and selling them to the trade. This proved so remunerative that two more factories began to compete with them: one, the Illinois Watch Company at Springfield, founded in 1870; and the Rockford Watch Company, established in 1874. The year 1865 also saw a large pottery works established at Peoria, the incorporation of the Union Stock Yards of Chicago, and the opening of a large stove factory at Quincy.

As the greatest manufacturing city of the West, Chicago had in 1879 a total of 2,271 establishments which produced $268,000,000 of manufactured goods in that year. It had 343 woodworking shops, 246 iron foundries and machine shops, 156 metal works, 111 breweries, together with packing houses, harvester works, and clothing factories, and produced 60 per cent of the manufactured goods of Illinois.

During this period of general expansion great impetus was given to coal mining, farm implement manufacture (*see Agriculture*), and meat packing. Three names are associated with the packing industry in the United States: Philip D. Armour, Nelson Morris, and Gustavus F. Swift. Before he came to Chicago, Armour had been first a partner in Jacob Plankington's packing house in Milwaukee, one of the largest in the country, and later became head of his own concern. When tremendous shipments of cattle and hogs began to pour into Chicago in 1865, the legislature incorporated the Union Stock Yards on 345 swampy acres south of the city limits. Foreseeing the rich future of the Middle West as a packing center, Armour, with his brothers, moved the headquarters of Armour and Company to Chicago from Milwaukee in 1875; soon the Armour brand of meat was known all over the world. Before Armour's rise, a young Bavarian Jew named Nelson Morris had conducted a flourishing meat business in Chicago. He had procured contracts for provisioning Union troops during the Civil War, and had amassed a fortune while still a comparatively young man. In 1875 an Easterner added his name to the meat barons of the West. Gustavus F. Swift, a Cape Cod Yankee, who had owned a large dressed-beef business in New England, came to Chicago and opened a big slaughter house. Swift subsequently revolutionized meat packing by the use of railroad refrigeration, which made it possible to ship fresh meat to the East.

Before the coming of the railroads coal mining was unimportant in the State. As there was no means of large-scale transportation of the bulky commodity except by water, mining before the 1850's was confined to the vicinity of rivers. But in the middle 1850's the industry in Illinois suddenly expanded; locomotives began to use coal instead of wood, and the railroads were showing a marked interest in coal transportation. Another factor was the introduction in 1873 of Bessemer furnaces, using bituminous coal, into the steel plants of Illinois. Related to the coal mining industry was the smelting of lead and zinc from Missouri in Illinois coal towns. Illinois was the third coal producing State in the Nation in 1917, with 810 mines, which produced more than 86 million tons of coal valued at $162,218,822.

Uniquely midwestern were the mail order houses which arose in Chicago. Montgomery Ward and Company was formed in 1872 during the Grange movement's fight against the profits of the middleman. It sold directly from its catalogue, and guaranteed "Satisfaction or Your Money Back." In 1939 it had 614 retail stores and 9 mail-order houses scattered throughout the country. Sears Roebuck and Company which had its beginning in 1886 as a C.O.D. watch business at North Redwood, Minnesota, is the largest business of its kind in the world. In 1937 and again in 1938, its sales exceeded half a billion dollars. The company operates 504 stores and 10 mail-order plants.

Chicago's State Street grew to be one of the most concentrated shopping areas in the world. One of the landmarks in Middle Western merchandising is Marshall Field and Company's retail store. Thirteen stories high, it occupies a whole city block, with a six-story annex. The store had its beginning in the dry goods business of Potter Palmer, established in Chicago in 1852; Marshall Field and Levi Z. Leiter came into the business later, and it expanded along with the phenomenal growth of Chicago. Among other State Street stores are the Fair, the Boston Store, Carson Pirie Scott & Company, Mandel Brothers, Goldblatt's, Sears Roebuck and Company, The Hub, Rothschild's, and Charles A. Stevens Company.

Despite the long period of depression in the 1890's, the rapid expansion of manufacturing continued in the State. While the population increased 26 per cent, the number of manufacturing establishments doubled, and the number of workers mounted from 312,198 to 480,643. In the next decade, however, the value of manufacturing products continued to grow at the same pace, but the number of establishments and the number of workers employed in them had a much slower growth. The dominant note in industry was large-scale production and centralization. The standardization of machinery, improved accounting systems, the appearance of the corporate form of organization, the use of stock and produce exchanges, the perfection of the telephone, telegraph, and typewriter, and the building of the railroads, all contributed to this development. The corporate form of organization grew steadily, from 1,090 units in 1873 to over 20,000 in 1914. Corporations manufactured 90 per cent of all the products and employed 85 per cent of all the workers in the State. Three hundred thirty-six establishments out of 18,388 in Illinois in 1914 had a production of $1,000,000 or more in value; these establishments, constituting less than 2 per cent in number, employed over two-fifths of all the wage-earners and turned out three-fifths of all products. Twenty-two per cent of all the wage-earners were employed in the six largest plants.

Along with this early twentieth century growth of centralization came a tendency to localize manufacturing in particular districts, dependent upon nearness to materials and markets, transportation facilities, and plentiful labor supply. Chicago, with all these advantages, became the unrivaled center, producing two-thirds of the State's manufactured goods. Peoria, an important center for distilled liquors, meat-packing, printing, agricultural implements, cooperage, cordage and twine, and food products, moved into second place. Joliet was third with its steel and rolling mills, its blast furnaces, its coke and wire. Next came East St. Louis with flour and grist mills, chemical and paint works, meat-packing plants, rolling mills, foundries, machine shops, and railroad repair shops. Though Rockford ranked fifth in the value of its manufactures, it was second to Chicago in the number of workers, of whom more than one-half were employed in furniture factories, knitting mills, foundries, and machine shops. Almost half the manufacturing output of Moline was farm implements. The other leading manufacturing cities in the new century were Chicago Heights, Granite City, Alton, Waukegan, Decatur, Springfield, Aurora, and Elgin.

This period saw the development of huge combinations, particularly in the three leading industries: meat packing, steel, and farm implements serve as examples. Immense plants in Chicago's "Packingtown" were turning out by 1914 one-quarter of all meat packing products in the country. In 1903 Morris, Swift, and Armour had organized the National Packing Company. In 1912 they dissolved voluntarily, Swift and Company taking over 46 per cent of the assets, Armour and Company about 40 per cent, and Morris and Company the remaining 14 per cent. Illinois steel furnaces had a greater capacity in 1914 than those of any other State. At first pooling agreements were entered into under the aegis of the National Steel Association, the Western Nail Manufacturers Association, and the Stove Manufacturers Association. But something more binding than pooling agreements became necessary, and after 1900 various Illinois companies were drawn into the American Can Company, the Republic Iron and Steel Company, the Federal Steel Company, and the American Steel and Wire Company. The United States Steel Corporation, largest in the industry, was formed in 1901. It combined the Federal Steel Company and the American Steel and Wire Company, both Illinois concerns, with the American Bridge Company of Chicago, and the American Tin Plate Company of Joliet.

In 1902 the International Harvester Company was formed, combining the McCormick Harvesting Machine Company, the Deering Harvester Company, the Plano Manufacturing Company, the Warder Bushwell Company, the Glessner Company, and the Milwaukee Harvester Company. The capital stock was $120,000,000, and its annual output more than 8,500,000 machines. The centralization of industry can be estimated on the basis of reports made in 1919 to the State of Illinois under the factory law: of the 18,593 establishments reporting, 799 each produced $1,000,000 of goods or more annually, turned out 75 per cent of the total products, and employed 389,686 wage-earners.

Under these circumstances the period following the World War witnessed a remarkable expansion in industry and commerce in the State. The value of manufactured goods rose from $5,041,113,314 in 1923 to $6,232,863,025 in 1929. But with the long years of depression that followed 1930, the manufacture of goods fell, and by 1937 recovery had been only partially achieved, with less than $4,000,000,000 of goods manufactured that year.

In the last two decades a tendency toward decentralization of industry has appeared. Factories are more and more frequently situated in the suburbs of large cities or in small towns. Two factors have contributed to this development. One is the technical improvement in the means of transportation, facilitating the moving of raw materials. The other is the rationalization of mechanical production and the increasing adaptation of electric power, permitting the use of lighter and more easily transported, installed, and operated machines. At present almost every small town in Illinois has at least one manufacturing establishment—making shoes, machinery, electrical goods, or foundry products —while the growth of manufacturing plants in large centers has not only failed to maintain its normal increase but has in many instances declined. The agrarian center has become transformed into the small factory town. This change has cultural as well as economic aspects. The rush to the cities is waning; younger people are remaining in their home towns. Statistics on the distribution of population in Illinois show that whereas 26.4 per cent of the inhabitants of the State lived in small towns in 1918, by 1925 that figure had risen to 39.3 per cent. In 1934 the Illinois State Planning Commission recommended "that ruralization of industry may be advantageous because of the lower living costs and cheaper lands and buildings where there is no need for a concentrated market, or where an industry is not bound to a producing center because of the perishability of the materials processed."

Thus, in less than a century, Illinois has grown from an undeveloped wilderness to a great economic empire. In 1937 the State had 12,090 manufacturing establishments which produced $3,818,213,281 of goods. It was first among the States in the processing of meats, and in the manufacture of farm implements, confectioneries, and corn refinery products. It ranked second in the Nation in printing and publishing, and in the manufacture of distilled liquors, furniture, pianos and musical instruments, and women's and children's wearing apparel, and third in the manufacture of men's and boy's clothing.

In the farm equipment industry alone more than 75,000 persons were employed.

Over three-quarters of the State's manufactured goods were produced in the metropolitan area of Chicago, whose six leading industries were food products, steel, machinery, printing and publishing, clothing, and agricultural implements. The Chicago area had 8,052 establishments which produced almost $2,500,000,000 of goods. Throughout the State manufacturing had become greatly diversified; thus, Elgin is best known for its watches, Moline for its farm implements, Kewanee for its boilers, and Rockford for its furniture. Because of the growing competition of petroleum from both local and national fields, coal mining had fallen from third to seventh place in the Nation.

Railroads have increased their accommodations to meet current needs. Streamlined passenger trains were introduced in 1935; Burlington's silverstreaked "Zephyr," Rock Island's "Rocket," Alton's "Abraham Lincoln," Illinois Central's "Green Diamond," the red and yellow "Hiawatha" of the Chicago, Milwaukee and St. Paul, the "Super-Chief" of the Atchison, Topeka & Santa Fe, and North Western's "400," are all capable of attaining a speed of 120 miles per hour. All have Diesel engines. Electric lines made their appearance in the State soon after 1900; although in 1927 there were 47 companies with over 2,000 miles of electrified tracks, ten years later there were only six companies with 536 miles of tracks, a decline due to the growth of bus, truck, and automobile transportation.

Forty-eight bus companies operated over 15,000 miles of routes in 1937, while trucking concerns with fleets of giant trucks and trailers engaged in inter- and intra-state commerce. With the development of the automobile road-building programs were undertaken; acts of Congress in 1916 and 1919, and State bond issues in 1918 and 1924, provided funds for construction; by 1937, exclusive of city streets, there were some 13,000 miles of concrete, brick, or bituminous-surfaced roads. Over a thousand miles of air lanes latticed the Illinois area, joining its 64 airports. Largest of the airports is that at Chicago, its runways laid out in the form of a Union Jack to enable planes to take off in eight different directions. Its 640 acres of land and brick hangars accommodating 800 planes have already become inadequate for the growing air traffic, necessitating adoption of a new expansion program with aid of the legislature.

The Illinois and Michigan Canal, completed in 1848, has fallen into disuse, as has the Illinois and Mississippi Canal from Hennepin to Rock River. A new route between the Illinois River and Lake Michigan was begun in 1890 by the Sanitary District of Chicago, and a canal from Chicago to Lockport on the Desplaines River was completed in 1900. In 1919, with funds provided by a State bond issue, the waterway was continued from Lockport to Utica. Finally, with Federal aid, the channel of the Illinois River was deepened to its confluence with the Mississippi River at Grafton, and the first barges from St. Louis arrived on March 4, 1933.

The spirit with which Illinois faces the future appears in the almost boastful tone with which the *Illinois Journal of Commerce* recently asserted that "although Illinois embraces less than 2% of the land area of the United States, it has 6.1% of the nation's population, 6.9% of its wealth, 5.4% of its improved farm land, 4.8% of its railway mileage, 7.1% of its bank resources, 8.1% of its life insurance, 8.9% of its telephones, and 6.3% of its motor vehicles."

The translation of this great economic wealth into material comfort for all the citizens of the State is one of the important problems for the future.

AGRICULTURE

FOR THOUSANDS OF YEARS human beings have cultivated the soil of Illinois, though the history of modern agriculture in the State extends over little more than a century. The ancient peoples who built the mounds probably were better farmers than the Indians whom the white men found, though the latter had extensive hand-tilled fields of corn, beans, squashes, and tobacco. The French who were the first white settlers added wheat and hops to the Indian crops, and used primitive wooden plows drawn by oxen. In this fashion they cultivated considerable areas in the vicinity of their towns, holding the cleared land—for the most part old Indian clearings—in common.

The first English-speaking settlers of the State followed the rivers and streams and utilized the clearings made by the Indians and the French. Very soon, however, they began the same slaughter of the hardwood forests along the rivers which had characterized the advance of settlement in Ohio, Indiana, and Kentucky. A generation later they swarmed out upon the prairies. In less than the span of an average lifetime, the whole area of the State was occupied and subdued. The log-cabin period of obvious pioneering was shorter in Illinois than in the neighboring states to the east and south, the transition to modern agriculture more rapid, and its expansion more violent.

The swiftness of the process of settlement and the subsequent agricultural development of the State was due most of all to the character of the land itself. It was stimulated, however, by certain factors which operated also in other states, but perhaps most clearly in Illinois.

First among these was the increasing liberality of the land policy during the period of settlement. The compromise which opened the Northwest Territory to settlement gave concessions to Revolutionary War soldiers, and opened the way to further inducements to settlers. Morris Birkbeck, who publicized Illinois effectively in the second decade of the nineteenth century, and organized the first agricultural society within its borders, was the foremost of many who proclaimed the richness of Illinois land and the ease of acquiring it. The Homestead Act of 1862, the final step in the liberalizing of the Federal land policy, was too late to benefit settlement in Illinois; but as late as the preceding decade, it was still possible to acquire rich land on

the Illinois prairie for as little as $1.25 an acre—and easy to pay for
it within a few years by the crops raised.

The liberality of the land policy was most evident in the treatment
of canals and railroads, which as parts of a developing transportation
system contributed to the second of the great factors in agricultural
growth. The first settlers depended on the rivers as means of transportation for their surplus. Peoria early assumed importance as a
shipping point for grain and cured meats, and other towns along the
Illinois, the Mississippi, and the smaller rivers of the State contributed
their flatboat loads of wheat, hams, whiskey, salted beef, beans, and
tobacco. As settlements pushed back from the rivers, these channels
became inadequate. The Illinois-Michigan Canal was heralded with
great enthusiasm, and encouraged with great gifts of public lands.
Hard on the heels of the canal diggers came the railroad builders, and
a network of rails was quickly laid over the State, to the immense
stimulation of farming. The canal and the railroads aided expansion
both directly and indirectly, for in order to sell land given them by
the State and to create business for themselves as carriers they resorted to extensive programs to attract and encourage settlers. The
railroad building of Illinois had been pretty well completed—so far
as agricultural interests were concerned—within the decade following
the Civil War. There was little further stimulating development of the
transportation system of the State until well into the present century,
when Illinois led the way in the Middle West in the creation of a system of hard-surfaced roads now totaling 13,000 miles. Almost all of
these roads are, from the farmer's point of view, "farm-to-market"
roads; and on them are transported, in thousands of trucks, more
than half of all the farm products marketed annually in the State.

Linked with the land policy and the growth of transportation facilities in stimulating agricultural expansion in Illinois, has been the
advance in farming machinery and farming methods. The preference
of the first settlers for the wooded areas along the river was not merely
a matter of habits acquired in wholly wooded areas, nor of the convenience of water, fuel, building material, and means of transportation. The first settlers would have had great difficulty in farming the
prairies had they tried. Their plows were not able to cope with the
sticky prairie sod. Intensive cultivation of the prairie waited on the
invention of the steel plow—an honor variously claimed for Harvey
H. May of Galesburg, for John Lane of Lockport, for Asahel Pierce,

and for John Deere, who certainly built a steel plow at Grand Detour in 1837, and built eight more the next year. As cultivated acreage increased, crops outran the scanty labor supply of the frontier State, and the demand for mechanical aids to harvesting became intense. In 1847 Cyrus Hall McCormick came to Chicago, and by 1856 was producing mechanical reapers at the rate of fifteen a day. The heavy enlistment from Illinois farms and rural towns during the Civil War greatly depleted the supply of farm labor, and combined with the high prices of war times to stimulate further the invention and use of machinery. The Illinois State Agricultural Society, formed in 1853, noted in the report of its Secretary in 1865: ".As men were withdrawn from the farms, improved implements . . . were introduced to supply their places." In 1862 this Society had conducted an extensive field trial of the new machines near Dixon, at which 22 different reapers and 13 mowers were demonstrated. Among the important Illinois manufacturers represented, in addition to McCormick, were John H. Manny of Rockford, H. H. Taylor of Freeport, George S. Curtis of Chicago, Thomas H. Medell of Ottawa. Barber, Hawley and Company of Pekin showed a heading machine called the "Haines Harvester," and W. W. Burson of Rockford demonstrated a pioneer grain binder. Barbed wire, a cheap and effective fence material, particularly adaptable to the prairie states, was also an Illinois invention.

The perfecting of farm machines and accessories went on in the decades after the Civil War, but it was not until the World War produced another critical coincidence of high prices and depleted labor supply that further revolutionary steps were taken toward mechanized farming. First of these was the wide adoption of the tractor, as a substitute for horse and mule power in the major farm operations, particularly in plowing and the cultivation of corn. High prices of the feed for horses helped to hasten this change, but the chief cause was the tractor's addition of many acres to the amount one man could farm—with perhaps a psychological element derived from the motor-mad spirit of the times. The extensive use of large tractors made possible the adoption of the mechanical corn-picker, the latest major innovation in Illinois farming methods.

From the beginning Illinois agriculture has been widely differentiated in different sections because of the variation in soil and the range of climate from north to south. In the extreme southern part of the State cotton has been grown extensively at different periods, and fruit and other specialized crops predominate today. In some sections, corn, other grains, and livestock are the chief interests on the majority of farms. A University of Illinois Experiment Station bulletin in 1934 established nine differentiated farming type areas in the State, each characterized by an easily recognizable type of farming.

Area 1, in the northeastern section, is primarily devoted to dairy and truck farming. Area 2, the northwestern, is a mixed livestock section, with much dairying. Area 3, the western, is devoted to livestock and grain, with hogs and beef cattle as the most important sources of income. Area 4, east central, is a rather sharply differentiated cash grain region. Two thirds of all farms in this area were primarily devoted to grain farming in the years covered by this study, and more than half of the income of these farmers was from cash sales of grain. Area 5, the west-central section, is devoted to general farming, with livestock ranking first in importance. The southwestern section, Area 6, is devoted to wheat growing, dairying, and poultry raising. Area 7, south central district, is a mixed farming area of small general farms with a variety of products. Area 8, southeastern, includes grain and livestock farms, but general farming predominates. Area 9 is the most important fruit and vegetable area. Characteristic of this section is the general farm from which a large part of the produce is fruit and vegetables.

Corn. The extent and productiveness of Illinois corn fields have been especially conspicuous in Illinois agriculture from the days of the first extensive settlements. Corn has been the major crop from the beginning. The varieties grown at first were those obtained from the Indians or brought from the New England states. Soon after the Civil War improved varieties of corn, especially adapted to Illinois soils and climate, were developed, most important of these being Reid's Yellow Dent. The result was a marked increase in the quantity and quality of the crop.

The area of corn in the State reached a peak of more than 10,500,-000 acres during the period 1900-05, but in the five years from 1925 to 1930, the average declined to 8,862,000 acres. The farm value of the Illinois corn crop usually amounts to more than one-half the value of all crops produced, and almost one-half of the cultivated acreage is planted to corn. Illinois is exceeded only by Iowa in corn production. In 1937 the corn production was 444,197,000 bushels.

Oats. Illinois is exceeded in oats production only by Iowa and Minnesota. The acreage of oats in-the State increased yearly until 1900, and since that time has remained around 4,000,000 acres. The eastern and northern parts of the State have the greatest acreage of oats. The 1937 yield was 162,208,000 bushels from 3,565,000 acres.

Wheat. Until the 1870's wheat was a major crop in Illinois; in 1860 the State led the Nation in wheat production. In 1880 the wheat acreage reached a peace-time peak of 3,000,000, but declined to 2,000,000 in 1890-1895. The demand created by the World War increased acreage to 4,000,000 in 1919, but subsequently it declined to 2,000,000. In 1937 Illinois ranked seventh among the States in wheat production, with a 45,724,000 bushel yield from 2,621,000 acres.

Soy Beans. Illinois threshes three times as many soy beans as any other State, and in 1937 about 57 per cent of the total national production of threshed soy beans was raised in Illinois. They are widely planted in many parts of the State as an emergency hay crop when clover does not survive the winter. Soy bean oil factories have been the principal market for the grain, though the amount of grain fed has increased during the last few years. Industrial uses of soy beans in automotive and other industries are fast increasing. Since soy beans grow well on soils too acid for alfalfa or clover, they are popular as hay and cash grain crops in the southern part of the State. In 1937 Illinois produced 22,800,000 bushels of soy beans.

Hay and Clover Seed. One-third of all the farm land in Illinois was sown in hay or pasture crops in 1929, and out of the 4,091,000 acres used for pasture crops, hay was harvested from 2,917,000 acres. The total area occupied by these two crops accounts for 27.7 per cent of all the tillable lands in the State, and in the production of tame hay Illinois ranks sixth among the states of the Union. In 1920 timothy and mixed hay made up 50 per cent of the total acreage of the State; clover hay made up 20 per cent, with the heaviest production in the western and northern sections of the State; and alfalfa hay 7 per cent, with a distribution similar to that of clover hay. From 2,487,000 acres of hay, 3,346,000 tons were cut in 1937, and 27,000 bushels of clover seed were produced on 30,000 acres.

Livestock. Since seed and pasture crops are grown on three-fourths of the farm lands of the State, and since a large part of this crop is fed on the farm, livestock holds an important place in the agriculture of Illinois. Sixty per cent of all agricultural sales in the State

AIR VIEW OF FARM

FARM YARD

HARROWING

BINDING

HOISTING HAY

COUNTRY AUCTION

HOGS

WHITE FACES

CULTIVATING SOY BEANS

ONE-MAN COMBINE HARVESTING WHEAT

COUNTRY SCHOOL

ROADSIDE STAND

APPLE GRADING

are derived from livestock or livestock products. Hog production alone accounts for one-fourth to one-fifth of the total cash farm income. In 1937 Illinois had 4,053,000 hogs, second only to Iowa. Excepting poultry and hogs, dairy cattle outnumber other livestock kept on Illinois farms. Beef cattle are most important in the area west of the Illinois River and north to the Wisconsin line. The number of cattle and calves in 1937 was 2,620,000, with a valuation of $107,479,000; this included 1,146,000 milk cows and heifers, valued at $63,030,000.

Exceeded only by Iowa and Minnesota, Illinois ranks third in the number of horses. The number of horses and mules, however, has been steadily declining; there was a drop from an average of 1,486,000 horses and mules during 1911-15 to 887,000 during 1926-30. In 1937 there were 732,000 horses and colts with a value of $77,592,000; and 108,000 mules and mule colts valued at $12,960,000.

The distribution of poultry in the State follows closely the distribution of milk cows. Flocks of 50 to 400 chickens are common in the corn belt. In 1935, 37,035,000 chickens were produced with a value of $24,072,750, while the egg production totaled 1,534,000,000 dozens, with a cash value of $27,995,500.

Yet farming is a way of life as well as a business, and statistics as to yields and income are an inadequate though important index to the character of rural life as a whole. Like all frontiersmen, Illinois farmers in the early days developed to a marked degree a social philosophy in which self-sufficiency under normal conditions was compensated by prompt and generous co-operation in emergencies.

To a considerable extent this spirit has survived the changes of a century and is still the basis of social attitudes in rural Illinois. Agricultural and horticultural societies existed as early as the founding of the State itself. Important co-operative action by farmers appeared in the 1870's when farmer-elected Representatives dominated the State legislature and obtained revision of freight rates. Today the farmers' appreciation of the advantage of working together is seen in the National Grange, which had its origin as the Patrons of Husbandry in the troubled years of the seventies; the Illinois State Farm Bureau; the Co-operative Livestock Producers Association; and numerous local co-operative elevators, creameries, and stores.

From the earliest day, rural churches and religious societies have made a profoundly important contribution to State culture. Circuit-riding preachers and missionaries were among the earliest settlers. In the decades before the Civil War, denominational academies and colleges sprang up all over the State, enriching the life of rural people as well as of those in the towns. Country churches played a large part in the maturing sense of community relationship and responsibility after the Civil War. In these days of hard roads and automobiles, rural churches have been threatened with extinction, and some have been abandoned; but a large number of rural churches in Illinois show marked vitality, and in some parts of the State the healthy condition of these churches reflects the permanence and value of a rural culture.

The State University of Illinois, through the Agricultural College and experimental station at Urbana, has played a very large part in the rural life of the State for half a century. The State University itself serves as a center from which many types of agricultural activity emanate. Over a period of years, the extension department has sponsored much education off the campus. One of its earliest steps was to place in each agricultural county a representative known as the "county agent," or "farm adviser," to provide first-hand contacts between the farmers and the college. In time this movement grew into what is now known as the American Farm Bureau Federation. This extension service encourages potential leadership in agriculture by boys and girls now on the farm. Into the cross-roads schoolhouse, the community church, the community house, go leaders who so encourage and inspire the youth that now it is not unusual for mother, daughter, father, and son to exhibit in their respective departments at local fairs, to attend shows together, and to enroll in the short courses given by the University.

Another important force in Illinois agriculture today is the State Department of Agriculture, which was made an executive branch of the State government in 1917 and is under the supervision of a Director of Agriculture, appointed by the Governor.

Agricultural magazines have been a powerful influence in the farm life of Illinois. The State is the home of the oldest farm magazine of the Middle West, the *Prairie Farmer*, founded in 1841 by John L. Wright and now published in Chicago. Another important Illinois magazine in this field was the *Breeder's Gazette*, established in 1881 by Alvin H. Sanders and enriched by the contributions of Joseph E. Wing.

Local agricultural fairs led to the establishment of the annual

State Fair, which has stimulated interest in the improvement of farm products and livestock. Chicago can boast of the most important stock show in the world, the annual International Livestock Exposition, held in its own huge building at the Stock Yards during the first days of December each year. For the coveted prizes in both the fat and purebred classes exhibitors come from all over the world. An impressive part of each year's exhibit is the large number of animals fattened and displayed by boys and girls who are members of the 4-H Clubs in Illinois and other states. These and other organizations are working for the rehabilitation and redirection of agriculture in Illinois and the Nation.

As one travels through the State today, he sees many farmhouses in need of paint and repairs, many evidences of soil depletion and erosion. These symptoms of a lack of health in rural society are in a part the results of the tremendous flow of wealth from farm to city in the last half century, as young workers reared and educated at the expense of rural districts have entered the shops and factories of the cities, as estates have been settled and money has followed the heirs to the cities, and as rents and interest have been paid by farmers to city people, directly or indirectly. This flow of wealth from country to city is an aspect of the general economy of the State, the importance of which has only lately been recognized. Recent improvements of rural roads and other comparable measures are as yet far from equalizing it, and in spite of the prosperity of many individual Illinois farmers, the difficulty of the general situation is sufficiently indicated by the low relative equity of the farmers in their land. The U. S. Census of Agriculture, as of Jan. 1, 1935, shows that of farm real estate in Illinois, valued at $2,205,899,576, more than half was operated by tenants. Less than one-third of the total—$637,387,867—was fully in the hands of owners.

Yet few in Illinois expect or believe that the rural society of the State will become wholly a tenant or a peasant society. Many in the cities as well as out of them, are resolved that this shall not come to pass. The most encouraging elements in the situation are such organizations as the 4-H Clubs, which are emphasizing to young farm people the values of farm life, and the steadfast example of the thousands of Illinois families who continue to find the good life on the farm.

LABOR

INDUSTRIALISM INVADED ILLINOIS in the 1870's when corn, wheat and pork were the predominating factors in the economic life of the state. Railroads marched into remote agrarian strongholds and, to the accompaniment of a heavy cannonade from iron and steel mills, the factory system took its place beside the plow and furrow. By 1890 Illinois was third among the States in manufacturing. In 1930, four decades later, the ranks of agricultural workers had dwindled to 351,977 or 23,430 less than in 1870, while the number of manufacturing workers had grown to 1,035,696, or 952,717 more than in 1870.

Like other States that underwent rapid industrialization, Illinois faced many problems in its period of transition from a purely agricultural state. The consequent gap between traditional procedure and actual circumstances fostered the growth of groups that created realistic means and blazed the way for the State's course of action. Labor unions, especially, performed that function and continue to perform that function in Illinois. The main body of law that specifically defines and protects the workingman's rights can invariably be traced to the "agitation" of organized labor. Thus labor unions in a great sense became the medium through which the individual workingman communicates his desires to his government.

In general, labor organization in Illinois dates from the 1850's. Among the thousands drawn west in the labor vacuum created by the construction of the Illinois and Michigan Canal (1836-1848) and the Illinois Central Railroad (1851-1855) were emigrants from European cities where workers' unions were common. When the canal and the railroad were completed, some laborers turned to homesteading, others were employed in newly opened coal mines, and others found jobs in urban industries. Among the latter were Germans who introduced principles of group action that had been evolved in their homeland. Clubs and societies were organized among the tailors, waggoners, and carpenters of Chicago. These so-called mechanics' unions participated in the successful movement to obtain free public schools (1855).

Shortly after the Civil War began, English miners from St. Clair County, Illinois, met in St. Louis and established the American Miners' Association "to mutually instruct and improve each other in knowledge, which is power, to study the laws of life, the relation of Labor to Capital, politics, municipal affairs, literature, science, or any other subject relating to the general welfare of our class." Branches of the A.M.A. were formed in Ohio, Indiana, and Maryland, but, owing to membership losses in the post-Civil War depression, the organization became inactive after 1868.

The decline in real wages incident to the Civil War contributed to the formation of a score of trade unions at Chicago in 1863. Strikes that year among the coal miners were answered with the La Salle Black Law which, as summarized by Earl R. Beckner in *A History of Illinois Labor Legislation,* "prohibited any person from preventing any other person from working at any lawful occupation on any terms he might see fit and from combining for the purpose of depriving the owner or possessor of property of its lawful use and management." During the two decades in which the Black Law was enforced, violaters were punished by fines and imprisonment. However, later attempts to revive the statute were frustrated by the courts.

The enaction of the La Salle Black Law spurred organized labor to consider political action. Formation of an independent party was forestalled, however, through appeasing measures, advanced in 1864 by the two major parties. In the following year the eight-hour day advocated by Ira Steward (1831-1883), a Boston mechanic, absorbed the workingman's attention. Eight-hour Leagues were organized throughout the State in 1866 to support those candidates for the General Assembly who endorsed the eight-hour working day. A sympathetic legislature was elected, and, in 1867, Illinois was the first State to declare that "eight hours of labor . . . shall constitute and be a legal day's work, where there is no special contract or agreement to the contrary."

This, however, was immediately offset by the development of a solid array of special contracts and agreements to the contrary. And, in a joint ultimatum employers warned they would discharge all employees unwilling to work ten hours a day. Defiant Chicago workers called a general strike on May 1st, the day on which the law was to be effective. Two days later, following disorders between strikers and non-strikers, Mayor John B. Rice of Chicago intimated that the La Salle Black Law would be invoked. Thus admonished, the strikers returned to work; the eight-hour law was hastily ushered into legislative limbo.

To complicate matters a practice destined to provoke a long time controversy was instituted in 1871 when arrangements were made to lease convict labor to private employers under the so-called "contract system." As a result of competition between the products of free and convict labor the wages of coopers, shoemakers, stonecutters, and, later, clothing and furniture workers were reduced. In 1884, for example, the work of shoemakers who received an average annual wage of $355 was duplicated by 766 convicts who were paid an average annual wage of $159. Although the contract system was countenanced by the General Assembly because of State revenues thus derived, many persons opposed it as a vicious mechanism for lowering the workingmen's standard of living.

The use of child labor also served to depress the wage level. Remedial legislation was opposed on the contention that initiative would be blighted; widows would be deprived of their sole support; and families would lose the added revenue required to augment the father's income. Notwithstanding these objections, the General Assembly in enactment of the general mining law of 1872 adopted a provision forbidding mine operators to employ children under 14 years of age; two years later the age limit was set at 12 years. An act of 1877 prohibited the employment of children under 14 years of age in "begging, peddling, acrobatics, gymnastics, singing [non-religious], playing musical instruments [non-religious], obscene exhibitions, or occupations that endangered life and health." Neither of the foregoing laws was thoroughly enforced.

In the hard times that followed the panic of 1873 labor unions, including the Sons of Vulcan (iron-puddlers) and the Knights of St. Crispin (shoemakers), underwent heavy membership losses. The subsequent upswing of business was marked by the formation of a socialist party in Chicago, four candidates of which were elected to the General Assembly (1878), and the renewal of labor organization on all fronts. Local assemblies of the Knights of Labor were chartered at Peoria, Chicago, and Springfield in 1877. In the same year delegates from 17 trade unions met at Chicago and formed a Trade Council which, renamed the Trade and Labor Assembly in 1879, was the forerunner of the Chicago Federation of Labor.

As production increased and profits mounted, workmen made determined efforts to raise wage scales that in many instances remained at depression levels. Strikes and lockouts occurred throughout the

State. In the nation-wide railroad strike of 1877, militiamen were detailed to Peoria, Chicago, Decatur, Galesburg, and East St. Louis. Shortly afterwards the General Assembly passed a law prohibiting any person or persons from impeding or obstructing the operation of railroads or any other business under penalty of fines and imprisonment.

A major objective of organized labor was attained in 1879 with the creation of the Illinois Bureau of Labor Statistics. Despite its limited authority and an insufficient appropriation, the bureau performed valuable services, furnishing data frequently used to substantiate abuses that otherwise might have been ascribed to mere chronic complaint on the part of workingmen. The General Assembly of 1879 also enacted the Armed Workmen Law, requiring all military organizations other than the State militia to be licensed by the governor. The law was meant to disband such groups in Chicago as the Labor Guards, the *Jaeger Verein,* the Bohemian Sharpshooters, and other military societies which bewildered workers had formed in reaction to overzealous police.

The first half of the decade 1880 saw renewed demands for the eight-hour day, the emergence of the Black International at Chicago, and the rapid growth of unions throughout the State. The Knights of Labor, its prestige enhanced by a series of successful railroad strikes, had enrolled an Illinois membership of 52,461 in 1886. The Federation of Organized Trades and Labor Unions, forerunner of the American Federation of Labor, experienced comparable gains. At the fourth convention of the federation, held in Chicago on May 7, 1884, the 25 delegates endorsed a general strike for the eight-hour day, beginning on May 1, 1886. Local assemblies of the Knights of Labor enthusiastically concurred in the movement, although T. V. Powderly, Grand Master Workman, sought to undermine their zeal by secretly disavowing the general strike.

The Black International, organized by anarchists at Pittsburgh in 1883 and immediately centralized at Chicago, injected martial temper into the Illinois labor movement. The conduct of the handful of converts won to its doctrine of violence and terrorism during the depression of 1884 was such as to support resentment aroused by the newspapers concerning the purposes of the International but the Central Labor Union, organized at Chicago in 1884 under the International's sponsorship, made rapid gains among butchers, carpenters, cigar makers, metal workers, cabinet workers, hodcarriers, and lumber-yard workers. Members of the *Lehr und Wehrverein,* which, though formed in 1875 had been unaffected by the Armed Workmen Act, allied themselves with the International and drilled secretly in preparation for open strife. Among the anarchists' propaganda agencies were the *Fackel,* the *Vorbote, The Alarm,* the *Budoucnost,* and the *Arbeiter-Zeitung.* The editor of *The Alarm,* the only English language paper in the group, was Albert Parsons, a veteran of the Confederate Army.

The militant Central Labor Union and the conservative Trade and Labor Assembly united their 40 affiliates behind the general strike for an eight-hour day. Alarmed employers met at Chicago in April and agreed, if necessary, to crush the eight-hour demand by hiring hordes of strikebreakers. About 100,000 workers, of whom 58,000 were in Chicago, struck on May 1. No immediate disorders occurred.

Two days after the strike began, August Spies, co-editor of the *Arbeiter-Zeitung,* spoke on the eight-hour day at a rally of striking lumber-shovers. The meeting was held near Cyrus H. McCormick's reaper works, where three months earlier 1,500 employees had been locked out and replaced with strikebreakers under the protection of 300 Pinkertons. As Spies neared the end of his address about 200 of his listeners moved off to the reaper works where they beset home-ward-bound strikebreakers. A detachment of police suddenly appeared at the scene of the disturbance. Curious to know what was happening, the remainder of Spies' audience started toward the reaper works. Evidently mistrusting the approaching crowd's intent, the police fired into its ranks, killing six and wounding others.

Infuriated by the tragedy Spies issued a call for a rally on the evening of May 4 "to denounce the latest atrocious act of the police." The meeting took place, not at the Haymarket, but two blocks away on Desplaines Street between Lake and Randolph Streets. The night was overcast and but 3,000 assembled; among them was the senior Carter Harrison, then mayor of Chicago. Referring to the dead of the previous day, Spies opened the meeting with a talk on "Justice"; Albert Parsons spoke next on the eight-hour day. As Samuel Fielden, popular labor orator, began the final address, rain fell and the crowd dwindled to about 500. Mayor Harrison, relieved by the moderate tone of the rally, strolled to the Desplaines Street police station and told Inspector John Bonfield that "nothing is likely to occur that will require interference." When the mayor departed, Bonfield marched

200 policemen to the gathering and ordered its dispersal. Fielden remonstrated: "But officer, this is a peaceable meeting." And, at that moment a dynamite bomb exploded, killing eight policemen and wounding about 65 others. The number of civilian dead was not determined, nor was the identity of the bomb-thrower ever learned.

Spies, Parsons, and Fielden were arrested, along with five other labor leaders, George Engel, Oscar Neebe, Michael Schwab, Louis Lingg, and Adolph Fischer. The legal philosophy that prevailed was expressed by State's Attorney Grinnell, who, in his concluding address to the jury on August 11, 1886, said: "These men have been selected, picked out by the grand jury and indicted because they were leaders. They are no more guilty than the thousands who follow them. . . ."

Seven were sentenced to death; the eighth, Oscar Neebe, received 15 years imprisonment. An appeal was made to the Illinois Supreme Court which, in a 273-page opinion, affirmed the lower court. On the eve of the execution Governor Oglesby commuted the sentences of Schwab and Fielden to life imprisonment; that same night Louis Lingg escaped the gallows by exploding a fusecap in his mouth. Spies, Engel, Parsons, and Fischer were hanged on November 11, 1887. Six years later Governor John P. Altgeld (1847-1902), aware that he was inviting political oblivion for himself, pardoned Neebe, Schwab, and Fielden. The *Pardon Message,* an 18,000-word document, charged gross irregularities in the trial procedure and scored the conduct of the presiding Judge, Joseph E. Gary.

In the wake of the Haymarket tragedy and the unfortunate association of anarchy and unionism thereby lodged in the public mind, organized labor's progress was halted and demands for an eight-hour day were temporarily relinquished. Branded as anarchistic on the basis of Fielden's membership in Local Assembly No. 1037, the Knights of Labor underwent decline. The major cause for the Knights' rapid extinction was, however, the skilled workers' increasing preference for trade separatism. Thus, while the power of the Knights' "one big union" waned between 1889-1894, membership in the craft unions of the Chicago Trade and Labor Assembly was more than tripled.

Genuine recognition of the rights and problems of labor occurred in the administration (1892-1896) of Governor Altgeld. A law enacted in 1893 forbade employers to prevent employees from forming, joining, and belonging to lawful labor unions; the Illinois Supreme Court, however, held this to be unconstitutional in 1900. A State

Board of Arbitration, empowered to investigate and make public its recommendations for settling industrial disputes, was established in 1895 and maintained thereafter until its duties were vested in the Industrial Commission (1917). In its 21 years of existence, the board arbitrated 138 strikes, 75 of which were successfully adjusted.

Although designed primarily to safeguard public health, the Sweatshop Law of 1893 was the first measure to attempt adequate regulation of child labor, the sweating system, and the working hours of women. Section 4 prohibited the employment of children under 14 years of age in factories, workshops, and manufacturing establishments; Section 5 limited women's working-day to eight hours and their work-week to 48 hours. Upon the removal of Mrs. Florence Kelley as chief factory inspector, following Governor Altgeld's failure to be re-elected in 1896, it was charged that Section 4 was flagrantly violated, especially by glass manufacturers. After a series of test cases sponsored by the Manufacturers' Protective Association (later the Illinois Manufacturers' Association) the Illinois Supreme Court found Section 5 to be unconstitutional on May 14, 1895.

Attacked by the press as an "Apologist for Murder" because of the pardons issued to Neebe, Schwab, and Fielden in the Haymarket riot case, Governor Altgeld had further vituperation heaped upon him as a result of the Pullman strike which began in May 1894 after a grievance committee of Pullman Palace Car Company employees interviewed Mr. George M. Pullman and asked restoration of wage cuts that ranged from 25 to 40 per cent. Several members of the committee were fired two days later and the Pullman employees, 3,700 of whom were members of the American Railway Union organized by Eugene Debs (1855-1926) in 1893, walked out. Following the Pullman Company's refusal to arbitrate the dispute, the American Railway Union instructed its 150,000 members to cease handling Pullman cars. The General Managers Association, a group of railroad executives controlling 40,000 miles of railroad, simultaneously came to the defense of the Pullman Company and ordered the dismissal of all employees who refused to switch Pullman cars. The strike spread from State to State, clogging the Nation's railway arteries.

Eager to preserve the railway union and aware that disorders would bring public disapproval, Debs cautioned the strikers to maintain peace, declaring that "A man who will destroy property and violate the law is an enemy and not a friend to the cause of labor." The Pullman Company and the General Managers Association, meanwhile, hired 2,000 strikebreakers, some of whom it was contended by strike leaders were instructed to destroy railroad property. "Outrages" began to echo in the press, but the strikers maintained their composure and, more important, a large share of public sympathy. According to Herbert Harris in his *American Labor,* strikebreakers attached mail cars to trains composed, otherwise, of Pullman cars; thus, when strikers stopped Pullmans they also stopped the United States mail.

Thus the Federal Government was involved, and the strike reached a swift denouement. About 3,400 men, later described by Police Superintendent Brennan of Chicago as "thugs, thieves, and ex-convicts," were sworn in as U. S. deputy marshals at the request of the General Managers Association. Clashes between strikers and deputies took place. On July 2, Judge Grosscup of the Federal Court at Chicago issued an injunction ordering Debs and the 150,000 members of the American Railway Union to cease and desist from interfering with the mails, interstate commerce, and the operation of railroad. Two days later President Cleveland detailed four companies of infantry to Chicago. Governor Altgeld immediately informed the President that "Local officials have been able to handle the situation. . . . The Federal Government has been applied to by men who had political and selfish motives 'for wanting to ignore the State government. . . . As Governor of Illinois, I protest against this, and ask an immediate withdrawal of Federal troops from active duty in this State."

Governor Altgeld's request was not heeded. On July 6 Federal troops attempted to start railroad traffic in Chicago but little progress was made. The strikers' morale suddenly snapped and frenzied rioting began. Enraged beyond control, they sought to block trains with their massed bodies; rails were torn up and hundreds of boxcars were fired. Governor Altgeld mobilized five regiments of militiamen, some of whom shot and killed seven strikers on July 7. On that day Eugene Debs was arrested and the strike was practically broken although it continued sporadically throughout the summer. The executives of the American Federation of Labor, in special session at Chicago, advised the strikers to return to work on July 12. Found guilty of violating Judge Grosscup's injunction, Debs was imprisoned at Woodstock, Illinois, for six months.

The Pullman strike and the Haymarket tragedy are notable, though sordid episodes in the history of American labor strife. Similar events of Chicago origin and nation-wide consequence include the formation of the Industrial Workers of the World in 1905 by Eugene Debs, Daniel De Leon, Vincent St. John, and "Big Bill" Haywood; the strike of 40,000 clothing workers in 1910, led by Sidney Hillman, a one-time resident of Jane Addams' Hull House; and the post-World War organization of steel-workers under the leadership of John Fitzpatrick and William Z. Foster. The latter movement culminated in the general steel strike of 1919, which was broken following issuance of a court injunction and the use of Federal troops. The clothing workers' strike, although lost, contributed to the development of the Amalgamated Clothing Workers of America, now one of the country's most powerful unions. The Industrial Workers of the World received a death blow at Chicago, the city of its birth, when, in 1919, more than a hundred of its leaders were tried before Federal Judge Kenesaw Mountain Landis and found guilty of criminal syndicalism.

The growth of the United Mine Workers of America in the Illinois coal fields has its roots in the successful coal strike of 1897, by which the miners won the eight-hour day, a 20 per cent increase in pay, abolishment of the company store, and recognition of their union. Repudiation of this agreement by the Chicago-Virden Coal Company in 1898 was the immediate cause of the so-called Virden riot (see Tour 17), a violent outbreak ending for the first time in victory for an A.F. of L. affiliate in a major strike. The Herrin massacre (see Herrin, Tour 4) occurred in the coal strike of 1922, which was ended by State and Federal troops. In 1929 the miners struck again and were again defeated. Three years later, a split in the ranks of the United Mine Workers of America led to the formation of the Progressive Miners of America. For several years thereafter the two unions fought bitterly throughout southern Illinois; later their feud was continued in the Federal courts. The Progressive Miners of America are now affiliated with the A.F. of L.

At the beginning of the present century, the numerical strength of miners and factory workers loomed large on the political horizon of Illinois. The Census of 1900 enumerated 450,614 agricultural workers and 405,319 miners and manufacturing workers. Rapid strides were made in labor legislation enacted in the succeeding thirty years. Following Altgeld's courageous precedent, subsequent governors, with the support of organized labor, attacked the evils of unbridled industrialism and sought to impart morality and fair play in dealings between employer and labor. In some instances the courts, meanwhile, retained outmoded viewpoints. A change in attitude may be dated from 1909, however, when following the decision of Judge Richard S. Tuthill of the Circuit Court of Cook County in which he ruled the recently enacted Ten-Hour Working Day Law for Women unconstitutional, he was vigorously berated on every side. "He permitted himself," said the Chicago *Evening Post,* on September 15, 1909, "to indulge in old-fashioned legal metaphysics that showed how unfamiliar he is with the evolution of social legislation. . . ."

Judge Tuthill's decision was reversed by the Illinois Supreme Court on April 12, 1910. The brief for the defense, a masterly work of some 600 pages, had been prepared by Louis D. Brandeis, later a United States Supreme Court Justice, who had volunteered his services to the working women of Illinois.

The State-Use Law of 1903 barred the products of convict labor from the open market, thereby silencing one of the workingman's chief complaints; night work by children under 16 years of age and the employment of children under 14 was also prohibited that year. An Occupational Disease Act was passed in 1911. The Illinois Mining Code, revised in 1879 and 1899, was given teeth in 1911 when inspectors were empowered to shut down the mines of operators who repeatedly failed to comply with safety regulations. The Workmen's Compensation Act became law in 1913. The use of injunctions to restrain peaceful picketing was prohibited in 1925. By an amendment of 1929, State certification was required for the employment of children over 14 and under 16 years of age. A minimum wage law for minors and women was enacted in 1933; three years later the working day of women, with the exception of nurses, cannery workers, and telephone and switchboard operators, was limited to eight hours.

The foregoing laws and various other statutes related to working conditions are enforced by the Illinois Department of Labor, established in 1917. The Illinois State Employment Service, instituted in 1899, and the Unemployment Compensation Act, passed in 1937, are administered in co-operation with the U. S. Employment Service and the Social Security Board.

Following its appearance in Illinois in 1935, the Committee for Industrial Organization succeeded in welding together vast groups of workers who had previously been unorganized. This was in part due to the aid lent by well-intrenched Illinois branches of the United

Mine Workers, the Amalgamated Clothing Workers, and the International Ladies' Garment Workers. The most formidable task undertaken by the Illinois unit of the C.I.O. was the drive to organize steel workers. Workers in three of the four largest plants in the Chicago area were organized in the spring of 1937. The subsequent C.I.O. victory was marred by the Memorial Day tragedy at the Republic Steel Company in which ten strikers were killed by the Chicago police. Although the police were exonerated by a coroner's jury, the La Follette Senate Civil Liberties Committee criticised their actions on the basis of newsreel films which had been taken of the riot.

The Illinois State Federation of Labor, grown strong and influential since its formation in 1884, has been unflagging in its efforts to improve the worker's circumstances. Among its major gains are the Child Labor Law of 1903, the State-Use Law of 1903, and the Workmen's Compensation Act of 1913. The Chicago Federation of Labor issues the weekly *Federation News* and maintains a full-time radio station, WCFL, and two short-wave stations. The Amalgamated Clothing Workers has operated a bank in Chicago since 1922; a related agency, the Amalgamated Securities Corporation, is maintained for small investors.

Illinois has made notable strides in settlement of its labor difficulties. Like other industrial centers it has had momentous struggles between the contending forces of employer and employee, although it can be truly said that in recent years, Illinois has had proportionately less labor strife than any other great industrial state of the Union. Meanwhile both capital and labor have advanced toward a new basis of understanding, and the outlook for the future is bright.

GOVERNMENT AND EDUCATION

In 1717 the Illinois country became a district of the French province of Louisiana, and was governed by a major commandant, who, besides exercising military powers, supervised fur trading and agriculture. Other district officers were a doctor, a notary, an interpreter, and a judge who administered the *coutume de Paris* or common law of Paris. Each village maintained a militia company, the captain of which was an agent of the district judge and the major commandant. Although there was no legal basis for local government, that function was admirably performed by *marguilliers* (church wardens), elected by the parishioners of the Catholic churches at Cahokia, Kaskaskia, and New Chartres. In addition to their accounting of church property, the *marguilliers* passed acts concerning the time of harvest, fence repair, and, in short, the general welfare of the village.

Under British rule the French system was discarded and the Illinois country was without civil government. Lieut. Col. John Wilkins, while commandant of the area, established a civil court in December 1768, but abolished it eighteen months later. In desperation the French colonists elected two delegates who went to New York in 1771 and petitioned General Gage, commander of the British troops in America, to organize a government. The general rejected this plea. The English parliament belatedly provided for the civil government of Illinois in the Quebec act of 1774, but plans to set up administrative machinery were disrupted by the Revolutionary War.

Following George Rogers Clark's campaign, the Illinois country was successively designated a county of Virginia (1778), part of the Northwest Territory (1787), part of the Indiana Territory (1800), a corporate territory (1809), and, finally, a member of the Union (1818). The first constitution was suitable for the rudimentary State, but its seams were soon split by social and economic expansion. Thus in 1848 a second constitution was adopted. It in turn became restrictive and a constitutional convention was called in 1862. The constitution it framed, however, was rejected by the voters of the State. Another convention met in December 1869, and, in sessions marked by acrimonious debate (43 delegates were Republicans, 44 Democrats), framed a new constitution which was ratified by the electorate on July 2, 1870.

The third and, to date, last Constitution of Illinois was designed to regulate a social order which, though it had railroads and developing factories, was predominantly agrarian. When industry outstripped agriculture in subsequent decades, the purposely rigid instrument was bound to a sphere of secondary importance. The existence of a dynamic society beyond the jurisdiction of static laws was recognized in 1893 when the State Senate passed a resolution declaring that "weighty social and economic issues persistently pressing upon us and demanding solution . . . cannot be squarely met and intelligently solved with the present constitution in the way."

Dissatisfaction with the document was not confined to the State Senate. A committee of the State Bar Association underscored its imperfections in 1902, particularly the amendment procedure which was said to be "entirely impracticable." The Chicago *Tribune* called for immediate action, asserting that the constitution "has outlived its usefulness. It is not the ark of the covenant. It has no sacred qualities. We may touch it without dropping dead." This exhortation received scant attention until 1918 when the electorate, in the general revaluation incident to the war, endorsed a constitutional convention by a vote of 562,012 to 162,206.

In a series of sessions beginning on January 6, 1920, the convention framed a constitution that abolished cumulative voting, granted Chicago a measure of home rule, authorized a general income tax on all net incomes, revised the procedure and organization of the judiciary, and allowed Cook County full representation in the House but limited its Senate membership to seventeen. The income tax provision militated against the proposed constitution, and, on December 12, 1922, it was crushed by a vote of 185,298 to 921,398. Twelve years later a proposal for a second constitutional convention was rejected.

Constitutional expansion through amendments, the seeming alternative, is a tedious process dependent on ponderous machinery. To emerge from the General Assembly, a proposed amendment must be approved by two-thirds of the elected members of that body. To be adopted as law, it must then receive the majority of all votes cast in a general election. The Gateway Amendment, which would liberalize the provision that prevents the General Assembly from proposing amendments to more than one article of the constitution in the same session or to the same article oftener than once in four years, has been defeated in four general elections. Of the seven amendments to the constitution, the last was made in 1908.

The elected executive officers of the State government are the governor, lieutenant governor, treasurer, attorney general, secretary of state, auditor of public accounts, and superintendent of public instruction. With the exception of the treasurer, who serves a two-year term, they hold office for four years. The governor has the power to call special sessions of the General Assembly, to grant pardons, commutations, and reprieves for all offenses against the State, and to veto legislation, including separate items or sections of appropriation bills.

Illinois was the first State to adopt a Civil Administrative Code. By means of this measure, enacted in 1917, more than a hundred State agencies were consolidated into nine departments (now ten) administered by directors whom the governor appoints with the consent of the Senate. The governor also appoints the members of certain boards and commissions beyond the scope of the code, notably the Illinois State Civil Service Commission, and, with the advice and consent of the Senate, he selects three judges who hear and determine claims against the State. The governor's annual salary is $12,000.

The General Assembly or Illinois legislature consists of a Senate and House of Representatives. Senators serve four years, representatives two years. The State is divided into 51 senatorial districts, the separate voters of which elect one senator and three representatives. Although the constitution provides for apportionments each decade to meet its further stipulation that districts shall contain "as nearly as practicable an equal number of inhabitants," both requirements have been disregarded since 1901 and inequalities in representation have developed. The 3,982,123 residents of Cook County, for example, elect 19 senators and 57 representatives; the remaining 3,648,531 residents of Illinois elect 32 senators and 96 representatives.

The General Assembly convenes for one regular session each biennium. The lieutenant governor presides over the Senate; the Speaker of the House is nominated at the caucus of the major party, and is formally chosen by vote of the House of Representatives. The members of both houses receive $5,000 for each two-year period. The powers of the legislature are distinct and more comprehensive than those of the judicial and executive branches. To override a veto, both houses must muster a two-thirds vote of their total membership.

Unique among the States is the Illinois system of cumulative voting, used to elect members of the lower house. The voter, as set forth in the constitution, may "cast as many votes for one candidate as there are candidates to be elected." Thus, instead of distributing his three votes among that many candidates, the Illinois voter can "plump" them all for one candidate. By virtue of concentrated "plumping" the minority party usually elects one representative in each district.

Cumulative voting was incorporated in the constitution as a result of the intense partisan spirit that prevailed in post-Civil War years. At that time delegations from southern Illinois were wholly Democratic, those from northern Illinois solidly Republican. Cumulative voting was adopted to provide representation for the minority in each section. It sometimes results, however, in a legislature so evenly balanced that neither party has the working majority required to accomplish its program.

The main branch of the State judiciary consists of the Supreme Court, the Apellate Courts, and the Circuit Courts. The Supreme Court is composed of seven judges, elected to serve nine years at an annual salary of $15,000. Each of the four Appellate Courts is administered by three judges appointed by the Supreme Court from judges of the Circuit Courts in their respective districts. Branch Appellate Courts may be created when a sufficient number of cases are pending. Excepting Cook County, the State is divided into 17 circuit court districts, each presided over by three judges elected to serve six years. At the base of the judicial pyramid are the county courts, one in each county; the probate courts, optional in counties whose population exceeds 70,000; and the various city courts, police magistrates, and justices of the peace.

The judicial system of Chicago and Cook County consists of a Circuit Court of 20 judges, a Superior Court of 28 judges, the Municipal Court of Chicago conducted by a chief justice and 36 associate justices, and the Cook County Probate Court presided over by one judge elected each four years. One of the circuit court judges presides over a juvenile court; a criminal court is maintained by judges of the circuit court and the superior court. The Municipal Court of Chicago, established in 1905, has been commended by students of jurisprudence for its swift precision. Among the 40 branches of this court are a renters' court, a boys' court, a woman's court, and a court of domestic relations.

County government originated in Illinois with Clark's conquest, which led the legislature of Virginia to organize the region as the "County of Illinois." In 1779 John Todd was appointed its "county lieutenant." The government that Todd established was short-lived. Later, when Virginia ceded the Illinois country to the Federal government, the area was administered by Gen. Arthur St. Clair who, in 1790, issued proclamations organizing the counties of Knox and St. Clair. These vast tracts were subsequently divided into 71 of the 102 counties in Illinois.

The present county structure of Illinois consists of 17 organized in the southern county manner, and 84 organized on the New England township basis. The two types generally indicate the region from whence the first settlers emigrated. Those organized in county fashion are each governed by three commissioners, one of whom is elected annually to serve on the county board for three years. Those organized on the township basis are governed by supervisors elected in the townships to serve on the county board for four years. Because of constitutional limitations on the taxing powers of counties, the General Assembly has created various units of government with functions that supplement those of the county board. Among these are districts for drainage, sanitation, fire protection, mosquito abatement, and forest preservation.

The organization of Cook County is based on the township plan and the county system. The eight townships within the limits of Chicago have been abolished. The outlying townships elect five commissioners, who, with ten commissioners from Chicago, constitute the county board. The president of the board receives $12,000 annually. His powers include the appointment of several important county officials, and the right to veto any appropriation in whole or in part. A four-fifths vote is required to over-ride his veto. The president and members of the board hold office for four years.

The Illinois Constitutions of 1818 and 1848 vested the General Assembly with the power to issue special charters for the organizations of towns and cities. This method was nullified by the constitution of 1870 and replaced, two years later, by a general cities and villages law under which all but a few communities were subsequently reincorporated. Villages are each governed by a board of six trustees, a president of the board, a clerk, and a police magistrate, all of whom are elected by popular vote. Cities are governed under the commission (74) and aldermanic (223) systems. The city manager plan may be

adopted by referendum in communities with less than 5,000 inhabitants; the more populous cities and villages may install a city manager
by ordinance.

Chicago is governed by a mayor, clerk, treasurer, and a city council
composed of 50 aldermen, one from each ward. These officials are
elected for four-year terms. The mayor's annual salary is $18,000.
With the advice and consent of the council, he chooses the members of
the Board of Education, the Chicago Park District, the Public Library
Board, and the trustees of the Municipal Tuberculosis Sanitarium. The
Sanitary District of Chicago, created in 1889, has jurisdiction over 440
square miles. Its executive board consists of nine trustees, three of
whom are elected every two years.

At the constitutional convention of 1870, Washburn of Jackson
County declared that "unless some compromise [is] agreed on, Chicago will soon wish to be outside of this state for want of a constitution
large enough to hold her." Washburn's warning went unheeded and
his prediction was fulfilled. By the end of the century Chicago was
clamoring for new powers to cope with its vast population and
tremendous industrial growth. The constitution was consequently
amended in 1904 so that the General Assembly could on occasion sub-
mit special legislation to the Chicago electorate. Save for this concession
the share of home rule desired by the city has been withheld. Indeed,
its representation in the general assembly, despite an enormous increase
in population, is the same as it was in 1901.

Chief among those who have sought to increase the autonomy of
Chicago is Professor Charles E. Merriam of the University of Chicago,
who, in *The Government of the Metropolitan Region of Chicago*
(1933), written in collaboration with Albert Lewpowsky and Spencer
D. Parratt, declares "That Chicago is neither bond nor free. If
Chicago were held as a ward, the principal would be responsible . . .
Or if the city were free, it could take care of itself. But as things
actually are, the city is crippled for lack of power to move, and, on
the other hand, the state will not assume the responsibility of guiding
the urban community."

As an alternative to the present diffusion of powers, it has been
suggested that Chicago be organized as a city-state, a status neither
impliedly nor specifically forbidden by the Federal Constitution. A
more feasible proposal is that which would combine the county government of Cook and the municipal government of Chicago, inasmuch

as 84 per cent of the county's taxable property and 85 per cent of its population are in Chicago. Consolidation of Chicago and Cook County was proposed in the 1899 session of the General Assembly, but the plan has never béen referred to the electorate.

The school system of Chicago is supervised by a Board of Education composed of eleven non-salaried members who serve for five years. They choose their own presiding officer and appoint an attorney, a business manager, and a superintendent of schools who holds office for four years. The city maintains a normal college, a parental school, a continuation school, a day school for adults, two schools for boys, two schools for crippled children, three junior colleges, four vocational and six pre-vocational schools, 37 high schools, and 332 elementary schools. The teaching staff numbers about 13,300; the average enrollment exceeds 500,000.

The educational system of Illinois has its historical basis in the Land Ordinance of 1785 and the Northwest Ordinance of 1787, the one of which reserved sections of public land for the maintenance of common schools, while the other declared that "schools and the means of education shall forever be encouraged." These conditions were accepted by Illinois upon its admission to Statehood, but implementation was delayed until the enactment of a law in 1825 that provided for the formation of school districts and the levying of a compulsory tax to support schools which were to be available to all white children between the ages of 6 and 21. The purpose of the law was all but abrogated four years later when, as a result of its condemnation as a "Yankee device," the compulsory taxation clause was revoked.

Throughout the 1830's and 40's Illinois had a rudimentary public school system, dependent on inconstant funds and the vicissitudes of local initiative. Its weaknesses extended beyond the usual log schoolhouse (of necessity, often little better than a barn) to include makeshift curricula, irregular school terms, and poorly paid teachers. Persons of means generally sent their children to private schools. Higher education was limited to denominational institutions, among which were the Rock Spring Seminary (1827), Lebanon Seminary (1828), Illinois College (1830), Jacksonville Female Academy (1835), and Knox Manual Labor College (1837). Rush Medical College, incorporated in 1837, graduated its first class of physicians in 1848.

A slight improvement was worked in 1845 by a legislative act that incorporated congressional townships as school townships, permitted school taxes to be levied in townships at the wish of the voters, and designated the secretary of state as the state superintendent of schools. Further amelioration came in 1854 when Governor Matteson (1808-1873) appointed Ninian W. Edwards as a special officer of public instruction. In the following year through the combined efforts of Edwards and various mechanics' unions, teachers' societies, library associations, and Sunday School organizations, the General Assembly enacted an enlarged version of the law of 1825. Its Magna Charta thus obtained, the public school system expanded steadily thereafter.

The office of Superintendent of Public Instruction was created by the Constitution of 1870. He supervises all elementary and secondary public schools, establishes educational standards, acts as chairman of the examining board that issues teachers' certificates, and serves as an *ex officio* board member of the State Teachers' Pension and Retirement Fund. His administrative staff, so to speak, is composed of the county superintendents of schools, one of whom is elected in each county. Their duties include the distribution of the funds derived from the county's school tax, and the issuance of advice to local school officials.

A survey of the Illinois public school system in 1936 enumerated 13,898 schools, 47,179 teachers and administrative officers, and 1,373,320 pupils. The system is financed by direct State and local taxes, the total of which amounted to 128 million dollars in 1938. The bulk of this sum (88.7 per cent) came from local taxes. Illinois ranks 35th among the States in the percentage of State funds allotted for education.

There are about 12,000 school districts in Illinois. These consist of special charter districts, township high school districts, community high school districts, community consolidated districts, districts controlled by school directors, and districts managed by boards of education. The excessive number of districts (Illinois has more than any other State), and the consequent inequality and duplication, has been challenged by the Illinois League of Women Voters and other responsible groups. A suggested remedy is the creation of a State Board of Education that would, with the State Superintendent of Public Instruction, assist the General Assembly in overhauling the district structure.

The State-supported facilities for higher education consist of the University of Illinois (1867), Illinois State Normal University (1857), Southern Illinois State Normal University (1874), Northern

Illinois State Teachers' College (1899), Eastern Illinois State Teachers' College (1899), and Western Illinois State Teachers' College (1900). The average enrollment of the University of Illinois exceeds 11,000; the average enrollment of the five normal schools is about 14,000. The latter are supervised by a Normal School Board, whose nine members are appointed by the governor. The University of Illinois is directed by nine trustees, elected by popular vote to serve six years.

The State university and colleges are supplemented by notable private institutions, of which there are 3 schools of drama and expression, 3 schools of physical education, 4 schools of kindergarten training, 5 schools of art, 6 technical schools, 8 schools of music, 14 junior colleges, and 34 colleges and universities. The foregoing are located mainly in central and northern Illinois, a circumstance that reflects settlement of those areas by Easterners and New Englanders.

Among the miscellaneous educational activities of the State are the Jacksonville schools for the blind and the deaf, and, in co-operation with the United States Office of Education, the maintenance of classes in vocational agriculture, home economics, trade and industry, which are attended annually by about 100,000 students. A law enacted in 1927 provides that classes for adult education may be established in any community, their expense to be defrayed by monies from the school fund. Although this phase of public instruction has advanced slowly, its eventual widespread adoption has been recently accelerated by the adult education program of the Works Progress Administration.

ARCHITECTURE

THE FACTORS in Illinois that produced a clear and distinct new stream of architectural innovations have never been fully explained. It was in Chicago, generally speaking, that the conflict was fought between dead classicism and direct, vigorous functionalism, but what placed the battlefield in the prairie metropolis is perhaps too complex a tangle of circumstances for unraveling. Both geography and the economics of the city played their part. Separated by a thousand miles from the seaboard cities and their traditions, and given a city that was building at an unprecedented rate, Illinois architects experienced a subtle freeing of spirit that within a generation was to permeate the whole of American building. That the innovations they brought forth are now widely accepted has tended to obscure the daring they required, but from the first problems of the skyscraper, through the " Chicago School" of Wright, and down to the ultimate solution of skyscraper design, the significance of Illinois architecture has been that it was creative rather than adaptive.

The early settlers of Illinois built hastily and with the materials at hand. Log cabins provided the first shelter. These the French *habitants* built with the logs vertical, as in Canada, while the English placed their logs horizontally, notching them at the corners and chinking the cracks with clay and straw. Throughout the early history of the State log structures served as houses, barns, schools, churches, and taverns. Fort Dearborn, a replica of which stands in Burnham Park in Chicago, is a good example of this type of construction. Its builder and first commander was Captain John Whistler, grandfather of the famous artist. Another excellent reconstruction from this period is New Salem (*see Tour* 21), where an entire log village has been faithfully rebuilt.

But log cabins were only a makeshift. As soon as the settlers could get sawed lumber they began to build frame houses. One of the first of the chain of innovations which came out of Illinois was developed in the construction of these dwellings, namely the "balloon" frame, so called because of its lightness and strength. Invented by George W. Snow of Chicago in 1832, this method, still in use, replaced heavy braced frames of large timbers by lighter studding closely spaced and held together by sheathing under the clapboards.

These frame houses were built in the Greek Revival style then popular in the East and South. This was an outgrowth of the Classical Revival style inspired by archeological research in Greece and by sympathy for the Greek revolt against the Turks in 1821. From the Atlantic seaboard, where it first flourished, it came to the Middle West through the books of designs that architect-carpenters brought with them. It reached its height in public buildings such as the old State Capitol in Springfield by Rague (still standing), which resembles a Greek temple with its pedimented Doric portico. The more pretentious houses also boasted porticos, but even the humblest showed a Greek character in their cornices, doorways, and molding profiles.

Most of Chicago before the Civil War followed the prevailing mode, judging from contemporary prints and from the Widow Clark house at 4526 S. Wabash Avenue, which survived the Great Fire. Records show that the first Chicago courthouse, built in 1830, had a Doric portico above a basement story of brick. The courthouse (once the State Capitol) at Vandalia is another interesting example of this style, and many fine Greek Revival houses still stand in Du Page county, the Lake towns north of Chicago, and throughout the Fox and Rock River valleys. A fine record of this work has been published by the Historic American Buildings Survey, compiled by Earl Reed.

In the settlements along the Mississippi are found building types brought up from New Orleans. Typical of these is the Pierre Menard house near Kaskaskia. It is low and broad, of one story with the attic lighted by dormers and the roof sweeping out over a columned porch the entire length of the house. The New Orleans influence persisted to a later date throughout the Mississippi valley, particularly in delicate cast-iron porches and balconies like those of the Vieux Carré. It mingled with the Greek Revival style in happy combinations in river towns such as Cairo, Shawneetown, and Alton; especially in the lead-mining boom town of Galena many charming examples of this union may be found.

Several Illinois towns were founded by groups directly from Europe or with a fresh European background, and these took on the character of their homelands. Thus the town of Highland testifies to the prevalent Swiss ancestry of its inhabitants. The Swedish religious community at Bishop Hill is noted for the Steeple Building, an example of the Scandinavian technique in molded stucco. The Dutch strain is represented by South Holland—the "New Holland" of Edna Ferber's *So Big*—with its "squat, many-windowed houses patterned after the north Holland houses of their European memories . . . . a geometric neatness like that of a toy house in a set of playthings." The considerable German contingent, particularly in the Amish settlements near Fairbury and Morton in Central Illinois, built along the same lines. Both at Nauvoo, the Mormon settlement, and at Albion, English immigrant craftsmen brought authentic Georgian architecture with them, and today among Albion's early structures there is the Public Library built in 1842 with a fine elliptical arched doorway.

Even during the Greek Revival period the Gothic style was often used for church buildings such as the Second Presbyterian Church in Chicago by James Renwick and Bishop Chase's Jubilee College near Peoria. But later it was developed into what was called "castellated" Gothic, exemplified by the Chicago Water Tower, and the Potter Palmer mansion by Cobb and Frost.

In the period of tremendous expansion following the Civil War and especially after the Great Fire in Chicago there evolved a restless striving for grandiose formality, expressing itself in distorted imitations of the styles then popular in Europe. Industrialists with newly amassed fortunes outdid each other in tasteless displays of extravagance that resulted in what some critics have called the "Parvenu period." Today all of this work is labeled Victorian, but in reality it falls into two main classes: the Gothic style mentioned previously and one similar to that used in France under Napoleon III. Hallmark of the latter was the mansard roof, such as may be seen on the old McCormick mansion in Chicago. This florid version of the late French Renaissance was especially popular for public buildings; the State Capitol at Springfield dates from this period, as do many county courthouses with their heavy brackets and cast-iron domes.

In the 1880's the influence of the Romanesque Revival was added to the prevailing styles, and gradually became the most important. Henry Hobson Richardson, the originator of this movement, designed in a rugged and powerful manner, as may be seen in his one surviving example in Chicago, the former Glessner House at 1800 Prairie Avenue. One of his pupils, John Root, almost caught the essence of his master's spirit in the Chicago Club at Michigan Avenue and Van Buren Street, but the great host of his imitators missed the spirit and merely copied the forms. Miles of crudely picturesque rock-faced façades with low arches and Romanesque carving testify to the popularity of the style, and when tall buildings began to be built they were with few exceptions in the Romanesque mode.

While the Romanesque was at its height the revolutionary story of the skyscraper began to unfold one of the most exciting chapters in the history of building. The skyscraper has come to be accepted as America's outstanding contribution to architecture, and contrary to popular belief, it was in Chicago, not New York, that the technique of the tall building was developed in the two decades after the great fire of 1871.

Directly after that disaster fireproofing became a public issue, leading to stricter building regulations and fire laws. In 1872 George H. Johnson built the first fireproof floor of hollow tile arches between wrought-iron beams in the Kendall building. The cast iron interior columns to which the beams were bolted were regarded as fireproof because they were incombustible, but experience showed they would yield in the heat of a fire with disastrous results. Columns subsequently were also fireproofed with hollow tile.

The Montauk Block built in 1882 by Burnham and Root was the first all-fireproof building and embodied new developments in foundation design as well. This was a serious problem because of the yielding bed of clay underlying Chicago. In a striking innovation Root hit upon the idea of embedding a crisscross of steel rails in concrete to make a rigid support distributing the load, and this system was used until the development of caissons in 1893 by Adler and Sullivan in the Stock Exchange building.

But the basis of skyscraper construction is the underlying steel frame—the "bones" which carry walls and floors, and which have given this method of building the name of "skeleton construction." At the beginning of this period cast-iron columns inside the building carried part of the floor loads, but the walls carried the rest. For low buildings this was practical, until the soaring prices of Chicago real-estate made tall buildings an economic necessity and the development of elevators made them a possibility. But in order to carry the weight of the additional upper stories the walls had to be so massive that they took too much space from the ground floor. This can be seen in the 16-story Monadnock building by Burnham and Root, the last example of this type of construction, where the ground floor walls are 6 feet thick. Its design, paradoxically, was admirably simple; ornamentation was renounced and a sharp flare at the roof replaced the traditional cornice.

The first step toward solving problems of height was the building of cast-iron columns into the walls to carry the ends of the floor beams. But in 1885 a more daring and satisfactory solution was achieved by William LeBaron Jenney in the 10-story Home Insurance building. There the outside columns of the two street-front walls and court carried not only the floor loads, but also the wall panels from floor to floor.

In 1887 Chicagoans were startled to see a building being built "from the top down." This structure, the Tacoma building by Holabird and Roche, developed the skeleton construction further, and the builders found it convenient to fill in the upper wall panels first. With the development of the Bessemer and open-hearth processes, rolled steel gradually displaced wrought and cast-iron, though the latter persisted until 1904. Elevators were rapidly improved and engineers soon solved the various other mechanical, electrical, and structural problems involved in a high building.

Culminating this period was the 22-story Masonic Temple (later renamed the Capitol Building) designed by Burnham and Root in 1892. Highest building in the world at that time, the throngs of visitors to the World's Fair the following year gasped at its awe-inspiring height.

The influence of the Columbian Exposition on both contemporary and subsequent building was tremendous. In one year it turned the tide of public taste away from the romanticism of the Romanesque revival to the white classicism of its Court of Honor, and sounded the death knell on the profuse elaborations of the Victorian Gothic and the Romanesque. That this transition, in itself, was salutary few have denied.

The exposition's architectural success was largely due to the genius of Daniel H. Burnham, Chief of Construction, who insisted that the work be distributed among several architects, and by the fire of his personality pushed the herculean task to completion. Though dominated by Burnham, a galaxy of genius in all the arts was assembled to contribute to the work. Architectural firms were chosen from the east and west about equally. Among the former group were McKim, Mead, and White, Richard M. Hunt, Peabody and Stearns, and Charles B. Atwood, whose lovely Palace of the Fine Arts has been preserved in Jackson Park. Chicago firms beside Burnham's (Root's death at the beginning of the work left him to carry on alone) included Solon H. Beman, Henry Ives Cobb, and Adler and Sullivan.

And yet there were other implications in the fair. An English architect, Banister Fletcher, expressed his disappointment in what he termed the fair's "collection of well-studied Parisian designs," and advised American architects to produce their own idiom. He wrote:

It is to be hoped that the imitative element will not cause these great Classic designs to be reproduced elsewhere for town halls, museums, and other buildings, but that American architects, already advancing so rapidly along certain new lines of departure will value the lessons they teach without copying their exact forms . . . it is certain that there is a great future for American architecture if only the architects will, as much as possible, express themselves in the language of their own times.

Unique among the exposition's buildings was Louis Sullivan's expression of exactly that credo. Sullivan bitterly condemned the architecture of the exposition as an unimaginative borrowing of dead forms to make a grandiose but fictitious stage set. However, he succeeded in obtaining a free hand in the design of his Transportation building, which stood out in warm colors amid the surrounding whiteness. In design it was fresh and original, though showing traces of Saracenic and Romanesque influence, and it was the one exposition building unanimously acclaimed by European critics, to whom the classic buildings were an old story.

At the time of the fair Adler and Sullivan were, next to Burnham and Root, the best-known architects in Chicago. Largest and most illustrious of their early commissions in Chicago was the Auditorium, built in 1887 and still used. This mammoth structure, combining a hotel, an office building, and a great opera house, was the boldest architectural conception of its time. Dankmar Adler successfully solved the difficult problems of structure and acoustics, while Sullivan was responsible for the design. On the exterior this showed a decided Romanesque influence, but in the interior Sullivan lavished his rich plastic ornament based on natural forms and imbued with a mystic symbolism.

Sullivan's chief contribution to architecture, however, lay in his all-embracing philosophy of design. To reduce it to the formula "form follows function" is to overlook the emotional and spiritual qualities which he held to be functions of a building as important as its utilitarian requirements. He pleaded for a living, democratic, American way of building, based on the laws of nature, and disregarding the forms of the past. His tall buildings before and after the fair embody these principles. First came the Wainwright building in St. Louis, then the Schiller Theater and the Stock Exchange in Chicago, all strongly vertical in feeling. The Carson Pirie Scott store, being lower, he treated in a horizontal pattern, with rich ornament around the show windows to enhance the displays.

Working in Sullivan's office up to the time of the fair was Frank Lloyd Wright, destined to become his disciple and chief exponent of the functionalist gospel. Wright first made his reputation in the residential field. Departing radically from previous styles, his houses first strike the eye by their strong horizontality achieved by low-pitched or flat roofs with widely projecting eaves and windows arranged in bands. By these devices Wright sought to make his houses appear to grow out of the prairie. Immediately the public spoke of his "prairie style," and evidently liked it, judging from the number of examples (and imitations) in Chicago's suburbs, especially Oak Park. But there was a principle underlying Wright's designs which proved to be more important than the more obvious external appearance. He objected to the current practice of regarding rooms as separate cubicles to be assembled into a house. His plans became more open; rooms had less definite limits; the outdoor and the indoor spaces "flowed" into each other in a more intimate way.

Wright experimented widely with new ideas in construction. Some he adapted from engineering practice for residential use, and some he himself developed. Many have since come into general use. Two examples are hollow walls of precast patterned concrete blocks, reinforced horizontally and vertically; and his method of supporting floors by the cantilever rather than the wall-to-wall principle.

For many years Sullivan and Wright were, in their own country, but voices in the wilderness. Sullivan's work dwindled to the vanishing point and Wright had to go to Germany to find a publisher for his books. Perhaps this was fortunate, for the drawings and text were hailed there with enthusiasm. His influence in Europe soon succeeded that of "L'Art Nouveau" (which many suspect was based on Sullivan's flowing ornament). Especially in Holland Wright's blocky forms were widely imitated.

Sullivan once exclaimed, "The damage wrought by the World's Fair will last for half a century if not longer." Certain it is that from then on architects turned to eclecticism, that is, a borrowing from the past, and the coincidence of eclecticism and the rise of the skyscraper could not have been more unfortunate. Of this paradox, Thomas Tallmadge has written:

There was one problem, however, that the lessons of the past could not help to solve, one Gordian knot that could not be untangled with Classic fingers, and that was the purely modern and American skyscraper. So we see a generation of distracted architects, vainly endeavoring to stretch the mantle of Phidias and the cape of Palladio to fit the gaunt form of the steel skeleton.

More than half of the tall buildings on Michigan Avenue facing Grant Park, built during the eclectic period, attempt to hide the fact that they are skyscrapers. Their skeletons are disguised, the vertical lines are broken at intervals, traditional cornices are used. And yet, in the early days of the skyscraper, Sullivan had indicated the ultimate solution. "What is the chief characteristic of the tall office building?" he asked. "And at once we answer, it is lofty . . . [which] must be in turn the dominant chord in the architect's expression of it, the true excitant of his imagination. It must be tall. The force and power of altitude must be in it . . . "

But in buildings where height did not intrude its troublesome head, the eclectic period fared well. A full account is impossible, and a few names, examples, and tendencies must suffice. The Boston firm of Shepley, Rutan, and Coolidge was responsible for two neoclassic buildings, the Art Institute and the Public Library, showing the influence of the fair. D. H. Burnham and Co. continued in importance, and after Burnham's death one of his designers, Pierce Anderson entered the partnership of Graham, Anderson, Probst, and White, whose best-known earlier work is the Wrigley Building, erected in 1921. Holabird and Roche were another important team, handling the Gothic vernacular in the University Club as skillfully as the Classic orders in the City and County building. Alfred S. Alschuler's outstanding building, the London Guarantee and Accident building, is decidedly classic, while Marshall and Fox's sumptuous hotels are French and Italian Renaissance.

The Gothic style's most accomplished exponents were Cram, Goodhue, and Ferguson in the East, who built the Fourth Presbyterian Church in Chicago. Gradually Goodhue developed a more personal and highly distinctive version of that style which reached a high point in the University of Chicago chapel. This was echoed to some extent by James Gamble Rogers in the Chicago campus of Northwestern University.

In 1922 a Gothic design by Raymond Hood and John Mead Howells of New York won the $50,000 first prize in the world-wide competition by the Chicago *Tribune* for its new building. Here, were it not for a strange quirk, the satisfactory solution of height was indicated; the shaft of the building was frankly vertical, and the Gothic detail and crown struck no incongruity and yet retained the note of traditionalism. The quirk was the second-prize design, the "building that was never built." The work of Eliel Saarinen of Finland, it followed no style but took Sullivan's creed and stated it more boldly than he had ever dreamed. It discarded the cornice, stripped the ornament away, and frankly exposed its structural plan, relying solely on set-back masses and strong vertical lines. The basic elements in the design were soon widely imitated, and the Gothic and Classic styles were completely discarded thereafter for skyscrapers.

Before long office-building architects began to work with even simpler surfaces and bold sculptural masses dictated by the set-back provisions of the zoning laws and the necessity of supplying light to as many offices as possible. Two firms led in designing a series of soaring, clean-limbed towers in this new style. One was Holabird and Root, beginning with 333 Michigan Avenue and ending with the Board of Trade and Palmolive buildings. The other was Graham, Anderson, Probst, and White with the Field building, Merchandise Mart, and Civic Opera.

While the new spirit revolutionized the design of skyscrapers, it was less felt in other fields. Residential architecture continued to be predominantly Colonial or Tudor in treatment, with occasional efforts in French or Mediterranean styles. However, there has been a strong tendency toward simplification, and now a few examples in the so-called International or functional style may be seen, harking back in principle to the teachings of Sullivan and Wright though in very different forms and not always with true understanding. Illinois architects have been experimenting also with methods of prefabricating houses for mass production.

Churches, schools, apartments, and public buildings have been for the most part eclectic, though many of their designers seem to have been obsessed with a desire to be startling and original. The net result is usually that ornament of the historic styles is replaced by "modernistic" ornament, but there is seldom a fresh approach to the problem as a whole. Fortunately signs of such an approach are here and there becoming evident.

The depression of 1929 put a stop to skyscraper building, but it saw another great Chicago fair, the Century of Progress Exposition of 1933-34. The need for economy dictated a light temporary form of construction and prevented lavishness in design. Intense colors were used instead, which produced an impressive effect until they weathered to pastel shades.

The architecture of this exposition was an attempt to crystallize the tendencies in modern design, but it was evident, as Frank Lloyd Wright was quick to point out, that to the designers "the modern" was just another style, and that the basic principles of functionalism were but half understood. He admitted, however, that the visitors might be impressed by the refreshing value of simplicity. This possibility and the experiments with new materials and methods of construction may prove to have been the main achievements of the fair architecturally.

But the architecture of a city applies to more than single buildings. The broader aspects of planning, namely the relation of buildings to each other and to the community, deserve mention. Until the World's Fair of 1893 few people were concerned with such questions. Cities "just grew" in chaotic haphazard patterns and the resulting evils of congestion and blight, as yet uncomplicated by the automobile, were taken for granted. But the openness and grandeur of the fair aroused some of Chicago's leaders to a desire for a greater civic orderliness, which Burnham stimulated by telling them how property values would begin to climb if the city were dressed up a bit. So from 1905 to 1908 the Commercial Club backed him while he worked on his famous city plan.

The plan was conceived along European lines with plazas, vistas, and radiating avenues. Some have called it "window dressing," but

Burnham studied the fundamental problems of Chicago: the need for better transportation both by highway and railway to relieve congestion, for better recreation facilities and parkways, and for the development of the lake shore waterfront into the show place of the country. All these things were incorporated in the plan. Though his proposals seemed at the time too visionary to admit of achievement, a host of them have been realized under the guidance of the Chicago Plan Commission, a perpetual advisory body appointed by the mayor. It seems probable that all of Chicago's future development will be around the basic scheme laid down by Burnham.

In recent years city dwellers have become more acutely conscious of another problem which the mushroom growth of the metropolis has produced. This concerns those once fashionable sections that have been left behind by the advancing waves of outward development. Early efforts by philanthropic agencies and limited-dividend groups to meet this problem proved inadequate. Recently, however, in answer to a growing demand for slum clearance and to demonstrate what can be done in group housing, the Public Works Administration has built several large open housing developments in run-down neighborhoods. It is possible that from a sociological point of view these projects may be more significant in the history of architecture than the towers of the Loop.

Now that America's population curve is flattening out, growth and development are likely to proceed more slowly. The problems of the future largely concern re-ordering the present situation, consolidating gains and rectifying mistakes. Builders of the future will perhaps find significance in the philosophy of Sullivan and in the oft-repeated exhortation of Daniel Burnham:

Make no little plans; they have no magic to stir men's blood and probably themselves will not be realized. Make big plans; aim high in hope and work, remembering that a noble and logical diagram once recorded will never die, but long after we are gone will be a living thing, asserting itself with growing intensity. Remember that our sons and grandsons are going to do things that would stagger us. Let your watchword be "order" and your beacon "beauty."

ART

SINCE ART HAS A BROAD as well as a narrow sense, the blacksmiths, carpenters, cabinetmakers, and housewives of early Illinois deserve to be called artists, for they designed and ornamented their products carefully. These folk arts and crafts reflect the cultural history of the State as enacted by the mixture of French, English, Scandinavian, Irish, and German pioneers who came to the fertile prairies, seeking new ways of life.

Of the French period, little remains. A few stone houses at Cahokia and Bourbonnais contain objects that recall the Jesuits and the *voyageurs,* but they are meager evidence of the former brilliant social life of these French towns. So completely did the English influence merge with the newly formed pioneer customs in Illinois that today, except at Albion, it is scarcely recognizable. This Anglo-Saxon pioneer-puritan union is perhaps best exemplified by the recently restored village of New Salem, significant in the early life of Abraham Lincoln. The Bishop Hill community, settled by religious dissenters from Sweden, has hoarded numerous examples of linen, furniture, and silverware representing its formative years. Nauvoo still shows traces in its furniture and tools of the Mormons; the Icarians, a French communistic group; and the Germans, who lived there in successive periods.

Pottery, a traditional form of folk art, was first made on an extensive scale at Galena; because of the proximity of the lead mines, the early jars, crocks, churns, and water pipes were lead-glazed. Stoneware was shaped at Anna, Peoria, Quincy, and Elizabeth, but these products were usually very crude.

Little else remains of pioneer folk-art in Illinois. Of the wooden figureheads that guided thousands of sailing ships through the Great Lakes, none has been preserved. The river-boat handicrafts that featured a great era in the history of the State are no longer to be seen. An occasional dusty cigar-store Indian and a few faded hitching-posts incite a passing glance, but other early examples of arts and crafts have been lost forever.

The history of Illinois art in the narrow and formal sense of painting and sculpture is largely confined to Chicago. In 1834 an assortment of French, English, and American engravings, and a number of still-life and landscape paintings were advertised in the Chicago *Democrat*. In 1840 an exhibition was held there of the work of Claude Marie Dubufe, the last of the David school, and another the following year by two English artists, Wilkins and Stevenson, who sought pupils and offered to paint miniatures and portraits.

Opportunities to make a living as a painter in Chicago were few at this time. Local fortunes, however, grew rapidly, and well-established merchants and manufacturers soon developed a prideful longing for the outward symbols of "culture." Art was hastily added to expensive garments, costly furniture, polished carriages, and imposing stone houses, as a symbol of elegant living. The first manifestation of this cultural urge was an intense interest in portraits, and into this picture stepped George Peter Alexander Healy (1813-1894), a Bostonian by birth. A great friend and disciple of Thomas Couture, French genre and historical painter, Healy introduced a certain French feeling into American portraiture. During the fifties and sixties Chicago was a dirty, mud-spattered, squalid town, yet Healy's portraits are of stately ladies and fashionably dressed gentlemen. Healy's art was conventional and highly competent; the section of society portrayed was self-conscious and, perhaps pardonably, a little vainglorious.

By the beginning of the Civil War, Chicago's patronage of art had expanded until it could boast an impressive number of well-attended and profitable exhibitions. Among local artists at this time were Leonard W. Volk, famous for his statues of Lincoln and Douglas, Howard Strong, George S. Collis, S. P. Tracy, and Daniel F. Bigelow.

The Chicago Art Union was formed in 1850, and in 1862 Volk and Jacob Antrobus opened an "Art Building" for exhibition purposes. Works of "local and foreign artists of repute" were displayed at fairs; art stores and picture-framing establishments were surprisingly numerous. The M. O'Brien and Son Gallery, founded in 1855, still supplies paintings and prints to Chicago's art collectors. A significant event in the art history of Illinois was the founding of the Chicago Academy of Design in 1866. This institution was incorporated in 1869 as a school of artists, and supported by tuition fees and membership dues.

Chicago, despite the devastating effects of the Great Fire in 1871, had become the art center of the Middle West. During the first half of the seventies, a severe financial depression slackened the progress of art in the State, but in 1879 the Chicago Academy of Fine Arts was founded as a school of art and design and "for the promotion and exhibition of objects of art, and the cultivation and extension of the arts of design by any appropriate means." The name of the institution was changed in 1882 to the Art Institute of Chicago, and in 1893 the present Institute building in Grant Park was completed.

In 1876 D. Knight Carter established the Vincennes Art Gallery, and in 1880 Frank C. Bromley, Henry Arthur Elkins, and other artists formed a syndicate to make it a permanent institution for the exhibition and sale of works of art. The syndicate erected luxurious buildings to house the collections and serve as a temporary home for artists. The gallery was an important influence in the art life of Chicago, but it has long since disappeared.

Oscar Wilde came to Chicago in 1882 as a lecturer on art. Many of his eastern audiences had jeered and hooted, but in Chicago only the newspapers were outwardly rude. While the people were vexed at his disrespectful allusions to the medieval architecture of the water tower and his scoffing at the American worship of European culture, some noted that he spoke well of the possibilities of American art, and were impressed by his advice that "You can make as good a design out of an American turkey as a Japanese out of his native stork."

Wilde visited Chicago in an era when all manner of knick-knacks covered the walls, mantels, and tables of luxurious houses, and the popular conception of decoration had become a matter of filling the available space in rooms with useless and frequently absurd trifles. Most well-bred young ladies painted flowers, birds, cats, and landscapes, not only on canvas, but on almost any substance that would take oil pigments. The fine homes in Illinois were museums of the curious, and the more they overflowed with "artistic" pictures, screens, medallions, plaques, marble statuary, stuffed birds, figurines, and vases, the more "tasteful" they were considered. A decade passed before a reaction occurred—a reaction that was influenced more than was generally realized by the critical comments of the long-haired velvet-clad Oscar Wilde.

The promoters of the World's Columbian Exposition of 1893, ignoring Wilde's advice to develop American art along indigenous patterns and to break with the traditions of Europe, procured what were considered the best of the classical masterpieces and housed them in the imposing Palace of Fine Arts of classic design. Innovation and experiment were felt to be unsafe and too iconoclastic for a fair that was to show the world how Chicago had overcome provincialism and how its citizens bowed to none in the appreciation of art. The neoclassical influence exerted by the exposition was felt for more than a generation. However unfortunate this may have been for the progress of indigenous art, it did establish an art-consciousness that was tempered by a high standard of appreciation.

Between 1893 and 1895 the Central Art Association sent exhibits of works by native painters throughout Illinois and the neighboring States. In 1896 the first annual exhibition of the Society of Western Artists was held, followed shortly by the organization of the present Chicago Society of Artists, composed of a union of several art groups. The year 1899 saw the formation of a Municipal Art League, and within a few years Chicago had a city art commission.

Lorado Taft (1860-1937) injected a fresh stream into the art current of Chicago, with his native and transitional sculptures. His great life-burdened figures, sorrowful and yet serene, cry out for comparison with Rodin. The similarity is not one of texture only, but of spirit and philosophy, a new-world outlook realizing both the tragedy and the dignity of life. Taft's classes in the Art Institute attracted many young men and women of Illinois, some of whom have since become well-known sculptors.

The School of the Art Institute of Chicago has contributed to art and artists of Illinois the stimulating influence of other celebrated artist-teachers. Just before the turn of the century its faculty included such men as Frank Duvenek and William Chase. Charles Francis Browne, Hermon Mac Neil and Albert Herter conducted classes at that time. The Spanish painter, Joaquin Sorolla came to the school early in the second decade of the present century. Indeed, through the years the faculty has included exponents of a wide variety of "schools." The student has had his choice of such outstanding masters as George Bellows, Randall Davys, Nicholas Roerich, Boris Anisfeld, and Francis Chapin. Albin Polasek in sculpture, and Louis Ritman and Edmund Giesbert in painting have been popular teachers for a number of years.

Until 1922 the director of the Institute was also director of the school but in that year Raymond T. Ensign became dean of the school. He was succeeded by Charles Fabens Kelley in 1927, and in 1938 Norman Rice succeeded to the deanship.

The permanent collections of the museum have consistently grown. At first limited only to plaster casts and a few nondescript originals, the Institute today owns one of the most notable collections of historic and modern paintings and exhibits a sequence of nineteenth century French painting unequalled elsewhere. Strong departments of Prints and Drawings, Oriental Arts, Decorative Arts, etc., have been created including many periods and civilizations. William M. R. French, Newton H. Carpenter, George W. Eggers contributed to the early development of both museum and school. In 1921, Robert B. Harshe was made director and under his brilliant leadership the Art Institute became one of the world's great institutions. Mr. Harshe's taste, knowledge and showmanship culminated in two great exhibitions of art for the Century of Progress Expositions in 1933 and 1934. After his death in 1938, the functions of directorship were divided. Mr. Daniel Catton Rich, who had assisted Mr. Harshe, became Director of Fine Arts and Mr. Charles H. Burkholder became Director of Finance and Operation.

Since the first American show in 1889 the exhibition of regional and contemporary art has become an increasingly important function of the Art Institute. The first exhibition of Artists of Chicago and Vicinity was held in 1897 and the first International Water Color Show, which is predominantly American, in 1922. More and more the Institute has been bringing the contemporary art of America and the world to Chicago. As a consequence the tendency among students to regard a period of study in Paris and New York as an indispensable part of a complete art education has been steadily diminishing.

Nevertheless, during the early 1900's, the attitude of most Chicagoans towards art was somewhat smug and complacent. Satisfaction with traditional forms lapsed into a kind of stagnation—a lethargy derived from too long familiarity with the great masters. So it was with the force of a bombshell explosion that the famous New York "Armory Show" descended upon Chicago in 1913. Here were the works of Picasso, Braque, Matisse, Kandinsky, and many others of the Expressionist and Cubist schools in all of their strange grotesqueness of color and form. This was the advent of modernism in Chicago, and its coming was heralded by jests and hoots, not only from the citizenry, but from established art critics. Only a few persons had the temerity to praise the vigor in these works, and to predict that they would have a salutary influence upon popular painting.

In 1915 Carl N. Werntz and Carl M. Newman staged in Chicago the "First Annual Exhibition of Independent Artists," a display which clearly demonstrated the effects of the Armory Show. In the same year the Cordon Club was organized by a group of artistic and professional women, and now holds continuous exhibitions of Chicago artists, and presents an annual show. The Arts Club of Chicago was founded in 1916; it had aided materially in bringing the best in modern art to Chicago, and has greatly encouraged artistic enterprise in the city.

During the great artistic and literary renaissance of the present century, numerous groups which fostered the creation and appreciation of art assembled in Chicago. Among these were the Renaissance Society, the Society of Artists and Sculptors, the Chicago No-Jury Society, the Chicago Professional School of Art, the National Academy of Design; and lesser but vigorous groups including the Neo-Arlimusc Art Club, the Dill Pickle Club, and the Seven Arts Club. Many new galleries and art stores that contributed to the creative ferment of the city sprang into life during this period, perhaps the most important of which is the Vanderpoel Art Gallery in Beverly Hills.

Instead of giving impetus to artistic production, the unprecedented prosperity between 1926 and 1929 caused many Chicago artists to turn to commercial work or enter the business world. The sale of a picture or two during those years was insufficient to combat the cost of living, and even lowly quarters in a run-down neighborhood were beyond the reach of many painters and sculptors. The ensuing depression brought even greater hardship. Artistic enterprise was almost at a standstill from 1929 to 1933.

Departing radically in architecture from the Columbian Exposition, the Century of Progress Exposition of 1933-34 accepted modernism in art. Sharing the spotlight with the old masters in the Art Institute were exhibits liberally sprinkled with works from the current "schools," and the fine photographic displays at the fair-grounds showed a strong preoccupation with experimental lay-out and design. American art was stressed in the exhibit of 1934, featuring Stuart, Trumbull, Copley, Melchers, Henri, Homer, Blakelock, Mary Cassatt, Inness, Whistler, Sargent, Weir, Eakins, Ryder, Bellows, and Luks.

The final influence of the fair on Illinois art is as yet undetermined. It brought to the Middle West the "International Style" in architecture and industrial arts. Some critics believe that it has had a deleterious effect upon interior decoration. Certain it is that the geometrical forms outlined in black and chromium have pervaded the shops, restaurants, saloons, night-clubs, beauty parlors, and dress shops in Chicago. But perhaps it is a mistake to attribute too much of this modernistic trend to the fair, for the already flourishing movement towards a revolution in painting and interior decoration was only boldly and uncompromisingly realized in the exhibition halls of the Midway.

Illinois' artists of the present period, unlike so many of her writers, have not migrated to the East or to Europe in search of more congenial atmosphere or better markets for their work. Although Chicago serves as an art center for the vast hinterland of surrounding States, the rest of Illinois has furnished its share of creative activity. As early as the eighties, a union of art clubs for the study and appreciation of art was organized in the central section of the State. Only a few of the smaller towns held exhibitions at this time, but artists and critics journeyed to Springfield, Decatur, Champaign, Lincoln, and other cities to read essays on art and literature before large and enthusiastic audiences. The All-Illinois Society of the Fine Arts, organized in 1926, has permanent galleries in the Stevens Hotel in Chicago, and holds annual shows in the towns and cities of the Middle West.

The public library at Bloomington exhibits the works of Illinois painters continuously from October to May. In 1919 the Decatur Art Institute was organized for the promotion of the fine and applied arts. Both the State House and the Centennial Building at Springfield house large collections of paintings. The Laura Davidson Sears Academy at Elgin and the Art Association of Peoria possess interesting canvases. Jacksonville, Aurora, and Rockford are supplied with exhibitions from the Grand Central Galleries of New York, the Federation of Arts in Washington, the All-Illinois Society of the Fine Arts, and other organizations.

Since its creation in 1933, the Federal Art Project has had the dual effect of encouraging impoverished artists and creating popular interest in painting and sculpture. By paying all non-labor costs of production, tax-supported institutions of Illinois can obtain the work done by the Project. This arrangement has enabled many public schools, colleges, and charitable institutions to own works of art which would otherwise have been beyond their means. The Federal art program for Illinois fosters regional art in its best and broadest sense. Under its influence, native artists have been led, as never before, to assert the peculiar qualities of their surroundings and to interpret their lives and experiences in thousands of easel paintings, murals, graphic works, sculpture models, dioramas, posters, and plates for the index of American Design. Among the most notable contributions of the Federal Art Project in Illinois are the frescoes, murals, and sculptures of the University of Illinois Medical Unit and the paintings selected by Mayor Edward J. Kelly for the Chicago city hall.

Present-day art in Illinois is absorbing the two main streams of American art; realism and modernism. It is becoming more socially conscious; it is becoming more experimental. In these two tendencies lies its future.

LITERATURE

To the left are beautiful lands. In various Places, the stream is Divided by Islands. Its Width is very unequal; sometimes it is three-quarters of a league, and sometimes it narrows to three arpents. We gently followed its course, which runs towards the south and south-east. Here we saw that its aspect was completely changed. There are hardly any woods or mountains; the Islands are more beautiful, and are Covered with finer trees. We saw only deer and cattle, bustards, and Swans without wings, because they drop their plumage in This country.

THE LITERARY RECORD of Illinois opens with these words, in which Father Marquette recorded his first impressions of the Illinois country, as he and Louis Jolliet with their companions journeyed southward down the Mississippi in 1673. It is one of the anomalies of American literary scholarship that the rich and dignified *Journal* of Father Marquette, and the beautiful letter in which an associate told of his death, are still unmentioned in histories of American literature, while materials from the Atlantic seaboard are exclusively and expansively treated.

But few of the French wrote as well as Marquette, and the long period of the three-sided conflict among French, Indians and English for possession of the Illinois country left little of literary importance. One narrative, however, deserves mention—George Rogers Clark's account of his expedition to oust the British from Vincennes and Kaskaskia in 1789. Clark had small respect for grammar and his orthography is amazing, but the directness and economy of his narrative give memorable expression to one of the noteworthy exploits of the history of the region.

In 1830 a young lawyer named James Hall had the temerity to establish a literary magazine in Vandalia, then the capital of Illinois, a prairie town containing perhaps 1,000 people. The *Illinois Monthly Magazine* was larger and relatively more expensive than any literary magazine published in Illinois today. Much of the material in the magazine was written by Hall himself, and these contributions included at least one story of permanent interest and delight, "The Philadelphia Dun"—an account of the initiation of a young Philadelphia lawyer into a frontier community. The *Illinois Monthly*

Magazine was suspended in 1832 and Hall moved to Cincinnati, where he engaged in other literary ventures. Among his writings on the West are a number of sketches and stories dealing with Illinois in a somewhat florid and formal literary fashion.

Chicago was an infant city of only 8,000 people when its first literary magazine was founded by a boy of 20. *The Gem of the Prairie* (1844) reflects the youthfulness of its editor, Kiler Kent Jones, and was much less substantial, judged by the literary standards of the times, than the *Illinois Monthly Magazine.* Its pages are enlivened, however, by a gossip column, signed "Man About Town," and by a series of entertaining sketches entitled *Slices of Chicago Life.*

In contrast to these self-conscious literary endeavors are the origin and growth of the talent through which Illinois gave world literature her first great gift, and still her greatest. It has been almost universally recognized that Abraham Lincoln was a great writer as well as a great man—that his letters and speeches, quite definitely unapproached in their kind in America, represent a literary achievement of the highest order. It has not been realized so generally that whatever nourished and sustained Lincoln, as a writer and as a man, he found in Illinois. He drew into himself and gave forth in supreme expression all that was best in a frontier society too often assumed to have been merely crude and ugly.

While Lincoln was being considered for the vice-presidency, in 1856, an old preacher sat at a table in his home at Pleasant Plains, Illinois, writing the story of his life. Peter Cartwright had been a Methodist circuit rider in Illinois for more than thirty years. He had traveled thousands of miles on horseback or on foot, baptized thousands of converts, organized scores of church societies. His autobiography, a frank and detailed account of day-by-day activities, with shrewd observation of the people he encountered and unstinting revelation of himself, is one of the minor classics of the American frontier. It belongs on the same shelf with David Crockett's autobiography and Timothy Flint's *Recollections of the Last Ten Years.*

After the Civil War Francis Fisher Browne, one of the most influential and least appreciated literary figures, appeared on the Illinois scene. In 1871 he founded the *Lakeside Monthly,* a periodical devoted to the cause of literary progress in the Middle West. Publishing stories and poetry as well as articles, this magazine replaced the less definitely literary *Western Monthly,* founded in 1869. After weathering the Chicago fire and other hazards through the efforts of its editor, the *Lakeside Monthly* suspended publication in 1874. In 1880 it was succeeded by a new magazine which Browne named the *Dial*. Throughout his editorship of more than thirty years the *Dial* maintained a high standard of thoughtful and informed critical comment on literature and literary affairs. The *Dial* left Browne relatively little time for the few books which bear his name. A characteristic achievement was his courageous and far-sighted defense of Governor Altgeld.

Perhaps as a result of the faithful endeavors of Browne as well as by the impact of other forces, Chicago and Illinois experienced in the last years of the nineteenth century an outburst of activity which justifies the description of this interval as the first major period of literary production in the State. During these and later years, many natives of Illinois won literary fame for work done elsewhere, dealing with other materials than those of Illinois life. Such writers will not be considered here.

Of all the writers in this Illinois movement of the 1890's, Hamlin Garland was the most conspicuous. Wisconsin born, product of Iowa farms and country schools and rural academy, Garland had gone to Boston and then returned to his early habitat to write the realistic stories of Middle Western rural life in *Main Traveled Roads*. Early in the 1890's he came to Chicago and continued his reporting of the Middle Western scene in *Jason Edwards,* a political novel, as well as in occasional short stories, and in the convention-challenging *Rose of Dutchers Coolly*. Born in Illinois, but never essentially orientated in the Middle West, was Garland's contemporary and friend, Henry B. Fuller, whose first novel, *The Chevalier of Pensieri-Vani,* a memorial of lyrical journeyings among the gardens and relics of the Old World, awed his western readers and threatened to brand him a condescending purist. But that he could deal objectively and uncompromisingly with Middle Western Life, Fuller soon proved by publication of another novel, *The Cliff Dwellers,* bristling with ironic and penetrating comments on the artistic Chicago of the 1890's. In the same vein are his *Under the Skylights, With the Procession,* and *On the Stairs.* In *Gardens of this World,* written shortly before his death in 1929, he resumed much of his early, nostalgic manner.

In this Illinois literary movement in the 1890's, Chicago publishing houses and newspapers played an important part. From 1880 until

1892 the *Dial* was owned and published by A. C. McClurg and Co.; after the purchase of the journal by Browne in 1892 it continued to be published by them. The firm of Stone and Kimball published for a time the *Chap-Book*, a Midwestern *Savoy*, or *Yellow Book*, later merged with the *Dial*. A new standard for literary columnists was introduced by the appearance of Eugene Field's "Sharps and Flats" column in the Chicago *Daily News*. Field's successive volumes of poems and essays won for him a loyal audience of discerning readers. A columnist of a different sort was Finley Peter Dunne, whose creation of Mr. Dooley in the pages of the Chicago *Times-Herald* added a new name to the brief and honorable list of homely commentators on the American scene. Also truly of America and of Chicago are George Ade's *Fables in Slang,* which present among other characters, the notable creations of Doc Horne and Pink Marsh.

Following the high standard set by Field, Dunne, and Ade, the Chicago *Tribune,* oldest newspaper of the city, brought zest to its pages through the wit of Bert Leston Taylor, a poet of genuine distinction who, as editor of *"A Line o'Type or Two,"* became the most beloved columnist of his day. Another *Tribune* columnist, albeit on the sports page, was Ring Lardner, who later attained a position of first rank among present day short-story writers. Also a noteworthy feature of the *Tribune* was the dramatic criticism of James O'Donnell Bennett and Percy Hammond. Literary supplements of Chicago newspapers have justified their existence under the editorship of authors and critics who gave them a weight and influence felt throughout the State and the entire Middle West. Identified with the old Chicago *Evening Post* were Francis Hackett, Henry B. Fuller, Floyd Dell, George Cram Cook, Lucian Cary, and Llewellyn Jones. Harry Hansen and Burton Rascoe made their reputations as literary critics in the 1920's while editing the book pages of the *Daily News* and the *Tribune*.

In things materialistic Chicago had attained, during the 1880's, a metropolitan prominence to be reckoned with throughout the State and the Nation. For many, in the city of over 500,000 population, business success had been swift and flattering. Economic security more assured, it was a time when the explicitly superior attitude of the East, with its cultural advantages and traditions, became for the clamorous market-metropolis a spiritual challenge. But in its struggle for material achievement, Chicago had not only become the central market for grosser commodities, it had also become the center of a vast book purchasing and book reading section of the country. By the beginning of the following decade there were rumors of a Middle Western school of literature; within the next few years Chicago was both censured and praised for its alleged pretensions of fostering the emerging school.

In the East criticism was carping, even vindictive; in England, sympathetic, encouraging, prophetic. In the opinion of the New York *Daily Tribune* there was something "funny" in Chicago's "getting up a school of literature over night," and in its "trying to establish a 'literary school' out of crudity and the froth and fury of the last new things, no matter what they may be . . . . Chicago needs a stiffening of her intellectual backbone." In 1896, Stanley Waterloo who in 1870-71 had been a reporter on Chicago newspapers, published a London edition of his *An Odd Situation*. For this novel Sir Walter Besant, the prominent English author, prepared a preface in which he declared ". . . . there has sprung up in the city of Chicago a new literary center and a new center of publishing. There exists in this city of a million inhabitants, which sixty years ago was but a kind of barbican, or advanced post against the Red Indian, a company of novelists, poets, and essayists, who are united, if not by associations and clubs, at least by an earnest resolution to cultivate letters. It may be objected that this is nothing but a provincial coterie . . . and that . . . it will presently disappear. I do not think that this will be the fate of the Chicago movement, for several reasons. First, the city is so huge that there must be continually born in it, or brought into it from the country, persons with the literary gift; next, there exists in the Northwest States an unbounded admiration for the literary calling—a feeling which ought by itself to raise up aspirants . . . ." In alluding to the *Dial,* he characterized it as "a journal of literary criticism, sober, conscientious and scholarly, from every point of view unsurpassed by any other literary journal in America or England." Further, he took account of Chicago's "daily papers by the dozens, which afford the aspirant the means of a livelihood while he is working at his real profession."

That Sir Walter Besant's reflections were indeed prophetic is borne out by the literary development that followed in less than twenty-five years. Perhaps by more than a coincidence, it was also in

London that Chicago came finally to be hailed as "the literary capital of the United States." H. L. Mencken's famous article, *The Literary Capital of the United States,* appeared in the English periodical, *Nation,* in 1920. He wrote:

It is, indeed, amazing how steadily a Chicago influence shows itself when the literary ancestry and training of present-day American writers are investigated. The brand of the sugar-cured ham seems to be upon all of them. With two exceptions, there is not a single novelist of the younger generation—that is, a serious novelist deserving a civilized reader's notice—who has not sprung from the Middle Empire that has Chicago for its capital . . . . All the rest have come from the Chicago palatinate: Dreiser, Anderson, Miss Cather, Mrs. Watts, Tarkington, Wilson, Herrick, Patterson, even Churchill. It was Chicago that produced Henry B. Fuller, the packer of the modern American novel. It was Chicago that developed Frank Norris, its first practitioner of genius. And it was Chicago that produced Dreiser, undoubtedly the greatest artist of them all . . . The new poetry movement is thoroughly Chicagoan ; the majority of its chief poets are from the Middle West ; *Poetry,* the organ of the movement, is published in Chicago. So with the little theatre movement. Long before it was heard of in New York, it was firmly on its legs in Chicago. And to support these various reforms and revolts, some of them already of great influence, others abortive and quickly forgotten, there is in Chicago a body of critical opinion that is unsurpassed for discretion and intelligence in America.

At the turn of the century, Frank Norris had returned to Chicago from his adopted California for the scenes and the actual writing of his most successful novel, *The Pit.* Theodore Dreiser, who had driven a laundry wagon and done his first reporting in Chicago, used Chicago settings and characters for his first two novels, *Sister Carrie* and *Jennie Gerhardt,* and returned to the same city for the settings and characters of *The Titan* and for parts of *The Genius.* Moreover, Chicago remained a symbol and a point of reference to Dreiser ; his work was profoundly affected by the coarse vitality of the city as he knew it in a brief but crucial period of his life.

More significantly identified with Chicago in his life, though not in his writings, was William Vaughn Moody, one of the greatest American poets of his time. Moody taught at the University of Chicago, and wrote during the period of his teaching most of his best work, including the great *Ode in a Time of Hesitation,* in which he denounced the American attitude in the Spanish-American War.

If, during the 1890's and even in the first decade of the new century, the literary impulse of the region was sporadic, with little to bring it to a focus, a definite force for direction was supplied by the establishment in 1912 of a magazine which was, and is still, unique in America—*Poetry: A Magazine of Verse,* founded by Harriet Monroe. With the inception of this magazine began a second important period in the literary history of Illinois. Miss Monroe was a fine poet in her own right. She had been chosen to write and recite a dedicatory ode for the Columbian Exposition in 1893. She published several volumes of verse. In 1917, co-editor with Alice Corbin Henderson, she published *The New Poetry, An Anthology of Twentieth Century Verse.* Revised and enlarged in 1923, and again in 1932, this anthology has done much to promote recognition of the younger poets of America.

Miss Monroe's greatest achievement, however, was *Poetry,* which she maintained by funds largely obtained through her personal efforts and which she edited with consistent courage and acumen. On the eve of *Poetry's* twenty-fourth anniversary, Miss Monroe wrote the editorial which was destined to be her last. "We shall remind people once more, as we did with quite a din twenty-four years ago, of the meager and lackadaisical support given to the finest of the fine arts, the art most powerful for making the story of our deeds immortal by telling it to the next age," the editorial declared. "We shall insist again, as many times in our history, that great poetry is not a creation *in vacuo,* but antiphonal between a poet and his audience, that it is not enough to sing—the song must be heard. . . . What a printing may mean to a struggling poet in the way of spiritual food and refreshment, hundreds of letters in our files would show. It is that realization which has impelled me to continue the effort to finance and run *Poetry* all these years." Miss Monroe died in South America in 1936. Her autobiography, published in 1938, is a rich record of literary activities in Chicago and elsewhere during a long and fruitful life.

Early in its career the magazine established several annual prizes for poets. The Helen Haire Levinson prize betokens *Poetry's* highest honor, and is not restricted to work published in its own pages. Among recipients of the Levinson prize, first awarded in 1914, are eight poets of Illinois: Carl Sandburg, Vachel Lindsay, Edgar Lee Masters, Cloyd Head, Lew Sarett, Margery Allen Seiffert, Mark Turbyfill, Maurice Lesemann. Lew Sarett has been a member of the faculty of Northwestern University for many years, following an earlier connection with the University of Illinois. Sympathetic insight and rich personal observation are evident in his poems, particularly in those dealing with nature and with Indian life. Glenn Ward Dresbach, a native of Lanark, Illinois, and long a resident of Chicago, is another poet of importance whose best work has consisted of the poetic recording of the experience of nature. Eunice Tietjens and Alice Corbin Henderson, both editorially associated with the magazine *Poetry,* have written about Chicago, but have 'found the material for their best work elsewhere—Mrs. Tietjens in China, Mrs. Henderson in New Mexico. Margery Allen Seiffert of Moline is a poet whose work is noteworthy for its variety and versatility, though she too has found relatively infrequent inspiration in the Illinois scene.

Of the Illinois poets who emerged into positions of recognized importance during the decade following the establishment of *Poetry,* one was not introduced by that magazine, though much of his later work appeared in its pages. This was Edgar Lee Masters, whose Illinois epitaphs in the *Spoon River Anthology* were first published in William Marion Reedy's *Mirror* in St. Louis. *Spoon River Anthology* was a landmark in regional literature. It revealed to writers the possibilities of a new approach to life in the Middle Western small town, and impressed publishers by becoming a best seller. The bitterness of some of the poems and the sensationalism of others have blinded some readers to the compensating beauty and soundness of such epitaphs as those of Lucinda Matlock, Emily Sparks, and Ann Rutledge. Masters, a Chicago lawyer, who had besieged the citadel of literary fame persistently and ineffectually before the success of *Spoon River Anthology,* has continued to write voluminously. His successive volumes of poetry since 1915, though containing some fine work, have never approached the stature of *Spoon River Anthology.* In recent years he has written chiefly in prose. In *Skeeters Kirby* he gave a memorable portrayal of an Illinois boyhood. One of his later contributions is a biography of his fellow poet of Illinois, Vachel Lindsay.

Masters rightly describes the life of Lindsay as tragic. After a childhood dominated by religious bigotry, Lindsay early achieved control of singularly fresh and vital rhythms. When those rhythms are applied to the expression of profound experience, as in "Abraham Lincoln Walks at Midnight" and "Sleep softly, eagle forgotten" (his tribute to Altgeld), the result is poetry of a very high order. Even when, as in such longer poems as "The Congo" and "The Chinese

Nightingale," the emotional content is slight and the intellectual element even slighter, the involved rhythms and colorful language are a perpetual delight. Lindsay was as erratic and impractical as poets are traditionally expected to be. He sought to add to the inadequate income from his writing by lecturing and teaching, but was unsuccessful in establishing himself in a workable relationship to his environment —though he steadfastly refused to remain long away from his native Illinois. He died penniless at Springfield in 1931, by his own hand.

Of the many writers whose early or first work was presented in the pages of *Poetry*, none was more truly a product of Illinois than Carl Sandburg, and none has made a greater contribution to Illinois literature. Born at Galesburg in 1878, Sandburg attended Lombard College, served as an organizer for the Socialist Labor party, and did newspaper work in various towns. His volume, *Chicago Poems* (1915), with its famous dedicatory "Chicago," was the first successful attempt to capture in verse the quality of life in a modern industrial metropolis. This work was followed by *Cornhuskers* (1918) in which Sandburg recorded with the same decisiveness and power the rural life he knew in Illinois. To the study of Abraham Lincoln and the interpretation of his life to the modern world, Sandburg has devoted the energies of his later years. His biography of Lincoln, begun in 1916 with *Abraham Lincoln: The Prairie Years,* is a unique achievement. Scholarly and authentic, it is at the same time a work of art, a genuine recreation in moving and appropriate words of the intimate experience of its subject. But Sandburg's preoccupation with the Lincoln biography has not interrupted his output of poetry. *The People, Yes,* his most recent volume of verse, shows a maturing and sharpening of his powers as a poet, and particularly a clarification of his faith in democracy. Though he now lives on a farm in Michigan, Sandburg is near enough to Chicago to play a part in the cultural life of the State. He is clearly Illinois' most distinguished man of letters in our time.

Sandburg was one of a brilliant group of writers who were employed by the Chicago *Daily News* under the editorship of Henry Justin Smith, himself a novelist, short-story writer, and historian of importance. Among the other members of this group were Ben Hecht, Harry Hansen, Keith Preston, and Howard Vincent O'Brien.

Sherwood Anderson was a resident of Chicago during this important period, and *A Story Teller's Story* contains an interesting reflection of his experience in the city. Much of his important work was written in Chicago; the city is expressed in *Marching Men,* and both city and country in *Mid-American Chants.* Another Anderson—Margaret —established the *Little Review* in Chicago in 1914, but after three years of weathering "no compromise with the public taste," took it to New York and later to Paris. While in Chicago the "no compromise" policy of the magazine was once expressed by an issue of blank pages, intended as a reproach to readers and writers alike; and later in New York by publication of the first chapters of the epoch-making *Ulysses* by James Joyce. Throughout its stormy career the pages of the *Little Review* were open to the most radical literary experiments that were being made in both America and Europe.

The colleges and universities of Illinois have shared in the creation of its literature both directly and indirectly. At the University of Chicago, Robert Morss Lovett was closely associated with the brilliant achievement of successive groups of students, among them Elizabeth Madox Roberts and Glenway Westcott. In its brief history Mundelein College has made an exceptional record in the encouragement and development of young writers. Among the careers of creative writers with academic connections, that of Robert Herrick is noteworthy. As the author of such novels as *Together* and *Homely Lilla* he became a nationally important figure in the field of fiction.

Since 1930 the creative literature of Illinois has entered a new phase, too little matured as yet to allow of definite evaluation, in which the novel seems to be the most favored medium. Magazines and publishing houses have played a relatively unimportant part in this most modern phase of Illinois' literary development. *Poetry,* edited by Morton Dauen Zabel after the death of Harriet Monroe, and more recently by George Dillon, whose volume of poems, *The Flowering Stone* won for him the Pulitzer Award, has continued to print poetry of real worth and has made a valuable contribution to criticism as well. *The Midland,* founded and edited in Iowa by John T. Frederick, and moved to Chicago in 1930, introduced Albert Halper and many other important writers, and printed James T. Farrell's first story in America, before its suspension in 1933. Short-lived magazines, chiefly radical in emphasis, such as *Left,* published at Moline, and *Direction,* published at Peoria, have contained some valuable work.

It is natural that this recent Illinois literature should reflect the thought and feeling of the times. Significantly a part of the main current of critical realism in American fiction at the present time are the novels and stories of such writers as James T. Farrell, Albert Halper, and Louis Zara. Farrell in *Studs Lonigan* and *A World I Never Made,* Halper in *The Foundry* and *The Chute,* and Zara in *Give Us This Day* have written about industrial Chicago from within in terms frequently denounced as too harshly critical, but marked by sincerity and power. There is indication that Illinois literature in its current phase will continue to express the preoccupation of writers with the social and economic problems reflected in the unhappiness and insecurity of many of the people of the State, in both urban and rural areas. Among examples of this preoccupation are Nelson Algren's *Somebody in Boots,* Stuart Engstrand's *The Invaders,* and Tom Tippett's *Horseshoe Bottoms.*

In fields other than the narrowly creative, members of the faculties of Illinois colleges and universities have made extremely important contributions to the literature of the State throughout the period since the nineties. The writings of such men as William Rainey Harper, James A. Breasted, Thorstein Veblen, and Richard G. Moulton did much to build the world-wide reputation of the University of Chicago. Stuart P. Sherman was a professor of English at the University of Illinois when his *On Contemporary Literature* and *The Genius of America* established him as one of the major critics of the country. Among the many contemporary Illinois teachers whose writings have possessed general literary importance are Charles E. Merriam, Harold W. Gosnell, T. V. Smith, Ferdinand Schevill, Bruce Weirick, and Baker Brownell. No record of Illinois literature would be complete without reference to Jane Addams' *Twenty Years at Hull House* and Clarence Darrow's *The Story of My Life.* Particularly valuable is the interpretation of their city by Lloyd Lewis and Henry Justin Smith in *Chicago: A History of Her Reputation.* At an opposite pole of interest are Donald Culross Peattie's studies of nature, particularly the fine *An Almanac for Moderns.* Excellent contributions in the field of biography and history are Paul Angle's *Here I Have Lived;* E. E. Calkins' *They Broke the Prairie;* and Harry Barnard's *Eagle Forgotten.*

Contemporary Illinois novelists are recognizing more and more the value of the State's historical background as subject matter for their work. Margaret Ayer Barnes introduced a noteworthy study of Chicago's development on one social level in her *Years of Grace;* in *Bright Land* and *The Smiths* Janet Ayer Fairbank used rich material from nineteenth-century Galena and Chicago. Harold Sinclair in *A Prairie Town,* Donald Culross Peattie in *A Prairie Grove,* and Gareta Busey in *The Windbreak* have given appreciative treatments of the early days in other cities and in a rural community.

But notwithstanding the creative exploration of Illinois' present and past in recent years, great areas of Illinois life still lie untouched by writers. The builders of canals and railways, the workers in mines and mills, the members of varied ethnic groups in cities and rural districts, all are waiting for novelists, poets, and dramatists whose vision and power are worthy of their material. It would be wrong to think of Illinois literature of today in any terms save those of opportunity, of praise, and of continued growth.

THEATER

THE THEATER was always an afterthought on the hard fighting frontier and the hardships of pioneer life in sparsely settled Illinois gave little encouragement either to the itinerant actor or the aspiring amateur. Perhaps the first amateur Illinois theatricals were presented in Springfield, on December 3, 1836, as announced in the *Sangamon Journal.*

One of the first professional actors to visit Illinois was Joseph Jefferson III, later beloved throughout the country in the rôle of Rip Van Winkle. "In the year 1838," wrote Jefferson in his *Autobiography,* "the new town of Chicago had just turned from an Indian village into a thriving little place, and my uncle had written to my father urging him to join in the management of the new theater which was then being built there." The Jefferson family traveled part of the journey through the Erie Canal on a packet-boat. Her name, as Jefferson noted, was the *Pioneer,* and it was most appropriate, for the Jeffersons were among the first players to migrate to the West.

Traveling in open wagons over the rough prairie roads, the venturesome players made their way to Galena, Illinois. Turning south again, they were forced to give their entertainment at Pekin in a porkhouse, accompanied by the squealing of pigs. In Springfield, where they arrived for a season during a session of the Legislature, they were disheartened by a prohibitive license fee demanded by the town.

In the midst of our trouble, [wrote Jefferson] a young lawyer called on the managers. He had heard of the injustice, and offered, if they would place the matter in his hands, to have the license taken off, declaring that he only wished to see fair play, and he would accept no fee whether he failed or succeeded. The case was brought up before the council. The young lawyer began his harangue. He handled the subject with tact, skill, and humor, tracing the history of the drama from the time when Thespis acted in a cart to the stage of today. He illustrated his speech with a number of anecdotes, and kept the council in a roar of laughter; his good-humor prevailed, and the exorbitant tax was taken off. This young lawyer was very popular in Springfield, and was honored and beloved by all who knew him. . . . He now lies buried near Springfield, under a monument commemorating his greatness and his virtues—and his name was Abraham Lincoln!

How other early Illinois actors, managers, and their creditors fared during their barnstorming is vividly described by the celebrated actor-manager, Sol Smith, in his delightfully rambling *Theatrical Management*. Smith, who began his long career in the Middle West in 1824, has this to say of Manager Potter, a male counterpart of the present-day sob-sister. Smith wrote:

It ought to be mentioned that P. has a weakness in a nerve of one of his eyes, from which a *tear* is always involuntarily starting. It is supposed that in this weakness consists Manager Potter's strength, no person having yet been found who could resist it. There is not a town on any of the Western waters from Fever River in Illinois, to the Bay of Mobile in Alabama, but has experienced him.

One of Potter's devices for moving from place to place without money was to "abolish the salary-list." Another was to borrow additional sums from his creditors when they came to collect what was already overdue. Enroute to Chicago in 1844, Potter and his company came to St. Louis on a steamboat from Memphis. The captain swore that no baggage would be taken off until the company paid its passage. But before nightfall Potter had the whole company and its properties on board a Galena boat; the captain who had brought him to St. Louis had a note for his debt, and had been persuaded to endorse other notes to pay not only the passage of the company to Galena, but across the country to Chicago!

During the frontier period productions in the larger cities differed little from those presented in the villages. To a measurable extent this· was due to the "star" system then practiced, for an actor's appearances were limited only by his opportunity to travel. Many of the famous actors of the day were well known in the remote parts of the State.

Essentially, however, the theater of the pioneer period was an imported product. The classics of the English stage, particularly the plays of Shakespeare, together with contemporary English offerings, held the boards. In his *Literature of the Middle Western Frontier*, R. L. Rusk, who has examined over seven thousand newspaper advertisements appearing between 1799 and 1840, states that of the Shakespearean plays, *Richard III., Othello,* and *Hamlet* were the most popular. American dramatists, according to Professor Rusk, were given slight attention, with the single exception of John Howard Payne, whose greatest successes were *Therese, Charles the Second, 'Twas I, or the Truth a Lie,* and *Clari.* Plays on Western life were not popular; *The Lion of the West,* and *The Kentuckian, or a Trip to New York,* for instance, had together less than a dozen performances. At first, melodrama, farce, opera, and pantomime proved slightly more popular than forms of greater literary pretension: later, they were much preferred to comedies, tragedies, and historical plays. But productions of any sort were events, and audiences usually represented a well-defined cross-section of frontier society.

During the pioneer period Chicago became the center of the theater in Illinois. In 1837, the year the city was incorporated, the first actors who came to Chicago, unlike the Jeffersons in Springfield, found no champion who "only wished to see fair play," and were restrained from performing because they could not afford to buy a license. Before long, however, two managers purchased a license, improvised a theater in the dining room of the Sauganash Hotel, and drew a crowd with their production of Kotzebue's *The Stranger.* The success of the venture encouraged the opening of a new theater in the upper story of a wooden building, and it was probably in this more pretentious house that the Jeffersons appeared in 1839.

A vivid description of one of Chicago's earliest playhouses appears in Jefferson's *Autobiography.*

And now for the theater, newly painted canvas, tack-hammer at work on stuffed seats in the dress circle, planing-boards in the pit, new drop-curtain let down for inspection, "beautiful"—a medallion of Shakespeare, suffering from a severe pain in his stomach, over the center, with "One touch of nature makes the whole world kin" written under him, and a large, painted, brick-red drapery looped up by Justice, with sword and scales, showing an arena with a large number of gladiators hacking away at one another in the distance, to a delighted Roman public. . . . There were two private boxes with little white-and-gold balustrades and turkey-red curtains, over one box a portrait of Beethoven and over the other a portrait of Handel. . . . The dome was pale blue, with pink-and-white clouds, on which reposed four ungraceful ballet girls representing the seasons, and apparently dropping flowers, snow, and grapes into the pit. . . . With what delight the actors looked forward to the opening of a new theater in a new town, where dramatic entertainments were still unknown—repairing their wardrobes, studying their new parts, and speculating on the laurels that were to be won!

In 1847 John Rice, soon to become Mayor of Chicago, erected the first theater building in the city on Randolph Street near Dearborn.

Theaters continued to multiply until ten or more were playing at a time. Players who appeared in Illinois found enthusiastic audiences. Such famous actors as Edwin Forrest, the Jeffersons, John Drew, Charlotte Cushman, the Booths, Charles Kean, and others were often seen.

Stock companies, composed of permanent groups, which often gained prestige by the presence of an actor of distinction, flourished during this period. Visiting stars from Europe and the East, traveling alone, found ensembles ready to support them in stock performances. Comedy, burlesque, light and grand opera, minstrel shows, and pantomimes were presented. Foreign groups, particularly the Germans, were active, and supported three companies in Chicago.

John H. McVicker, a popular actor of the day, built the third theater in Chicago in 1857, at a cost of $85,000, and named it after himself. Crosby's Opera House, famed throughout the Midwest, was built in 1865 at a cost of $600,000. Two years later, this huge structure was won by an individual on a lottery ticket. Other well-known theaters were Wood's Museum, North's Amphitheater, Aiken's, the Academy of Music, the Globe, and the Dearborn. In 1871 the Chicago fire destroyed some fourteen showhouses.

Between 1871 and 1894 literally dozens of theaters arose in the city. Entertainment adjusted itself to the social stratum of its audience. For the well-to-do, sentimental melodrama was offered. A type of burlesque for the entire family appealed to those of lesser means. It was at this time that the burlesque houses of Sam T. Jack appeared. Although eastern companies toured the Middle West, competent local stock companies continued to thrive, and as Chicago took on the proportions of a metropolis, stars gradually confined their performances to its well-attended theaters.

Chicago, however, was not the only scene of the theater in Illinois. Though the drama presented along the rivers was unimportant from the viewpoint of literature, it merits attention as a phenomenon in the history of the American stage. In his *Theatrical Management,* Sol Smith states that the Chapman family "established and carried into operation that singular affair, the 'Floating Theater,' concerning which so many anecdotes are told. . . . It is said of this Floating Theater that it was cast loose during a performance at one of the river towns in Indiana by some mischievous boys, and could not be landed for half a dozen miles, the large audience being compelled to walk back to their villages."

Because of its depth and placid waters, the Illinois River became an early favorite of show boat operators. These craft ascended the stream as far as it was navigable, stopping at such towns as Morris, Marseilles, Ottawa, La Salle, Peru, Peoria, Pekin, and Beardstown. Along the Mississippi they docked at Galena, Rock Island, Moline, Quincy, Alton, and Cairo. Along the Ohio their itinerary included Shawneetown and Metropolis. Among the show boat plays were comedies, with the shrewd Yankee as hero; sentimental melodramas, like *Uncle Tom's Cabin,* effective as "tear-jerkers"; and dramas of horror. These three types formed the core of the repertory.

Outstanding "floating theaters" were the *Cotton Blossom,* the *Golden Rod, French's New Sensation,* and the *Princess.* The nineties were the big years for them, and whenever one of these "singular affairs" tied up at a town, it was a sign that festive days were to begin. Among the popular companies known in Illinois were those headed by Mencke and Billy Bryan. When the show boats became outmoded and their audiences small, the stock companies of the twentieth century followed a route that had as its basis the old river itinerary.

Between 1810 and 1830 James H. Caldwell, an English actor with several years' experience in the South, controlled a theatrical monopoly in the Mississippi Valley. The Cincinnati *Daily Gazette* of November 16, 1836 commented,

Mr. Caldwell of New Orleans, not satisfied with owning all the theaters between the falls of St. Anthony and the Balize, and managing two or three of them, with being the proprietor of a bank, and the largest bathing establishment in the Union—and with holding contracts for lighting three or four cities with gas, has a new project on foot—the formation of an Ocean Steam Company for running a line of packets between New Orleans and Liverpool.

But the shrewd English actor's monopoly was only a hint of what was to come. Following the trend of the industrial revolution, the season of 1895-96 saw the formation in New York of "The Syndicate," controlled by Charles Frohmann, Marc Klaw, Abraham Erlanger, Sam Nixon, Al Rayman, and Fred Zimmerman, which began at once to dominate the American stage. Some managers and players, however, refused to capitulate to the dictatorship of this new monopoly, among them David Belasco, Mrs. Fisk, Richard Mansfield, and Sarah Bernhardt. Because of her defection, Mrs. Fisk was forced to

appear in halls, and Madame Bernhardt was reduced to playing in a
tent. In the opinion of many observers, the effect of the trust on the
theater was devastating. Dating from its origin, the theater in Illinois
began to decline, and has now become but a catch-all for the conventional drama produced in the East.

Eastern managers shielded good plays by sending them on tour
with their own companies, and as a protection against high rentals,
gained control of a number of theaters in various cities. By 1880 the
old style stock company was dead in the major houses. New York
became the producing center, and the rest of the country served as a
"road" for its productions. A successful play was regarded as a formula, and worn thin through repetition. This stifled initiative and
originality, and also produced a revolt, out of which came the first
drama in America that had any pretensions at all toward greatness.

In Illinois the theater trust touched only the larger cities, particularly Chicago, and as a consequence local stock companies, suffering
from the impact of the eastern invasion, took on new form. Just as
New York became the producing center for the commercial theater on
a large scale, so did Chicago function for Illinois and its environs
on a small scale. Stock companies which had been permanently situated took to the road, and nearly every settlement and village in the
State saw one or another of them in at least a "one-night stand." A
more or less standardized theatrical bill-of-fare—including such old
favorites as *East Lynn* and *Uncle Tom's Cabin*—was served alike to
cities and villages; the smaller communities, however, received an
extra measure of emotional seasoning. Stock companies toured Illinois
until the World War period, and most were successful financially.

About the turn of the century Illinois produced a few dramatists
who strove to create a vital native drama, and chose their themes from
the chaos of the rising industrial order. William Vaughn Moody, Robert Herrick, Edward Sheldon, among others, dramatized the malad-
justments of this new society. But theirs was a short-lived battle, and
the theater became more and more the genteel art of convention. As
the independent companies in Illinois gradually disbanded, the better
actors, playwrights, and technicians migrated to the East, drying up
still further the sources of an indigenous Midwest theater.

With the establishment of New York as the theatrical producing
center of America, a movement of protest began almost immediately.
Although directed primarily against the type of drama presented by

the commercial theater, and stressing its interest in "art," the revolt was at the same time an attempt to reincarnate the local theater. In Illinois many groups sprang up with these objectives; the most important were organized in Chicago. A theater was formed at Hull House with the aim of presenting dramas that reflected the problems of contemporary society.

The second movement of revolt against commercialism came in 1912, when Maurice Browne established the Little Theater in Chicago. Among the plays produced by Browne on the tiny stage in the Fine Arts Building were: *Trojan Women* and *Medea* by Euripides; *Creditors* and *The Stronger* by August Strindberg; *Joint Owners in Spain* by Alice Brown; *The Fifth Commandment* by Stanley Houghton; and *Grotesque* by Cloyd Head. This Little Theater venture lasted about four years, stimulated the local theater throughout the Middle West, and fostered native talent.

In 1913, asked to write an article on the book *The Ideals and Accomplishments of Little Theaters* by the late Theodore B. Hinckley, editor of the *Drama,* Mr. Browne replied, in part:

It is nearly half a generation since Laura Dainty Pelham established the Hull House Players and laid the first foundation stone in America of what is known as the Little Theater, in England as the Repertory Theater, movement. Our future dramatic historian . . . will certainly record the fact that Chicago was the first city in America where the movement came into active being, not only with the work of Mrs. Pelham, but also, a few years later, with the plucky and thorough pioneering of Donald Robertson and the earliest experiments of The Chicago Theater Society, which were none the less interesting and profitable for their being temporarily abortive.

In 1916 a theater was formed to produce experimental dramas and to encourage local playwrights. Kenneth Sawyer Goodman and Alice Gerstenberg were members of this organization, which started with great promise but dissolved with the coming of the World War. The Goodman Theater was the next important advance in the crusade. It introduced a number of talents, but was forced by the depression to close its doors as a repertory company. It now exists as a school of dramatic art. A short-lived venture in Shakespearean productions came to an end in 1931 with the closing of the Repertory Company.

Today a number of "little" and semi-professional groups, among them the Jewish People's Theater, the Mummers, the Chicago Repertory, and the Group, are actively engaged in theater work. They have been producing plays that deal with the more basic issues of present-day society. Among the dramatic schools in the State are the School of Speech at Northwestern University, the Goodman Theater, the De Paul Little Theater, and the Barnum School of Drama.

When, as a result of the depression, the Federal Government turned its attention to the rehabilitation of actors, technicians, and the many assistants necessary in the operation of playhouses, it offered a new hope for a professional theater in the Middle West. From the beginning the Federal Theater has neither sought to compete with nor rival the type of virtuosity displayed in the commercial theater. Along with the educational phase of the vast undertaking, the aim has been to bring a living theater to those people who could not afford to attend the regular offerings.

Recent offerings of the Federal Theater have been the highly successful, *The Mikado,* a modern swing version with an all-Negro cast; the ballets, *Frankie and Johnnie, Ballet Fedre,* and *Guns and Castanets;* and the plays, *Power, The Copperhead,* and *Prologue to Glory.* At present the Federal Theater is using two playhouses, the Great Northern and the Blackstone.

Although no great drama has come from Illinois, the State has had its prominent critics, the most influential of whom were associated with Chicago. The names of Burns Mantle and Percy Hammond received Nation-wide recognition. Amy Leslie stood out as one of the most competent critics in the country, and her authority was undisputed in the Midwest from the early nineties until the late twenties.

MUSIC

Despite her meager inheritance in the realm of music, Illinois has made a praiseworthy artistic contribution to the rapidly focusing national musical picture. Unfortunately America has not afforded her music-lovers the stimulation to be found in native ballads and ancient folk tunes. Since the songs of the American Indians have never struck a responsive chord in our nature, they have exerted a minute influence upon our cultural development in comparison with the music imported from Europe. But from the assimilation of the melodies of other countries has sprung an intense desire for a music of our own, and Illinois has produced a number of compositions conceived in an idiom recognizably American.

Eastern settlers, trappers, and hunters, who pushed westward into the Illinois wilderness, brought with them the tunes, hymns, and ballads from which much of our music of today has logically progressed. In New England, whence came many of the Illinois pioneers, an organized effort had been made to confine music to church use. But the traditional ballad singing and fiddle playing had persisted, and plays with music similar to our comic operas had been given since Revolutionary time. This type of music was further encouraged by the freer life of the migrants. In his *American Songbag,* Carl Sandburg has included several songs which were brought to Illinois directly from New England. "Down, Down Derry Down" is one of these colorful many-versed ballads.

From about 1800 to 1830, the unadorned struggle for food, shelter, and clothing fully occupied the Illinois pioneers. But eventually they picked up the threads of their former modes of life. Among the new settlers were ministers and missionaries. Churches were established, and soon the hymns of Wesley, Mason, Billings, and others floated out upon the prairie air. Singing schools also appeared. Often the teacher did not live in the settlement, but went about from post to post, encouraging groups to cultivate a love and appreciation of music.

In 1834 the Beaubien brothers, John and Mark, possessed two of the earliest musical instruments in the State. Mark owned the first violin recorded in Illinois, and John had the first piano in Chicago, if not in Illinois. One year later the Old Settlers' Harmonic Society was founded at Chicago; its opening concert was given within a year at the Presbyterian Church. In 1837 a theater was opened in Chicago. This brought to Illinois a ballad singer and a group of minstrels who were soon followed by others.

In the 1840's and 1850's families of strolling singers and musicians were extremely popular throughout the State, and monopolized the musical entertainment field. The Sable melodist, the Negro minstrels, the Algerines, the Antoni, the Newhall, and the Peak families were welcomed warmly wherever they performed. In 1853 the Swiss Bell Ringers appeared before an overflow crowd of eight hundred persons at the Springfield courthouse. The trend toward musical self-expression also thrived at Alton, where "Professor" Van Meter conducted a music course attended by five hundred pupils, one hundred and fifty of whom appeared in graduation recitals. By the end of the period, bands and choral societies had been organized in many Illinois towns. Grierson's Band at Jacksonville, founded at this time, gained wide attention for its unique method of playing by notation instead of "by ear." The number of music lovers increased so rapidly that in 1852 a two-day State-wide convention was held at Springfield. A *Sangerbund* was organized in Belleville in 1865, followed by a Philharmonic Society in 1867.

Between 1840 and 1850 American music was further stimulated by the arrival of immigrants from Europe. Early music in Illinois had a distinctly German flavor. Hans Balatka, once a choral conductor in Vienna, was appointed to lead the newly organized Philharmonic' Orchestra at Chicago in 1860. His first program included the Second Symphony of Beethoven and a chorus from Tannhauser, the first Wagnerian music to be played in the region. The Germania Orchestra of New York was one of the first large orchestras to tour Illinois. Among visiting artists at this time were Richard Hoffman, Gottschalk, and Rubenstein.

It is not to be supposed, however, that the arrival of the works of Wagner, Beethoven, and other European composers effected an immediate leavening of the musical taste in the cities of the Prairie State, much less in the rural districts. Music of another sort—robust, not to say coarse—played its part in both pastime and manual labor. An idea of the place occupied in Illinois by popular and utilitarian music is given in Charles Edward Russell's *A-Rafting on the Mississip'*.

If in the face of . . . fairly eloquent testimony, I continue to maintain that my rascals of the raft had sometimes a redeeming substratum of sentiment and poetry under their rowdyism, I may be judged merely eccentric . . . . Of a sudden, there would float over the water the sounds of a fiddle, or maybe an accordion, playing "Buffalo Gals," and we could easily make out the crew sitting in a semi-circle rapt upon the solitary musician. . . . It was not always hymnody of a kind to edify the youthful mind, but I am bound to say that, when there were children about, the raftsmen, if they happened to be sufficiently sober, would put some restraint upon both their language and their lyric offerings. They had a singular and absorbing passion for music— crude music, but still something approaching melody. Most rafts carried fiddlers as conscientiously as they carried cooks.

Of the old songs and tunes, Mr. Russell has said,

Those that provided a chorus or an opportunity to dance a few steps between the stanzas were the favorites. "One-Eyed Riley" went like this:

> He was prime fav'rite out our way,
> The women folks all loved him dearly;
> He taught the parsons how to pray,
> An' he got their tin, or pretty nearly.
> He's the man they speak of highly!
>   W-a-h-hoop!
> Riddle, liddle, linktum!
> *Pause—then all together, fortissimo*
> One-Eyed Riley!

. . . When "tum" is reached, all the boot-soles must slap the floor together. Then the dancers remain rigid until the refrain, which they deliver with roaring enthusiasm, "One-Eyed Riley!"

The "Big Maquoketa" and "Raftsman Jim" were other favorites of the period. The former, according to Russell, was the "flowerage of an undiscovered river laureate," although the tune, like that of "Raftsman Jim," was not composed in Illinois. Of "Buffalo Gals" Russell stated that he printed the text "with a sense of humiliation," but had "found this song on old Broadway programs as having been sung to audiences that ought to have known better, and there is evidence that East and West, it was the darling of its times."

Although music was steadily gaining the collective fancy of early Illinoisans, choruses and instrumental groups in the towns and cities

almost entirely suspended their activities during the Civil War. Only
minstrels singing war songs were popular with audiences at that time.
But with Lee's surrender and peace, Chicago, Jacksonville, Peoria,
Rock Island, Alton, Cairo, and many other growing places were again
visited by musicians. Louise Kellog sang, and Camilla Urso came
with her violin. A traveling artist, Gunge, spoke of the smaller towns
as being quite as appreciative of music as Chicago, although he found
the American taste was far below the European. Said Gunge, "In
music he [the American] likes best—waltzes, the galop, quadrilles,
and best of all, polkas. There are only a few exceptions. Minstrels
have the best business."

Perhaps these "exceptions" were responsible for the establishment
of music schools in Alton, Moline, Rockford, Elgin, and Chicago.
Some of the foreign and local teachers who conducted early schools
earned but a pittance; others received a thousand dollars a year, which
was considered a good salary in a profession that twenty years earlier
had been able to reward its followers with only a meager existence.

Soon conservatories were created to meet a definite need: the
Chicago Conservatory of Music in 1866; the Illinois Conservatory of
Music at Jacksonville in 1871; the Department of Music at Northwestern University, with Peter Christian Lutkin at its head, in 1873;
the Knox Conservatory of Music at Galesburg in 1883; and the Chicago Musical College, founded in 1887 by Dr. Florenz Ziegfeld, father
of the late producer of the Follies. These forerunners were followed
by many others.

The development of music in the public schools was at first slow
and difficult. With no American folk songs handed down from generation to generation, the early settlers from the East had only the
European tunes and words their parents had taught them. But this
music held little meaning in a frontier atmosphere, where an exotic
culture might be remembered but could not thrive. The only hope lay
in transplanting music training from the singing school. This was
done gradually, a town here and there fusing music with academic
study. As early as 1872 the State school laws provided that music and
drawing might be insisted upon in the various districts by their
respective boards.

In 1885 questionnaires were sent to the public schools throughout
Illinois. Twenty towns and cities in the State were found to be teaching music. Freeport and Sycamore were not among these because of

the expense. The Carlyle school was too crudely organized to admit of anything but compulsory subjects. Mount Vernon was hampered by the inability of its teaching force and want of money to pay a special music teacher. In Dwight only music by rote and some instrumental accompaniment were taught.

Twenty years later the situation was vastly different. Statistics taken in 1905, covering the whole of the United States, indicated that approximately 97 per cent of the cities in Illinois that answered the questionnaires taught music in their schools. By 1908 twenty-six conservatories, colleges, and universities throughout the State, offered courses in music. The State university credited music toward a degree. The course of study prepared in 1915 by the committee of county superintendents' section of the Illinois State Teachers' Association included an outline for music in elementary grades. Today the study of music is widespread in Illinois public schools, although no law exists forcing them to include it in their curricula.

School glee clubs and orchestras are as numerous today in the small towns as in the cities. Music festivals have become legion, beginning with competition in each town, then narrowing to a number of towns vying for honors in a district meet, and finally centering in a State contest. Winners from the various States meet in the early summer for national competition. The entries include vocal and instrumental solos, choruses of all kinds, orchestras, bands, and ensemble groups.

By 1885 nine Illinois towns boasted of large singing societies. A few years later Jacksonville had an excellent chorus; the Peoria Oratorio Society, during its first season, performed with seventy-five voices. The Northwestern University musical groups were giving well-attended chamber music recitals.

Opera made a start in Chicago in 1850 at the Rice Theater, but when a fire destroyed the building, enthusiasm waned until the Crosby Opera House was built in 1865. Several good productions were presented there. At the same time chamber music concerts under the management of the Briggs House were being given. About 1887 the city enjoyed a season of German opera, and an opera festival held soon afterwards in the Exposition Building encouraged the construction of Chicago's famous Auditorium Theater.

Shortly before 1890 the Auditorium was formally opened by President Harrison. The evening was momentous. Harriet Monroe's dedicatory ode was read, and Adelina Patti sang with the Apollo Musical Club. On the next night *Romeo and Juliet* was presented, the first of twenty-two operatic performances to be given that year. From then until 1914 Chicago enjoyed a succession of well-known singers, including Lillian Nordica, Schumann-Heink, Caruso, John McCormick, Mary Garden, and Carolina White.

Soon after the outbreak of the World War the Chicago Grand Opera Company went into bankruptcy. But a year later a new organization, the Chicago Opera Association, headed by Harold F. McCormick, was organized; Galli-Curci sang with this company in 1916. The Opera Association was disbanded in 1922, and its functions taken over by the Chicago Civic Opera Company.

In 1929, under the direction of Samuel Insull, a $20,000,000 Civic Opera House was built on Wacker Drive in Chicago. But what had seemed a triumph, presaging a brilliant future, turned out to be a finale, for in a few years the inverted pyramid of Insull finance suddenly collapsed, and with it went the Civic Opera Company. Several smaller groups were formed to carry on. Of these the Chicago Grand Opera Company is the most prominent today. Until 1931 opera stars from the Metropolitan and Chicago Opera companies appeared annually during the summer season in the open air pavilion at beautiful Ravinia Park, twenty-five miles north of Chicago's Loop.

Orchestral music paralleled the growth and struggle of opera in Chicago. From 1859 until 1905 the name of Theodore Thomas was synonymous with orchestral development in the Middle West. Thomas, often referred to as "Chicago's Father of Music," toured the region in 1859 with the operatic company of Karl Formes, the famous German basso. On October 9, 1871, the young violinist led his own symphony orchestra in a concert at the Crosby Opera House in Chicago, playing one of Beethoven's overtures to Fidelio, a scherzo from a Schumann symphony, and music by Chopin, Gounod, Schubert, and Wagner. Later that night the Chicago Fire began its furious assault upon the city, forcing the musicians of the Thomas Orchestra to flee from a North Side hotel. Despite this harrowing experience the popular Thomas was induced to settle in Chicago, and in 1891 he organized the Chicago Orchestra. With nearly 8,500 Chicagoans contributing to a popular subscription fund, the present Orchestra Hall building was erected on Michigan Avenue in 1904, but Thomas lived only long enough to direct three concerts there. He was succeeded in 1905 by

Frederick Stock, the present conductor (1939). In 1906 the orchestra was named the Theodore Thomas Orchestra and kept this name until 1912, when it was changed to the Chicago Symphony Orchestra.

Orchestral music flourished in Chicago following the World War. The Chicago Civic Orchestra was established in 1919; and the Woman's Symphony Orchestra in 1925. Ravinia Park was again opened to the public in 1936, with the Chicago Symphony Orchestra a major attraction. That same year symphony and band orchestras co-operating with city officials inaugurated a series of free summer concerts, in Grant Park on Chicago's lake front, which attracted thousands of music-lovers.

An organization unique in the Middle West was the Chicago Allied Arts, Inc., founded in 1924. The Chicago Allied Arts comprised a ballet company of about twenty-five dancers, under the choreographic direction of Adolph Bolm, formerly of the Diaghileff *Ballets Russes,* and Eric DeLamarter's Solo Orchestra of about twenty-five pieces. An air of novelty distinguished the organization's performances. The orchestral concerts, preceding the ballets, presented the works of John Alden Carpenter, Leo Sowerby, Honegger, Milhaud, Stravinsky, Schonberg, and many others. The ballets, too, their settings and costumes designed by Nicholas Remisoff, were mostly modern in treatment. An interesting feature of the organization was its presentation of guest artists. Among a number of guest dancers who appeared with the company was the distinguished ballerina, Tamar Karsavina, upon her first visit to America. Ruth Page, later ballet mistress of the Ravinia Opera Company and the Chicago Opera Company, was *première danseuse* throughout the three seasons of the Allied Arts, and introduced some characteristically American choreography. John Alden Carpenter acted as president of the organization during its first season. The Allied Arts closed its brilliant Chicago career in December 1926. The following year the entire company was invited to give joint performances with the League of Composers in New York. Among the ballets presented were the Chicago creations, *The Tragedy of the Cello,* with music by Alexander Tansman, and *The Rivals,* composed by Henry Eichheim.

At the close of the World War a new musical phenomenon, jazz, captured the entire entertainment field. Jazz, as every one knows, was once regarded as "an underground waif," a low noise in the scale of music, but some forget that Chicago made jazz its protegé, and gave it a vibrant send-off that imparted prestige. Paul Whiteman wrote:

There !s considerable discussion over exactly who did invent the term "jazz band," with many authorities giving the honor to Bert Kelly of Chicago who described a group of musicians that he hired out to the Boosters' Club at the Hotel Morrison in Chicago as a "jazz band." The Boosters' club promptly raised all its prices, alleging that the new-fangled jazz came high.

But long before this, Brown's orchestra (a group Mr. Gorman had recently discovered in a frenzy of syncopation on the streets of New Orleans) had been taken over by Mr. Gorman and placed at the Lamb's cafe, also in Chicago. The players burst upon the unsuspecting pork-packer world with a bang that nearly shattered the roof. . . . This, so far as I can discover from cabaret history, was the honest-to-goodness beginning of jazz.

"Hot" bands appeared also in Peoria, Springfield, and East St. Louis; saxophones whined, banjos strummed, and drums beat a new kind of rhythm. Crowds filled the night clubs and ballrooms, dancing to the jazz of Wayne King, Ben Bernie, Duke Ellington, and Cab Calloway. Paul Ash and his orchestra enlivened the Oriental Theater in Chicago's Loop with his jazz renditions, while on Chicago's South Side the Negro jazz band of Erskine Tate, experimenting with new forms of rhythmic music, elevated from its ranks one of the Nation's foremost jazz composers, Louis Armstrong. Negroes also found an eager audience with such famous spirituals as "Go Down, Moses," "Steal Away," and "Swing Low, Sweet Chariot."

With the organization of the Federal Music Project in 1935, music in Illinois has for the first time been brought within reach of the masses of the people. Symphony orchestras and bands, choral groups and music classes, have kindled a desire for cultural development in communities weighed down by economic depression. This has been particularly true in the mining area of southern Illinois, where in the Negro settlement of Colp, paralyzed by unemployment, a chorus of twenty-five was assembled to travel about the countryside, singing their spirituals before enthusiastic crowds. In Chicago the Illinois Symphony, a WPA unit, presents weekly concerts, and encourages the work of native composers.

Of recent development is the working-class song. To the tune of "Jacob's Ladder," a Negro spiritual, the miners of southern Illinois, after the formation of the Progressive Miners' Union in 1932, sang

"We are Building a New Union." During a strike in the steel mill area of South Chicago, the labor song "Beans" was composed. These songs, together with older ones like "John Brown's Body," sometimes with new words, have been adopted by groups of industrialized and urban Illinois workers.

A number of composers in the State have contributed to the dignity and musical importance of Illinois. John Alden Carpenter is the author of many beautiful songs. In his "Adventures in a Perambulator" and in his ballet *Krazy Kat,* he has struck a persuasively American and original note. Leo Sowerby was the first American winner of the *Prix de Rome* musical scholarship. Hamilton Forrest's opera, *Camille,* was produced by the Chicago Civic Opera Company, with Mary Garden singing the principal rôle. The ballet, *Play of Words,* composed by David Van Vactor in 1932, was produced at the Goodman theater for the Originalists, a group whose members represented all of the arts and professions. Among many distinguished compositions by Eric DeLamarter, formerly associate conductor of the Chicago Symphony Orchestra, is his ballet *The Dance of Life.* Other well-known Illinois composers include: Frederick Stock, Felix Borowski, Robert Sanders, Rosseter G. Cole, Arne Oldberg, Dr. Albert Noelte, Wesley La Violette, Robert Whitney, Irwin Fischer, Max Wald, Edward Collins, William Lester, Radio Britain, and Daniel Protheroe.

Music critics and journals of music have rendered a valuable service to the art in Illinois. Both the *Musical Leader* and the *Music News* are published in Chicago. The late Edward Moore was author of *Forty Years of Opera in Chicago.* Karleton S. Hackett was vice-president of the American Conservatory of Music at the time of his death. Among the music critics writing today for the Chicago press are Eugene Stinson, Glenn Dillard Gunn, Herman Devries, Claudia Cassidy, Edward Barry and Cecil Smith.

Part II

ILLINOIS:

Cities and Tours

ALTON

ALTON (488 alt., 30,151 pop.), just above the confluence of the Mississippi and the Missouri, and just below that of the Illinois and Mississippi, rises on the bluffs where they retreat from the river to mark the head of a vast river plain known as the American Bottom. From this point south to East St. Louis, in a great thirty-mile arc that follows the river, is an almost continuous manufacturing area. Although it benefited, along with East Alton, Wood River, and Granite City, from the great industrial expansion of the first part of the twentieth century, Alton differs sharply from its sister cities in that its growth was spread over more than a century.

Alton works in the valley and lives on the hill. The main business district fronts on the river at the west part of the city; at the eastern limits, where the valley flares wide, lies a cluster of sprawling plants that manufacture glass, lead, steel, chemicals, box-board, and scores of other products.

Residential Alton lies chiefly back from the river on the bluffs. Here the expression "going downtown" has literal meaning, for the streets that run to the river drop abruptly on a steep grade from immediately above the business district. The central section, with its unusually wide streets (many still surfaced with brick) and Victorian houses that give each other elbow room, retains the spaciousness and faintly lavender scented dignity of the nineteenth century. Many of the older houses, built during steamboat days, are surmounted with lookout platforms that vary from a mere fenced-in rectangle to elaborate circular and octagonal cupolas. In the middle of the last century crack steamboats, such as the *Golden Eagle,* the *Gossamer,* and the *Kate Kearney,* vied with each other on the stretch between St. Louis and Alton, where a rich load of freight usually awaited the first steamer to dock. The lookout stations were an architectural outgrowth of this racing mania. Merchants awaiting shipments and persons who gambled on the races built observation towers on their stores and houses from which, even at a distance, to view the outcome. At length the observation platforms became ornamental rather than functional, and many of them today cap houses completely out of sight of the river.

Although the site of Alton had been passed by Marquette and Jolliet on their voyage down the Mississippi in 1673, the first known settler, Jean Baptiste Cardinal, did not come to the vicinity until 110 years later. By the beginning of the nineteenth century an Indian trading post had been established. The site was obviously suitable for a permanent settlement, for above it the bluffs closed in on the river and for miles there was no sufficient setback for a boat landing. The confluences of the two great rivers nearby marked the spot as an eventual focal point for river traffic. Between 1816 and 1818 three towns, hoping to capitalize these advantages, were founded in the area now included in the Alton city limits. One of these, now the downtown business district, was planned by Col. Rufus Easton and named Alton for one of his sons. Proving to be the most satisfactory for river trade, his town eventually absorbed the other two, and Alton was incorporated as a city in 1837.

The first major period in its development coincided with the ascendancy of steamboat transportation, and for a time its wharfs teemed with white steamboats and Alton rivaled St. Louis as a river port.

Lying just north of a section where slavery was favored, Alton felt many of the repercussions from the slavery dispute; here, in 1837, Elijah Lovejoy, noted Abolitionist editor, was murdered while protecting his press from the onslaught of a pro-slavery mob.

Alton was again the focus of the slavery question in 1858, when the last of the Lincoln-Douglas debates (*see below*) was held here. Altonians were already familiar with Lincoln because of the serio-comic Lincoln-Shields duel of 1842. Mary Todd, whom Lincoln later married, had lampooned State Auditor of Accounts James Shields in a Springfield paper ; and Lincoln assumed responsibility for the article and was challenged by Shields. Lincoln chose broadswords, and Alton as the duelling ground. With a crowd of the curious they rowed to a sandbar in the river. The lanky Abe practiced swings and told stories while the seconds conferred at great length, but the duel did not take place. Shields finally accepted a formal statement that although Lincoln "did not think . . . that said article could produce such an effect," he had not intended "injuring the personal or private character or standing of Mr. Shields."

Alton has seen a steady increase in population each decade for more than 100 years. The decline of steamboating at the end of the nineteenth century was offset by the rise of industrial plants, notably that of the Owens-Illinois Company, which grew from a one-building concern tucked way in the bluffs to its present position as the dominant corporation among the nation's glass-producers. And as other plants began to smoke on the river plain, Alton listened to the gradual diminishing of the steamboat's hoot with only the regret occasioned by the passing of a colorful era.

In recent years one resident of Alton has done more than all the city's notables of the past to make the world at large aware of Alton. He is Robert Wadlow, the young giant who had achieved by his 21st birthday in 1939, the height of 8 feet 8¼ inches. Weighing more than 490 pounds, wearing a size 36 shoe, Wadlow is the tallest human of whom there are authentic measurements in the annals of medical science.

POINTS OF INTEREST

The OWENS-ILLINOIS GLASS FACTORY, Broadway and Washington, (*guides furnished at the employment office, 8-4, week-days*), is said to be the largest bottle-producing unit in the world. Visitors see first the power plant building, which, like those housing the pattern and repair shops, has walls of hollow glass blocks, immensely strong, translucent but not transparent. This building has frequently been publicized as initiating a new development in industrial architecture, the windowless building. The blocks were used in the glass House of Tomorrow at the Century of Progress Exposition in Chicago.

Next the visitors see the enormous glass-blowing machines, each with some 10,000 moving parts, and the annealing ovens. Machines that produce small bottles spin like a merry-go-round and spit out the finished product at the rate of two a second, while those that make large bottles and demijohns have a ponderous, jerky motion, like giant robots. The largest of these, which blows 2 to 12-gallon carboys, weighs 120 tons and is considered the most advanced bottle-blowing unit in the trade. From the blowing machines the bottles are carried on steel belts through long ovens, where in a period of three hours their temperature is lowered from over 1,000° to that of the room. As they come from the annealing ovens, they are inspected and packed. The tour of the factory ends with an inspection of the box factory, in which are made the cartons used in shipping.

The ELIJAH LOVEJOY MONUMENT, at the north end of Monument Ave., stands at the entrance to Alton City Cemetery. Visible from the greater part of Alton, it was erected in 1897 by the State of Illinois and by the city in memory of the anti-slavery editor. A slim granite column, 93 feet high, supports a 17-foot bronze figure of *Victory,* flanked with two shorter columns, each bearing an eagle with outstretched wings.

Lovejoy came to Alton in 1835 from St. Louis, where he had begun his anti-slavery agitation, after a mob had destroyed his press. In Alton, before he had printed a single issue of his paper, the *Observer,* another mob threw his press into the Mississippi. He obtained a third press and continued publication for more than a year. Although Alton was nominally an anti-slavery town, it was sufficiently near the slavery line to harbor many anti-Abolitionists. Late in 1837 the third press was destroyed. Undaunted, Lovejoy obtained a fourth, and stored it in a warehouse on the river bank, where next day a mob besieged him and his friends, gathered to protect the press. Shortly after nightfall the warehouse was attacked, and in the exchange of shots Lovejoy and some of the attackers were killed. A few days later both sides were acquitted in a trial denounced as a travesty on justice.

The ALTON DAM, on the Mississippi River at the foot of Easton St., is best viewed from the approach to the Lewis-Clark Bridge, Broadway and Langdon. Largest of the series of 26 dams under construction between Alton and Minneapolis, the dam helps provide a 9-foot channel, solving the navigation problems caused by the unpredictable shifting of the Mississippi's current. The lake formed by the dam will eventually be developed as a recreation spot.

The SITE OF THE FIRST STATE PRISON IN ILLINOIS, at Broadway and Williams Sts., now a vacant lot, is marked only by a fragment of one cell tier. The first Illinois State Prison became the center of a violent controversy that eventually ended in a legislative investigation and the construction of a new prison at Joliet.

Badly situated in a spot too near the river, undrained and ungraded, it aroused the insistent criticism of Dorothea Dix, pioneer in prison reform, and others. With the outbreak of the Civil War the plan to discontinue its use was abandoned, and it became a military detention camp. Overcrowding and the lack of sanitation culminated in a smallpox epidemic in 1863, which raged uncontrolled for weeks for want of prison doctors. Prisoners died at the rate of six to ten a day. At the demand of citizens all stricken prisoners were transported to an uninhabited island in the Mississippi, where a deserted dwelling was converted into a hospital. There is no evidence that any of the victims ever returned, and although no record of deaths was kept, it has been estimated that several thousand persons died and were buried on the island during 1863-64. Many of the Confederate soldiers who died during the epidemic are buried in the CONFEDERATE SOLDIERS' CEMETERY, Rozier and State Sts., in North Alton. After the war the prison was evacuated, sold, and razed.

The SITE OF THE LINCOLN-DOUGLAS DEBATE, Broadway at the foot of Market St., is now occupied by a large municipal parking area. Here, on October 15, 1858, Stephen A. Douglas and Abraham Lincoln met in their campaign for election to the United States Senate. From a platform erected on the east side of the old City Hall they addressed a crowd estimated at 5,000 to 10,000 people. Douglas, his voice worn with continual public speaking, maintained, as in previous debates, that each State should decide the slavery question for itself, and told the audience that Lincoln believed that a Negro was as good as a white. Lincoln restated his belief that a house divided against itself could not stand, that the States must be all slave or all free, and that a crisis was approaching which would swing the country one way or the other.

The reproduced painting of the PIASA BIRD, on the bluffs half a mile northwest of the downtown area, is reached by following Broadway along the base of the bluff, but is best viewed from the river. Paintings of the Piasa Bird in this location, first mentioned in Pere Marquette's account of his trip down the Mississippi in 1673, have been the basis for several fantastic legends of Indian origin. The pictures that Marquette saw were blasted away during quarrying operations in 1870, and the present reproduction was made in 1934 with funds raised by private subscription. Marquette thus described the pictures:

As we were descending the river we saw high rocks with hideous monsters painted on them, and upon which the bravest Indians dare not look. They are as large as a calf, with head and horns like a goat; their eyes red; beard like a tiger; and a face like a man's. Their tails are so long that they pass over their heads and between their fore legs, under their belly, and ending like a fish's tail. They are painted red, green, and black.

The next account follows Marquette's description closely, but mentions only one bird. The Alton *Evening Telegraph* of September 28, 1836, gave what was perhaps the first published account of the story of the Piasa bird. In this version, the popularly accepted one, the Piasa bird lived in a cave in the bluffs, and came winging down the river to carry off any Indians it encountered. Chief Quatoga of the Illinois prayed to the Great Manitou for some means of delivering his people from this scourge and was told that the arrows of Quatoga's tribe alone could kill the monster. Accordingly, the chief exposed himself on the bluff and hid 20 of his warriors in the bushes behind him. When the bird swooped down on him, the warriors shot it with poisoned arrows, and it fell screaming into the river. The writer of the newspaper story goes on to say naively that he had observed the supposed cave-home of the Piasa, and found it ample to house such a monster.

LOVERS' LEAP, a huge rock on the edge of the bluffs at the end of Prospect St., is associated with another legend. This tale, recounting the tragedy of Lovers' Leap, is the same story found in hundreds of such precipitous spots about the United States. It is interesting to note that it involves the same chief who figures in the Piasa bird story.

The tale is that Quatoga's young daughter, Laughing Water, fell in love with a young man, Black Otter, from a hostile tribe, and met him secretly here on the bluffs. The chief discovered the affair and in attempting to shoot Black Otter killed his daughter, whereupon the lover took her body in his arms and leaped to death in the river below.

SHURTLEFF COLLEGE, College and Seminary Aves., grew out of the Rock Spring Seminary, founded in 1827 by the Rev. John Mason Peck, near O'Fallon, Illinois.

The Reverend Mr. Peck was appointed in May 1817, by the Triennial Baptist Convention as a missionary to the Missouri Territory. He first established a school in St. Louis in 1818, but found conditions there unfavorable, and decided to move. During his search for a suitable location he looked at and rejected the present site of the college, finally deciding on Rock Spring, where for four years the school struggled for existence with an enrollment of about 50. In 1831 he was prevailed upon to move to Alton.

The first charter was granted under the name of Alton Seminary, but a new and more favorable charter obtained in 1835 renamed it Alton College of Illinois. In the same year Dr. Benjamin Shurtleff of Boston donated $10,000 to the school, which was renamed in his honor.

The buildings occupy a campus of 35 acres. The first building, Academie Hall (1832), still in use, gives a pleasantly archaic air to the whole group. The college grants the Bachelor of Arts degree, the Bachelor of Music degree, and offers preparatory training in medicine, law, engineering, and journalism. A one-year secretarial course and a two-year commerce course are also offered.

POINTS OF INTEREST IN ENVIRONS

Monticello Seminary, 4 *m.;* Principia College, 18.4 *m.;* Pere Marquette State Park, 25.4 *m.* (*see Tour 7*).

AURORA

Railroad Stations: 175 S. Broadway for Chicago, Burlington & Quincy; 51 S. Broadway for Chicago, Aurora & Elgin (electric).

Bus Station: 51 S. Broadway for Burlington Transportation Co.; White Star Motor Coach; Joliet, Plainfield & Aurora Transportation Co.; and Deluxe Stages.

Intra-City Buses: Fare 5c.

Taxis: Intra-city rate 25c first mile, 20c thereafter.

Accommodations: 12 hotels; municipal tourist camp at Phillips Park.

Information Service: Chamber of Commerce, 71 Stolp Ave., and Chicago Motor Club, 48 Galena Blvd.

Golf: Municipal links, Phillips Park. Two commercial courses.

Swimming: Non-commercial pools, Y.M.C.A., 205 Fox; Y.W.C.A., 31 Downer Place. One commercial pool.

Tennis: Municipal courts, Phillips Park, Parker Ave.; East High School Athletic Field, Jackson St., between Benton and Fox.

AURORA (638 alt., 46,580 pop.) lies on both sides of the Fox River, spreading over the broad and gentle valley through which once rushed a wide glacial stream. Although only an hour from Chicago, Aurora is no suburb, but serves rather as an outpost of the metropolitan industrial area, at the border where factories make their last stand against the checkered prairie. Meeting point of the two areas, Aurora is best described as a farm town with 140 factories.

The river that divides the city into what were once East and West Aurora has many islands; on the major one, Stolp's, lies the civic center, with the city hall, postoffice, and library. Although water power is now of inconsiderable importance, many of the industrial plants lie along its banks.

When the first settler, Joseph McCarty of Elmira, New York, came to this region in 1834, he found a large Potawatomi village on the river. "It was not a wild, desolate, unpopulated region," he wrote, "for we had plenty of neighbors in the red men. The village and vicinity contained from 300 to 500 Indians, and we had many visits from them. Quite a commercial trade sprang up, especially swapping bread and tobacco for fish, of which we soon found they had much the larger supply. We could give but one slice of bread for a fish weighing from three to five pounds."

After beginning work on his cabin, McCarty took a short jaunt eastward to look over the little village of Chicago. Deprecating the place as "more promising for the raising of bullfrogs than humans," he returned with satisfaction to the site he had chosen on the Fox River. There he was shortly joined by his brother, Samuel, who aided in damming the river and erecting a mill. The McCartys were the first of the small but steadily growing stream of settlers that came to the valley after the Black Hawk War had rid Illinois of Indians. When the sawmill was finished in 1835, there were more than a dozen pioneers to join in the celebration. Platted in 1836, the little community had thirty families and a postoffice within a year.

For a decade and a half Aurora grew along both sides of the river, bound to it because it was the only suitable power source for the first crude industrial plants. Then, in 1848, the forerunner of the Chicago, Burlington and Quincy Railroad extended its lines into town. It is difficult to appreciate, today, the effect the absurd little locomotives and their diminutive cars had upon towns in the fifties. Illinois at that time was entering a period of expansion, but in those towns that lay in the route of the railroad the expansion was intensified. And Aurora not only got her railroad early, but the line also later established its shops here. Today the "Q" shops remain the city's largest employer.

Like many a river community, Aurora grew up as two towns, and it was not until 1857 that East Aurora and West Aurora incorporated as a unit. Rivalry at one time was intense, and urchins from one side of the river crossed to the other only with great caution, 'fearing chauvinistic urchins from the opposite side who looked upon them as foreigners. Fierce verbal battles were fought, even after the towns were united, over the location of the postoffice, railroad station, and other public or semi-public buildings. Streets underwent a change of name in crossing the river; for a long time the mayor was chosen alternately from the east and the west sides. Eventually a convenient solution for the left and right bank rivalry was found in the middle of the river—at Stolp's Island. The civic center was established there, and citizens wondered why they hadn't thought of it before.

In 1881 Aurora became the first town in Illinois, and among the first in the nation, to light its streets with electricity. Aurorans were impressed by the yellow glow on top the high steel towers, although a few cynics remarked that "the heavens were better illuminated than the streets." Later there arose a persistent fiction that Aurora took its name from this pioneering in illumination, but the town was named long before Edison began to putter with filaments. The early settlers had wanted to name the town Waubonsie, for the friendly Indian chief who once lived here. When it was found that the name had already been given to a town, "Aurora" was chosen as the best philological substitute, since the meaning of Waubonsie was also "morning light."

In 1893 all Aurora was arguing over its last mayoralty election. No one was sure who was mayor; on the first count John Murphy defeated James Brattle by one vote, and then a recount gave the victory to Brattle by five votes. The election was then thrown into the courts, and was fought to the State Supreme Court, which eventually decided in Brattle's favor. But his victory was little more than a technical one, because when he finally took office, only four months remained of his two-year term.

By 1890 Aurora had reached 20,000 population, and its subsequent history was that of an even-paced expansion of its industrial basis. The booming years of the new century saw a steady growth, not as spectacular as that of many another industrial town, but subject to little fluctuation. For the 1890-1900 period its percentage of increase in population varied less than 3 per cent from decade to decade, remaining near 20 per cent.

The diversity of Aurora's products in the 1930's included belt conveyors, excavation machinery, elevators, pumps, office supplies, fire escapes, balloons, parachutes, and deep well machinery. When, in 1937, it celebrated its centennial, erecting reproductions of the first store, the blacksmith shop, McCarty's cabin, the small crude buildings stood in strange contrast to the appurtenances of a new era. Linked now with the breadth of the country, Aurora's commerce had, in a hundred years, hugely overshadowed its simple beginnings, when Samuel McCarty sallied forth up the Fox to barter "one slice of bread for a fish weighing from three to five pounds."

POINTS OF INTEREST

The AURORA PUBLIC LIBRARY (9-5 *weekdays;* 2:30-5 *Sun.*), 1 Benton St., is an ivy-covered building containing more than 75,000 volumes. On the second floor are overflow exhibits of the historical society, most important of which is the Blanford Clock. Nine feet high and three feet wide, it is elaborately carved, depicting the Roman Forum and other scenes. The clock shows the time of day, the phases of the moon, the earth's revolution about the sun, and the calendar day, month and year. Clockwork automatically switches on lights at the approach of night, dutifully turns them off again in the morning. The clock was conceived and executed by William Blanford of Aurora, who worked intermittently on the clock during the greater portion of his life.

MEMORIAL BRIDGE spans the Fox River on US 34, just beyond the end of Stolp's Island. Designed by Emory P. Seidel, Chicago sculptor, it was dedicated on Armistice Day, 1931, "to the past, present, and future defenders of American ideals." Almost 700 feet long, the bridge cost $300,000. Piers at either end bear seated female figures, illuminated by lights concealed in helmets held in their laps.

The AURORA HISTORICAL SOCIETY BUILDING (*open weekdays* 10-4), Oak Ave. at Cedar St., was a gift to the city from the daughters of W. A. Tanner, early settler. Built in 1857, the 17-room house contains a grandfather's clock, Aurora's first piano, and other pieces of early furniture brought by boat from Buffalo to Chicago and then hauled overland to Aurora. Home utensils, ornaments, intimate letters, and other exhibits are arranged throughout the rooms to portray, in warmly personal terms, living conditions of early days. There is an excellent collection of pioneer portraits, an original Lincoln letter, and a group of legal documents and memoirs of local historical significance.

JENNINGS SEMINARY, 276 S. Broadway, is a Methodist girls' school founded in 1859. The original limestone building, now covered with ivy, stands with impressive dignity high on the slope of a shaded lawn. The enrollment of the school averages 100.

AURORA COLLEGE, bounded by Gladestone Ave., Randall Ave., Kenilworth Pl., and Marseillaise Pl., was founded by the Advent Christian faith at Mendota in 1893, and moved to Aurora in 1912. Its courses lead to B.A., B.S., and B.Th. degrees. The college owns a good collection of fossils and archeological specimens gathered locally.

The UNSTAD COLLECTION OF ANTIQUE WEAPONS (*open upon convenience of owner*), 1109 Fifth St., is housed in the owner's home. The collection comprises more than 200 weapons, ranging from a crossbow of the 11th century, a German wheel-lock gun of the 17th century, down to an assortment of Kentucky rifles. Indian weapons include a number of fine axes, as well as the ubiquitous arrowhead.

PHILLIPS PARK, Parker and Hill Aves. on US 30, contains a museum and zoo (*open daily* 9 *a.m.*-10 *p.m.; free*). On exhibit are three mastodon skulls and many other archaeological specimens. In the open park, near the greenhouses, are old millstones, a prehistoric grain mortar and other early stone-work. The small zoo specializes in native birds and mammals. The park, which lies on several levels, contains ponds, formal flower beds, and rock gardens.

BLOOMINGTON and NORMAL

Railroad Stations: Union Station, foot of Washington St. for the Alton, Peoria & Eastern branch of the Cleveland, Cincinnati, Chicago & St. Louis Ry., the New York, Chicago and St. Louis R. R.; 800 E. Grove St. for Illinois Central R. R.; 220 N. Madison St. for Illinois Terminal R. R. Co. (electric).

Bus Station: Union Bus Station, 217 S. Main St. for Illini Coach Co., Central Trailways, and Greyhound Lines.

Taxis: Intra-city rates, 25c, each additional passenger 10c.

Intra-city buses: Fare 5c.

Accommodations: Seven hotels.

Radio Station: WJBC (1200 kc.).

Motion Picture Houses: Five.

Golf: Highland Park (18 holes), S. Main St.

Swimming: Non-commercial pools, Y.M.C.A., Washington at East St., Y.W.C.A., Jefferson and Roosevelt; Miller Park, W. Wood and Summit Sts.; 3 outdoor commercial pools.

Picnic Grounds: Miller Park; Forest Park, adjoining Miller Park on the S.

Tennis: Municipal courts, Miller Park.

Annual Events: Presentation of *The American Passion Play,* Palm Sunday and continuing for 10 consecutive Sundays.

BLOOMINGTON (830 alt., 30,930 pop.), seat of McLean County, and its sister city, Normal (790 alt., 6,768 pop.), lie a little to the north and east of the geographical center of the State, in the heart of the corn belt and near the northeast limits of the coal fields. The gentle hill of the town site—uncommon in the central prairie—is a portion of the Bloomington Moraine, the long ridge of drift left by the Wisconsin glacier. Well wooded, with the courthouse crowning its top, it affords pleasant contrast to the flat geometry of towns that have clustered around the railroads on the unrelieved prairie. Normal, an independent municipality with its own waterworks, fire department, and police force, scorns the appellation of "suburb" and maintains its individuality, centered on State Normal University.

Leisurely paced, in keeping with its rôle as a university town, Bloomington serves as a trading center for a wide and fertile farm area, and gives little evidence of its industrial underpinning, although its products range from candy bars to heating equipment, from stoves and air-conditioning plants to grain elevators. Its residential area is in a large part gracefully Victorian, but the business section was largely rebuilt after the fire of 1900, when elaborate cornices, deco-

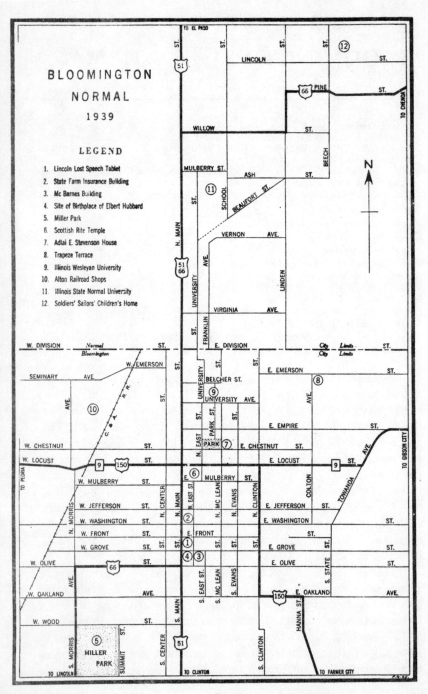

BLOOMINGTON
NORMAL
1939

LEGEND

1. Lincoln Lost Speech Tablet
2. State Farm Insurance Building
3. Mc Barnes Building
4. Site of Birthplace of Elbert Hubbard
5. Miller Park
6. Scottish Rite Temple
7. Adlai E. Stevenson House
8. Trapeze Terrace
9. Illinois Wesleyan University
10. Alton Railroad Shops
11. Illinois State Normal University
12. Soldiers' Sailors' Children's Home

rated façades, and machined gee-gaws were replaced by a soberer functionalism.

In the earliest years of the nineteenth century the large grove at this point, focus of several Indian trails, was known to a few stray trappers and traders. Legend has it that a small party of these rovers of the forests cached a keg of liquor here and inadvertently played absent host to a hilarious party of Indians. It is known, at least, that the site was called Keg Grove when the first permanent settlers came in 1822. The name was shortly changed, because of the profusion of flowers, to Blooming Grove, which prompted a citizen years later to express due gratitude. "Suppose Keg Grove had become transformed into Keg Town," he said. "How do you suppose Joe Fifer could have ever been elected governor of this State? Or how could Adlai Stevenson, of Keg Town, have been chosen Vice-President of the United States?"

Blooming Grove's early settlers were largely of British stock, and they brought a desire for the appurtenances of stability. Their community's name altered decently, they established a school of a sort, and a church with its own pastor, all within two years.

Although Bloomington traces its growth from Blooming Grove, it is not strictly a natural outgrowth of that village. In 1830 James Allin, subsequently ranked first among the city fathers, entered a quarter section of land on the north side of Blooming Grove. Formerly a commissioner of Fayette County, Allin undoubtedly had foreknowledge of the impending subdivision of that county; in December of the same year the legislature at Vandalia created the county of McLean. The following year the county commissioners accepted Allin's offer of land for the court house, and the town of Bloomington was laid out, adjoining Blooming Grove.

Of all the factors that gave rise to Illinois towns the possession of the county courthouse was far and away the most dependable. Bloomington grew slowly, in a complacent security, until the 1850's, when three events in quick succession forecast Bloomington's destiny as a little "big town" rather than as a sleepy and static county seat. In 1853 Illinois Wesleyan University was organized; the following year the rails of both the Illinois Central and the Chicago and Mississippi Railroads were extended through the town. The latter, now the Alton line, subsequently established its repair shops here, still the industrial mainstay of the city. Then, in 1857, residents remarked their "incredible good fortune" at the awarding of the Illinois State Normal University to North Bloomington, which shortly changed its name to Normal.

In the late 1800's Bloomington spread its name abroad with Wakefield's *Almanac,* published by a patent-medicine king whose specifics stood in rows of vari-colored bottles on the shelf above the wash basin in every kitchen in the Middle West. The publication reached readers of four languages, and made Bloomington the first word to pop into the mind when malaria or chilblains threatened.

Bloomington had its finger in many a State political pie. The State Republican party was organized here in 1856, at the Anti-Nebraska convention that heard Lincoln's "Lost Speech." Speaking extempore, he declared that those who deny freedom to others could not hope to retain it for themselves, that the abolitionists would never withdraw from the Union, that secession by the South would be met by forceful preservation of the Union by the North. The speech made Lincoln a power in the new party, a key-noter of the cause whose popularity swept him inevitably onward to the Presidency. Aligned with Lincoln from the first was the Bloomington *Pantagraph,* which has been published continuously since 1846.

Bloomington has had rather more than a fair representation of distinguished citizens. Two of her sons, John M. Hamilton and Joseph Fifer, were governors of the State; the portly Judge David Davis was one of Lincoln's most potent political allies; and Adlai Stevenson became Vice President of the United States under Cleveland. The late Margaret Illington, actress, compounded her stage name of syllables in the names of her native State and city, a city that has long had an inexplicable talent for nurturing artists of the world of amusement *(see below).*

POINTS OF INTEREST

1. The LINCOLN LOST SPEECH TABLET, SW. cor. East and Front Sts., commemorates the first State Convention of the Illinois Republican Party, May 29, 1856, at which Lincoln delivered his outspoken denunciation of slavery.

2. The STATE FARM INSURANCE BUILDING, 112 E. Washington St., 12 stories high, the tallest in Bloomington, is the home of the large fire and life insurance company that now ranks second among the city's employers.

3. The McBARNES BUILDING (*open weekdays, 10-9*), 201 E. Grove St., is an ornate 3-story brick building with Bedford trim. A memorial to the soldiers and sailors of all wars, it is the State headquarters of the American Legion and other patriotic organizations. On the first floor is the McLEAN COUNTY HISTORICAL SOCIETY MUSEUM (*10-12, 1-5 weekdays*), with much local material pertaining to Lincoln, old furniture and farm implements, and war relics. A plaque on the exterior commemorates this as the site of the first courthouse in the county.

4. The SITE OF THE BIRTHPLACE OF ELBERT HUBBARD, SE. corner of Grove and S. Main Sts., is marked by a tablet in memory of the native son who founded the Roycroft Shops at East Aurora, New York, published *The Philistine*, and wrote the *Message to Garcia*.

5. MILLER PARK, W. Wood and Summit Sts., Bloomington's main recreation ground, has 66 wooded and landscaped acres. A small Zoo and an AQUARIUM (*free 9-5*) are the principal attractions; in addition, Crystal Lake offers boating and bathing. The pavilion overlooking the lake has a roof-garden, concessions, and other accommodations. Near the northeast entrance stands the *Soldiers' Monument*, designed by Dwight Earl Frink, commemorating McLean County's dead in all wars previous to the World War.

6. The SCOTTISH RITE TEMPLE, 110 Mulberry St., built in the Italian Renaissance style, is headquarters for the Scottish Rite Order in central Illinois. Here, on one of the largest stages in the Middle West, are given performances of Bloomington's *American Passion Play*, which for almost two decades has been an annual event (*performances each Sun. from Palm Sun. until the first of June*). Carefully following the Biblical account, and lavishly staged, it has been attended by more than 500,000 persons from all parts of the country.

7. The ADLAI E. STEVENSON HOUSE (*private*), 901 N. McLean St., a two-story-and-a-half brick residence, Tudor in style is now occupied by the Sigma Alpha Iota sorority. Adlai Stevenson (1835-1914), a Kentuckian, came to Bloomington in 1852, practiced law, and served two terms in Congress before his election in 1893 to the vice-presidency of the United States. In 1900, running on Bryan's ticket for the same office, he was defeated, and returned to his law practice in Bloomington, where he resided until his death.

8. TRAPEZE TERRACE, 1201 E. Emerson St., has been termed "the Ecole des Beaux Arts of . . . that strange breed of human bats who soar, *sans* wings, far above the gaping crowds in circus tents and on county fair ballyhoo boulevards." Here are the winter quarters of many of the greatest aerial artists of the country, a large percentage of whom are natives of Bloomington. Both here and at Ward's Barn, the Flying La Vans, the Flying Concellos, and all the flying troupes of circus fame meet and set up their rigging under the watchful eye of "Pap" La Van, reigning patriarch. Tradition avers that no proper infant in the colony should leave its mother's arms for a swing less than 20 feet high. Although they do not care to have an audience while practicing, during the season Bloomington trapezists are to be seen in almost every circus.

9. The ILLINOIS WESLEYAN UNIVERSITY occupies six blocks in Bloomington's north side residential area, bounded by University Ave. and Park, Beecher, and University Sts. Comprising two divisions, the College of Liberal Arts and the School of Music, it is accredited by the North Central Association of College and Secondary Schools. Although it is supported by the Illinois Conference of the Methodist Episcopal Church, the university is non-denominational, enrolling some 800 students.

The university was first proposed in 1849 at the Illinois Methodist Episcopal conference here, but full classes were not held until 1851 and the charter was not granted until 1853. Listed among the early trustees of the University were such prominent persons as Judge Davis and Peter Cartwright, the great pioneer preacher. Encountering financial difficulties, the school suspended operations between 1855 and 1857, when it was reopened with a new president, the Rev. Oliver Munsell. An intensive drive for funds conducted by the president soon put the university on a sound basis, and it has since operated continuously. In 1930 it absorbed Hedding College, another Methodist Episcopal institution, which had long functioned at Abingdon, Illinois.

The university centers around HEDDING HALL (1871), which contains class rooms and the chapel. Nearby are OLD NORTH HALL, completed in the 1850's, and SCIENCE HALL, a modern laboratory. In adjacent squares are the MEMORIAL GYMNASIUM, with a swimming pool; BUCK MEMORIAL LIBRARY, housing 55,000 volumes; and PRESSER HALL, newest building, in which is the school of music and the auditorium.

10. The ALTON RAILROAD SHOPS, the largest industrial establishment in Bloomington, cover 124 acres of land between W. Chestnut St., N. Morris Ave., and Seminary Ave., employing more than 1,500 people. Here the entire process of the rehabilitation of railroad rolling stock can be observed.

11. ILLINOIS STATE NORMAL UNIVERSITY (*open; 8-4, Mon.-Fri.*) occupies a 56-acre campus bounded by University Ave. and Mulberry, School, and Beaufort Sts., in Normal. Oldest teachers' university in Illinois, it requires only a registration fee of thirty dollars for students pledging themselves to teach in Illinois. Its courses comprise a two year junior college course for teachers of elementary schools, and a four year course leading to a degree of Bachelor of Education.

The university, which now enrolls some 1,900 students, was among the first normal schools established in the United States, and grew out of the movement for free higher education that closely followed the establishment by Horace Mann of the first State Normal School in Massachusetts in 1839. A State convention of teachers at Bloomington in 1853 advocated the establishment of a normal school; in 1856, after side-tracking a motion to make the school a branch of the proposed Industrial University, they successfully petitioned the State legislature for a grant of funds.

Throughout the State newspapers announced that the school would go to the city offering the greatest inducement. When the contest narrowed to Batavia, Peoria, and Bloomington, local residents, led by Jesse Fell, increased their bid from $100,000 to $145,725, only to learn that their original bid had topped the next highest by $20,000; $70,000 of the bid was underwritten by a guarantee drafted by Abraham Lincoln and signed by 85 citizens.

Construction of the main building, begun in 1857, was soon halted by the panic, and classes were held in temporary quarters in Bloomington. When it became evident that some citizens would be unable to make good their pledges, additional funds were raised, largely through the efforts of Charles E. Hovey, first head of the school.

OLD MAIN, housing the administration offices and classrooms, is still the nucleus of the university. The other nine buildings are grouped informally about the wooded campus, laid out by a Philadelphia landscape architect early in the school's development. The LIBRARY, remodeled in 1917, was the second building erected. OLD

CASTLE, a gray stone building of medieval design, houses the commerce department and radio station WJBC. East of Old Main is the TRAINING SCHOOL, a practical teaching laboratory, with classes ranging from kindergarten to high school. The INDUSTRIAL ARTS BUILDING, which contains a large auditorium, is headquarters for the departments of industrial arts, home economics, and fine and applied arts. The DAVID FELMLEY HALL OF SCIENCE (1930) is the newest university building. FELL HALL, the women's dormitory, and McCORMICK GYMNASIUM complete the main buildings. One block west of the campus is the university's experimental farm, 95 choice acres in one of the richest sections of the State.

12. The SOLDIERS' AND SAILORS' CHILDREN'S HOME, Beech and Lincoln Sts., Normal, provides a home and education for about 650 children in ideal surroundings. On the 160 acres of land, mostly under cultivation, are 34 buildings; those for the younger children are designed in Norman style to represent a Mother Goose village. A special feature of the care afforded is an experimental school for retarded children of pre-school age. A placement bureau arranges adoptions in certain cases.

POINTS OF INTEREST IN ENVIRONS

Lake Bloomington, 15 *m.* (*see Tour 4*).

CAIRO

Railroad Stations: Commercial Ave. and 2nd St. for Cleveland, Cincinnati, Chicago and St. Louis Ry. (Big Four); Commercial Ave. and 14th St. for Illinois Central System (bus to North Cairo); Jefferson Ave. and 8th St. for Mobile and Ohio; 904 Commercial Ave. for Missouri Pacific (bus to Poplar Bluff, Mo.).

Bus Stations: Greyhound Terminal at 904 Commercial Ave. for Gibbs Bus Line, Missouri Pacific Transportation Co., Dixie Greyhound Lines, Inc., and Tri-City Transportation Co., Inc. (also at Big Four Cafe, Commercial Ave. and 2nd St.).

Taxis: City rates 10c per person.

Accommodations: Five hotels in business district.

Golf: Egyptian Golf Club (*daily fee*), 10 m. N. on US 51.

Swimming: Municipal pool, 2400 Sycamore St.

Tennis: Municipal courts, St. Mary's Park, 23rd St. and Park Place West.

For further information regarding this city, see the *Cairo Guide,* another of the American Guide Series, published November 1938 by the Cairo Public Library.

CAIRO (315 alt., 13,532 pop.), southernmost city of Illinois and seat of Alexander County, stands on the tip of a narrow peninsula where the Ohio pours its gray waters into the yellow Mississippi. Somewhat exotic for Illinois are Cairo's ginkgo and magnolia trees, its nearby canebrakes and cottonfields. Many Illinoisans and others blink on learning that the city is farther south than Richmond, Virginia, or Tunis, Africa.

Cairo is encircled by a huge levee that rises from the river delta like the ramparts of a walled town. Steamboats have whistled for a landing on the Ohio side since the 1840's. But most of the whistles have been stilled by the railroad, and today the levee, its revetted slope scoured clean by the river, has no more than a half-dozen sternwheelers moored along its mile-length. The street fronting the levee is lined with hotels, shops, and taverns, many of them deserted and falling to ruin, their weathered façades embellished with bracketed cornices, rows of dentils, and balconies of wrought iron. Of this quiet street, in which grass now sprouts between its pavement bricks, the Cairo *Gazette* reported in 1863: "Every house, cellar, and shed is occupied as a place of business and every occupant is doing well."

But gentle decay is not all of Cairo. Directly west of the Ohio Levee is Commercial Avenue, its south end solid with business houses, their modern first-floor fronts belied by the Victorian pomposity of

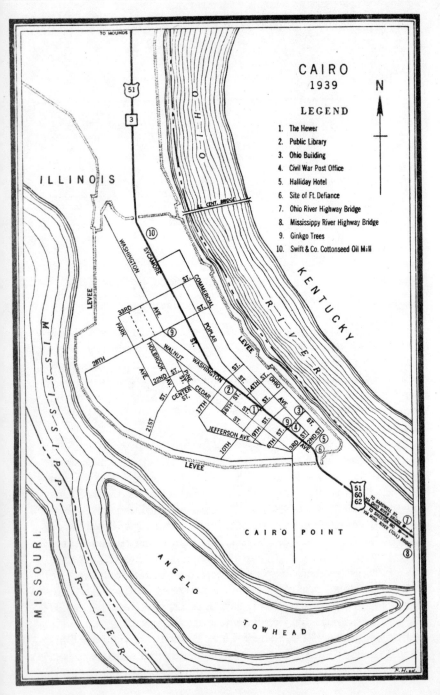

CAIRO
1939

LEGEND

1. The Hewer
2. Public Library
3. Ohio Building
4. Civil War Post Office
5. Halliday Hotel
6. Site of Ft. Defiance
7. Ohio River Highway Bridge
8. Mississippy River Highway Bridge
9. Ginkgo Trees
10. Swift & Co. Cottonseed Oil Mill

the upper stories. On Saturdays Commercial Avenue is astir with growers of corn, cotton, and apples, who arrive in clay-spattered cars to shop, see a movie, and observe the city sights. At such times Negro boys jig on the levee for the pennies of the passersby, and Negro jug bands play on street corners for pitched coins. The hot-tamale man appears at dusk, pushing his wares in a box fixed on a perambulator chassis.

Except for the industrial area at the north and the business section at the south, Cairo is largely residential. Most of the houses are frame structures of conventional design. Because early land promoters set high values on property near the confluence of the rivers, lots in the southern part of the city are noticeably small. Lawns here are minute, and porch fronts are within a few yards of the street. But in the central and northern sections, built when Cairo's hopes of becoming a steamboat metropolis were fading, there are spacious lawns planted with mulberry, sycamore, cottonwood, and magnolia trees.

Negroes compose 34 per cent of Cairo's population. They have a moving picture house, their own churches, restaurants, and small places of business. As in southern towns, separate schools are maintained for Negro children. Some Negroes are employed as longshoremen, others in cottonseed processing plants, and a smaller group as field-hands. Sharecropping is practised to some extent.

The processing of cottonseed is the chief industry of Cairo. Four mills produce cottonseed oil and cottonseed livestock feed. Ten firms deal in lumber, two in lumber milling. The lumber was originally obtained from nearby forests but is now shipped here from Southern States. The rivers continue to play a part in Cairo's economy. Three barge lines maintain local terminals, the largest of which is the rail-to-water terminal of the Federal Barge Line, at the east end of 18th Street.

The first attempt at settlement here occurred in 1818 when John G. Comegys, a St. Louis merchant, obtained from the Territorial Legislature an act incorporating the city and the bank of Cairo. The projected city was so named because its site was presumed to resemble that of Cairo, Egypt. When Comegys died about 1820, his scheme perished with him, but he had made a lasting contribution to Illinoisana in his choice of the name Cairo, for as a result "Egypt" has become the popular name of southern Illinois.

A second and successful attempt at settlement began in 1837 when the State legislature incorporated the Cairo City and Canal Company, with Darius B. Holbrook, "a shrewd Boston Yankee," as president. Holbrook hired several hundred workmen to build a levee, shops, and houses. The settlement was widely advertised in England, where the bonds of the Cairo City and Canal Company found eager purchasers through the London firm of John Wright & Company. This latter concern failed on November 23, 1840, and Cairo immediately declined, its population dropping from a thousand to less than a hundred within two years. Those who remained conducted shops and taverns for steamboat travelers. Charles Dickens visited Cairo on April 9, 1842; several historians have suggested that his interest in the settlement was inspired by his unprofitable investments in Cairo City bonds, but this is not established. In any case, he damned Cairo vigorously in *American Notes* (1842), using it as the prototype of the nightmare City of Eden in *Martin Chuzzlewit* (1843).

The discredited Cairo City and Canal Company was reorganized as the Cairo City Property Trust in 1846. Plans were laid to make Cairo the main depot of a trade route running south to the Gulf by water and north to the Great Lakes by rail. This necessitated the construction of a railway through Illinois, the cost of which was to be defrayed by a Federal land grant. In response to pressure generated by the Cairo City Property Trust, Congress gave Illinois more than 2,000,000 acres of public land in September 1850. The Illinois Central Railroad Company, beneficiary of the grant, was incorporated in 1851, and four years later a track between Cairo and Chicago was opened to traffic.

Cairo took root at once and prospered; its population had increased to 1,756 by 1857, the year in which a city charter was obtained. Each succeeding month increased the volume of products transported along the north-south route. This route might have become part of the basic economic pattern of the Middle West, with Cairo as a commercial capital, had not the Civil War dammed up the developing trade route. When gunboats drove the packets from the lower Mississippi, the corn and pork of central Illinois began to move in increasing amounts to Chicago, as they have continued to do, and Cairo ultimately ceased to be of importance as a regional commercial center.

Throughout the war Cairo was a concentration point of the Union Army and the base of the Western Flotilla, later renamed the Mississippi Squadron. One week after the fall of Fort Sumter, Cairo was garrisoned by 2,000 Illinois volunteers to prevent its seizure by Confederate troops, who had advanced within twenty miles of the city. The point at the junction of the rivers was fortified as Camp Defiance. Anthony Trollope, the English author, who visited Cairo in the winter of 1862, later reported in *North America* that the "sheds of soldiers" at Camp Defiance were "bad, comfortless, damp, and cold," but that they did not "stink like those of Benton barracks at St. Louis."

Ulysses S. Grant, then commander of the district of southeastern Missouri, established his headquarters at Cairo in September 1861. Here he massed men and gunboats for an arrow-like offensive that began early in February 1862, and resulted in the capture of Fort Henry, February 6, and Fort Donelson, February 16. Fourteen thousand Confederates were transported to Cairo to await confinement in Northern prisons. Later, when Vicksburg fell, some 30,000 Confederates were brought here.

By the end of the war Cairo had an estimated population of 8,000. In 1867 more than 3,700 steamboats docked at the city, a figure that made predictions about the decline of the steamboat seem absurd. Later, when the supremacy of the railroad was established, Cairo offset the loss in part by developing local plants to process cottonseed oil and mill lumber. In the last quarter of the century seven railroads were built into the city. Mark Twain, most notable of the steamboatmen who had gone "booming down to Cairo," observed in *Life on the Mississippi* (1883) that "Cairo is a brisk town now and is substantially built and has a city look about it . . ."

The spotlight focused on Cairo during the fifties and sixties was again trained on the city in 1937. In February of that year the Ohio River swelled to record heights, inundating Paducah, Louisville, Cincinnati, and scores of smaller communities. As the huge crest moved downstream to the Mississippi, newsreel cameramen and newspaper correspondents rushed to Cairo to report the anticipated catastrophe. Women and children were evacuated from the threatened city, and a three-foot bulwark of timbers and sandbags was hastily built on top of the levee. The water rose swiftly to within four inches of the untested bulwark, wavered there for several hours, and then began slowly to recede. Of all the cities on the lower Ohio, Cairo alone withstood the flood.

POINTS OF INTEREST

1. THE HEWER, between 9th and 10th Sts., a heroic bronze nude by George Grey Barnard, was presented to Cairo in 1906 by Miss Mary H. Halliday and her family, in memory of her father, William Parker Halliday, who died in 1889. Prior to its unveiling at Cairo, *The Hewer* had been exhibited at the St. Louis World's Fair. In 1910 Lorado Taft declared *The Hewer* to be one of the two best nudes in America.

2. The CAIRO PUBLIC LIBRARY *(open 9-6 weekdays)*, 1609 Washington Ave., is a two-story brick structure, built in 1883, housing 31,000 volumes. Near the entrance is the *Fighting Boys,* an original by Janet Scudder. The Cairo group differs from Miss Scudder's *Fighting Boys* in the Art Institute of Chicago in that its figures are of bronze and garlanded; those at Chicago are nude and of lead.

A MUSEUM on the second floor of the library contains statuary, geological specimens, Indian artifacts, Civil War memorabilia, various relics and curios, and a complete file of Cairo newspapers between 1848-60. Other Civil War relics, including soldier's uniforms and a Confederate flag, are in a glass case on the landing of the stairway to the second floor.

3. The OHIO BUILDING, 609 Ohio St., a three-story stone structure built about 1858, was the headquarters of General Grant between September 1861, and April 1862. Grant's office was at the second-floor front. During part of his stay in Cairo, Grant's wife and children lived in the rooms opposite his office.

4. The CIVIL WAR POST OFFICE OF CAIRO was housed in the two-story brick structure at the SW. corner of Commercial Ave. and Sixth St. Now occupied by a cafe, the building was constructed in 1855 by S. Wilson and his brother, who advertised, "Our store will be kept open Day and Night for the accommodation of steamboats."

5. The HALLIDAY HOTEL *(15¢ guide fee for non-guests)*, Ohio and Second Sts., is a five-story brick structure, with a mansard roof and a cupola. With the exception of the south half of the wing that fronts Ohio Street, the Halliday was built in 1857-59. When Cairo became an Army depot in 1861, a correspondent for *Harper's Weekly* reported that "the officers . . . occupy the hotel from cellar to garrett." Most important of the hostelry's wartime guests was Gen. U. S. Grant, who lodged in Room 215. From the window at the south of this chamber the General could keep an eye on Camp Defiance and the gunboats

that commanded the confluence of the Ohio and Mississippi. This view has been obstructed by an addition made to the hotel in 1908.

On the walls of the hotel lobby are photographs of Camp Defiance, Civil War Cairo, gunboats of the Western Flotilla, and various Union officers, including Generals Grant and McClernand. In the hotel tap-room is the so-called "Grant's bar," manufactured in 1859.

In the cellar, under the east sidewalk, are eight cells; according to tradition, they were used to conceal fugitive slaves and later to quarter Rebel prisoners; research fails to substantiate either of these claims. In all probability the chambers were used merely as storage places.

6. The vacant lot about 350 yards south of the Halliday Hotel is the SITE OF CAMP DEFIANCE. The confluence of the Ohio and Mississippi, which the camp once commanded, is now about three-fourths of a mile farther south.

7. The OHIO RIVER HIGHWAY BRIDGE, left from the south end of Washington Ave., joins Illinois and Kentucky. It was built in 1937-38 at a cost of $3,000,000. The total length, including approaches, is 6,229 feet.

8. The MISSISSIPPI HIGHWAY BRIDGE, right from the south end of Washington Ave., connects Illinois and Missouri. A cantilever structure 3,720 feet long, designed by Dr. J. A. Waddel, it was opened to traffic in 1929.

9. GINKGO TREES, a species indigenous to China and Japan, grow on the lawns of houses at 608 Washington Ave., the SE. corner of Washington Ave. and 28th St., and elsewhere. These delicately leafed trees, commonly planted near Chinese temples, thrive at Cairo, some of them reaching a height of 100 feet. The date and circumstances of their introduction locally are unknown.

10. The SWIFT AND COMPANY COTTONSEED OIL MILL (*generally closed during growing season; at other times open between 8-4 weekdays; free guide service*), 4210 Sycamore St., is representative of Cairo's chief industry. Visitors are shown the process of extracting oil from cottonseed. The seed is conveyed from the storage place by a work screw to an apparatus where jets of compressed air blow away extraneous matter. The seeds then enter linters, which function like cotton gins, to be stripped of fleecy fibers that escaped the teeth of the gin; the "linters" thus obtained are used in manufacturing paper, films, fabrics, batting, cellophane, lacquers, and varnishes. The cleansed seeds are cracked and screened to separate the hulls from the kernels.

The hulls are used as stuffing, livestock feed, and as a base for explosives. The kernels are rolled, cooked, and reduced to pulp, which is subjected to a pressure of 4,200 pounds per square inch. The crude oil that emerges is refined and used in salad oils, shortening, oleomargarine, candles, miners' lamps, and glycerin. The caked kernels that remain are fed to livestock.

POINTS OF INTEREST IN ENVIRONS

Horseshoe Lake, 16 *m.* (*see Tour 8*). Mound City Marine Ways, 8 *m.* (*see Tour 4*).

CHAMPAIGN and URBANA

Railroad Stations: Champaign—116 N. Chestnut St., for Illinois Central System; 804 N. Randolph St., for Wabash R. R.; 719 N. Neil St., for Cleveland, Cincinnati, Chicago and St. Louis Ry. (Big Four); 804 N. Randolph St., for Illinois Traction System (electric). *Urbana*—223 N. Broadway, for Cleveland, Cincinnati, Chicago and St. Louis Ry. (Big Four); 220 N. Broadway, for Wabash Ry. and Illinois Traction System (electric).

Bus Stations: Champaign—Union Bus Depot, 213 S. Neil St., for Illini Coach, Illinois Greyhound, and Swallow Coach. *Urbana*—107 N. Broadway, for Greyhound and Swallow Lines.

City Buses: Same rate both cities—5c.

Taxis: Same rate both cities; 25c first m., 5c each additional ¼ m.

Accommodations: Champaign—three hotels. *Urbana*—two hotels.

Information Service: Champaign—Champaign Chamber of Commerce, 318 N. Neil St., and Chicago Motor Club, Virginia Theatre Building. *Urbana*—Urbana Association of Commerce, 201 W. Main St.

Radio Stations: Champaign—WDWS (1370 kc.). *Urbana*—WILL (890 kc.).

Motion Picture Houses: Champaign—Five. *Urbana*—Two.

Golf: Champaign—Kenwood Links, 2½ m. W. of city on State 10; 9 holes; 25c fee. *Urbana*—Urbana Golf and Country Club, N. of city on Broadway; 18 holes; $1.00 fee.

Tennis: Champaign—University courts, bordering Memorial Stadium on First and Fourth Sts.; no fee; use courts marked Public. *Urbana*—University courts, Springfield Ave. and Wright St.; no fee.

Indoor Ice Skating: Champaign—University Rink, Armory and Fifth Sts., November to April.

Swimming: Urbana—Crystal Lake Park, 601 N. Broadway, 15c.

Horseback Riding: Urbana—Crystal Lake Park, 601 N. Broadway, 50c per hour.

Annual Events: For University of Illinois events consult University calendar, posted in all campus buildings.

CHAMPAIGN (740 alt., 20,348 pop.) and URBANA (750 alt., 13,060 pop.) lie in the east central section of the State in the center of a fertile prairie. Although they are divided by no more than a street, they are individually incorporated and preserve a vigorous independence.

The campus of the University of Illinois, which lies largely in Urbana at the dividing line of the two cities, is the heart of the two cities, both physically and economically. Interposing what is virtually a third city between the two, it far surpasses any single local industry in importance. Here the rivalry of town and gown founders on the rock of commerce. For nine months of each year the population is increased by fourteen thousand or more; merchants watch the registration figures closely, and dress their shops to cater to the youthful taste.

Should a volcanic upheaval cover Champaign and Urbana, future

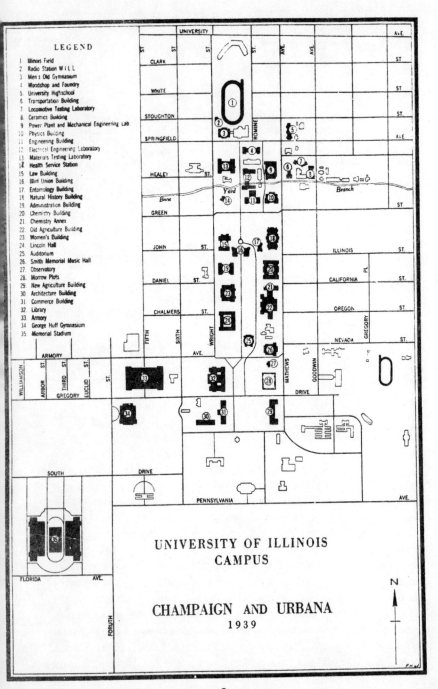

LEGEND

1 Illinois Field
2 Radio Station WILL
3 Men's Old Gymnasium
4 Woodshop and Foundry
5 University Highschool
6 Transportation Building
7 Locomotive Testing Laboratory
8 Ceramics Building
9 Power Plant and Mechanical Engineering Lab.
10 Physics Building
11 Engineering Building
12 Electrical Engineering Laboratory
13 Materials Testing Laboratory
14 Health Service Station
15 Law Building
16 Illini Union Building
17 Entomology Building
18 Natural History Building
19 Administration Building
20 Chemistry Building
21 Chemistry Annex
22 Old Agriculture Building
23 Women's Building
24 Lincoln Hall
25 Auditorium
26 Smith Memorial Music Hall
27 Observatory
28 Morrow Plots
29 New Agriculture Building
30 Architecture Building
31 Commerce Building
32 Library
33 Armory
34 George Huff Gymnasium
35 Memorial Stadium

UNIVERSITY OF ILLINOIS
CAMPUS

CHAMPAIGN AND URBANA
1939

N

archaeologists would encounter little difficulty in piecing together the mosaic. Although not an industrial town, Champaign is the worldlier of the two, with its railroads, its bustling business district, and its 20-odd factories that manufacture tiles, concrete mixers, gloves, soy bean products, and a dozen others. Urbana, which is heavily wooded, gives the impression of being more leisurely and maintains that subdued dignity characteristic of a Midwest county seat. Certain features would identify the campus section even if its university buildings were completely razed. At the campus edge cluster numerous "coke 'n smokes," elaborate confectioneries, counterparts of which are to be found only in university towns. And deep into both towns, north, east, and west of the campus, runs street after street of student rooming houses, varying in size from seven to thirty rooms, each with the ubiquitous double-decked bed, goose-neck study lamp, and capacious book rack. Interspersed are the fraternity and sorority houses, individual in architectural style and more elaborately furnished, but unmistakably indigenous to the American university. It was the fraternity houses of Illinois that inspired *Fraternity Row,* a popular novel of the 1920's by Lynn and Lois Montross, both of whom were students here.

Settled in 1822 by Willard Tompkins, Urbana is some 30 years older than Champaign. In 1833 it was designated seat of newly formed Champaign county, and settled back in anticipation of a leisurely and steady growth. In 1854 came a rude awakening. The Illinois Central Railroad, first line of any importance in the State, was pushing south with its rails. At Urbana the engineers laid out three possible routes, two through the city and one about two miles west. To Urbana's dismay, the last route was chosen. What prompted this choice lies buried in rumor and counter-rumor, which hint at covert real estate deals. Swarms of laborers swung their hammers and eventually moved on, leaving new rails glistening on the prairie two miles out of town.

Urbana, faced with the choice of moving to the depot or attempting to maintain its existence without a railroad, chose the latter. Almost immediately a town referring to itself as West Urbana sprang up around the depot, but farmers avoided confusion by calling the two towns the Depot and Old Town. In a bill for incorporation as a city in 1855, Urbana included a clause authorizing the annexation of the new town. Indignant Depot residents successfully fought the bill and in 1860 incorporated under the name of Champaign. The cleavage thus established has since been maintained.

Champaign boomed as a trade center and soon passed Urbana in population. The rich prairies, opened for cultivation by the railroads, poured their bumper crops into the railroad town. Upstart and flushed with prosperity, Champaign attempted to wrest the county seat from Urbana, which, realizing that the courthouse was its chief asset, met the assault with successful vigor.

In the middle of the nineteenth century arose a great clamor from the people of Illinois for an industrial college, at which their children could receive practical training as well as a classical education. In 1862 Congress passed the Morrill Act, providing generous land grants to the several States for the establishment of schools "to teach such branches of learning as are related to agriculture and the mechanic arts." A scramble for the new college immediately ensued. A few years earlier Champaign and Urbana, with the aid of several eastern promoters, had begun constructing between the two towns a seminary for higher education. The rival cities buried the axe in the log of expediency, and collaborated on a plan to obtain the new "Agricultural College" by proffering the seminary building as its nucleus. A powerful lobby was sent to Springfield; in 1867, to the surprise of older communities, Urbana was named the home of the new State college. The choice was bitterly assailed by Chicago and other cities, but by the end of the century the new institution was functioning smoothly and criticism had turned to praise.

The population curve of the two cities has largely followed the registration of the university. In the summer months, following the student exodus, the importance of the school to both cities becomes graphic. As the campus undergoes the annual exodus and is turned over to the comparative handful of summer students, many of the campus stores and restaurants close for the vacation period, and Urbana and Champaign turn to their internal affairs until the middle of September when the trains and buses, running special schedules, again pour their young thousands into town.

The University of Illinois

The University grew out of the Illinois Industrial College, chartered in 1867 and opened on March 2, 1868. Confused for many years over its proper function, the school did not begin to exert much influence in the State until the closing years of the century. One group stoutly insisted that the Morrill Act limited the scope of the school to agriculture and purely vocational subjects. Derisive pictures were painted of farmboys coming, muddied from their plowing lesson, to study Plato.

The school received little aid from the State until Governor Altgeld's term (1892-1896), when expansion enabled it to compromise between plow and Plato, to the satisfaction of the supporters of each. Among the last of the State universities established in the Old Northwest Territory, Illinois grew rapidly in the early 1900's and by 1938 ranked eighth in enrollment (13,587) among the Nation's colleges and universities. Huge, versatile, and democratic, Illinois might well be studied as the prototype of Midwest universities. Particularly known for its efficient College of Agriculture, the university has also done notable work in the fields of chemical and physical research. Seven colleges and four schools comprise the Champaign-Urbana campus; the medical, dental, and pharmaceutical colleges are in Chicago.

The campus lies largely north and south of Green Street, and east of Wright Street, the line between Champaign and Urbana. It is divided roughly into two quadrangles, with the exception of the southern portion, which spreads over the broad South Campus. North of Green Street, dividing the two, are the crowded older buildings, the woodshops, foundries, and laboratories. The main quadrangle with its newer buildings encloses an open mall. Beyond the Auditorium, the south limit of the main quadrangle, are the newer buildings, carefully planned in relation to each other and consistent in their Georgian architecture.

CAMPUS TOUR

(Points of interest are listed geographically and are numbered to correspond with the accompanying map. Motorists are cautioned that classes change during the last 10 minutes of each hour. Unless otherwise specified, buildings may be inspected between 8 and 5.)

(1)   ILLINOIS FIELD is the oldest site of the university. Here stood the Champaign and Urbana Seminary, first building to house the old Industrial College. Later the football field, where Robert Zuppke first put into practice many of his theories, it is now used for university baseball games. At the south end of the field is (2) RADIO STATION WILL, owned and operated by the university. Around the corner on Springfield Ave. is (3) the MEN'S OLD GYMNASIUM,

formerly the main gymnasium, but now used for physical education classes. In one of the older buildings (4), the WOODSHOP AND FOUNDRY *(guide; apply Room 3)*, is offered vocational training typical of that proposed by certain early educators as the sole function of the college.

(5)   The UNIVERSITY HIGH SCHOOL co-operates with the College of Education, which uses it as a training school. The College of Engineering directs the activities carried on in (6) the TRANS-PORTATION BUILDING *(guide; apply Room 101)*. On the second floor is a mining exhibit, showing different types of lamps and a display of assaying methods. Behind the Transportation Building is (7) the LOCOMOTIVE TESTING LABORATORY, containing a complete locomotive for practical training of students in railway engineering.

(8)   The CERAMICS BUILDING houses one of the finest schools of ceramics in the United States, and is completely equipped with a laboratory for making brick, tile, pottery, enamels, glazes, etc. The building, which contains a small museum on the second floor, was constructed entirely of material obtained in Illinois.

(9)   The POWER PLANT and the MECHANICAL ENGI-NEERING LABORATORY are in the same building. An open mez-zanine on the main floor overlooks the welter of pumps, boilers, and other equipment, on which students make practical application of engineering theory. Fronting on Green St. is (10) the PHYSICS BUILDING *(guide; apply Room 201)*, containing classrooms and the offices of the College of Physics. There are numerous specialized laboratories in the building for advanced research by staff members and student assistants. Notable among the achievements of this staff is the development of a ray for the treatment of lukemia.

Immediately to the west is (11) the ENGINEERING BUILD-ING *(guide; apply Room 201)*, with the offices of the College of En-gineering. Opposite the entrance is a scale model of a reinforced concrete arch bridge, typical of those prepared by the college to aid construction engineers in the planning and building of real bridges. Behind the Engineering Building is (12) the ELECTRICAL EN-GINEERING LABORATORY, with electric motors, dynamos, and other apparatus for training in electrical engineering. Here, once a year, is given the department's big "E. E." show of popularized experi-ments with electricity.

(13)   The MATERIALS TESTING LABORATORY contains the testing equipment of the engineering school, including an Emery-Tatnall machine, one of the largest in the world, which can exert a push or pull of 3,000,000 pounds. It is used for testing full-sized concrete and steel columns, and other units of heavy construction.

(14)   The HEALTH SERVICE STATION, formerly the president's home, is occupied by the hygiene department. Here, in the early days of September each year, come thousands of new entrants to the university for the required medical examination. Behind the Health Station flows the Bone Yard Branch, a small stream, once the sophomores' favorite receptacle for brash freshmen.

(15)   The LAW BUILDING, formerly the University Library, houses the College of Law and the department of mathematics. It has been commended as one of the finest examples of Romanesque architecture in the Middle West. Sharpest of many a graduate's memories of Illinois are the solemn Westminster notes, echoing from its chimes tower over the deserted campus at midnight. The inner court of the building faces on the receiving desk of the law library, and is decorated with four lunettes by Newton Wells. In the mathematics annex is a large collection of physical models of mathematic equations, curiously resembling cubist or surrealist sculpture.

(16)   The ILLINI UNION BUILDING, the student center, is the newest of the campus structures, replacing University Hall, which was demolished in 1938.

Immediately east is (17) the little ENTOMOLOGY BUILDING, which was once large enough to house the Law School; beyond is (18) the NATURAL HISTORY BUILDING, containing a Museum of Natural History scattered throughout its three floors. Facing Wright St. is (19) the ADMINISTRATION BUILDING, housing the offices of the President, the Dean of Men, the Registrar, and the Bursar. It is the business heart of the University, where the immense detail of running the huge institution is handled. Just north of the building is the grave of Dr. John Milton Gregory, first Regent of the University, marked by an inconspicuous granite monument with the following inscription: ". . . if you seek his monument look about you."

Across the open quadrangle is (20) the CHEMISTRY BUILDING and (21) the CHEMISTRY ANNEX, with the offices of the department of chemistry, classrooms and laboratories. The chemistry department has long been noted for the research achievements of its members, important among whom is B. F. Hopkins, who isolated the rare element illinium in 1926.

(22)   The OLD AGRICULTURE BUILDING, formerly the offices of the College of Agriculture, now has the offices of several departments, classrooms, and laboratories. Directly across the mall is (23) the WOMEN'S BUILDING, with the offices of the Dean of Women. Adjoining is (24) LINCOLN HALL, with the offices of the College of Liberal Arts and Sciences, classrooms, and a little theater for student productions. On the fourth floor is a Museum of European culture *(open weekdays 3:30-5:30, except Sat. 1-3, Sun. 2:30-5:45)*. The exhibits are in the main, illustrative of the medieval period: manuscripts, arms and armor, costumes, and coins. Across the end of the quadrangle is (25) the AUDITORIUM, containing a large lecture hall, also used as a theater. In the lobby is a journalistic Hall of Fame, instituted to commemorate outstanding Illinois editors, but since expanded to include those of national and international importance. On the steps of the building, in late spring and early fall, are held twilight band concerts and interfraternity and intersorority sings. Behind the building is the *Alma Mater Group,* the work of the late Lorado Taft, a graduate of the university in 1879.

(26)   SMITH MEMORIAL MUSIC HALL houses offices of the School of Music, an excellent recital hall, and sound-proof practice rooms. Behind the hall is (27) the OBSERVATORY *(not open to the public)*. Immediately south lie (28) the MORROW PLOTS, oldest soil experimental plots in America. The three tiny strips of land have been under controlled cultivation and observation since 1876.

Just beyond is (29) the NEW AGRICULTURE BUILDING, housing the classrooms, laboratories, and offices of the university's great College of Agriculture. From it is directed the extensive research that reaches, either through the school's graduates or its numerous extension services, almost every farm in Illinois. South of the Agriculture Building are subsidiary buildings, under the control of the College of Agriculture, such as greenhouses, laboratories, stables and dairies, and beyond them, the broad stretches of the experimental farms.

(30)   The ARCHITECTURE BUILDING is the home of the College of Fine and Applied Arts, and contains, on the first floor, a gallery where work of students is exhibited. Making an L with the

Architecture Building, (31) the COMMERCE BUILDING contains the offices and classrooms of the College of Commerce.

Immediately north, at the end of Wright St., stands (32) the LIBRARY, one of the newer buildings. The call desk, on the second floor, opens on the low ceilinged stacks, which are ten floors in height and contain 800,000 volumes. The reference room, directly opposite the call desk, has windows decorated with the colophons of distinguished printers of the past. Above the main stairway are four distinguished murals by Harry Faulkner.

Down Armory Street from the Library is (33) the huge ARMORY, home of the university's Reserve Officers' Training Corps. When the building was first erected, it was suggested that provision be made to convert it into a ballroom for university dances, and the enormous size of the Armory prompted a campus wag to recommend that chaperones be provided with motorcycles and binoculars.

(34) The GEORGE HUFF GYMNASIUM was named for the long-time director of athletics at the university. Here are held the home games of the varsity basketball team, and many Big Ten swimming meets. Beyond it rears the great bulk of (35) MEMORIAL STADIUM, dedicated in 1924, the gift of some 20,000 graduates and students. On the east and west sides are great colonnades bearing the names of 183 Illinois students and alumni who died in the World War. The stadium, seating approximately 70,000, was the scene of Harold "Red" Grange's swift rise to national fame in 1925. The Big Ten Conference football games begin in October and end the Saturday before Thanksgiving.

OTHER POINTS OF INTEREST

The CHAMPAIGN CITY BUILDING, Neil St. and University Ave., was finished in 1937. Its design, an adaptation of the widely publicized City Building in Los Angeles, departs sharply from the classic and neo-classic forms prevalent throughout the Midwest. The lower portion is two stories in height, severely simple in treatment, and at the west end a six-story tower rises in a receding shaft to an octagonal, five-stepped crown.

WEST SIDE PARK, corner Church and Elm Sts., is the oldest of Champaign's parks. At its center is the bronze statue, *Prayer for Rain*, executed by Edward Kemeys, sculptor of the Chicago Art Institute's noted lions. The statue depicts an Indian brave praying for rain, while a panther and a deer join him in attitudes of supplication.

CARLE PARK, Iowa St. and Carle Ave. in Urbana, about ten acres in extent, is distinguished by Lorado Taft's statue of heroic size, portraying Lincoln as a young lawyer on the old Eighth Judicial Circuit.

The CHAMPAIGN COUNTY COURT HOUSE, corner Main St. and Broadway, was dedicated in 1901, the fourth courthouse to stand on this site. A memorial at the north entrance attests the fact that Lincoln traveled this way as he rode the Eighth Judicial Circuit. In the third building, one spring day in 1853, Lincoln argued a railroad case as attorney for the Illinois Central Railroad, receiving $25 for successfully prosecuting a condemnation suit. In the fall of 1854, no longer an obscure lawyer, he spoke again in the old building, assailing Senator Stephen Douglas and the Nebraska Bill. A marble tablet on the second floor of the present courthouse commemorates this occasion.

CRYSTAL LAKE PARK, W. Park and Lake Sts., Urbana's largest park, contains wooded sections, a spring-fed lake used for boating in summer and skating in winter, a swimming pool, and an amusement hall. Within the park traces of the old Kickapoo Trail can still be seen.

POINTS OF INTEREST IN ENVIRONS

Chanute Field, 17 *m.* (*see Tour 3*).

CHICAGO

Steam Railroad Passenger Stations: North Western Station, Madison and Canal Sts., for Chicago and North Western Ry.; Dearborn Station, Polk and Dearborn Sts., for Santa Fe Ry., Chicago and Eastern Illinois Ry., Chicago Western Indiana R. R., Chicago, Indianapolis, and Louisville Ry. (Monon Route), Erie R. R., Grand Trunk Western R. R., and Wabash Ry.; Union Station, Canal St., Adams St., and Jackson Blvd., for A ton R. R., Burlington R. R., Chicago, Milwaukee, St. Paul and Pacific R. R., and Pennsylvania R. R.; Central Station, 11th Pl. and Michigan Ave., for Illinois Central System, Cleveland, Cincinnati, Chicago and St. Louis Ry. (Big Four), and Michigan Central R. R.; Grand Central Station, Harrison and Wells Sts., for Baltimore and Ohio R. R., Chicago Great Western R. R., Minneapolis, St. Paul, and Sault Ste. Marie Ry. (Soo Line), and Pere Marquette Ry.; La Salle St. Station, Van Buren and La Salle Sts., for Chicago, Rock Island and Pacific Ry., New York Central R. R., and New York, Chicago and St. Louis R. R. (Nickel Plate).
There are many stations in outlying neighborhoods for both suburban and through trains. For various ticket offices and agencies, see Chicago Classified Telephone Directory.

Steam Railroad Interurban Service: Chicago, Burlington & Quincy R. R., Chicago, Milwaukee, St. Paul and Pacific R. R., Alton R. R., and Pennsylvania R. R.: Chicago, Rock Island and Pacific Ry., New York Central R. R., Chicago and North Western Ry., Chicago and Eastern Illinois Ry., Chicago and Western Indiana R. R., and Wabash Ry.

Electric Interurban Stations: Wells and Quincy Sts., for Chicago, Aurora and Elgin R. R.; Wabash Ave. and Adams St., for Chicago, North Shore and Milwaukee R. R.; Michigan Ave. and Randolph St. for Chicago, South Shore and South Bend R. R., and Illinois Central Suburban System.

Bus Terminals: New Trailway Bus Terminal, 20 E. Randolph St., for National Trailways System, Southern Limited, Bluebird System, Yankee Trailways, and South Suburban Safeway Lines; 514 S. Wabash Ave. for All American Bus Lines, and De Luxe Motor Stages of Illinois; 746 S. Wabash Ave. for De Luxe Motor Stages, and Sioux Ltd. Lines; Union Bus Depot, 1157 S. Wabash Ave. for Greyhound Lines and Chicago, North Western Stages. Many other sub-stations and ticket offices in Loop and in outlying areas. Shore Line, 6309 South Park Ave.

Airport: Municipal Airport, 6200 S. Cicero Ave., for American Air Lines, Braniff Airways, Chicago and Southern Air Lines, Eastern Air Lines, Northwest Air Lines, Transcontinental and Western Air Lines, United Air Lines, and Pennsylvania Central Air Lines. Taxibus to Loop in 35 minutes, 75c.

Piers: Navy Pier, foot of Grand Ave., for Chicago, Duluth and Georgian Bay Transit Co., Chicago-Milwaukee Steamship Line, Cleveland and Buffalo Steamship Co., and Chicago, Roosevelt Steamship Co.

Taxis: 20c first 1/3 m.; 10c for each additional 2/3 m.; 5c for each additional passenger.

Local Transportation: Surface lines, 7c fare; buses, 10c, elevated lines, 10c. Transfers issued from surface cars and buses to elevated, and vice versa; no transfers between surface lines and buses. The Illinois Central electric suburban system serves the south side and south suburbs with downtown stations on Michigan Ave., at Randolph St., Van Buren St., and Roosevelt Rd.

Street Numbering System: Madison St. is the dividing line between the north and south numbers, State St. between the east and west numbers; 800 numbers to a mile, except first three miles south. For direction and location of streets see Chicago Classified Telephone Directory.

Accommodations: Ample accommodations in all sections of the city; no seasonal rates; first-class Loop hotels are sometimes filled during large conventions. Tourist homes are found along some of the through routes in the city.

Public Information Services: Chicago *Tribune* Public Service Office, 1 S. Dearborn St.; Chicago *Daily News* Personal Service Bureau, 400 W. Madison St.; Chicago Motor Club, 66 E. South Water St.; Illinois Automobile Club, 3401 S. Michigan Ave.; Marshall Field and Co. Personal Service Bureau (main floor), and Information Bureau (3rd floor), State and Washington Sts. Other department stores and newspapers also maintain information offices.

Radio Stations: WAAF (920 kc.), WBBM (770 kc.), WCBD (1080 kc.), WCFL (970 kc.), WCRW (1210 kc.), WEDC (1210 kc.), WENR (870 kc.), WGES (1360 kc.), WGN (720 kc.), WJJD (1130 kc.), WLS (870 kc.), WMAQ (670 kc.), WMBI (1080 kc.), WSBC (1210 kc.).

Theaters and Motion Picture Houses: Legitimate theaters downtown; about four plays usually run concurrently during the winter, with a few scattered productions during the summer. First run motion picture theaters are in the Loop; there are many large neighborhood theaters.

Recreation: The Chicago Park District offers facilities for wide variety of sports in parks and field houses throughout the city, including free tennis courts, beaches, and small fee golf courses. Call Harrison 5252 for information. The Forest Preserve District provides facilities for picnicking, tobogganing, and other forms of recreation. Call Franklin 3000.

Annual Events: Theodore Thomas Memorial Concert, Jan. 4th or first Thurs. following, Orchestra Hall. Exhibition by Artists of Chicago and Vicinity, Feb.-Mar. (4-6 *weeks*), Art Institute; Chinese New Year, Jan.-Mar. (1 *day*), Wentworth Ave. and Cermak Rd.; Golden Gloves Boxing Tournaments, Feb.-Mar., Chicago Stadium; Civic Orchestra Concerts, 3 or 4 Sundays in Jan.-Mar., Orchestra Hall; Chicago Singverein Concert, early Spring, Orchestra Hall; Flower Show of the Garden Club of Illinois, Mar.-Apr. (1 *week*), Navy Pier; Swedish Choral Club Concert, Apr., Orchestra Hall; Apollo Musical Club Concert, Apr. and Dec., Orchestra Hall; Paulist Choristers Concert, Apr., Orchestra Hall; Sunrise Service, Easter Sun., Soldier Field; Easter Flower Show, Easter or Palm Sun., (2 *weeks*), Garfield and Lincoln Park Conservatories; Greek Orthodox Good Friday Procession, Halsted St. at Blue Island Ave.; International Exhibition of Water Colors, Apr.-May (4-6 *weeks*), Art Institute; Polish Constitution Day Parade, first Sun. before or after May 3, Kosciusko Statue, Humboldt Park; Norwegian Independence Day Celebration, May 17, Humboldt Park; Exhibition by Students of the School of the Art Institute, May-July (4-6 *weeks*), Art Institute; Outdoor Concerts, July 1-Labor Day, Grant Park Band Shell; Italian Church Fiestas, summer, streets about various Italian churches; Chicago-Mackinac Race, one Sat. in July, Belmont Harbor; Summer Flower Show, July and Aug., Garfield and Lincoln Park Conservatories; Chicagoland Music Festival, 3rd Sat. in Aug., Soldier Field; Mexican Independence Day, Sept. 16 or Sat. preceding, Ashland Boulevard Auditorium; Chicago Camera Club Exhibition, Oct., Art Institute; Exhibition of American Paintings and Sculpture, Oct.-Nov. (4-6 *weeks*), Art Institute; Chicago Civic Opera, Oct.-Dec., at Civic Opera House; Chicago Symphony Orchestra Concerts, Oct.-Apr., Orchestra Hall; Woman's Symphony Orchestra of Chicago, Oct.-Jan., 3-6 concerts, Orchestra Hall or Auditorium; Chicago Sunday Evening Club Lectures, Oct.-May, Orchestra Hall; Florence Dibell Bartlett lectures on art, Thurs. 6:30; Oct.-May, Art Institute; International Exhibition of Etching and Engraving, Nov.-Jan.; even numbered years (6-8 *weeks*), Art Institute; Annual Automobile Show, 3rd week in Nov., International Amphitheater; International Live Stock Show, 4th week in Nov., International Amphitheater; St. Andrew's

Banquet ("piping in the haggis"), Nov. 30, Palmer House; Chrysanthemum Show, Nov., Garfield and Lincoln Park Conservatories; Christmas Flower Show (2 *weeks*), Garfield and Lincoln Park Conservatories; International Exhibition of Lithography and Wood Engraving, Dec.-Jan., odd years, (6-8 *weeks*), Art Institute. During the summer many boat races are held in the harbors on weekends. See Park District schedules for tournaments, regattas, and various exhibitions held throughout the year.

CHICAGO (598 alt., 3,376,438 pop.), vibrant, noisy, every inch alive, is the youngest of the world's great cities, and has the optimism, the exuberant and often rather self-assertive pride of youth. But there is more than youthful swagger—there is a legitimate sense of triumph for achievements in the past, a boundless self-confidence as it faces the future, in the challenging ring of its civic motto, I WILL!

Gargantuan alike in size and rate of growth, the New World's second largest metropolis, the seventh largest on the globe,

> Stormy, husky, brawling,
> City of the Big Shoulders . . .

it lies at the point where the long finger of Lake Michigan pushes deep into the continent through the North woods and touches the fertile open prairie, the granary and stock farm of the Nation. Of that contact Chicago was born.

Toward the blue waters of the lake, fringed with a green ribbon of parks, Chicago presents its most impressive front. South from Evanston to the Indiana line, in a 25-mile arc, the lake front is lined with many of its finer mansions and apartment hotels; in and around the Loop, rising high above great museums housed in vast marble piles, looms a serrated mass of towers, spires, shafts, and huge cubes, a jagged mountain range of brick, stone, steel, concrete, and glass. To the south, beyond the busy docks along the Calumet River, are great black mills, factories, and furnaces, filled with the roar and rumble of machinery, their gaunt stacks belching black clouds by day, red flames by night.

Behind this façade, for a depth of almost 10 miles, lies not so much a city as a sprawling plexus of industrial towns, local shopping districts, crowded tenement neighborhoods, green and spacious settlements, spread unevenly on 212 square miles of flat and once marshy lowland. By the North and South Branches of the Chicago River, the city is divided into three sections—the North Side, the West Side, and the South Side, each with its own characteristics. Beyond, in an unbroken line of settlement, extend other cities, towns, villages, and subdivisions, with nothing but road signs to indicate where one stops and another begins.

Known to millions as the Windy City, although many American communities excel it in this respect, Chicago remains essentially a prairie town. Like every other, it is laid out in a rigid gridiron pattern, with a few diagonals. Some of its longer streets stretch straight ahead for more than 20 miles, flat gray bands tying horizon to horizon. Prairie-like, too, are the clumps of trees in occasional parks, and the raw scars of erosion in its poorer sections. But there is nothing bucolic in the roar and smoke and quick pace of its activities.

Chicago is the heart of a great arterial system of steel rails, concrete roads, waterways, and airways, radiating in all directions. No railroad line passes through the city. Freight trains are shunted around belt lines connecting the various roads, and passengers shift from one to another of the six stations that border the downtown district. A popular portage in its earliest days, Chicago remains in a sense the world's busiest portage. Only New York with its export trade transacts a larger volume of business than the Midwest Titan, "half-naked, sweating, proud to be Hog Butcher, Tool Maker, Stacker of Wheat, Player with Railroads and Freight Handler to the Nation."

But Chicago is also something more, a city of Protean shapes eluding any single formula, any simple characterization. It has sat for its portrait in more than 400 novels, in many poems and plays, but none has succeeded in catching all of its aspects and moods. Any full-length portrait would have to include State Street, with its glittering shops, and Clark Street, with its flophouses and cheap gin mills—the Stock Yards and the tower built by chewing gum—the Chicago Club and the shrill babel of "Bughouse Square"—Hull House and the bulging arsenals of the Al Capone and rival "mobs," private armies waging private war. On the canvas there would have to be room, too, for the Field Museum and the "World's Greatest Newspaper"—for Samuel Insull's "tallest opera building in the world" and the spectacular collapse of his holding-company empire—for Harriet Monroe, poet and critic of international reputation, and William Hale ("Big Bill, the Builder") Thompson, who for years has carried on a valiant and almost single-handed combat with the ghost of King George III. And no Chicagoan would admit a picture of his city to be complete without the curious horrendous charm of the old castellated Water Tower, about which buzzes local Bohemia, or without the stately Gothic structures of the University of Chicago.

All of these reflect other basic patterns. Along no street in the world live so many different nationalities and races as along Halsted Street in its long course across the city. There is a German Chicago, and a Polish Chicago, and a Swedish, Italian, Jewish, Lithuanian, Czech, Greek, Negro, Chinese, and New England Puritan Chicago, each within rather sharply defined limits. The bawdy roisterers of James Farrell's *Studs Lonigan* and milady of the "Gold Coast" are equally at home in Chicago.

He who would reduce the city to a common denominator will perhaps approach it closest in economic functionalism, and may find Chicago's slogan of more pertinence than is expected from civic catchphrases. A city of action, Chicago has been not only a peculiar focus for almost all of the major currents that have swirled across the continent, but also the spring from which not a few of them have welled. The figures of the city's census reports kept pace with the rapid expansion of the country. With the large scale cutting of the nation's forests and the breaking of the prairie, Chicago became the greatest grain and lumber market in the world. The spreading railroad lines of a national network converged here as nowhere else in America. The Great Fire of 1871 pointed warningly to the inflammable condition of a country filled with wooden buildings, the violence and hysteria of the Haymarket affair and the Pullman strike were the strongest expressions of the "riotous" eighties and nineties, and in the periods of mass European immigration, Chicago became the country's largest settlement for many foreign nationalities. The symbolism of the Columbian Exposition sharply revealed the imperialism of the nineties, while the first appearance of the skyscraper, the changing voice of American literature, and the inspiration of American city planning were among the significant prophecies. The scandalous political graft and antidotal reform movements around the turn of the century were indications of wide-spread corruption. The figures of Capone and Insull are, respectively, epitomes of the later period of American gangsterism and speculation.

One fourth of Chicago's heterogeneous population is foreign born. A large number of Jews is included in the three most numerous groups: 149,622 Poles, 111,366 Germans, and the 78,462 Russians. Next in order of size are the groups from Italy, Sweden, Ireland, and Czecho-

Slovakia. There are 233,903 Negroes. Among the smallest groups are the 8,766 French and French-Canadians.

In September 1673, there were seven Frenchmen here, but only for a day—Louis Jolliet, Father Jacques Marquette and five canoe-men—first white men known to have been at the site of Chicago. Returning to Mackinac after exploring the Mississippi as a possible route to the Pacific, they had ascended the Illinois and Des Plaines Rivers, portaged across a short swampy tract in the southwest section of the present city, and paddled down the South Branch and the Chicago River into Lake Michigan. They had failed of their original quest, but they had discovered something quite as important—the Chicago portage, a principal key to the continent—and they immediately appreciated the value of their find. Jolliet envisaged a canal penetrating the heart of the immense expanse of New France, reporting that it would be necessary to dig through only "half a league of prairie," to provide a continuous water route between the Great Lakes and the Mississippi Valley.

Curiously, no Indian settlement appears to have been made here until 1696 when Father Pinet, a Jesuit, established the Mission of the Guardian Angel and came periodically during the next four years to minister to the Miami, recent arrivals. The stream was known to the Indians as the Checagou, signifying anything big, strong, or powerful. But as the river was ever a small and sluggish stream, the "strong" probably referred to the pungent wild garlic that grew in profusion along its banks.

La Salle's ambitious schemes to colonize the Illinois Valley failed; hostile Indians closed the Chicago portage for long periods. When possession of the entire region passed to the British in 1763, there remained in Chicago no permanent marks of the 90 years of French rule. Twenty years later the country became part of the infant American Republic, but actual control was exercised by the British and their redskin allies until they abandoned their posts following Jay's Treaty, signed in 1794. The next year, by the Treaty of Greenville, the Indians ceded, among other territories, "a piece of Land Six Miles Square at the mouth of the Chickago River," recognized by the military authorities as a strategic point from which to command the farther reaches of the Northwest Territory, but no attempt was made to occupy it for almost a decade.

At length, in 1803, Capt. John Whistler, grandfather of the famous

painter, arrived with a company of infantry from Detroit to take
possession. At the point of a narrow bend in the river, which then
curved sharply southward from where the Michigan Avenue bridge
now stands, Whistler and his men built log blockhouses, barracks, and
stores, enclosed within a strong stockade, and named the fort for
Henry Dearborn, veteran of the Revolutionary War, then Secretary
of War in Jefferson's Cabinet. Opposite the fort, on the north bank,
stood four cabins; three were occupied by Frenchmen with their
Indian or half-breed wives; the fourth, a large cabin of squared logs
surrounded by numerous outbuildings, stood vacant. It had been
erected about 1783 by Jean Baptiste Point Sable, an industrious and
cultivated Negro of Santo Domingan origin, who had prospered in
trading with the Indians and in outfitting occasional travelers using
the portage, but who had suddenly vanished in 1800.

The Sable trading post was taken over in 1804 by John Kinzie,
a Scotch-Canadian, the first English civilian settler, who in search of
beaver pelts and shaved deerskins energetically extended his field of
operation to the north and west. The settlement in the shadow of Fort
Dearborn grew slowly until by 1812 it had a dozen or more small
cabins sheltering some 40 persons—the Frenchmen and their families,
the Kinzies, several farmers, a cattle dealer, and a few discharged
soldiers with their families. The War of 1812 aroused uneasy fears
in this isolated outpost, especially after the news came that the British
and their Indian allies had easily captured Mackinac at the head of
the lake in July 1812. General William Hull, commander of the
American forces in the Northwest, reported to the Secretary of War
that he was ordering the evacuation of Fort Dearborn, "provided it
can be effected with a greater prospect of safety than to remain," but
this conditional proviso was omitted in the order (not in Hull's handwriting) sent to Capt. Nathan Heald, Whistler's successor at the fort.

Black Partridge, a friendly Potawatomi chief, argued against
removal, saying that he had been warned of trouble by "linden birds,"
but on the morning of August 15, 1812, the fort was evacuated, and
the group, numbering approximately 100, started south along the beach
on their way to Fort Wayne, led by an experienced scout, Captain
William Wells. The nondescript column had not marched two miles
when, with a whoop, a large band of Indians in their war paint came
swarming down the dunes and fell upon the party, killing more than
half—all of the dozen militiamen, twenty-six of the fifty-five regulars,

two women, and most of the children. With the exception of the Kinzies, to whom the Indians were friendly, all survivors were taken and held captive until they were freed by ransom or death. The next day, the Potawatomi set fire to the fort in revenge for the many indignities the "Long Knives" had inflicted upon them in the past.

Four years elapsed before the fort was rebuilt. Kinzie and a few other survivors returned and some new settlers arrived. The growth of the powerful Astor's American Fur Co. monopoly absorbed the individual traders and led, after lobbying in Congress, to the abolition of the government trading factory system in 1822. But the rapid decline of the fur trade in the depleted region had already set in. Although an election was held in 1826 to select state and national officers, Chicago remained a somnolent settlement of squatters, evincing more vigorous signs of life only when the State Canal Commissioners surveyed and started the sale of a few blocks on both sides of the river as the terminal site of the projected Illinois-Michigan Canal. The date of the filing of the survey plat, Aug. 4, 1830, is the first in Chicago's corporate history. The following year Chicago was designated as the seat of Cook County.

The enormous mushroom growth of the modern city began in 1833, the year Chicago was incorporated as a town with a population of less than 200. The surrounding area had been cleared of Indians by the removal of the tribes following the Black Hawk War, and a harbor was opened by cutting through the sand-bar from the bend in the river to the lake. Glowing reports about the potential fruitfulness of northern Illinois and southern Wisconsin were eagerly received in the East—by farmers wearied of scratching the stony New England fields for an existence in competition with the more productive Ohio lands, discontented workers in the growing factories of New York and New England, and unsettled immigrants from western Europe in search of virgin soil on which to build new homes and an entire new life. The way was clear—the Erie Canal through the Mohawk pass to Buffalo, schooners and steamboats on the Lakes, and the harbor at Chicago.

Twenty thousand swept into Chicago from Buffalo in the first year (1833) of a wave that was years in passing. Many others came over eastern turnpikes. All but a few went on, in wagons, into the "plains without end."

Realizing that Chicago's marshy acres rested on economic bedrock, merchants early established the foundations for the vast trade to come. It was an era of wild speculation throughout the land-hungry country, but the fever raged nowhere more vehemently than in Chicago, climaxed in 1836 with the sale of lands along the projected Illinois and Michigan Canal. Harriet Martineau, in her *Society in America,* remarked amazement at finding in Chicago that "wild land on the banks of a canal, not yet even marked out" was selling for more than rich and improved lands "in the finest part of the valley of the Mohawk, on the banks of a canal which is already the medium of an almost inestimable amount of traffic."

Incorporated as a city in 1837, Chicago suffered severely in the financial panic and deflation of that year, but on his arrival by steamboat the next summer, Joseph Jefferson, destined to become one of the great actors of his day, found Chicago in a typically buoyant mood: "Off we go ashore and walk through the busy little town, busy even then, people hurrying to and fro, frame buildings going up, board sidewalks going down, new hotels, new churches, new theaters, everything new. Saw and hammer—saw, saw, bang, bang—look out for the drays!—bright and muddy streets—gaudy-colored calicos—blue and red flannels and striped ticking hanging outside the dry-goods stores—bar-rooms—real-estate offices—attorneys-at-law—oceans of them!"

And he might have noted, but for his tender years, gamblers, horse-thieves, holdup men, prostitutes, ruffians, and "rogues of every description, white, black, brown, and red," the usual riffraff of a booming frontier town. To combat sin and discourage even innocent ribaldry, the more pious organized "seasons of prayer," but with no appreciable effect.

It was the payment of eastern money for canal construction and harbor improvement that helped sustain the city until the flow of an agricultural surplus in 1841 from the rapidly developing surrounding region forced Chicago's first rooted growth. From three States in a radius of 250 miles, canvas-covered wagons, laden with wheat—200 a day by 1847—trundled prairie wealth into Chicago. Elevators rose along the river banks, holding grain until the spring arrival of dozens of steamboats and propellors "and an almost endless number of large brigs and schooners" from Buffalo. Half a million bushels in the second year of surplus (1842), 25 times as much a dozen years later, and Chicago became the world's largest grain market. Hogs and cattle were driven through prairie grass to Chicago abattoirs; barreled pork and beef reached markets as far as London.

In 1847 there were more than 450 stores, centering mainly about Lake and Clark Streets. Lumber yards, elevators, shipyards, warehouses, and factories lined the docks of the river jammed with sail and steam craft.

Industry in the main was handmaiden to the extractive economy of the period. Field and forest fed tannery and packing plant, flour and wood-work mill; fabrications of farm machine works and wagon factories helped to cultivate and garner. But a small surplus of manufactured goods produced by the more than 200 concerns began to find an eastern market.

Most of the 16,859 residents of 1847 lived in frame or "balloon" houses, painted white; successful business men built large houses, some of brick, in green squares on the North Side (now the Near North Side). Hotels and taverns housed hordes of travelers and unmarried residents and provided centers for town conviviality.

Social life was a melange of the "humbug and frippery of an eastern city" and backwoods crudities, of New England ideals of education and religion, and frontier ribaldry. Churches were established as soon as congregations could be formed. Including the newly-arrived Irish, German, and Scandinavian groups, who composed more than one-third of the population, there were 20 congregations, all but one in their own buildings and nearly all self-supporting. Methodism had the earliest start, in 1831. Catholics, Baptists, Presbyterians, formed congregations in 1833, followed the next year by Episcopalians, and by Universalists and Unitarians in 1836, Swedenborgians in 1842, and Jews in 1847. Private and semi-private schools preceded the first permanent establishment of free schools in 1841. Rush Medical College, initiated in 1837, soon had a city hospital.

Beginning in 1848, canal and railroad penetrating the fertile farmlands gushed torrents of city-building nourishment into Chicago. The city had quadrupled in size in its seven years of plenty, fed only by the comparatively trickling flow through its prairie roots, the crude wagon trails. The Illinois and Michigan Canal, opened in 1848, tapped the navigation head of the Illinois River 100 miles southwest and connected it with the Chicago River and Lake Michigan. This reversed the flow of grain and pork that had been draining southward to the Gulf of Mexico and thence to the eastern seaboard. Two years later,

New Orleans, "once the emporium and mart of the immense empire of the west" began to decline in commercial rank. By 1860 Chicago's grain receipts were nearly ten times as large as those of New Orleans. Lumber was brought down the lake by a fleet of 500 brigs, and carried into the treeless prairies by canal boat, supplying farms and towns as 'far as Fort Leavenworth, Kansas. Chicago became the largest lumber market in the world.

Total imports and exports quadrupled in the first year of the canal, which carried an increasing tonnage until the early eighties. But when rail replaced trail and striped the country with bands of steel, Chicago's growth rocketed to dizzy heights. A stub running a few miles to the west in 1848, then the lines of the Illinois Central and the Rock Island, and the Michigan Southern from the east in 1852, were the first of the strands that were soon tied into a knot that gripped the Middle West to Chicago.

Lake Michigan, in its dual rôle as barrier and carrier, strengthened the hold. Interposing its 307 miles of deep water between East and West, like a huge lens, it focused to a point the railroad lines between the entire Northwest and the East. Chicago became the greatest railroad center in the world. For many years interchange of cargo between waterway and railway boomed both forms of transportation. In 1869 the 13,730 arrivals at the Chicago Harbor exceeded the combined number of vessels entered at the ports of New York, Philadelphia, Baltimore, Charleston, Mobile, and San Francisco.

Local merchants had vigorously opposed the building of railroads in Chicago, arguing that trade would be ruined if farmers did not drive their produce into town and there fill up their wagons with supplies to carry home; they soon saw the transformation of their city into a vast wholesale mart, supplying entire towns and cities. Chicago's population increased six-fold between 1840 and 1850, rising from 4,470 to more than 28,000, and during the next decade vaulted to almost 100,000.

By 1856 the city embraced 18 square miles, and was trying desperately to pull itself out of the mud. Its streets had been little better than swamps—beloved by hogs, dogs, and small boys, but a terror to horses and pedestrians—and a serious menace to health, for the slops of the city were poured into these "noisome quagmires." A few streets had been paved with planking as early as 1849, and five years later the city had 27 miles of such pavement. It represented a considerable improvement, but was not without its disadvantages: laid on marshy ground only a few feet above the water level of the river, the planks rotted quickly and snapped under the weight of straining horses, or even pedestrians, and the loose ends flew up to deliver them a stunning slap in the face. Sand and then cobblestones were laid, but were immediately swallowed by the ubiquitous mud. At last, with heroic resolve, Chicago decided to raise the level of its streets 12 feet, a herculean task undertaken in 1855. Sand was dredged from the river, which accomplished the double purpose of deepening the channel and providing fill not only for the streets but for 1,200 acres of low ground between them. The new streets were huge ramps that ran level with second-story windows until people either jacked up their houses or converted their original ground floors into cellars. For years the sidewalks climbed and dipped like roller coasters. In 1859 a mile of track for horse cars was laid on State Street, which soon replaced Lake Street as the business center. A few four-story brick buildings began to replace flimsy wooden structures in the downtown section, but the Chicago of 1860 was described in its day as "one of the shabbiest and most unattractive of cities .... Half the town was in process of elevation above the tadpole level and a considerable part on wheels —a moving house being about the only wheeled vehicle that could get around with any comfort to the passengers."

Part of its shabbiness could be attributed to the depression that followed the panic of 1857, which struck the city a staggering blow. One-tenth of its 1,350 business establishments closed their doors; many thousands were thrown out of work to face starvation. In the midst of this distress Chicago built the Wigwam, a huge wooden shed, to accommodate the Republican National Convention, at which Lincoln was nominated for the presidency. Then came the Civil War to provide such stimulation of business as the always slightly feverish city had never known. To feed great armies in the field, farmers broke new ground and grain shipments from Chicago more than doubled in two years, rising to 65,400,000 bushels in 1862. In 1864 the mile-square Union Stock Yards were built. The McCormick and other factories were humming in their effort to satisfy the apparently insatiable demand for reapers, steel plows, agricultural implements of all kinds, harness, wagons, and a miscellany of wood and metal products.

In 1864 George Pullman built his first sleeping car, *The Pioneer*, marking the birth of another great local industry. Business transacted through the banks swelled to such a volume that the Chicago Clearing House was established in 1865. By 1870 Chicago's population numbered some 300,000, a three-fold increase within a decade. It had now outstripped Cincinnati, an old rival, and was hot on the heels of St. Louis, with whoops of joy and taunts of derision, which were repaid in kind. Chicago had to reach greedily for trade in all directions in order "to support its fast horses, faster men, falling houses, and fallen women," was the acid comment.

Times were indeed lush at the tip of the lake. Typical of the almost Hollywoodian order of things in that period was the case of the bankrupt backwoods tailor who came to Chicago, sold trousers for a few years, and built one of the largest and most celebrated hostelries of its day. Race tracks, gambling saloons, and bawdy houses multiplied. Lavish "marble" mansions went up along Michigan Avenue to 12th Street. Theaters, hotels, shops, and business buildings crowded into what is now the Loop. Coal yards, warehouses, flour mills, factories, foundries, and distilleries lined the river banks and the lake front. Scattered through the city were 170 churches—25 Catholic, 21 Methodist, 19 Presbyterian, and 5 Jewish, a partial reflection of the fact that half the Chicagoans of that day were foreign-born.

In 1867, after years of violent protest that the entire community was being poisoned by "filthy slush, miscalled water . . . a nauseous chowder" of fish and filth, which was taken from the lake into which the city poured its sewage, a sanitary water system was installed and immediately reduced the appallingly high death rate. The flow of "Garlic Creek" was reversed in 1871, and some of its foul waters were carried down the Illinois into the Mississippi, but not in sufficient quantity, so that sewage continued to pour into the river and the lake, to be thrown back at Chicago by the winds and waves.

Public high schools and evening schools, industrial and professional schools, including one of the first art schools in the country, two colleges, three theological seminaries, the Chicago Historical Society, and the Academy of Sciences were established in this period. In 1869 a ring of unimproved parks with boulevard connections surrounded the "Garden City." Beyond, in suburban subdivisions, carpenters were hammering out miles of houses that were to be swallowed in the city's growth within two decades. "More astonishing than the wildest vision of the most vagrant imagination!" visitors exclaimed, and Chicagoans agreed, although they felt that a more accurate index of the city's superiority over all others was provided when the White Stockings, its professional baseball team, defeated the Memphis nine, 157 to 1.

But, born in the haste to put wall and roof around home and business as quickly and cheaply as possible, a large part of the city's construction ran to "shams and shingles." Of the estimated 40,000 Chicago buildings in 1868, more than seven-eights were wooden. In 1871 the total increased 50 per cent, and while the 40 new stone buildings on State Street and many brick and iron-front structures elsewhere were promising improvements, solid blocks knew nothing but flimsy pine.

After months of severe drought a fire of unknown origin started in such a block, in a cow barn behind the cottage of Patrick O'Leary on DeKoven Street, Sunday night, October 8th, 1871. It soon spread beyond the control of the firemen, who were wearied by fighting and celebrating the defeat of a blaze that burned four blocks the previous day. A powerful wind swept flames to the north and northeast and hurled brands in advance of the roaring columns of fire, which destroyed the notorious "Conley's Patch" and practically everything north of Van Buren Street in the areas now designated as the Downtown District and the Near North Side. So intense were the flames that hot blasts were felt in Holland, Michigan, 100 miles across the lake. Tapering to a point near the lake at Fullerton Avenue, the boundary with the then suburban Lake View, the fire stopped after consuming 17,450 buildings in 27 hours. At least 250 persons perished. Homes of one-third the population, about 1,600 stores, 60 manufacturing establishments and 28 hotels, railroad structures, government and other public buildings, and bridges became three and one-third square miles of ashes and debris. Thousands were penniless, stripped of their last possession.

The embers were scarcely cool before rebuilding began. Generous contributions of money and supplies came from the entire country and from Europe. Thousands of temporary structures provided for immediate needs while more than 100,000 artisans were reconstructing the city under stricter construction codes, although the latter were frequently violated. Extensions of credit and payment of about half of the $88,634,022 insurance on the $192,000,000 loss helped rebuild the business district within a year. In another two, scarcely a scar of the fire remained anywhere. Many buildings, particularly hotels and depots, were replaced by far costlier structures. Fashion took over Michigan Avenue south of 12th Street, and Prairie Avenue, and brought in granite and brownstone. Chicago dumped its debris within the lake breakwater, forming subsoil for a future park, and went about its increasing business. Local manufactures doubled between 1870 and 1873; Chicago banks, alone of those in the larger cities, continued steadily to pay out current funds during the acute financial panic of 1873.

The germ of American industrialism found the Chicago of the middle seventies an ideal medium. A circle of 500 miles contained the principal ingredients. Around western Lake Superior lay one-fifth of the world's richest iron-ore reserve, yielding at the slightest scratch, easily loaded on lake freighters after a short land haul, and carried away by the most economical form of transportation on the continent. In Illinois, Indiana, Kentucky, West Virginia, and Pennsylvania, Chicago's railroads clutched at a trillion tons of coal. Blast furnaces and large factories forged tremendous wealth that filled Prairie Avenue and spread into Lake Shore Drive.

Nationwide labor unrest, following the wave of western settlement that had "broken against the arid plains" became particularly acute here. The line between wealth and poverty, cutting sharply into a single generation of workmen with rapidity unequalled elsewhere, drew Chicago into the forefront of "radical" cities. In 1877, led by Albert R. Parsons, workers in the factories and on the railroads struck for increased wages and the 8-hour day. Federal troops broke the strike, but without removing the causes of discontent. Industrial warfare over wages and hours grew increasingly bitter and culminated in the Haymarket bombing of 1886. Although no adequate evidence was produced that they had thrown the bomb, Parsons and three other labor leaders were hanged for the crime. Two others escaped death by having their sentences commuted to life imprisonment, and a third received a sentence of 15 years in prison. These three were pardoned seven years later by Governor John P. Altgeld, ". . . eagle forgotten" in Vachel Lindsay's phrase, who denounced the trials as unfair and illegal and was himself denounced as little better than a criminal for daring to doubt highly questionable evidence. Again large strikes broke out in the depression years that followed 1893, notably that which began in the local Pullman shops and spread to the railroads; once more Federal troops broke the strike.

Meantime, as one result of the Haymarket tragedy, the Civic Federation was founded by Lyman C. Gage, a banker, to provide free and open discussion of controversial questions. In 1889 Jane Addams opened Hull House in the worst slum district on the West Side. By 1890 Chicago had more than 1,000,000 people, having added 200,000 the previous year by the annexation of several surrounding municipalities. The Newberry Library, and The Public Library, had been founded, and in 1892 the University of Chicago began with the most auspicious program in university history. Theodore Thomas had organized the Chicago Orchestral Association and had long been presenting the popular concert series that brought the city renown as a musical center. W. L. B. Jenny, Daniel H. Burnham, John W. Root, William Holabird, and other architects were constructing huge new buildings on steel frames and evolving a new architectural form. In Maitland's *Dictionary of American Slang,* published in 1891, the new term "skyscraper" was defined as "a very tall building such as are now being built in Chicago."

Commerce, manufacture, labor, and these new cultural developments united to bring the city one of its great triumphs, the World's Columbian Exposition of 1893, in celebration of the 400th anniversary of the discovery of America. Jackson Park was developed out of swamp land on the South Side and here were built the great white buildings of the Fair in accordance with a master plan drawn by Daniel H. Burnham. The "White City," as it was soon known on five continents, was hailed as the miracle of the day, the "miniature of an ideal city . . . built as a unit on a single architectural plan . . . a symbol of regeneration." Millions crowded into the Fair to stare at and be equally impressed with "the most beautiful building since the Parthenon," a knight on horseback made of California prunes, cannons by Krupp, the Tower of Light, and the Parliament of Religions—the whole providing "matter of study to fill 100 years."

Remembrance of the genuine triumph of the Fair helped buoy up the spirit of Chicago during the hungry winters that followed, when thousands of unemployed walked the streets, hungry and homeless. The city joined the farmers of the Midwest in the Populist campaign against monopolies and the high finance of Wall Street, cheering William Jennings Bryan to the echo when he delivered his "Cross of Gold" speech here during the Democratic National Convention of 1896. George E. Cole organized the Municipal Voters League and launched a frontal attack on the brazen corruption in the City Hall, on the organized vice and violence in the almost ducal kingdoms ruled

LOOP NIGHT SCENE

CERES OVER LA SALLE STREET

PALMOLIVE BUILDING

WRIGLEY BUILDING

CONTINENTAL HOTEL

TRIBUNE TOWER

MICHIGAN AVENUE IN THE NINETIES

VIEW OF MODERN MICHIGAN AVENUE

OUTER DRIVE BRIDGE

GOLD COAST

JOHN D. ROCKEFELLER

MEMORIAL CHAPEL,

UNIVERSITY OF CHICAGO

SHEDD AQUARIUM

THE MUSEUM

OF SCIENCE

AND INDUSTRY

ART INSTITUTE
OF CHICAGO

STANLEY FIELD HALL,

CHICAGO NATURAL

HISTORY MUSEUM

ADLER

PLANETARIUM

MERCHANDISE MART

DAILY NEWS BUILDING

by such potentates as "Bath House John" Coughlin and "Hinky Dink" Kenna, and on the local traction king, "Yerkes the Boodler." A determined and finally successful effort was made to solve, once and for all, the distressing sewage problem; in 1900 the Sanitary and Ship Canal was opened, a wide channel some 28 miles long, and 20 feet deep. The Drainage Canal, as popularly known, served a triple purpose; it entirely reversed the polluting flow of the Chicago River, served as a link on the Lakes-to-Gulf Waterway, and by a generating plant built at Lockport, provided electricity to light the city's streets and parks.

By 1900, Chicago, which already had more Scandinavians and Dutch than any other city in the United States, became the Nation's largest Polish, Lithuanian, Bohemian, Croatian, and Greek settlement.

After a long battle the first Juvenile Court in the country was established, and it was soon adopted as a model by other cities. New parks and playgrounds were laid out to bring breathing space into crowded tenement areas. A comprehensive plan for the physical and cultural development of the city was drawn up by Daniel H. Burnham and presented to the city by the Commercial Club. Although much of it was characterized by what Lewis Mumford later called "municipal cosmetic," it was accepted by the city, and the Chicago Plan Commission, an advisory body formed in 1909, has used it with important modifications, to guide civic improvements since that time. Streets were widened and bridges were built to facilitate movement in the city, which had been growing at a rate of more than 500,000 each decade since 1880.

The World War found Chicago somewhat divided in counsel, for Mayor William Hale Thompson was vigorously opposed to American intervention. When the die was finally cast, however, Chicago contributed more than her quota to the armies in the field. The war greatly stimulated production in almost all local plants, particularly in the food-processing and metal industries, and incidentally created a grave new problem. Thousands of workers were drawn from the factories to the military training camps, and with immigration from Europe cut off, 65,000 Negroes poured in from the South to fill the demand for labor. Sporadic clashes occurred as the newcomers rapidly filled up the constricted Negro areas and spilled over into neighborhoods in which they "did not belong." In July 1919, an incident on a South Side beach precipitated five days of rioting which took a death toll of 22 Negroes and 16 whites; more than 500 persons were more or less seriously injured. A voluminous study of the psychological, social, and economic causes of the outbreak was made, but no effective steps were taken to improve conditions, which grew more acute as Negroes continued to move into the already overcrowded Black Belt.

During the fantastic 1920's Chicago boomed as never before. By 1930 it had passed the 3,000,000 mark in population, and it was manufacturing or processing $4,000,000,000 of goods a year—meat and meat products, books and printed matter of all kinds, machinery, clothing, and steel leading among thousands of products. Within three years it expended $1,000,000,000 on new buildings, erecting more than 90 miles of them in one year. Field Museum, a massive marble pile, and the great oval of Soldier Field took form in Grant Park, extended and improved as "Chicago's front yard." On the fringes of the city the chain of forest preserves expanded to approximately 30,000 acres of recreational areas. Downtown streets became deep canyons with sheer limestone walls as skyscrapers, one more aspiring than the other, shot up toward the heavens. The financial structures of the buildings and other enterprises soared to even dizzier heights, reaching an apogee in the huge inverted pyramid of public utility holdings assembled by Samuel Insull.

But with the lavish abandon of a booming frontier touched with a kind of Continental *laissez faire,* Chicagoans on the whole cared not about the financial soundness of these structures, nor about how the city was run. The traction muddle, the wasteful multiplicity of governmental units, the archaic taxing system—for each of these and other pressing problems solutions were offered, but were turned down by the electorate.

The chauvinistic clowning of Mayor William Hale Thompson (1915-23 and 1927-31) was climaxed by the emergence of the "wide open town." The enormous trade in alcohol and beer, gambling and prostitution, and the various "rackets" preying on legitimate businesses moved smoothly; the conviction of a gangster was extremely rare. The blazing sub-machine guns and sawed-off shotguns that were heard around the world were employed by rival gangs in the battle for control of the business whose sales ran into scores of millions annually. Of the several combines resulting from this warfare, Alphonse Capone's was the largest.

Although its effects were not immediately apparent, the knell of this gawdy period sounded with the stock market crash of 1929.

Prices of commodities in which Chicago had a vital interest tumbled disastrously; the Insull utilities empire and other elaborate financial edifices collapsed with a roar, while the "underground" empire shriveled to a remnant after the removal of Capone for income tax evasion, and later, the repeal of the eighteenth amendment. Unemployment spread in ever widening circles; teachers and other city employees endured long periods of payless pay days.

In the midst of the world-wide depression, Chicago courageously proceeded with plans for A Century of Progress Exposition, which opened in 1933 in a striking group of modern, plainly geometrical structures erected in newly-made Burnham Park and Northerly Island. Its central theme was applied science, and its exposition at the fair was guided by data furnished by the National Research Council. Hard times accounted in large part for the fact that the exposition was a financial disappointment in its first year, but Sally Rand and her fan dancers accomplished what applied science had failed to do, and the exposition closed in 1934 with a net profit, which was donated to participating cultural institutions, excluding Sally Rand.

Although its mood was somewhat sobered by the depression, Chicago still retains the tremendous vital energy that enabled it to grow from an isolated frontier post to a giant metropolis within a century. In its boisterous youth it was not inclined to stop for self-appraisal, but now, more mature, it is beginning to turn a critical eye upon itself and its problems. In the Midwest Titan's I WILL! is the assurance that these problems, too, will be solved, as those in the past.

The Loop and Vicinity

The Loop, the crowded rectangle between Wabash Avenue and Lake, Wells, and Van Buren Streets, is bound round with a steel band of elevated tracks, upon which converge trains from all parts of Chicago. The commercial center of the city since the beginning, it received its name in 1897 when the elevated lines were linked and routed to "loop" the district. At the present time the term is used loosely to designate the bustling commercial section that lies around as well as within the steel frame of tracks.

The cluster of towers at the Loop is the expression of Chicago as Big Town, with all the attributes of Big Town: the roar of traffic, on the street and overhead; sidewalks crowded with restless throngs;

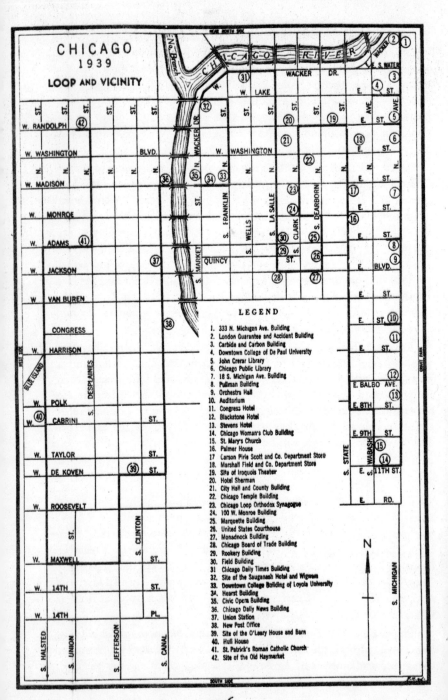

CHICAGO
1939
LOOP AND VICINITY

LEGEND

1. 333 N. Michigan Ave. Building
2. London Guarantee and Accident Building
3. Carbide and Carbon Building
4. Downtown College of De Paul University
5. John Crerar Library
6. Chicago Public Library
7. 18 S. Michigan Ave. Building
8. Pullman Building
9. Orchestra Hall
10. Auditorium
11. Congress Hotel
12. Blackstone Hotel
13. Stevens Hotel
14. Chicago Woman's Club Building
15. St. Mary's Church
16. Palmer House
17. Carson Pirie Scott and Co. Department Store
18. Marshall Field and Co. Department Store
19. Site of Iroquois Theater
20. Hotel Sherman
21. City Hall and County Building
22. Chicago Temple Building
23. Chicago Loop Orthodox Synagogue
24. 100 W. Monroe Building
25. Marquette Building
26. United States Courthouse
27. Monadnock Building
28. Chicago Board of Trade Building
29. Rookery Building
30. Field Building
31. Chicago Daily Times Building
32. Site of the Sauganash Hotel and Wigwam
33. Downtown College Building of Loyola University
34. Hearst Building
35. Civic Opera Building
36. Chicago Daily News Building
37. Union Station
38. New Post Office
39. Site of the O'Leary House and Barn
40. Hull House
41. St. Patrick's Roman Catholic Church
42. Site of the Old Haymarket

great movie palaces, and vast department stores. But in the Loop
stands a reminder that its economic roots are in the prairie, its primary
source of wealth: crowning the Board of Trade Building, the highest
elevation in the city, stands a gigantic statue of Ceres, goddess of
grain, whose cornucopia of plenty symbolically pours a golden shower
of wheat and corn on the city.

In the buildings of the Loop can be clearly traced the architectural
evolution of Metropolis. Within its bounds stand great masonry buildings, in their day among the tallest in the world; some of the first
structures built with steel framework; many buildings plainly revealing the painful struggle of architects to adapt old styles to new structural forms; and many newer buildings of simple modern functional
design, unadorned and starkly vertical, with no strivings to disguise
them as Greek temples, French chateaux, or Chinese pagodas.

Chicago lies on land easily dug for subways but unsuited for heavy
building construction, but, paradoxically, it was the first to build skyscrapers and the last of the large cities to tunnel passenger subways.
With bedrock in places more than 100 feet below the soft and marshy
surface, engineers had to erect the first large buildings on "floating"
foundations; caissons were sunk to bedrock to provide footing for
modern towers. After many years of planning and public clamor, construction of a subway began in 1938. For more than 30 years, however,
Chicago's traffic congestion has been considerably relieved by an unusual system of freight tunnels. Some 60 miles of narrow gauge track
have been laid 40 feet under downtown streets and carry a large part
of coal and other heavy shipments between the freight terminals and
downtown buildings.

TOUR 1 — 5 m.

S. from the Chicago River on Michigan Ave.

MICHIGAN AVENUE, from the river to Randolph Street, is a wide
thoroughfare between towering buildings. South of Randolph Street
the lake side of the avenue opens on Grant Park, but on the west side
the line of buildings continues unbroken in the "Splendid Mile," best
known part of the Chicago skyline. Here, in sharp contrast, are spread
many of Chicago's finest buildings, the old, for the most part, in the
southern portion, the new northward, near the river. Bordered with
smart shops, fine hotels, and office buildings, Michigan Avenue is

somewhat reminiscent of Gotham's Fifth Avenue, but has a vigorous, breezy character all its own.

1. The 333 N. MICHIGAN AVE. BUILDING commands the northern approach to downtown Michigan Avenue. Designed by Holabird and Root (before 1928 Holabird and Roche), its slender mass, seen edgewise from the bridge, soars to a height of 435 feet in clean unbroken lines.

2. The LONDON GUARANTEE AND ACCIDENT BUILDING, SW. corner of Michigan Ave. and Wacker Drive, was erected in 1923 on the approximate site of Fort Dearborn, a fact commemorated in a bronze relief over the entrance. Designed by Alfred S. Alschuler, the 21-story building has a concave façade, in the center of which the imposing entrance resembles a Roman triumphal arch. Surmounting the building is an adaptation of the Athenian Choragic Monument.

3. The CARBIDE AND CARBON BUILDING, 230 N. Michigan Ave., a 40-story tower completed in 1929, presents a striking color scheme with its black marble base, dark green terra cotta walls, gilded trim, and green-eyed campanile.

R. from Michigan Ave. on Lake St.

4. The DOWNTOWN COLLEGE OF DE PAUL UNIVERSITY, 64 E. Lake St., consists of the university's Colleges of Commerce and Law, School of Music, Secretarial School, Department of Drama, and Graduate School. Here, too, are held the late afternoon, evening, and Saturday classes of the College of Liberal Arts and Sciences.

Retrace Lake St.: R. on Michigan Ave. R. on Randolph St.

5. The JOHN CRERAR LIBRARY (*open 9-6 weekdays, non-circulating*), 86 E. Randolph St., an internationally known scientific library, occupies ten of the fifteen floors of a building that outwardly resembles a dignified office block. The library was established in 1894 with a bequest of $2,500,000 by John Crerar, Chicago railway magnate. Until 1920, it was housed in the Marshall Field store building. Its many valuable collections include 600,000 volumes and more than 225,000 pamphlets, as well as thousands of periodical publications. Especially noteworthy are the Senn Medical Collection (12th floor), the DuBois Raymond Collection on comparative physiology, the Martin Collection on physiology, the Lane Collection on histology, the Gradle Collection

on ophthalmology, the Baum Collection on historical medicine, the Huntington Jackson Collection on constitutional law, and the Chanute Collection of aeronautics.

In addition to these, definitive collections in other fields of study attract thousands of general readers and many scholars doing advanced research work in the various sciences.

Adjoining Crerar on the west, and reached from the fourth floor, is the LIBRARY OF INTERNATIONAL RELATIONS (*open* 9-5:30 *weekdays*), a separate organization founded in 1932. The library contains a specialized open-shelf collection of source material on current international affairs.

6. The CHICAGO PUBLIC LIBRARY (*open* 9 *a.m.*-10 *p.m. weekdays*; 1-6 *Sun.*), Randolph St. between Michigan Ave. and Garland Ct., and extending to Washington St., a massive structure of Bedford limestone designed by Shepley, Rutan, and Coolidge, and completed in 1897 at a cost of $2,000,000, combines Renaissance and Neo-Greek features. The Washington Street side of the interior is decorated with favrile glass mosaics and marble, executed by Tiffany of New York. They are seen at their best in the curved surface of the pendentives supporting the glass dome of the delivery room.

After the fire of 1871 a movement was fostered in London by Thomas Hughes, a member of Parliament and author of *Tom Brown at Rugby,* to provide bookless Chicago with the nucleus of a library. Several thousand volumes, donated by Queen Victoria, Darwin, Huxley, Carlyle, Disraeli, Tennyson, Browning, Ruskin, and others, arrived in 1872. The first library quarters were in an iron water tank which had escaped the flames. The present collection of some 1,750,000 books and 400,000 pamphlets forms the core of a city-wide library system of 45 branches, with numerous sub-branches and deposit stations.

On the first floor are the newspaper room, the A. W. Swayne collection of 80,000 lantern slides, and a library for the blind that includes books phonographically recorded and some 20,000 volumes in Braille and Moontype. On the second floor are the offices of the Illinois department of the G. A. R., a Memorial Hall housing Civil War relics, and an assembly hall. The delivery room on the third floor is flanked by the open shelves and the foreign book section. On the fourth floor are the reference and general reading rooms, the children's department, the periodical department, and the Civics Room. The Music Room, containing 22,000 volumes and an extensive file of sheet music, and the Arts and Crafts Room, are on the fifth floor.

Retrace Randolph St. R. on Michigan Ave.

7. The 18 S. MICHIGAN AVE. BUILDING houses on its upper floors the University College of the University of Chicago, where afternoon and evening courses are conducted by members of the university faculty. The exquisitely modeled ornament on the front of the building was designed by Louis Sullivan.

R. from Michigan Ave. on Adams St.

8. The PULLMAN BUILDING, 79 E. Adams St., built in 1884, typifies the Victorian brownstone period of architecture, in which medieval details were combined in restless, fantastic patterns. S. S. Beman was the architect. Formerly housing "highly respectable bachelors" in its upper six floors, the building became known as an "Eveless Eden." Now the Pullman Company uses all nine floors, but with its arrangement of rooms, cherry woodwork, and four small elevators, the interior retains its early charm.

Retrace Adams St. R. on Michigan Ave.

9. ORCHESTRA HALL, 216 S. Michigan Ave., is a dignified brick and limestone building in the French Renaissance style. It was designed by Daniel H. Burnham and completed in 1904 at a cost of $1,000,000. Approximately one half was underwritten by the music-loving public as an expression of its regard for Theodore Thomas, founder and first conductor of the orchestra now known as the Chicago Symphony Orchestra. After Thomas's death in 1905, the baton passed to his violinist, Frederick Stock, who is its present conductor (1939). The auditorium seats 2,600; in addition to its use during the regular concert series and for special musical events, is the meeting place of the non-sectarian Sunday Evening Club, and the Central Church. The church was founded by the Reverend David Swing in 1875, after his noted heresy trial before the Presbyterian Synod.

R. from Michigan Ave. on Congress St.

10. The AUDITORIUM, Congress St. between Michigan and Wabash Aves., in its day "the most famous building on the American

continent," houses a great theater, and also incorporates a hotel and offices, income from which was intended to aid in the support of a grand opera company.

This is perhaps the best known of Louis Sullivan's buildings. Begun in 1887 and completed three years later, it is of masonry construction. Although Sullivan denied that he was influenced by H. H. Richardson, the Romanesque style is evident in the exterior, and Sullivan's partner, Dankmar Adler, admitted that alterations in the original plans were inspired in part by the Auditorium directors' admiration for Richardson's newly completed Marshall Field Wholesale Building. The Auditorium is an excellent example of Sullivan's ambivalent theory of design. The massive and rather simple exterior illustrates his tenet that form should follow function, but throughout the interior examples of his intricate and graceful surface decorations abound. The main dining room, the bar, and the lobby are enriched with plaster reliefs in foliage designs; ornamentation is especially rich in the great series of arches in the auditorium proper. Of these, Hugh Morrison wrote in his biography of Sullivan:

Even the borders of the arched panels are enriched by relief bands and an inner lace-like pattern delicately stencilled in gold. Rarely has there been such a wedding of large and majestic simplicity with refined and subtle detail. The effect is superb.

Both the structural plans of the building and the complex acoustical design were drawn by Dankmar Adler. His solution of the construction problem posed by the massive tower was particularly ingenious. The foundation of the building is not on bedrock, and Adler feared that the imposition of the heavy tower might cause uneven settling that would crack the masonry. By loading pig iron and bricks equal to the weight of the finished tower on the lower floors, he obtained an even settling before the masons had finished the body of the building and begun to erect the huge tower.

On the opening night, Dec. 9, 1889, 5,000 of Chicago's elite crowded into the Auditorium to hear Adeline Patti sing. Governor Fifer of Illinois and President Harrison, accompanied by a large party, sat in special boxes. In following seasons, the theater rang with the voices of the operatic great. In 1929, the Chicago Civic Opera Company, an outgrowth of Chicago's first permanent opera company, moved to the new Civic Opera House. But the Auditorium, its acoustics unsurpassed, is still used for leading musical events.

Retrace Congress St. R. on Michigan Ave.

11. The CONGRESS HOTEL, Michigan Ave. between Congress and Harrison Sts., built as an annex to the Auditorium Hotel, now functions separately. Designed by Holabird and Roche, it dates from the Columbian Exposition of 1893, and has been the headquarters of the Democratic and Republican parties during all national conventions held in Chicago.

12. The BLACKSTONE HOTEL, Michigan Ave. at Balbo Ave., completed in 1910, was designed by Benjamin Marshall, who received the gold medal of the American Institute of Architects for his plans. One of the swankiest Chicago hotels, it has frequently housed visiting royalty. Its red and white shaft, crowned with a green mansard roof, is a prominent landmark on the lake front.

13. The STEVENS HOTEL, Michigan Ave. between Balbo Ave. and 8th St., is the largest hotel in the world, having 3,000 rooms. French Renaissance in decoration, it was designed by Holabird and Roche, and completed in 1927. Part of the third floor corridor is used as a permanent gallery by the All Illinois Society of the Fine Arts.

R. from Michigan Ave. on 11th St.

14. The CHICAGO WOMAN'S CLUB BUILDING (*apply two days in advance for club room tour*), 72 E. 11th St., was designed by Holabird and Root and completed in 1928. Graceful ornament in a sophisticated modern style gives the building a distinctly feminine character. Notable features of the interior are the little theater, and the Tudor Gallery (*open 9-5 weekdays*), used for one-man shows by Chicago artists. A limited-membership organization, the club has done notable pioneer work for compulsory education legislation, birth control, social hygiene, and other progressive social measures.

R. from 11th St. on Wabash Ave.

15. ST. MARY'S CHURCH, 9th St. and Wabash Ave., erected in 1865, one of the few churches antedating the Great Fire, is the center

of worship for the oldest Roman Catholic parish in Chicago, organized in 1833. The three o'clock mass is popular with late Loop crowds.

L. from Wabash Ave. on 8th St. R. on State St.

STATE STREET, between 8th and Van Buren Streets, is a short stretch of cheap taverns, men's hotels, lady barber shops, pawnshops, dime burlesque and peep shows, tattoo parlors, and penny arcades. As the street passes under the elevated at Van Buren, it undergoes a remarkable transformation. Northward, to Lake Street, it is the shopping center of Chicago, lined with huge department stores and small retail shops. Most metropolitan of Chicago's streets, State Street is the heart of the Loop, said to be the most brilliantly lighted in the world; the corner at State and Madison Streets is one of the world's busiest intersections.

16. The PALMER HOUSE, State and Monroe Sts., completed in 1925, succeeded the hostelry that enjoyed an international reputation for its splendor. When Lake Street was the principal business thoroughfare, Potter Palmer (1826-1902) bought a mile of State Street frontage and pioneered its commercial development.

17. The CARSON PIRIE SCOTT AND CO. DEPARTMENT STORE, SE. corner of State and Madison Sts., is housed in a building designed by Adler and Sullivan and erected in 1899. Unusually large windows light the store well while expressing naturally the steel frame. On the lower stories the lacy ornament which Sullivan intended to be "a rich frame for a rich picture" seems too ornate for present tastes.

18. The MARSHALL FIELD AND CO. DEPARTMENT STORE (*tours arranged at the Information Bureau, third floor*), covers the entire block bounded by State, Washington, Randolph Sts., and Wabash Ave., with an annex occupying the northeast quarter of the block to the south. It is one of the largest and best known retail stores in the world. Marshall Field, born in 1834 near Conway, Massachusetts, began his business career in Chicago in 1856 as a dry goods clerk. In 1865, together with Levi Z. Leiter, he bought an interest in Potter Palmer's Lake Street dry goods store. In 1881, after the retirement of Field's partners, the present firm name was adopted. Marshall Field developed many new practices and policies in department store management and invested heavily in Chicago real estate. At his death in 1906 he had accumulated a fortune which has since become one of the largest in the world.

L. from State St. on Randolph St.

RANDOLPH STREET in the Loop is the Rialto of Chicago, ablaze at night with theater, night club, hotel, and cafe signs. In the four blocks between State and Wells Streets, and at short distances on intersecting streets, are most of the first-run movie and legitimate theaters in Chicago.

19. The SITE OF THE IROQUOIS THEATER, N. side of Randolph St. between State and Dearborn Sts., is occupied in part by the modern, fireproof Oriental Theater. At the newly completed Iroquois, on December 30, 1903, occurred one of the most horrible disasters in the nation's history. While a matinee performance of *Mr. Bluebeard* was playing to a crowded house, the stage curtain caught fire, probably from an incompletely enclosed electric arc floodlight. The elaborate stage sets went up in flames, and a draft from the opened stage door swept a gale of fire over the audience. In a few minutes the locked gallery exits were further barred by piles of trampled bodies. When the flames were finally curbed, 596 persons were dead or dying—more than twice the toll of the Great Fire of 1871. The investigation disclosed the guilt of responsible persons and led to drastic reforms in theater regulations, both here and abroad. Annually, on the anniversary of the disaster, memorial services are held in the City Council Chamber.

20. The HOTEL SHERMAN, NW. corner of Randolph and Clark Sts., was completed in 1925, the latest of a succession of hotels that have occupied this site since 1837. The noted Tony Sarg cartographic ceiling in the Old Town Room depicts Chicago in 1852.

L. from Randolph St. on Clark St.

21. The CITY HALL AND COUNTY BUILDING, Clark St., between Randolph and Washington Sts., and extending to La Salle St., is actually two buildings, uniform in style; the section facing Clark was erected as the County Building in 1907; the west half, the city section, was added in 1910. Simple in design and ponderous in size, it represents a compromise between functional and classic styles; its long rows of huge columns, which support nothing but the cornice, are insufficient to make a temple out of what is obviously a city hall. The City Council Chamber, on the second floor, is an impressive oak-paneled room with murals by Frederick Clay Bartlett.

\

The Municipal Reference Library (*open* 9-5 *Mon.-Fri.;* 9-12 *Sat.*), on the 10th floor, contains over 150,000 books and pamphlets, including reports, proceedings, and treatises on the government of Chicago and other cities.

22. The CHICAGO TEMPLE BUILDING, SE. corner of Clark and Washington Sts., houses commercial offices and the First Methodist Episcopal Church, an outgrowth of Chicago's first church society, organized in 1831. For 100 years, with the exception of a short period after the Chicago Fire, the site has been occupied continuously by the various churches of the congregation. The present building, Gothic in detail, designed by Holabird and Roche and completed in 1923, rises 568 feet above the street. The delicately illuminated cross-tipped spire is a soaring note of beauty in the night sky. The tubular carillon, one of the largest in the world, sounds on the quarter hour, and in season fills the air with holiday tunes.

23. The CHICAGO LOOP ORTHODOX SYNAGOGUE, 16 S. Clark St., has walls decorated with murals, each symbolizing one of the Ten Commandments. Symbols were employed by the artist, Raymond Katz, because of the traditional Jewish ban on the depiction of figures in art.

R. from Clark St. on Monroe St.

24. The 100 W. MONROE BUILDING contains, of all things, a cowpath Ten feet wide, 18 feet high, and 177 feet deep, it opens on Monroe Street at the west end of the building, and leads nowhere. The functionless path is maintained in accordance with deeds drawn by Willard Jones, original owner of the land. When the growing city forbade cows and pigs to use the streets in the 1840's, Jones provided in the sale of his property for a perpetual 10-foot easement whereby his cows could plod to and from their pasture, which lay where the Board of Trade Building now stands. When the present building was erected in 1926, a reputed $350,000 was sacrificed because of the unusual cantilever construction and loss of rentable property.

Retrace Monroe St. R. on Dearborn St.

25. The MARQUETTE BUILDING, 140 S. Dearborn St., an office building notable for its decorations representing early historic figures and events, has bronze reliefs over the entrance depicting Father Mar-

quette's journey, and bronze medallion portraits of other explorers and of several Indian chiefs in the rotunda, the work of Hermon A. MacNeil. Martin Roche designed the mosaics around the mezzanine balcony to illustrate scenes from the journeys of discovery of Jolliet and others in this region.

26. The UNITED STATES COURTHOUSE, Dearborn St. between Adams St. and Jackson Blvd. and extending to Clark St., which served until 1934 as the main post office, now houses a large branch post office, a number of local Federal offices, and United State District Courts. The courtrooms, adorned by William B. Van Ingen's murals depicting the development of Law, have been the scene of many famous trials. It was here that the Standard Oil Company was fined $29,000,000, and Al Capone was sentenced. The Weather Bureau (*open 9-4 weekdays*), on the fourteenth floor, has a display of instruments used in its work, and a library of climatological data for the entire country. The cross-shaped building surmounted with an octagonal dome derives a certain grim splendor from its ornate design in the Roman Corinthian style. It was planned by Henry Ives Cobb and completed in 1905. In 1851, part of the site was occupied by the first Jewish house of worship built in Illinois.

R. from Dearborn St. on Jackson Blvd.

27. The MONADNOCK BUILDING, 53 W. Jackson Blvd., was studied and highly praised by European critics during the Columbian Exposition. Last and largest of the old type masonry buildings, it has walls 15 feet thick at the base. Its lines are as pleasing now as in 1892 when John Root erected the building. Not only is it devoid of ornament, but all the angles are rounded in a manner that would be called "streamlined" today. This is especially noticeable in the flaring base, the lower parts of the soaring bay windows, and the subtle swelling at the top that replaces the usual heavy cornice of the period.

28. The CHICAGO BOARD OF TRADE BUILDING (*observatory, 10-9 daily, 25c*), Jackson Blvd. and La Salle St., the tallest building in Chicago, has also the most dramatic location. Typifying the Board of Trade's importance in Chicago's economy, it stands as a climax to La Salle Street, at the apparent end of its long gorge. Designed by Holabird and Root and completed in 1930, the building towers in huge set-back masses to a statue of Ceres, goddess of grain,

a 31-foot aluminum figure by John Storrs. Ornament throughout the building contains symbols of the harvest.

Organized in 1848, the Board of Trade, with a present membership of more than 1,500, is by far the largest grain exchange in the world. More than 85 per cent of the United States trade in grain futures and approximately one-half of the world total, is transacted here.

On the trading floor of the immense Exchange Hall (*visitor's gallery on 5th floor open 9:30-1:15 Mon.-Fri., 9:30-12 Sat.*), are the grain pits, bordered with batteries of telephones and telegraph instruments, and the small sections for trading in cotton, provisions, and stocks. Quotation boards cover three walls; at the north side of the hall nine huge windows open on La Salle Street. The tables at the windows contain samples of cash grain, each bag representing a carload on hand and available for immediate delivery. Trading in futures constitutes the principal function of the Exchange. Shouting, gesticulating traders crowd the grain pits, as messengers scurry back and forth between the wire desks and the pits. Trading usually opens briskly and closes in a brief frenzy. The gong that marks these periods was used for many years in the old Board of Trade, the scene of Frank Norris' *The Pit*. A free pamphlet, available at the gallery entrance, explains the intricate system governing the apparent bedlam. In Room 740 are exhibited working models of grain elevators and handling equipment.

R. from Jackson Blvd. on La Salle St.

LA SALLE STREET, north of the Board of Trade Building, is the most canyon-like of the city's streets, a stone-walled gorge cut through Chicago's richest stratum of finance.

29. The ROOKERY, SE. corner of La Salle and Adams Sts., maintains the name and occupies the site of the ramshackle structure that served as a temporary city hall after the Fire. The name was inspired, it is said, by the hundreds of pigeons that roosted on the eaves of the old building. Designed by Burnham and Root and erected in 1885, the Rookery reflects the Romanesque vogue of the period, but its profuse ornamentation is of Hindoo inspiration. It has been commended as the first tall building to solve intelligently the problems of grouping and lighting a large number of offices.

30. The FIELD BUILDING, NE. corner of La Salle and Adams St., newest of Chicago's skyscrapers, was designed by Graham, Anderson,

Probst, and White, and completed in 1934. Its clean soaring masses ascend to a height of 535 feet. The building stands on the site of the Home Life Insurance Building, erected in 1883, the first in the world of steel skeleton construction.

L. from La Salle St. on Wacker Drive

WACKER DRIVE, a wide double-decked boulevard of architectural beauty, follows the south bank of the Chicago River, where Chicago's earliest development took place. One of the chief units of the Chicago Plan, the drive was named for Charles H. Wacker, late chairman of the Chicago Plan Commission. The massive driveway, resting on 598 caissons sunk to hardpan, is a distributive artery for eight north-south streets, and has an express highway for freight traffic on the lower level. The construction of Wacker Drive, completed in 1926, displaced the fascinatingly chaotic South Water Street Market, which cluttered the Loop for many years with a creaking confusion of wagons.

31. The CHICAGO DAILY TIMES BUILDING, 211 W. Wacker Drive, designed by Holabird and Roche, was completed in 1928 for the old Chicago *Evening Post,* which sold it to the tabloid *Times* four years later.

32. The SITE OF THE SAUGANASH HOTEL AND THE WIGWAM, is at the SE. corner of Wacker Drive and Lake St. Here, in the early 1830's, convivial Mark Beaubien kept one of the first hotels in Chicago, a political and entertainment center of the pioneer community. The inn burned in 1851; later the Wigwam, a large wooden structure, was erected in its place to accommodate the second national convention of the Republican Party, at which Abraham Lincoln was nominated for the Presidency.

L. from Wacker Drive on Lake St.; R. on Franklin St.

33. The DOWNTOWN COLLEGE BUILDING OF LOYOLA UNIVERSITY, 28 N. Franklin St., houses the Loop departments of the Jesuit university: the Graduate School, the University College, and the Schools of Law, Social Work, and Commerce.

R. from Franklin St. on Madison St.

34. The HEARST BUILDING (*tours by arrangement*), 326 W. Madison St., houses the two Chicago newspapers of William Randolph

Hearst, the Chicago *Herald and Examiner,* a morning tabloid, and the Chicago *American,* an evening journal. The newspapers maintain separate editorial offices, but share the same press and composing rooms. The building also houses the International News Service and other affiliated Hearst corporations.

R. from Madison St. on Wacker Drive

35. The CIVIC OPERA BUILDING, 20 W. Wacker Drive, was designed by Graham, Anderson, Probst, and White, and completed in 1929 to house the Chicago Civic Opera Company and offices for the support of opera. The building, 555 feet in height, is best viewed from the plaza of the *Daily News* building across the river. From that point it appears to be a huge throne, which won it the newspaper soubriquet of "Insull's Armchair." The late Samuel Insull, who occupied a penthouse suite in the building, was the chief promoter in the erection of the immense opera house. The gilded auditorium, seating 3,800 persons, with an immense stage 13 stories in height, departs from the usual opera house design in that it replaces the "Golden Horseshoe" with 31 boxes arranged in a barely perceptible curve.

TOUR 2 — 3.5 m.

W. from the river on Madison St.

36. The CHICAGO DAILY NEWS BUILDING (*tours by arrangement*) 400 W. Madison St., houses the plant and offices of the Chicago *Daily News.* A $10,000,000 Indiana limestone structure, designed by Holabird and Root and completed in 1929, it was one of the first Chicago buildings constructed in a large measure over a railroad right-of-way and the first to develop the river front aesthetically as well as commercially. The vast plane of its block-long façade rises from a balustraded plaza. Exterior stone panels depict the evolution of printing; murals by John W. Norton, on the ceiling of the main floor concourse, illustrate the gathering, printing, and distributing of news.

The Chicago *Daily News,* noted for the many authors developed on its staff, was published by the late Victor Lawson from 1876 to 1925. Control has been in the hands of Col. Frank Knox since 1931.

L. from Madison St. on Canal St.

37. The UNION STATION, on both sides of Canal St. between Adams St. and Jackson Blvd., is composed of two large units con-

nected below street level. Although the exterior is treated in Roman Doric and the monumental waiting room is distinguished in its ornamental detail, the concourse is frankly functional in its deliberately unconcealed steel girders. The vast station, designed by Graham, Anderson, Probst, and White, and opened in 1926, serves four large railroad systems.

38. The NEW POST OFFICE (*tours by arrangement*), Van Buren St. from Canal St. to the river and extending to Harrison St., is the largest post office building in the world, a bulky Indiana limestone structure designed by Graham, Anderson, Probst, and White, and completed in 1934 at a cost of $21,500,000. The building is constructed over railroad tracks which permits the direct handling of one-third of the daily mail. On May 15, 1938, an autogyro landed on the roof of the two-block long structure, with mail from the Municipal Airport, in a test flight of transfer service. In addition to the postal plant, the building houses the regional offices of several Federal Departments.

R. from Canal St. on DeKoven St.

39. The SITE OF THE O'LEARY HOUSE AND BARN, 558 DeKoven St., is occupied by a three-story flat-building. Here, as the inscription on the stone front indicates, began the Chicago Fire of 1871. Legend ascribes the cause of the fire to a lantern shattered by Mrs. O'Leary's cow.

L. from DeKoven St. on Jefferson St. R. on Maxwell St.

The MAXWELL STREET MARKET, frequently called the Ghetto, centering at Halsted and Maxwell Sts., is a confusion of wagons, stalls, pushcarts, and boxes, a littered jungle of used umbrellas, festoons of shoes, high-piled vegetables, and wind-swung underwear. The sidewalks run between a solid line of stalls and stores, along which salesmen solicit the custom of passers-by. Few of the stores have fixed prices; extended bargaining is the rule. The crescendo is reached on Sunday mornings, when Poles and others of European extraction come to bargain with the Jewish merchants for their incredibly varied stores of goods.

R. from Maxwell St. on Halsted St.

HALSTED STREET, between the Maxwell Street and the Randolph Street markets, is a cosmopolitan mile, a shabby commercial corridor through the old settlements of several foreign-language groups. Large numbers of Mexicans, Italians, and Greeks inhabit other parts of the city, but nowhere is there such a concentration of stores displaying the native goods of these people. Gypsies winter here in scattered stores along the street, gaining a livelihood ostensibly by fortune telling.

LITTLE ITALY, largest of the settlements, spreads westward from Halsted St. near Taylor St. Here, in stores marked by curbside pyramids of tinned olive oil, are displayed deviously wrought spaghetti and macaroni, Romane and Provolone cheeses, many varieties of olives, spices, fish, and sausages. Some of the larger stores are wholesale establishments, catering to outlying districts. In other shop windows are bundles of spindly black cigars, paper-backed novels, "art" calendars, and huge wedding cakes. The residents of Little Italy hold street festivals in spring and summer at nearby churches.

LITTLE MEXICO centers on Hull House, Halsted St. at Polk St., where shops sell native handicrafts, particularly pottery, and restaurants serve *tacos, enchiladas, tostadas,* and tender vinegar-soaked cactus.

40. HULL HOUSE (*open* 11-8 *daily; other hours by arrangement*), 800 S. Halsted St., one of the first settlement houses in America, has become one of the most famed institutions of its kind in the world. About the original plant, the old Charles J. Hull residence, built in 1856, are clustered a dozen buildings. Some of the buildings provide living quarters for the large resident staff, most of whom engage in self-sustaining occupations, devoting their leisure time to the House programs. Activities include classes in English for foreigners, group discussions and investigations of social problems, instruction in the manual and fine arts, and gymnasium classes. Among the exhibits at Hull House are the Labor Museum, displaying various spinning and weaving devices formerly found in the homes of the foreign groups living in the surrounding area; the Benedict Art Gallery; and the Octagon Room, Jane Addams' study, furnished as it was during her lifetime, and containing memorabilia of her achievements. In the House are the offices of such co-operating organizations as the Juvenile Protective Association, Immigrants' Protective League, Visiting Nurse Association, United Charities, and Infant Welfare Society.

Hull House won its fame as a social center largely through the devoted and indefatigable efforts of Jane Addams, who, together with her Rockford College classmate, Ellen Gates Starr, founded the insti-

tution in 1889. Miss Addams remained head resident until her death
in 1935. A visit to Toynbee Hall, the London settlement house, and a
study of London slums, were the immediate inspiration for her
pioneering work in Chicago.

Immigrants constituted about half of Chicago's population when
Hull House was chartered "to provide a center for a higher civic and
social life, to institute and maintain educational and philanthropic
enterprises, and to investigate and improve the conditions in the industrial districts of Chicago." The splendid accomplishments of Hull
House are modestly revealed by Miss Addams in her *Twenty Years
at Hull House* (1912) and *The Second Twenty Years at Hull House*
(1930), and in James Weber Linn's *Jane Addams* (1935).

LITTLE GREECE is bounded by the delta formed by Halsted and
Polk Sts. and Blue Island Ave. The colony has dwindled sharply in
recent years, but it retains much of its color. At the approach of the
Greek Orthodox Easter the store fronts are gayly decorated with banners. The Good Friday procession, the Funeral of Christ, draws thousands of participants, many of them carrying lighted candles. Market
fronts are filled with live lambs; on Easter Sunday they are barbecued
in a vacant lot on Polk Street, with much dancing and drinking of
sweet wines and *mastika*.

R. from Halsted St. on Adams St.

41. ST. PATRICK'S ROMAN CATHOLIC CHURCH, Adams and
Desplaines Sts., dedicated in 1856, is the oldest church building in use
in Chicago. The interior is notable for its windows of colored glass,
designed in 1912 by Thomas O'Shaughnessy. The window patterns
follow fifth century precepts formulated by St. Bride (St. Bridget),
and employ symbolism used in the ancient Book of Kells. Save for the
faces of the saints, the windows are of pot-metal glass, some pieces of
which are one-thousandth of an inch thick. The main window, composed of 250,000 pieces, is valued at $100,000.

L. from Adams St. on Desplaines St. to Madison St.

WEST MADISON STREET, for several blocks on either side of Desplaines Street, is a sordid "Skid Row," lined with missions, pawnshops, flop houses, saloons, dime movies, and cheap lunch rooms. From
the railroad yards come the transient worker, the bum, the veteran

cadger, the down-and-outer. Here, for half a century, a ragged army has shuffled in bewildered frustration, moving into breadlines at dawn, kneeling in missions during rain, wandering in and out of "cake flops," where the price of a pallet includes a lump of stale pastry.

L. from Desplaines St. on Randolph St.

The RANDOLPH FARMERS' MARKET, Randolph St. between Desplaines and Sangamon Sts., expands westward to Union Park during the harvest season. Large numbers of farmers and truck gardeners from northern Illinois gather in the wide street to sell their fruits and vegetables. One block is utilized by flower growers.

42. The SITE OF THE OLD HAYMARKET, the scene of the tragic bombing of May 4, 1886 (*see Labor*), is at Desplaines and Randolph Sts.

Grant Park

Central link of Chicago's chain of lake 'front parks, Grant Park lies between the most imposing section of Michigan Avenue and the inner basin of the Chicago Harbor. Known as the Front Yard of Chicago, it contains many of Chicago's finest museums and monuments, and its 303 acres provide the mile-long Loop with an open view of the lake.

Practically all of the land in the park has been reclaimed from the lake; in 1852 the Illinois Central tracks, only 100 yards east of Michigan Avenue, were laid on trestles in the water. Subsequent filling created new land on both sides of the Illinois Central, which raised the grade around the tracks, so that the railroad right-of-way is now hidden some 20 feet below the level of the park.

Before the Columbian Exposition in 1893, many attempts were made to secure the embryo park for private use. Largely through the persistent efforts of A. Montgomery Ward, the "Watchdog of the Lake Front," it was kept free of buildings, except for the Art Institute. Later, Field Museum and Shedd Aquarium were built on a southeast extension of Grant Park, beyond the Loop area.

The pattern of the park, broken by the railroad right-of-way, the two major boulevards, and the connecting extensions of several downtown streets, is essentially formal. But the park is not merely a formal showpiece. On warm days students pore over books in the shadow of the peristyle, where passers-by feed the great flocks of pigeons. After

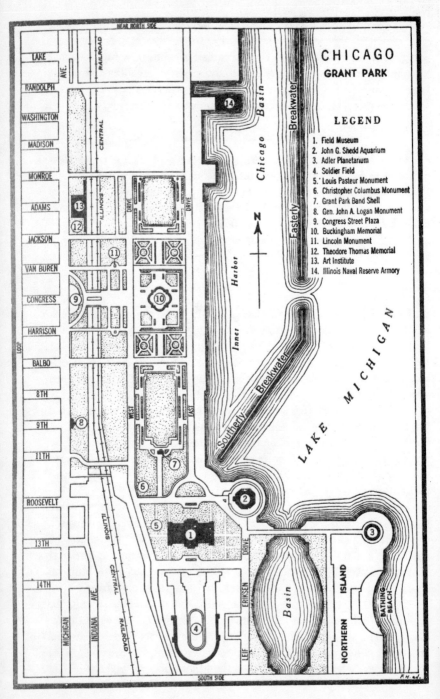

CHICAGO

GRANT PARK

LEGEND

1. Field Museum
2. John G. Shedd Aquarium
3. Adler Planetarium
4. Soldier Field
5. Louis Pasteur Monument
6. Christopher Columbus Monument
7. Grant Park Band Shell
8. Gen. John A. Logan Monument
9. Congress Street Plaza
10. Buckingham Memorial
11. Lincoln Monument
12. Theodore Thomas Memorial
13. Art Institute
14. Illinois Naval Reserve Armory

working hours in summer months, the ball fields and tennis courts are crowded with players and spectators from Loop offices. At dusk, dense throngs converge on the band shell for the open air concerts, and always, the year round, visitors cross the viaducts to view the exhibits in the museums.

Facing Roosevelt Road, overlooking the entire length of Grant Park, is the broad façade of (1) the FIELD MUSEUM OF NATURAL HISTORY. (*Open* 9-4 *Nov.-Feb.; 9-5 Mar., Apr., Sept., and Oct.; 9-6 May-Aug. Children, students, and teachers free; others free, Thurs., Sat., and Sun.; other days, 25c. Tours 3 p.m., Mon.-Fri., also 11 a.m. July-Aug., and by arrangement at other times. Cafeteria, ground floor; guidebooks and other publications for sale at main entrance. Wheel chairs, 25c per hour; visitor must furnish attendant. Free parking*).

The Field Museum, one of the renowned scientific museums in the world, houses a vast and constantly growing collection of exhibits on anthropology, zoology, botany, and geology. Founded in 1893 after the Columbian Exposition, it was endowed by a number of prominent citizens, chief among whom was the late Marshall Field, Chicago merchant. To his initial gift of $1,000,000 he added more than $400,000 during his life, and at his death in 1906 bequeathed $8,000,000. Until 1921, when the present building was opened, the Museum was housed in the Palace of Fine Arts in Jackson Park. Nucleus collections were exhibits transferred from the Exposition, purchases, and private gifts, notably an anthropological collection by Edward E. Ayer.

Most of the objects have been collected by expeditions, of which the Museum has had as many as eighteen at work in one year. Their scientific reports, as well as the findings of the local research staff, are published and circulated internationally by the Museum. The vast research collections are open to scholars, on application. New acquisitions, improvements in the permanent exhibits, and the extensive lecture activities create recurring interest in many of the 1,000,000 annual visitors to the Museum.

The massive white Georgia marble building, one of the largest marble structures in the world, was designed by Daniel H. Burnham, but the work was completed after his death by Graham, Anderson, Probst, and White. Its architecture is pure Greek Ionic, with some of its details following the Erechtheum in Athens. A great flight of steps leads to the majestic pedimented portico, two rows of columns in depth. This is flanked by long wings, four stories high, that are decorated with Ionic colonnades ending in transverse halls.

The main hall, known as Stanley Field Hall, rises unbroken to the roof. The heart of the Museum, it contains exhibits, frequently changed, drawn from the various divisions of the Museum. Two African elephants mounted in fighting pose, and bronze groups of African natives in the act of spearing lions, all the work of the late Carl Akeley, are permanent exhibits. Sculptor, author, and naturalist, Akeley became chief taxidermist in 1896, and for fourteen years his research, exploration, and taxidermy brought renown to him and to the Museum.

The Department of Anthropology occupies the first floor of the east wing, most of the exhibition space on the ground floor, and the five second-floor halls around the nave. Its exhibits include, in Hall 3, east of the entrance, Malvina Hoffman's widely known *Races of Mankind*, 101 statues and busts based on six years of research among the races of the world. A bronze group of a white, a yellow, and a black man, indicates that humanity is a single species; statues and busts of various racial types surround this central composition. South of this exhibit are seven halls devoted to the anthropology of American races, with an extensive exhibit of the works of North American Indians and Eskimos, past and present. Collections in Halls D and E, on the ground floor, illustrate the ethnology of Africa and include the only Madagascar collection of importance in the United States. Polynesia, Micronesia, Malaysia, and the Philippine Islands are represented in Halls F, G and H; Hall A contains the most comprehensive Melanesian collection in America.

The Egyptian collection, in Hall J, includes reproductions of the Rosetta Stone and papyri, but most of the articles are originals, including a funeral barge 3,800 years old. One of the rare items is the body of a woman preserved in sand for more than 6,000 years. It antedates the period when bodies were mummified. Hall C, devoted to Stone Age relics, contains dioramas of prehistoric scenes, with life-size figures. Adjacent to each diorama are authentic artifacts, and animal and human remains of the period, including the Cap Blanc skeleton.

The H. N. Higinbotham Hall of gems and jewels, west of the main stairway on the second floor, contains examples of almost every known gem, including the famous Sun God opal and the De Vrees engraved diamond. Most of the other exhibits on this floor are devoted to China and Tibet, with a fine jade collection in Hall 30.

The Department of Botany occupies the second floor of the east wing. Few other general natural history museums have attempted to cover this subject. The Hall of Plant Life offers a general view of the entire range from the lowest orders, such as bacteria and fungi, up through the many varieties of flowering plants. Two halls are devoted to general economic botany—food products, palms, and plant raw materials. Nearby are halls showing varieties of wood from all over the world. Many of the botanical exhibits, skillfully processed in wax, glass, and celluloid in the museum's laboratory, cannot be distinguished from natural specimens.

The Department of Geology occupies the second floor of the west wing. Crystals, meteorites, and a systematic display of minerals are in Hall 34; the meteorites, with specimens from more than two-thirds of the known meteorite falls, includes one weighing 3,336 pounds. In the Ernest R. Graham Hall of Historical Geology is traced the development of life from earliest times to the present. A huge skeleton of a dinosaur of the species *Apatosaurus,* surrounded by other fossil reptiles, as well as mammals and birds, forms one of the exhibits. A series of murals by Charles R. Knight around the hall depicts various prehistoric animals as they probably appeared in life. There are also several life-size three-dimensional restorations by the sculptor Frederick Blaschke. Exhibits in Hall 35 illustrate geologic processes. Relief maps in the corridor represent the Chicago area in various stages following the glacial period. Specimens and models in Hall 36 and 37 illustrate the occurrence, processing, and utilization of petroleum, coal, clay, and various ores.

The first floor of the west wing and Hall N are occupied by the Department of Zoology's systematic and habitat groupings of animals. The sculptural methods of taxidermy, principally devised by Akeley, account for the life-like appearance of the specimens. Hall 22, which includes some of Akeley's best work, contains all major African species of mammals. Several series of habitat groups, in many respects more spectacular than the African series because of their more elaborate scenic backgrounds, include the groups of American mammals in Hall 16, the Asiatic group in Hall 17, and the birds in Hall 20. In the Hall of Domestic Mammals, west of the main stairway, is an unusual exhibit of quarter-sized statues, modeled by Herbert Haseltine from prize-winning livestock.

The Museum library (*open weekdays; closed Sat. at 12*) contains more than 100,000 scientific books and pamphlets. There are many rare volumes, as well as current scientific periodicals and publications of institutions throughout the world.

The Department of the N. W. Harris Public School Extension circulates 1,200 special exhibit cases among 500,000 school children to stimulate their interest in local natural history. Through the James Nelson and Anna Louise Raymond Foundation for Public School and Children's Lectures, lectures and pictures are presented in the schools, and in the James Simpson Theatre of the Museum on Saturday mornings in spring and autumn. On Saturday afternoons during these seasons, illustrated lectures are given here for adults by eminent naturalists and explorers.

At the east end of Field Museum a pedestrian subway leads under Lief Eriksen Drive to (2) the JOHN G. SHEDD AQUARIUM (*open 10-5 daily; children free, adults free Thurs., Sat., and Sun., other days, 25c. Guidebooks at information desk, 50c*).

The Aquarium was endowed in 1924 with a gift of more than $3,000,000 by the late John G. Shedd, a Marshall Field executive. The displays of live fish and aquatic animals attracted 4,700,000 visitors in 1931, the first year after the aquarium was completed.

The many-sided white Georgia marble building, of simple Doric design, is effectively set in a terrace at the water's edge. The architects, Graham, Anderson, Probst, and White, used marine symbols throughout the decorations. Outside, this is seen in the wave-like cresting and the trident of Neptune on the pyramidal roof. Inside, a marble wainscoting has markings that give a wave effect and the clock in the foyer, which substitutes aquatic figures for numerals, is typical of the imaginative use of water symbols. In the center of the rotunda is a rockery with a swamp pool, in which carp wind in and out among tree stumps that serve as resting places for turtles and frogs.

Six main galleries radiate from the rotunda. The symbols that identify the majority of the exhibits are coded with the comprehensive guidebook; the numbers indicate the family and species of the fish; the colored oblong denotes the kind of water from which it was taken. Special attention is given to reproducing the appearance and conditions found in the natural habitats of the specimens. As many of them cannot live long in captivity, there is constant fluctuation in the number and kinds of fish exhibited, but there are always many varieties of gorgeously colored and curiously shaped specimens from the warmer waters, American game fish, and the odd rays, eels, sharks, lungfish, and sea horses. Such invertebrates as shrimps, star fish, and sea anemones, are usually represented.

The balanced aquariums, in which the water is oxygenated by growing plants, occupy a separate room to the left of the entrance foyer. The room, in colorful Japanese style, is illuminated with lanterns on bamboo poles, and contains many small tropical fishes, including those commonly kept in homes.

Southeast of the Aquarium over a causeway is Northerly Island, officially a separate park of 91 "made" acres; on its northeast corner stands (3) the ADLER PLANETARIUM AND ASTRONOM-ICAL MUSEUM. (*Open* 10-5 *Mon., Wed., Thurs., and Sat., demonstrations at* 11 *and* 3; 10-9 *Tues. and Fri., demonstrations at* 11, 3, *and* 8; 2-5 *Sun., demonstrations at* 2:30 *and* 3:30. *Free Wed., Sat., and Sun.;* 25c *other days; children free every morning. Descriptive booklets at entrance,* 20c.)

The approach to the building is along a broad esplanade, which has a series of twelve cascading pools in the center. On the bottom of each pool is the zodiacal symbol of one of the twelve months. The building, designed by Ernest Grunsfeld, Jr., follows no historical style but achieves a monumental effect by its mass and its plain surfaces of rich rainbow granite. It is in the form of a regular dodecagon, topped with a circular dome of green copper. Bronze plaques of the twelve signs of the zodiac by Alfonso Iannelli are inset at the exterior corners. The gift of Max Adler, Chicago merchant-executive, the Planetarium was dedicated in 1930, the first in the western hemisphere. It is operated by the commissioners of the Park District.

In the planetarium chamber are reproduced the intricate phenomena of the heavens. Chairs arranged in concentric circles provide a comfortable view. The projection instrument, a fantastic and highly complex machine weighing more than two tons, was manufactured by the Carl Zeiss Company of Germany. More than 100 lenses stud its exterior and cast images of all visible heavenly bodies on a linen screen shaped in the form of a dome. The motor-driven projector, moving on its various axes, enables the lecturer to show four types of apparent celestial motion: the change of latitude; the diurnal motion; the interlocked motion of the sun, moon, and planets; and the precessional cycle. Thus the heavens can be viewed as they appear from any spot on earth, at any time. The day, year, and even the precessional cycle can be shortened to seconds by means of controls on the lecturer's desk.

For sheer drama and realism the demonstrations are superb. As the lecture begins, the chamber lights are slowly dimmed until the dome assumes the lambency of twilight. On the apparent horizon— the base of the dome—the silhouette of Chicago's skyline enables spectators to orient themselves. The light fades lower, the hum of the great stilted projector is heard, and gradually the first and brightest stars appear. When the room is black as night, the illusion is complete. At the end of the lecture, when the lights come on slowly to reveal the prosaic domed screen, spectators invariably blink for a moment in astonishment. The demonstrations are changed monthly, and include the Calendar, the Seasons, the Annual Journey of the Sun, the Winter and the Summer Constellations.

Seventy-two large transparencies from negatives made by the world's largest telescopes are mounted in niches along the walls of the corridors. Here, also, is displayed the fine collection of old instruments gathered by the Strozzi family of Florence, Italy; nocturnals, armillae, globes, sundials, and telescopes dating from 1479 to 1800. On the lower floor are modern astronomical instruments and exhibits to illustrate their use.

Directly behind the Field Museum in Burnham Park is (4) SOLDIER FIELD, begun in 1922 and named in tribute to Chicago's fallen soldiers. Seating approximately 80,000, with provisions for adding many thousands of temporary seats, it has been the scene of such events as the 28th Eucharistic Congress in 1926, and the second Dempsey-Tunney fight in 1927. Enclosing the north end of the horseshoe stadium is the Chicago Park District Administration Building, completed in 1939.

West of Field Museum is (5) the LOUIS PASTEUR MONUMENT, a bronze bust of the great scientist by Leon Hermant.

To the north stands (6) the CHRISTOPHER COLUMBUS MONUMENT by Carlo Brioschi, presented by citizens of Italian ancestry.

(7) The GRANT PARK BAND SHELL faces the entrance of the Field Museum (*concerts 8 p.m. nightly, except Tues., 7:30 p.m.,*

July 1-*Labor Day.*) The Park District and the Chicago Federation of Musicians sponsor concerts by various bands and orchestras.

West of the Band Shell, on Michigan Ave., at the foot of Ninth St., is (8) the GENERAL JOHN A. LOGAN MONUMENT, an equestrian work by Augustus Saint-Gaudens. The small grassy mound supporting the statue is often humorously referred to as the only hill in Chicago.

Northward is (9) the CONGRESS STREET PLAZA, formal entrance to the park. The broad concourse is marked by stone pylons, bronze eagles by Frederick C. Hibbard, and two immense symbolic equestrian Indian monuments, the work of Ivan Mestrovic.

At the end of the concourse stands (10) the BUCKINGHAM MEMORIAL FOUNTAIN (*operated May-Sept.*), formally landscaped as the "centerpiece of Grant Park." Dedicated in 1927, the pink Georgia marble fountain is the gift of the late Miss Kate Buckingham, in memory of her brother, Clarence Buckingham, a former trustee of the Art Institute. The main pool, 300 feet in diameter, contains four pairs of sea horses, dedicated to and facing each of the four states bordering Lake Michigan. For creating these fine large figures, N. Marcel Loyau won the *Prix National.* In the center of the pool three concentric basins rise to a height of 25 feet, and from their outer rims spouts a series of diminishing water domes. A central column of water rises almost 100 feet above the apex of the highest dome. At night, hidden lights of 45 million candlepower concentrate a blaze of color, constantly shifting in pattern, on the cascades of spray. The intricate control mechanism is housed in an underground room. During displays the fountain shoots 15,500 gallons of water per minute from its 134 jets. It is twice the size of the Latona Fountain at Versailles, which in a measure inspired its design. The architects were Bennett, Parsons, and Frost, with Clarence Farrier and J. H. Lambert as associates.

In an imposing architectural setting is (11) the SEATED LINCOLN MONUMENT, across Columbus Drive at the pedestrian extension of Van Buren St. One of the last of Augustus Saint-Gaudens' statues, it was completed in 1907, but was not placed until nineteen years later.

On Michigan Ave., just south of the Art Institute, is (12) the THEODORE THOMAS MEMORIAL, half-draped figure in bronze symbolizing Music. Behind it a long granite seat bears a bas-relief of an orchestra grouped around a profile of Chicago's great conductor. The memorial was designed by Albin Polasek and un-veiled in 1924.

(13) The ART INSTITUTE OF CHICAGO faces Michigan Ave., at the foot of Adams Street. (*Open weekdays 9-5; Sun. and holidays 12-5. Free Wed., Sat., Sun., and holidays; other days 25c; children under 14 always free. Libraries open weekdays 9-5 and Mon., Tues., and Fri., 6-9:30. Guidebooks and catalogues for sale in the Department of Reproductions. Guides by appointment. Cafeteria on ground floor. See Calendar of Events for lecture series and annual exhibitions.*) This building, with its warm smoky-toned patina, has long been the Mecca of artists in the Middle West. Designed by Shepley, Rutan, and Coolidge in the Italian Renaissance style, it is notable for its delicate and fine proportions. Broad steps guarded by Edward Kemeys' bronze lions lead from the avenue to the main entrance, above which is a deep loggia sheltering statues of Minerva, Mercury, and Augustus Caesar. The bareness of the second story gallery walls is relieved by sections of the Parthenon frieze and on the north and south façades by a fine Palladian arcade. Lorado Taft's *Fountain of the Great Lakes,* at the south terrace, is composed of five female figures, the topmost symbolizing Lake Superior. From the shell in her hand water spills to the figures representing the other Great Lakes. The fountain memorializes Benjamin Franklin Ferguson, donor of a $1,000,000 trust fund, the income from which is used by the Institute trustees to erect and maintain monuments throughout Chicago. One of the eleven monuments already constructed by this fund, a replica of Jean Antoine Houdon's bronze of George Wash-ington in regimental dress, stands at the entrance doors.

The Institute, incorporated in 1879 as the Chicago Academy of Fine Arts, is an outgrowth of one of the first art schools in the country, the Chicago Academy of Design, founded in 1866. The organization received its present name in 1882 and a few years later achieved international recognition when it purchased the Demidoff Collection of fifteen old Dutch Masters. At this time the Columbian Exposition authorities, instead of building a temporary structure to house the Parliament of Religions, cooperated financially with the Institute trustees in erecting the present permanent building. The Institute has since used the building and constructed large additions, notably Gunsaulus Hall spanning the Illinois Central right-of-way, and Hutchinson Wing, east of the tracks.

The Institute is supported largely by endowment and trust funds, together with Park District tax funds, membership dues, and entrance fees. For the past three decades there has been an annual average of one million visitors. Approximately seventy exhibitions held every year, ranging from international to one-man shows, make the Institute a constant source of fresh interest.

In the chronologically arranged galleries on the second floor of the main building are works by masters of almost every great school of painting from the thirteenth century to the present. But the Institute is richest in French paintings of the late nineteenth and early twentieth centuries. Many of the exhibits were gifts from Chicagoans. Earliest of these was the Henry Field collection, forty-one canvasses representing some of the best work of the Barbizon School and including Breton's popular *Song of the Lark*. Other notable collections include the Palmer French Impressionists; the Kimball British and Dutch paintings: the Ryerson loan group of Monets and Renoirs, primitives, and eighteenth and nineteenth century works; the Birch-Bartlett Post-Impressionists; the Butler Innesses; the Munger nineteenth century paintings, and the De Wolf and Schulze American canvasses. El Greco's *Assumption of the Virgin,* Rembrandt's *Young Girl at an Open Half-Door,* Seurat's *Sunday on the Island of Grand Jatte,* Constable's *Stoke-by-Nayland,* Manet's *Jesus Mocked,* and Renoir's *Two Little Circus Girls,* were selected by Robert S. Harshe, director of the Institute from 1921 until his death in January 1938, as perhaps the most valued of all the canvasses.

American and European drawings, water colors, and sculptures line the corridor galleries in the center of the second floor. The entrance hall, on the first floor, is devoted to modern sculpture, and is flanked by galleries of Egyptian and classical arts. The north half of the floor contains Fullerton Hall, the center of the extensive lecture activities of the Institute, and the print galleries. In these galleries exhibits are frequently arranged from the Institute's collection of 25,000 European and American prints; the important International print exhibitions are also held here. The Print Department Library is a general collection of 1,200 works on prints and drawings, and portfolios of reproductions of drawings.

In the south half of the first floor are the Children's Museum, filled with objects of interest to children, and the main libraries. Ryerson Library contains more than 35,000 volumes on the fine and decorative arts, including many monographs on individual painters and sculptors, and an exceptional series of Japanese and Chinese illustrated books. In addition, it receives 200 magazines and museum bulletins in English and other languages, even the Oriental. The 7,700 volumes and the 45 current issues of magazines in Burnham Library embrace the fields of architecture, town planning, housing, and landscape architecture. The unusually complete files of bound periodicals in both libraries make them especially valuable for research. The Photograph and Slide Department has 80,000 photographs and color prints, and 34,000 lantern slides, loaned free to educational and religious institutions in Chicago, and for a nominal fee to individual Chicagoans and to institutions outside the city.

Blackstone Hall, extending to the ground floor in the rear of the main building, houses interior architectural casts and the imposing cathedral fronts exhibited by the French government at the Columbian Exposition.

Some of the decorative arts collections are found in lower Gunsaulus Hall. Here the galleries are bright with English and Continental glass, pewter, American pottery, porcelain, wallpaper, and printed cottons. The fine collection of English lustreware includes rare specimens of "resist" and "stencil" processes.

The Alexander McKinlock, Jr. Memorial Court, in the center of the Hutchinson Wing, surrounds Carl Milles' *Triton Fountain,* a bronze group of four mythological figures returning from the sea with marine trophies. The south half of the wing, together with the most recent addition, the Allerton Wing, is given over mostly to European period rooms, furniture and rugs, metal and wood work, and textiles from the Coptic Period to the present. Rotating exhibitions are drawn from extensive groups of woven fabrics, lace, and needlework.

The north half houses the Oriental collection, one of the finest in America. The ceremonial bronze vessels, chiefly of the Chou and Han dynasties, are among the oldest existing works of Chinese art; other treasures are rare Cambodian sculptures, fine ceramics of various dynasties, and Mohammedan art objects. The history of Japanese prints is illustrated in the Buckingham collection, one of the most complete in existence. Frequently changed exhibits from it are shown in the Japanese gallery.

The School of the Art Institute, progenitor of the entire institution and one of the largest art schools in America, occupies part of the ground floor of the main building. Enrolling some 3,000 students, it awards degrees in fine arts, art education, and dramatic art.

In 1925 a School of Drama, offering a 3-year course of professional training in all branches of theater work, was added to the Schools of Fine Arts and Industrial Art. Connected with Hutchinson Wing is the KENNETH SAWYER GOODMAN MEMORIAL THEATER. Designed by Howard Van Doren Shaw, the theater is largely below surface level; for this reason it has no loft, and sets are wheeled into place. The arrangement of the main auditorium, seating 800, is an adaptation of the Continental type; the rows of seats, reached by longitudinal aisles on either side, stretch unbroken in their full width. Several productions are given for the public by the Goodman Theater players during the year.

The CHICAGO HARBOR is formed by inner and outer breakwaters extending the length of Grant Park to a point a mile north of the mouth of the river. In the second half of the nineteenth century, the Chicago River was one of the busiest ports in the world, constantly crowded in the shipping season with grain and lumber boats. Breakwaters were first built in 1874 to protect the mouth of the river and provide basins for boats waiting to enter it. Today, except for an occasional tramp steamer from Norway or a few barges, there is little shipping to be seen in the river. The large tonnage still registered for Chicago is handled mainly near the southern limits at Calumet Harbor, which receives iron ore, coal, and limestone, and exports grain. The inner basin of the Chicago Harbor is now an important part of the city's recreational facilities, providing free anchorage for hundreds of boats, ranging from tiny sail boats to sleek yachts. Some of the boat owners are members of the Chicago and Columbia yacht clubs, which have clubhouses at the piers north of Monroe Street.

The pier at the north end of Grant Park is occupied by (14) the ILLINOIS NAVAL RESERVE ARMORY. The training ship *Wilmette,* usually tied up alongside, is, as few Chicagoans know, the remodeled excursion steamer, *Eastland,* on which occurred Chicago's most appalling disaster. On July 24, 1915, loaded with a holiday crowd, the *Eastland* capsized as it was about to leave the dock at the Clark Street bridge, drowning 812 persons.

The Near North Side

The Near North Side, the birthplace of Chicago, lies almost within the shadows of the Loop. Within its two square miles, which extend from the Chicago River to North Avenue, from Lake Michigan to the North Branch of the Chicago River, is a jumble of the diverse elements of Chicago life. A spearhead of smart shops and office buildings thrusts up Michigan Avenue past the old Water Tower, the center of Towertown, the "Gold Coast" of the late nineteenth century; here, in old mansions and converted coach houses, live many of Chicago's artists, and a number of young professional and business people who prefer high ceilings, old fireplaces, and "atmosphere" to modern conveniences. Farther north is the present "Gold Coast," with its mansions and apartments along the lake front. A few blocks inland lie the desolate tenements and shacks of Italians and Negroes, bounded by factories and warehouses along the river. Moody Bible Institute neighbors on "Bughouse Square"; the sombre, mansard-roofed mansions on lower Rush Street end abruptly at the towering Wrigley Building; the chili parlors and cheap saloons on Clark Street are a few steps from swank restaurants and cocktail lounges; from a corner of the Seminary that he founded, Archbishop James Edward Quigley fixes a stony gaze on two elaborate night clubs across the street.

A century ago the great bulge of land south of Oak Street and east of Michigan Avenue did not exist. In 1886 a small craft, manned by Capt. George Wellington Streeter, grounded on a shoal off the foot of Superior Street. Unable to float the boat, Streeter decided to make his home on it. The shoal gradually filled in; eventually Streeter's boat stood on solid ground; to the amazement of Chicago, the Captain claimed it for himself as the District of Lake Michigan, renouncing allegiance to the State of Illinois. In his *Captain Streeter, Pioneer,* Everett Guy Ballard describes the long series of battles, legal and physical, between the Captain and city authorities in their efforts to evict him. Title to the land was eventually cleared, and the valuable section, now the site of some of Chicago's finest apartment buildings and hotels, remembers the Captain only in its name, Streeterville.

TOUR 1 — 1.2 m.

N. from the Chicago River on Michigan Ave.

1. The MICHIGAN AVENUE BRIDGE, a massive double-decked

bascule structure, spans the Chicago River between the sites of Chicago's earliest settlements—that of Fort Dearborn on the South bank and of its first houses, four log cabins, on the north bank. Until the bridge was built in 1920, Michigan Avenue north of the river was a narrow lane lined with old-fashioned mansions. All but one of the old houses on the west side of the Avenue were removed when it was widened; a few remain on the east side, overshadowed by modern buildings. The bridge replaced the old Rush Street span, and until the Outer Drive bridge was opened in 1937, carried the major traffic stream between the North Side and the downtown district.

Bas reliefs adorn the four bridge pylons. *The Pioneers* and *The Discoverers*, at the north end, are by J. E. Fraser; at the south end are *Defense* and *Regeneration,* symbolizing Chicago's recovery from the Great Fire, by Henry Hering. At the memorial services commemorating the 300th birthday of Father Marquette in May, 1937, nine years after the erection of *The Discoverers,* it was noted that the figure of Marquette, a Jesuit, was wearing Franciscan robes.

2. The WRIGLEY BUILDING (*observatory 9-5 daily, 25c includes a package of gum and use of telescopes*), NW. plaza of Michigan Avenue bridge, a terra-cotta office building designed by Graham, Anderson, Probst and White, French Renaissance in style, is visible for miles, immaculately white by day and incandescent at night. From the south its oblique façade resembles a partly opened gate, inviting entrance to the modernized north section of Michigan Avenue, the development of which it pioneered. From a certain angle across the street the building appears to flatten into an elaborate stage prop. Its four-faced tower clock furnishes small talk for Chicagoans who know that its figures are really not Roman numerals but simply single keystone strips of tile, 3½ feet high. The Arts Club of Chicago maintains clubrooms and galleries on the second floor; at intervals, exhibitions by well-known artists are shown here.

3. The TRIBUNE TOWER (*open; tours 2:30, 3:30, 4:30, and 8:00 Mon.-Fri.; reservations for evening tour; observatory 9-5 daily, 25c*), 435 N. Michigan Ave., contains the plant and offices of the Chicago *Tribune.* Cathedral-like, its vertical shaft of soft-toned Indiana limestone terminates in a crown reminiscent of the Butter Tower in Rouen. At the 25th floor a setback provides a promenade enclosed within a Gothic cloister of delicate tracery, above which soaring arches simulate flying buttresses.

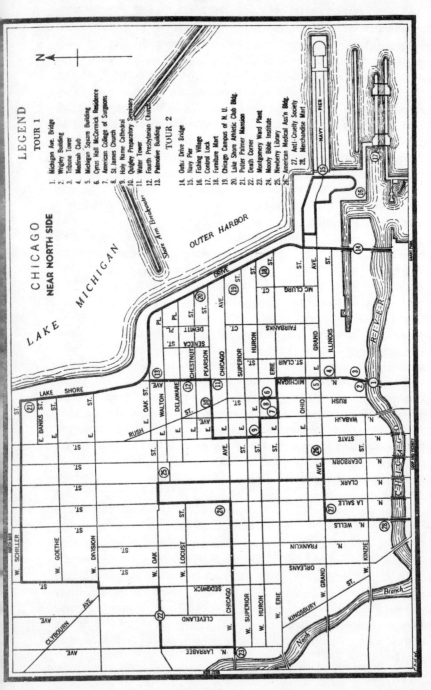

LEGEND

CHICAGO
NEAR NORTH SIDE

TOUR 1

1. Michigan Ave. Bridge
2. Wrigley Building
3. Tribune Tower
4. Medinah Club
5. Michigan Square Building
6. Cyrus Hall McCormick Residence
7. American College of Surgeons
8. St. James Church
9. Holy Name Cathedral
10. Quigley Preparatory Seminary
11. Water Tower
12. Fourth Presbyterian Church
13. Palmolive Building

TOUR 2

14. Outer Drive Bridge
15. Navy Pier
16. Fishing Village
17. Control Lock
18. Furniture Mart
19. Chicago Campus of N. U.
20. Lake Shore Athletic Club Bldg.
21. Potter Palmer Mansion
22. Death Corner
23. Montgomery Ward Plant
24. Moody Bible Institute
25. Newberry Library
26. American Medical Ass'n Bldg.
27. Anti-Cruelty Society
28. Merchandise Mart

Flanked by built-in stone fragments from celebrated buildings, the richly carved entrance arch is three stories high; light enters the lobby through a pierced stone screen of fanciful design. Entwined in foliage are figures from Æsop's fables and facetious representations of the architects—a howling dog for John Mead Howells, a figure of Robin Hood for Raymond M. Hood—whose design won the $50,000 award in the world-wide competition held by the *Tribune* in 1921 for "the most beautiful and distinctive office building in the world." The second prize was won by the Finnish architect, Eliel Saarinen, whose severely vertical design has had a more profound and extensive influence on skyscraper architecture.

On the travertine walls of the spacious lobby are quotations on the freedom of the press, a mural depicting man's struggle for freedom of speech, letters written by Abraham Lincoln to Joseph Medill, founder of the *Tribune,* and several weather recording devices.

The Chicago *Tribune,* occupying a large part of the building, was established in 1847. Oldest and most widely circulated newspaper in Chicago, it is one of the most profitable publishing enterprises in the world. Col. Robert R. McCormick, grandson of Joseph Medill, has been editor and publisher since 1925. Tours of the plant take visitors through the news room, engraving and composing rooms, and other offices associated with the production and distribution of the newspaper, including the great press room. Here, in the lower levels of the building, some of the largest and fastest presses in the world roar out 2,500 miles of newsprint daily. Adjoining the tower is WGN RADIO STATION (*tours* 10-4:30 *weekdays;* 11-4:30 *Sun.*), with rich portals and decorations in flamboyant Gothic style.

4. The MEDINAH CLUB OF CHICAGO (*observatory* 10-10 *daily,* 25c), distinguished by its exotic Moorish dome and minaret, is a residential club, formerly for Shriners but now unrestricted. The 42-story structure, designed by Walter W. Alschlager, incorporates a miscellany of architectural styles and was completed in 1928 at a cost of $10,000,000.

5. The MICHIGAN SQUARE BUILDING, 540 N. Michigan Ave., within a severe exterior, contains a striking blend of commerce and art. Holabird and Root turned the disadvantages of an uneven lot into an architectural triumph by planning a number of small shops on different levels. Concentric semi-circular floors and flying stairways radiate from the Fountain of Diana. Sculptured by Carl Milles in a

technique resembling archaic Greek, the central statue and secondary figures of the fountain reveal strength and movement rather than grace, creating an impression of wild forest life. The illusion is furthered by the details of the court, the lighting of which suggests a forest glade; massive striped pillars symbolize tree trunks.

L. from Michigan Ave. on Erie St. R. on Rush St.

RUSH STREET became a dead-end street when its old bridge was superseded by the Michigan Avenue bridge. The first building erected on new Michigan Avenue, the Wrigley, turned its back on Rush Street with its line of mansard-roofed mansions south of Chicago Avenue. Rush Street's brownstone gentility has been further invaded by restaurants and modernistic night clubs.

6. The CYRUS HALL McCORMICK RESIDENCE (*private*), 675 Rush St., a Victorian mansion designed by Cudell and Blumenthal, was built in 1879 for the inventor of the reaper, and is owned by his son, Harold Fowler McCormick. An iron-railed mansard roof and tower crown the three-story brownstone structure.

The McCormick Historical Association Library (*open to research workers on application*), in the former coach house, contains more than 1,500 printed and 1,500,000 manuscript items concerned with the activities and interests of the McCormick family: the history of agriculture, the evolution of farm machinery, early Virginiana, the development of the Presbyterian church in the Midwest, and records of the McCormick reaper companies.

Retrace to Erie St. R. on Erie St.

7. The AMERICAN COLLEGE OF SURGEONS (*open 9-4:30 Mon.-Fri., 9-1 Sat.*), 40 E. Erie St., is the national headquarters of a fellowship of 12,000 surgeons. The gray stone building, formerly the mansion of S. M. Nickerson, a banker, was completed in 1883; the great entrance hall is entirely of marble; carved alabaster openwork graces the stair-rail.

An enclosed passageway leads to the JOHN B. MURPHY MEMORIAL, 50 E. Erie St., an auditorium dedicated to the memory of one of the great surgeons of the early twentieth century. From the street the colonnaded façade appears to be wedged between the adjoining buildings. Panels in the imposing bronze entrance doors picture epoch-making discoveries in the history of medicine.

R. from Erie St. on Wabash Ave.

8. ST. JAMES CHURCH, Wabash Ave. at Huron St., was rebuilt around parts of the tower and rough stone walls that withstood the flames of 1871. The Episcopal Parish of St. James, established in 1834, built the original Gothic structure in 1857. At the north end of the church is the Chapel of St. Andrew, a beautiful bit of Gothic architecture, designed in 1913 by Bertram Goodhue; the chapel commemorates James L. Houghteling, founder of the Brotherhood of St. Andrew.

L. from Wabash Ave. on Superior St.

9. HOLY NAME CATHEDRAL, Superior and State Sts., a Victorian Gothic structure of limestone, dominates six diocesan and parish buildings. Containing the cathedra of the archbishop of the diocese, it is the center of Roman Catholic worship in metropolitan Chicago. At the Sunday noon high mass the Cardinal's cathedral choristers sing; the Cardinal himself celebrates the Pontifical high masses. The music of the cathedral is in authentic liturgical form. In the library (*private*) are the complete works of Palestrina, said to be one of only two such collections in the United States.

R. from Superior St. on State St. R. from State St. on Pearson St.

10. The QUIGLEY PREPARATORY SEMINARY, Pearson and Rush Sts., prepares some 900 youths for the Roman Catholic priesthood. Regarded by some as the most picturesque Gothic group in Chicago, the seminary buildings, designed by Zachary Davis, surround a quadrangle court. The Chapel of St. James is reminiscent of Sainte Chapelle, Paris, in the delicacy of its design. Its windows, designed by Robert Giles, are composed of many thousands of pieces of antique English glass with fused pigments; the rose window was patterned on that in Notre Dame de Paris.

11. The WATER TOWER (*closed*), Michigan Ave., between Chicago Ave. and Pearson St., was one of very few Near North Side buildings that survived the Chicago Fire. It again escaped destruction when streets were widened in 1928 because it had endeared itself to Chicagoans as a favorite landmark. Built in 1869, it performed an important function in the water system for many years. An ornamented standpipe, the tower absorbed the pulsations caused by the old style

pumps in the station across the street, steadying the water flow in the city mains. The 186-foot tower of rough-hewn Lemont limestone is now a buffer between the old and the new in Chicago. In style it is "goldfish castle" Gothic, striking an anachronistic note in the midst of trim modern buildings. The tower stands like a hoop-skirted matron in a garden, majestically deflecting the surging flow of Michigan Avenue traffic; at night it is bathed in the amber glow of concealed lights.

The WATER WORKS (*open 8 a.m.-9 p.m. daily*), opposite the tower, is the oldest link in the chain of twelve stations pumping Chicago's water supply. In 1842 the first station was built at Lake Street and Michigan Avenue to pump water through hollowed cedar logs. The first municipally owned plant was built on Chicago Avenue in 1854. Of the plant that replaced it in 1867, the Chicago Fire left only the walls, which were used in the present building.

The tank-like structures in the lake, about two miles offshore north of Chicago Avenue, are two of the six cribs, or intakes, where approximately a billion gallons of water per day enter tunnels under the bed of the lake and flow to the pumping stations for distribution through the mains. The system was designed by E. S. Chesborough in 1864.

L. from Pearson St. on Michigan Ave.

12. The FOURTH PRESBYTERIAN CHURCH, Michigan Ave. and Delaware Pl., designed by Ralph Adams Cram, is a fine example of English Gothic in beautifully carved Bedford stone. With the parish house and manse adjoining, it encloses a grass plot on three sides. The fourth side of the rectangle is an arcade through which passers-by glimpse the cloister garth and fountain. The church is a massive edifice with pinnacled gables, slender spire, and generous buttresses. The beautiful stained-glass windows were designed and executed by Charles Connick. For many years the Fourth Presbyterian has been a focal point of Chicago's fashionable Easter Sunday parade.

13. The PALMOLIVE BUILDING, 919 N. Michigan Ave., an impressive modern office structure designed by Holabird and Root, faces the Gold Coast on one side and the downtown district on the other. Rising 37 stories in a series of setbacks, the building is topped with a slender aluminum tower supporting the Palmolive Beacon, formerly known as the Lindbergh Beacon. Flood lights on the setback terraces project interesting patterns on the smooth limestone walls.

The beacon, the most powerful in the world, a high-intensity arc of two billion candlepower, rotates twice a minute. At an altitude of 45,000 feet it can be seen 500 miles; the average visibility is 250 miles. Newspapers have been read by its light in planes 27 miles away. Below it, a directional light of 11,500,000 candlepower points to the Municipal Airport.

TOUR 2 — 6.5 m.

N. from mouth of the river on Lake Shore Drive

14. The OUTER DRIVE BRIDGE, at the mouth of the Chicago River, together with the smaller bridge immediately north over Ogden Slip, connects the express highway systems between the north and the south lake shore, diverting through traffic from the downtown area and providing another artery between the Loop and the North Side. The largest bascule bridge in the world, it was dedicated October 5, 1937 by President Franklin D. Roosevelt in a memorable address castigating aggressor nations.

R. from Lake Shore Drive on Ohio St. leading into Grand Ave.

15. NAVY PIER, at the foot of Grand Avenue, extends 1,000 yards into the lake as a terminal for freight and pleasure craft, and as a summer playground. Recreational facilities at the east end include picnic and dining pavilions, children's playground, dance hall, auditorium, excursion landing, and promenades. Garden clubs and others use the long sheds for periodic displays. From the far end of the pier is an excellent view of Chicago's skyline.

16. The FISHING VILLAGE, SW. of the Navy Pier, is one of the two commercial fishing centers of Chicago. Shacks, with store fronts, house the fishermen and provide a market for their catch, principally perch and lake herring. Smokehouses process chubs and other fishes shipped in from northern points. Linen gill nets, wound on reels, dry in the sun along the wharf, to which gasoline launches are tied. Early each morning the fishermen first set miles of nets on the lake bottom several miles offshore and then reel in the nets set the previous day.

17. The CONTROL LOCK, SE. of the village, forms an anteroom to the mouth of the river through which all boats passing between the lake and the river must go. It was built in 1938 to prevent the possibility of the river flowing into the lake, as it did before the Drainage

Canal reversed the flow in 1900. The Supreme Court ordered a reduction in the diversion of lake water from a maximum of 10,000 cubic feet per second to 1,500, beginning January 1, 1939. It was feared that this reduced withdrawal might at times be insufficient to maintain the delicately balanced westward flow of the river, which would then back its polluting waters into the lake. At such times, the lock will hold the river back until the control gates at Lockport, which regulate the rate of diversion, are opened wide.

Retrace Ohio St. R. on Lake Shore Drive

18. The AMERICAN FURNITURE MART (*open to wholesale trade only*), 666 Lake Shore Dr., reflects the current merchandising trend toward centralized wholesale markets. The largest building in the world at the time of construction in 1924, its huge utilitarian bulk is the most massive structure on the lake front. Gothic entrances and ornamentation, as well as a blue campanile tower, somewhat mitigate the heaviness of this great block of pressed brick, 28,000,000 cubic feet in volume. Housing the national showrooms of the country's leading manufacturers of home furnishings, it provides a convenient year-round market for buyers, and semi-annually makes Chicago the greatest wholesale furniture market in the United States. The building was designed by Henry Raeder and associates, N. Max Dunning and George C. Nimmons.

WCFL BROADCASTING STATION (*open 9 a.m.-10 p.m. daily*), on the 20th floor of the Mart tower, is the largest independent radio broadcasting unit devoted to the interests of organized labor in the United States. It is owned and operated by the Chicago Federation of Labor.

19. The CHICAGO CAMPUS OF NORTHWESTERN UNIVERSITY, formerly McKinlock Memorial Campus, Lake Shore Drive at Chicago Ave., is the Chicago group of professional and part-time schools under the general administration of Northwestern University in suburban Evanston. The cluster of six Tudor Gothic structures, designed by James Gamble Rogers, with Frank A. Childs and William J. Smith as associates, stands on a 14-acre landscaped tract, secured in 1920. The schools enroll about 1,300 full-time and 9,000 part-time students.

The MONTGOMERY WARD MEMORIAL BUILDING, tallest of the group, gift of Mrs. Elizabeth J. Ward in memory of her husband, houses the medical school on its lower floors and the dental school above. The medical college was the first in the United States to establish a certain standard of preliminary education as a prerequisite to enrollment. Its list of alumni includes such illustrious names as Mayo, Billings, and De Lee. The Frederick Robert Zeit Museum of Pathology (*open* 9-5 *Mon.-Fri.;* 9-12 *Sat.; apply room* 694 *for guide*), one of the finest of its kind in the country, contains approximately 3,000 labeled specimens showing changes produced by disease in the various organs of the human body. The William Bebb Library and Museum (*open* 9-5 *Mon.-Fri.,* 9-12 *Sat.*), on the 10th floor, contains rare and comic prints and etchings of dental practice, busts and biographical placques of famous dentists, old instruments, and pathological and normal animal and human dentures.

East of the Ward building is WIEBOLDT HALL, in which are held the evening classes of the School of Commerce, the second largest in the United States, and of the Medill School of Journalism. Clubrooms and a large commerce library serve the largest group of students on the campus.

LEVY MAYER HALL and the ELBERT H. GARY LIBRARY BUILDING, east of Wieboldt Hall, are used by the Law School, established in 1859, oldest in Chicago. A cloistered garden between the ivy-covered buildings is enclosed within an arched wall connecting the wings. Hundreds of illustrations of the history, customs, and leaders of the legal profession, and facsimiles of historically interesting documents line the corridors.

THORNE HALL, on Lake Shore Drive, contains an auditorium and a social room. The Alexander McKinlock Memorial Gate, at the south entrance, is a high and massive archway of ornamental bronze and wrought iron, with two beautifully designed gates.

20. The LAKE SHORE ATHLETIC CLUB BUILDING (*private; apply for permission to view murals*), 850 N. Lake Shore Drive, is a dignified 18-story building of buff brick. The fifty panels on the walls of the five private dining rooms on the second floor were designed by Otto E. Hake, and depict Chicago scenes and historical events from Indian days to the present.

21. The POTTER PALMER MANSION (*closed*), Lake Shore Drive between Banks and Schiller Sts., designed by Henry Ives Cobb, was completed in 1885, first of the Drive's imposing houses. Battlemented turrets and towers, brown sandstone walls trimmed with gray

granite, and a stone balcony, create the impression of a feudal castle. The mansion was the scene of many brilliant social events.

L. from Lake Shore Drive on Schiller St.
L. on Sedgwick St. R. on Oak St.

22. DEATH CORNER, Oak St. and Cleveland Ave., in the heart of the crowded Italian slum area, was the scene of more slayings during the prohibition era than any other point in the city. The numerous shootings and stabbings of men engaged in the "alky" trade, were invariably "unwitnessed," although many occurred in broad daylight.

L. from Oak St. on Larrabee St. R. on Chicago Ave.

23. The MONTGOMERY WARD AND CO. PLANT (*tours by arrangement*), sprawls along the North Branch at Chicago Ave. The three huge eight-story buildings, each a block long and half as wide, are a far cry from the 12- by 14-foot room, at 825 N. Clark Street nearby, in which A. Montgomery Ward and George R. Thorne started the first mail-order house in the world in 1872. The present catalogue issues, grown from a few 8- by 12-inch single sheets to millions of voluminous books, are familiar throughout the country.

The company, the second largest mail-order house in the world, maintains eight other plants and approximately 500 retail stores in the United States. The building on the south side of Chicago Avenue, surmounted with the symbol of the institution, a figure of the *Spirit of Progress,* houses the general administrative offices and a large department store. In the north buildings, mail orders are speedily assembled and shipped, as many as 200,000 a day.

Working out of St. Louis as a traveling salesman in the late 1860's, Montgomery Ward recognized the merchandising limitations of the small stores in rural areas. When he conceived the idea of mail order selling, he came to Chicago, and initiated the business with a capital of less than $2,500.

Retrace Chicago Ave. L. from Chicago Ave. on La Salle St.

24. MOODY BIBLE INSTITUTE (*open 8:30-5 Mon.-Fri., 8:30-12:30 Sat., evenings by arrangement*), La Salle St. at Chicago Ave., is a coeducational, interdenominational, Christian training school sup-

ported largely by contributions from friends throughout the world. Twenty-eight buildings serve the needs of 2,700 resident and evening students, prospective teachers, and preachers of the Gospel. The curriculum emphasizes Biblical doctrine and the ministry of music. The activities of Dwight L. Moody gradually expanded from his Sunday School class, his North Market Mission, and the Illinois Street Church, to this "West Point of Christian Service," founded in 1886.

The ADMINISTRATIVE BUILDING, 812 N. La Salle Street, a 12-story Gothic structure of red brick and Bedford stone, was designed by Thielbar and Fugard and completed in 1938. In the tower of the building is the Institute's radio station, WMBI, devoted entirely to religious programs. The MOODY EXHIBIT, 830 N. La Salle Street, contains various Bibles and relics from Moody's home and office.

R. from La Salle St. on Oak St. R. on Clark St.

BUGHOUSE SQUARE, Walton St. between Dearborn and Clark Sts., separates Newberry Library from Washington Square, the oldest park in the city. This is the outdoor forum of garrulous hobohemia. On summer nights local and visiting intellectual hoboes and hobophiles expound unorthodoxy, socio-political and sexual. Tourists in the many sight-seeing buses that tarry in the square frequently find themselves the target of a verbal barrage.

25. The NEWBERRY LIBRARY (*main reading and genealogy rooms open 9 a.m.-10 p.m. weekdays; Edward E. Ayer, John M. Wing and rare book collections, 9-5; non-circulating*), Clark, Walton and Dearborn Sts., was named for Walter Loomis Newberry, pioneer Chicago merchant and financier, whose bequest forms the principal part of its endowment. Established in 1887, it contains more than 500,000 books, bound pamphlets, and manuscripts on Americana, British history, English and American literature, typography, genealogy, music, and comparative philology.

The library is notable for its rare books and source material. It contains some 1,700 books issued before 1500, many of them superb examples of early printing, such as the *Hypnerotomachia Poliphili*, Venice, 1499, regarded as the most beautiful of early illustrated books. Its collection of European and Oriental manuscripts contains examples dating from the ninth century. The music collection, one of the best in the country, contains autographed scores by Richard Wagner, Edward MacDowell, Robert Schumann, Franz Schubert, and Johann Sebastian

Bach. The philological library, assembled by Prince Louis Lucien Bonaparte and acquired in 1900, ranks as one of the finest collections on linguistics in the world. The Edward E. Ayer Collection is particularly rich in materials on the archaeology and ethnology of the North American Indian, the native races of Mexico, and the Hawaiian and Philippine Islanders. The collection is increased from year to year, with emphasis on South American archaeology, ethnology, and colonial history, and the general subject of cartography. Another distinctive collection, provided by the John M. Wing Foundation, is devoted to typography and provides a comprehensive view of the history of book-making.

The Library holds periodic exhibitions of its rare books, prints, maps, and manuscripts. There is a regular annual exhibition of the fifty books of the year, under the auspices of the American Institute of Graphic Arts, and of Chicago fine printing, under the joint auspices of the Library and the Society of Typographic Arts.

The five-story building constructed of Connecticut granite in Spanish-Romanesque style, designed by Henry Ives Cobb, occupies the site of the Mahlon Ogden residence, the only Near North Side house saved during the Chicago Fire. About the various rooms and corridors hang thirty-four portraits, painted and presented to the library by G. P. A. Healy.

CLARK STREET, for a few blocks on either side of Grand Ave., provides a night life section for the down-at-the-heeler. Taverns, five and six to a block, advertise whisky and gin for 5 and 10 cents a shot, and incredibly large schooners of beer for a dime. Conveniently interspersed between the taverns are pawnshops. The street is lined with ornate red brick buildings, once pretentious family hotels. Some still function as hotels but serve a much less moneyed clientele.

North from Chicago Avenue, Clark Street was formerly the center of the "Nort Seit" of early German immigrants. The celebrated Turner Hall was recently demolished, but on and near North Avenue, at Clark Street, remain a number of German restaurants and food shops, and the old Germania Club.

L. from Clark St. on Grand Ave.

26. The AMERICAN MEDICAL ASSOCIATION BUILDING (*open* 8:30-4:30 *Mon.-Fri.,* 8:30-12 *Sat.*), NE. corner of Grand Ave. and Dearborn St., is the headquarters of the co-ordinating organiza-

tion of some 100,000 doctors whose delegate sessions shape the policies of the medical profession. The eight-story building contains laboratories, libraries, assembly rooms, and the editorial and production rooms of *Hygeia*, the *American Medical Directory*, and the *Journal of the American Medical Association*.

Retrace Grand Ave.

27. The ANTI-CRUELTY SOCIETY (9-5 *Mon.-Fri.*, 9-1 *Sat.*), 153 W. Grand Ave., maintains an establishment that would delight the most ardent zoophile. For the unfortunate among the animals of Chicago, the Society provides in its beautiful limestone building and grounds such modern comforts and conveniences as a clinic with X-ray equipment, and an exercise yard with trees and running water. Ambulances pick up stray, crippled, and unwanted animals at all hours. The placement service and free counsel by veterinarians are widely used.

L. from Grand Ave. on Wells St. R. on North Bank Drive

28. The MERCHANDISE MART (*commercial exhibits open to wholesale trade only*), 222 N. Bank Dr., is the largest building in the world. An enterprise of Marshall Field and Company, it was completed in 1930 as a wholesale market; more than 5,600 lines of department and general store goods are displayed here by wholesalers, manufacturers, and importers from all parts of the country. Built in part over the Chicago and North Western tracks, the $30,000,000 structure, designed by Graham, Anderson, Probst, and White, covers two city blocks. Six and one-half miles of store front corridors give access to 93 acres of floor space, an area almost two-thirds as large as the Chicago Loop. This concentrated commercial city houses a working population of 25,000, and has its own "L" station, bank, post office, telegraph and railroad ticket offices, large restaurants, and retail shops.

Set back from the river bank along a wide private street, its southern façade is visible for blocks, an example of dignified beauty in modern business architecture. Concealed lighting of the massive symmetrical structure forms a beautiful composition of light and shadow in the Chicago night scene. Fifteen murals by Jules Guerin depicting market scenes in foreign countries decorate the lobby walls. In the Home Building Exhibit (*open 9-5 Mon.-Fri., 9-1 Sat.*), on the seventh floor, are model homes and a great variety of building materials.

The National Broadcasting Company studios and offices, and stations WMAQ and WENR (*open 9-5 daily; after 5 by appointment or by special ticket to a specific broadcast*), occupy the 19th and 20th floors of the Mart. There are eleven studios and five public observation rooms; Studio A is one of the largest in the world. The operations in the main control room include the amplification of programs for transmission to network stations, over some 45,000 miles of special telephone lines.

Lincoln Park

Along the lake shore between North and Foster Avenues stretches Lincoln Park, more than a thousand acres of rolling woodlands, bridle paths, quiet lagoons, yacht basins, grassy playgrounds, golf courses, and gardens, dotted with monuments and museums. For diversity of use the park is unequalled in Chicago. Originally a 120-acre city cemetery, the tract was designated as a park in 1864, and most of the graves were moved to outlying cemeteries. Adjacent lands were acquired, but the largest part of the park was created with sand from the lake in the present century.

At the south end of the park, commanding the Dearborn Parkway entrance, is (1) the STATUE OF ABRAHAM LINCOLN, by Augustus Saint-Gaudens, unveiled on October 22, 1887, regarded by many as the noblest portrait statue in the country. It captures in bronze the mood of the Gettysburg address. The simple base and the spacious exedra, backed by the foliage of the park, are the work of Stanford White.

West of the statue is (2) the CHICAGO HISTORICAL SOCIETY MUSEUM (*open 9:30-5 weekdays, 1-6 Sun.; children, students, and teachers free; adults free, Mon., Wed., Fri., other days, 25c; handbooks, 25c; guide service by arrangement*). Georgian in style the red brick building with limestone trim has two stories and a basement (which on the west is at ground level) and a flat balustraded roof; a broad flight of steps sweeps down from the Doric portico. Opened in 1932, the museum is the fourth home of the society, founded in 1856 to collect and preserve materials pertaining to the history of the United States, particularly those relating to Chicago and the Northwest Territory.

On the main floor, (east entrance) adjoining the foyer, which is patterned after that of Independence Hall, are the Marine Room, illustrative of the merchant marine and the Navy, and the Chicago Diorama Gallery, with eight scenes from the city's history.

The dozen period rooms on the main floor pictorialize the story of America from the days of Columbus through the World War; several reproduce famous old rooms. Objects range from anchors used by Columbus to messages sent by carrier pigeon from the "Lost Battalion" in the Argonne Forest. The George Washington collection includes several noteworthy paintings of Washington, the velvet suit he wore at his inauguration, and other personal effects. In the Chicago rooms are women's costumes of various periods, illustrations of the Chicago Fire, and miscellaneous relics.

On the top floors are other period rooms more specifically Illinoisan; among others, the Pioneer Room, containing a reproduction of the Lincoln log cabin and three store buildings of the 1840's and 1850's. The Illinois Room has a mask of Stephen A. Douglas and some of his effects, a first edition of the Book of Mormon, and part of the Lovejoy press. Lincoln Hall, lined with portraits and sculptures of the martyred President, contains his blanket shawl, the penholder with which he signed the Emancipation Proclamation, and the clothes he wore at the time of his assassination. His deathbed is preserved in a room that reproduces the one in which he died. The Lincoln Parlor, a reproduction of that in his Springfield house, has the original furniture.

In an adjoining large room portraits and busts of men and women prominent in the history of the city gaze down upon a huge model of contemporary Chicago. Constructed of balsa wood on a scale of one inch to 300 feet, the model accurately reproduces Chicago's 445,000 buildings as seen from an altitude of 8,000 feet. The work was done as a WPA project under the direction of Col. M. O. Kasson. Also on the top floor is the Gilpin Reference Library (*for research only; closed Sun.*), containing 75,000 volumes, and files of maps, newspapers, and documents pertaining largely to Chicago.

In the foyer of the ground floor (west entrance) is the dynamic *Massacre Monument,* by Carl Rohl-Smith. Behind it are logs from the second Fort Dearborn and various relics of pioneer days. The Carriage Room contains a Conestoga wagon and other early types of vehicles. Also on the ground floor is the Pike collection of American city prints, and the Auditorium, where lectures on Chicago history are

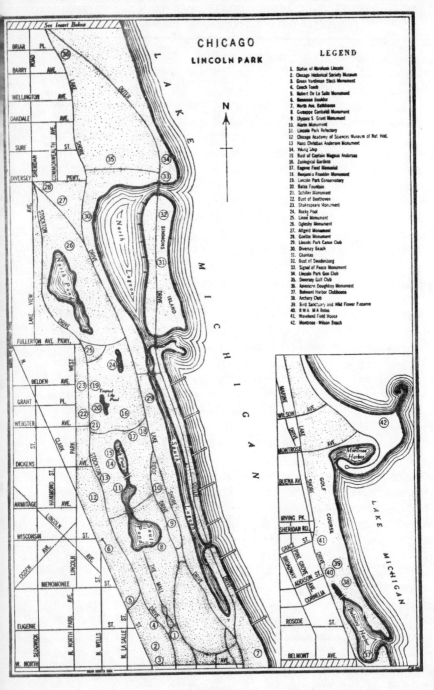

CHICAGO

LINCOLN PARK

LEGEND

1. Statue of Abraham Lincoln
2. Chicago Historical Society Museum
3. Green Vardiman Black Monument
4. Couch Tomb
5. Robert De La Salle Monument
6. Rosenson Boulder
7. North Ave. Bathhouse
8. Giuseppe Garibaldi Monument
9. Ulysses S. Grant Monument
10. Alarm Monument
11. Lincoln Park Refectory
12. Chicago Academy of Sciences Museum of Nat. Hist.
13. Hans Christian Andersen Monument
14. Viking Ship
15. Bust of Captain Magnus Andersen
16. Zoological Gardens
17. Eugene Field Memorial
18. Benjamin Franklin Monument
19. Lincoln Park Conservatory
20. Bates Fountain
21. Schiller Monument
22. Bust of Beethoven
23. Shakespeare Monument
24. Rocky Pool
25. Linné Monument
26. Oglesby Monument
27. Altgeld Monument
28. Goethe Monument
29. Lincoln Park Canoe Club
30. Diversey Beach
31. Charitas
32. Bust of Swedenborg
33. Signal of Peace Monument
34. Lincoln Park Gun Club
35. Diversey Golf Club
36. American Doughboy Monument
37. Belmont Harbor Clubhouse
38. Archery Club
39. Bird Sanctuary and Wild Flower Preserve
40. R W A M A Relns
41. Waveland Field House
42. Montrose - Wilson Beach

given Saturdays (10:30 *a.m.*) for school children and popular movies of historical background are shown on Sundays (3 *p.m.*), except during the summer months.

The Thorne Miniature Rooms (*adm. 25c, children, 10c on museum free days; otherwise no charge; lectures 3 pm. Mon., Wed., Fri.*), designed by Mrs. James Ward Thorne of Chicago, are architectural models of various rooms in American, Italian, Spanish, French, and English homes of different periods. Most of the miniature objects were collected in European shops or made by wood-carvers and iron-workers. Scaled one inch to the foot, they are so exact in detail that tiny books can be read with the aid of a magnifying glass.

South of the Historical Museum is (3) the GREEN VARDI-MAN BLACK MONUMENT, a memorial to the "Father of Modern Dentistry," by Frederick C. Hibbard (1918). North of the building, a dense growth of shrubbery screens (4) the COUCH TOMB. Many legends concerning this incongruous remnant of the old cemetery exist; actually, it escaped removal by order of the Illinois Supreme Court, because the stone blocks, fastened with copper rivets, could not be taken apart without completely demolishing the mausoleum. Ira Couch, owner of the old Tremont House, several members of his family, and a stranger who died in the old hostelry, are interred at this spot. (5) The ROBERT DE LA SALLE MONUMENT, by Count Jacque de la Laing (1889), faces the street that bears the explorer's name. (6) The KENNISON BOULDER, at the foot of Wisconsin Street marks the approximate location of the only other known grave in the park. Here lies David Kennison (1736-1852), veteran of the Revolutionary War, and last survivor of the Boston Tea Party.

Lake Shore Drive, which throughout most of its length marks the former shore line of Lake Michigan, enters the park east of the Lincoln statue and the adjoining play fields. In 1938-39 sand was pumped in between North and Fullerton Avenues to form a beach a mile long. The NORTH AVENUE BATHHOUSE (7) stands in the southeast corner of the park.

North of the Lincoln statue, the Mall runs through the heart of the old park. It divides into paths to skirt South Pond and continues north to the Zoo. At the southeast corner of the pond is (8) the GUISEPPE GARIBALDI MONUMENT, a memorial (1901) to the Italian patriot, by Victor Gherardi. Between Ridge and Lake Shore Drives,

(9) the ULYSSES S. GRANT MONUMENT, a heroic equestrian bronze, stands on a massive stone arch. The work of Louis Rebisso, it was erected by popular subscription and unveiled with elaborate ceremony on October 7, 1891. Northward, along Ridge Drive, is (10) the ALARM MONUMENT, a memorial (1884) to the Ottawa Indians, the work of John Boyle. (11) LINCOLN PARK RE-FECTORY, at the northwest corner of South Pond, contains the Cafe Brauer (*open summer only*) and a rowboat concession.

West of the refectory, at Clark St. and Armitage Ave., is (12) the CHICAGO ACADEMY OF SCIENCES MUSEUM OF NATURAL HISTORY (*open weekdays* 9-5, *Sun.* 1-5), which portrays the natural history of the Chicago region. The ivy-mantled building, designed by Patton and Fisher in Italian Renaissance style, was made possible by a gift from Matthew Laflin. Gov. John P. Altgeld laid the cornerstone in 1893. Collections include plants and animals of Chicago's dune and marsh regions, arranged with large tinted photographs of their habitats as backgrounds. Geological and paleontological specimens, systematic exhibits of flora and fauna—some once common but no longer found in the Chicago area—are labeled with cards bearing interpretive data. Collectors of edible fungi frequently use the mushroom case to check doubtful specimens.

The Academy of Sciences, founded in 1857, is one of the oldest scientific bodies in Chicago. The original collections, later destroyed by fire, were secured by the first director, Robert Kennicott, on the Western Union survey for a telegraph-line route between Alaska and Russia in 1865. The Academy, supported by endowments, gifts, and memberships, not only maintains the museum and a library, but engages in field studies, extension work, and laboratory research. The vast study collections, particularly rich in invertebrates, are open to qualified students. Illustrated talks on natural history, travel, and exploration are given in the lecture hall (3 *p.m. Sun., Oct.-Mar.*). The Academy publishes scientific bulletins and the *Chicago Naturalist*, a quarterly; it also distributes gratis a map of the Chicago region of interest to naturalists.

Eastward, across Stockton Drive, is (13) the HANS CHRIS-TIAN ANDERSEN MONUMENT, a bronze by Johannes Gelert (1896) to the memory of the Danish author of fairy tales. (14) The VIKING SHIP, northeast of the monument, is a reproduction of the vessels used by the Norse in crossing the North Atlantic 1,000 years ago. In this ship Captain Magnus Andersen and a crew of eleven crossed the Atlantic for the Columbian Exposition in 1893. (15) The BUST OF CAPTAIN MAGNUS ANDERSEN, at the prow of the ship, is the work of Carl Paulsen (1936).

(16) The ZOOLOGICAL GARDENS, frequently visited by 100,000 people a day, occupy 25 acres between Stockton and Lake Shore Drives, and center upon a group of five animal houses (*open 9-5 daily; feeding hours 1:30-4*). In the LION HOUSE are lions, tigers, jaguars, and leopards; to the south is the REPTILE HOUSE, formerly the Aquarium. Eastward, in the SMALL ANIMAL HOUSE, are the primates; the trained chimpanzees and Bushman, a gorilla acquired in 1930 when two years of age, attract large crowds. Across the parkway is the BIRD HOUSE, riotous in color and sound, and the ELEPHANT HOUSE, sheltering Deed-a-day, an Indian pachyderm donated by the Boy Scouts of Chicago. In the outdoor pens, cages, and shelters are bears, foxes, camels, llamas, zebras, buffaloes, and animals from all over the world.

Near the center of the Zoo buildings is (17) the EUGENE FIELD MEMORIAL, by Edward McCartan (1922). Depicted in bronze are the Dream Lady with two drowsy children, and inscribed on the granite base below are the poems of "Wynken, Blinken, and Nod" and the "Sugar Plum Tree in the Garden of Shut-Eye Town." End panels represent "The Fly Away Horse" and "Seein' Things." Northeastward is (18) the BENJAMIN FRANKLIN MONUMENT, by Richard Parks (1896).

West of the Zoo rise the glass buildings of (19) the LINCOLN PARK CONSERVATORY (*open 8-6 daily; 8 a.m.-10 p.m. July-Aug. and show periods; see Annual Events for show dates*). The Palm Room and Fern Room are lush with tropical foliage; exotic plants fill the Stove Room. The Show Room, brilliant with flowers at all times, are at their best during the four annual major shows, when thousands of blossoms are arranged in symphonies of color and form. About 650,000 persons visit the Conservatory annually.

In the Main Garden in front of the conservatory is (20) the BATES FOUNTAIN, designed by Saint-Gaudens and MacMonnies (1887). Nearby is (21) the SCHILLER MONUMENT, a memorial to the German poet and dramatist, by Ernst Raus (1886). Across Stockton Drive, in a planting of old-fashioned perennials known as Grandmother's Garden, are (22) a BUST OF BEETHOVEN, the

work of Johannes Gelert (1897), and (23) a SHAKESPEARE
MONUMENT, by William Ordway Partridge (1894). Northeast of
the Conservatory is (24) the new ROCKY POOL, resembling a small
limestone canyon, around which grow native wild flowers, hawthorns
and willows. Overlooking the Conservatory from the north is (25)
the LINNE MONUMENT, an impressive bronze memorial to the
Swedish botanist, Karl Von Linne (Linnaeus), by C. Dyfverman
(1891), with four allegorical figures surrounding the pedestal.

North Pond, with a casting pool at one end, lies across the parkway
from the monument. On a wooded eminence at the northeast corner of
the pond is (26) the OGLESBY MONUMENT, dedicated to the
memory of Richard James Oglesby, three times elected governor of
Illinois (1865, 1872, 1885); it is the work of Leonard Crunelle (1919).
To the north, across the drive, is (27) the ALTGELD MONU-
MENT, by Gutzon Borglum (1915), a memorial to Gov. John Peter
Altgeld (1892-96); opposite the Elks Memorial (*see North and
Northwest Sides*) is (28) the GOETHE MONUMENT, the work
of Herman Hahn.

Eastward in this section of the park are the North and South
Lagoons, between Lake Shore and Outer Drives. On South Lagoon
is (29) the LINCOLN PARK CANOE CLUB (*private*); on North
Lagoon is (30) DIVERSEY BEACH. On Simmons Island, east of
North Lagoon, is (31) CHARITAS, a statue by Ida McClelland
Stout (1922), symbolizing the humanitarian work of the Chicago
Daily News Fresh Air Sanitarium, which for years occupied the
adjoining building. At the north end of the island is (32) a BUST
OF SWEDENBORG, the Swedish religious leader, by Adolph
Jonsson (1924).

Across the bridge is (33) a SIGNAL OF PEACE MONU-
MENT, depicting a mounted Indian with upraised hand, by Cyrus
Dallin (1894). On the lake shore is the whitewashed concrete block
building of (34) the LINCOLN PARK GUN CLUB, members of
which practice trap and skeet shooting on the adjoining ranges (*range
open to public; rates slightly higher than for members*). Northward
stretches (35) the DIVERSEY GOLF COURSE (*9-hole*); at its
northwestern end, on Lake Shore Drive, is (36) the AMERICAN
DOUGHBOY MONUMENT, by E. M. Viquesney (1927), enclosed
within a barbed wire fence.

To the north, on Belmont Harbor, a 53-acre basin, is (37) the

BELMONT HARBOR CLUBHOUSE, the two-story houseboat of the Chicago Yacht Club. The harbormaster's office and slips for power boats line the east bank. This harbor is the starting point for the Chicago to Mackinac race, the longest fresh-water course in the world (*see Annual Events*). North of the harbor, beyond the range of (38) the ARCHERY CLUB, is (39) a BIRD SANCTUARY AND WILD FLOWER PRESERVE; facing Addison St. is (40) the KWA MA ROLAS, Haidan Indian totem pole from the Queen Charlotte Islands. Beyond is (41) the WAVELAND FIELD-HOUSE, with the Wolford chimes which announce the quarter-hours. Athletic fields and tennis courts adjoin the building, and a 9-hole golf course lies to the north.

Into the lake, north of Montrose Avenue, juts a huge peninsula, from the end of which is a fine view of the entire Chicago skyline and part of the North Shore. A hook of land on the south shore shelters Montrose Harbor for pleasure craft; on the north side spreads (42) the MONTROSE-WILSON BEACH; one of the largest in the world made by man. To the north the drives through the park turn abruptly westward on Foster Avenue to Sheridan Road, but some day may continue as far as Evanston over land yet to be made.

North and Northwest Sides

Coursing southeasterly into Chicago, the North branch of the Chicago River divides the section north of North Avenue into the North Side and the larger Northwest Side. Together they contain more than a quarter of the area and the population of Chicago. Up to the nineties this section was made up of farmlands, truck gardens, hamlets and villages, subdivisions, and suburban towns. The settlements were focused along the railroads and along the former plankroads now followed in general by Clark Street and Milwaukee Avenue.

Only a small corner of the present area was a part of Chicago until the contiguous City of Lakeview (pop. 46,164) and the Town of Jefferson (pop. 11,600) were annexed in 1889. Jefferson consisted of many hamlets scattered about what is now the Northwest Side. Around the borders, the former villages of Rogers Park, West Ridge, Edison Park, and Norwood Park, annexed to the city at later dates, comprise most of the rest of the section.

Least industrialized of the principal divisions of Chicago, the North

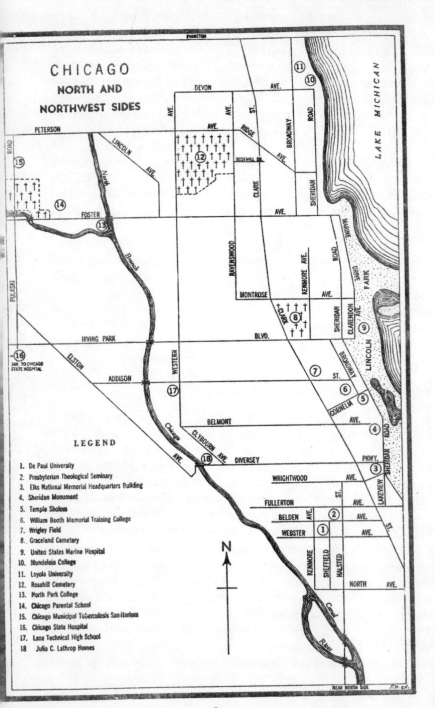

CHICAGO
NORTH AND
NORTHWEST SIDES

LEGEND

1. De Paul University
2. Presbyterian Theological Seminary
3. Elks National Memorial Headquarters Building
4. Sheridan Monument
5. Temple Sholom
6. William Booth Memorial Training College
7. Wrigley Field
8. Graceland Cemetery
9. United States Marine Hospital
10. Mundelein College
11. Loyola University
12. Rosehill Cemetery
13. North Park College
14. Chicago Parental School
15. Chicago Municipal Tuberculosis Sanitarium
16. Chicago State Hospital
17. Lane Technical High School
18. Julia C. Lathrop Homes

N

and Northwest Sides contain the full range of types of residences, with few blighted areas and more cemeteries and institutions, such as colleges and hospitals, than any other part of Chicago. The line of large homes, apartments, and hotels opposite Lincoln Park, which borders two-thirds of the North Side lake shore, is continued along the lake through Rogers Park to the city limits. The developments along the river provide typical cross-sections of the entire inland district. The lower half of the river is improved for navigation and heavily industrialized on both banks. To the east are small houses in the old German and Swedish settlements, and several Polish groups live westward. Beyond Addison Street the river winds past many small parks, and, above the entrance of the North Shore Channel at Argyle Street, becomes a small stream in open subdivisions and forest preserves, passing the city border near the still village-like Norwood Park and Edison Park.

POINTS OF INTEREST

1. DE PAUL UNIVERSITY, occupying the block formed by Kenmore, Belden, Sheffield, and Webster Aves., was founded in 1898 as St. Vincent's College by the Fathers of the Congregation of the Mission. The coeducational institution enrolls approximately 400 students. The Downtown College Building houses professional and evening classes for 7,000. North of the new HALL OF SCIENCE, Kenmore and Belden Aves., is the COLLEGE OF LIBERAL ARTS AND SCIENCE BUILDING, a four-story modern Gothic structure. The ADMINISTRATION BUILDING, 2235 Sheffield Ave., contains the 25,000 volumes of the Liberal Arts Library. On the domed ceiling of the UNIVERSITY AUDITORIUM, south of the Administration Building, are murals illustrating the history of education. The university church, ST. VINCENT'S, 1010 Webster Ave., a massive Romanesque stone structure, stands next to DE PAUL UNIVERSITY ACADEMY.

2. The PRESBYTERIAN THEOLOGICAL SEMINARY, Halsted St., between Belden and Fullerton Aves., and extending to Sheffield Ave., was founded in 1829 at Hanover, Indiana, and established here in 1859 when endowed by Cyrus H. McCormick. About 130 students are enrolled for the three year course leading to the Bachelor of Divinity degree. On the west half of the large campus are the English Gothic limestone GYMNASIUM and the COMMONS. Long rows of dormered red brick residences face on Belden and on Fuller-

ton Avenues. Between them, opening on a square, are the faculty residences. At the east end stands a group of age-scarred dormitory and classroom buildings. EWING HALL, erected in 1863, contains a small museum of Palestinian archeology. The VIRGINIA LIBRARY, a classical structure of Indiana limestone, has more than 70,000 volumes and a museum of objects from various mission fields.

3. The ELKS NATIONAL MEMORIAL HEADQUARTERS BUILDING (open 10-5 daily: guide at entrance), Lakeview Ave. at Diversey Parkway, a shrine to the 70,000 Elks who served in the World War, designed by Egerton Swartwout and completed in 1926, consists of a domed rotunda surrounded by a Roman Doric colonnade above a high base; narrow wings connect the rotunda with end pavilions and house the national offices. The symbols of the order, a pair of reclining elk, by Laura Gardin Fraser, flank the entrance stairway. The frieze under the colonnade illustrates the theme, "The Triumphs of Peace Endure—The Triumphs of War Perish." The frieze and *Patriotism* and *Fraternity*, symbolic groups by Adolph Weinman, fill niches in the ends of the wings.

The impressive marble Memorial Hall is decorated with murals by Eugene Savage, inspired mainly by the Beatitudes, and with statues by James E. Fraser and panels by Edwin Blashfield. Peace is the theme of the panels, also by Savage, in the Grand Reception Room.

4. The SHERIDAN MONUMENT, Sheridan Road, Belmont Ave., and Lake Shore Drive, a dynamic bronze designed by Gutzon Borglum, represents Gen. Philip Sheridan mounted on his galloping stallion.

5. TEMPLE SHOLOM, Lake Shore Drive at Cornelia Ave., an impressive modern Romanesque structure of ancient-looking Lannon stone, designed by Coolidge and Hodgdon, with Loebl, Schlossman, and Donnuth as associate architects, was built in 1930 for the North Chicago Hebrew Congregation, a reform Jewish congregation organized in 1867. The temple has a seating capacity of 1,500, which can be doubled on holidays by moving a huge sliding partition separating it from the Frankenstein Memorial Center.

6. The WILLIAM BOOTH MEMORIAL TRAINING COLLEGE (open by arrangement), Brompton Ave. at Broadway, occupies the former Joseph E. Tilt mansion, built in 1914. One of the four colleges of the Salvation Army in the United States, it trains young men and women to be officers in all branches of the service; the

seventy students are taught orders and regulations, doctrine and Bible.

Designed by Holabird and Roche, the Tudor Gothic structure, with pitched roof and buttressed chimneys, stands in grounds enclosed within a 7-foot wall and has the air of a secluded English country home. The block-long servants' quarters have been converted into a men's dormitory.

7. WRIGLEY FIELD, Clark and Addison Sts., home of the Cubs, Chicago's National League baseball club, seats approximately 45,000 people.

8. GRACELAND CEMETERY (*open* 8-5 *daily*), Clark St. and Irving Park Blvd., organized in 1861, contains many re-interments from the old city cemetery, now part of Lincoln Park. John Kinzie, Chicago's first white civilian settler, is buried here. Within the 119 landscaped acres are a crematory, and many family tracts and imposing mausoleums, particularly around the artificial lake near the east border. The Carrie Getty and the Martin Ryerson tombs are among Louis Sullivan's finest works.

9. The UNITED STATES MARINE HOSPITAL (*not open to the public*), 4141 Clarendon Ave., operated by the U. S. Public Health Service, provides hospitalization (300 beds) and clinical treatment mainly for men in the merchant marine, coast guard, and lighthouse services. Constructed in 1873, the long Lemont limestone building is a distinctive Lakeview district landmark. Several new buildings house the hospital staff.

10. MUNDELEIN COLLEGE (*tours* 2-5 *Sun. except last Sun. of month*), 6363 Sheridan Road, was founded in 1930 by the Sisters of Charity of the Blessed Virgin Mary on the initiative of George, Cardinal Mundelein, as a center of the higher education for Catholic young women. The student body of 500 is instructed by nuns, and lay and clerical professors. The student publications of the college are well known. The bi-weekly *Skyscraper,* a news sheet, has won All-American Collegiate Press Association honors. *Mundelein College Review,* a literary magazine, is a quarterly; *Quest,* an anthology of verse, is published annually.

Designed by Joe W. McCarthy and Nairne Fisher, the college building, striking in the long sweeping lines of its Indiana limestone walls, rises fourteen floors above the lake shore campus. Setbacks provide terraces used as recreation courts and roof gardens.

The LIBRARY, a white Italian marble building with a wide carved porch, contains 35,000 volumes, including many vellum-bound volumes of early church history, and early Aldines, Elzevirs, Bodinis, and other rare editions.

11. LOYOLA UNIVERSITY, 6625 Sheridan Road, grew from Saint Ignatius College, which, founded by the Jesuit Fathers in 1870, became the College of Arts and Sciences of Loyola University in 1909, and was removed to the present 23-acre shore campus in 1922. Six hundred of the 6,000 Loyola students attend classes on this campus. Others receive instruction in the Downtown College Building, and at the medical, dental, and nursing schools in the West Side Medical Center.

The ELIZABETH M. CUDAHY MEMORIAL LIBRARY (*open* 8:30-5, *Mon.-Fri.;* 8:30-12 *Sat.*) designed by A. N. Rebori in modern Romanesque style, is a finely modeled structure of Indiana limestone. The interior is lined with pink-striped Mankato stone. The mural on the west wall, by John Norton, depicts cartographically the activities of the Jesuit missionaries in the Great Lakes and upper Mississippi Valley regions. Among the 71,000 volumes are incunabula, rare editions, and an extensive collection of Jesuitica. The MADONNA DELLA STRADA CHAPEL, constructed in 1939, harmonizes with the library building. Between them stands the ADMINISTRATION BUILD- ING, which houses the Jesuit members of the faculty.

To the west are CUDAHY SCIENCE HALL, with classrooms, labora- tories, and a seismographic observatory; DUMBACH HALL, housing the Loyola Academy; and the ALUMNI GYMNASIUM, in which the national Catholic high school basketball tournament is held annually.

12. ROSEHILL CEMETERY (*open* 9-5 *daily*), Ravenswood Ave. at Rosehill Drive, the largest in Chicago, was developed privately after the city closed its cemetery. Beyond the castellated Gothic entrance are 331 park-like acres containing more than 110,000 graves, including many of Chicago's great of the past century. An immense marble and granite mausoleum (*not open to the public*) stands at the west end of the cemetery.

13. NORTH PARK COLLEGE, Foster and Kedzie Aves., has the appearance of a small town college, with its seven modest buildings clustered on an 8-acre campus in a quiet residential section on the North Branch of the Chicago River. The Evangelical Mission Cove- nant of America, organized in 1885, controls the college, which had

its beginnings in Minneapolis and moved to Chicago in 1894. Offering 2-year courses in liberal arts and commerce, North Park, one of the largest privately owned junior colleges, has an enrollment of more than 500 students. With the exception of the Theological Seminary, the institution is non-sectarian and coeducational. The Music School offers a four-year course leading to the senior diploma.

14. The CHICAGO PARENTAL SCHOOL (*grounds always open; tours by arrangement*), 3600 Foster Ave., trains boys and girls of school age committed to its charge for truancy by the Juvenile Court. Organized in 1902 and conducted by the Chicago Board of Education, the school attempts to provide normal home conditions by use of the cottage plan. Its red brick buildings are clustered on a 75-acre tract, partly landscaped, partly used as a farm, and seem far removed from the Chicago scene.

15. The CHICAGO MUNICIPAL TUBERCULOSIS SANITARIUM (*open 2-4 Mon., Wed., Fri., Sat.*), 5601 N. Pulaski Road, has contributed much to Chicago's fight against the "White Plague." Since the erection in 1915 of the first red brick buildings here on the 160-acre grounds, the city's tuberculosis mortality rate has dropped from 170.6 to 55.7 per 100,000. Although more than 1,200 patients are admitted annually, there remains a long waiting list. Eight dispensaries throughout the city treat thousands of additional cases. The institution has won renown for its pioneer work in the field of home pneumothorax.

16. The CHICAGO STATE HOSPITAL (*open 9:30 and 1:30 Mon.-Fri.*), 6500 Irving Park Road, an insane asylum commonly known as Dunning, was founded as a county institution in 1869. Its various buildings house 5,100 inmates and employees.

17. LANE TECHNICAL HIGH SCHOOL, Western Ave. at Addison St., one of the largest school buildings in the world, accommodates approximately 9,000 students. The modified Tudor Gothic structure of red brick, designed by Paul Gerhardt, spreads like a double-barred H on a 31-acre tract. The murals in the cafeteria and at the auditorium entrance are by the Federal Art Project.

18. The JULIA C. LATHROP HOMES, Diversey Parkway at Damen and Clybourn Aves., named in honor of the revered social worker, provide low cost modern housing for 925 families of limited income. The 29 reinforced concrete and brick buildings were constructed by the Public Works Administration in units of 2 to 5 rooms.

Central conveniences include a laundry and ample storage space; seven large social rooms and as many recreation rooms are the center of community activities. The grounds were laid out by Jens Jensen and occupy more than three-quarters of the 37-acre site, which embraces gardens, lawns, and playgrounds.

The West Side

The West Side lies between the two branches of the Chicago River, but it is commonly limited on the north by North Avenue. Chicago has grown and flowered most conspicuously along the lake front, with the result that the "inland" West Side is sometimes called the city's neglected back yard. But from this soil has sprung much of the vitality and color for which Chicago is known, for here have come thousands of persons from foreign lands, year after year. Scandinavians and Germans and Irish, no longer found in the West Side in great number, had their roots here; still flourishing are the later arrivals, the great colonies of Poles and Jews, Italians and Czecho-Slovakians and many others. But the West Side is more than a nursery in which various groups have established themselves and then been transplanted to other sections of the city. Although the east half of the district is spotted with slums and the whole is streaked with rail lines and grey manufacturing zones, there is a belt of fine parks and boulevards in the center from north to south, and farther west, such sections as Austin, a village annexed in 1899, resemble the adjoining prosperous suburbs.

The West Side, like the North and the South Sides, had its rows of expensive houses close to the downtown district. Brownstones and mansard-roofed mansions line the streets leading west from the Loop for about two miles, and the streets intersecting them. Although the mansions spared demolition have been cubicled into rooming houses, their exteriors are reminders of nineteenth century magnificence.

POINTS OF INTEREST

1. CHICAGO COMMONS (*open 8 a.m.-10 p.m. daily*), Grand Ave. at Morgan St., a social settlement in an Italian and Polish neighborhood, was founded in 1894 by Graham Taylor, widely known for his civic work. The many outgrowths of its work are revealed in his publications, *Pioneering on Social Frontiers* (1930) and *Chicago Commons Through Forty Years* (1936). A monthly leaflet first published

by the institution later became the nationally known social service magazine, *The Survey.*

2. NORTHWESTERN UNIVERSITY SETTLEMENT (*open* 9 *a.m.*-10 *p.m. daily*), 1400 Augusta Blvd., was founded in 1891 by Charles Zueblin and Mrs. Henry Rogers. The neighborhood, largely Polish, is one of the most densely settled in the city.

3. HUMBOLDT PARK, Augusta Blvd. at Sacramento Ave., with its lagoons, islands, hills, and large variety of trees, is a 207-acre tract containing some of the most beautiful park landscapes in the city. Near Division Street is the STABLE, a park maintenance building erected in 1896 from plans drawn by Emil H. Frommann and Ernst Jebsen. The building rambles near a stream and rustic bridge. In style it resembles a German hunting lodge, with a foundation of rock boulders, half-timbered walls of red brick, and a tile roof, romantically gabled. Little known, even to Chicagoans, the charming building is markedly appropriate in its park setting.

North of Division Street, bronze bison by Edward Kemeys flank the entrance to the ROSE GARDENS. Fountain figures by Leonard Crunelle rise from the four corners of the garden pool. Opposite the entrance is a STATUE OF FRITZ REUTER, German poet, by Frederick Engelmann. HOME, a modest little sculpture of a miner and his child, at the east end of the park, is by Charles J. Mulligan. A STATUE OF ALEXANDER VON HUMBOLDT, German naturalist, by Felix Gorling, stands in the center of the park beside the old boathouse. Westward, near the garish Refectory Building, is the LEIF ERIKSEN MONUMENT by Sigvald Asbjornsen. The equestrian STATUE OF THADDEUS KOSCI-USKO, Polish hero of the American Revolution, by Casimir Chodinski, at the north entrance, is the center of the Polish Constitution Day cele-bration on the Sunday nearest May 3, when thousands of neighboring Poles parade to the park.

4. In GARFIELD PARK, Central Park Ave. at Lake St., is an immense CONSERVATORY (*open* 8-4:30 *daily*, 8-6 *summer*, 8 *a.m.*-10 *p.m. special show periods; tours by arrangement*). Erected in 1907, it has 8 exhibition halls for the display of more than 5,000 varieties of plants. At the entrance to the Palm House is a shadowy pool flanked with marble figures, *Pastoral* and *Idyl,* by Lorado Taft, and displays of orchids and other exotics. Opposite the pool lies a sunken garden of tropical ferns, with delicate fronds of tree-ferns and cycads arching over tufa rock formations and ponds. In the cool dry Succulent House,

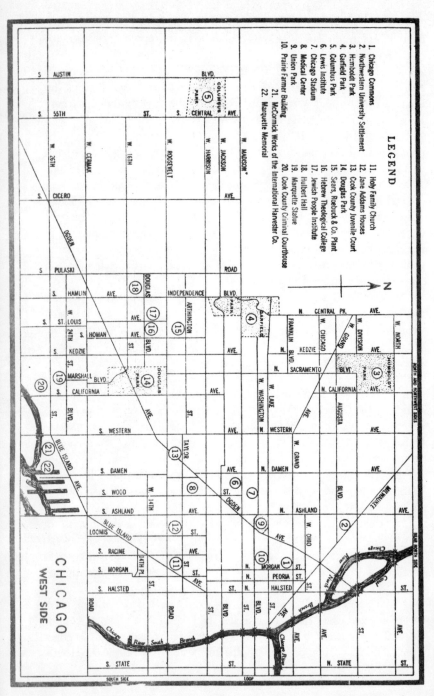

LEGEND

1. Chicago Commons
2. Northwestern University Settlement
3. Humboldt Park
4. Garfield Park
5. Columbus Park
6. Lewis Institute
7. Chicago Stadium
8. Medical Center
9. Union Park
10. Prairie Farmer Building

11. Holy Family Church
12. Jane Addams Houses
13. Cook County Juvenile Court
14. Douglas Park
15. Sears, Roebuck & Co. Plant
16. Hebrew Theological College
17. Jewish People Institute
18. Hulbert Hall
19. Marquette Statue
20. Cook County Criminal Courthouse
21. McCormick Works of the International Harvester Co.
22. Marquette Memorial

CHICAGO
WEST SIDE

DIANA COURT, MICHIGAN SQUARE BUILDING

LONGSHOREMEN

STOCK YARDS

STATE STREET

CORNER OF MILWAUKEE AND CHICAGO AVENUES

MODEL'S EYE VIEW

CONTRAST, NEAR NORTH SIDE

HULL HOUSE

BRONZEVILLE SLUM

MAXWELL STREET

JANE ADDAMS HOUSES

NAVY PIER

MANSIONS—ONCE

cacti extend their spiny arms in weird postures. The Warm House and the Aeroid House, high in temperature and humidity, contain colored and variegated foliage plants, and vines that curtain the hall with their long, free-hanging aeroid roots. Another hall is devoted to economically useful plants, each labeled with pertinent information. The Easter, Mid-summer, Chrysanthemum, and Christmas Flower Shows fill the Show House and Horticulture Hall with thousands of blooms raised in adjoining propagating houses, and attract a large part of the 500,000 people who visit the conservatory each year.

The ADMINISTRATION BUILDING stands on a knoll between two lagoons south of the conservatory, a gold-domed Spanish Renaissance structure with a rotunda containing casts of classical statuary. Immediately south is the bronze MONUMENT OF LINCOLN, THE RAIL SPLITTER, by Charles J. Mulligan; a few yards west stands the bronze ROBERT BURNS MONUMENT, by W. Grant Stevens, a replica of the monument in Edinburgh, with bas-reliefs on the pedestal depicting scenes from Burns' poems. Formal flower gardens surround the tropical WATER-LILY POOLS, at Madison Street.

5. COLUMBUS PARK, Jackson Blvd. at Central Ave., newest of the large West Side parks, is a tract of 144 acres landscaped by Jens Jensen in his naturalistic style. The prairie motif is carried out in the long horizontal sweep of meadow threaded by running streams. Subtly adorned with sun-loving flowers, accented by thickets of hawthorn and other native trees and shrubs, the park is particularly charming in the autumn. Additional attractions are the waterfalls near the Refectory, and a 9-hole golf course.

6. LEWIS INSTITUTE, Madison St. at Damen Ave., endowed by Allen C. Lewis, was opened in 1896 as an academy and junior college. Now a four-year college, housed in two 6-story buildings, it is known principally for its engineering, home economics, and pre-professional courses. About two-thirds of the 3,000 students attend evening classes. The Psychological Museum (*tours by arrangement*), opened in 1937, contains psychological testing devices of all kinds.

7. The CHICAGO STADIUM, Madison St. at Honore St., an indoor amphitheater seating more than 25,000 persons, was erected in 1928 as a center for sports, circuses, and conventions. Here Franklin D. Roosevelt was nominated for President of the United States in 1932.

8. The MEDICAL CENTER (*arrangements for inspection must be made with each institution*), extends south from Congress St. to Tay-

lor St., and west from Wood St. to Wolcott Ave. Some 30 buildings, old and new, form Chicago's largest grouping of public and private hospitals; medical, dental, pharmacy, and nursing schools; research institutes and nurses' homes. Dominating the group is COOK COUNTY HOSPITAL, founded in 1866 to provide medical aid for the poor of the county, now one of the largest in the world, capable of caring for more than 3,000 patients. In addition to the florid white terra cotta and brick GENERAL BUILDING facing Harrison Street at Honore Street, the County group includes the MORGUE; the CHILDREN'S DENTAL CLINIC; the PSYCHOPATHIC, and TUBERCULOSIS, CONTAGIOUS, and MEN'S HOSPITALS; and the CHILDREN'S HOSPITAL, widely known for its Mothers' Milk Bureau. The County Hospital is known, too, for its Blood Bank, in which the four types of blood are stored for emergency use in transfusions.

LOYOLA UNIVERSITY SCHOOL OF MEDICINE, 706 S. Wolcott Ave., has a collection of human embryos and foetuses in various stages of development, and a comprehensive series of sections of the human body. The school enrolls more than 300 students.

The COOK COUNTY SCHOOL OF NURSING, 1910 Polk St., an imposing 17-story brick structure, was completed in 1935. The school succeeded the Illinois Training School for Nurses, founded in 1880, first institution of its kind west of the Alleghenies.

In the block south of the County group are the new medical buildings of the University of Illinois and the State Department of Public Welfare. The College of Medicine, enrolling more than 600 students, and the College of Dentistry, both started as proprietary schools, are housed in the MEDICAL AND DENTAL COLLEGE LABORATORIES BUILDING, fronting on Polk St. The medical unit was occupied in 1931; the dental unit, with its commanding 15-story tower on the Wood Street corner, in 1937. On the south, the parallel ILLINOIS RESEARCH and EDUCATIONAL HOSPITALS are joined to form a rectangle, from which extend in series to the south, the PSYCHIATRIC, ORTHOPAEDIC, and JUVENILE RESEARCH INSTITUTES. Designed in the collegiate Gothic style by Schmidt, Garden and Erikson, associated with Granger and Bollenbacher, the Illinois buildings are constructed of red brick trimmed with limestone. Artists of the Works Progress Administration Federal Art Project have decorated them with frescoes, stained glass windows, sculptures, mosaics, and canvases.

RUSH MEDICAL COLLEGE, Harrison St. and Wood St., Chicago's first medical school, was founded in 1837 by Dr. Daniel Brainard and named for Dr. Benjamin Rush, eminent Philadelphia physician. In 1923, Dr. Arthur Bevan, a Rush professor, performed the first operation in which ethylene-oxygen was used as an anaesthetic. In 1924, Rush became part of the University of Chicago. Offering the last two years of the regular medical course, the school enrolls more than 200 students.

9. UNION PARK, Ogden Ave. at Washington and Ashland Blvds., is a bit of green landscape at the north end of "Labor Row," a section of Ashland Boulevard with old mansions and new buildings housing various labor unions. The park is the starting point of the annual May Day parade and contains a STATUE OF CARTER H. HARRISON, the "martyred mayor," by Frederick C. Hibbard, and a HAYMARKET RIOT MONUMENT by Johannes Gelert, commemorating the policemen who lost their lives in the Riot of 1886. In a flat opposite the park lived the prototype of the heroine of Theodore Dreiser's novel *Sister Carrie*.

10. The PRAIRIE FARMER BUILDING (*open 9-5 Mon.-Fri., 9-1 Sat.*), 1230 Washington Blvd., contains the editorial offices and radio station, WLS of the journal devoted to the interests of farmers. Founded in 1841 by John Stephen Wright as *The Union Agriculturist and Western Prairie Farmer,* it has a circulation of 400,000. One of the paper's noteworthy campaigns was its successful agitation for a free school system in Illinois. West of the building is the site of the house where Mrs. Abraham Lincoln and "Tad" lived in 1866.

The SOUTH WATER MARKET, 15th St. between Racine Ave. and Morgan St., supplanted in 1925 the noisy picturesque market that for decades had occupied the south bank of the Chicago River. The 225 commission firms in the six, long, efficiently-planned buildings of the market, functioning independently under the guidance of the Market Service Association, supply the city with fruits and vegetables.

11. HOLY FAMILY CHURCH, 1080 W. Roosevelt Road, a large brick Gothic structure designed by Dillenburg and Zurber, and John Van Osdel, was dedicated in 1860. The parish, founded three years earlier by a Jesuit, Father Arnold Damen, the "Father of the West Side," in what was then largely open country, eventually numbered a congregation of 20,000 people. With the exodus of the Irish and Germans from the neighborhood, the membership has declined.

12. The JANE ADDAMS HOUSES (*open; apply at office*), 1002 S.

Lytle St., are a group of fireproof buildings erected in 1937 by the
Public Works Administration. Built of brick in austere, well-arranged
groups, the 52 houses of 4 and 5 rooms, and 975 apartments of 2 to 5
rooms provide low-cost modern housing in the midst of one of the
most poverty-stricken areas of the West Side. More than three-fifths
of the total ground area is devoted to lawns, gardens, and playgrounds. There are 20 recreation and social rooms, and a shower yard
ornamented with sculptured animals.

13. The COOK COUNTY JUVENILE COURT (*open by appointment*), Roosevelt Road and Ogden Ave., was established in 1899 as
the first children's court in America.

14. DOUGLAS PARK, Roosevelt Road at Sacramento Ave., a 182-
acre retreat for the large Jewish and Bohemian population of the
adjacent neighborhoods, has lily ponds and flower gardens, a lake for
boating, an open-air natatorium, athletic fields, and an outdoor gymnasium. Near West Douglas Park Drive and Ogden Avenue stands a
heroic bronze STATUE OF KAREL HAVLICEK, nineteenth century liberal
writer, sculptured by Josef Strachovsky. Annually, on Rosh ha-Shanah
(New Year's Day), which occurs on a variable date in early autumn,
orthodox Jews gather at the lagoon for a ritualistic casting away of
their sins.

15. The SEARS, ROEBUCK AND COMPANY PLANT (*tours
9:45, 10:45, 1:45 and 2:45 Mon.-Fri.*), Homan Ave. and Arthington
St., houses the main offices of the nation-wide chain of retail stores
and the largest mail-order system in the world. One of the bulkiest
structural groups in the city, the building shelters the largest of the
company's 10 mail-order plants. The precisely timed assembling of
orders in the 2-block long merchandise building is a marvel of efficiency, as packages stream constantly along conveyor belts to cascade
down chutes. Seven million catalogs, each 1,000 pages long, distributed
semi-annually by the company have done more, perhaps, than any
other one factor toward building the company's sales volume to hundreds of millions of dollars annually.

The business was originated in 1886 by Richard W. Sears, station
agent of North Redwood, Minnesota. When a shipment of watches
was refused by a local firm, Sears requested permission to sell the
watches by mail to station agents along the railroad. The venture was
successful, and led to the founding of the present firm. The man most

prominently identified with the company was the late Julius Rosenwald, philanthropist.

16. The HEBREW THEOLOGICAL COLLEGE (*open 9-8 Sun.-Thurs., 9-12 Fri.*), 3448 Douglas Blvd., a large three-story building with a classic façade, is an institution of higher Jewish learning, combining Jewish tradition and advanced methods of instruction. It trains young men to become modern orthodox Rabbis, teachers, and leaders of American Jewry. Its 400 students are drawn from all parts of the country. The LIBRARY BUILDING, dedicated in 1938, contains approximately 30,000 volumes, being noteworthy in the fields of Hebraica, Judaica, and Rabbinica. Included are many rare and out-of-print books.

17. The JEWISH PEOPLE'S INSTITUTE (*open 9 a.m.-10:30 p.m. Sun.-Thurs., 9-5 Fri., 6 p.m.-10:30 Sat.*), 3500 Douglas Blvd., is a social, recreational, and educational center in the heart of the Lawndale district. Largest Jewish community in Chicago, the section is portrayed in novels and stories by Meyer Levin, Albert Halper, Louis Zara, and others. Educational activities from grade school to college, instruction in the various arts, and a wide range of physical activities make the Institute an extraordinarily active place throughout the year.

In addition to numerous class and club rooms, lounges, gymnasium, theater, and roof garden, the four-story brick and stone building contains the Herman Schur Reference Library, with 16,000 volumes on Judaica and the social sciences, and a Museum of anthropology and natural history specimens gathered by Samuel Bornstein in his worldwide wanderings. Architects of the building were Eugene Klaber and Ernest A. Grunsfeld, Jr. The Museum of Antiquities, in the Spinoza Study, decorated with murals by A. Raymond Katz, exhibits ceremonial objects, rare books, and scrolls. Unique in Chicago is the mural-walled Blintzes Inn, a kosher restaurant with separate kitchens and dining sections for meat and for dairy dishes. An impressive wooden statue of Moses, by Enrico Glicenstein, stands in the center of the main hall.

18. HULBERT HALL, 1530 S. Hamlin Ave., (*open 6:30 p.m.-9 daily*), is the clubhouse of the Boys' Brotherhood Republic. With its novel plan of preventing juvenile delinquency by developing social relations by a form of municipal self-government, the organization, formed in 1914 by Jack Robbins, has been successful in providing for the recreational needs of thousands of underprivileged boys. Along

with a council, courts, and welfare departments, the Republic maintains a co-operative store and a bank.

19. The MARQUETTE STATUE, Marshall Blvd. and 24th St., is a bronze group of three figures representing Father Marquette, Jolliet, and an Algonquin Indian, sculptured by Hermon A. MacNeil.

20. The COOK COUNTY CRIMINAL COURTHOUSE (*jail open by warden's permission*), California Ave. and 26th St., includes the Criminal Court Building, the Cook County Jail Building, and four cell blocks. Designed by Eric E. Hall in rectangular neo-classic pattern, the Indiana limestone group was completed in 1929 at a cost of $7,500,000. Inmates of the jail are persons awaiting trial, transfer, or execution, and prisoners whose sentences for any single charge do not exceed one year.

The HOUSE OF CORRECTION (*tours arranged for groups*), immediately south of the Court House, is the municipal prison established in 1871 to supplant the old Bridewell. Around the castellated Gothic buildings are formal flower beds and an artificial stream.

21. The McCORMICK WORKS OF THE INTERNATIONAL HARVESTER COMPANY (*tours by arrangement*), 26th St. and Western and Blue Island Aves., occupying about 100 acres, produces a large part of the country's farm implements. It was established in 1872 after the destruction of the first harvester plant in Chicago, built in 1847 by Cyrus Hall McCormick near the north end of the present Michigan Avenue bridge. The plant normally employs about 4,500 men.

22. The MARQUETTE MEMORIAL, Damen Ave. Bridge on the South Branch of the Chicago River, marks the site of Marquette's dreary sojourn during the winter of 1674-75. E. P. Seidel modeled the bronze relief from a sketch by Thomas A. O'Shaughnessy.

Jackson Park

Through the 543 heavily wooded and informally landscaped acres of Jackson Park, which extends along Lake Michigan between 56th and 67th Streets, wind placid lagoons dotted with tiny islands and lined with cattails and other aquatic plants. Originally a swamp, it was converted into a park under the direction of Frederick Law Olmsted to be used first as the site of the World's Columbian Exposition of 1893, which was built here and along the Midway Plaisance joining

Jackson with Washington Park. Among other facilities in this third largest park in Chicago, the chief recreational area of the South Side, is an 18-hole golf course, first public course in Chicago.

At its narrow northern end the park is flanked with large apartment hotels. Facing them is (1) the MUSEUM OF SCIENCE AND INDUSTRY (*open 10-6 daily; guides for groups by appointment; special evening tour for groups of 500 or more by arrangement*).

The museum building incorporates a part and throughout closely follows the design of the Fine Arts Building of the World's Columbian Exposition. Designed by Charles Atwood, who adapted its detail from the Erechtheum, the Fine Arts Building won acclaim for its purity of style and excellence of composition. Two pavilions flank the great domed central pavilion, which they resemble in miniature, and are separated from it by transverse halls with free-standing Ionic columns. On each side of the main portico are caryatids, and the sides of the minor pavilions bear similar figures. The building, more than one-fifth of a mile long, has 600,000 square feet of floor space.

From the close of the Columbian Exposition until 1920, the original building was occupied by the Field Museum of Natural History, but as it had been erected for temporary use, it began to deteriorate rapidly. Agitation for the preservation of this sole major survival of the Exposition began and a $5,000,000 bond issue was floated for the purpose. In the reconstruction only part of the original structure was retained; wood and plaster were stripped away and replaced with Indiana limestone.

The present museum was conceived by the late Julius Rosenwald as a result of his young son's interest in the Deutsches Museum at Munich. When the bond issue proved insufficient to restore the building completely, Rosenwald donated funds and also provided a sum of $3,000,000 if the building would be used as a scientific and industrial museum. The first section was opened during the Century of Progress Exposition in 1933-34, and after the Exposition closed, many of its industrial exhibits were transferred here.

The museum stresses education, and many of the exhibits are elaborate working models; spectators set machinery and apparatus in motion by pushing a button. Such exhibits include a model airplane that realistically banks, zooms, and dives, controlled by a remote joystick. Elsewhere, steel ball bearings drop from a runway and bounce neatly one after another, all day long, through a revolving hoop, to

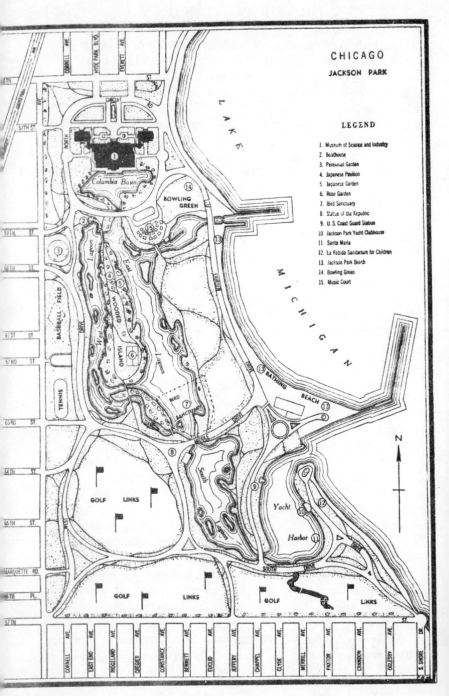

CHICAGO

JACKSON PARK

LEGEND

1. Museum of Science and Industry
2. Boathouse
3. Perennial Garden
4. Japanese Pavilion
5. Japanese Garden
6. Rose Garden
7. Bird Sanctuary
8. Statue of the Republic
9. U. S. Coast Guard Station
10. Jackson Park Yacht Clubhouse
11. Santa Maria
12. La Rabida Sanitarium for Children
13. Jackson Park Beach
14. Bowling Green
15. Music Court

show the precision of machine-made bearings. In a large egg-shaped room principles of acoustics are demonstrated. Two people can carry on a whispered conversation from opposite ends of the room without being overheard by a third person standing between them. Other models graph the sound of a voice, transmit music on a beam of light, and X-ray the contents of a purse.

Lecturers operate more complicated apparatus at regular intervals, including demonstrations of the use of high-frequency electricity in lighting an electric bulb by wireless and of intermittent illumination, making readable the inscription on an airplane propellor revolving 1,400 times a minute. The full-sized coal mine, manned with miners and equipped with modern machinery, is the only exhibit for which there is a charge (*adults* 25c; *children* 10c).

In the theater, seating 1,000, motion pictures and popular lectures on scientific subjects are held (*hours vary; consult schedule posted weekly*). The library contains 25,000 volumes on science and industry.

Immediately behind the Museum is Columbia Basin, its waters lapping the rear steps of the great white building. Around it, to the right, a path leads to the West Lagoon and (2) a BOATHOUSE (*motor launches* 50c *a half-hour; row boats* 25c *an hour*). At the Midway Plaisance is (3) a PERENNIAL GARDEN. To the left of the boathouse a camel-hump bridge leads to WOODED ISLAND, planted with a large variety of trees and shrubs, many of them labeled. On the island are (4) the JAPANESE PAVILIONS, restored survivals of the Columbian Exposition. The three connecting pavilions, a gift of the Mikado, are patterned after the temple of Hoo-do, a shrine to the Phoenix bird. The central building symbolizes the body of the bird; the flanking pavilions, its wings. Tea is served in summer at the central pavilion. Adjoining the pavilions is (5) a JAPANESE GARDEN, with two small lily pools fed by a stream that splashes into it over boulders. Around the pools are junipers, dwarf pines, stone lanterns, and a tea house built of straw matting.

On the island, near the East Lagoon, is (6) the ROSE GARDEN, laid out during the Columbian Exposition and since expanded. Immediately south of the Wooded Island is (7) the BIRD SANCTUARY. An 8-foot fence keeps out predatory small animals; some domestic birds are kept here, but the majority are wild. In the shallow waters near the shore, many food plants have been set out for the birds.

The Middle Drive, which skirts the sanctuary, leads to (8) the

STATUE OF THE REPUBLIC, a gilded bronze of heroic proportions. The work of Daniel Chester French, it marks the site of the Administration Building of the Columbian Exposition.

The statue faces the South Lagoon, which provides anchorage for motor launches and small craft. Adjoining the South Lagoon is the Yacht Harbor for larger boats. On its shores are (9) the U. S. COAST GUARD STATION, a white building with an inclined runway leading to the water's edge, and (10) the JACKSON PARK YACHT CLUBHOUSE (*private*).

Anchored at the clubhouse is (11) the SANTA MARIA (*open when caretaker is available*), a copy of Columbus' flagship, built in Spain, for the Columbian Exposition, together with reproductions of its sister ships, the *Nina* and the *Pinta,* and sailed to America over substantially the route followed by Columbus. In 1915, on its way to the San Francisco Exposition, through the Great Lakes and St. Lawrence River, the *Santa Maria* was damaged in a storm near Halifax, Nova Scotia. Held by the Canadian government for repair bills, the boat was returned in 1918. Carrying 5,000 feet of canvas, it has an over-all length of 100 feet. With its high bow and high poop over the cabin aft, with clumsy masts and rigging, it contrasts sharply with the trim modern sailboats in the harbor. The *Nina* sank in 1918; the *Pinta* burned the following year.

On the rise of ground behind the clubhouse stands (12) LA RABIDA SANITARIUM FOR CHILDREN (*open by arrangement*). The original building, built for the Columbian Exposition, was a copy of the monastery at Palos, Spain, where Columbus found shelter before he secured aid for his expedition. Burned after more than 20 years of service, it was replaced in 1932 with the present building, designed by Graham, Anderson, Probst, and White; it accommodates 100 patients, offering free treatment to children suffering from rheumatic heart.

North, across the harbor inlet, is (13) JACKSON PARK BEACH (*bathhouse and pavilion, with picnicking facilities*), one of the most popular in Chicago.

Farther north, beyond the beach, is (14) a BOWLING GREEN, occupying the site of the Columbian Exposition's German Building. Behind it stretches (15) the MUSIC COURT, an outdoor amphitheater, in which concerts are held during the summer.

University of Chicago

The University of Chicago, the youngest of the world's great institutions of higher learning, is less than a half century old. Unlike its rivals, it attained almost full stature at once, for it did not grow by slow degrees from a small college. Rather, it sprang fully fledged into the world as a large and splendidly equipped university, its entry smoothed by the oil millions of the Rockefellers. Today, it ranks among the best American universities in its scholastic standards, the scholarly attainments of its faculty, and its contributions to modern life and thought.

Founded in 1890 by John D. Rockefeller through the American Baptist Education Society, the university was placed in charge of the distinguished Hebraic scholar, William Rainey Harper. The latter gathered a most distinguished faculty of eminent scholars by offering them much higher salaries than any university was paying and by promising them freedom to carry on original research. The original faculty included nine college presidents and scores of younger scholars who had already made a name for themselves, or who were soon to do so. On the roster appeared the names of Thomas C. Chamberlin, noted geologist and collaborator with F. R. Moulton in developing the planetesimal hypothesis that revolutionized astronomical theory; Paul Shorey, perhaps the greatest of our classical scholars; Albion W. Small, a founder of modern sociology; John M. Coulter, a pioneer in the field of plant ecology; and Albert A. Michelson, the first American to win the Nobel prize in science, awarded for his measurement of the speed of light. By October 1, 1892, Cobb Lecture Hall was half completed, and the university opened its doors.

"President Harper's fondest wish was realized when the University started upon its practical life of instruction yesterday morning with the same confidence and absence of parade as if it had been running half a century," reported the Sunday *Inter Ocean,* October 2, 1892, adding that young men and young women, with books under their arms walked with lively steps and soon "everybody was working as industriously and earnestly as bees in a hive."

> John D. Rockefeller, wonderful man is he,
> Gives all his spare change to the U. of C.—

sang the students, as the faculty smiled, as well they might, for the "spare change" mounted to a $35,000,000 total and has since been

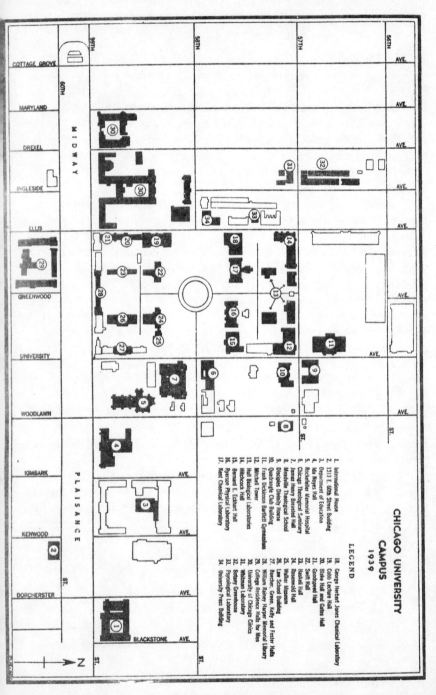

CHICAGO UNIVERSITY
CAMPUS
1939

LEGEND

1. International House
2. 1313 E. 60th Street Building
3. Department of Education
4. Ida Noyes Hall
5. Rockefeller Memorial Hospital
6. Chicago Theological Seminary
7. James Henry Breasted Hall
8. Meadville Theological School
9. Disciples Divinity House
10. Quadrangle Club Building
11. Frank Dickinson Bartlett Gymnasium
12. Mitchell Tower
13. Hull Biological Laboratories
14. Hitchcock Hall
15. Bernard E. Eckhart Hall
16. Ryerson Physical Laboratory
17. Kent Chemical Laboratory
18. George Herbert Jones Chemical Laboratory
19. Cobb Lecture Hall
20. Blake Hall and Gates Hall
21. Goodspeed Hall
22. Swift Hall
23. Haskell Hall
24. Rosenwald Hall
25. Walker Museum
26. Law School Building
27. Beecher, Green, Kelly and Foster Halls
28. William Rainey Harper Memorial Library
29. College Residence Halls for Men
30. University of Chicago Clinics
31. Whitman Laboratory
32. Botany Greenhouse
33. Psychological Laboratory
34. University Press Building

N

278

more than doubled by grants from the several Rockefeller foundations. John D. Rockefeller, Jr., personally contributed more than $5,000,000. Other gifts and bequests were received, many from Chicagoans, including a $4,500,000 donation by Julius Rosenwald, and the university's endowment today exceeds $125,000,000.

From the start the university has been noted for its reforms in the field of education. President William Rainey Harper created the university summer school by introducing the quarter system. He also pioneered in university extension work and in establishing a university press. The incumbent president, Robert Maynard Hutchins, instituted the "New Plan," with a curriculum designed to give students a comprehensive background in arts and sciences during their first two years, followed by more specialized work later. Under this plan compulsory class attendance has been abolished. Accomplishment is measured by comprehensive examinations taken whenever the student feels himself prepared. Approximately half of the 6,000 students are enrolled as undergraduates. There are six professional schools on the quadrangles. The downtown University College enrolls an additional 1,600.

The university grounds have expanded from 17 acres of sandy ridges and mucky swales, dotted with scrub oaks, to 110 trim landscaped acres. The 85 university buildings are in compact but uncrowded quadrangles and in single units on the Midway Plaisance, a mile-long parkway, lying between 59th and 60th Streets and connecting Washington and Jackson Parks. Built of Indiana limestone, almost all buildings are designed in late Gothic style, and possess an architectural unity rare among Midwestern universities; their mature dignity belies their age. Most of them are ornamented with symbols of their functions and bear the names of their donors.

CAMPUS TOUR

(Tours for groups by advance arrangement at the Information Office, 5758 Ellis Ave. Most buildings open 8-5 weekdays; permission to visit classes, except where otherwise noted, must be obtained from the appropriate dean. Information concerning lectures open to the public can be obtained from the weekly university calendar, posted on the bulletin boards of various buildings and in Chicago libraries. The university is closed in September. Official university guidebook 50c; chapel guidebook $1.00 at the University Bookstore, 5802 Ellis Ave.)

Easternmost of the university buildings on the Midway is (1) INTERNATIONAL HOUSE (*see announcements for activities open to public*), 1414 E. 59th St., an immense club with 507 dormitory rooms, lounges, assembly and dining halls, and national rooms, designed by Holabird and Root and completed in 1932. It is one of four such houses established by John D. Rockefeller, Jr., to promote mutual understanding among students of various races and nationalities as a means of fostering world peace. Thirty-six countries and 46 states are represented in the present membership (1939) of the House.

(2) The 1313 E. 60th STREET BUILDING, on the south side of the Midway, is owned and maintained by the university. It contains the national offices of such organizations and agencies interested in public administration as the American Society of Planning Officials and the International City Managers' Association.

(3) The DEPARTMENT OF EDUCATION occupies the second block to the west, on 59th St. between Kenwood and Kimbark Aves. A consolidation of several institutions formerly headed by such educators as Col. Francis W. Parker and John Dewey, the school conducts a complete pedagogical program from kindergarten through graduate work. EMMONS BLAINE HALL, on 59th St., houses the elementary school and some of the high school classes; HENRY HOLMES BELFIELD HALL, at the north end of Scammon Court, contains the University High School (*visitors welcome in laboratory school classrooms*). These buildings were designed by James Gamble Rogers, and completed in 1903 and 1904. The GRADUATE EDUCATION BUILDING, on Kimbark Ave., and the BERNARD E. SUNNY GYMNASIUM (high school) on the west side of Kenwood Ave., complete the group.

(4) IDA NOYES HALL, one of the most gracious of the campus buildings, designed by Shepley, Rutan, and Coolidge, and dedicated in 1916, rises like a great Tudor manor house from a flowered terrace, on 59th St., between Kimbark and Woodlawn Aves. Richly appointed and decorated, the hall is a clubhouse, refectory, and gymnasium for women. Murals by Jesse Arms Botke, the *Spirit of Youth,* adorn the walls of the theatre.

(5) The ROCKEFELLER MEMORIAL CHAPEL (*non-denominational services 11 a.m., Sun.*), 59th St., between Woodlawn and University Aves., designed by Bertram Grosvenor Goodhue and associates, is an original interpretation of Gothic architecture, extra

ordinarily massive, simple and vigorous. The immense striding 40-foot bays, the glazed tile in the vaulted ceiling, and the placement of the tower over one of the transepts, are striking and unusual. Of solid masonry construction, the walls of the 207-foot tower are eight feet thick at the base.

A rich array of sculpture relieves the severity of the exterior. Designed by Lee Laurie and Ulric Ellerhausen, the 24 free standing and 53 demi-figures are, in general, archaic in style and symbolic in character, suggesting the religious continuity of the present with the past. The exquisite interior wood carvings were done by Alois Lang.

The LAURA SPELMAN ROCKEFELLER Carillon in the tower (*tours* 1-3:30 *Wed.*, 1-5 *Sat.*, 12-3:30 *Sun.*) ranks with the largest in the world; the tuning of the 72 bells (ranging from 10½ pounds to more than 18 tons in weight) is said to be the finest ever achieved.

North of the Midway, on 58th St., between Woodlawn and University Aves., is (6) the CHICAGO THEOLOGICAL SEMINARY, affiliated with the Divinity School of the University. It was founded in 1855 by the Congregational Church. The main buildings, designed by H. H. Riddle, and completed in 1928, are dominated by the graceful Lawson Tower. Hammond Library contains an important collection of source materials for the history of American Christianity. The Thorndike Hilton Chapel and Graham Taylor Hall have stained glass windows modelled on those of Chartres Cathedral. The WOMEN's RESIDENCE HALL, on the east side of Woodlawn Ave., was originally designed as a private house by Frank Lloyd Wright in 1909.

(7) JAMES HENRY BREASTED HALL (*open* 10-5 *Mon.-Sat.*; 11-5 *Sun.*, *June-Nov.*; 9-5 *Mon.-Fri.*; 10-5 *Sat.*; 11-5 *Sun.*, *Dec.-May*), SE. corner of 58th St. and University Ave., contains the museum and the offices of the Oriental Institute, a great center of research on the rise of civilization. Named for the professor who directed the Institute until his death in 1935, the building was designed by Mayers, Murray, and Phillip, and completed in 1931. Most of the objects in the museum were unearthed by the 12 expeditions sent by the Institute to the Near East. The sites of present field operations are marked on a map in the lobby, where the publications of the Institute are displayed.

The exhibits in the Egyptian Hall, left of the lobby, illustrate the life story of the Egyptians—their dress and tools; the masterful craftsmanship of their artists revealed in delicate glass and pottery ware, carvings, paintings, and writings; their ways of life; and their manner of burial. The exhibits, arranged chronologically except for two topical alcoves, range from pre-historic implements taken from terraces along the Nile to Greco-Roman portraits of the second century A. D.

Dominating the Egyptian Hall near the entrance to Assyrian Hall stands a 40-ton stone figure of an Assyrian winged bull with human head, discovered in the ruins of the palace of King Sargon II (724-705 B. C.) near ancient Nineveh. A colossal red quartzite statue of Tut-ankhamen (Thebes 1350 B. C.) stands to the right of the bull. In the Assyrian Hall are relief sculptures from Sargon's palace, fine examples of the Assyrians' gift for portraying movement and force. The screen cases in this and the next hall illustrate the work of the Institute's various field expeditions by means of photographs, diagrams, maps, and color plates.

The gateway at the entrance of the Assyro-Babylonian Hall reproduces the style of the palace of Nebuchadnezzar at Babylon (sixth century B. C.). The objects in this hall represent some of the most important archeological work of the Institute. The Sumerian cult statues, with large noses and big eyes, are the only ones yet discovered. The cylinder seals in the same collection are ornamented with animals unknown to the Babylonians—the elephant and rhinoceros—and significantly link the history of the Sumerians with that of India.

In the Iranian-Moslem Hall are ancient Persian pottery and bronzes; manuscripts in Arabic, Persian, Syriac, and Hebrew; and Egyptian Arabic tombstones and book-bindings. Soon to be installed (late 1939) are decorations from the palace of Xerxes—a massive bull's head, and reliefs still black with smoke from fires set by Alexander the Great in the fifth century B. C.

The Hittite-Palestinian Hall exhibits are from excavations at Alishar in Anatolia, and Megiddo in Palestine. In the collection are gold jewelry, carved ivory objects, and the oldest extant Biblical document—a stamp seal dating from early Christian centuries containing a verse of scripture from the Book of Jeremiah.

(8) The MEADVILLE THEOLOGICAL SCHOOL, 57th St. at Woodlawn Ave., founded in Pennsylvania in 1844, is associated with the Divinity School of the University; there is no denominational control. The Wiggin Library contains more than 50,000 volumes, being rich in source material on the liberal movement in religion.

(9) The DISCIPLES DIVINITY HOUSE, NE. corner of 57th St. and University Ave., is a residence hall and social center for Disciples of Christ students registered in the Divinity School and affiliated institutions.

(10) The QUADRANGLE CLUB BUILDING, SE. corner of 57th St. and University Ave., was designed by Howard Van Doren Shaw and opened in 1922. Membership is drawn chiefly from the Faculties.

(11) The FRANK DICKINSON BARTLETT GYMNASIUM, NW. corner of 57th St. and University Ave., provides athletic facilities for the men of the university. The murals in the entrance hall, by Frederic Clay Bartlett, depict medieval athletic contests. The window above the main door, designed by Edward D. Sperry, portrays the crowning of Ivanhoe by Rowena. The remainder of the block is occupied by Stagg Field, a stadium seating 57,000. Professor Amos Alonzo Stagg, known affectionately as "The Old Man," was athletic director of the university for forty-one years, and was the first football coach to achieve faculty status. The immense new Field House stands north of the Stagg Field on University Ave.

The central Quadrangles occupy four blocks extending south from 57th St. to 59th St. and west from University to Ellis Ave. The entrance through Mitchell Tower, at the SW. corner of 57th St. and University Ave., is the busiest traffic artery on the campus. In the other corners of the Quadrangles are all of the university dormitories, except the College Residence Halls. All but one were completed before 1900; they were designed by Henry Ives Cobb, university architect of that period.

(12) MITCHELL TOWER closely reproduces the tower of Magdalen College, Oxford. From the studios on the second floor is broadcast the discussion around the Sunday Round Table, one of the first university programs with a national hook-up. The Alice Freeman Palmer Chimes peal the close of each college day, 10:05 p.m., with "Alma Mater." HUTCHINSON HALL, opening on the main floor of the Tower, is patterned on Christ Church Hall, Oxford. On the wood paneling of this great dining hall hang the portraits of benefactors and members of the university; above, are the shields of English and American colleges.

Also connected with the Tower are the Reynolds Student Clubhouse for men, and the Leon Mandel Assembly Hall. The entire

Tower group was designed by Shepley, Rutan, and Coolidge in 1903, and decorated by Frederick Clay Bartlett; the buildings stand on two sides of Hutchinson Court, a sunken English garden, scene of the popular "University Sing" in June.

Westward, (13) the HULL BIOLOGICAL LABORATORIES (1897) stand on three sides of Hull Court; connected by cloistered walks are the BOTANY, ZOOLOGY, and ANATOMY BUILDINGS, and CULVER HALL, formerly the Physiology Laboratory, the first in America, now occupied by the Biology Library and various laboratories. Entrance from 57th St. on the north is through the massive stone Cobb Gate, richly ornamented with grotesques; from the south, through a delicately arched iron gate. Landscaped Botany Pond is one of the most charming spots on the Quadrangles, except during the annual muddy melée of the Freshman-Sophomore tug-of-war in Homecoming Week.

(14) HITCHCOCK HALL, designed by D. H. Perkins, (1902) and SNELL HALL, men's dormitories, stand in the NW. corner of the Quadrangles. Easternmost of an imposing row of Physical Science Laboratories, facing south on the Circle, at the center of the Quadrangle, is (15) BERNARD A. ECKHART HALL, designed by C. Z. Klauder and completed in 1930 for use of the Mathematics, Astronomy, and Physics Departments.

(16) The RYERSON PHYSICAL LABORATORY (1894) has rooms specially designed for control of sound, temperature, humidity, and vibration. Much of the work of the three Nobel prize winners of the university was performed here.

(17) The KENT CHEMICAL LABORATORY (1894) contains a large theater.

(18) The GEORGE HERBERT JONES CHEMICAL LABORATORY, at the west end of the row, was designed by Coolidge and Hodgdon and completed in 1929. Graduate and research work is carried on in the Laboratory, which contains student social halls.

(19) COBB LECTURE HALL, westernmost of the row of buildings on the south side of the Circle, houses various administrative offices and college classrooms. Named for its donor, Silas B. Cobb, the Hall and adjoining dormitories, extending south along Ellis Avenue in a solid row to the Midway, were the first of the university buildings.

(20) BLAKE HALL and GATES HALL, originally men's dormitories, are now women's residence halls.

(21) GOODSPEED HALL, at the corner, was a dormitory for divinity students until 1938, when it was taken over by the Department of Art. In the Gallery (*open* 2-5 *daily*), on the first floor, the Renaissance Society of the University of Chicago exhibits the collections and works of its members, and those drawn from other sources. In the Art Reference Library are some 200,000 reproductions of paintings and drawings, duplicating the collection of Sir Robert Witt of London, most notable in the world.

(22) SWIFT HALL, facing north on the Circle, east of Cobb Hall, is used by the Divinity School of the university. The school was originally organized in 1867 as the Baptist Union Theological Seminary but its present faculty and student body include representatives of all the leading Protestant churches. Connected with Swift Hall by a stone cloister is the charming JOSEPH BOND CHAPEL. Both structures were designed by Coolidge and Hodgdon and were completed and dedicated in 1926.

(23) HASKELL HALL (1896), south of Swift Hall, formerly the Oriental Museum, now houses the School of Business.

(24) ROSENWALD HALL, east of Swift Hall, designed by Holabird and Roche and completed in 1916, is occupied by the Departments of Geology and Geography. The first floor contains a museum with collections of minerals and rocks, and one of the largest map libraries in the country. The official Chicago station of the U. S. Weather Bureau (*open* 9-4 *Fri.*, 9-12 *Sat.*) is in the tower. The seismograph in the basement rests on a concrete pier sunk 62.5 feet below floor level to bedrock.

(25) WALKER MUSEUM (1893) adjoining Rosenwald Hall (*open* 9-5 *Mon.-Fri.*, 9-1 *Sat.*), is the foremost center for materials relating to Permian reptiles and Paleozoic invertebrates. Each of the alcoves on the first floor exhibits specimens of a particular geologic period. The fossil invertebrate collection on the second floor containing over a million specimens, is especially rich in Paleozoic material from the Mississippi Valley region. The paleobotanical collection on the third floor, gathered from all continents, includes extensive exhibits of specimens from the coal regions of southern Illinois.

(26) The LAW SCHOOL BUILDING, south of Rosenwald

Hall, was designed by Shepley, Rutan, and Coolidge. The cornerstone was laid by President Theodore Roosevelt in 1903.

(27) BEECHER, GREEN, KELLY and FOSTER HALLS, women's dormitories, extend south along University Ave. to the Midway.

(28) The WILLIAM RAINEY HARPER MEMORIAL LIBRARY (*open 8 a.m.-10 p.m., Mon.-Fri.; 8-6 Sat.*), facing the Midway, is the central unit at the south end of the Quadrangles. One of the great libraries of the world, it contains more than 1,250,000 volumes. The impressive main reading room is on the third floor. The American drama collection, among the best in the United States, includes a large group of Chicago playbills. Many collections of rare books and manuscripts, totaling 23,000 items, are housed in the west tower. The Lincoln Library (*open 9-11:45 and 1-5 Mon.-Fri.; 9-1 and 2-5 Sat.*), on the second floor, has 5,000 volumes, and 14,000 manuscripts and facsimiles of Lincolniana, one of the nation's largest collections. Notable among the Lincoln portraits are two original oils by George Frederick Wright. The principal motif of the elaborate interior and exterior decorations is based on the coats-of-arms of eminent universities and the devices of famous European printers. The building was completed in 1912.

The SOCIAL SCIENCE RESEARCH BUILDING (1929) opening into Harper Library from the east, is unusual among university structures in its provision of facilities for cooperative research on social problems by members of various departments. Many of the public lectures offered by the university are given in the Assembly Room; musical recordings are played here (*12:30-1:15 Tues.-Fri.*).

WIEBOLDT HALL (1927), forming a west unit of the library building, is the center of modern language study. The Modern Poetry Library, on the second floor, has as a nucleus the collection of books and manuscripts gathered by Harriet Monroe during her editorship of *Poetry* magazine.

The CLASSICS BUILDING: HIRAM KELLY MEMORIAL (1915), at the west end of the library group, is devoted largely to the study of classical languages and literatures. The small Classics Museum on the fourth floor contains architectural models and ancient pottery. The Classics and Harper Memorial Library Buildings were designed by Shepley, Rutan, and Coolidge; Wieboldt Hall and Social Science Research Buildings by Coolidge and Hodgdon.

(29) The COLLEGE RESIDENCE HALLS FOR MEN, on 60th St. between Ellis and Greenwood Aves., are stately dormitories, surrounding Judson Court and Burton Court. They were designed by Zantzinger, Borie and Medary, and completed in 1931.

(30) The UNIVERSITY OF CHICAGO CLINICS, on 59th St. between Ellis and Maryland Aves., are dominated by the ALBERT MERRITT BILLINGS HOSPITAL, for medical and surgical cases; included are the Max Epstein Clinic for out-patients, and the Walter G. Zoller Memorial Dental Clinic. The north wings house the laboratories of the Departments of Medicine, Pathology, and Surgery. Across the court on 58th Street stands the PHYSIOLOGY AND BIOCHEMISTRY BUILDING. East of Billings is the HOME FOR DESTITUTE CRIPPLED CHILDREN, conducted in affiliation with the university; to the west is the BOBS ROBERTS MEMORIAL HOSPITAL FOR CHILDREN. Across Drexel Avenue is the CHICAGO LYING-IN HOSPITAL; founded by Dr. Joseph B. De Lee, noted obstetrician, the hospital has been a part of the university since 1938. The building was designed by Schmidt, Garden, and Erickson. Coolidge and Hodgdon planned the other buildings of the group. All were built between 1927 and 1931. The hospitals have 630 beds in all. Maintenance and operation of clinics constitute the largest single item on the university budget.

(31) The WHITMAN LABORATORY, a block north of the Clinics, on the SW. corner of 57th St. and Ingleside Ave., is devoted to experimental zoology. Hundreds of chickens and guinea pigs are kept in the surrounding pens.

(32) The BOTANY GREENHOUSE occupies a quarter acre at the NW. corner of 57th St. and Ingleside Ave. The cycad collection is the largest in the world. At the north end of the greenhouse is the C. R. BARNES BOTANY LABORATORY.

(33) The PSYCHOLOGICAL LABORATORY, 5730 Ellis Ave., is flanked on either side of the two units of the HOWARD TAYLOR RICKETTS LABORATORIES, used in the study of bacteriology and parasitology.

In (34) the UNIVERSITY PRESS BUILDING, NW. corner of Ellis Ave. and 58th St., are printed various departmental journals, books and pamphlets, and all official documents of the university. More than 1,000 books and pamphlets have been published and 16 departmental journals are issued regularly. On the main floor are the Faculty Exchange and the Information Office.

The South Side

A varied and complex city in itself, comprising more than half of Chicago, the South Side lies between the South Branch of the Chicago River and 138th St. Up to 1889 it extended only as far as 39th Street, embracing less than 10 square miles, but in that year the municipalities of Lake and Hyde Park were annexed, adding 84 square miles and shifting the geographical center of the city close to the stock yards, previously outside the city limits. Later, an additional 23 square miles of towns were added so that today, in area, the South Side is larger than the District of Columbia by some 40 square miles, and in character, is a plexus of highly diverse communities, many of which have retained their original names.

Edged by the landscaped lake shore in the north half of the South Side, are some of the most elegant houses in Chicago, including the old and frequently dilapidated mansions of the former Gold Coast along Prairie, Calumet, Ellis, Lake Park, and Michigan Avenues, some occupied by institutions of various kinds, others converted into rooming houses. Southward are the communities of Kenwood, Hyde Park, and South Shore, laid out in fine avenues, and dotted with impressive schools and churches, and swank apartments.

In a narrow north-south belt known as the Black Belt, extending the length of the north half of the South Side immediately west of the lake shore communities, live most of Chicago's Negroes. Many of them find employment in the vast central manufacturing districts, packing plants, and switch-yards to the west. Monotonous acres of cottages of Polish, Lithuanian, and Czecho-Slovakian workingmen fill much of this industrial district, which is bordered on the south by the boisterous Irish section pictured in James T. Farrell's *Studs Lonigan* trilogy, and by Englewood, a middle-class community with a commercial center second only to the downtown district in magnitude.

From 79th Street to the southern limits of the city, the lake shore near the Calumet River, and the area along the Indiana border, are covered with the black clutter and confusion of industry. Great hulks of mills and furnaces and grain elevators rise along the banks and slips of the Calumet River. In spite of heavy industrialization, parts of the grimy but impressive Calumet region are still marshy and untamed, particularly in the neighborhood of Wolf Lake; its reedy waters are frequented by countless birds and contain many rare species of aquatic plants.

Pullman and the old Dutch community of Roseland occupy slightly higher ground west of Lake Calumet. Farther west lies the Blue Island Ridge, a thick glacial deposit about two and one-half miles long, the most conspicuous elevation in Chicago. It was an island left high and dry before the waters of glacial Lake Chicago receded from the rest of the Chicago area. Spreading among the huge oaks on the ridge are the leafy residential communities of Washington Heights, Morgan Park, and Beverly Hills.

POINTS OF INTEREST

1. The COLISEUM, 1463 S. Wabash Ave., retains the battlemented stone façade of the Civil War Libby Prison, removed from Richmond in pieces and rebuilt here in 1888. The structure served as a war museum; in 1900 it was replaced, and the façade incorporated in the present building, an indoor stadium seating 13,000. Here Taft, Theodore Roosevelt, and Harding were nominated for the presidency, and the notorious First Ward Balls were held in the early part of the century.

2. The HUMAN ENGINEERING LABORATORY (*open* 9-5 *weekdays; closed every fourth Sat.*), 1800 Prairie Ave., was established here in 1938 by the Armour Institute of Technology; people are here tested for vocational aptitudes. The laboratory, a branch of the organization created by Dr. Johnson O'Connor at Stevens Institute of Technology, occupies the John J. Glessner House, built in 1886 for the late director of the International Harvester Company. The Glessner House is the only remaining work in Chicago of H. H. Richardson. Its low lines, rugged construction, and crisply carved ornament are characteristic of the Romanesque Revival that he introduced.

3. The ARCHITECTS CLUB OF CHICAGO (*open daily*), 1801 Prairie Ave., occupies the W. W. Kimball house, the home of one of Chicago's pioneer piano manufacturers. Designed by Solon S. Beman after the 16th century Chateau de Josselin in Brittany, and built in 1887, it is a fine example of the Francis I style. Its many pinnacles and high gabled roof make a singularly romantic silhouette. The interior of the house has a sedate grandeur, with its rich oak and

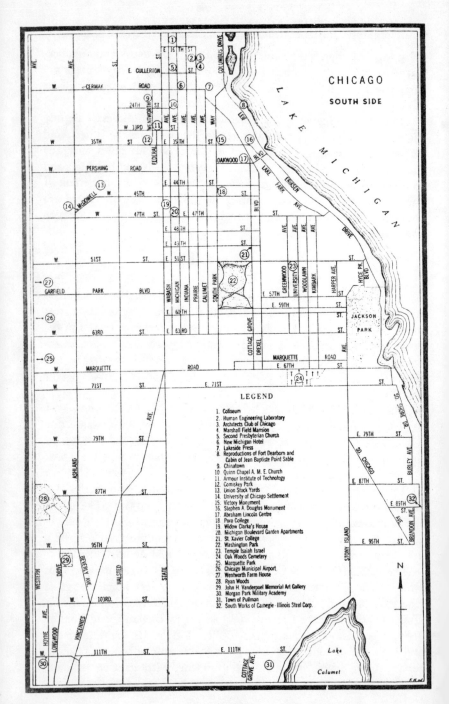

CHICAGO
SOUTH SIDE

LEGEND

1. Coliseum
2. Human Engineering Laboratory
3. Architects Club of Chicago
4. Marshall Field Mansion
5. Second Presbyterian Church
6. New Michigan Hotel
7. Lakeside Press
8. Reproductions of Fort Dearborn and Cabin of Jean Baptiste Point Sable
9. Chinatown
10. Quinn Chapel A. M. E. Church
11. Armour Institute of Technology
12. Comiskey Park
13. Union Stock Yards
14. University of Chicago Settlement
15. Victory Monument
16. Stephen A. Douglas Monument
17. Abraham Lincoln Centre
18. Poro College
19. Widow Clarke's House
20. Michigan Boulevard Garden Apartments
21. St. Xavier College
22. Washington Park
23. Temple Isaiah Israel
24. Oak Woods Cemetery
25. Marquette Park
26. Chicago Municipal Airport
27. Wentworth Farm House
28. Ryan Woods
29. John H. Vanderpoel Memorial Art Gallery
30. Morgan Park Military Academy
31. Town of Pullman
32. South Works of Carnegie - Illinois Steel Corp.

N

mahogany panelling, majestic staircase, and many fine fireplaces. The base of the monument *The Fort Dearborn Massacre* stands a few feet to the east, near the site of the massacre of 1812.

4. The MARSHALL FIELD MANSION (*closed*), 1905 Prairie Ave., was designed by Richard Morris Hunt and erected in 1879. The interior was extensively remodeled and a wing in the modern "International" style was added during its occupation by the New Bauhaus in 1937-38.

5. The SECOND PRESBYTERIAN CHURCH, Michigan Ave. at Cullerton St., was designed by James Renwick, and completed in 1874. Two small windows, executed by William Morris from designs by Sir Edward Burne-Jones, flank the front entrance.

6. The NEW MICHIGAN HOTEL, Michigan Ave. at Cermak Road, known during prohibition days as the Lexington Hotel, gained wide renown as the headquarters of Alphonse Capone, from whose suite the powerful Capone vice and alcohol ring operated.

7. The LAKESIDE PRESS, 350 E. Cermak Road, a handsome 8-story brick and stone building, is one of the largest in the United States devoted to the production of printing. The Press is noted for its typography and color work; the Exhibition Hall on the eighth floor (*open* 9-5 *Mon.-Fri.*) has displays of fine binding, printing, and illustration.

BURNHAM PARK, newest and second largest of Chicago's major parks, was envisaged by Daniel Burnham as a connecting link between Grant and Jackson Parks at least ten years before he drew up the comprehensive Chicago Plan, but construction was delayed until 1920 by negotiations for riparian rights held by the Illinois Central Railroad. Sand was pumped in and debris dumped to raise above the lake waters this strip of land one-eighth of a mile wide and five miles long, 598 acres in extent. Northerly Island, also "made" land, consists of 91 acres facing the north end of the park. In 1933-34 the park and island were the scene of the Century of Progress Exposition. Extensive grading and landscaping have since been carried out by Works Progress Administration.

There are striking views of the Chicago skyline from Leif Eriksen Drive, which traverses the length of the park, unimpeded by cross traffic. Southward, in Hyde Park, rises the sharp, bright cluster of towering apartments; along the shoreline curving to the east spread the gaunt black stacks of the Calumet district, overhung with a pall of smoke. The view northward is rivalled in magnificence in few other cities of the world. Angling in towards the open front of the downtown district, the drive affords a line of vantage for the greatly varied but somehow harmoniously grouped towers of central Chicago. Particularly splendid is the night scene approached along the light-streaked drive.

8. REPRODUCTIONS OF FORT DEARBORN AND THE CABIN OF JEAN BAPTISTE POINT SABLE (*not open*) stand in Burnham Park at Leif Eriksen Drive and 26th St., nearly three miles southeast of the original sites. Built for the Century of Progress Exposition, the reproduction of Fort Dearborn, complete with stockade, blockhouses, powder house, and barracks, is based on sketches of the first fort drawn in 1803 by its builder, Capt. John Whistler, later discovered in the War Office files.

9. CHINATOWN extends about three blocks from the corner of Cermak Road and Wentworth Ave., mainly along these two streets. Commercial and social center of Chicago's 6,000 Chinese, and the home of half of them, it ranks next in size to the settlements in San Francisco and New York. At first glance little distinguishes Chinatown from many other small outlying business sections. Cermak Road has been widened into one of the broadest streets in Chicago, and Wentworth Avenue resounds with the rumble of one of the most heavily used car-lines in the city. Architecturally, most of the district is old, consisting of a miscellany of two- and three-story shop and flat buildings, but some of the brick structures have been interestingly remodeled with recessed balconies, and the new Chinese "City Hall" is one of the finest examples of Chinese architecture in America. The numerous Cantonese, some slipper-shod, gliding along the sidewalks, and the store fronts with Chinese names and inscriptions in Chinese characters advertising Oriental foods and merchandise, attract thousands of visitors to Chinatown.

Jade and soapstone ornaments, incense, back scratchers, and all manner of charms and baubles are found in dim little shops, in the brightly lighted CHINESE EMPORIUM, Cermak Road at La Salle St., and in the LING LONG MUSEUM, 2238 Wentworth Ave., which contains a score of dioramas depicting the history and customs of China. Many food markets display a curious assortment of preserved foods from China and strange Chinese vegetables. Barbecued pork loins hang near boxes of succulent lotus roots; bright bitter-greens with yellow blossoms and fat bitter-melons nestle in window trays beside baskets of butter fish; flaky birds' nests, mud-caked "thousand year" eggs, shark fins, and beetles rest in jars and tins on store shelves.

The center of the district is the CHINESE CITY HALL (*open except during Tong meetings*), 2216 Wentworth Ave., headquarters of the On Leong Tong, an association of prosperous Chinese merchants. Adjoining the reception hall is the shrine room, with portraits of George Washington and Sun Yat Sen, father of the Chinese Republic. Teakwood chairs along the walls have backs of striped marble, selected to suggest seascapes, landscapes, and fantastic creatures of Chinese folklore. An elaborate memorial shrine to Quan-Kung, a teacher of the third century who emphasized honest dealings in business, has a painting of Quan-Kung half hidden in its gilded recesses. Here joss sticks are burned, and a perpetual oil light glimmers on ceremonial objects and ornaments symbolizing various qualities and virtues of the good life. In the building are meeting halls, a courtroom for settling business disputes between tong members, and a schoolroom for the instruction of Chinese youth in the language and customs of China.

On a variable date, between the end of January and the beginning of March, the Chinese celebrate their New Year. Fireworks pop, a 30-foot paper dragon and a grotesque lion dance in the streets, and the tables of the many good restaurants in Chinatown groan under the weight of 27-course dinners.

10. QUINN CHAPEL A. M. E. CHURCH, Wabash Ave. at 24th St., a massive Gothic structure of rough cut stone, houses a congregation that was organized in 1847, and in 1853 built Chicago's first Negro house of worship, the race's civic and social center, near Jackson Boulevard and Dearborn Street. Many of the members are descendants of the founders.

11. The ARMOUR INSTITUTE OF TECHNOLOGY, 3300 Federal St., founded in 1892 by Philip D. Armour, offers college courses in various branches of engineering in the red brick and sandstone laboratory buildings of modified Romanesque design. The Department of Architecture is housed downtown in the Art Institute. The school enrolls some 1,300 full-time students and about twice as many in its evening courses.

12. COMISKEY PARK, 35th St. and Shields Ave., is the home of the White Sox, Chicago's American League baseball club. Here Joe

Louis knocked out James J. Braddock for the world's heavy-weight boxing championship, in June 1937.

13. The UNION STOCK YARDS, Halsted St. and Exchange Ave., and PACKINGTOWN, Racine Ave. and Exchange Ave., the world's largest unit for the marketing of livestock and the processing of meat, consist of a square mile of pens and packing plants, in which some 12,000,000 animals, valued at $250,000,000, are received annually. Livestock is the chief source of cash income for the American farmer, and the Union Stock Yards handle approximately one-fifth of the total sales. About 75 per cent of the animals received are slaughtered and processed here. The remainder are shipped largely to feeders in the corn belt and to packers in the East. Most shipments of cattle and lambs go to Jewish packing houses in New York City, for by Mosaic law kosher meat must be eaten within a few days of slaughter.

Hundreds of latticed freight cars rattle into the yards each night with their noisy cargo. Transferred to the pens that fill the east half of the square mile, the animals are watered, fed, and prepared for sale in the morning. Cattle buyers, frequently mounted, representing large and small packers, traders, butchers, and feeders, inspect the day's offerings and bargain with the commission men to whom the livestock is consigned.

In busy seasons the streets within and around the yards swarm with men who have accompanied their stock to market—drawling Texans with wide-brimmed Stetsons, bearded men of rural religious sects, and Midwest farmers in ordinary business clothes.

The LIVE STOCK NATIONAL BANK BUILDING, 4150 S. Halsted St., is a reproduction of Independence Hall in Philadelphia. The STOCK YARDS INN, 4178 S. Halsted St., Tudor in design, with dormered roof and overhanging gables, contains paintings of animals and hunting scenes. The INTERNATIONAL AMPHITHEATRE, adjoining the Inn, is the scene of the International Live Stock Exposition, held annually during the last week in November.

From the roof of the EXCHANGE BUILDING, Exchange Ave. and Laurel St., is a fine view of the pens and barns, the connecting alleys, the chutes and platforms along the network of rails, and the overhead driveways leading into the solid wall of Packingtown buildings to the west. The CHICAGO DAILY DROVERS JOURNAL BUILDING, 836 Exchange Ave., houses a newspaper for the livestock farmer, and radio station WAAF.

Slaughter houses were established early in Chicago's history, but there were no centralized stock yards until John B. Sherman opened the Bull's Head Stock Yards at Madison Street and Ashland Avenue in 1848, from which the several packing plants along the Chicago River and its branches drew their supplies. In 1856 Sherman replaced the Bull's Head with yards along the Illinois Central Railroad at 29th Street, and in 1865 organized the Union Stock Yard and Transit Company and opened the present yards. Within a few years, Philip D. Armour, Gustavus F. Swift, Nelson Morris, and others built their plants adjacent to the stock yards. The rapid growth of the packing industry was stimulated by the development of the refrigerator car in the 1870's and by the utilization of by-products after 1885. But the poor working conditions in the plants and the unsanitary methods of waste disposal took their toll in human misery. Upton Sinclair's novel of protest, *The Jungle,* caused a public reaction; the report of an investigating committee, appointed by President Theodore Roosevelt in 1906, led to effective reform legislation.

Meat packing is Chicago's chief industry in value of its products. The Armour, Swift, and Wilson plants, largest in Packingtown, do most of the business.

The SWIFT PLANT (*tours* 9-2:30 *Mon.-Fri.;* 9-12 *Sat.*), Exchange and Racine Aves., normally employs 7,000 workers in its cluster of more than 100 buildings. The ARMOUR PLANT (*tours* 8:30-11, *and* 12:30-3:00 *Mon.-Fri.;* 8:30-11 *Sat.*), Racine Ave. and 43rd St., is comparable in size. Both of these companies provide 90-minute tours of their plants, which include the slaughter rooms if desired. The rapid "disassembling" operations—the conversion of cattle, calves, hogs, and sheep into wholesale cuts of meat, canned and smoked products, and by-products—are as smooth as on the production line of an automobile factory. But "Judas goats," trained rams, are still used to lead lambs from their pens to the slaughter.

14. The UNIVERSITY OF CHICAGO SETTLEMENT (*open* 9 *a.m.*-10 *p.m. daily*), 4630 McDowell Ave., was founded in 1894 by William Rainey Harper and a group of Christian Union workers. The "back of the yards" district was chosen as the best field near the University of Chicago for actual social service work and for study. Mary McDowell, selected by Jane Addams to head the settlement, won wide renown for her militant welfare work. Opened in a 4-room tenement apartment, the institution now covers most of a city block.

The BLACK BELT, known also as Bronzeville, forms a narrow rectangle from about 16th St. to 67th St. Although members of the Negro race have been identified with Chicago's earliest history, it is only since the World War that they have come in sufficient numbers to make the city the world's second largest metropolitan settlement of Negroes. In these few years they have developed a large and successful professional and semi-professional class, welfare organizations, modern hospitals, hotels, manufacturing concerns, department stores, and from time to time a score or more newspapers, one of which is known as the "World's Greatest Weekly." Extensive settlement began at the north end of the belt and spread rapidly southward. White residents in the path of expansion abandoned substantial dwellings in many cases, particularly along South Park Way. As a result, much of Bronzeville compares favorably in outer aspect with the rest of Chicago. But the low income of most of the Negroes, the terrific pressure of some 250,000 people living in an area of six square miles designed for a much smaller population, and the resistance to the expansion of the district by the owners of adjacent property, have created serious housing and racial problems.

The desolation in the older part of Bronzeville contrasts sharply with the gay, cornucopia air of the business section. The largest shops, theaters and ballrooms center on South Park Way at 47th Street, a corner alive with people most of the time. On adjoining side streets are small shops selling mystic charms and potions; curbstone stands with smoke rising from wood fires over which chicken and spareribs are being barbecued; lunchrooms serving hot fish, sweet potato pie, gumbo, and other Southern dishes, markets bulging with turnip tops, mustard greens, and chitterlings; taverns and night clubs that resound with blues-singing and hot-foot music. The SAVOY BALLROOM, 4733 South Park Way, is a counterpart of its more famous namesake in New York City. Once a week the ballroom is converted into an arena in which ambitious pugilists, their mind's eye on Joe Louis, jab warily at each other. Louis' victory over Max Schmeling on the night of June 22, 1938, catapulted thousands of Bronzeville's residents onto the streets to participate in one of the wildest celebrations ever witnessed in Chicago.

15. The VICTORY MONUMENT, 35th St. and South Park Way, the work of Leonard Crunelle, was dedicated in 1927 to the memory of soldiers of the old Eighth Infantry of the Illinois National Guard who died in France. Around the central shaft stand three heroic

figures in bronze symbolizing the tragedy and the glory of war. The bronze statue of a Negro doughboy surmounts the monument.

16. The STEPHEN A. DOUGLAS MONUMENT, foot of 35th St., memorial to the "Little Giant," overlooks the tracks of the Illinois Central Railroad, which he helped to organize. In the small square a tall granite pillar supports a heroic bronze statue of Douglas. The base of the monument, adorned with four seated figures representing *Illinois, Justice, History,* and *Eloquence,* contains the Douglas sarcophagus. The oldest sculptured monument in Chicago, it was executed by Leonard W. Volk in 1879. Nearby are the sites of Camp Douglas, famous Civil War training camp and prison, and the first university in Chicago (1857-1886), built on land given by Douglas.

17. The ABRAHAM LINCOLN CENTER (*open 7 a.m.-12 p.m. daily*), 700 Oakwood Blvd., occupies a massive, foursquare brick building designed by Frank Lloyd Wright. Founded in 1905 by the Reverend Jenkin Lloyd Jones to foster international, inter-religious, and inter-racial fellowship, the institution is an outstanding educational and recreational center. Among the noteworthy activities are the Friday Morning Forum (*Oct.-March*), and the Sunday Evening Discussion Club.

18. PORO COLLEGE, 4415 South Park Way, headquarters of a nation-wide chain, is a Negro school of beauty culture, occupying approximately half a city block. The plant includes four three-story buildings, housing dormitories, cafeteria, beauty shop, and school. The college faces on a beautiful lawn, available to the public for entertainment, as are the parlors. The college, accredited by the Illinois State Board of Education, was founded by Mrs. Anne Pope Malone, known for her philanthropy and work for the social betterment of her race.

19. The WIDOW CLARKE'S HOUSE (*private*), 4526 S. Wabash Ave., the oldest in Chicago, is a spacious two-story house of oak and Georgia pine. Built in 1836, it is in good repair and is still used as a residence. The original porch, with its columns and balcony, has been removed, but the cupola remains. The house was erected near Michigan Avenue and 16th Street for Henry B. Clarke, who died in 1849. His widow sold the house in 1872 to John Chrimes, merchant tailor, who moved it almost four miles south to its present site, then beyond the city limits.

20. The MICHIGAN BOULEVARD GARDEN APARTMENTS, Michigan Ave. and 47th St., is a group of modern brick buildings erected in 1928 by the late Julius Rosenwald, widely known for his philanthropic work among American Negroes. The development covers six acres, three of which are given over to gardens and courts. Other features include a playground and day nursery for children of the families occupying the 421 apartments. Klaber and Grunsfeld were the architects.

21. ST. XAVIER COLLEGE, Cottage Grove Ave. at 49th St., founded in 1912, is an outgrowth of Chicago's first Catholic private school, opened by the Sisters of Mercy in 1846 as the Saint Francis Xavier Female Academy. About 350 women are enrolled for courses which lead to the standard degrees of a liberal arts college. The college building of tan brick and limestone, approached by a semi-circular drive through a landscaped block, rises four stories to a steep sloping slate roof with dormer windows.

22. WASHINGTON PARK, S. from 51st St. to 60th St., and E. from South Park Way to Cottage Grove Ave., is the largest inland park in Chicago, embracing 371 acres. In the eighties and nineties gay parties of Chicago's elite rode through in polished carriages and tallyhos to attend the races at the former Washington Park Racing Course, a block south of the park. With the extension of the Negro district in the last decade, the park is now used largely by this group. Large crowds of spectators and participants are attracted to the archery ranges; football, baseball, and cricket fields; tennis and roque courts; bridle paths, casting pools, and bowling greens. Pathways wind around the beautifully landscaped lagoons in the south half of the park.

The STATUE OF GEORGE WASHINGTON, South Park Way at 51st St., sculptured by Daniel Chester French and Edward C. Potter, pictures Washington taking command of the American Army at Cambridge. The statue is a replica of one presented to the government of France by the Daughters of the American Revolution.

Behind the Refectory at 56th St. and South Park Way are the SWIMMING POOLS, built by the Works Progress Administration.

The FOUNTAIN OF TIME, Midway Plaisance at Cottage Grove Avenue, masterpiece of Lorado Taft, illustrates in sculpture the line of Austin Dobson's poem:

"Time goes, you say? Ah, no!
Alas, Time stays, *we go.*"

The figures of people in various stages and stations of life appear to move from the surging waters at the right to the engulfing waves at the left—a procession of mankind from birth to death crossing a bridge along the border of a quiet pool, under the brooding gaze of Father Time.

The Washington Park Open Forum, an outgrowth of the historic "Bug Club," meets near 56th St. and Cottage Grove Ave. Crowds gather on Sunday afternoons to hear noted speakers and to discuss the problems of the day. In the SUNKEN GARDENS, a block northward, stands a monument, sculptured by Albin Polasek, of the philosopher Gotthold E. Lessing, holding a book and a pen. The new ARMORY, Cottage Grove Ave. at 52nd St., one of the largest buildings of its kind in the United States, houses the 124th Field Artillery, 33rd Division, Illinois National Guard.

23. TEMPLE ISAIAH ISRAEL, Hyde Park Blvd. and Greenwood Ave., one of the most impressive houses of worship in Chicago, was designed by Alfred Alschuler for a reform Jewish congregation. Built of tawny brick of interesting texture and pattern and trimmed with limestone, the octagonal auditorium is roofed with a gold-tiled dome, behind which rises a slender minaret. The whole effect is early Byzantine. Interior and exterior ornamentations were based on photographs of fragments of a second century synagogue unearthed at Tiberias, Palestine.

The JACKSON PARK ART COLONY, 57th St. between Stony Island Ave. and Harper Ave., is a forlorn row of sagging barn-like shacks erected during the Columbian Exposition to serve as souvenir stores and popcorn stands. After the turn of the century they were taken over by artists and writers. In *Midwest Portraits*, Harry Hansen tells of the carefree but productive life of the colony, and of the inspiration he derived from association there with Floyd Dell, Margaret Anderson, Theodore Dreiser, Edgar Lee Masters, Carl Sandburg, Sherwood Anderson, and many more. Later, there arrived lesser but no less industrious figures. Many of them live and work in GOUDICH CASTLE, an old apartment house at 5642 Harper Avenue, another relic of the fair.

24. The OAK WOODS CEMETERY (*open* 8:30-5 *daily*), 1035 E. 67th St., is one of the oldest of Chicago's cemeteries. Within this 187-acre garden spot rest 123,000 dead. In the southwest corner of the cemetery, in a small mound, are buried some 6,000 Confederate

soldiers who died while imprisoned in Camp Douglas. A large shaft of Georgia granite, surmounted with the bronze statue of a sorrowing Confederate infantryman, commemorates them. The names, companies, and regiments of 4,275 are inscribed on bronze plates around the base of the monument.

25. MARQUETTE PARK, Marquette Road and California Ave., second largest inland park in Chicago, contains 322 acres, extensively improved by the Works Progress Administration. Recreation facilities include a nine-hole golf course. At the entrance on California Avenue stands a red granite monument of striking modern design by the sculptor Raoul Josset, commemorating Captain Steponas Darius and Lieutenant Stasys Girenas, and their attempted flight from New York to Kaunas, Lithuania, July 17, 1933. In the form of a faceted irregular pyramid suggesting the broken wing of an airplane, the front face bears a bronze globe with the figures of ten airplanes tracing the route of the flyers, who crashed to their deaths just short of their goal.

26. The CHICAGO MUNICIPAL AIRPORT, a square-mile tract near the edge of the city at Cicero Ave. and 62nd St., is one of the busiest airfields in the world. Eight lines operate more than 100 schedules daily; the total of scheduled passengers carried to and from the field exceeds 250,000 annually.

27. The WENTWORTH FARM HOUSE (*private*), NE. corner of 55th St. and Harlem Ave., is a rambling white 19-room frame structure, once the seat of the vast country estate of "Long John" Wentworth (1815-88). Wentworth who arrived in Chicago in 1836, barefoot, as legend has it, was closely identified with the rapid transition of Chicago from a mudhole to a metropolis. Editor of the *Democrat,* mayor, congressman, he was also the largest landholder in the city.

28. RYAN WOODS, 87th St. and Western Ave. is one of the few tracts of the magnificent 33,000-acre Cook County forest preserve system that lies within Chicago. A bit of native woodland, it covers the north end of the Blue Island Ridge.

29. The JOHN H. VANDERPOEL MEMORIAL ART GALLERY (*open* 9-5 *weekdays;* 2-5 *Sun.*), occupies a wing of the Ridge Park Fieldhouse, Longwood Drive and 96th st. Vanderpoel was an instructor, artist, and author; three years after his death in 1911, his friends organized an association to perpetuate his memory, and

bought one of his paintings, *The Butter Makers,* as the beginning of a permanent collection.

Largely through the efforts of John A. Campbell, volunteer curator, who invited artists to contribute some of their work, the collection includes 600 paintings, water-colors, etchings, and sculptures. The collection, only part of which is shown at a time, includes works by Maxfield Parrish, Ralph Clarkson, Lorado Taft, Louis Betts, and Albin Polasek.

30. The MORGAN PARK MILITARY ACADEMY, 111th St. and Hoyne Ave., attracts thousands of visitors to its full dress parades and military maneuvers on Sunday afternoons during the school year.

31. The TOWN OF PULLMAN, centering around 111th St. and Cottage Grove Ave., at the northwest edge of Lake Calumet, is the result of a grandiose experiment in town planning, and its still beautiful old houses and public buildings give evidence of the proprietary Utopia that briefly flourished here. In 1881 George M. Pullman, inventor and manufacturer of the Pullman sleeping car, hired a group of experts, including the architect Solon S. Beman, to build a model settlement within the municipality of Hyde Park for the employees of his immense new manufacturing plant. This gigantic enterprise attracted world-wide attention as an "extension of the broadest philanthropy to the working man, based on business principles." Some of the employees, however, resented what they considered undemocratic town management. Shortly after the great strike of 1894, the Illinois Supreme Court ruled that the Pullman Company was exceeding the rights of its charter in leasing houses to its workers, and thereafter the cottages and apartments passed into the hands of private owners.

North of 111th Street are the CAR SHOPS, low rambling buildings, strangely ornate in contrast with the austerely practical factory buildings to be seen across Lake Calumet. Above the gabled roofs rises the old campanile-like Water Tower that once supplied water for Pullman. Rows of staunchly built brick cottages, simple in design, gracious and homelike, extend south to 115th Street. Some are well kept, with garden plots bright with zinnias and balsam. Interesting among the dwellings are the "blockhouse tenements," large apartment buildings designed for Pullman's lower-wage workers.

At Cottage Grove Avenue and 111th Street stands the FLORENCE

HOTEL, completely Victorian in the furnishings of its public rooms. Several fine houses, once occupied by executives of the Pullman Company, are grouped near the hotel square. The MARKET HOUSE, in the center of a tiny square at 112th Street and Champlain Avenue, is surrounded by curved arcades with apartments above. The old GREEN-STONE CHURCH at 112th St. and St. Lawrence Ave., with its gabled roof and towering spire, is perhaps the handsomest building in Pullman. Its serpentine stone walls, of a faded green, delicately complement the subdued red tones of the surrounding houses.

32. The SOUTH WORKS OF THE CARNEGIE-ILLINOIS STEEL CORPORATION (*tours by arrangement*), 3426 E. 89th St., occupy 591 acres along the lake front at the mouth of the Calumet River. Established in 1880 by the Chicago Rolling Mill Company, it is the second largest steel plant in America, chiefly manufacturing stainless steel for all U. S. Steel Corporation subsidiaries.

By daylight the external aspect of the plant is grimly dark and cold, a rather confusing, heavy conglomeration of materials and equipment: huge cranes that scoop Mesabi ore out of block-long boats, 11 bulky furnaces capable of reducing mountainous cocoa-colored ore piles and coke and limestone heaps to 10,000 tons of pig iron each day, 43 open-hearth furnaces and 3 Bessemer converters that purify and convert the iron into thousands of tons of steel daily, long black sheds that mill slabs, rails, blooms, plates, and bars; and thick nets of rail-lines, that remove the finished products.

At night, like a huge fireworks sparkler almost instantaneously consumed, fountains of sparks leap from the Bessemer converters into the sky, projecting a weird quavering glow on the clouds, visible for miles along the lake shore.

POINTS OF INTEREST IN ENVIRONS

Baha'i House of Worship, 16 *m.*, Ravinia Park, 26.9 *m.*, Dunes Park, 48 *m.* (*see Tour 2*); Chicago Zoological Park, 13.4 *m.*, Morton Arboretum, 26.1 *m.* (*see Tour 13*); Illinois and Michigan Canal Parkway, 44 *m.* (*see Tour 14*).

DECATUR

Railroad Stations: Wabash Depot, 700 East Cerro Gordo St., for Wabash Ry. and Baltimore & Ohio R. R.; Illinois Central Depot just east of the Wabash Depot at Cerro Gordo and Front Sts. for Illinois Central R. R. and Pennsylvania R. R.; Illinois Terminal Depot (electric) North Van Dyke at Packard St.

Bus Station: Transfer House at Lincoln Square for Santa Fe, Illinois Transit, De Luxe Stages, and All American Lines.

Intra-City Bus: 5c fare.

Taxicabs: 25c for the first two miles and 10c for each mile thereafter.

Accommodations: Five hotels; eight privately conducted tourist camps.

Information Service: Decatur Motor Club, Hotel Orlando, Association of Commerce, Decatur Club Building, 158 West Prairie.

Radio Station: WJBL (1200 kc).

Motion Picture Houses: Six.

Golf: Municipal links, Nelson Park, S. 22nd and E. Wood Sts.

Swimming: Non-commercial pool, Y.M.C.A., West Prairie at Church St. Commercial beach, Nelson Park Beach, Lake Decatur; rate 15c.

Tennis: Courts at most city parks, no charge.

Annual Events: Ice Carnival at Lake Decatur, midwinter.

DECATUR (682 alt., 57,510 pop.), seat of Macon County, lies on a bend in the Sangamon River, which was dammed here in 1923 to form Lake Decatur. An important railroad center, Decatur is the home of the Wabash Railway's repair shops, which are the city's second largest employer. The northeast section of the city is a welter of tracks bordered by roundhouses where locomotives are periodically dismantled and refurbished, and by shops where coaches are overhauled. Near the tracks rise the buildings of Decatur's largest employer, the Staley Company, dependent on the railway to feed the maws that annually swallow 13,000 carloads of corn and soybeans.

And yet Decatur is not a "factory" town, although its 12,000 workers fabricate products ranging from fly swatters to steel bridges. Neither is it essentially a college town, despite its Millikin University, nor a farm town, although it is hedged in by a limitless stretch of farms in all directions. In part it is all of these; students liven its streets and the university lends its academic dignity to the west part of the city; on Saturdays farmers descend on the city in large numbers for their weekly shopping; the fortunes of its industrial plants concern a large portion of the citizenry.

Certainly Decatur is a prairie town. It rests on a long swell of the

Illinois grass land, which rises gently from the Sangamon River, carries the business district on its crest, and drops again to the prairie level north of the Wabash tracts. Prairie grasses and flowers push against the doorsteps of the outermost houses, and each spring brighten the vacant lots. The swell imparts to the streets a sense of affinity with the land; the blocks of low weathered buildings seem a part of the prairie, in no way foreign to it, having the horizontal line emphasized in Frank Lloyd Wright's conception of prairie architecture. Neon-lighted store fronts in downtown Decatur fail to hide the fact that the buildings are old; even the "new" ones, with the exception of the Citizens Bank, were built before the World War. The others date back to the nineteenth century and have been stained as much by time as by smoke.

In 1829, although there were small settlements nearby, a 20-acre tract of prairie with no inhabitant, house or footpath was named Decatur and made seat of Macon County. Later in the year James Renshaw built the first cabin within the town site.

In the spring of 1830, when the town consisted of a few log houses, a store, a tavern, and a courthouse, Abraham Lincoln, just twenty-one, drove through town with his family and took up residence on the Sangamon River a few miles west of town. At the home of Major Warnick, the county's first peace officer, young Lincoln pored over borrowed books; in what is now Lincoln Square he made extemporaneous public speeches; and on surrounding farms he hired out as a plow boy and rail splitter.

In 1836 arrived another farm boy, Richard J. Oglesby. After spending many years of his boyhood in Decatur working at whatever job came his way, and sporadically attending country school, he went to Springfield to study law. Later he became a State senator, a United States senator, three times Governor of the State, and Major General during the Civil War. A friend of Lincoln from the time they met in Springfield, he was at the bedside of the President when he died.

The wealth of Decatur until 1854 was almost entirely dependent on agriculture. But with the arrival of the railroads in that year manufacturing began; the first factories were small and mainly supplied the immediate needs of the town and neighboring countryside. Their demand for labor steadily increased the town's population and the great need for goods and farm products during the Civil War further stimulated industrial growth. From 600 in 1850 the population rose to 3,839 in 1860 and more than doubled in the next two decades. Outstanding among the men who developed local commerce and industry was James Millikin, who established the Millikin Bank and amassed a fortune, part of which later was used to endow Millikin University.

In 1874 the city's economy was broadened when coal veins under the city were tapped, and with the opening of the new century the population had passed 20,000. In 1903 the university was opened, with President Theodore Roosevelt present at the dedication. Four years later the processing of corn products began here and has expanded continuously. By 1914 Decatur was among the few Illinois cities producing more than $10,000,000 of goods annually, much of which found markets in foreign countries.

Through the booming twenties the city prospered. In 1923, realizing that an inadequate water-supply would soon restrict her industries and prevent the establishment of new ones, Decatur replaced its archaic little dam with the present one, which impounds enough water for a city three times its present size. In 1925, 800 new homes were built, and in 1927 almost $6,000,000 went into commercial and residential construction.

The stock market crash of 1929 did not immediately affect Decatur as a whole; the year 1930 was a prosperous year for the entire county and agricultural products were valued at $11,000,000. But soon the great depression that moved across the world came to the corn belt and Decatur. Farm products fell in value; wages decreased; men were thrown out of work; for a time almost all of the major plants in the city were closed. During these years of depression Decatur experienced its first serious strike. In February, 1935, the employees of Decatur's several garment factories walked out to fight wage cuts. On several occasions pickets and police officers clashed; by October, 1937, with the issues still unsettled, many of the workers had returned to their jobs.

Although in 1938 industry and farming in Macon County approached their former prosperous levels, hope for the future lay not entirely in them. Oil has been found in southern Illinois, and reports of geologists have strengthened the belief that "liquid gold" underlies western Macon County.

POINTS OF INTEREST

The M. L. HARRY MEMORIAL FOUNTAIN (*operated nightly, May-Oct.*) in Central Park, in the downtown business district, was named in memory of a local utility executive. Set in a symmetrical pool 70 feet in diameter, the fountain rises in a series of ever-shifting formations; constantly changing lights illuminate it from beneath the glass floor. The lighting display executes a complete cycle every 10 minutes. In front of the fountain stands a weather-beaten Civil War statuary group, in dramatic military pose, executed by Sigvold Asbjornsen, Chicago, and erected in 1904.

At the SITE OF THE WIGWAM CONVENTION HALL, 200 E. Main St., marked by a plaque, the State Republican Convention convened on May 9, 1860, to decide which candidate Illinois would support at the forthcoming national convention. John Hanks, cousin of Lincoln, was present with several fence rails that were placarded "from a lot of 3,000 made in 1830 by Thos. Hanks and Abe Lincoln." With little ceremony the convention passed the following resolution:

That Abraham Lincoln is the choice of the Republican part of Illinois for the Presidency, and the delegates from this State are instructed to use all honorable means to secure his nomination by the Chicago Convention, and to vote as a unit for him.

The DECATUR CIVIC ART INSTITUTE BUILDING (*open, 2-5, 7-9 weekdays; 2-6 Sun.*), NE. corner W. Main St. at Pine St., was constructed in 1863 as the home of James Millikin University. The two-and-a-half-story structure of red brick is set in a wide expanse of lawn. The interior of the building is finished entirely in walnut, and original furnishings of the Millikin home are still in use.

Three rooms and the hallway on the first floor are used for exhibiting visiting collections of etchings, lithographs, and paintings. Permanent exhibits of the Institute include *Grandmother*, by Eugene Speicher; *Indian Girl in Blue Wrap*, by Robert Henri; and *Apples* by Emil Carlsen. A large part of the collection is largely of local interest; portraits of local figures done by local artists, and the work of students in secondary schools. In the southeast room on the second floor is a stationery box used by Charles Dickens and a letter written by him. In the southwest room is a stamp collection of the Decatur Philatelic Society. The northeast room houses a small collection of vases and statuary.

JAMES MILLIKIN UNIVERSITY, 1100 block on W. Main St., which supplements an excellent city educational system, was named for James Millikin, Decatur business pioneer, whose initial gift of $200,000 and a tract of land encouraged the founding of the school in 1902. Citizens added $100,000, and the Illinois-Indiana-Iowa Presbyterian synod gave a like amount. The dedicatory speech in 1903 was delivered by Theodore Roosevelt.

The small hills and valleys of Millikin's 35-acre campus offer a pleasing vista. The structures are widely spaced, interspersed with winding walks and expanses of well-tended lawns, and flanked by old shade trees. The three buildings of the original group, of Elizabethan design, are connected by corridors and appear as one. LIBERAL ARTS BUILDING opens on the west into ENGINEERING HALL and on the east into HOUSEHOLD ARTS HALL. Directly north is MACHINERY HALL, which contains a foundry and shops. ANSON HALL, the women's dormitory, the ORVILLE B. GORIN LIBRARY, the UNIVERSITY GYMNASIUM, and the MILLIKIN CONSERVATORY OF MUSIC were all added later, but preserve a style consonant with the original group. In addition to the usual college courses, advanced study in music is offered. Approximately 500 students were enrolled in 1938.

FAIRVIEW PARK, McClelland and W. Eldorado Sts., comprises 180 acres. On a slight eminence in the southwest section stands the LINCOLN LOG CABIN COURTHOUSE (open, 8-5). Originally built at the southwestern edge of what is now Lincoln Square, in the heart of Decatur's business district, the cabin passed into the hands of the Decatur Park District, was restored, and moved to its present site.

This was the first courthouse in Macon County; its construction was started in 1829. John Hanks, cousin of Abraham Lincoln's mother, received $9.87 for "chinking and daubing" the building. Two stories high, it is constructed of notched, hewn logs, chinked with concrete, and has a concrete and stone foundation. After 1839, when a new courthouse was built, the old structure was used as church, school, and a camping place for movers. At present it is used for Boy Scout Meetings, and is not furnished in the period.

The A. E. STALEY MANUFACTURING COMPANY PLANT (open 9-4 except Sundays; guides furnished), N. 22nd and E. Eldorado Sts., comprises the administration building and 40 other buildings on a 380-acre tract. The 14-story administration building, rising 206 feet, is built of Indiana limestone, with gold-crowned dome, bronze doors, and bronze exterior trimmings. Completed in 1929, it was designed by Aschauer and Waggoner of Decatur. The lighted building is visible for miles at night, and the changing colors are so striking that cars frequently line the adjacent State highway. White lights are thrown on the building, then an almost imperceptible shade of pastel pink is added, changing slowly to red; two huge pillars become a powder blue; then the lights dim, and the dome appears, as emerging from a thinning mist, in green or gold. The plant normally employs 1,600 workers, and operates 24 hours daily, producing starches, unmixed corn syrups, crude corn sugar, gluten feed, germ meal, crude and refined corn oil, soy bean meal, soy bean flour and oil, and soy bean sauce.

LAKE DECATUR, on the Sangamon River, SE. edge of the city, has 12 miles of shoreline drive. Decatur organized a stock company and spent $1,000,000 damming lazy Sangamon River, creating a lake 13 miles long and a half mile wide, which impounds eight billion gallons of water. The lake, with its natural setting, provides Decatur with facilities for sail-boating, swimming, and fishing not available elsewhere in the vicinity; it is spanned by several bridges.

POINTS OF INTEREST IN ENVIRONS

Site of First Lincoln Home in Illinois, 12 *m.* (*see Tour* 21).

EAST ST. LOUIS

Railroad Stations: Relay Depot, 14 Missouri Ave., for Alton R. R., Baltimore & Ohio R. R., Burlington R. R., Cleveland, Cincinnati, Chicago & St. Louis Ry. (Big Four), Illinois Central System, Louisville & Nashville R. R., Missouri Pacific Lines, Mobile and Ohio R. R., Pennsylvania R. R., St. Louis Southwestern Railway Lines (Cotton Belt Route) and Southern Railway System; Nickel Plate Station, Spring Ave. and Front St., for New York, Chicago and St. Louis R. R. (Nickel Plate). (More frequent service on most lines at Union Station, 18th and Market Sts., St. Louis, Mo.)

Steamboat Landing: Foot of Eads Bridge in St. Louis for local excursion lines.

Airports: Curtiss Airport, 2 m. S. of city and E. of State 3, for American Air Lines to Chicago daily during summer; Parks Airport, 3 m. S. on State 3, sightseeing only.

Bus Stations: 505 Missouri Ave., for Greyhound, Egyptian Motor Lines, Jacksonville Bus Lines, and St. Louis-Red Bud-Chester Bus Co.; 500 Missouri Ave. for Santa Fe Trailways, Vandalia Bus Line, and De Luxe Motor Stages; 628 Missouri Ave., for Illinois Terminal System and St. Clair Bus Line.

Local Buses: Intra-city rate, 2 tokens for 15c; to St. Louis, 15c.

Taxis: 10c per person anywhere within city limits.

Accommodations: 10 hotels.

Information Service: Chamber of Commerce, 8th floor, Spivey Bldg.

Radio Station: WTMV (1500 kc.).

Motion Picture Houses: 15.

Swimming: Lake Park, 43rd St. and Lake Drive; Jones Park, 25th St. and Lynch Ave.; Lincoln Park (Negro), 16th St. and Piggott Ave.

Boating: Jones Park; canoes 50c per hr., rowboats 25c per hr.

Fishing: Lake No. 3, Lake Park.

Golf: 18-hole municipal course, Lake Park.

Tennis: Jones Park; Lincoln Park (Negro).

Trapshooting: Jones Park, free, apply Park Board Office, 10th St. and Missouri Ave.

Horse-racing: September meet at Fairmont Jockey Club, 4 m. N. of city on US 40, pari-mutuel betting.

Annual Events: Lady of the Lake Festival, water carnival and historical pageant, at Lake Park, several evenings in early autumn.

EAST ST. LOUIS (418 alt., 74,347 pop.), railroad and industrial center, lies opposite St. Louis, Mo., on the Mississippi flood plain known as the American Bottom. Steep bluffs rise several miles east, but within the city there are neither hills nor valleys. Warehouses and railroad yards crowd the riverfront. At the northwest is one of the country's largest stockyards, its borders outlined by huge packing plants. Mills manufacturing iron, steel, glass, aluminum, and some sixty other products sprawl through the south length of the city. Lusty, smoky, and virile, East St. Louis takes more pride in its industries than in any other phase of its civic life.

To thwart overflows that did frequent damage before a system of levees was installed, the main streets were graded from eight to fifteen feet above the flood plain. This accounts for the present pock-marked appearance of the business district, centered at Missouri and Collinsville Avenues. Vacant lots along side streets resemble shallow quarry pits and the roofs of houses that antedate elevation of the streets are but a few feet higher than the pavement. Elsewhere, the streets are built on the ground level, and house foundations are of ordinary height.

Missouri Avenue, from 10th Street southeast to its terminus, is the division point between the Negro and white residential sections. For the most part, the latter lie north of this avenue beyond the area of heavy industry. Architectural styles range from houses of the late 1880's, with mansard roofs, to scores of brick "flats" of pre-World War and contemporary construction. Outnumbering these are conventional frame or brick structures, with gable roofs and wide front porches. The Lansdowne section near Jones Park is beautifully landscaped, but scarcely less attractive is the Alhambra Court neighborhood at 35th and State Streets. The latter street is the main thoroughfare of the white residential area, its four-mile length lined with chain stores, restaurants, filling stations, and automobile repair shops.

Most of the city south of Missouri Avenue and 10th Street, excepting the Alta Sita region on Bond Avenue southeast of 21st Street, is occupied by Negroes, who comprise 15.5 per cent of the population. Negroes have their own schools, churches, grocery stores, and motion picture theaters. Industrial plants have begrimed the section; its sole strip of green is Lincoln Park, 16th Street and Piggott Avenue. An intermixed Negro and foreign born population lives in the "Bad Lands" along Missouri Avenue, between 21st and 31st Streets, while the remnant of a once-sizeable Armenian colony dwells near 16th Street and Broadway.

The farms on the bluffs and bottom land around East St. Louis produce abundant crops almost within the shadow of the industrial plants. At dusk during the harvest season hundreds of trucks laden with corn and vegetables file across the Municipal Bridge to the curb markets of St. Louis. In autumn the farmers' trucks give way to larger vehicles piled high with coal from the mines of southern Illinois. These caravans enliven the city's aspect, but add little to its income. Of much greater consequence are the freight trains that rumble in at all hours, carrying livestock from the West and goods from the East. About 14 per cent of the working population is employed in transportation.

East St. Louis owes its origin to Cahokia, the historic village several miles south of the city, where the French established an Indian mission in 1699. Cahokia became the chief trading center on the Illinois frontier in the eighteenth century, and then declined quickly as the result of floods and the commercial rivalry of St. Louis. Although an attempt at settlement opposite St. Louis had been made in 1770 by Richard "English" McCarty, the first permanent foothold was gained by Capt. James Piggott some 25 years later when he established a ferry service across the Mississippi. The ferry helped hasten settlement of the region. In 1816 McKnight and Brady, St. Louis land operators, auctioned lots in Illinoistown, a newly platted village near the ferry station.

Aided by the westward flow of pioneers and the rise of steamboat commerce, Illinoistown's permanence was further secured through an early development of natural resources. Coal deposits in the nearby bluffs were mined in 1837 by a company organized by ex-Governor John Reynolds. The coal was freighted to the river in cars drawn by horses along wooden rails; some historians cite this contrivance as the first railroad in Illinois. The first steam railroad from the East was the Ohio and Mississippi, in July 1855, followed in a decade by ten other lines. All terminated at Illinoistown, connected with St. Louis by the Wiggins Company ferries, which had replaced Capt. Piggott's crude *pirogues*. Freight handling became Illinoistown's chief economic function.

Although the plat of Illinoistown was recorded in 1818, the town was not incorporated until January 1859. Several months later a town named East St. Louis was platted northeast of Illinoistown. In 1861 the State legislature presented a new charter to Illinoistown, proposing that its corporate limits be extended and its name changed to East St. Louis. The charter was approved in a bitterly contested referendum, and Illinoistown, in growing larger, lost the name it had borne for almost half a century.

The opening of the Eads Bridge to rail traffic in 1874 impaired the ferry business but did not destroy it. Continuous rail passage was limited to certain roads, and the majority of companies, rather than pay heavy tolls for each box car sent over the bridge, used ferries or wagon vans. The construction of the Municipal Bridge in 1917 afforded cross-river passage to all railroads, but by that time warehouses and miles of track had been built at the East St. Louis riverfront. Today many railroads still break carload lots into bulk at East St. Louis and transport the goods to St. Louis by motor trucks. Ferry boats are no longer used.

Because of its low site on the flood plain, East St. Louis has been constantly threatened by the Mississippi. The severest flood on record was that of 1844 when the American Bottom was so completely inundated that a steamboat was able to load a cargo of coal at the bluffs east of the present city. To ward off possible disaster, John B. Bowman, many times mayor of East St. Louis, proposed in 1870 that the streets be elevated above the 1844 high-water mark. The city split into vociferous camps of "High-Graders" and "Low-Graders"; the latter group charged that the "High-Graders" were the cat's-paw of profit-hungry construction companies. After considerable bickering the "high-grade" was established by the city council in 1875.

During the last decades of the nineteenth century, East St. Louis declined as a river town and gradually assumed its present industrial profile. Then, on May 27, 1896, a tornado struck the city, demolishing the business district, killing more than 100 people. Buildings were splintered, fires raged unchecked, and the entire east approach of the Eads Bridge was ripped away. With the aid of a $90,000 relief fund contributed by neighboring communities, East St. Louis entered the new century with the scars of this calamity effaced.

The opening years of the twentieth century brought an era of great industrial expansion to East St. Louis. New industries created jobs faster than houses could be built for incoming workers. Although 2,600 new dwellings went up in 1903, an acute housing shortage existed and more than a thousand workers were forced to commute between St. Louis and East St. Louis.

In June 1903, despite frantic efforts of levee workers, the swollen Mississippi poured into East St. Louis, flooding one-fourth of the city. Eight thousand refugees were housed in St. Louis; although no lives were lost, the flood was a bitter reminder that the problem of control had not been solved by "high-grade" streets and the construction of a few makeshift levees. Public demand for protection resulted in the formation of the East Side Levee and Sanitary District in 1907. The levees and canals built by that agency have sent subsequent floods swirling harmlessly past the city.

During pre-World War years the foreign and Negro population, drawn by the city's rapid industrial growth, became important elements in political and labor struggles. Negroes were used as strike breakers in at least one instance. Competition for jobs sharpened racial prejudices and fanned the mob spirit. Race riots of shocking ferocity occurred on May 28 and on July 2, 1917, when more than 100 Negroes were killed. Property damage exceeded $400,000. Seven thousand panic-stricken Negroes fled to St. Louis where they were quartered in the municipal lodginghouse. An investigation by a committee of the House of Representatives found much municipal corruption, and the electorate abandoned the aldermanic for the commission form of government on November 5, 1917.

POINTS OF INTEREST

The 640-acre NATIONAL STOCKYARDS, main entrance at First St. and St. Clair Ave., is one of the largest in the country. It has a daily capacity of 5,000 horses and mules, 25,000 sheep, 25,000 cattle, and 50,000 hogs. About 8 per cent of East St. Louis' working population is employed in herding, processing, and merchandising livestock. Although considered a part of East St. Louis, the stockyards are actually in National City (pop. 262). When the yards were opened in 1873, an agreement was concluded whereby East St. Louis was restrained from future attempts to annex the area.

Of the several packing houses in the yards, the two major plants are those of Armour and Company (*1 hr. tours, 9; 10; 11; 1; 2; Tues.-Sat.*), and Swift and Company (*1 hr. tours, 9:30; 10:30; 1:30; 2:30; Tues.-Sat.*) The tours conducted by the two plants are similar. In the Swift plant the tour begins in the beef-boning department and continues through the beef-cooling house, thence to the fourth floor, from which point there is an excellent view of the yards. On this floor cattle are slaughtered with amazing speed and dexterity. Passing from the abattoir the visitor enters successively the sheep cleaning, paper-box, and bacon departments, the smoke-house, the refrigeration room, and finally the loading dock.

The EAST ST. LOUIS LEVEE parallels the Mississippi between the villages of Mitchell on the north and East Carondelet on the south. The embankment is part of the drainage and flood control system maintained by the East Side Levee and Sanitary District. Two drainage canals, flanked with levees built of the excavated earth, extend from the extremities of the Mississippi levee to bluffs at the east. The area thus enclosed is 96 square miles. The levees rise 45 feet above the low water mark of 1860 and provide a 3.6 foot margin of safety against the highest authentically recorded stage of the river, 41.4 feet in 1844. The total cost of the system exceeded that of the Galveston Sea Wall.

BLOODY ISLAND is bounded by Front St., Spring Ave., Trendley Ave., and the approach to the Eads Bridge. This area, now occupied by freight terminals and warehouses, was formerly an island in the Mississippi. The island, a sandbar that shouldered its way above the water in the early nineteenth century, soon grew to be a mile in length and about 500 yards wide. Its dense willows and cottonwoods made it a favorite arena for illegal boxing bouts, cock fights, and duels. The most tragic combat was that between Maj. Thomas Biddle and Spencer Pettis, member of the 21st Congress. Armed with pistols and stationed but five feet apart, the men killed each other here on August 25, 1831.

As Bloody Island continued to enlarge, the Mississippi was diverted from the Missouri shore and the St. Louis harbor became dangerously shallow. Urged by alarmed St. Louisans, Congress appropriated funds in 1836 for the construction of diversion dikes. Under the supervision of Robert E. Lee, then a lieutenant, a dike was built between the upstream tip of the island and the Illinois shore; another was built from the downstream end of the island. The current was consequently deflected toward the Missouri side, the St. Louis harbor rapidly deepened, and in time the space between Bloody Island and the mainland was filled with silt. In reward for his work, Lee received a captain's commission.

Charles Dickens, the novelist, saw Bloody Island in 1842 and afterwards wrote in *American Notes:* "Bloody Island . . . so designated in honor of the last fatal combat fought there, which was with pistols, breast to breast. Both combatants fell dead upon the ground; and possibly some rational people may think . . . that they were no great loss to the community."

EADS BRIDGE, named for its builder, James B. Eads (1820-87), spans the Mississippi between Washington Ave., St. Louis, and Broadway, East St. Louis. Completed in 1874 after five years' work, the Eads Bridge was one of the engineering marvels of its day. It marked the first use of steel in a truss-bridge and embodied the longest fixed-end metal arch in the world. In building the piers on bedrock under the river, Eads was the first engineer in America to employ the compressed-air caisson. Twelve workmen lost their lives in the air chambers. Other caisson-workers wore bands of zinc and silver to ward off attacks of the then mysterious "bends."

Hailed by the *Encyclopedia Britannica* (1875) as the "finest example of a metal arch yet erected," the Eads Bridge still merits a share of that description. Contrasted with the other bridges across the Mississippi at St. Louis, it appears to skip lightly where they stoop and plod. The central arch is 520 feet long, the two others are 18 feet shorter. The upper deck is used by vehicles and pedestrians; the lower deck—screened by diagonals—carries railroad traffic.

MUNICIPAL BRIDGE *(private cars 10¢, commercial cars, 15¢)*, Illinois approach at 10th St. and Piggott Ave., is one of the largest double-deck steel span bridges in the world. Its overall length is about two miles; the main span is 668 feet long. Approximately 70 per cent of the vehicle traffic between St. Louis and East St. Louis is borne by this structure. Owned by the city of St. Louis, the bridge was completed in 1917 at a cost of $6,000,000.

JONES PARK, a 128-acre tract centered at 25th St. and Lynch Ave., has an aviary, picnic grounds, 6 athletic fields, 10 tennis courts, children's playgrounds, a swimming pool, a lagoon for boating, and a trap-shooting range. Argonne Drive, the park's principal thoroughfare, branches east from 25th St., past extensive flower beds to the parking lot. Immediately south is a large lily pond, shaded by Lombardy poplars.

LAKE PARK, 43rd St. and Lake Dr., comprises 1,110 acres of what was formerly swampland. The site was purchased by the East St. Louis Park Board in 1927. Its subsequent development has been financed in part by agencies of the Federal government. At present the park contains three lakes, a fish hatchery, and an 18-hole golf course. Plans for completion include a 9-mile bridle path, tennis courts, athletic fields, a grandstand, a boathouse, and a pavilion.

Lake No. 1, NW. corner of the park, is used for boating; Lake No. 2, entered by Kingshighway, for swimming; Lake No. 3, largest and southernmost of the group, for fishing. The densely wooded island at the center of Lake No. 3 will serve as a picnic grounds. The FISH HATCHERY *(open daily, 8 until sundown),* on Lake Dr. near 59th St., supplies Lake No. 3 with bass, crappie, sunfish, and bluegills.

POINTS OF INTEREST IN ENVIRONS

Old Church of the Holy Family and the Jarrot Mansion, 3.9 *m.* (*see Tour 8*). Cahokia Mounds State Park, 6.3 *m.* (*see Tour 19A*).

ELGIN

Railroad Stations: 156 Douglas Ave. for Chicago & North Western Ry.; W. side of river at foot of Chicago St. bridge for Chicago, Milwaukee, St. Paul and Pacific R. R.; 3 E. Chicago St. for Chicago, Aurora, and Elgin R. R. (electric).

Bus Stations: Union Motor Coach Station, 9 N. Grove Ave., for Northland Greyhound Lines and Fox Valley Coach Line.

City Buses: 5c fare, transfer 1c.

Accommodations: Three hotels.

Information Service: Elgin Motor Club, 109 S. Grove Ave. and Elgin Association of Commerce, 164 Division St.

Golf: Municipal links, Wing Park, on Wing Blvd., 9 holes, daily fee.

Swimming: Wing Park, South Elgin Quarry Pool on State 31, and Y.M.C.A., 2 E. Chicago St.

Tennis: Municipal courts at Wing Park and at Lord's Park, E. end of Park Ave.

Annual Events: Elgin Industries Week, second week in May; Elgin Agricultural Fair and Old Settlers' Picnic, latter part of August; motor boat races on Fox River, Labor Day.

ELGIN (717 alt., 35,929 pop.), an industrial town in the midst of wide farmlands, lies on the gentle bluffs of the Fox River. Although only an hour's ride from Chicago, Elgin is sufficiently self-contained so that only 2 per cent of her wage earners commute to Chicago, and yet her industrial plants are not of the sort that cluster in an industrial wasteland. A few blocks from Fountain Square—described by Elgin wits as a triangle without a fountain—rises the city's major factory, while some of the finest houses are no greater distance down other radial streets. Concerned with more than industry, Elgin possesses an excellent art museum, a small zoo, and an extensive park system. "A midwest factory town," remarked an anonymous Boston reporter, "is not the place where one would ordinarily look for such things."

To Protestant ministers throughout the country, Elgin is the source of many of their Sunday School pamphlets; to Emerson Hough it is the city in which he wrote *The Covered Wagon;* to midwestern creameries it is the place their butter-tubs come from; but Elgin is known to the world at large as the manufacturer of the watches that bear the city's name. The seven-story clock tower of the watch factory, visible for miles, rises high above the central section, and the factory with its related industries employs the major portion of the city's workers.

The Black Hawk War was over when the first settlers, James and

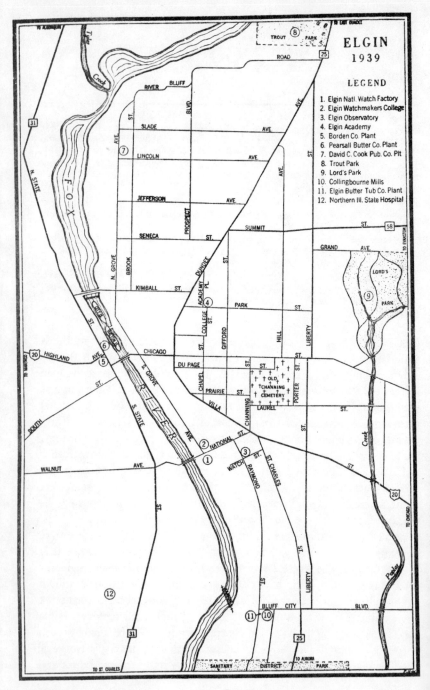

ELGIN
1939

LEGEND

1. Elgin Natl. Watch Factory
2. Elgin Watchmakers College
3. Elgin Observatory
4. Elgin Academy
5. Borden Co. Plant
6. Pearsall Butter Co. Plant
7. David C. Cook Pub. Co. Plt
8. Trout Park
9. Lord's Park
10. Collingbourne Mills
11. Elgin Butter Tub Co. Plant
12. Northern Ill. State Hospital

Hezekiah Gifford, came here from New York in 1835. An Indian ferried them over the Fox River on their way here, but by the following year northern Illinois was cleared of the red men, and the Giffords built up their little settlement without interference. Intent upon having the Chicago-Galena stage routed past his cabin, James Gifford laid out a road, with the assistance of Samuel Kimball, to Belvidere. "Anyone would think," scoffed his wife, "that you expected this farm to become a city, with stagecoaches going through." Within a year they were, twice weekly, with a great blare of horns.

Elgin's industry from the first was bound to the river. Kimball and James Gifford co-operated again in 1837 in damming the river, and a sawmill was built on one side and a gristmill on the other. Hezekiah occupied himself running a tavern for the stagecoach passengers, who noted with "astonishment" that he ran it according to the new-fangled temperance plan then gaining strength in the East.

In 1838 B. W. Raymond purchased a portion of Gifford's tract, and although he lived in Chicago and served as its third mayor, soon interested himself in the development of Elgin. Throughout the forties he invested in several local enterprises, and by 1847 Elgin was able to incorporate as a village. The following year Raymond, by pledging much of his property, had the Chicago and Galena Railroad routed into Elgin. For two years the village was the terminus of that road, and the great stream of west-bound pioneers here transferred to covered wagons. In 1854 Elgin was incorporated as a city.

Elgin began to ship milk to Chicago in 1852, and soon processed a growing surplus into cheese and butter. The city's importance as a dairying center was greatly enhanced by Gail Borden. During his youth he had observed the difficulty encountered by Western travelers in transporting food and began experimenting with condensed foods. Following a stormy trans-Atlantic voyage, during which the ship's cows refused to give milk, he concentrated on condensed milk, and soon had a successful plant running in Elgin. By 1875 it was using the milk from a thousand cows, and the product was being hawked from push-carts in New York and other metropolitan centers.

The watch industry came here in 1866, and by the application of new principles of manufacture soon rivaled dairying. Adopting much the same methods that Ford later used in the automobile industry, the Elgin plant standardized parts and introduced a modified assembly-line whereby craftsmen ceased to be watch-makers and became watch-workers. Low prices had widened the market, and the plant began to turn out thousands of watches monthly.

The booming dairy trade resulted in the formation of a local Board of Trade, in 1872, and for forty years Elgin served as the Midwest marketing center. The Board was an important factor in setting the national prices of butter and cheese; the Elgin *Dairy Report* bore the slogan "Elgin makes the price—We tell you what it is." The peak year for cheese was 1883, when board members marketed 12,500,000 pounds; in 1911 they reached a high in butter sales with 57,000,000 pounds. During the World War the Food Administration requested the Board to suspend operations, and after the Armistice it was not reorganized.

Because of changes in transportation, Elgin no longer manufactures butter, but some 5,000,000 pounds of milk are handled annually, half of it as fluid milk for Chicago, the rest processed as dried and malted milk or used in the manufacture of margarine, mayonnaise, and spreads.

In 1935 the city celebrated the beginning of its second century. A reproduction of James Gifford's log cabin was built, and descendants of the founders told stories of pioneer life. One of the floats in the parade carried an old Frink and Walker stagecoach of the type that James Gifford, laying out his road to Belvidere a century before, had hoped could be lured past his little log cabin.

POINTS OF INTEREST

1. The ELGIN NATIONAL WATCH FACTORY (*reception room only open, 8-4*), National St. and Grove Ave., is set in spacious landscaped grounds along the Fox River. In the reception room is displayed every model produced, from the first in 1867, a railroad movement named the B. W. Raymond for the company's first president, through the key-winders of the late sixties, down to the current models. The factory interior, which has a special dust-removal system, resembles a huge watch itself, what with the whir of belting, miles of shafting, and the myriad wheels running in precise synchrony to the master ticks transmitted from the observatory. Much of the work is done under high-powered lenses, because some of the screws used are so small that 20,000 would barely fill a thimble. Weighing a pencil mark on a piece of paper would be a comparatively rough operation

for some of the balances employed. The plant has produced more than 40,000,000 watches since its establishment.

2. The ELGIN WATCHMAKERS COLLEGE (*open to members of the trade only*), 267 S. Grove Ave., was established in the 1920's in response to a demand for skilled watch-makers, particularly in repair departments of jewelry stores. A non-profit institution controlled by the Elgin National Watch Company, it provides training in clockmaking, watchmaking, engraving, and jewelry work. The courses of 12 to 15 months' duration teach the drawing of patterns, toolmaking, and the manufacture of parts. Every type of clock and watch a watch-maker would be called upon to service is available.

3. The ELGIN OBSERVATORY (*apply Elgin National Watch Company for permit*), Watch and Raymond Sts., is housed in a small white stone building that caps a green hill. The observatory was built in 1909 by the Elgin Company to obtain sidereal time for the regulation of Elgin watches. From a list of 800 fixed stars, 10 or 12 are chosen nightly, and are followed across the heavens. An automatic electric recording device graphs time on a revolving drum. Variations of one-thousandth of a second in the master clocks can be checked. These clocks, of the Riefler type, are mounted on a concrete pier, separate from the building, in vacuum glass cases maintained at a temperature varying not more than one-tenth of a degree from 85° F. Secondary clocks relay the impulses by which workers time watches in the factory. A direct line conveys the impulses to the Chicago office of the company in the Pure Oil Building, where they are relayed to radio stations, utility companies, and other agencies requiring exact time.

4. The ELGIN ACADEMY, Park and College Sts., one of the oldest preparatory schools in Illinois, was chartered in 1839 but did not open until 1856. The spacious campus is on the highest ground in the city, and the academy is popularly referred to as "The School on the Hill." The curriculum includes a two-year junior college course. Only boys are boarded, but girls may enroll as day students. The main building, a three-story Greek Revival structure, was built in 1855.

The LAURA DAVIDSON SEARS ACADEMY OF FINE ARTS (*open 2-5 daily except Mon.*), a Georgia marble building with Doric columns, is an adjunct to the academy. The bulk of its exhibits were drawn from the private collection of the late Judge Nathaniel Sears, donor of the building. Some 250 canvases hang in five rooms, four of them devoted to American artists, arranged chronologically. There is a Gilbert Stuart equestrian portrait of Washington, and one by Charles Wilson Peale (c. 1770) picturing Washington in the uniform of a British colonel. Others include a portrait by Samuel Morse, who gave up painting when forty years old to tinker with telegraphy, Whistler's *On the Beach at Ostend,* and work by John Singleton Copley and Winslow Homer. The small but distinguished foreign gallery has a representative collection of the Barbizon School, and several paintings by early Italian masters, including Parmigiano and Bellini. Rosa Bonheur's *An Old Buffalo* was painted when "Buffalo Bill" Cody took his Wild West show to France.

5. The BORDEN COMPANY PLANT, 16 N. State St., erected in 1911, is one of the largest malted milk and dried milk plants in the country.

6. The PEARSALL BUTTER COMPANY PLANT (*tours by advance arrangement*), 31 N. State St., is one of the few plants still using the water power of the Fox River. Formerly a major factor in the production of Elgin butter, and purchaser of the entire output of 300 dairy farms, the firm now manufactures butter at branch plants elsewhere, and at Elgin produces mayonnaise, margarines and similar products.

7. The DAVID C. COOK PUBLISHING COMPANY PLANT (*tours by advance arrangement*), Grove and Lincoln Aves., has 13 acres of one-story buff brick units. Publishers of 37 religious periodicals and many pamphlets, with an annual production of over 100,000,-000 copies, and distributors of 7,000 mail order items, ranging from handkerchiefs to clocks and razor blades, the company accounts for half the income of the Elgin postoffice.

8. TROUT PARK, on State 25 at the NE. city limits, was a trout preserve on a private estate before it was acquired by the city in 1922. A large portion of its 57 acres is purposely untended, save for the paths that make it accessible. Trees blown down by the great storm of 1920 lie where they fell, clothed now in mosses and ferns. Throughout, the section is substantially as it was found by the pioneers. Many of the trees are tagged, and botanical classes from the University of Chicago and elsewhere frequently use the park as an outdoor laboratory.

9. LORD'S PARK, E. end of Park Ave., 110 acres in extent, was given to the city by Mr. and Mrs. G. P. Lord in 1892. Poplar Creek,

which winds through the park, has been dammed to produce lagoons on three levels, willow-shaded and connected by splashing little falls. The small Zoo, containing monkeys, black bears, coyotes, deer, raccoons, and snakes, was built into the side of a bluff, so that the animals may be viewed from above as well as from cage level. The AUDUBON MUSEUM *(open 1-5 daily during summer months)* contains a varied collection of mounted animals, including both American and foreign specimens, and historical relics associated with the pioneer history of the Fox Valley region.

10. The COLLINGBOURNE MILLS *(apply at office)*, Grace St. just off Bluff City Blvd., employ about 500 mill-workers in the spinning of silk, wool, and rayon threads and yarns.

11. The ELGIN BUTTER TUB COMPANY PLANT *(apply at office)*, Bluff City Blvd. and Raymond St., ships five carloads of tubs daily during the peak months. One of the by-products, a fine wood dust known as "flour," is sold to manufacturers of bakelite and linoleum.

12. The NORTHERN ILLINOIS STATE HOSPITAL *(9-11:30 and 1-4:30 for friends of patients only)* occupies 820 acres bordering S. State St. at the southern city limits. The three-story main building, opened in 1872 for 300 patients, now serves as the nucleus of a group of buildings housing 4,600 mental cases. The institution applies occupational therapy in its attempt to cure rather than merely incarcerate its patients.

POINTS OF INTEREST IN ENVIRONS

Yeoman City of Childhood, 4 *m.;* Illinois Pet Cemetery, 8.7 *m. (see Tour* 11).

EVANSTON

Railroad Stations: Main St. and Custer Ave., Dempster St. and Sherman Ave., Davis St. and Maple Ave., Central St. and Green Bay Road for Chicago and North Western Ry.

Interurban Stations: North Shore Line, running between Chicago and Milwaukee, five stations; Rapid Transit Line (elevated) to Chicago, nine stations.

Bus Stations: 305 Howard St. for Greyhound.

Local Buses: 7c fare.

Taxis: 5c to 15c per half mile.

Accommodations: 12 hotels.

Information Services: Chamber of Commerce, 518 Davis St.; Chicago Motor Club, 1011 Davis St.; Illinois Automobile Club, 1233 Chicago Ave.

Street Directions: Avenues and Courts run N. and S., Streets and Places E. and W.

Motion Picture Houses: Three.

Golf: Community course, 9 holes, Central St. and the canal, 50c fee.

Tennis: Bent Park, Central St. and Hastings Ave.; Ackerman Park, Central St. and McDaniels Ave.; Mason Park, Hamilton St. at Lake Michigan; Foster Park, Foster St. and Dewey Ave.; Leahy Park, Central St. and Simpson St.

Swimming: Free beaches at foot of Greenwood St. and of Davis St. Five fee beaches.

Annual Events: North Shore Music Festival, Dyche Stadium, variable date in May.

EVANSTON (601 alt., 63,338 pop.), fronting largely on Lake Michigan, and with an extension stretching westward at the northern edge of the city, is roughly L-shaped. It is the first of the North Shore suburbs, divided from Chicago only by Calvary Cemetery. Although its development hinged somewhat on the tremendous expansion of Chicago, Evanston retains a distinct individuality and runs a temperature at being referred to as an off-shoot of that city. Aristocratic and self-sufficient, it considers its proximity to Chicago little more than a geographic accident. In appearance it is almost an Illinois anomaly, the dignity and spaciousness of its residential districts contrasting sharply with the noisy, virile metropolis on the south. Untouched by the peculiar tumult that Sandburg calls the "harr and boom" of the early 1900's, Evanston felt no need to conform its city plan to the intense concentration of the new industrial age. The through traffic boulevard system that traverses Chicago's lakeside parks stops short at the threshold of Evanston. Here the lake front is given over to quiet streets that wind through small parks and past brick walls enclosing spacious city estates.

Despite its rather sentimental regard for the narrower streets of the pre-automobile era, Evanston has been able to maintain an amazing traffic-safety record; in 1936 it had been named America's safest city in three of the four preceding years. Its system offers no formula, and functions by scrutinizing each general type of traffic problem closely and applying the best research methods to its solution. From 42 traffic deaths per 100,000 in 1928, the rate was reduced to 2.9 in 1935, in spite of the heavy burden of through traffic to the suburbs farther north. The Traffic Safety Institute, established at Northwestern University in 1932, works with and helps train the city police.

Pere Marquette and his Indian companions landed in 1674 in the natural harbor formed by the 25-foot bluff now named Grosse Point. Marquette's diary has an account of the incident and a sketch of his fleet of ten canoes drawn up on the sands. In pioneer days, as lake traffic increased, Grosse Point assumed some importance as a port, and a village grew up around it, settled by those who followed the inland seas. For some time a faint maritime atmosphere clung to the community; a number of families at the present time trace their descent from the early Great Lakes captains.

The first dwelling on the "Point" was built in 1826, but it was not until 1854, the year before Northwestern University opened, that the town was platted. At that time it was renamed Evanston, honoring John Evans, one of the university founders and a prominent early citizen. The subsequent blend of the maritime (enhanced by the Grosse Point lighthouse) and the academic, won Evanston the sobriquet of "the finest New England village in the Middlewest."

In the year 1855 Northwestern University opened, after its founding fathers had considered Chicago sites and rejected them. Although it was under the control of the Methodist Episcopal Church, the school proclaimed that it was "not intended to be sectarian, but the minds committed to its care will be induced to the practice of virtue and religion." In its second year the school charter was revised to prohibit the sale of liquor within four miles of the campus (Evanston is still dry). Shortly afterward, in nice coincidence, Frances E. Willard came here with her family from Janesville, Wisconsin. In the following forty years she became Evanston's most famous citizen, serving as Dean of Women and Professor of Æsthetics at Northwestern, and

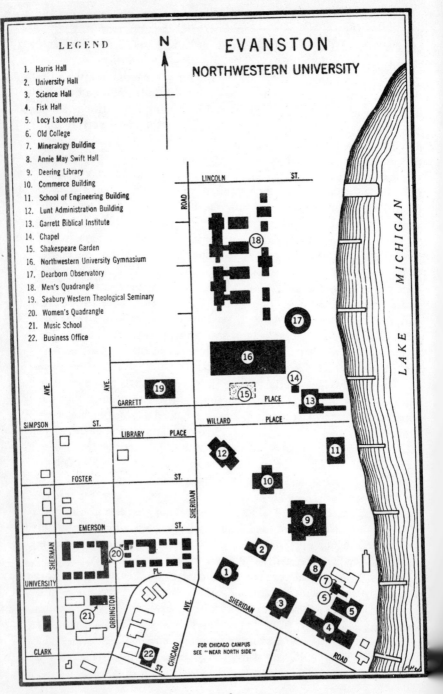

LEGEND

1. Harris Hall
2. University Hall
3. Science Hall
4. Fisk Hall
5. Locy Laboratory
6. Old College
7. Mineralogy Building
8. Annie May Swift Hall
9. Deering Library
10. Commerce Building
11. School of Engineering Building
12. Lunt Administration Building
13. Garrett Biblical Institute
14. Chapel
15. Shakespeare Garden
16. Northwestern University Gymnasium
17. Dearborn Observatory
18. Men's Quadrangle
19. Seabury Western Theological Seminary
20. Women's Quadrangle
21. Music School
22. Business Office

N

EVANSTON

NORTHWESTERN UNIVERSITY

LAKE MICHIGAN

LINCOLN ST.

ROAD

GARRETT PLACE

WILLARD PLACE

SIMPSON ST.

LIBRARY PLACE

AVE.

AVE.

FOSTER ST.

EMERSON ST.

SHERIDAN ST.

SHERMAN

UNIVERSITY

PL.

ORRINGTON AVE.

SHERIDAN

CLARK

CHICAGO ST.

ROAD

FOR CHICAGO CAMPUS
SEE "NEAR NORTH SIDE"

later organizing the World Women's Christian Temperance Union. Among her many writings was a glowing tribute to Evanston, entitled *The Classic Town*.

Early Evanston was a tiny town concerned largely with its university. Twenty-five years after the school was founded Evanston's population was only a scant four thousand, and not until 1892, when it annexed South Evanston, was it incorporated as a city. But after the turn of the century the city began to emerge as a suburb. Already cheap and efficient transportation had welded it economically to Chicago, and the booming of the metropolis could not help but be felt here. From twenty thousand in 1900, the population doubled in twenty years, and then almost doubled again in the decade ending in 1930.

In that last decade the city's economy underwent a sharp change. Today Evanston ranks twelfth among United States cities in per capita retail sales. Although a measure of this is consumed in good living by Evanstonians, the true significance of the statistics is the revealing of Evanston's lately acquired commercial importance. In the twenties large Chicago department stores began establishing branches in Evanston, local stores grew, and new ones were started. Increasingly Evanston has become the shopping center for much of the North Shore. But somehow this development has not greatly changed Evanston's suburban aspects; now and then, among the sleek modern cars of the North Shore shoppers, an archaic electric brougham still sedately whirs its way along.

Northwestern University

Northwestern University extends from Clark Street on the south to Lincoln on the north, and from Sherman Avenue on the west to Lake Michigan. Chartered in 1851 and opened in 1855, Northwestern was among the first institutions of higher learning in the Chicago area. The small group of founders, including Orrington Lunt, Grant Goodrich, and John Evans, were of the Methodist Episcopal faith, but the university is non-denominational. The first class, five in number, was graduated in 1857. The present enrollment of the university is about 12,000, which includes those enrolled on the Chicago campus, the majority of whom attend night classes.

The buildings of the Evanston campus are scattered informally about a wooded sward. Likewise informal is the architecture, from the stodgy red brick Romanesque of the Commerce Building, the eclecticism of Harris Hall, to the exquisite Gothic detail of the Deering Library. Back of the campus spreads Lake Michigan, its shore divided into beaches restricted to the University personnel. The pathways between the beach and the university buildings have an extra-curricular tradition as Lovers' Lanes.

CAMPUS TOUR

(The following walking tour [2 *hours*] begins at the main entrance, Sheridan Road and Chicago Avenue. A guide will be furnished for special groups upon application at the Administration Building. Buildings may be inspected between 8 *a.m.* and 5 *p.m.*)

One of the newer buildings, (1) HARRIS HALL, houses the social studies classes. Nearby rise the grey gables and spires of (2) UNIVERSITY HALL, effectively creating the intellectual atmosphere absent in some of the newer buildings, which are box-like and many windowed. It is given over to the departments of English and geology.

(3) SCIENCE HALL houses the departments of chemistry and physics. Here Winford Lee Lewis, professor of organic research, conducted the research leading to the discovery of lewisite, most deadly of poison gases. Immediately east is (4) FISK HALL, with the departments of classic and romance languages, and of botany.

In (5) LOCY LABORATORY is the department of zoology. Between it and the Mineralogy Building stands (6) OLD COLLEGE, a frame building, oldest on the campus. Its small rooms, still used by the School of Education, are connected by steep, narrow stairways, and lighted by many-paned high windows. In its tower is a huge candle, symbolic of the light of education, which is lighted once a year by the president of the university in a ceremony shared by alumni all over the world, who light similar candles at the same hour.

In (7) the MINERALOGY BUILDING there is a collection of specimens (*open daily during class hours*). The School of Speech, whose founder, John L. Cumnock, was widely known as a pioneer in his field, is in (8) ANNIE MAY SWIFT HALL.

(9) The beautiful new DEERING LIBRARY, from its central location above a sloping lawn known as the Meadows, presides aloofly over the campus. Its plan is an adaptation by James Gamble Rogers of the cathedral style of King's College at Cambridge, and is executed

in white limestone and marble. An interesting and unusual detail of its Gothic design is the omission of gables over the three exquisitely molded and carved arches of the porch, its dominating architectural feature. The entrance doors open into a broad, low-roofed hall, with groined arches decorated in mosaic of delicate colors. Two stairways mount to the second floor, where stained glass, the lofty ceiling and the fine Gothic carvings of the reading room give a grave and ecclesiastical air.

A million dollars of the initial cost of $1,250,000 came from the harvester fortune of the Deering family, who have contributed heavily to the university's endowment funds.

In (10) the red brick COMMERCE BUILDING, once the home of the Garrett Biblical Institute, are the School of Commerce and the Medill School of Journalism. East of this is (11) the SCHOOL OF ENGINEERING BUILDING. In (12) LUNT ADMINISTRATION BUILDING are the president's office and other administrative offices.

Across Willard Place and east toward the lake is (13) GARRETT BIBLICAL INSTITUTE, a school of divinity maintained by the Methodist Episcopal denomination, co-operating without affiliation with the university. The building is an exceptionally fine example of the perpendicular Gothic style of the Tudor period, finished in beautiful detail. On the first floor (L) is the BENNETT MUSEUM OF CHRISTIAN ARCHEOLOGY, with many reproductions of objects of use and beauty of early Christian and pre-Christian eras, vases, amphorae, chalices, and a large group of reliquary panels. To the west of the building is (14) a small CHAPEL, seating only 30, and open day and night for meditation and prayer. Its design is very early English Gothic. The entrance to (15) the famous SHAKESPEARE GARDEN is at the northwest corner of the Institute. Landscaped by Jens Jensen, it was the first in the country planned, like the one at Stratford-on-Avon, to display the flowers and herbs mentioned by Shakespeare in his plays. A double row of hawthorn encloses an oval in which there is an unbroken succession of bloom from earliest spring to fall. At one end is a tiny fountain inscribed with the quatrain from Midsummer Night's Dream beginning:

"I know a bank where the wild thyme blows."

North of the garden rises the great bulk of (16) NORTHWEST-

ERN UNIVERSITY GYMNASIUM. In it is a playing field large enough for football and baseball games, but the University's expansion now taxes even these ample facilities. Here are held the University's basketball games, between stands seating 5,000 spectators.

Behind the gymnasium is (17) DEARBORN OBSERVATORY (*open Thurs. evenings in clear weather*) used by the department of astronomy. Beyond the gymnasium on Sheridan Road is (18) the MEN'S QUADRANGLE, a group of houses for fraternity and non-fraternity men.

Across from the Shakespeare Garden stands (19) SEABURY WESTERN THEOLOGICAL SEMINARY, a handsome group of buildings of rough limestone in modernized Gothic. Offering training for the Episcopal priesthood, it is friendly but not affiliated with Northwestern.

(20) The WOMEN'S QUADRANGLE is bounded by Emerson Street, Sherman Avenue, University Place, and Sheridan Road. Here live the majority of Northwestern's women students, whose traditional beauty has given rise to the description of the university as a seminary that admits male students solely to provide escorts for her beautiful women.

Across University Place is (21) the MUSIC SCHOOL, whose long-time dean, Peter Christian Lutkin, built it into national prominence. At the end of the tour is (22) the BUSINESS OFFICE, which houses the offices of the university's business manager and the trustees' room. Here also is the ticket office for all major athletic events.

OTHER POINTS OF INTEREST

The EVANSTON PUBLIC LIBRARY, 1703 Orrington Ave., built in 1904 after a conventional Roman design, houses the exhibits of the Evanston Art Center, and those of the EVANSTON HISTORICAL SOCIETY MUSEUM (*basement: 1:30-5 weekdays except Sat. 9-12; closed from June 30 to Labor Day*). The society owns a notable body of historical material from Chicago and the North Shore, and scattered items from all over the country.

REST COTTAGE (*open weekdays 9-5 except Sat. 9-12*), 1728-30 Chicago Ave., is also known as the Frances E. Willard Home. A national shrine of the Women's Christian Temperance Union, Rest Cottage was the girlhood home of Frances Willard, second president of the organization and organizer of the World W.C.T.U. On the lawn behind the house, in a three-story brick building, are the national W.C.T.U. headquarters and the school of temperance instruction.

Rest Cottage consists of the Willard family residence, 1728, built in 1865, and No. 1730, which was added somewhat later to accommodate Miss Willard's brother and his family. Inside and outside, the cottage is a survival of another era. Gabled and with vertical weatherboarding instead of the usual horizontal, the house is surrounded by the same vines and shrubs which were planted by Miss Willard's father.

The sitting room of the Willard family has been dedicated to Miss Anna Gordon, Miss Willard's lifelong companion and later world W.C.T.U. president. The room contains, in addition to several pieces of the Willard furniture, a cup and saucer of John Wesley and a pair of earrings worn by Susannah Wesley.

The Willard parlor is at the left of the entrance. Archaic and prim, it appears much as it did in the days of the family's occupancy. Here are portraits of Miss Willard, her parents, her brother, and her sister Mary, whose biography Miss Willard wrote in *Nineteen Beautiful Years*. In the dining room, to the rear, stands the bicycle which Miss Willard learned to ride when she had passed fifty. A banjo clock, dated and signed by Simon Willard, eighteenth century clock-maker of Boston and an ancestor of Miss Willard's, hangs on the wall.

Miss Willard's study, upstairs, is the inner sanctum of the shrine. In an alcove is her ink spotted desk, and her bookshelves, filled with annotated books and faded family photographs. Nearby is the rocker where she held a tablet on her lap while writing her books and speeches. The grandfather's clock, still ticking, was also made by Simon Willard. On the wall is framed a piece of cloth used by Queen Victoria, as a child, for a doll's wrap. An inscription above the fireplace reads, "Let something good be said."

LEVERE MEMORIAL TEMPLE (9-5 *weekdays except Sat.* 9-12; 3-5 *Sun.*), 1856 Sheridan Road, houses the national headquarters of Sigma Alpha Epsilon and serves as a memorial to the fraternity's war dead. To the right of the entrance is a reference library chiefly devoted to fraternity books and publications. The chapel, Gothic and austere, has windows by Tiffany, and an everburning memorial light. The museum, on the second floor, contains S.A.E. relics, among which is the first saxophone owned by Rudy Vallee.

The EVANSTON CRADLE (10-4 *weekdays*), 2039-49 Ridge Ave., occupies three buildings, the newest of which was completed in 1939. Organized in 1923 by Mrs. Florence Walrath and others, the Cradle has become an internationally known child placement agency. The efficiency of its management and its innovations in the care of infants has won it the patronage of many headline names here and abroad; its waiting list usually tops 2,000. Despite its small capacity (28 cribs) by the beginning of 1936 it had admitted 2,904 infants. It is supported by contributions, and among its sponsors, most of whom are social leaders, the annual Cradle Ball is an event of first importance.

The EVANSTON WATER FILTRATION PLANT (*open; 8-5 daily*) is at Sheridan Road and Lincoln Street. Ultra modern and distinctive in appearance, the Evanston plant is widely recognized by engineers as a model of efficiency. Using a system adapted from the tank type domestic filter, it daily treats 75,000,000 gallons of water supplied by submarine pipes from a crib a mile and a quarter off-shore. Visitors are shown the entire process of treatment.

The GROSSE POINT LIGHT HOUSE (*not open*) does much to heighten the New England atmosphere of Evanston. Built in 1860, it was the indirect result of the wreck of the *Lady Elgin,* in which nearly 300 persons lost their lives in the lake off Evanston. In recent years the old Fresnel light, installed in 1874, has been replaced by an electric beacon visible for 20 miles and needing no tender.

The NATIONAL COLLEGE OF EDUCATION, 2770 Sheridan Road was established in 1886 as the Chicago Kindergarten College, and moved to Evanston in 1926 under its present name. It trains teachers for kindergartens, nursery and elementary schools, and also for children's social and religious work. The demonstration school, maintained as a laboratory in child training methods, may be visited by educators.

DYCHE STADIUM, Central St. and Asbury Ave., was named for William A. Dyche, long time business manager of Northwestern. Dedicated in 1926, it was designed by James Gamble Rogers and Gavin Hadden, and has a capacity of 48,000.

POINTS OF INTEREST IN ENVIRONS

Baha'i House of Worship, 3 *m.*; Ravinia Park, 13.9 *m.*; Fort Sheridan, 18.9 *m.*; Great Lakes Naval Training Station, 26.7 m. (*See Tour 2*).

GALENA

Railroad Station: Foot of Bouthillier St. for Illinois Central R. R. and Chicago and North Western Ry.

Bus Station: Main St., between Warren and Green Sts., for Greyhound Lines.

Accommodations: Three hotels, three tourist camps.

Information Service: Galena branch of Chicago Motor Club, S. Main at Perry and Franklin Sts.; American Automobile Assoc., Commerce and Perry Sts.

Motion Picture Theaters: One.

Golf: Galena Golf Club, two miles W. on US 20, nine holes, greens fee $1.00.

Tennis: Grant Park, Park Ave. at Johnson St.

Swimming: Galena Recreational Park, E. side of river near US 20.

For further information, see the *Galena Guide,* another of the American Guide Series, published 1937 by the City of Galena.

GALENA (603 alt., 3,878 pop.), in the extreme northwest corner of the State, perches on the terraces cut by the old Fever River, a novel sight to eyes accustomed to the prairie flatness. Its streets climb tortuously from level to level of the ancient river bed, and the houses cling to the hills like chalets in an Alpine village. Deserted warehouses and granaries line the old course of the river. On the middle slopes the church spires rise above masses of trees along winding cobbled roads; many steep flights of steps climb the bluffs; on the heights is the high school, the clock of which marks the time for the countryside. Typical of the long flights of steps that scale the bluffs are those between Main and Prospect Streets, leading to the high school. In the valley trickles the stream, now called the Galena River, which cut the terraces on which the city is built; its once strong current bore to Galena's wharves the freight of the northwest, but Galena is now the ghost of a metropolis, the relic of the first major industrial development of the region.

The most vivid reminder of Galena's past is its architecture. The diversity of background of Illinois' pioneers brought about the great variety of styles in which they designed their houses and public buildings. Because of this diversity, Illinois has never developed a style distinctively its own, as have most of the eastern seaboard states. But in Galena survive more examples of good American building than perhaps anywhere else in Illinois, a résumé of the nation's architectural experience. Along the terraces of Bench, Prospect, and High Streets, are stately Greek Revival mansions of brick, imposing in size and romantic in setting. On the scrambled byways the range runs from a Cape Cod cottage to a number of tiny Greek temples, both in the Doric order and in the Ionic. New Orleans galleries, colonnaded porticos, iron grilles from French foundries, the forthright gable ends of Pennsylvania, and the double galleries of the Carolinas, all are here. The Victorian era swept over Galena lightly, and the scourge of gingerbread brackets and scrolls so prevalent through newer sections of the State is less virulent here than elsewhere. In the main, the churches hark back to New England, an exception being the Grace Episcopal Church, in early English Gothic style, built of rough gray stone hewn from the hollow in the bluff in which the church is tucked away. The elegance of the De Soto House, a 200-room hotel built in 1855, was unparalleled in the State for many years.

The old air of opulent luxury has mellowed with time to a gentle and decorous decay. The great houses seldom blaze with the festive lights of other years, the once teeming streets are placid now, and the shouts of the roustabouts have long since been stilled on the wharves. Galena is now distinguished among its neighbors mainly by reason of its topography, and for the story of pioneer achievement still documented on its streets.

For more than half a century before the Revolutionary War, when such settlements as existed in the Illinois country were either missions or trading posts, the lead deposits of the Galena district, in what was then called the Fever River Valley, excited the ambition and avarice of the French adventurers. The existence of lead in what is now southern Wisconsin was probably known before the explorations of Marquette and Jolliet, who mentioned it in their reports. The Indians mined it, but were unfamiliar with its use, except as a medium of exchange with the whites. It was of such interest to France that a party of 30 men under Le Sueur and Iberville was sent out in 1699 to investigate. Le Sueur is credited with the discovery of the Galena River in August 1700. He called it the River of Mines, and it was so named on a map published in Paris in 1703 by Delisle, geographer of the French Academy of Sciences. The Galena district was included in John Law's unfortunate promotion scheme of 1717, since known as the Mississippi Bubble. There are accounts of widespread prospecting by an expedition under Phillippe François de Renault in the second or third decade of the eighteenth century. This party, said to have num-

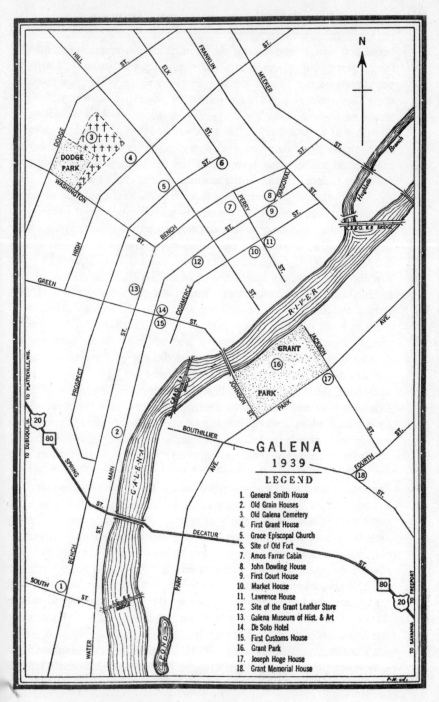

GALENA
1939
LEGEND

1. General Smith House
2. Old Grain Houses
3. Old Galena Cemetery
4. First Grant House
5. Grace Episcopal Church
6. Site of Old Fort
7. Amos Farrar Cabin
8. John Dowling House
9. First Court House
10. Market House
11. Lawrence House
12. Site of the Grant Leather Store
13. Galena Museum of Hist. & Art
14. De Soto Hotel
15. First Customs House
16. Grant Park
17. Joseph Hoge House
18. Grant Memorial House

bered 200 miners and 500 slaves from Santo Domingo, was probably the largest group to come into the region up to that time, when the population of the Illinois country is given as 500. Perhaps some of these men remained and were joined by others, for in 1743 Le Guis wrote of finding along the Fever River 18 or 20 miners, whom he describes as a "fast lot." Although there is little information concerning the next 75 or 80 years, the theory has been advanced that during that period soldiers and trappers of the Mississippi Valley used lead from the Galena district in the manufacture of their bullets.

After years of plundering by these freebooters, Congress passed a statute in 1807, which took the mines under government protection; mineral lands could be occupied and worked only on lease. The opening of steam transportation on the Mississippi River about 1816 spread the fame of the diggings through the land, and the subsequent 15 years saw the transition to a semblance of order. In 1826 the post office was established, the first in northern Illinois, and the town was laid out and named for the sulphide of lead for which the region was noted.

The peak of the Galena rush occurred in 1828 and 1829 when squatters swarmed into the region, and trading became concentrated at what is now Galena. The first lease under the new protective statute was granted in 1822, the first steamer entered the Fever River in 1823, and in the same year the first licensed smelter began operations. That first year's output was 210 tons of metal; production rose rapidly to 27,000 tons in 1845, when Galena produced 83 per cent of the country's supply, which made the town the unchallenged metropolis of the region. River traffic made Galena a trading center also. Many warehouses were built along the river; the retail and wholesale stores which filled the business district in the lowest level of the town were stocked with all the necessaries for every domestic and commercial undertaking. The early thirties saw the beginning of agricultural development, and granaries were built along the river. These granaries ingeniously solved the elevator problem, for wagons simply unloaded from streets level with the top stories into chutes that carried the grain to the water's edge.

The people, largely drawn from Virginia and the South, brought with them the habits and standards of their slave-holding forebears. While other settlements were building log cabins, Galena was erecting the mansions of stone and brick which still mark a high level in America's architectural development. While settlers in other regions were concerned primarily with the struggle for existence, Galena's citizens were building churches and schools, founding a library, publishing the widely read Galena *Gazette*, forming societies for "moral and intellectual development," and altogether living a life unmatched in the Middle Border.

This order of things was not to endure. After the prosperous days of the forties and fifties a gradual decline set in. Galena, like many boom towns, had enjoyed a prosperity based on factors as evanescent as they were brilliant. The lead in the surface veins was finally exhausted; the mines could no longer be operated at a profit. Her supremacy as a market center vanished with the completion of the railroad in 1855, for the road diverted traffic from the river and gave every village through which it passed an advantage equal to that of the city which had so vigorously promoted its construction. The river contributed to the downfall by silting in, and the heavily laden cargo boats of earlier days could no longer navigate the channel. The gold rush to California in 1849 drew off the more adventurous of the mining population, and the town turned slowly from the glamor of fortunes made and lost overnight to the slow processes of farming. The country as a whole fell on evil days with the panic of 1857, and Galena, which had survived an earlier panic untouched, suffered seriously under the national calamity.

With the outbreak of the feeling which led to the Civil War, Galena was divided in its political faith. A large proportion of its citizenry being of Southern origin, it had been definitely a slave-holding community until the adoption of the State Constitution of 1848 put a ban on the ownership and sale of human lives. If the decline of river traffic had not loosened the town's bonds with the South, the situation would have been even more critical. President Lincoln's appeal for troops after the fall of Fort Sumter brought a local crisis; considerable wrangling ensued, but those who favored the Union prevailed, and two companies were formed to support the President.

Ulysses S. Grant, a veteran of the Mexican War, had recently come to Galena from St. Louis. Grant declined the captaincy of one of the Galena companies, but consented to act as drillmaster, and accompanied the troops to Springfield. Six weeks later he was commissioned colonel of the 21st Illinois Volunteers; in August 1861, he was appointed brigadier general. As he came from a State with marked Southern sympathies, his appointment was questioned, but finally confirmed through the influence of his friend, Congressman Washburne.

He rewarded his supporters by appointing eleven of them to high commands in the Union forces, the town's roster of generals surpassing that of any comparable community in the country. Galena's hero eventually led the Federal armies, and brought the town greater glory when he was elected to the Presidency.

Since those days Galena has changed little in appearance. Modern fronts screen 80- and 100-year-old stores; creameries and a cheese factory have replaced the lead smelters; several small manufacturing plants maintain the industrial tradition. But to the visitor Galena is primarily a symbol of life of a century ago when it was a cultural and commercial capital of the old Northwest.

POINTS OF INTEREST

1. The GENERAL SMITH HOUSE (*private*), NW. corner of Bench and South Sts., designed in 1846 by Henry J. Stouffer, is one of Galena's architectural gems. Only one story high, its graceful Ionic portico gleams white against the warm red brick. The spacing of the four fluted columns is noteworthy, and their scrolled capitals are especially graceful. In the interior, the moldings around windows, doors, and fireplaces spread widely at the base in an exaggeration of the ancient Greek treatment. Most unusual feature is the S-scroll newel-post at the foot of the fine walnut staircase.

2. The OLD GRAIN HOUSES, Bench St., almost midway between Spring and Green Sts., now abandoned, once stored much of the grain raised in the Northwest. Built into the cliff between Bench Street on the high level and Main Street below, the unloading platforms were reached by bridges from the former street into the third story of the buildings.

3. The OLD GALENA CEMETERY, Washington St. between High and Dodge Sts., contains the graves of many pioneers, including a number of the Cornish miners who came here in large numbers in the 1830's and 40's. The land was given by Capt. Hezekiah H. Gear, who made a lucky strike in the lead mines after the Black Hawk War, and became the region's wealthiest man; his memory is kept alive by many benefactions.

4. The FIRST GRANT HOUSE (*private*), 121 High St., is a simple two-story brick and stone structure with shuttered windows and a side-lighted doorway. Grant, newly arrived in Galena with his wife and four children, was its first occupant, just before the Civil War.

5. GRACE EPISCOPAL CHURCH, Prospect St. near Hill St., was built in 1847 by C. W. Ottis, a Buffalo, N. Y. architect. Its design is in the early English Gothic style, which was then being revived, concurrently with the Greek. Later it was remodeled by William LeBaron Jenney, father of the skyscraper, at which time the apse was enlarged and the original steeple removed. Simple lancet windows contain stained glass imported from Belgium. The furnishings are of local walnut, and members of the early congregation carved the altar, choir stalls, and lecturn. The one-manual organ, brought from Philadelphia by sailing vessel to New Orleans in 1838 and relayed to Galena by steamboat, was the first in the Middle West.

6. The SITE OF THE OLD FORT, corner of Prospect and Elk Sts., is marked by a boulder placed by the Daughters of the American Revolution to designate the spot on which stood the watch tower built in 1832.

7. The AMOS FARRAR CABIN, which stood within the stockade built during the Black Hawk War as a refuge for women and children, is now incorporated within the structure of the Gardner residence (*private*), Perry St. between Bench and Main Sts.

8. The JOHN DOWLING HOUSE, Main St. near Diagonal, the oldest structure still standing in Galena, was perhaps the first (1828) to use local stone. Today its windows are gaping holes, its roof sags, and the long high porch across the front is gone.

9. The FIRST COURTHOUSE, Main St. between Perry and Franklin Sts., built in 1838 as a store and later rented by the county, housed for a time the first theater of the district, in which played a company led by the elder Joseph Jefferson; his later famous son Joe attended the Campbell school next door to the courthouse. The two-story gray stone building, now a monument works, is distinguished by six portholes on the second floor.

10. The MARKET HOUSE, corner of Commerce and Troy Sts., remodeled for use as a city hall, is a Greek revival building erected in 1845 by Henry J. Stouffer. The two-story brick center section is surmounted by a square cupola, which contained offices and a meeting hall. On each side were the market stalls, one story high, with colonnades to shelter the customers. The flagged square on which it faces was the old public market, where all commodities were bought and sold, including slaves.

11. The LAWRENCE HOUSE, NW. corner of Commerce and

Perry Sts., now a garage, is a three-story brick building, erected in 1831. One of the well-known hotels of the old Northwest, it entertained many who made history on the Middle Border, but unfortunately its register was lost some years ago.

12. The SITE OF THE GRANT LEATHER STORE is occupied by a building at 120 S. Main St. Here Grant went to work for his father when he came to Galena in 1860.

13. The GALENA MUSEUM OF HISTORY AND ART (9-5 *daily; adults* 10c, *children free*), 207 S. Bench St., occupies a 15-room brick building that the city has leased to it for two hundred years at a dollar a year. Opened in 1938, the museum has five rooms of paintings; the remainder is devoted to Galena relics. Outstanding among the canvases is Thomas Nast's *Peace and Union,* depicting Lee's surrender to Grant at Appomattox.

14. The DE SOTO HOTEL, corner of Main and Green Sts., built in 1855, was in its day the finest hotel in the Northwest. Among the notables entertained in its spacious drawing rooms and elegant bars, were James Russell Lowell and Horace Greeley. From its balcony Lincoln made a speech in 1856 which did much to change the political complexion of the community. Grant maintained headquarters here. The fourth and fifth stories and the iron balcony of the original building have been removed.

15. The FIRST CUSTOMS HOUSE and FORMER POST OFFICE (now a beer parlor) is at the corner of Commerce and Green Sts.

16. GRANT PARK, on the east bank of the river, reached from the post office by the Johnson St. Bridge, is Galena's recreational center and a memorial to her illustrious son whose statue, *Grant Our Citizen,* stands there, the gift to the city of another son, publisher Herman Kohlsaat.

17. The JOSEPH HOGE HOUSE (*private*), 512 Park Ave., was built a year before the General Smith House, by the same architect, Henry J. Stouffer. Hoge, a lawyer from Baltimore, instructed Stouffer to build a house that would be strongly reminiscent of the South, so the architect designed a low Doric portico with four white columns, despite the diminutive size of the house. Inside are marble fireplaces, woodwork of elegant profile, and a walnut staircase; the fourteen panels of Russian engraved glass around the doorway to the vestibule were made with a hand-engraving technique now almost lost.

18. The GRANT MEMORIAL HOUSE (*open 9-5 daily*), above

the park on Bouthillier St., was presented to the General by the city on his return from the war. This sturdy two-story house of red brick has some of the earmarks of the Victorian period in its wide bracketed eaves and heavy porch, but somehow escapes being clumsy. It stands on a height overlooking the valley in an expanse of broad lawn. Maintained by the State as a permanent memorial, it is furnished with authentic Grant heirlooms, including the dishes and silver service used in the White House during Grant's administration.

POINTS OF INTEREST IN ENVIRONS

Mississippi Palisades State Park, 29 *m.* (*see Tour* 6). Apple River Canyon State Park, 41 *m.* (*see Tour* 5).

JOLIET

Railroad Stations: Union Depot, Jefferson and Scott Sts., for Chicago, Rock Island, and Pacific, the Alton, and the Atchison, Topeka, and Santa Fe.

Bus Stations: 301 N. Ottawa St. for Bluebird Coach, Gold Star, and Greyhound Lines; Union Bus Depot, 32 E. Jefferson St., for Joliet, Plainfield, and Aurora Lines, Kankakee Bus, National Trailways System, and Santa Fe Trailways.

City Buses: 5c fare.

Taxis: Rates from 15c per person to 15c for first half-mile.

Accommodations: Seven hotels.

Information Services: Association of Commerce, 436 Clinton St.; Illinois Motor Club, 224 Van Buren St.; Chicago Motor Club, 615 Van Buren St.

Radio Station: WCLS (1310 kc.).

Motion Picture Houses: Five.

Golf: One municipal, five commercial courses.

Tennis: Joliet High School courts, Jefferson and Eastern; Highland Park, Cass St., West Park, West Park Ave., Nowell Park, US 66 at Mills Road.

Swimming: Y.M.C.A. pool, 409 Ottawa St.; Michigan Beach, Rowell Ave. ½ m. S. of intersection with Second Ave.; Nowell Park and Pilcher Park.

JOLIET (607 alt., 42,993 pop.), the seat of Will County, lies 35 miles southwest of Chicago, on the Des Plaines River and the Illinois and Michigan Canal, a part of the Great Lakes to Gulf Waterway. Here the outer belt freight lines shunt much of the through freight around Chicago. Concerned with its freight handling and possessed of early transportation advantages, Joliet has developed as a self-dependent unit; here one senses little or no dependence upon the metropolis looming a scant hour's drive to the northeast. Joliet reveals its economic independence from almost every approach, in railway yards, warehouses, shipping platforms, quarries, factory stacks, and mountains of coal.

This is the Joliet of which Sandburg wrote, years ago:

> On the one hand the steel works
> On the other hand the penitentiary.
> Santa Fe trains and Alton trains
> Between smokestacks on the west
> And gray walls on the east . . .

But this is not all of Joliet; the man-of-the-street scarcely gives a thought to the penitentiary, so little does it intrude upon the life of the town. Across the north side of town stretches the Joliet park system, which, although planned too late to include areas in the city proper, is one of the finest among the small cities of the State. If the average resident were asked what is the most outstanding thing about his town, he would probably say the high school band, followed by the park system, and mention the penitentiary as an afterthought.

The city is one of the largest wall paper producers in the country, manufacturing enough daily to reach to New York and back. One hundred and fifty other factories produce more than 1,700 different articles. This diversification of products is the third stage of an industrial development that began some ninety years ago.

The first settler here was Charles Reed, who came in 1831. The following year he, along with numerous settlers in the vicinity, fled the region when the Black Hawk War broke out, but before the war was over they returned, and by 1834 a town was laid out and the first public sale of lots was held. By some unexplained quirk, the town was known as Juliet for years, and a nearby village romantically took the name of Romeo. When Will County was laid out in 1836, the designated county seat was referred to under the name of Shakespeare's heroine, and a year later it was incorporated with that name.

For ten years the fortunes of Joliet rose and fell as work went forward or languished on the canal. The first boat arrived here April 11, 1848, and was met by the entire population, with bands, booming cannon, and much oratory. With its new transportation means, Joliet entered into its first industrial era, based on the large-scale shipping of local limestone. In the fifties and sixties Joliet shipped blocks as far as New York, and its quarries provided the Middle West with material for such public structures as the Rock Island Arsenal, the Indiana penitentiary, and the State House and Lincoln monument at Springfield.

The first railroad, the Rock Island, came here in 1852, followed by five other lines. Although the railroad was eventually to cause the decline of the canal it brought, in the seventies, the new industry of steel manufacture, which was further attracted by the soft coal in the vicinity. The earliest mill manufactured spikes, track bolts, and other railroad items. Bessemer plants, rail and rod mills, blast furnaces followed, and then plants that made galvanized wire, barbed wire, nails, and other products for the growing agricultural west.

In 1894 Joliet pioneered notably in the elimination of grade crossings, seeking to require the railroads to elevate their tracks in the major portion of the city. In and out of courts the battle was fought, with the lines objecting strenuously to the ordinance that had been passed. Finally, in 1904, a compromise plan was effected, and within the next decade the work was completed. The program, which eliminated a score of dangerous crossings and consolidated all passenger service in one station, brought numerous queries from other cities that were spurred to emulate the plan.

The rise of the Chicago area as a steel-producing center wooed away from Joliet some of the mills engaged in heavier manufacture. But the lighter processing mills remain, surrounded by a plexus of plants that manufacture power corn shellers, soap, jewelry, packaging machines, flyspray, ink, sulphuric acid, steel washers, and shoes with which horses all over the world are shod. The outer belt railroad is still Will County's largest employer, but the glinting waterway, which Sandburg saw as "stripes of silver or copper or gold" still moves its freight through town, its quaint donkeys long discarded for power-boats as efficient as the factories they slip past.

POINTS OF INTEREST

The JOLIET WALL PAPER MILLS (*guides by arrangement*), 223 Logan Ave., is one of the six Joliet mills, which produce one-third of the country's wall paper. The visitor is first taken to the damp, warm boiler room, where dynamos generate electricity for the entire factory; from there to the raw material warehouses, which are piled high with chalky Georgia clay and huge bales of white paper already cut to wall paper width. Next visited is the color room, stacked with barrels of pigment and equipped with large grinding and mixing machines in which the colors are prepared in dry form.

In the actual printing room the air is pungent with the ammonia used to treat the soy bean color oils. Here are the printing machines, extending in vertical rows, a city block in length. The paper, fed from rolls in slow-moving festoons, is given a ground coating of the desired tint, picked up in loops by wooden fingers resembling broom handles, and slowly carried along drying units in a current of warm, dry air. Fed back into the machines, it is imprinted with as many as 12 different designs and colors. Carried back in dense scallops over the heaters, through a washing fluid, and into a long drying room, it is caught up by reels and wound into regulation rolls.

The AMERICAN INSTITUTE OF LAUNDERING VOCATIONAL TRAINING SCHOOL (*guides at main office*), Chicago St. and Doris Ave., was established in 1930. It conducts research for members of a national laundry association, and maintains a separate training school that gives a 40-week course in modern laundrying methods.

In OAKWOOD CEMETERY, 1919½ Cass St., is the OAKWOOD MOUND, situated on a steep rise of 30 ft., a conical structure 8 ft. high, extending over an area 64 by 67 feet. Excavations conducted by the University of Chicago in 1928, yielded 100 skeletons, in addition to weapons, ornaments and implements, all now exhibited at the University. There is revealed a preponderance of women and child burials, and five instances where the mother and child were clasped in an embrace. The mound, dating back some 1,000 years, contained the scattered skeletal remains of over 300 persons. The confusion in placement and the lack of uniformity of the burials, which were characterized by both flexed and full length positions, indicate a great number of sudden deaths, and a hurried disposal of the bodies, which were probably gathered in a heap and covered with earth.

BIRD HAVEN is a 75-acre strip of land, reached by driving out Cass St., through Hobbs Parkway and the south drive of Pilcher Park. The dense natural growth of hawthorn, to which 300 evergreen species have been added, serves as natural protection of small birds from hawks and owls. Over two hundred kinds of birds, by count, have nested here. The area includes a greenhouse with a desert room containing about 170 kinds of cactus, and a chrysanthemum show is given each fall.

PILCHER PARK ARBORETUM, US 30, from Maple to Gauger Road, was presented to the people of Joliet by Robert Pilcher in 1922 with the stipulation that it should remain in its natural state. About 75 species of trees, including 9 kinds of oak, are native, as well as many shrubs, bushes, and almost innumerable wild flowers. A collection of imports started by John Higginbotham, original owner, includes southern magnolia, sweet gum, cypress, tulip-tree, white fringe, pecan, black birch, and hickories and black cherry trees. Plans for development envisage introduction of trees from all over the world. A five-acre picnic camp, across Hickory Creek, is connected with the main park by foot bridge. One-way motor lanes are supplemented by five miles of narrow footpaths and several miles of bridle paths.

The OLD PRISON, 1900 Collins St., functions as a unit under the same warden, with the new Stateville prison (*see Tour* 17). Its construction was begun in 1857 after long and bitter criticism of the first State prison at Alton by Dorothea Dix. Built on an impregnable limestone stratum from the stone quarried for the foundation, the prison was the model of its day. Corbelled walls five feet thick at the base surround the cell-block, which had a capacity for almost 3,000. Until 1928, much prison work, ranging from quarrying to match-making, was done by inmates, but income producing work has been discontinued. At one time one-hundred cells were reserved for women, but the entire prison is now given over to men.

The JOLIET HIGH SCHOOL, Jefferson St. and Eastern Ave., is a Tudor-Gothic building, constructed in 1899. The school band is nationally famous; so frequently did it win the national band competition that it was eventually barred and now attends the contests on an honorary basis only. On the main floor is a series of six murals by William Panhallow Henderson, painter, architect, and muralist. The murals depict the activities of Marquette and Jolliet among the Indians. Presented by the graduating class of 1906, they are considered among the finest of Henderson's mural work.

The COLLEGE OF ST. FRANCIS, 303 Taylor, is a Catholic senior women's college, and the only such one in Illinois outside of Chicago. Opened in 1925 as Assisi Junior College, it was rechartered in 1930 as an accredited college, awarding a bachelor's degree. It is conducted by the Sisters of St. Francis of Mary Immaculate, and is an outgrowth of the St. Francis Academy, a resident and day preparatory school for girls, established in 1869 and still functioning. The present enrollment of the academy is approximately 400, and that of the college, 500.

POINTS OF INTEREST IN ENVIRONS

Brandon Road Lock and Dam, 2.7 *m.* (*see Tour* 14). Illinois and Michigan Canal at Channahon, 11 *m.* (*see Tour* 14). Stateville State Prison, 4 *m.* (*see Tour* 17).

NAUVOO

Ferry landing: Foot of Water St. for ferry connecting with the Chicago, Burlington & Quincy R. R. at Montrose, Iowa. No ferry service in winter months.
Accommodations: One hotel; rooms available at Mansion House.
Guide Service: Tour of the Mormon dwellings can be arranged at Mansion House; small fee, depending on size of party.
For further information regarding this city, see the *Nauvoo Guide,* another of the American Guide Series, published January 1939 by the Unity Club of Nauvoo.

NAUVOO (620 alt., 966 pcp.), the city built up by Joseph Smith, stands on a promontory around which the Mississippi River flows, some fifty miles north of Quincy, Illinois. Here, when Chicago was a stripling village of less than 5,000, stood the largest city in Illinois, the headquarters for the newly established Church of Jesus Christ of Latter-day Saints, popularly known as the Mormons.

In no sense of the word is Nauvoo a ghost town, but the bones of a greater past show starkly, here and there, in the living town of today. Scattered throughout are empty foundation pits, with elms and maples leaning over, and here and there the shell of a house, its windows boarded and its collapsed roof spilling a great crest of trumpet flowers. Occupying two levels, which residents call the Hill and the Flat, the town sprawls loosely over an area capable of housing a community twenty times its size. Extending almost to the back doors of its business establishments are vineyards and garden plots, as though a dam that once had barred country fields from the town had fissured and let the fields come seeping in.

The Flat graphically presents the fact that Nauvoo occupies the framework of a larger and older community. The checkerboard streets laid out by the Mormons are still discernible, although many of them are now delineated only by the fences of bordering farms. A scant two score of houses remain in what was once the most populous section of the city. Main Street and Parley Street have but few buildings facing them, although the former was the business street of old Nauvoo, and the latter, according to a visitor in the 1840's, was lined solidly with houses for more than a mile back from the river.

The living city, which centers around the crest of the hill, is a quiet, stable little community almost wholly dependent upon agricul-

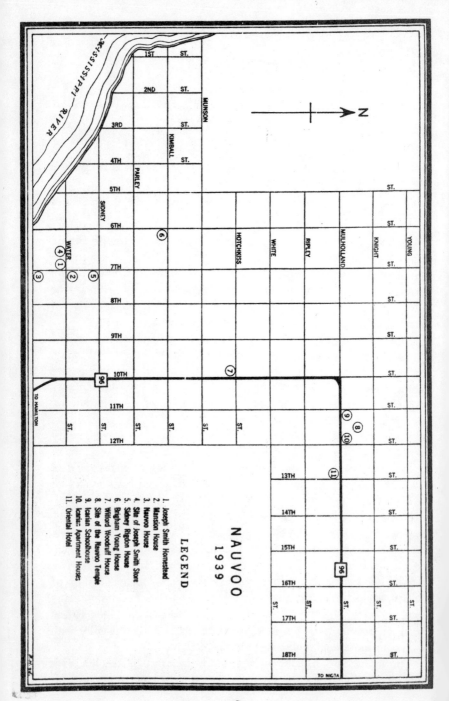

NAUVOO
1939

LEGEND

1. Joseph Smith Homestead
2. Mansion House
3. Nauvoo House
4. Site of Joseph Smith Store
5. Sidney Rigdon House
6. Brigham Young House
7. Wilford Woodruff House
8. Site of the Nauvoo Temple
9. Icarian Schoolhouse
10. Icarian Apartment Houses
11. Oriental Hotel

ture and horticulture. A recently established aeronautical school strikes an anachronistic note; there are two Roman Catholic boarding schools, a cheese factory, and a winery, but most of Nauvoo's citizens look to the soil for their livelihood. Grape culture, instituted by the French communists who occupied Nauvoo after the expulsion of the Mormons, remains the most important source of income. Many thousands of gallons of wine and grape juice are pressed annually; the remainder of the crop—as many as 150 carloads a year—is shipped out. Most of this leaves by truck or ferry, since Nauvoo has no railroad.

Today there are only some sixty members of the Reorganized Church of Jesus Christ of Latter-day Saints in Nauvoo. They differ sharply from the larger Utah branch on several important tenets of dogma, the chief of which is the succession to the presidency. The Reorganized Church holds that leadership has properly descended from father to son, for their present head is a grandson of Joseph Smith; the Utah group maintains that at the death of Smith the Twelve Apostles became the presiding quorum. But since both look on Joseph Smith as true prophet and founder of their church, Nauvoo increases yearly in importance as the Mormon Mecca.

When the Mormons, harried out of Missouri by an irate citizenry, came to this place in the spring of 1839, there was nothing here but half a dozen buildings in what pretentiously called itself the town of Commerce. "The place," wrote Joseph Smith, "was literally a wilderness . . . but believing that it might become a healthy place by the blessing of Heaven to the Saints, and no more eligible place presenting itself, I considered it wisdom to make an attempt to build up a city." Shortly he renamed the town Nauvoo, to which many writers and others have properly added the phrase—"the beautiful."

Smith had founded his church nine years before, at Fayette, New York, shortly after he had published the *Book of Mormon,* which he offered as an addendum to the Bible. The book, he claimed, was a divinely inspired translation of a set of gold plates that he had dug up, under the guidance of an angel, on a hill near Palmyra, New York.

By shrewdly bargaining their political support, the Saints obtained a highly favorable charter for Nauvoo from the legislature. Nauvoo was made virtually an autonomous state, empowered to pass any laws not in direct conflict with the State or Federal constitutions, and to maintain its own militia and city court.

While bricklayers and carpenters were fashioning a city out of the wilderness, Smith dispatched missionaries to the East and to Europe. In England they began publishing the *Millenial Star,* still in existence, and distributed thousands of copies of the *Book of Mormon.* Hundreds of immigrants began pouring into the new Zion, and by the fall of 1842 the new Mormon paper, *Times and Seasons,* estimated that Nauvoo contained "between 7,000 and 8,000 houses, with a population of 14,000 or 15,000." In 1841 the Saints began work on a great temple and a hotel, the Nauvoo House, as dictated in a revelation to Smith. At its peak, in 1845, the city had more than 20,000 inhabitants.

As the city spread over the promontory, opposition began to rumble among the Gentiles, as the non-Mormons were called. The Saints usually voted as a bloc and their neighbors feared political domination. Opposition grew when John C. Bennett, an opportunistic politician who had lobbied for the city charter, broke with the Saints and published in 1842 a lurid booklet, *History of the Saints; or an Exposé of Joe Smith and Mormonism,* which made the first detailed charges of polygamy against the Mormons.

Polygamy was never openly practiced at Nauvoo; not until 1852, in Utah, did Brigham Young announce the "plural wives" revelation, which he claimed Smith had received at Nauvoo on July 12, 1843. The Reorganized Church has consistently denied the authenticity of this revelation, but it is incontrovertible that rumors of polygamy at Nauvoo were rife in this region long before Smith's death.

The Prophet reached the height of his career in 1844, when, following unsuccessful attempts to secure reparation from Missouri for the confiscation of Mormon property, he announced himself as a candidate for the presidency of the United States. Some historians have questioned the seriousness of his intentions, although hundreds of the most eloquent church leaders were sent out to preach their religion and to electioneer for him.

Then suddenly occurred a schism that rocked the church. William and Wilson Law, Dr. R. D. Foster, Sylvester Emmons, and a few of their friends unexpectedly broke with the church, and on June 7, 1844, published the first and only issue of the *Expositor.* "We are aware," ran the preamble, "that we are hazarding every earthly blessing, particularly property, and probably life itself, in striking this blow at tyranny and oppression." They attacked polygamy and the political aspirations of Smith, and called for repeal of the powerful city charter.

The city marshal, on Smith's order, immediately destroyed the press, pied the type, and burned the remaining copies of the *Expositor*. The Laws fled to Carthage and procured a warrant for the arrest of Smith and other Mormon leaders. The Prophet and his brother surrendered themselves and were jailed. Mobs began to form, wild rumors circulated among both Gentiles and Mormons, and Governor Ford hurried to Carthage to quiet the unrest.

On June 27, while Ford was at Nauvoo assuring the uneasy Saints that Smith would receive justice, a mob stormed the jail at Carthage and murdered the Prophet and his brother Hyrum, the Patriarch.

The Mormon leaders preaching and campaigning in the East hurriedly returned to Nauvoo, and Brigham Young soon took command. But opposition to the Saints abated only temporarily. In January 1845, the Nauvoo charter was repealed, and armed clashes continued throughout the summer. Then, on September 24, Young announced that "as soon as grass grows," the Saints would leave Illinois and migrate to a distant place.

Nauvoo was transformed into a gigantic wagon shop, and the town echoed continually with the sound of hammer and saw. Property was disposed of at a fraction of its value; horses and oxen were at a premium. In February, 1846, Brigham Young led the first body of Saints across the Mississippi, and by spring the number of emigrants averaged one thousand a week. But rumors persisted that many of the Saints were planning to remain, and an armed force of Gentiles attacked the town. For several days there was open warfare, which ceased only when the remaining Mormons agreed to leave immediately. "The ferry boats were crowded," wrote an eye-witness, "and the river bank was lined with anxious fugitives, sadly awaiting their turn to pass over and take up their solitary march to the wilderness." Out of this epic march came the settlement of Utah and the final achievement of peace and prosperity by the Saints.

Nauvoo was left deserted. Weeds took root in the streets, and rats scurried fearlessly through the open doors of Saints' houses. The Temple, which had been almost completed, stood mute and staring above the abandoned city. Late in 1848 it was fired by an incendiary, and only the walls were left standing.

Then, in 1849, a small band of French communists, the Icarians, came to Nauvoo from Texas, where they had made a brief and unsuccessful attempt to found a colony. At their head was Etienne Cabet, prominent French jurist, author of *Voyage to Icaria*, and *True Chris-*

tianity, in which he had advocated a communistic society based on the moral teachings of Christ.

The Icarians soon set up a community governed by a president, elected annually, and by a cabinet of directors for each division of activity. The workshops and labor gangs were supervised by foremen elected monthly by the workers. Possession of money was restricted to the director of finance; shoes and clothing were supplied from the common fund. Icarian children, who entered the colony's school at the age of seven, were permitted to visit their parents on Sundays only, and were trained to manage the dormitories where they lived.

Fascinated by the ruins of the Temple, Cabet decided to reconstruct it. After a considerable sum of money had been spent, a terrific storm struck Nauvoo, and seeming to single out the Temple, felled the walls with a roar that was heard miles away.

Already saddled with considerable debt, the Icarians began to grumble against Cabet. Shirking became contagious, production slackened, and individualism crept into the colony. "The beast began to show itself," wrote Emile Vallet. "Having been raised under the influence of individualism, we could not be expected to fulfill the requirements of such a mode of life." In winter the coal that was to be equally divided among all was carried away by a few as soon as it arrived; a greedy few at the table would consume the butter intended for all.

Steadily Cabet lost his followers' esteem, and in 1856 he was defeated for the presidency. When he organized a strike, the majority locked the dining hall door, and finally, realizing that the breach could not be healed, Cabet and his followers withdrew to St. Louis. There, unattended and brooding over the failure of his plans, the Utopian died. The majority group sold their property and joined forces with a branch colony established in 1853 at Corning, Iowa. This group, faring somewhat better, held together for about twenty years.

Thus ended the unconventional days of Nauvoo. Gradual resettlement, much of it by Germans, began in the late fifties and sixties, but not in sufficient numbers to occupy the community left by the Mormons. Most of the frame buildings fell into ruin and were torn down, and by degrees Nauvoo scaled itself down to its present size. The façade of the Temple, somber and ruined on the crest of the Hill, was at last condemned and torn down. The limestone blocks went into the construction of many a house and commercial building, thus diffusing throughout the city the Temple that Joseph Smith had planned as the spiritual center and material glory of Nauvoo.

POINTS OF INTEREST

1. The JOSEPH SMITH HOMESTEAD *(open daily)* consists of three sections; the original log cabin into which Smith moved on coming to Nauvoo, the frame addition on the west, and the addition on the rear. The log cabin is the oldest structure in Nauvoo (1823). Maintained by the Reorganized Church as a shrine to the Prophet, the homestead is furnished with many pieces that belonged to the Prophet's family. On the river side of the house are the GRAVES OF JOSEPH, EMMA, AND HYRUM SMITH. The bodies of the Prophet and his brother were moved several times after the murder at Carthage, and were finally secretly buried in a springhouse near the homestead. Knowledge of their location was for years a family secret; the springhouse fell into ruin; and in 1928 the bodies were found only after considerable search. A hole in one of the skulls identified it as that of Hyrum Smith, shot through the head at Carthage jail. The bodies, with that of Joseph Smith's wife, Emma Smith Bidamon, were reinterred on January 20, 1928.

2. The MANSION HOUSE *(open daily)*, a two-story frame with a hip roof, served as Joseph Smith's home from August 1843 until his death a year later. Originally it extended much deeper, having 22 rooms, 15 of which were bedrooms. The portion of the interior that remained after the remodeling is substantially the same as it was when Smith lived here. Maintained by the Reorganized Church as a museum, it contains foreign editions of the *Book of Mormon,* early editions of *Doctrine and Covenants,* the book of Smith's revelations, bound volumes of *Times and Seasons,* and Joseph Smith's desk.

3. The NAUVOO HOUSE *(open upon application at Mansion House)* was begun in 1841 when Smith had a revelation commanding the erection of "a delightful habitation for man, and a resting place for the weary traveler, that he may contemplate the glory of Zion." The original plans called for a building 120 feet by 40 feet here on Seventh Street, with an ell of similar size along the river. Smith's death halted construction, and Emma Smith's second husband completed the building as it stands today. The foundation as originally planned still stands on the Seventh Street side.

4. The National Women's Relief Society marker designates the SITE OF THE JOSEPH SMITH STORE, still delineated by the foundation and cellar. In an office here, on March 17, 1842, Joseph Smith founded the relief society, one of the oldest such organizations in the country.

5. The SIDNEY RIGDON HOUSE (*private*), a story-and-a-half frame dwelling, served as the first postoffice in Nauvoo. Rigdon, according to a somewhat dubious theory, aided in drafting the *Book of Mormon*. After Smith's death he attempted to gain control of the church, but was read out of the ranks and "delivered over to the buffeting of Satan." He retired to Pittsburgh, gathered a few followers about him, and organized his own church. "I will cross the Atlantic," he wrote, "encounter the Queen's forces, and overcome them . . . . demand a portion of her riches and dominions, which if she refuse, I will take the little madame by the nose, and lead her out. . . ." His church soon died out.

6. The BRIGHAM YOUNG HOUSE (*private*), a two-story red brick in good repair, is flanked by two great maple trees. Young, a Vermonter, became one of the Twelve Apostles of the Mormon church in 1835. After leading the Mormon trek to Utah he became Territorial Governor, and although he lost that position when the Federal government began to war on polygamy, he exercised great authority over the Utah branch until his death in 1877.

7. The WILFORD WOODRUFF HOUSE (*private*) is a two-story brick with large double chimneys at either end. Woodruff, one of the early Twelve Apostles, became fourth president of the Mormon church. On September 25, 1890, he issued at Salt Lake City, the famous proclamation calling upon the Saints to abandon the practice of polygamy. Approved by the Church in general conference eleven days later, the proclamation officially ended the practice.

8. The SITE OF THE NAUVOO TEMPLE, on the crest of the Hill, has nothing to mark the imposing structure that once dominated the whole of Nauvoo. The style of the Temple was a mixture of Romanesque, Egyptian, and Greek; 83 by 128 feet, it was adorned with 30 hewn pilasters that cost $3,000 each. Topping the structure was a gilded statue of the angel Moroni, who, according to the Prophet, had revealed to him the burial place of the golden plates bearing the *Book of Mormon*. The Temple was not quite completed

when the Mormons were driven from Nauvoo, although it had been used for a few months after October 5, 1845.

9. The ICARIAN SCHOOLHOUSE was built of Temple stone by the French communists, and now serves as a Roman Catholic school.

10. The TWO ICARIAN APARTMENT HOUSES (*private*) are two-story frame structures, gray and weather-beaten. Originally there were four of them here along Mulholland Street. A ground floor room in the corner house is occupied by Miss Rose Nicaise, last of the first-generation descendants of the Icarians, who still lives in the room to which her parents were assigned by Cabet; the doors are marked with the original numerals and bear the locks fashioned by her father at Cabet's directions. Although she recalls nothing of the experiment, save that it removed her father from France and thereby broke his heart, she declares that her father bore no malice toward Cabet and retained until death his faith in the Utopian's principles.

11. The ORIENTAL HOTEL (*small fee for inspection of relics*) is Nauvoo's only hotel. Filling its lobby, corridors, rooms, and overflowing into a barn in the rear is an astonishing collection of Mormon and Icarian relics. Currier and Ives prints and Seth Thomas clocks hang on the walls. Among the deeds, manuscripts, and books, are copies of the *Expositor*, letters of Joseph Smith, and a bound volume of *Times and Seasons*. The rooms are furnished with canopy beds, rope-net beds with trundles, complete suites in cedar, walnut, and cherry, many of which antedate the Icarian years. One room is furnished with Joseph Smith's furniture; in the yard stands one of the stones from the base of the Temple, the finest specimen in existence.

POINTS OF INTEREST IN ENVIRONS

Old Carthage Jail, 25 *m*. (*see Tour 7*).

PEORIA

Railroad Stations: Rock Island Station, foot of Liberty St., for Chicago, Rock Island & Pacific Ry., and Minneapolis & St. Louis R. R. Union Station, foot of E. State St., for Alton R. R., Chicago, Burlington & Quincy R. R., Chicago & Illinois Midland Ry., Chicago & North Western Ry., Cleveland, Cincinnati, Chicago & St. Louis Ry., Illinois Central R. R., and New York, Chicago & St. Louis R. R. Illinois Terminal Station, 542 S. Adams St. for Illinois Terminal Railroad Co. (electric).

Steamboat Landing: Landing for local excursions just south of Main St.

Bus Stations: United Bus Depot, 212 North Adams St., for Santa Fe Trailways, Black Hawk Motor Transit Co., Burlington Trailways, Central Trailways, Jacksonville Trailways, Illini Coach Co., Sterling Stages and Bartonville Bus Co. (service to Pekin only); Peoria Bus Center, 306 Hamilton St., for Greyhound Lines, and White Star Lines; De Luxe Station, 128 N. Adams St., for De Luxe Motor Stages; 342 Fulton St. for Illinois Highway Transportation Co. (service to Pekin only).

Airports: Municipal Airport, on Jacob Harmon Highway, and Mount Hawley Airport, on State 88, sightseeing and charter planes only.

Street Cars: 10c. 3 tokens for 25c; feeder buses connect with cars over certain streets; no extra charge.

Taxis: 25c first m., 10c each additional m.

Accommodations: 14 hotels.

Information Services: Peoria *Star*, 119 E. Madison, Peoria *Transcript*, 125 S. Jefferson, Association of Commerce, 408 Main, Chicago Motor Club, 239 S. Jefferson St.

Radio Station: WMBD (1440 kc.).

Athletics: Madison Park, Junction of 7th and Lincoln Aves., Bradley Park, 2700 N. Main St., Glen Oak Park, N. Perry Ave. & Abingdon St., Proctor Recreation Center, Allen & Martin Sts.

Golf: Madison Park Municipal Links, Bradley Park, North Moor.

Swimming: Non-commercial pools; Y.M.C.A., 6th and Franklin, Y.W.C.A., Fayette and Jefferson St., Glen Oak Park Pool, Proctor Pool, Logan Pool, Starr and Livingston Sts., South Park Pool, Montana and Idaho Sts. (for commercial pools and beaches see tel. directory).

Tennis: Glen Oak Park Municipal Courts, Bradley Park, South Park, Proctor Recreation Center.

PEORIA (608 alt., 104,969 pop.), named for an Indian tribe, is the seat of Peoria County and Illinois' second largest city. Slightly north and west of the center of the State, the city lies on three levels along the northwest bank of the Illinois River, where it widens into a broad basin known as Lake Peoria. The river has been a notable factor in both the early settlement and the present industrial prominence of Peoria.

On the river's narrow alluvial plain are many of Peoria's 174 major industrial plants, grouped there partly because of their early dependence on water power, but largely to make use of cheap water transportation. A river and rail terminal maintained by the city serves as a ligature between its 14 railroads and the barge lines that connect upstream with Chicago, by way of the Sanitary and Ship Canal, and downstream with the Gulf of Mexico, along the Mississippi.

Paralleling the band of industrial establishments in the lowlands is a second bench, higher and wider, anciently the river's bed. On it lie the business district and an extensive residential section. This level runs back from one to two miles to the Bluffs, the earliest bank of the river. From the Bluffs residential Peoria commands a view of the clustered business district, the serrated line of mills and factories along the curving river, and, far beyond the industrial suburbs, the checkered farm fields. Grand View Drive and the Galena Road, both branching from the end of Adams Street at the entrance to Grand View Park, offer fine views of the region.

From neighboring fields and from countless more throughout the Corn Belt, Peoria's four distilleries draw a considerable portion of the corn crop. With five rectifying plants, the distilleries produce a greater volume of spirituous liquors than any other city in the United States, and together yield $50,000,000 annually to the Internal Revenue Department. Because of Peoria's supply of pure water and its nearness to corn and coal, it has been a distilling center since the middle of the nineteenth century. Unusual for an inland city, Peoria paid $4,000,000 in import duties in 1937, most of which was for imported liquors used in blending. Other major industries include the manufacture of tractors, agricultural implements, and barrels, as well as meat packing and coal mining.

The first white men to reach this site were Father Marquette and the explorer, Jolliet, who passed through Lake Peoria in the fall of 1673, returning from their exploratory trip down the Mississippi. In his *Recite* Marquette mentions meeting the Indians "of Peourea," but this encounter did not occur here. The expedition erected no buildings, but the teachings of Marquette and his promise of the French king's protection against the Iroquois warriors from the north established mutual friendliness and confidence. But early quarrels among the French, Jesuits on the one side and imperialists on the other, later conflicts between the French and English, and finally the war between the American Colonists and the English, shifted protection of the

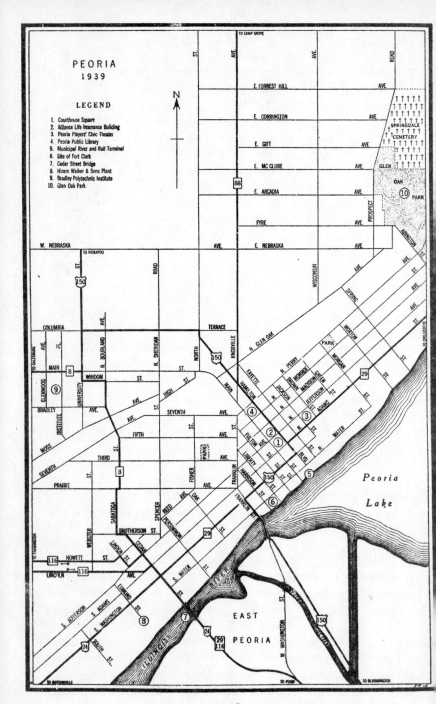

tribes from group to group until they lost all confidence in the "Great White Father," whose identity was always changing.

Marquette did not return, but in 1680 Robert Cavelier, Sieur de La Salle, with Henri de Tonti, Père Louis Hennepin, a group of Recollect friars and artisans, about 33 men in all, descended the Illinois River to Lake Peoria. At the outlet of the lake, on the left bank of the river, they erected Fort Crèvecoeur, "the refuge of the broken heart." Despite romantic legends to the contrary, the fort was probably so named to commemorate the then recent French capture of Fort Crèvecoeur in the Netherlands. Its name, however, foreshadowed its history, for within three months it was plundered and abandoned by its forces during La Salle's absence.

In 1691 Fort St. Louis, upstream from Peoria on Starved Rock, was abandoned, and the post moved to Lake Peoria, where it was usually referred to as Fort Pimiteoui (Ind., fat lake). On the settlement that grew up about it, Peoria bases its claim to being the oldest city in Illinois against the claim of Cahokia, founded in 1699. Settlement at this spot was not continuous after 1691, but certainly this was the first Illinois settlement on a site that is occupied today.

Center of a large tribe of friendly Indians, and possessing excellent transportation to key French settlements, the trading post thrived, and soon was ranked among the most important in this new country. In 1763 the British wrested control of the area from the French, but the treaty which concluded the French and Indian War exerted little influence here. Although the settlement was virtually abandoned during the Revolutionary War, the French returned, took up residence at a new village on the right bank of the river, and continued their trading well into the period of American jurisdiction. Historically unique among Illinois towns, the village at Peoria Lake was visited by two military expeditions during the Revolutionary War. The first, a group of George Rogers Clark's men, destroyed the Indian village here. In 1781 a company of Spaniards, French, and Indians came up the Illinois river to Peoria Lake, and from here crossed by land to the British post of St. Joseph, in Michigan, which they captured without a battle.

The new village to which the French returned was variously referred to as Au Pé, Le Pé, Opa, and Au Pay, and as early as 1790 there is reference to it as Piorias—the "s" was not pronounced—but it is not known when that name achieved common usage.

During the War of 1812 a military blunder on the part of the American forces resulted in the partial destruction of Au Pé. Alarmed at the depredations of the Indians, Governor Ninian Edwards led troops up from Edwardsville and destroyed the village of Black Partridge, unaware that the chief was rendering assistance in the attempt to recover Americans kidnapped at the Fort Dearborn massacre. Shortly afterward, another part of the same force, under Capt. Thomas Craig of Shawneetown, destroyed a large part of the French village and carried off its inhabitants. Subsequently the friendliness—or at least the neutrality—of the French was proved, and they were released.

On the site of Au Pé late in 1813 the Americans erected Fort Clark, and about it grew up the nucleus of modern Peoria, although the name of Fort Clark clung to it for more than 10 years. In 1819 the first American civilians arrived, a party of seven, forerunners of the swarm of land-seekers soon to follow. The river that had borne French traders and their cargoes for more than a century now helped bring in the tide of "movers," of New England farmers eager for cheap rich land, and the smattering of professional men who followed the first contingent of ground-breakers.

In 1825 Peoria County was created, and the community of Fort Clark, with the French-Indian name of Peoria officially restored, was designated county seat. Although Putnam County was laid out at the same time, comprising almost all of Illinois north of Peoria, no governmental machinery was set up for that county and business was transacted at Peoria. From here, for a period of six years, jurisdiction was exercised over one-fourth of Illinois, including the stripling village of Chicago.

Largely because of the broad river at its door, Peoria had almost a decade's lead in appreciable settlement over other large cities in North Central Illinois, antedating Galesburg and Bloomington. When the first steamboat came up the Illinois about 1828, it found a sizeable cluster of cabins at the lake. In 1835, when Peoria was incorporated as a town, it had a population of more than 500. A decade later it had grown to 2,000, and by 1845 had adopted a city charter.

In 1854 the bustling young village was the scene of a highly important event in the career of Lincoln. On October 16, after Stephen Douglas had spoken all afternoon, Lincoln rose and requested that the crowd return after supper to hear his rebuttal. That evening he addressed to them a longer version of a speech he had given 12 days earlier at Springfield. Concerning the speech, Albert Beveridge says, in his *Abraham Lincoln,* "Thus did Lincoln, for the first time in his life, publicly and in forthright words denounce slavery, and assert that it was incompatible with American institutions." The speech was not one of the series known as the Lincoln-Douglas Debates, which it antedated by four years.

Pork packing was one of the earliest industries; beef packing came later, and both are still carried on. In the 1840's began the first stirrings of the intense industrialization that quadrupled the population between 1850 and 1870. Early entering the profitable industry of farm implement manufacture, Peoria was making plows, threshing machines, and fanning mills by 1844. By 1860 the city had seven distilleries, with a capital investment of $700,000. At first highly competitive, the distilleries became part of the Cattle Feeders' and Distillers' Trust—the "Whiskey Trust"—organized by Joseph Greenhut of Peoria in the 1880's. Small distilleries were closed, and the trade was concentrated at 12 large plants, 6 of which were in Peoria. So effective was this combine that between 1870 and 1890 the number of distilleries in Illinois declined from 45 to 7, while the average output rose in value from $175,300 to $7,448,000 annually. The organization continued in existence until the early 1900's, when the wave of "trust-busting" effected its dissolution.

Peoria weathered the era of Prohibition with unexpected strength; other industries, expanding with the national boom of the 1920's, readily absorbed the workers rendered unemployed by the Eighteenth Amendment. Thus, when Repeal reopened the distilleries, Peoria faced the 1930's with one of the brightest prospects, economically, in Illinois.

POINTS OF INTEREST

1. The COURTHOUSE SQUARE, bounded by Main and Adams Sts., Jefferson Ave., and Hamilton Blvd., is landscaped with shrubs and small trees. Long the focus of town activities, it has seen the drilling of Civil War soldiers and heard the brilliant oratory of political leaders. Near the south portico of the courthouse is a bronze tablet marking the SITE OF LINCOLN'S PEORIA SPEECH. On the southeast corner of the square stands the SOLDIERS' AND SAILORS' MONUMENT, the work of Fritz Triebel, Peoria sculptor. Its dedication, on October

6, 1899, was attended by President McKinley and a large official party. One member of the crowd of 30,000, a war veteran named John McGinnis, eyed the monument critically, scurried home, and wrote a letter to the sculptor.

I have never seen a captain after a battle hold up the regimental flag and cheer, that being the job of the color bearer or his guard; that the lieutenant holding up the wounded captain is untrue to real life because these two officers should be at opposite ends of the line; that [I] never saw a drummer boy with a pistol chasing one of the enemy; . . . and never heard of a trumpeter mixing in with the infantry and tooting signals in the midst of battle.

Triebel's reply, written on a scrap of wrapping paper, was blunt and brief: "Poor John McGinnis—To speak of art to you is the same as speaking to a jackass."

The PEORIA COUNTY COURTHOUSE, a domed cruciform structure in Italian Renaissance style, was built in 1876. In the dome is a four-faced Seth Thomas clock, still functioning after sixty years of service, and the halls are hung with paintings memorializing men and events of Peoria's early history.

2. The ALLIANCE LIFE INSURANCE BUILDING, NW. corner Main St. and Jefferson Ave., was erected by the Peoria Life Insurance Company in 1919. Standing out white among its somber neighbors, it is the best-known work of the firm of Hewitt, Emerson, and Gregg. In design it conveys much the same feeling as the Wrigley Building in Chicago. Its style is French, of the late Renaissance, its front façade extending into a square six-story tower, with typical steep French roof, and a lantern on which an airplane beacon burns. The exterior facing of terra cotta lends itself admirably to the delicacy of French decorative treatment, and the interior is finished in marble, with floors of terrazzo and coffered ceilings in rich tones.

3. The PEORIA PLAYERS' CIVIC THEATER (*open; ring custodian's bell*), 209 Jackson St., was converted from a firehouse for the use of the players, an incorporated group of amateurs. It has an auditorium seating 360, 12 dressing-rooms, a club-room, and a well-equipped workshop. The players' group, formed in 1919, now has a membership of more than 500, and plays an important rôle in the cultural life of the city. Play direction is in the hands of qualified members, rather than of a paid director, and this circumstance, combined with the enthusi-

DICKSON MOUND EXCAVATION

PEORIA

AURORA

TOBOGGAN SLIDE, PALOS PARK

FOREST PARK SWIMMING POOL AND BATHHOUSE,

OLD BANK, SHAWNEETOWN

ST. PETER'S EPISCOPAL CHURCH, GRAND DETOUR

PRAIRIE DU ROCHER

PRE-EMPTION HOUSE. NAPERVILLE

MAIN STREET

CAIRO LEVEE

VACHEL LINDSAY BRIDGE, NEAR SPRINGFIELD

astic co-operation of the membership, results in performances of unusual merit.

4. The PEORIA PUBLIC LIBRARY (*open 9-9 weekdays; 2-5 Sun.*), 111 W. Monroe St., was the first iibrary organized under the Illinois Free Public Law of 1872. The library's lists were substantially increased in 1881 and 1882 by donations of the collections of the German and Mercantile Libraries, which had been in existence for some time. In 1894 the Mercantile Library Association offered the proceeds of the sale of its building to assist in the erection of a new library building. Completed in 1897, the building now houses educational, art, and children's departments, and collections numbering 216,000 volumes.

5. The MUNICIPAL RIVER AND RAIL TERMINAL (*best viewed from balcony at Main St. entrance*) lies on the river front between Main St. and Hamilton Blvd. Here the business that in the old days lent charm and color to all river towns, with the stevedores "toting" cargo from wharf to hold, is completely mechanized. Cranes and overhead conveyors swing huge loads between boat and train; tractor-drawn, rubber-tired trucks supply the conveyors.

6. The SITE OF FORT CLARK, Liberty and Water Sts., is marked by a bronze plaque on the wall of the power plant. The fort, erected by American troops to overawe hostile Indians, was constructed with great difficulty, for logs had to be hauled by man-power or rafted from across the river. Unfriendly Indians made it dangerous for the workers to venture out singly, and a mass attack by 150 Indians before the completion of the structure was beaten off with some loss to the defenders. It was garrisoned intermittently, and the first permanent American settlers, arriving in 1819, found it partially destroyed by Indians.

7. The CEDAR STREET BRIDGE spans the Illinois River between Cedar St., Peoria, and Washington Ave., East Peoria. Completed in 1933, it received the Award of Merit plaque of the American Institute of Steel Construction as the most beautiful bridge in class A (costing more than $1,000,000) for that year. Ninety-seven feet above high water, it is one of the few bridges over the Illinois that do not have a lift or draw span. Its length is almost one and a quarter miles, its longest span 296 feet.

8. HIRAM WALKER AND SONS PLANT (*tours 9:30 and 2, Mon.-Fri.; 9:30 Sat.*) at the foot of Edmund St., is the world's larg-

est distillery, being a subsidiary of the original Hiram Walker and Sons, Ltd., of Walkerville, Ontario, which incorporated in the United States after Repeal. With the acquisition of this plant, Peoria became a ranking city in the production of spirituous liquors. The lecture tour of the plant reveals the processes of manufacture from the initial transfer of grain from railroad car, or river boat, to the final detail of bottling and labeling the finished product. Operations are largely automatic.

9. BRADLEY POLYTECHNIC INSTITUTE, 2300 Main St., is more commonly known as Bradley College. Privately endowed by Mrs. Lydia Bradley, the institute has eight divisions; the College of Arts and Sciences, the School of Fine and Applied Arts, the College of Music, the Industrial and Trade Schools, the School of Horology, the Evening Division, the Summer School, and an Extension Division. Accredited as a degree-granting school, Bradley enrolls some 700 students. When founded, the institute included a four-year academy, but in 1922 the academy was discontinued and the school concentrated on collegiate courses. The school, chartered in 1876, absorbed Peoria Musical College in 1920 and the School of the Peoria Art Institute in 1933. During the World War the institute was used extensively by the army in training mechanics, when the technical division of the school was converted into Camp Bradley.

BRADLEY HALL and HOROLOGY HALL, both constructed in 1897, are the school's oldest buildings. The School of Horology, which offers courses in all phases of watch-making, is the only endowed school of its kind in the country. Of the other buildings on the 28-acre campus, several were adapted from other purposes; the Manual Arts department, for example, occupies two converted factory buildings.

10. GLEN OAK PARK, covering 106 acres on the Bluffs, bounded by Springdale Road, Abingdon St., Prospect Road, and Springdale Cemetery, has facilities for tennis, baseball, softball, archery, bait-casting, and skating; an annual flower show is held at the conservatory. At the Perry Avenue entrance stands a bronze STATUE OF ROBERT INGERSOLL, lawyer and agnostic. The statue was designed by Fritz Triebel, who, when asked why he combined a youthful face with a large-girthed figure, replied that the face was the one well known in Peoria when Ingersoll practiced law here, but the waist line was taken from one of Ingersoll's suits of clothes furnished him.

BOULDER MONUMENT, erected in the park by the Peoria County

Old Settlers Association, honors the early residents of Peoria. Nearby is the OLD SETTLERS' LOG CABIN, headquarters of the organization. Near the McClure Street entrance, and a trifle incongruous in its setting, stands an ALASKAN TOTEM POLE, brought from Sitka, Alaska. A tablet gives its history and an interpretation of the symbols.

POINTS OF INTEREST IN ENVIRONS

Fort Crève Coeur State Park, 4.5 *m.;* Jubilee College State Park, 11.5 *m.;* Metamora Courthouse, 17 *m.* (*see Tour 16*).

ROCKFORD

Railroad Stations: 815 S. Main St. for Illinois Central R. R.; 515 S. Main St. for Chicago and North Western Ry.; 609 S. Main St. for Chicago, Milwaukee, St. Paul and Pacific R. R., and for Chicago, Burlington & Quincy R. R.

Bus Stations: Union Bus Depot, 330 Elm St., for Northland Greyhound Bus Co., Interstate Transit Co., and Peoria-Rockford Bus Co.; 609 S. Main for Chicago, Milwaukee, St. Paul and Pacific Bus Line and the Burlington Line.

Intra-City Buses: 4 tokens for 25c.

Taxis: 25c for first m. and 10c for each additional ½ m.

Accommodations: Three first class hotels; 17 others.

Information Services: Chamber of Commerce, 208 Chestnut St.; Chicago Motor Club, AAA Branch, 318 N. Main St.

Radio Stations: WROK (1410 kc.).

Theaters: Ten motion picture houses.

Golf: Sinnissippi (9 holes, 20c) 3100 N. Second St.; Ingersoll Memorial Park (18 holes, 35c) 4300 W. State St.; Sandy Hollow (18 holes, 35c) Sandy Hollow Road.

Tennis: John Andrews Memorial Park, N. Central, Ashland, and Sunset Aves. and Sherman St.; Beattie playground, 605 Hall St.; C. E. Brown Park, 2019 N. Main St.; Churchill Park, Eighth Ave. and 18th St.; Fair Grounds Park, 900 W. Jefferson St.; Garfield Ave. Playground, 1000 Garfield Ave.; Ingersoll Memorial Park, 4300 N. State St.; Oxford St. playground, 2400 Oxford St.; Sinnissippi Park, 1600 N. Second St.; South Park, 1500 Rock St.; Southeast Park, 1700 Eleventh St.; Sunset Park, 1800 W. Jefferson St.

Bowling Green: Fair Grounds Park.

Swimming: Fair Grounds Park Pool, free; Tenth Ave. Playground Pool, 10c in evenings; Levings Park lake, 2100 Montague St., free.

Annual Events: Chrysanthemum show in the Sinnissippi Park greenhouse in October; Mendelssohn Club, the Rockford Symphony Orchestra, the Rockford Men Singers, and many other musical organizations give frequent concerts; consult information service (above).

ROCKFORD (742 alt., 85,864 pop.), seat of Winnebago County and third largest city in Illinois, is bisected by the Rock River 18 miles south of the Wisconsin Line. It was named for the shallow rock-bottomed ford used by the Galena-Chicago stagecoach line before any settlement existed here. Crowded by fine elms and oaks along the river banks with a background of extensive beds of colorful prairie flowers, the ford presented a natural beauty that touched even the gruffest pioneer; one early traveler exclaimed enthusiastically, "I've lived in nineteen states and three territories and been whipped a thousand times, but I'm damned if I ever see so pretty a country as that." Only one day's journey from Chicago and Galena, the ford was unmistakably marked by geographic determinism as a city site. But when Galena declined and Chicago boomed, Rockford utilized its natural advantages of water power and fertile prairies to the full, and continued its growth unaffected.

Since the erection of the pioneer saw mill that buzzed with activity in the early days, the city's industrial growth has been steady; the major industries of half a century ago—the manufacture of agricultural implements and furniture—rank among the first four today. Unblighted by mushrooming industrialism, Rockford has a pleasant informal appearance, heightened by rolling heavily wooded terrain, and scattered business districts, and a notable park system. In designating their community "The Forest City," Rockford's citizens substantiated the phrase by a census that disclosed an average of 122 trees to a block. The city's streets lend a further informality to the general scene, for they were laid out to humor the vagaries of the winding river, without heed of the future visitor who might have difficulty in finding his way. As a result, tiny, variously shaped parks, formed as two or more streets veer suddenly to avoid others, appear in unexpected places; street numbers frequently have no continuity; wide boulevards narrow surprisingly and dead-end against a wall or group of buildings. Self-contained, Rockford has developed but one purely residential suburb, and has kept its finest estates within the city limits along with its manufacturing plants.

Rockford's self-sufficiency appears also in its cultural activities, especially music. Although only two hours from Chicago, Rockford maintains a seventy-piece symphony orchestra and a supporting choral group. The Mendelssohn Club sponsors a concert series that has presented such singers as Lawrence Tibbett, Helen Jepson, and Nelson Eddy. The Svea Soner Society and Lyran Society, Swedish organizations, have their own halls and have toured the country in recitals.

It is estimated that 40 per cent of Rockford's population is of Swedish descent, and the Swedish accent colors much of the conversation heard on the streets. The Swedes have maintained their racial consciousness to some extent; mostly they live in the southeastern section of the city, where their neat homes are interspersed among the industrial plants. Early settlement of the community was centered in the area now known as South Rockford, but as the chief residential section moved northward this neighborhood was left isolated by the intervening industrial district. For some time it was occupied by the

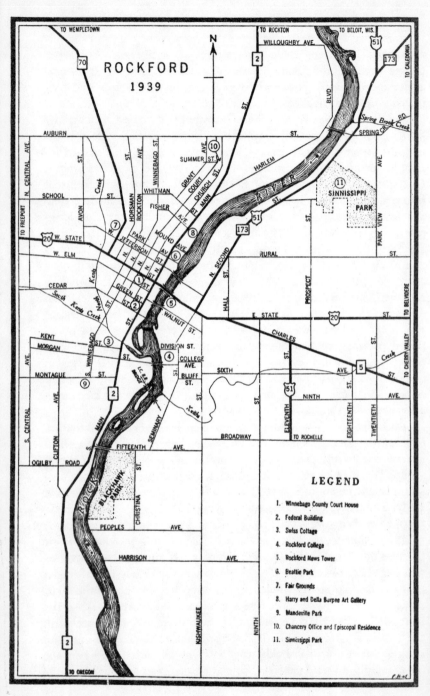

LEGEND

1. Winnebago County Court House
2. Federal Building
3. Swiss Cottage
4. Rockford College
5. Rockford News Tower
6. Beattie Park
7. Fair Grounds
8. Harry and Della Burpee Art Gallery
9. Mandeville Park
10. Chancery Office and Episcopal Residence
11. Sinnissippi Park

Irish, but in the early 1900's they too moved northward, and South Rockford was taken over by the Italians, who occupy it today, preserving a closely knit racial integrity.

Founded in 1834 by Germanicus Kent and Thatcher Blake of Galena, Rockford was settled mainly by New Englanders. Kent dammed a tributary of the Rock River, and erected a sawmill to cut the virgin timber that was to become homes for the settlers. Unconsciously he was basing Rockford's first industry on the factor that was to dominate the town for more than half a century—cheap water power. Kent and Blake were followed in 1835 by Daniel Haight, who founded a small rival settlement across the river. The two communities incorporated as the town of Rockford in 1839, but their rivalry persisted for many years.

Winnebago County was organized in 1836, and Rockford chosen as the seat in 1839 after a spirited contest with other settlements. It was fortunate that the town had a steady income from the agricultural lands around it, for the men who were guiding its destinies had accepted the major premise that the Rock River was navigable. Because of rapids and shallow water between Rockford and Rock Island, only two steamers ever docked here, and the little city's plans of becoming an important river port proved abortive.

The first years of the 1850's marked the beginning of Rockford's industrialization. Four major events baptized this new era: the Chicago and Galena Union Railroad reached the town; the Rockford Water Power Company was founded; the make-shift wooden dam across the bed of the old ford was replaced by a permanent one; and an L-shaped millrace was constructed that greatly increased space for factories and warehouses.

Perhaps equally important to Rockford's progress was the arrival in 1853 of John H. Manny. Inventor of a combination reaper and mower, Manny was brought from the East by the local firm of Clark and Utter, and turned out 150 machines for them the first year. The following year the machine was considerably improved by a new method of tempering knife sections in oil. Producing 1,100 reapers and mowers in 1854, the Rockford plant became a sizeable thorn in the side of Cyrus H. McCormick, the Chicago reaper king, who sued Manny in 1855, charging patent infringements. A silent member of Manny's successful defense staff was Abraham Lincoln.

Since the reaper had an enormous effect in increasing the agricultural output of Illinois, industrial Rockford benefited materially from its manufacture. As the acres in grain widened farther and farther across the prairies, a similar expansion of local foundries and factories occurred. When the original Manny Company was absorbed by the J. I. Case Company in 1928, it was capitalized at 50 million dollars.

Other firms manufactured plows, pumps, cultivators, and horse-power threshing machines. After the Civil War, however, the industrial make-up of Rockford shifted sharply, becoming more diversified. In 1870 John Nelson and W. W. Burson improved upon a hosiery machine they had seen in Chicago 4 years earlier, and founded Rockford's hosiery business. Important inventions in the trade, including the first fully automatic machine, have come out of Rockford, and one firm alone now produces over 12 million pairs of hose a year.

Swedish settlement dates from 1852, the year the Chicago and Galena Union Railroad was completed to Rockford. The story goes that the Swedes bought tickets for as far West as the train would take them, but, whatever prompted them to come, the city has profited much by their presence. Following their native craft and working on a co-operative basis, they established Rockford's furniture industry. The depression of 1893 wiped out the co-operatives, but the industry was re-established with private capital, and continues to thrive today.

Only a few oldsters can remember the days when Rockford's name was being sounded throughout the East because of her amateur baseball team, "The Forest City Nine." The Chicago *Evening Post* remarked in 1870:

If Chicago has no cause for local rejoicing over the achievements of her professional baseball representatives she can at least join heartily in the State pride resulting from the remarkable record made by the club of amateurs residing in the flourishing town of Rockford. . . . We consider the Forest City Nine the champion club of America.

In 1869 the club, which included A. G. Spaulding, Adrian "Pop" Anson, John Kling, and Roscoe Barnes, won 21 games and lost 4, all to the Cincinnati Red Stockings. Vindicating itself the following year by trouncing the Cincinnati team 12 to 5, the team turned professional, comprising one of the original teams of the newly formed National Association. But Spaulding and Barnes joined eastern teams, local interest died, and the affiliation with the association lasted only a year.

As Rockford firms gained State- and Nation-wide markets, they inevitably moved to the river for their power. But with the advent of modern methods of distributing electricity, the bond of the river was broken, and factories spread loosely over the southeastern portion of the city where they had more room for expansion. Mass production methods, made possible by precision instruments, inaugurated in the 1900's another of Rockford's major industries—the manufacture of machines that make machines. Multiple drills, boring and honing devices, and precision machine tools of innumerable varieties are produced here to facilitate the swift flow of the Nation's production lines.

In addition to its industrial importance, Rockford still serves as trading center for a large area of farms and small towns, in which dairying and the raising of grain and livestock are the chief sources of income.

POINTS OF INTEREST

1. The WINNEBAGO COUNTY COURTHOUSE, on the public square facing W. State St., is a hybrid structure, representing the architectural tastes of two centuries. The main part of the building, in yellow limestone of French rococo design, was completed in 1878. The modern addition, built in 1918, is of white limestone, anticipating in color and design the building which will some day replace the old structure.

On May 11, 1877, during the course of construction, the entire dome of the structure collapsed, killing seven workmen and fatally injuring two others. The coroner's jury roundly condemned the architect for incompetence and the board of supervisors for laxity in examining the architect's qualifications. Work was soon resumed, but before the building was completed, the streets of Rockford were again buzzing with talk about the courthouse. In bas-relief above the entrance appeared a group of unclothed cherubs; their presence led a committee of citizens to remark sharply in a resolution to the authorities:

Whereas, History teaches us that high attainments in Science, Agriculture and Mechanism are not, and never were, attendants of a nude civilization, making the emblems on the vestibule of the Court House inappropriate. . . . Therefore, We the undersigned, Citizens of Rockford, of Winnebago County, Would respectfully petition your honorable body to order such changes in said emblems as shall remove all occasion of offense and save the City and County from further reproach.

In the presence of the committee, workmen hastily mounted ladders and wielded chisels and hammers so that none might further reproach the City and County.

2. The FEDERAL BUILDING, S. Main and Green Sts., completed in 1933, is a three-story structure of white limestone and granite, adorned with graceful Corinthian columns. The floors of the main and outer lobbies are of Tennessee marble; walls of the main lobby of St. Genevieve rose marble. The first floor is occupied by the postal department; the remaining floors, by the army, navy, and other governmental offices.

3. The SWISS COTTAGE (*private*), 311 Kent St., faithfully follows the model of a Swiss chalet. Robert Tinker built it in 1870 following a sojourn in Switzerland. Reached by a suspension bridge across Kent Creek, the 26-room cottage contains curios collected by Tinker in Europe and the South Seas, as well as many early American pieces from the Manny home. The circular library, with its finely carved spiral stairway, is patterned after that in Sir Walter Scott's home, visited by Tinker in his travels. Given to Rockford by its owner, the house will not be opened to the public until the death of its present occupant, a niece of Tinker.

4. ROCKFORD COLLEGE for women, Seminary St. at College Ave., established as Rockford Seminary in 1849, occupies semi-Colonial, vine-covered buildings in a U-shaped group. Addams Hall stands to the north of the drive leading to the Commons, about which are grouped Sill, Lathrop, Emerson, Barnes, Chapel, Middle, and Linden Halls, built at various dates since 1852. South of these, on Morgan St., are other buildings, including the Music Hall and Maddox House, the social center on the campus.

A college course was added to the seminary curriculum in 1883, and the institution was renamed Rockford College in 1892. The college, which ranks high among Midwestern girls' schools, has long been known for its sociology courses. Jane Addams, founder of Chicago's Hull House, received the first degree to be conferred, and recently a professorship in sociology was endowed in her honor by alumnae. The enrollment of the school approximates 300 and is limited; applications for admission are usually made several years in advance.

5. The ROCKFORD NEWS TOWER (*tours for groups*), 98 E. State St., an impressive unit in the riverfront improvement program, consists of a two-story, L-shaped, main section, surmounted with a six-story tower. On the river level are the news and press rooms of the Rockford *Morning Star* and the Rockford *Register-Republic*. On the second floor are the broadcasting studios of radio station WROK.

6. BEATTIE PARK, bounded by Park Ave., N. Main St., Mound Ave., and the river, contains Turtle Mound, of the rare effigy type, and two small round mounds and an oblong one. In accordance with the donor's wishes none has been excavated. Turtle Mound is an unexplained misnomer, as the mound has the form of a lizard. The sprawling 150-foot figure stands 6 feet high, despite erosion, and is surpassed in size only by the great serpentine mound in Ohio. The Smithsonian Institution explains the absence of a head with the theory that a structure of wood or other material was used for the purpose.

7. FAIR GROUNDS PARK, 900 W. Jefferson St., was transferred to the city in 1904 by the Winnebago County Fair authorities. A boulder in the park marks the spot where General Grant made an address on September 16, 1880. The park contains a swimming pool, a bowling green, and sunken gardens that attract many visitors, especially during the early summer months when most of the flowers are in bloom.

8. The HARRY AND DELLA BURPEE ART GALLERY (*10-5 weekdays; 2-5 Sundays; free*), 737 N. Main St., the headquarters of the Rockford Art Association, provides a meeting place for handicraft, literary, and little theatre groups. Surrounded on three sides by a broad veranda and surmounted with a cupola, the Victorian house has been adapted to its present use with but little alteration from what it was when the home of John Nelson, local hosiery mill executive. Its exhibits include a small collection of paintings; the most important function of the gallery is to provide rooms for traveling exhibitions.

9. MANDEVILLE PARK, Montague and Winnebago Sts., contains the RICHARD MANDEVILLE HOUSE (*open by appointment only; apply to Mrs. Thomas Whelan, curator, 1003 N. Court St.*), built in 1837, and given to the city in 1911. It has been remodeled and serves as a house museum, containing natural history specimens collected and classified by the Nature Study Society of Rockford.

10. The CHANCERY OFFICE AND EPISCOPAL RESIDENCE (*private*), North Court and Sumner Sts., the headquarters of the

Catholic diocese of Rockford, is a Georgian building of Trenton limestone.

11. SINNISSIPPI PARK, 1600 N. Second St., comprises 123 acres in the northeast section of the city. Winding drives traverse the natural woods that overlook Rock River, and the park contains a perennial garden, a rosarium, and a lagoon, which seasonally shelters wild fowl. The greenhouses and nursery supply other Rockford parks with flowers and shrubs. An annual chrysanthemum show is held here, and the blossoming of the park's native crabapple trees attract thousands of visitors during the last part of May and the first part of June. Near the clubhouse is Lookout Point, offering an excellent view of the city.

POINTS OF INTEREST IN ENVIRONS

Camp Grant, 4 *m.* (*see Tour* 4). Black Hawk Monument, 23.7 *m.* (*see Tour* 4A). White Pines Forest State Park, 34 *m.* (*see Tour* 15).

ROCK ISLAND and MOLINE

Railroad Stations: Rock Island—31st St. and 5th Ave. for Chicago, Rock Island, and Pacific; 20th St. and 2nd Ave. for Chicago, Burlington, and Quincy; 1st Ave. and 17th St. for Chicago, Milwaukee, St. Paul and Pacific. *Moline*—1929 4th Ave. for Chicago, Burlington, and Quincy; 2016 3rd Ave. for Chicago, Milwaukee, St. Paul and Pacific; 1800 block on 4th Ave. for Rock Island Lines.

Buses: Rock Island—824 2nd Ave. for Black Hawk Motor Transit Co., and Burlington Trailways; Fort Armstrong Hotel for Chicago and North Western Stages and Illinois Transit Lines. *Moline*—1814 5th Ave. for Black Hawk, Burlington Trailways, Chicago and North Western Stages, and Interstate Transit Lines.

Airport: Moline Airport, 7 *m* SE. on US 150, for United Air Lines.

Streetcars: One line, between Davenport and Rock Island only.

City Buses: Several routes connect Rock Island and Moline.

Taxis: Rates 25c and 50c in limits; higher between cities.

Accommodations: Rock Island—five hotels. *Moline*—two hotels.

Information Services: Rock Island—Chamber of Commerce, 1910 3rd Ave.; Chicago Motor Club, Hotel Armstrong. *Moline*—Association of Commerce, 5th Ave. Bldg.; Chicago Motor Club, 1218 5th Ave.

Radio Station: Rock Island—WHBF (1210 kc.).

Motion Picture Houses: Five in each city.

Golf: Rock Island—Saukie, 38th St. and 31st Ave. and Black Hawk Hills Country Club, Coal Valley Road, both public fee. *Moline*—

Swimming: Rock Island—Y.M.C.A. pool, 20th St. and 5th Ave., men only. *Moline*—Y.M.C.A. pool, 1730 5th Ave., Riverside Park, 4th Ave. between 27th and 34th Streets, 20c adults, 10c children.

ROCK ISLAND (563 alt., 37,953 pop.) and MOLINE (586 alt., 32,236 pop.) comprise, with East Moline and cross-river Davenport, Iowa, an extensive metropolitan area known as the "Quad Cities." All four are separately incorporated and maintain their own business districts, but there is a strong rapprochement between them, stemming from proximity and nurtured by the fact that a long-time resident of Moline may well be one of the oldest employees of a Rock Island plant, and vice versa.

Both the cities face the Mississippi River, which here, for the only instance in its course down the State, runs almost due west. A short distance back from the river front, which is given over largely to factories and railroad tracks, lie the business districts of the two cities. The faintly sloping plain they occupy rises markedly just beyond the the outskirts where stores and other business houses dwindle, and the residential districts lie almost wholly on the rolling bluffs. Southward the broad valley of the Rock River marks the back yards of the two cities, and save for a narrow neck at the eastern edge of Moline, the cities are entirely surrounded by the two rivers. At the crest of the bluffs are fine views of both rivers, and here the well-to-do of the past century built their Victorian houses in spacious tree-shaded blocks.

The cities are much alike, for although the formal history of Rock Island runs farther back than that of Moline, the cities as they are today grew up hand in hand. From census to census Moline has dogged the heels of Rock Island, and once (1910) moved to within 137 persons of capturing the lead. And their parallel growth is a natural thing, since their economies are almost identical. Moline is the John Deere town, and Rock Island the home of the International Harvester, but both boom when the farmers are buying implements, and slacken when farm prices are low.

The other important factor in the lives of the cities is the Rock Island Arsenal, and the long limestone island that it occupies flanks much of both communities. Although Rock Islanders may tend, because the island is their city's namesake, to look upon it with a little possessiveness, the budget of the Arsenal is a matter of concern for Moline as well. The Arsenal can bring prosperity overnight; in peace time it averages 2,000 employees, but all except those of the newest generation remember the war years when 15,000 were working on the Island. Periodically the newspapers of both cities run editorials advocating an increased appropriation for the Arsenal.

Various Indian tribes occupied this region back into time beyond memory. The Illinois had their villages here when Marquette and Jolliet came down the Mississippi in 1673, but seven years later they were driven out by the Sauk and Foxes. When, in 1805, Zebulon Pike came up the river on an inspection trip for the government, he found 5,000 members of these tribes here. The Sauk chief, Black Hawk, described his visit:

A boat came up the river with a young American chief and a small party of soldiers. . . . He gave us good advice; said our American father would treat us well. He then requested us to pull down our British flag. . . . This we declined, as we wished to have two fathers.

The naivete of the Indians was to have a bloody result. Already their title to the land east of the Mississippi had been obscured by several treaties that they had signed with little understanding. In 1816

Rock Island was fortified by the government, and Colonel George Davenport (from whom the Iowa city took its name) became the first resident-settler. Not until 1828 did settlers come here in any numbers, but when they came trouble began before a year had passed. The settlers and the Indians claimed the same land. The whites callously plowed the ancient burial grounds of the Indians; apart from these indignities, the tribes loved this region with a fierce passion, and shortly they retaliated. The alarmed settlers finally petitioned the governor to send aid, complaining that the Indians "threaten our lives if we attempt to plant corn, and say that we have stolen their land from them, and they are determined to exterminate us."

Out of the dispute came the Black Hawk War (*see The Land and the People*), which resulted in the virtual extermination of the Sauk and Foxes, and opened all of Northern Illinois for settlement. Black Hawk was captured, and taken on a tour of the country to show him the extent of its settlement, and the folly of planning future resistance. Aged and broken, he dictated his fine simple *Autobiography,* with its dedication to the general who had defeated him in war. "That you may never experience," he wrote, "the humility that the power of the American Government has reduced me to, is the wish of him, who, in his native forests was once as proud and bold as yourself."

Rock Island County had been set up shortly before the war, but no organization was attempted until 1833. There were several small communities here then; and one of them, Farhamsburg, became county seat, only to lose that honor two years later to Stephenson. From the latter town grew the present city of Rock Island, but not until 1841 did it receive its present name.

In the meantime, an inconspicuous Negro servant had spent two years on the island with his master, a doctor at the garrison. When in later years he sued for his freedom and fought the case to the Supreme Court, the famous Dred Scott decision was handed down, ruling that "Scott was not made free by being taken to Rock Island in the State of Illinois." The implications of this decision hastened the country into the Civil War.

The forties and fifties saw the height of the steamboat era, and as many as 1,900 steamboats docked here annually. At the same time, the stripping of the northern woods began, and great rafts of logs came down to the mills for sawing. Rafts as long as a third of a mile were common, and frequently they were a hundred yards in width.

At times the broad Mississippi was so jammed with the log "islands" that upbound steamboats had to follow a tortuous course to keep in clear water.

Moline was platted in 1843 and incorporated as a town five years later. The year before Moline became a town, John Deere had come here from Grand Detour, where he had had some little success in fashioning plows that would scour clean in the gummy prairie soil. The first one he made used an old mill-saw blade, but blades were scarce and Grand Detour was a little town ten miles from nowhere. Moline was on the Mississippi, with steel readily available by boat from Pittsburgh and St. Louis, and water-power for his mills. When Moline incorporated as a city in 1872, much of its 4,000 population had come there because of the expanding Deere plants.

The railroads came in the fifties; the Rock Island was the first. In 1855 it completed its railroad bridge, the first span across the Mississippi in its entire length. The bridge became a symbol in the bitter fight between water and rail carriers. Boat after boat crashed on its piers and sank; pilots named it "Hell-gate" . . . "the invention of Satan and the Rock Island Railroad Company." Finally, in 1856, after the *Effie Afton* struck the bridge and burned, its owners brought the first suit against the railroad company, charging obstruction of navigation. "A distinguished lawyer who is employed by the bridge company to defend that mammoth nuisance," reported a local paper, "is expected in Davenport in a few days, for the purpose of examining that huge obstruction to the free navigation of the river." The "distinguished lawyer" was Abraham Lincoln, and after careful examination he prepared his defense, affirming that the steamer's starboard wheel had gone dead shortly before the crash. When the jury reached a deadlock, the steamboat company dropped the suit.

Not until 1862, after long hesitation and debate, was the arsenal located on Rock Island. At first it served as a prison for Confederate prisoners, and more than 12,000 were confined here at a time. When the Civil War ended, the Island was gradually converted to its present use.

The later stories of the two deal largely with the rise of industry to replace the declining steamboat traffic, and the lumber-milling that shortly followed the great white boats into oblivion. That their decline was crucial is evidenced in the fact that as late as the seventies 1,500,000 persons still used the Mississippi packets annually, while one local company alone milled 150,000,000 feet of lumber each year. But while the river dwindled in importance, the Deere Company was building new plants in Moline; today six of their eleven plants are located in Moline and East Moline. And Rock Island, which already had a venerable and prosperous plow company, acquired the tractor plant of the International Harvester Company. Implement making is the chief concern of the cities, but each possesses an underpinning of some ninety other industrial concerns.

POINTS OF INTEREST

ROCK ISLAND is connected with the cities of Rock Island and Moline by three bridges. More than two miles long, it is composed of solid limestone, and rises but a few feet above the river level since the dam has impounded the flow at its western edge. At the north west tip of the island stands a REPRODUCED BLOCKHOUSE, a copy of one of the buildings of old Fort Armstrong.

The ROCK ISLAND ARSENAL (*open daily; pass needed after night-fall*) occupies the greater portion of the island. Here, in rows of squat stone buildings, are stored a portion of the Nation's war supplies; in others civilian workmen produce small arms, artillery vehicles, and 1,600 other military items. The $21,000,000 property is owned by the Federal government; although visitors may walk around the grounds, none of the buildings are open to inspection except the WAR MUSEUM (*2-4 daily*). The museum contains a wide range of weapons, from early spears to modern artillery.

On the northern edge of the island stands the COLONEL DAVENPORT HOUSE, built in 1833 by the first white settler of this region. Davenport was connected with the garrison at Fort Armstrong, and not until the Indians were driven from this area did he venture up the island and build this house. Well preserved, the white frame building is the oldest in this region.

LOCK AND DAM NO. 10 span the Mississippi between the island and Davenport, Iowa. Completed in 1934, the unit cost $6,000,000, and helps to maintain a nine-foot channel in the Mississippi. Eleven great gates, each weighing 220 tons, control the stream by permitting the water to run under them, rather than over them as in ordinary dams.

VILLA DE CHANTAL, 200 13th Ave. in Rock Island, a day

and boarding school for girls, occupies a pleasant 15-acre campus. Founded in 1864 as the Francis de Sales Academy, it is now supervised by the Roman Catholic Sisters of the Visitation.

AUGUSTANA COLLEGE, bounded by 5th and 8th Aves. and 35th and 38th Sts. in Rock Island, was founded in 1860 by the Augustan Lutheran Synod. Enrolling 750 students, it comprises a theological seminary, a college department, and a school of music. Located at first in Chicago, it moved to Paxton, Illinois in 1863 and to Rock Island in 1875. The college is coeducational except for its theological department, which sends missionaries throughout the world upon graduation. The Augustana Choir, of mixed voices, has a national reputation, and annually gives a concert at Orchestra Hall in Chicago, followed by an extensive tour through the East. The DENKMAN LIBRARY (*open daily except Sun.*) houses the collections of the Augustana Historical Society, which include files of almost all the Swedish-American newspapers of North America.

The MODERN WOODMEN OF AMERICA BUILDING, (*open daily*), 318 16th St. in Rock Island, houses the national headquarters of the popular fraternal organization.

The ROYAL NEIGHBORS BUILDING (*open daily*), 230 16th St. in Rock Island, a three-story building of Bedford limestone, is the "supreme office" of the largest beneficiary society for women in the country.

BLACK HAWK STATE PARK, between 15th and 24th Sts. at the southern limits of Rock Island, covers some 200 acres of virgin woodland overlooking the confluence of the Rock and the Mississippi Rivers. The park centers on Watch Tower Hill, where in the days before the whites came Black Hawk would retire in contemplation to consider the problems of his people. At the lower end of the hill is the old graveyard of the Sauk tribe, and high on the bluff Black Hawk's two children are buried. From a fine vantage point the HAUBERG MUSEUM looks down into the valley. The rough-hewn stone building has three rooms, one devoted to Black Hawk items, including several portraits of the chief, another depicting the daily lives of the Sauk and Foxes, and a third with a gallery of Indian chiefs and the soldiers who opposed them in the Black Hawk War.

The FARMALL WORKS OF THE INTERNATIONAL HARVESTER COMPANY (*guides furnished*), 3rd Ave. between

40th and 44th Sts. in Rock Island, is one of the largest tractor plants in the world. Some 4,600 employees work in the 30-acre plant, which employs the assembly-line method.

The DEERE AND MANSUR WORKS (*apply for permit*), 5th St. and 3rd Ave. in Moline, began to manufacture corn-planters in 1877. Its range has been expended to include cotton-planters, disk harrows, end-gate seeders, alfalfa cultivators, and stalk cutters.

The JOHN DEERE WAGON WORKS (*apply for permit*), 9th St. and 3rd Ave., in Moline, is one of the largest wagon manufactories in the world. In addition to a wide range of wagons, it makes teaming gears, cotton harvesters, beet and bean harvesting equipment, and many other implements.

The JOHN DEERE PLOW WORKS (*apply for permit*), 13th St. and 3rd Ave. in Moline, employs mass production methods that can turn out a plow every 20 seconds. Parent concern of the far-flung Deere enterprises, it manufactures harrows, listers, and tillers as well as plows.

The SCOTTISH RITE CATHEDRAL, SE. corner of 18th St. and 7th Ave. in Moline, is a great modern Gothic building with a steep Bangor slate roof. Completed in 1929, the building cost a half-million dollars.

POINTS OF INTEREST IN ENVIRONS

International Harvester Company Plant, 5 *m.;* East Moline State Hospital, 5 *m.;* Campbell's Island State Park, 5 *m.* (*see Tour* 14).

SPRINGFIELD

Railroad Stations: Third St. between Washington and Jefferson, for Alton R. R., and Baltimore & Ohio R. R.; Madison St. between Fifth and Sixth Sts. for Illinois Central System. Fifteenth St. and North Grand Ave., for Chicago & Illinois Midland Ry.

Electric Interurban Station: 2015 Clear Lake Ave. for Illinois Terminal.

Bus Stations: Union Bus Station, 611 East Jefferson St., Black Hawk Lines, Greyhound Lines, Santa Fe Trailways, Western Coach Lines, Illinois Transit Lines and Central Illinois Bus Lines.

City Buses: 10c, 2 tokens 15c.

Taxis: Intra-city rates 25c, 1-5 passengers.

Street Numbering: Starting with number 100, East and West from First St.; North and South from Washington St.

Accommodations: 9 hotels; numerous tourist camps on outskirts of city.

Information Service: Springfield Chamber of Commerce, 406 S. Fifth St.

Radio Stations: WCBS (1420 kc.) and WTAX (1210 kc.).

Motion Picture Houses: 11.

Golf: Municipal links at Bunn, Bergen, and Pasfield Parks.

Swimming: Soldiers Memorial Pool, Ninth St. and Converse Ave.; Y.M.C.A., 317 South Seventh St.; Y.W.C.A., 425 South Fifth St.; Lake Springfield Beach, admission 10c, towel 10c, suit 10c.

Tennis: Municipal courts at Washington Park, Lincoln Park, Lanphier Park, and Lake Springfield.

Bridle Paths: Washington Park, West South Grand Ave., 5 miles of path.

Annual Events: Illinois State Fair, State Fair Grounds, eight days, Sat. to Sat., during the last half of Aug.

SPRINGFIELD (71,864 pop., 598 alt.), capital of Illinois, and the State's fifth largest city, lies some 20 miles west of the geographic center of the State. From the softly rolling prairies that stretch for miles in all directions the dome of the Capitol can be seen, announcing Springfield long before the first scattered homes come into view. Large farms, shadowed here and there with a mine tipple, extend to the city's door. For Springfield, capital of a farming and coal mining State, reflects its basic industries.

The city proper manifests both the well-ordered spaciousness typical of capital cities, and the disorder of smokestacks and railroad yards that attend factories and mines. Ninth Street, a north and south thoroughfare paralleling a railroad, divides Springfield roughly into capital and industrial areas. West of Ninth Street lie the business section, the great landscaped quadrangle of State buildings that center on the Capitol, and the wide shaded streets of fine houses that border and stem from the State group. East of Ninth Street are the bulk of Springfield's industrial plants and railroad yards, and the homes of 3,324 Negroes.

No other city in the United States, with the possible exception of Washington, D. C., is such a tribute in itself to a national hero. More than three-quarters of a century ago Lincoln left here for Washington, never to return alive, and at the old Great Western station told a farewell party, "My friends, no one not in my situation can appreciate my feelings of sadness at this parting. To this place and the kindness of this people I owe everything. Here I have lived a quarter of a century, and have passed from a young to an old man. . . ." The mark of Lincoln upon the city is now well-nigh ineradicable *(see Man of Illinois)*. Bronze placques mark the sites of many of his activities, his name graces one of the finest hotels, his tomb and his home are maintained by the State as public shrines, and notable contributions to American poetry—especially by the late Vachel Lindsay, long a resident, and Carl Sandburg—have dealt with Lincoln and Springfield.

The city that was to become the capital of Illinois did not exist when the State was admitted to the Union in 1818. In that year Elisha Kelly of North Carolina came to the Illinois country and wandered north to the beautiful valley of the Sangamon River in search of game. Finding the region abounding with deer and wild turkeys, and being greatly impressed with the fertility of the soil, he returned at once to North Carolina, and persuaded his father and four brothers to accompany him to this land of plenty. The Kellys erected a sturdy log house, cultivated a small plot of ground, feasted on the fish from the streams and the game at their very back door. Gradually other adventurers joined the group, and before long a tiny settlement had taken root around the Kelly home.

When Sangamon County was created in 1821, the Kelly colony was deemed the only one large enough to provide board and lodging for the county officials. On April 10, 1821, Springfield received both its name, from nearby Spring Creek and one of the Kellys' fields, and designation as temporary county seat. The county dignitaries drove a stake in the corner of John Kelly's field, and commissioned him to build a courthouse with "logs twenty feet long . . . a door and window cut out," for which the commissioners agreed to pay "the said Kelly forty-two dollars and fifty cents."

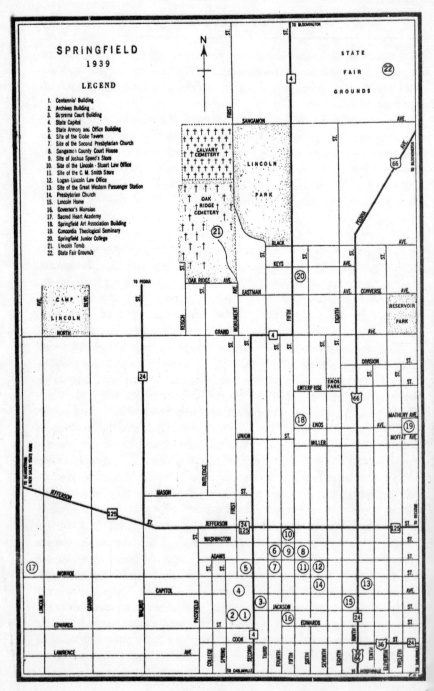

SPRINGFIELD
1939

LEGEND

1. Centennial Building
2. Archives Building
3. Supreme Court Building
4. State Capitol
5. State Armory and Office Building
6. Site of the Globe Tavern
7. Site of the Second Presbyterian Church
8. Sangamon County Court House
9. Site of Joshua Speed's Store
10. Site of the Lincoln - Stuart Law Office
11. Site of the C. M. Smith Store
12. Logan-Lincoln Law Office
13. Site of the Great Western Passenger Station
14. Presbyterian Church
15. Lincoln Home
16. Governor's Mansion
17. Sacred Heart Academy
18. Springfield Art Association Building
19. Concordia Theological Seminary
20. Springfield Junior College
21. Lincoln Tomb
22. State Fair Grounds

384

When the question of a permanent county seat arose in 1825, Springfield found a rival in Sangamo Town, 7 miles to the northwest. The legislative committee from Vandalia, having surveyed Springfield, decided to withhold judgment until they had seen its rival. Andrew Elliott, an experienced local woodsman, volunteered to guide them to the neighboring settlement, but led the party by a circuitous route through oozing swamps, across swollen creeks, and into dense patches of underbrush. By the time the weary, muddied, exasperated committee finally got back to Springfield, they had long before decided that Sangamo Town was far too difficult of access to be a county seat. Their vote for Springfield was unanimous; Sangamo Town soon declined, and no trace of it remains today.

Its future assured, Springfield rapidly expanded around the new courthouse—a "magnificent frame structure," for designing which one Robert Thompson was paid $2.25. In the spring of 1832 the *Sangamo Journal,* which had been established in Springfield the preceding November, excitedly reported the arrival of the steamboat *Talisman.* The venturesome little steamer had fought its way up the Sangamon River from St. Louis, conquering sand bars, shallows, deadheads, and leaning trees that lined the shore. "Springfield can no longer be considered an inland town," exulted the *Journal.* "We congratulate our farmers, our mechanics, our merchants and professional men, for the rich harvest in prospect, and we cordially invite emigrating citizens from other states, whether they be poor or rich, if so be they are industrious and honest, to come thither and partake of the good things of Sangamo." Unfortunately, the river fell while the *Talisman* was moored at Springfield; unable to turn around, she was forced to the ignoble expedient of backing down the river, and Springfield remained, henceforth, an inland town.

In the 1830's Springfield was experiencing the growing pains that had gripped the whole central section of the State. Settlers from the East and South were daily being lured to homesteads on these beautiful prairies by almost fabulous tales of the land's fertility and glowing accounts of unlimited water power. After the Erie Canal opened and the tide of settlement began to sweep north, agitation was begun for the transfer of the State capital from Vandalia to some town nearer the area of new settlement. Captained by Abraham Lincoln, "the Long Nine" from Sangamon County, seven representatives and two senators whose aggregate height was 54 feet, composed a formidable Springfield-for-capital bloc. This group so shrewdly traded their votes in favor of various public improvements that on February 25, 1837, the legislature awarded the prize to Springfield. In April of the same year Lincoln moved into the new capital city, then a prairie community of 1,500.

After a quarter-century of practicing law Lincoln left Springfield for the White House on February 11, 1861. During his stay the town had grown with him: in 1840 it had been incorporated as a city, a square mile in extent, with the statehouse in the center; by 1860 its population had reached 9,400. Following the ill-fated Northern Cross Railroad (see Transportation) in 1842, other lines came in and began transporting corn, wheat, and flour to Chicago and the East. Factories and mills were built rapidly. In 1853 Springfield held its first State fair, later to be an annual event. Although some crude mining of surface coal had been carried on sporadically for years, the first shaft mine was sunk in 1867, the beginning of an important industry. Today 22 mines employ 2,500 workers.

In 1865 a bill was introduced in the legislature to remove the capital to Peoria. Although the bill was tabled, anxious Springfield citizens hastily offered to purchase the capitol for $200,000; this sum was to finance the construction of a new building. In 1868 the cornerstone of the new statehouse was laid, and in 1875 the State offices were transferred to its commodious quarters. But legislative squabbles over the appropriation of supplementary sums delayed the completion of the building until 1887.

Since the closing decades of the nineteenth century Springfield has closely paralleled the State in growth. In 1914 the capital was chosen for one of the several sociological surveys made by the Russell Sage Foundation; the detailed findings of this work, published in 1918, proved of great aid to local social welfare organizations.

A comprehensive plan, making numerous suggestions for a long-range program of civic improvement and stressing Springfield's function as State capital in its city layout, was drawn up by Myron Howard West and a staff of the American Park Builders in 1924. At present the plan has been fulfilled only partly, but the work is progressing. The major civic project in Springfield's history, the creation of artificial Lake Springfield (see Tour 19), was approved in 1930, a bond issue was voted, and the immense job was carried out with the aid of Federal funds.

POINTS OF INTEREST

1. The CENTENNIAL BUILDING (*open 8-5 weekdays; Sun., 2-5*), 500 block on S. Second St., is connected with the capitol by a broad esplanade, and commemorates the first hundred years of Illinois' statehood. The cornerstone of the $3,000,000 building was laid in 1918; work was completed in 1923. Covering the site of the house where Lincoln and Mary Todd were married, the structure was intended as a museum and library, but many State offices have moved into it from the crowded capitol, and in 1930 a $1,000,000 addition was made to the south end.

From the esplanade the north façade rises 5 stories, with 12 Corinthian columns supporting a frieze inscribed with the names of prominent Illinoisans. Bronze gates guard the entrances at either end of the flower-bordered promenade. On the first floor is the Hall of Flags, lined with the standards and colors of Illinois regiments in all wars. In the basement are the NEWSPAPER ROOMS (*8:30-5 Mon.-Fri., 9-12 Sat.*), with extensive files of Illinois newspapers, including the *Illinois State Journal*, complete from 1831, the *Illinois State Register*, and the Alton *Observer*, an abolitionist periodical published by Elijah P. Lovejoy.

On the third floor is the ILLINOIS STATE HISTORICAL LIBRARY (*8:30-5 Mon.-Fri., 8:30-12 Sat.*). The Library proper contains the most comprehensive collection of Illinoisiana extant; a notable Lincoln collection covers the entire north wall. The walls in the library divisions on this floor are paneled in beautifully carved American walnut.

In the card catalogue room stands the old-fashioned walnut desk used by President-elect Lincoln in writing his first inaugural address. Here, also, is a group of graceful figurines, portraying prominent Illinois women; the figures are accurate in period costuming, and include personages from the Territorial period down to modern times.

Adjoining the catalogue room is the LINCOLN ROOM, with valuable pictures, manuscripts, and relics, vividly tracing the course of Lincoln's life. Designed especially for the Lincoln collection, the style of the room is of the Civil War period. The exhibit is arranged in chronological sequence, from the ancestry of Lincoln to his assassination and death, and includes a signed copy of the Emancipation Proclamation and many original letters. Brooding over the quiet hallowed room are two fine portraits from life, the works of William Cogswell and George H. Story.

The ILLINOIS STATE LIBRARY (*8:30-5 Mon.-Fri., 8:30-12 Sat.*), adjoins the Historical Library. Organized in 1938 to serve the legislature and the supreme court, it has grown until its various types of service reach all communities in the State. The library has three divisions, the General Library, the Archives (*see below*), and the Library Extension, which supplies books to individuals and small communities. The General Library Division serves as an intelligence agency for the State offices and the State as a whole, hence its collection is used chiefly for reference purposes.

On the fifth floor is the STATE MUSEUM (*open 8:30-5 Mon.-Fri., 8:30-3 Sat., 2-5 Sun.*), an outgrowth of the State Geological Survey, which in 1851 began to collect specimens of Illinois rocks, minerals, and fossils. In 1875 the State Historical Library and National Historical Museum was organized to care for the specimens. The Museum became a separate institution in 1889 and the scope of its collections has been broadened to embrace ethnology, botany, zoology, painting, and sculpture. The east section contains the Thomas Condell Indian handicraft group; the Clayton anthropological collection from West Africa; rhinoceros cups from the Yung Cheng dynasty; and a large number of Japanese inro, small carved medicine cases. In the main room is a systematic zoological exhibit, ranging from single-celled creatures to reptiles, including a good display of foreign and domestic birds, with all known Illinois species. The remarkably accurate habitat group of Illinois Indians, executed by Henri Marchand, was modeled from life at an Indian reservation in New York. In the west section is the Frank Grover collection of firearms; the geological collection, which includes the largest piece of copper (1,606 lbs.) ever discovered in Illinois; numerous mastodon bones found near Golconda and Chester; and an excellent group of miniature reproductions of the prehistoric monsters that once roamed the Middle Western prairies. The botanical collection has one particularly ambitious exhibit of 1,200 wax and plaster mushrooms, representing the 200 species known to exist in Illinois.

On the mezzanine, encircling the museum, is the STATE ART GALLERY. Organized in 1925, the museum opened with 12 paintings; only the works of Illinois artists are exhibited.

2. The ARCHIVES BUILDING (*adm. to first floor only*), directly west of the Centennial Building, was completed in 1937. This stone

structure, with classic detail and huge Corinthian pilasters, has 15 miles of steel cabinets and shelves, conditioned with washed and filtered air, to protect the official State and county records. Twelve floors of vaults contain records more than 10 years old, and other floors house semi-current records. The sole access to the vaults is through watchman-controlled elevators, and employees admitted may consult only their department's records, as defined by their identification key. Automatically operated steel doors can isolate any section of the vaults in the event of fire. Topping the building is a penthouse—so situated to minimize danger from explosion—containing film copies of important historical records.

3. The squat stone SUPREME COURT BUILDING *(8:30-5 weekdays)*, 400 S. block on 2nd St., stands on a terraced lawn that commands a good view of the capitol. Its Roman-Ionic columns, pedimented lower windows, and balustraded roof are consonant in style with the Centennial and Archives Building, in accordance with the Springfield plan *(see above)*.

The first floor is occupied by the offices of the clerk of the supreme court, the clerk of the appellate court, and the attorney general. A wide marble stairway leads to the second floor, with its law library, the marshal's office, and the courtrooms of the supreme and appellate courts. The third floor *(no adm.)* houses the living quarters of the justices, each of whom has a three-room suite.

4. The STATE CAPITOL *(building always open; offices open 8-5 weekdays; restaurant on 4th floor)*, 300 S. block on 2nd St., was designed by John C. Cochrane, and constructed between 1868-87 at a cost of $4,000,000. It is a cruciform limestone structure of Renaissance design, topped with a lofty dome. The octa-style façades are identical in their sandstone pediments and polished granite columns, save for the east wing, where the portico is flanked by twin turrets. At the base of the dome are four groups of Corinthian columns supporting balustrades. Twenty large circular-headed windows light the rotunda. The observation tower *(not open)* on the ribbed dome is 361 feet high.

The interior of the building is decorated with marble, blue limestone, and Missouri granite. State offices and assembly rooms open on corridors radiating from the rotunda, which extends upward six stories to the inner dome. On the first floor, facing the Second Street entrance, stands the bronze figure of *Illinois Welcoming the World,* brought from the Illinois Building after the World's Columbian Exposition in

Chicago in 1893; along the south corridor are murals depicting scenes and events of Illinois history. Above the landing of the grand staircase that leads to the second floor is a large canvas portraying George Rogers Clark negotiating a treaty with the Indians. On the second floor are the offices of various State officials, including the auditor, treasurer, secretary of state, and Governor. In the latter's reception room hang portraits of former Governors. The third floor contains a large legal library, the assembly rooms of the Senate and House of Representatives, and the offices of the Lieutenant Governor and the Speaker of the House. On the fourth floor are the galleries of both legislative branches *(legislature convenes the first Wed. after the first Mon. in odd years; sessions by special call only in even years)*.

Near the peak of the rotunda are eight statues of prominent Illinoisans, identified by plaques. A frieze depicting scenes from State history encircles the base of the inner dome. Both frieze and statues were designed by F. Nicolai, who died before the work was completed. Each statue was planned to supplement a panel of the frieze. After Nicolai's death it was discovered that the panels had not been placed in proper sequence. No realignment has been made because the artist left no key to his work.

From its slightly elevated site the capitol overlooks the whole of Springfield; its dome is visible for miles from all directions. Dominating the broad walk that leads to the Second Street entrance is Andrew O'Connor's statue of Lincoln, backed by a granite slab inscribed with his Farewell Address. Farther along the walk is the short sturdy figure of Stephen A. Douglas, U. S. Senator from Illinois, and opponent of Lincoln in the debates of 1858; the statue is the work of Gilbert Riswold. Statues of other Illinois statesmen—Richard Yates, John M. Palmer, and Pierre Menard—adorn the spacious lawn. Since the completion of the Armory to the north, the capitol is surrounded on three sides by a harmonious group of buildings, classic in design.

5. The STATE ARMORY AND OFFICE BUILDING, Monroe and 2nd Sts., the home of the Illinois National Guard, also houses a number of State offices. Constructed in 1937, it replaced the old arsenal destroyed by fire in 1934. The building is of neo-classic design and, except for the rear wall, is faced with Indiana limestone. A rusticated one-story base and a three-story row of pilasters emphasize the simplicity and virility of the structure, and at the same time complement the Centennial Building across the plaza.

The entire north and south wings are occupied by State offices and quarters of the Illinois National Guard. The drill hall, which occupies the main part of the building, also serves as an auditorium. The drill floor is surrounded by a balcony seating more than 2,500 people; when the entire floor space is utilized, the capacity is 6,000.

6. The SITE OF THE GLOBE TAVERN *(marked)* is at 315 E. Adams St. Here Lincoln lived from the time of his marriage to Mary Todd in November 1842, until May, 1844, paying $4 a week for their room and board.

7. The SITE OF THE SECOND PRESBYTERIAN CHURCH, 217 S. 4th St., is marked by a tablet. Here the House of Representatives, of which Lincoln was then a member, held its first session after the removal of the State offices to Springfield. As the statehouse had not been completed, several large churches offered to house this and other State bodies; the Senate met in the First Presbyterian Church and the Supreme Court convened in St. Paul's Episcopal Church.

8. The SANGAMON COUNTY COURT HOUSE *(open)* occupies the center of the public square bounded by Fifth, Sixth, Washington, and Adams Streets. Begun in 1837, it served as the State capitol for nearly 40 years, and was a focal point for Lincoln's activities during his residence in Springfield.

The old statehouse was built in what was then the center of town. The business district grew up around it, and so it remains today with modern office buildings dwarfing the small dignified structure. At the time of its construction the building was believed to be adequate for any demands ever likely to be made upon it, but the tremendous growth of Illinois soon disproved this supposition. Indeed, it later proved too small for the needs even of Sangamon County, to which it was sold when the new capitol was constructed. In 1899 a concerted move was begun to raze the building and build a new courthouse. Because of the old capitol's historical associations, this plan was defeated and the need for additional space was met by jacking up the entire building and sandwiching another story under it. The feat was considered an engineering miracle. The bald contrast between the relatively new lower story and the time-scarred original edifice is frequently commented on, but residents of Springfield accept it as the result of a necessary compromise.

The yellowish brown stone building is Greek Revival in style, following the mode for public buildings in the early nineteenth century.

On the Washington and Adams Street sides are porticos supported by massive Doric columns. The interior decorations are typical of the period. Stripped of modern fixtures, it would revert to the archaic political arena in which young Lincoln trained and won his first battles. The chambers of the supreme court, then housed here, echoed with his voice as he pleaded cases before the bench; in this same building he thumbed through the books of the State and supreme court libraries. It was in the present Circuit Court Room, then the Hall of Representatives, that he made his famous "House Divided" speech, and here his remains lay in state on May 3-4, 1865, prior to interment in Oak Ridge Cemetery.

9. The SITE OF JOSHUA SPEED'S STORE and the SITE OF THE LAST LINCOLN-HERNDON LAW OFFICE *(marked)* 101-103 S. 5th St., are now occupied by the Myers Building. Lincoln, an old acquaintance of Speed, moved in with him on his arrival in Springfield, and always considered him one of his most intimate friends. Lincoln's partnership with Herndon continued from 1844 until Lincoln left for the White House.

10. The SITE OF THE LINCOLN-STUART LAW OFFICE *(marked)*, 109 N. 5th St., was, for the lanky Lincoln, just a few steps from the old statehouse. Shortly after arriving in Springfield in 1837, Lincoln formed a partnership with Stuart which continued until 1841.

11. The SITE OF THE C. M. SMITH STORE *(marked)* is at 528 E. Adams St. In a room over the establishment here of his brother-in-law, Lincoln wrote, in great secrecy, his momentous First Inaugural Address.

12. The LOGAN-LINCOLN LAW OFFICE *(marked)* was on the third floor of the building at 203 S. 6th St. His partnership with Stephen T. Logan lasted from 1841 until 1844. Here also was the first law office of Lincoln and Herndon.

13. The SITE OF THE GREAT WESTERN PASSENGER STATION *(marked)*, Monroe and 10th Sts., is now occupied by the Wabash Freight Depot. On a drizzling morning, Feb. 11, 1861, President Lincoln entrained here for Washington, full of forebodings about the future of the Union.

14. The PRESBYTERIAN CHURCH, 7th St. and Capitol Ave., contains the pew rented by Lincoln's family from 1850 until 1861.

15. The LINCOLN HOME *(open 9-5 daily)*, 8th and Jackson Sts., was the only one ever owned by Lincoln; here he lived from 1844 until his departure for Washington in 1861. Built in 1839 for the Reverend Charles Dresser, who later performed Lincoln's marriage ceremony, the house is now maintained by the State. When Lincoln purchased it, there was a mortgage on it of $900, which was not mentioned in the deed. Characteristically, Lincoln remarked that he "reckoned he could trust the preacher that married him."

The frame of the building is of oak; the laths are hand-split hickory and oak; the doors, window frames, and weather-boarding are of walnut. The iron nails are all hand-wrought. The original story-and-a-half structure was remodeled in 1856 and enlarged to two full stories. The house is remarkably well preserved.

Within these walls Lincoln spent the greater portion of his much-discussed married life, moving here from the Globe Tavern as soon as the limited income from his law practice would permit. In this house three of his four children were born; the eldest, Robert, was born at the Globe Tavern a few months before the Lincolns' removal. Here, also, Lincoln's second son, Edward Baker, died.

The comfortable interior contains a number of Lincoln memorabilia, although most of the furniture is simply of the period. Among other prized pieces are his favorite rocking chair, a cupboard used as a bookcase, Mrs. Lincoln's sewing chair, and a photograph of Lincoln, known as the Ross picture, taken in 1860 for campaign purposes. The wallpaper in the south front room is an exact reproduction of the Lincolns' paper, and that in the other rooms is as similar to the original as could be procured. The two front rooms on the north side can be opened and made into one; at a grand levee here on February 6, 1861, the President-elect and his wife bade farewell to their Springfield friends.

16. The GOVERNOR'S MANSION *(open to general public on New Year's Day only)*, bounded by 4th, 5th, Jackson, and Edwards Sts., stands on a small knoll surrounded by shrubs, shade trees, and rose gardens. Begun and finished during the term of Governor Matteson (1853-1857), it quickly became a center of Springfield's social life. The two-story brick and stone structure rises from a high basement to a shingled hip roof, topped with a flat deck and balustrade. A pleasant spacious front veranda suggests the leisure and charm of the South. The ground floor contains the Governor's private office and

reception rooms; the main floor, the chambers of state, reception rooms, and the state dining room; on the upper floor are the living quarters of the Governor and his family.

17. SACRED HEART ACADEMY, Lincoln Ave. from Monroe to Washington Sts., a Roman Catholic high school for girls, was founded in 1895 by the Dominican Sisters, who have a convent here. On the grounds is a notable Grotto of Our Lady of Lourdes.

18. The SPRINGFIELD ART ASSOCIATION BUILDING *(open 10-12, 2-5 daily)*, 801 N. 5th St., is the former home of Benjamin S. Edwards, prominent Springfield lawyer and contemporary of Lincoln. Presented to the association by a descendant, the building is unchanged except in its interior. On the first floor is a permanent gallery of paintings, and space for traveling exhibits. Studios and classrooms of the association occupy the second floor.

19. CONCORDIA THEOLOGICAL SEMINARY, 12th St. and Enos Ave., was moved to Springfield from Fort Wayne, Indiana, in 1874. A training school for the Lutheran ministry, it offers a 6-year course, with a high school education prerequisite.

20. SPRINGFIELD JUNIOR COLLEGE, 1500 N. 5th St., and SAINT JOSEPH'S URSULINE ACADEMY, 1400 N. 5th St., are adjoining Roman Catholic schools. The college is coeducational and offers 2 years of accredited college work. It admits non-Catholics, as does the academy, which is a 4-year high school for girls, accredited by the State Department of Education.

21. The LINCOLN TOMB, at the end of Monument Ave. in Oak Ridge Cemetery *(open 7:30-6 daily)*, contains the bodies of Abraham Lincoln, his wife, and three of his children, Edward, William, and "Tad." Erected at a cost of $200,000 and dedicated October 15, 1874, the tomb was financed in part by small voluntary contributions from citizens throughout the country, and was designed by Larkin Meade. The exterior is unchanged, but in 1930 the interior was extensively remodeled; on June 17, 1931, the tomb was rededicated by President Hoover.

The obelisk rises 100 feet above a simple square building which stands on a beautiful headland. Around the top of the building and the polished shaft are groups of statuary in bronze, representing Infantry, Artillery, Cavalry, and Navy. In front of the entrance is a heroic bronze head of Lincoln, by Gutzon Borglum. The entrance opens into a rotunda, in which is a small model of Daniel Chester French's *Seated Lincoln*.

With the exception of the entrance rotunda and the sarcophagus chamber, this ground floor room is essentially a corridor around the base of the obelisk. In the right hand passage are many statuettes: *Lincoln the Ranger*, by Fred M. Torrey; *Lincoln the Soldier*, by Leonard Crunelle; *Lincoln as a Circuit Rider*, by Torrey; *Standing Lincoln*, by Augustus St. Gaudens; *The Freeport Lincoln*, by Crunelle, picturing Lincoln as a debater; *Seated Lincoln*, by Adolph Weinman; and *Standing Lincoln*, by Daniel Chester French.

Halfway around the passage, directly opposite the entrance rotunda, is the sarcophagus chamber, a semi-circular room of St. Genevieve Golden View marble, with black pilasters and frieze. The sarcophagus itself bears a marker of Red Arkansas Fossil granite, with the simple inscription, "Abraham Lincoln 1809-1865." Beyond is a bronze grill admitting light; above the grill are inscribed, in black marble, the words of Secretary Stanton, "Now He Belongs To The Ages." In a semi-circle around the tomb are nine flags, the grouping of which is based on Ida M. Tarbell's *In the Footsteps of the Lincolns*. The first seven flags are the banners of those States through which the family passed in successive generations, from that Samuel Lincoln, who in 1637 came from England to Hingham, Mass., down to Abraham Lincoln's generation.

In the south wall are vaults containing the bodies of Mrs. Lincoln and the children. The entrance and exit to the sarcophagus chamber have bronze grills which reveal the cornstalk motif, typical of Illinois and the prairie States that nurtured Lincoln.

Eleven years after Lincoln's death a fantastic attempt was made here to steal his body. Ben Boyd, engraver for "Big Jim" Kenealy's gang of counterfeiters, had been caught and sentenced to Joliet for ten years. Unable to replace Boyd, an excellent craftsman, the gang decided to "kidnap" Lincoln's body, bury it in the Indiana dunes, and then secretly inform Boyd of the burial place. With this knowledge Boyd was to force the Governor to "ransom" the body by granting him a pardon. The Secret Service learned of the plot and decided to catch the ghouls actually desecrating the tomb. The attempt was made the night of November 7, 1876, and was permitted to progress to the point where the gang had removed the casket from its stone covering. Then one of the service men accidentally discharged his gun;

in the confusion the officers began shooting at each other, and the gang escaped. Two of them, John Hughes and Terence Mullen, were later caught and given the maximum sentence for grave-robbing—one year in the penitentiary. Kenealy was subsequently sentenced for counterfeiting.

22. The STATE FAIR GROUNDS occupy 376 acres at the junction of Peoria and Sangamon Aves., at the northern city limits. Here, during eight days in the last two weeks in August, is held the Illinois State Fair, one of the largest in the country. From all parts of the State farmers come to display their prize stock and crops, to watch the trotting and pacing horse races, to examine exhibits of agricultural implements, to hear political speakers. The grounds are equipped with show stalls, exhibition halls, a large race track and grandstand. The fair is sponsored by the State Agricultural Association, and has been held here annually since 1893.

POINTS OF INTEREST IN ENVIRONS

Camp Butler, 6.7 *m.;* New Salem State Park, 24 *m.* (*see Tour 22*); Lake Springfield, 4.4 *m.* (*see Tour 17*).

TOUR 1

CHICAGO—CHICAGO HEIGHTS—WATSEKA—DANVILLE—
PARIS—MARSHALL; 183 m., STATE 1

Hard-surfaced roadbed throughout.
Chicago and Eastern Illinois Ry. roughly parallels the route between Chicago
and Danville, the Cleveland, Cincinnati, Chicago & St. Louis Ry. between
Danville and Marshall.
Usual accommodations throughout.

BETWEEN CHICAGO and Chicago Heights the metropolis dwindles
across a lake plain, its weakening impulse relayed from suburb to
suburb by intervening industrial plants and the weedgrown plots of
thwarted subdivisions. South of Crete, State 1 traverses farmlands
that were settled early in the nineteenth century. The trade center
villages rising from the cornfields owe their founding either to the
Hubbard Trail, the Chicago-Vincennes State Road, or the Chicago
and Eastern Illinois Railway, built between Chicago and Danville in
1871. The Hubbard Trail, which State 1 approximates, was marked
off in the 1820's by the wagon wheels of the fur-trader Gurdon S.
Hubbard (1802-1886). The Chicago-Vincennes State Road was routed
along the Hubbard Trail in 1833 and 1834.

CHICAGO, 0 m. (598 alt., 3,376,438 pop.) (see Chicago).

Points of Interest: Chicago Board of Trade Building, Union Stock Yards, Field
Museum of Natural History, Art Institute of Chicago, Museum of Science and
Industry, Adler Planetarium, Shedd Aquarium, University of Chicago, and others.

Chicago is at the junctions with State 42 (see Tour 2), US 41
(see Tour 2A), US 12 (see Tour 9), US 14 (see Tour 10), US 20
(see Tour 11), US 330 (see Tour 12A), US 66 (see Tour 17), and
the Illinois Waterway (see Tour 22).

CALUMET PARK (R), 15.7 m. (604 alt., 1,429 pop.), a suburb,
extends along the highway for half a mile.

Right from Calumet Park on Vermont Avenue to BLUE ISLAND, 2.1 m.
(605 alt., 16,534 pop.), a residential suburb centering about Vermont and Western Avenues. First settled in 1835 and organized as a village ·in 1872, Blue
Island has a population largely of German and Italian extraction. Its name
indicates the nature of its site on a glacial ridge, the only appreciable hill on
the Chicago lake plain. Rising like an island from the marshland that surrounds
it, the ridge was named by settlers for the blue haze that cloaked its dense
woods. The LIBBY, McNEIL & LIBBY PACKING PLANT (*open* 8:30-4 *daily; conducted tours*), 13635 S. Western Ave., is the main canning plant of a company
with branches throughout the world.

Left from Blue Island on Western Avenue (Dixie Highway) to a junction with 139th Street, 1.5 *m*.

Right on 139th Street to ROBBINS (602 alt., 753 pop.), 1 *m.*, one of the two all-Negro communities in Illinois (*see Tour 7*). Incorporated as a village in 1917, Robbins was named for Eugene S. Robbins, the realtor who developed the site expressly for Negroes. Save for a lumber yard and a dozen shops on Claire Boulevard, Robbins is wholly residential, its houses ranging from neat cottages to jerry-built structures of scrap materials. Despite a low per capita income, 15 churches and a public school system are maintained.

On Western Avenue (Dixie Highway) is POSEN, 2 *m.* (605 alt., 1,329 pop.), a community of industrial workers whose homes are surrounded by garden plots and small farms. Its homogeneous population (98 per cent Polish) reflects the enterprise of a Chicago realtor, whose 75 Polish salesmen sold 12,000 lots to their countrymen during 1893. Incorporation was in 1901 when neighboring Harvey attempted to extend prohibition to Posen.

RIVERDALE, 16.7 *m.* (597 alt., 2,504 pop.), a railroad center with a steel plant, had its genesis in a ferry operated across the Little Calumet River between 1836 and 1842 by George Dolton and J. C. Matthews.

HARVEY (R), 19 *m.* (608 alt., 16,374 pop.), is a manufacturing city, its industrial east side begrimed with smoke, its residential west side bordered by Kickapoo Grove, a forest preserve. When Turlington W. Harvey, Chicago lumberman and capitalist, bought this site in 1889, it was swamp and prairie, with one factory, a hotel, and a few dwellings. Two years later the village of Harvey had several factories, new schools and churches, and 5,000 inhabitants. Diesel engines, highway machinery, ranges and stoves, and railroad equipment are manufactured.

PHOENIX (L), 19.8 *m.* (605 alt., 3,033 pop.), a residential outgrowth of Harvey, is economically dependent on the factories of the latter city.

At 20.5 *m.* is a junction with US 6 (*see Tour* 14).

The 250-acre WASHINGTON PARK RACE TRACK (*racing in Aug. and Sept.; adm.* $1 *and* $2), 23 *m.*, is the annual scene of the American Derby; the CLUBHOUSE (R) is a reproduction of Mount Vernon.

HOMEWOOD, 23.3 *m.* (659 alt., 3,227 pop.), a residential suburb that adjoins Washington Park on the south, was originally named Hartford for James Hart, who platted the site in 1852.

On a 430-acre farm (L) is the GLENWOOD MANUAL TRAINING SCHOOL (*open*), 23.8 *m.*, established for underprivileged boys between the ages of 8 and 16. The institution is maintained by tuition fees and private philanthropy. The 345 pupils, enrolled on the recommendation of juvenile courts and social service agencies, receive grade school instruction and military and vocational training. There are 12 dormitories, a chapel, a schoolhouse, a clubhouse, a dining hall, and an administration building.

The route climbs the Valparaiso Moraine, 25 *m.*, which it crosses here at its widest point (15 miles). Deposited by the Wisconsin glacier, it is one of the largest terminal moraines in the world. It extends crescent-wise to the south shore of Lake Michigan, rising to a height of 200 feet above the lake plain on which Chicago is built. In contrast with the table-like lake plain, the moraine consists of low hills and marshy depressions.

CHICAGO HEIGHTS, 27.5 m. (694 alt., 22,321 pop.), is built on the comparatively high ground of the Valparaiso Moraine. In the days of exploration and settlement, the site was a meeting point for travelers from the east and south. Here the Hubbard Trail from Vincennes to Fort Dearborn crossed the Sauk Trail, along which the Indians had for generations traveled between their hunting grounds and the fur post and garrison at Detroit. The Sauk Trail became the westward artery for trappers, soldiers, settlers, and the mail. Covered wagons traversed it to lands beyond the Mississippi; the forty-niners followed it to California; New Englanders hurried over it to settle Kansas with abolitionists; and Negro slaves used it to escape from Missouri to Indiana.

The settlement at the junction of the trails became known as Thorn Grove in the 1830's. German settlers renamed it Bloom in 1849, honoring Robert Bluehm, a German patriot executed at Vienna in 1848. The present name and industrial character of Chicago Heights date from 1890 when the Chicago Heights Land Association induced manufacturers to establish plants here, bringing with them hundreds of workmen and their families. Chicago Heights was the earliest and, for a time, the most important of the steel-making communities of the Chicago district. But the blast furnaces have since been transferred to newer centers on Lake Michigan, reducing local production to steel fabrication.

Industrial plants and millworkers' houses occupy the east side of the city; the west side consists of the more spacious residences of mill officials and Chicago commuters. Many plants, including OWENS-ILLINOIS GLASS FACTORY, welcome visitors; others—among them INLAND STEEL, AMERICAN MANGANESE, and COLUMBIA TOOL AND STEEL PLANTS—owing to inherent occupational dangers, may be visited by special permission only.

Chicago Heights is at the junction with US 30 (see Tour 12).

SOUTH CHICAGO HEIGHTS, 29.7 m. (708 alt., 1,691 pop.), is a residential suburb of comfortable houses whose occupants—largely of Polish, German, and Italian ancestry—are employed in Chicago Heights industries. West of the community is the SAUK TRAIL FOREST PRESERVE.

STEGER, 30 m. (712 alt., 2,985 pop.), was named for John V. Steger around whose piano factory the town was built. The factory (L), a series of three-story brick structures, sections of which are closed, is now used for the manufacture of radio cabinets.

CRETE, 31.2 m. (720 alt., 1,429 pop.), a farm center and residential community, was platted in 1849 by William Wood, who operated a tavern here for travelers on the Chicago-Vincennes Road. Wide-girthed trees line the streets. In spring, front yards are bright and fragrant with lilacs. Crete is in the public spotlight each September when the season opens at the LINCOLN FIELD RACE TRACK (L), 34.5 m.

In the late 1820's droves of hogs owned by Gurdon S. Hubbard roamed the prairie between Crete and Danville. At intervals Hubbard and a crew of what might be termed "pigboys" rounded up the half-wild animals and drove them to Chicago where they were slaughtered.

BEECHER, 38.2 m. (723 alt., 772 pop.), named for Henry Ward Beecher (1813-87), noted divine and leader of the anti-slavery forces, provides retail facilities for the surrounding farm country. The village was platted in 1870 as a shipping point on the Chicago and Eastern Illinois Railway, then in construction. On Beecher's east side is the SHADY LAWN GOLF CLUB (18 *holes; 50c weekdays, $1 Sun. and holidays*).

South of Beecher State 1 crosses an agricultural district of orchards, truck farms, and cornfields. The farmhouses are overshadowed by silos, windmills, and red barns.

ST. JUDE'S SEMINARY (*open 2-6 Sun. and holidays*), 50.3 m., is a two-story brick structure (L) of neo-Romanesque design, built in 1938. The loggia contains a heroic marble STATUE OF ST. JUDE. The institution is maintained by the Claretian Missionaries, a Roman Catholic order, as a high school and preparatory seminary for boys.

MOMENCE, 52.7 m. (626 alt., 12,236 pop.), on the Kankakee River, was platted in 1844 by Dr. Hiram Todd and named for Isadore Momence, half-breed husband of Jeneir, daughter of a Potawatomi chief. Momence was an important point on the Hubbard Trail and the Chicago-Vincennes Road. As many as 200 wagons and pack trains sometimes camped here overnight. A flour mill was built on the island in the river in 1844. Today Momence has a dog-food plant, a textile mill, and an enamel-brick factory that makes use of local deposits of clay.

The Kankakee crossing often presented serious problems to pioneer travelers. Gurdon S. Hubbard was unable to ford the stream in November 1830 because of floating chunks of ice. "My wagon," he relates, "was one of those heavy, large-box vehicles called a 'Pennsylvania wagon,' the box of which we chinked with snow, over which we poured water, which soon froze and made it water tight. Into this we put our harness, blankets, and utensils, and using it for a boat passed safely over, the horses being made to swim. . . ."

For his memorable ride between Chicago and Danville in 1827, Hubbard has been likened to Paul Revere. Informed that the warring Winnebago might attack Chicago, Hubbard volunteered to get help. He left Chicago in the afternoon and arrived at Danville the next day.

There he raised a force of 50 men who returned with him. The attack did not occur; later the Winnebago signed a truce and the elated garrison at Chicago celebrated with a drinking bout.

ST. ANNE, 65 *m.* (678 alt., 1,078 pop.), built in a grove of maples planted by the first settlers, was founded by Father Charles Chiniquy, who, suspended from his pastorate in Bourbonnais, came here in 1852, accompanied by most of his French-Canadian parishioners. Father Chiniquy was excommunicated in 1856, and many of his congregation joined the Presbyterian Church; the log church he had built became a mission. The inhabitants of St. Anne are still largely of French-Canadian stock. French names predominate and the French language is spoken to some extent, as it is throughout this section. St. Anne's income is derived from dairying, the manufacture of brick and tile, and the canning of asparagus raised in the neighborhood.

St. Anne's Church (Roman Catholic), one block east of the highway, was built in 1872 to replace Father Chiniquy's log church, and was restored after a fire in 1893. A stone structure of Gothic design, topped with a bell tower, the church contains a shrine to St. Anne, established in 1888 to provide parishioners with a counterpart of the shrine at Beaupré, Canada. The shrine is now known throughout the Middle West and several miraculous cures have been reported. St. Anne's Day, July 26th, brings hundreds of visitors to venerate the relic of *la bonne Sainte Anne.*

MARTINTON, 73 *m.* (627 alt., 261 pop.), named for Porter Martin, a settler from Vermont, was platted in 1871 as a shipping point on the Chicago and Eastern Illinois Railway.

At 75 *m.* is the junction with US 52 (*see Tour* 15), and at 80.7 *m.* is the junction with US 24 (*see Tour* 16), which unites with State 1 for 2.7 miles (*see Tour* 16).

MILFORD, 96.5 *m.* (666 alt., 1,442 pop.), a rural trading center, was platted in 1836 by William Pickerel, proprietor of a mill near the ford where the Hubbard Trail crossed Sugar Creek, and was incorporated as a village in 1874.

At 107.7 *m.* is a junction with State 9.

Left on State 9 is HOOPESTON, 0.5 *m.* (717 alt., 5,613 pop.), a canning center. Following the construction of the Chicago and Eastern Illinois Railway in 1871, which here intersected the Lafayette, Bloomington & Muncie Railroad (now the Nickel Plate Road), three land companies platted townsites on the Hoope farm. By January 1872 there were 70 buildings and 245 inhabitants. Residents of the boom town were so confident of its rise to metropolitan stature that the first copy (January 11, 1872) of the local paper, *North Vermilion Chronicle,* was auctioned off for $32.50. Hoopeston has a can manufacturing plant, a canning machinery plant, and two canneries with an annual output of more than 30 million cans of corn, lima beans, and red beans. In addition to such crops, local farmers raise poultry and Hampshire hogs.

Near the entrance (L) to 30-acre McFERREN PARK (*swimming, boating, small zoo, and picnic grounds*), 107.8 *m.*, a bronze plaque marks the Hubbard Trail.

ROSSVILLE, 113.4 *m.* (700 alt., 1,453 pop.), entered on a street flanked with fine trees and large comfortable houses, was named for Jacob Ross, an early settler. Platted in 1857 at the junction of the Chicago-Vincennes and the Attica-Bloomington roads, the site had previously been known as Henpeck. On the lawn of the TAKE-A-REST MASONIC HOME (R), a two-story brick house with a mansard roof, is a marker designating the course of the Hubbard Trail.

At 118.7 *m.* is a junction with State 119.

Left on State 119 to ALVIN, 3 *m.* (663 alt., 322 pop.), a grain elevator village platted in 1876; L. from the north of Alvin on a graveled road to an OLD MILL, 4.2 *m.*, built in 1838. The weatherbeaten frame structure contains much of its original machinery, including stone burrs imported from France; the mill was operated until the early 1930's.

Southward the route traverses the eastern Illinois coal mining region; the terrain is broken by river valleys and the broad ridges of the Bloomington Moraine (*see Tour* 4).

In a small grove, 126.5 *m.*, is a ROADSIDE PICNIC PARK, the first (1936) to be established on a principal route by the Illinois State Planning Commission.

LAKE VERMILION (*boating, fishing, swimming*), 129 *m.*, impounded by a dam across the North Fork of the Vermilion River, is eight miles long and nearly a mile wide. Although an artificial lake, it has the appearance of a natural body of water, with summer cottages along its heavily wooded banks. At the northern end of the lake is 233-acre HARRISON PARK, a gift of the late John H. Harrison of Danville; in it are a fully equipped community clubhouse, a bridle path, and a 9-hole public golf course.

DANVILLE, 132 *m.* (601 alt., 36,765 pop.), at the junction of the north and south forks of the Vermilion River, occupies the site of an Indian village visited by Col. George Croghan, a trader, in June 1765. The Vermilion River, Croghan noted, "is so called from a fine red earth found here by the Indians, with which they paint themselves." Croghan made no mention of salines a few miles west of the village, which the Indians had tapped by means of shallow wells. The first white man to learn of the salines was Joseph Barron, interpreter of Indian dialects for Gen. William H. Harrison. Barron is said to have inspected the salines in 1801, but, as the region was inhabited by the Kickapoo, he made no attempt to claim them.

In the summer of 1819 the Kickapoo ceded a large area, including what is now Vermilion County, to the Federal government. Barron immediately went to the salines with three white companions and tested the brine for its salt content; satisfied with his find, he returned to Fort Harrison. Truman Blackman, one of Barron's party, hastily organized a secret expedition and returned to the salines in October 1819. There he left two of his men, sent two others back to Fort Harrison for equipment, while he continued on to Vandalia where, contrary to an agreement with his fellow claim-jumpers, he sought full title to the salines.

The complaints of Barron and the duped partners of Blackman created a legal snarl that was not untangled until 1824 when Maj. John W. Vance (1782-1857) obtained a lease on the salines. He imported 80 iron kettles from Louisville, Kentucky, employed nine workers, and began manufacturing salt, for which settlers traveled as much as 200 miles. When Vermilion County was organized in 1826, the Salt Works —grown to a settlement of a tavern and 12 cabins—was selected as the county seat. The county's citizens disapproved of the site, however, and in 1827 Guy W. Smith and Dan Beckwith (1795-1835), a trader at the Salt Works, offered to donate 100 acres for a new county seat a few miles to the east. Their offer was accepted. Beckwith, in his capacity as county surveyor, platted a new site, which was named Danville in his honor. Forty-two lots were sold in the new town on April 10, 1827. Beckwith built a trading post near the North Fork, in what is now Ellsworth Park. A post office and a grist mill were established in 1828; five years later Danville consisted of 81 houses and cabins.

Foremost resident of the new county seat was Gurdon S. Hubbard, who established a trading post in 1828 (changed to a "white goods store" in 1831), and led an unsuccessful movement to provide the settlement with a trade outlet on the Vermilion River. To demonstrate the feasibleness of the latter, he sent a flatboat loaded with corn, pork, and flour from Danville to New Orleans in 1831. But Danville did not hold him long; in November 1833, Hubbard sold his store and pack train of 50 horses, bundled his possessions into four Conestoga wagons, and drove across the prairie to Chicago. A month later in a letter to his brother-in-law, Dr. William Fithian of Danville, he declared: "So far I have no regret for having moved to the smaller town."

Ward Hill Lamon, a Virginian, settled at Danville in 1847. In the following year he met Abraham Lincoln, then making his first round of the Eighth Judicial Circuit. The two men became friends; in 1852 they formed a law partnership which lasted for five years. According to Judge David Davis of the circuit court, "Abe trusted Lamon more than any other man." In Danville, as in other towns on the circuit, Lincoln had a reputation as a wit and a story-teller. Here he is said to have amused fellow lawyers by wielding a lath to demonstrate the cuts he intended to use in his duel with Shields (*see Alton*).

Present day Danville is the trade center of a farming, dairying, and coal mining area. Local manufactories produce candy, bricks, butter, textiles, hardware, paper boxes, and mining machinery. The business district contains both shops of contemporary design and heavily corniced structures of the 1890's. REDDEN SQUARE, at the junction of Main and Vermilion Sts., was named for Col. Curtis Redden, a resident who was killed in the World War. The First National Bank, northwest corner of Redden Square, is on the SITE OF THE BARNUM BUILDING, in which Lincoln and Lamon maintained a law office. The Palmer Bank Building, southeast corner of Redden Square, is on the SITE OF GURDON S. HUBBARD'S TRADING POST, operated by Hubbard (*see above*) between 1828 and 1833.

Joseph Gurney Cannon (1836-1926), the distinguished representative in Congress from Illinois, resided in Danville the latter half of his life. "Uncle Joe," as he was familiarly known to the country, came to Illinois from North Carolina, and in 1861 succeeded Ward Hill Lamon as district state's attorney. In 1873 he was elected to the House of Representatives. Except for two defeats occasioned by the Populist and Progressive uprisings, he served continuously until 1923. Between 1901 and 1911 he was Speaker of the House.

The CANNON HOUSE (*private*), 418 N. Vermilion St., a two-story brick structure of Victoria style, was built in 1876. The library on the first floor, its walls hung with political cartoons, remains as it was when used by Uncle Joe. The Grier-Lincoln Hotel, 103 W. Main St., is on the SITE OF THE McCORMICK HOUSE, in which Lincoln and his circuit-riding colleagues lodged on their visits to Danville. Here Lincoln was tried before an "Orgmathorial Court" of fellow lawyers on the charge that his law fees were too low. Found guilty, Lincoln paid his fine with a gallon of whiskey.

The FITHIAN HOUSE (*private*), 116 N. Gilbert St., a two-story brick structure, was built in 1830 for Dr. William Fithian. On September 21, 1858, a large crowd met Lincoln at the railroad depot and escorted him to Dr. Fithian's home. Lincoln expressed his thanks for the reception in a brief speech delivered from the balcony at the south side of the house, as attested by a LINCOLN MEMORIAL BOULDER on the lawn.

The VICTORY MONUMENT, W. Main St. and Gilbert Ave., was designed by Lorado Taft, and dedicated in 1922 to the men of Vermilion County who died in the World War. At the base of the heroic bronze statue of Victory are granite figures of a sailor, a marine, a soldier, and a Red Cross nurse. A short distance south of the Victory Monument is the MEMORIAL BRIDGE, a reinforced concrete structure, built across the Vermilion River in 1922.

The DANVILLE VETERANS ADMINISTRATION FACILITY (*adm. by pass*), E. Main St. near the city limits, was established by Act of Congress in 1897 for disabled soldiers. Neuro-psychiatric hospitalization has been the institution's primary function since 1934. On the 535 acres of lawn and woodland are 14 barracks arranged informally around the central buildings. Grounds and buildings are valued at $3,000,000.

BELGIUM, 137 *m.* (670 alt., 484 pop.), incorporated as a village in 1909, was named for the homeland of its predominant racial group. Prior to the exhaustion of local coal seams in recent years, mining was the chief industry here and in adjoining WESTVILLE, 138 *m.* (671 alt., 3,901 pop.), which was platted in 1873 by W. P. and E. A. West. The mine-workers of both communities now travel to shafts and "strippers" five to fifteen miles distant.

GEORGETOWN, 142.5 *m.* (676 alt., 3,407 pop.), laid out in 1827, has a town square and maple-shaded streets. Among the first settlers were Quakers who emigrated from Tennessee and North Carolina because of their anti-slavery sympathies. The STAR MILL, 224 Mill St., a huge frame structure painted red, was built in 1850 and operated until 1929.

OLIVET, 144.5 *m.*, consists of OLIVET COLLEGE (*apply at office*), a coeducational Bible School and college maintained by the Church of the Nazarene. The student body, numbering about 300, is housed in two three-story brick structures (L) on a 14-acre campus.

At 145.5 *m.* is a junction with a graveled road.

Right on this road is VERMILION GROVE, 0.4 *m.*, site of the first Quaker settlement in Illinois (1820).

RIDGE FARM, 147.5 *m.* (694 alt., 888 pop.), a trading center, was platted in 1853 and incorporated as a village in 1874.

Left from Ridge Farm on Main Street to a junction with a graveled road, 2 *m.*; R. to the HARRISON PURCHASE MARKER, 2.3 *m.*, a boulder placed by the Women's Club of Ridge Farm in 1927. At this site in 1809 Gen. William Henry Harrison (1773-1841) negotiated a treaty whereby the United States obtained more than 2,000,000 acres from the Indians in return for $4,000.

The highway skirts CHRISMAN, 154.6 *m.* (645 alt., 1,092 pop.), a rural shipping point and trading center, platted by Matthias Chrisman in 1872.

At 155 *m.* is a junction with US 36 (*see Tour* 18).

The highway passes TWIN LAKES, 166.7 *m.*, and 100-acre TWIN LAKES PARK (*cabins, picnic grounds, swimming, fishing, boating*).

PARIS, 168 *m.* (739 alt., 8,781 pop.), seat of Edgar County, was platted in 1853. Here, while attending the county fair, Lincoln's kinsman, Dennis Hanks (*see Tour* 21) was run down and killed by a team of horses. Lincoln addressed an enthusiastic Paris audience in 1856 on behalf of presidential candidate John C. Fremont (1813-90). Two years later, returning as a candidate for the United States Senate, Lincoln spoke from 3 to 5 on the afternoon of September 17; that evening Owen Lovejoy, brother of the martyred Elijah Lovejoy (*see Alton*), denounced slavery from the same platform. Throughout the Civil War, Edgar County was beset with "Copperheads," several hundred of whom had a rendezvous near Paris. Their plans to attack the city in February 1864 were put down by Union troops, following minor clashes.

Present-day Paris, built around a public square, has tree-shaded streets and generously proportioned houses. Local manufactories produce shoes, brooms, broomcorn harvesters, buses and coaches, and advertising novelties.

Southward the highway traverses farming country. The old expression "everything's lovely and the goose hangs high" is claimed by old residents to have originated in the robust pioneer sport of "goose pulling," once popular in this region. A live goose, its neck stripped of feathers and greased, was suspended from a tree barely within reach of a man on horseback. Contestants, mounted bareback, galloped down a gauntlet of shouting spectators who spurred on the horses with hearty thwacks. The rider who succeeded in tearing off the goose's neck was declared the winner and awarded the remainder of the fowl.

MARSHALL, 183 m. (606 alt., 2,368 pop.) (*see Tour* 19), is at a junction with US 40 (*see Tour* 19).

TOUR 2

(MILWAUKEE, WIS.) —ZION—WAUKEGAN—WILMETTE— CHICAGO; STATE 42.

Wisconsin Line to Chicago, 53 m.

Hard-surfaced roadbed throughout.

The Chicago & North Western Ry. and the Chicago, North Shore and Milwaukee R. R. (electric) parallel the route throughout.

Ample accommodations.

BETWEEN THE Wisconsin Line and Chicago, State 42 (Sheridan Road) follows the shore of Lake Michigan, which stretches toward the eastern horizon. Traversing a brief agricultural area, the route crosses the heavy industrial region of Waukegan and North Chicago and, winding and dipping through thickly forested sections, proceeds south past Chicago's wealthy North Shore suburbs.

State 42, a continuation of Wisconsin 42, crosses the Wisconsin Line, 0 m., 8 miles S. of Kenosha, Wisconsin (*see Wisconsin Guide*).

WINTHROP HARBOR, 1 m. (598 alt., 661 pop.), grew out of the acquisition in 1892 of 2,700 acres of dairy farm land by the

Winthrop Harbor and Dock Company, which planned to develop a harbor and establish an industrial town. With the collapse of the plan, dairying continued as the chief occupation of the community, and today its sole industrial plant is an ultra-modern dairy near the North Western station.

ZION, 3 m. (633 alt., 5,991 pop.), was founded by a man who believed the world to be flat despite his having taken a trip around it. The town enforces one of the most stringent sets of blue laws in the country.

In 1899 Chicago real estate offices were buzzing with rumors of a big land deal on the North Shore. On the night that marked the end of the nineteenth century, the man behind the deal revealed himself as John Alexander Dowie (1847-1907), Scottish faith-healer who, four years before, had founded the Christian Catholic Apostolic Church. He announced his plan for the city of Zion, a community where the tenets of that church would govern every phase of life. "Our motto," affirmed Dowie, "the unalterable and unassailable truth that where God rules, man prospers . . . our object, the establishment of the rule of God in every department of the government."

To the hastily erected town flocked hundreds of Dowie's followers, and within a few years Zion's population reached 10,000. Although Dowie planned the physical features of the town before a spade of earth was turned, he ignored the economic structure, except to establish a lace factory, for the operation of which he imported skilled workers from Nottingham, England. The real industrialization of Zion was largely the work of Wilbur Glenn Voliva, who succeeded Dowie upon his death in 1907.

Under Voliva, Zion has had a roller-coaster existence. Bankrupt in 1906, redeemed from bankruptcy in 1910, booming with prosperity in the 1920's, into receivership again in 1933, Zion had not, until recently, modified the essential structure of theocratic government. The church, under the tight control of its overseer, owned all industries and commercial establishments but one. The use and sale of liquor, tobacco, playing cards, oysters, pork, and clams are prohibited. Through a special ruling obtained from the Illinois Commerce Commission, no trains stop in Zion on Sunday. In 1939 Voliva lost his control as overseer; titles to real estate were being transferred to individuals; and other modifications of the theocratic government and managed economy seemed imminent.

In ZION AUDITORIUM, 27th St. and Enoch Ave., a 3-story, gray stone building, an elaborate Passion Play is given annually (*Sundays, Palm Sunday through June,* 3 P.M.). Research for the settings was done by the play's conductor, who made a special trip to Palestine for that purpose. ZION HOME, on Elijah Avenue, a gray frame, block-long building erected in 1904, serves as a hotel and divine healing home. A ground-floor porch extends along the entire front exposure, and an upper porch in the center of the structure separates a belfry and a short, square, box-like tower. A green Moorish turret, supported by pillars, guards the southern end of the building. Zion Home, the only available eating place on Sunday, strictly observes the ban on oysters, clams, and "swine's flesh," offering for the latter a substitute called "Zion beef bacon." The square, gray frame Zion Administration Building, across the street from the Home, has a gray-green roof with gables, and is faced by a porticoed entrance. The building houses the offices of Zion Industries, Inc., and serves as the general administrative quarters for the town.

The Zion Lace Industries Plant (*open only to those affiliated with the trade*), on 27th Street, is the sole Zion industry operated by outsiders. It was acquired by the Marshall Field Company of Chicago following the bankruptcy of 1906.

At 5.5 *m*. is a junction with a graveled road.

Left on this road is the entrance to Dunes Park (*adm.* 10c), 0.5 *m.*, 1,500 acres of duneland along three and a half miles of beach. This typical dune region, with pine and oak woods, cactus, juniper, and bearberry clinging to windblown sandhills, has been kept in its natural state.

WAUKEGAN (Ind., fort or trading post), 10 *m*. (669 alt., 33,499 pop.), the seat of Lake County, is on the site of an Indian village that was known to seventeenth-century explorers. La Salle and Hennepin are reported to have recommended the establishment of a trading post in the village. The post, listed on eighteenth-century maps as Little Fort because of the small stockade that the French erected, remained a minor French outpost until about 1760. Potawatomi continued to occupy the Little Fort region long after the area became part of the United States (1783). Pioneers who would have attempted settlement were restrained by an Act of Congress and an Indian treaty that forbade the entry of white men until after August 1836, and, in turn, provided for the evacuation of Indians from the territory before that date.

Thomas Jenkins of Chicago, anticipating the departure of the Potawatomi, came to Little Fort in 1835 and set up a general store. The decayed timbers of the old French fort were still visible near what is now the intersection of Water Street and Sheridan Road; for that reason the flourishing settlement that arose around Jenkins' establishment retained the traditional name.

Little Fort superseded Libertyville as county seat in 1841. As totaled several years later the community had "three commodious public houses, seven stores, two blacksmith shops, one chair and cabinet factory, one pier, and a second being constructed, and two brickyards." Designated as a United States port of entry in 1846, Little Fort became the chief outlet for the region's abundant furs, hides, pork, oats, wheat, and wood. When it was incorporated as a village in 1849, the inhabitants voted to change the town's name to Waukegan. A decade later, caught up in the same expansion that boomed Chicago, Waukegan was organized as a city.

The shops and residences of Waukegan are on a bluff overlooking Lake Michigan. The lowlands between the base of the bluff and the waterline of the city harbor are jammed with factories that back the piers and railroads. Here are produced gas, tool steel, locks, chemicals, machinery, sausage, babbitt, envelopes, asbestos products, outboard motors, refrigerating units, ornamental and industrial steel fences, ignition contacts, and pharmaceuticals. Coal, coke, and raw materials comprise the bulk of the cargoes landed at Waukegan.

On April 2, 1860, Abraham Lincoln visited Waukegan and spoke at Dickinson Hall. His speech here was the only one he did not finish. While addressing the audience of 400 people, he was interrupted by a fire alarm from outside. One of his listeners arose and stated his belief that the alarm was a Democratic plot to break up the meeting. However, the uneasiness among the people continued and Lincoln finally stopped and said, "Well, gentlemen, let us all go, as there really seems to be a fire, and help to put it out."

NORTH CHICAGO, 12 m. (673 alt., 8,466 pop.), and Waukegan constitute a continuous industrial area with 65 diversified industries manufacturing more than 200 commodities. In North Chicago, State 42 is the main business street, along which are the more important shops and restaurants and the City Hall. Along the lake-shore east of the business district is Foss Park (*May 30-Sept.* 15; *camp sites 50c a night or $2 a week, including stoves, tables, chairs, and running water*), a 34-acre recreational tract. The stretch of wooded bluffs and sandy beach has complete playground equipment, with facilities for boating, tennis, baseball, dancing, and swimming.

From the Fansteel Metallurgical Corporation Plant, 2200 Sheridan Rd., a long, two-storied brick building of modern industrial design, 63 sit-down strikers were driven by tear gas in 1937. Two years later, in March 1939, the U. S. Supreme Court, by reversing an order of the National Labor Relations Board that the strikers be rehired, ruled, in effect, that sit-down strikes are illegal.

The GREAT LAKES NAVAL TRAINING STATION, 13.3 m. (9 *to sunset; guides at entrance gates*), only major naval unit in the Middle West, is one of four in the United States. In 1937, 2,943 recruits, ranging in years from 18 to 25, trained here. About 245 men leave the station each month, after 12 weeks of intensive training, for assignment to ships or naval trade schools. The station was first designed to accommodate 1,500, but during the World War (1918) the area and structures were increased to receive and train 50,000 men. Closed for some time after the war, it was reopened in July 1935.

The station is in a wooded area, an excellent setting for the Colonial style of its architecture. The grounds cover 507 acres, with

117 buildings, including barracks, marine hospital, field house, swimming pool, bowling alleys, auditorium, and library. Dress parade is held during the summer months on Wednesday, at 3 P.M., with music by the Great Lakes Band. The HOSTESS HOUSE (*open to public*) contains a restaurant and rest rooms. The Navy Day celebration, October 27, is the station's chief "show" day.

At 13.6 *m.* is a junction with a paved road, reached by a sub-pass.

Left into this sub-pass; R. on the road to the VETERANS ADMINISTRATION FACILITY HOSPITAL (2-4 *Tues., Thurs., Sat., Sun., and holidays*), 0.6 *m.* The hospital, maintained and operated by the Veterans' Administration of the Federal Government, is for the care of veterans afflicted with mental illness necessitating hospital care. In a wooded area of 590 landscaped acres, the hospital is an almost self-sufficient unit, with its own slaughter house, laundry and power house.

The entrance, 14.6 *m.*, to ARDEN SHORE, a year 'round recuperative center operated by the Gads Hill settlement of Chicago for underprivileged mothers and children of the settlement neighborhood, also leads to the THORNE DONNELLY EXPERIMENTAL RADIO STATION W9TZ (*private*), on Mr. Donnelly's estate.

In June of each year scientists, amateur radio operators, and owners of amateur stations gather as Mr. Donnelly's guests for what they call a "hamfest," to interchange ideas and discuss matters pertaining to the development of radio. The station was in direct contact with Commander Eugene F. McDonald, Arctic explorer, on his last polar expedition, and was one of the key stations in the pick-up for the McMillan and Byrd expeditions.

LAKE BLUFF, 15.6 *m.* (683 alt., 1,452 pop.), is the most northern of the North Shore suburbs, separated by the Great Lakes Naval Station from the nearby industrial districts of North Chicago and Waukegan.

Lake Bluff first became generally known in 1874, when it was chosen as a camp-meeting ground by a group of Methodist ministers and laymen. A tabernacle in the campground was the scene of an important State W.C.T.U. convention in 1881 and of a conference of the Prohibition Party in 1885. The campgrounds and buildings were disposed of in 1898, but residents exhibit as relics garden benches made of the tabernacle wood.

LAKE FOREST, 18 *m.* (713 alt., 6,554 pop.), is known as the wealthiest of the North Shore suburbs. Magnificent estates, many surrounded by high iron fences, border both sides of State 42. Large groves of timber outline beautifully landscaped lawns; statues, formal gardens, pavilions, and stone benches are placed with an eye to beauty and functional use; occasionally a tennis court or swimming pool is visible from the road. The architecture of the costly homes, many silhouetted against the blue waters of Lake Michigan, ranges from the elaborate pre-World War styles to the straight-line modernity of Frank Lloyd Wright.

Lake Forest was first settled in 1835. Deerpath Avenue, once an actual deer and buffalo path leading to the lake, made a convenient portage track to the Des Plaines River and was a thoroughfare for trappers, traders, and explorers in early days. Green Bay Road, west of the North Western tracks, was once an Indian trail to the Green Bay region. In 1856, two years after the railroad went through, a company of Chicago businessmen bought 1,300 acres of land and planned the town. David Hotchkiss, a St. Louis landscape architect, laid it out, making use of the beauty of the deep ravines and wooded bluffs. The winding streets through which Sheridan Road twists are part of his handiwork.

Fifty-two acres were reserved for school purposes and every alternate lot was assigned as an endowment for LAKE FOREST COLLEGE, Sheridan Rd. and Deerpath Ave. The college is divided into two campuses; the most outstanding building on the North Campus, at Deerpath Avenue, is of ivy-covered red stone, with a red roof; the South Campus, a few blocks away, comprises a group of gray stone and red and yellow brick buildings, set among handsome trees and well-kept lawns. The first unit of the college, a preparatory school for boys, LAKE FOREST ACADEMY, 677 E. Rosemary Rd., was opened in 1857. The second unit, a school for girls, FERRY HALL, 541 N. Mayflower Rd., was opened in 1869. The coeducational college, opened in 1876, provides higher education for graduates of the two lower schools. In 1925 the Academy and Ferry Hall withdrew from the college and became independently controlled.

Across Sheridan Road from the college stands the PRESBYTERIAN CHURCH, organized in 1859 in connection with the college. The bituminous limestone used in the construction of the present building, erected in 1871, was salvaged after the Chicago fire from the Second Presbyterian Church in that city. The PUBLIC LIBRARY, 360 Deerpath Ave., of pink Holland brick and white stone, won the 1931 Craftmanship award of the Chicago Architects Club. The building is surmounted with a large glass dome that serves as an effective skylight. North two blocks from Deerpath on Western Avenue is MARKET SQUARE, a group of stores housed in Elizabethan styled buildings surrounding a village green.

At the intersection of Sheridan and Westleigh Rds. is the entrance (R) to the grounds of SACRED HEART ACADEMY and BARAT COLLEGE. The preparatory school and liberal arts college operate in connection with a convent, vicariate headquarters for the order. The red stone main building, all but hidden from the road by trees, dates from 1904.

FORT SHERIDAN, 21.1 m. (*grounds open to public during day*), a United States Army post, consists of about 725 acres of wooded bluffs rising in places 100 feet above Lake Michigan. The fort was used as a camp during the Spanish-American War, and 3,000 officers were trained here during the World War. For two years after the war the post was given over to the rehabilitation of wounded soldiers; thousands passed through the hospital and received vocational training. In addition to serving as an Army post, Fort Sheridan is now used to train reserve officers, CMTC recruits, and ROTC members during the summer months.

HIGHLAND PARK, 24.1 *m.* (691 alt., 12,203 pop.), one of the largest residential suburbs of the North Shore, stands on the site of two Potawatomi villages. White settlement began with the construction of the Green Bay House (1834), a tavern on the Chicago-Milwaukee post road, now Waukegan Road. The name Port Clinton was used in 1850, during the city's brief career as a lake port. The railroad company named its station Highland Park in 1854, and the town was incorporated under that name in 1867. It was laid out to take full advantage of the natural beauty of its lake shore, bluffs, woods, and ravines. Cottages of modified Colonial and English designs are features of the residential districts.

On Sheridan Road, opposite the entrance to Lake Shore Country Club, is an INDIAN TRAIL MARKER, a bent tree that the Potawatomi twisted as a sapling to mark one of their trails.

The DEERFIELD-SHIELDS TOWNSHIP HIGH SCHOOL, Vine and St. John's Sts., is an L-shaped, red brick building, with white trim around its windows. The functional design of the original building has been duplicated in the large annex, which forms the north portion of the ell. Each year the students of the vocational training department build a five- or six-room house, which is sold to finance a similar undertaking the following year.

In Highland Park along the highway (R) is RAVINIA PARK (*adm. 75c, reserved seats in the roofed pavilion 75c add.; free parking*), long the summer music center for the Chicago area. Like a faded diva, Ravinia has seen great days. Begun as a privately operated amusement park, it was taken over in 1910 by North Shore residents who promoted a series of symphony concerts each summer. After 1916 the burden of sponsorship was largely assumed by Louis Eckstein, Chicago real estate dealer and mail order executive, who changed the programs from symphony to grand opera. Audiences of 10,000 were common, but the policy of maintaining popular prices while presenting top-rank opera stars resulted in a deficit each year. Year after year Eckstein met the deficits, which often exceeded $100,000, but in 1931 the burden became too great and the programs were discontinued. Five years later the park was reopened with a series of more modestly budgeted symphony concerts, which were repeated in 1937 and 1938.

GLENCOE, 27.9 *m.* (673 alt., 6,295 pop.), was first settled about 1836, and was incorporated as a village in 1869. The name is a compound of "glen," suggestive of the site, and "Coe," the maiden name of the wife of Walter S. Gurnee, one of the founders. The GURNEE HOUSE (*private*), a three-story yellow brick building with elaborate porches and gables, still stands on Green Bay Road, opposite the North Western station. It was built in the 1870's. Glencoe's public schools are rated among modern educators as models of progressive teaching. The method of study guidance draws a close parallel between the subjects studied and the daily life of the community.

WINNETKA, 31 *m.* (651 alt, 12,166 pop.), a suburban village incorporated in 1869, also is known for its public school system. The Winnetka schools were organized in 1919 under the direction of Carleton Washburne, superintendent. The program advocates self-reliance and allows children a great deal more freedom than is customary in the average school system. The child studies arithmetic and spelling by himself, sets his own pace, checks his own work, and receives aid from his teacher only when necessary. Social ideals are obtained through group activities, during which the pupil translates many of his studies into action. The child thus in large part educates himself, and his own goal card, which he keeps and on which he records his progress and social attitudes, becomes more important to him than the record kept by his teacher.

The NORTH SHORE COUNTRY DAY SCHOOL is a private organization for children from kindergarten through high school. It occupies the former Garland Mansion, 310 Center St., and Leicester Hall, 301 Forest Ave., the latter built in the 1880's to house a preparatory academy for the original Chicago University.

The HADLEY CORRESPONDENCE SCHOOL FOR THE BLIND has headquarters at 584 Lincoln St. Organized and incorporated in 1922, it offers extension courses to the blind free of charge. The school was founded by William A. and Jessie H. Hadley, and is conducted by the former, now blind, a prominent educator once connected with the Chicago public schools. Directors of education for the blind throughout the country make up the advisory board, and the school is supported by donations and a community chest.

On Tower Road, L. of the highway, is the WATER TOWER (1893) of the community-owned and operated water plant. The plant, at the base of the steep bluff on which the tower stands, is integrated with the municipal electric plant, resulting in numerous economies in the operation of both.

KENILWORTH, 33.2 *m.* (615 alt., 2,501 pop.), is named for Sir Walter Scott's novel, and many of the streets in its hilly residential section commemorate places or characters in the book. In the cloistered yard of the CHURCH OF THE HOLY COMFORTER (Episcopal), 333 Warwick Rd., is the GRAVE OF EUGENE FIELD. The remains of the "children's poet" were brought here from Graceland Cemetery, Chicago, in 1925. Those of Mrs. Field, his survivor by more than forty years, were buried beside him in 1936.

No MAN'S LAND, 33.7 *m.*, offers a brief and sharp contrast to the remainder of the North Shore. Brightly colored stucco buildings with Spanish names provide commercial recreation—dancing, drinking, dining, and movies. Access to the lake and beach, exclusive elsewhere in the North Shore, may be had here for a nominal price. This bright spot, which on a summer's day contrasts strikingly with the quiet of the residential suburbs, is so named because a strip of lake shore frontage was not included in the corporate limits of either Kenilworth or Wilmette.

WILMETTE, 34.7 *m.* (614 alt., 15,233 pop.), the largest of the residential North Shore suburbs, was named for its first white settler, Antoine Ouilmette, a French-Canadian whose Indian wife received the land under a Government treaty in 1829.

Visible along the North Shore from a distance of several miles is the graceful white dome of the BAHA'I HOUSE OF WORSHIP (*visiting, 10-4 daily; open meetings, 3:30 Sun.*), R. of the highway at Linden Avenue. Designed by the late Louis J. Bouregeois, the temple is the sole North American house of worship of the faith founded in the 1860's by Baha'u'llah (1817-92), a Persian religious leader. The Baha'i faith correlates the major religions with the tenet that God has periodically revealed, through such prophets as Buddha, Zoroaster, Moses, Christ, and Mohammed, such of the truth as man has been capable of assimilating. Members of the faith believe that Baha'u'llah was the latest of these prophets, or "Manifestations." The unity of all religions and peoples is taught, as well as universal education, world peace, the equality of the sexes, and a universal language; a simple life of service is advocated. There is no clergy; teachers of the faith work without remuneration; no formal services are held; contributions are accepted from members only, and only from those members who are free of debt. The faith spread to America in the early 1900's through the teachings of the son of Baha'u'llah, Abdu'l-Baha (1844-1921), who laid the cornerstone of the temple. Actual construction was not begun until 1930.

The building, in process of construction, employs the elements of many architectural styles, blended into a harmonious pattern that is distinguished for its lightness and grace. A nine-sided structure, it rests upon nine caissons of steel and concrete; the nine sides of the clerestory and of the dome are staggered upon the nine sides of the base. Glass, mounted in metal, is used extensively, both in the dome and clerestory and in the lower part of the building. When completed, the steel and concrete of the structure and the metallic forms that hold the glass will be concealed by delicate traceries in molded materials that will overlay the exterior walls and dome and cover the interior as finely traced grills. The design of the ornamentation is geometric; the symbols employed are largely astronomical. The color will shade from white on the dome to light buff at the base.

From the auditorium, beneath the great dome, open nine chambers separated by nine hallways. These smaller rooms, which will be used for study and meditation, are comparable to the chapels of a cathedral. The numbers nine and nineteen, recurrent throughout the structure, illustrate, according to a Baha'i publication, the "basic principle of Unity—nine being the number of perfection, containing in itself the completion of each perfect number cycle, and nineteen representing the Union of God and man, as manifested in life, civilization and all things."

In the financing of the temple, the East has contributed to the West, the coppers of impoverished Persians supplementing the generous gifts of affluent Americans. Eventually the grounds will be landscaped in the Eastern manner, and the temple will be the center of a group of Baha'i buildings which will include a hospital and a school.

EVANSTON, 40 *m.* (603 alt., 63,338 pop.) (*see Evanston*).

Points of Interest: Northwestern University, Gross Point Lighthouse, the Cradle, and others.

CHICAGO, 53 *m.* (598 alt., 3,376,438 pop.) (*see Chicago*).

Points of Interest: Chicago Board of Trade Building, Union Stock Yards, Field Museum of Natural History, Art Institute of Chicago, Museum of Science and Industry, Adler Planetarium, Shedd Aquarium, University of Chicago, and others.

Chicago is at the junctions with State 1 (*see Tour* 1), US 41 (*see Tour* 2A), US 12 (*see Tour* 9), US 14 (*see Tour* 10), US 20 (*see Tour* 11), US 330 (*see Tour* 12A), US 66 (*see Tour* 17), and the Illinois Waterway (*see Tour* 22).

TOUR 2A

(MILWAUKEE, WIS.)—CHICAGO—(HAMMOND, IND.); US 41
Wisconsin Line to Indiana Line, 64 *m.*

Concrete road-bed throughout; four lanes divided by parkway.

The Chicago & North Western Ry.; the Chicago, Milwaukee, St. Paul and Pacific R. R.; and the Chicago, North Shore and Milwaukee R. R. (electric) parallel the highway at varying distances throughout.

Limited accommodations.

US 14 crosses the Wisconsin Line, 0 *m.*, 38 miles S. of Milwaukee, Wisconsin (*see Wisconsin Guide*).

Compared with State 42 (*see Tour* 2), the lake-shore route to the east, or US 45 (*see Tour* 3), the scenic road to the west, US 41 is an uninteresting express highway. Such charm as it may possess lies more in its clean-cut lines and freedom from dangerous intersections than in beauty of scene or history of settlement. It is the direct through traffic highway between Milwaukee and Chicago.

Points of scenic or historic interest in the region are largely along the highways that parallel US 41 to the right and left. Yet the route is not devoid of aesthetic appeal. South of the Wisconsin Line the valley of the Des Plaines is followed for 10 miles. Then the road rises to the upland to sweep over gentle grades from the crests of which broad pasture lands and vast estates stretch to the wooded horizon. Southward for 30 miles, the embanked road runs down the center of Skokie Valley, until recent decades a continuous marsh that resisted settlement. Today much of the valley remains in wild lands, but some sections have been drained, and small suburban communities or rich, black farm lands have replaced quaking bogs and peat beds. Near Chicago, country clubs and golf courses are numerous.

Entering Chicago from the north, the highway quickly reaches the lake shore, and follows outer drives through lake shore parks, past Chicago's skyline, to the intersection of Michigan Ave. and Jackson Blvd., in the heart of the city.

CHICAGO, 49.5 *m.* (598 alt., 3,376,438 pop.) (*see Chicago*).

Points of Interest: Chicago Board of Trade Building, Union Stock Yards, Field Museum of Natural History, Art Institute of Chicago, Museum of Science and Industry, Adler Planetarium, Shedd Aquarium, University of Chicago, and others.

At Chicago are junctions with State 1 (*see Tour* 1), State 42 (*see Tour* 2), US 12 (*see Tour* 9), US 14 (*see Tour* 10), US 20 (*see Tour* 11), US 330 (*see Tour* 12A), US 66 (*see Tour* 17), and the Illinois Waterway (*see Tour* 22).

Southward from the Loop US 41 follows lake shore drives past several parks and crosses the Indiana Line, 64 *m.*, at Hammond, Indiana (*see Indiana Guide*).

TOUR 3

(Union Grove, Wis.) —Libertyville—Kankakee—
Champaign and Urbana—Mattoon—Norris City—
(Paducah, Ky.) ; US 45
Wisconsin Line to Kentucky Line, 430 m.

Hard-surfaced roadbed throughout.

The route is paralleled by the Minneapolis, St. Paul & Sault Ste. Marie Ry. between the Wisconsin Line and Des Plaines; the Illinois Central R. R. between Kankakee and Effingham; the Baltimore & Ohio R. R. between Louisville and Norris City; the Cleveland, Cincinnati, Chicago & St. Louis Ry. between Norris City and Vienna; and the Chicago, Burlington & Quincy R. R. between Vienna and Metropolis.

Usual accommodations throughout.

US 45, longest highway in Illinois, extends from lake-studded dairy lands in the north, past suburbs of Chicago, through cities and towns and interminable prairie cornfields, across the coal mining district of southern Illinois, through the wooded hills of the Ozarks, to the historic valley of the Ohio.

Section a. Wisconsin Line to Kankakee, 103 m.

BETWEEN THE Wisconsin Line and Kankakee US 45 crosses the rolling hills of the Valparaiso and associated moraines, the most vigorously glaciated part of Illinois. In the extreme north is the Chain-O'-Lakes of the Fox River system, a summer playground of Chicago; along the Des Plaines River are the forest preserves of Cook County; throughout are dairy farms producing for the urban market. In summer the green meadows and woodlands, and the ripening fields of hay, oats, corn, barley, and alfalfa are varied with the black and white of Holstein herds. In winter snow covers the scene; cows and crops are moved into the spacious red barns and tall silos that dominate the farmsteads, and the process of producing Chicago's milk goes on.

US 45 crosses the Wisconsin Line, 0 m., 14 miles S. of Union Grove, Wisconsin (see Wisconsin Guide).

MILBURN, 6 m. (744 alt., 155 pop.), a century-old village, was so named by Scottish settlers. At the principal intersection is a two-story brick store (R), built in the 1840's.

Right from the old store on a graveled road to HASTINGS LAKE, 1 m., surrounded by a 267-acre tract in which the Chicago Y.M.C.A. maintains three summer camps. Pheasant and other small game abound; the lake is stocked with fish.

South of Milburn the highway sweeps up and down easy grades through high rolling country.

On the shores of DRUCE LAKE (*boating and swimming*), 9 *m.*, are 300 cabins, cottages, and year-round homes; southward is the summer colony of LEWIN PARK (*cottages for rent*), 10 *m.* In the vicinity of the latter are many INDIAN MOUNDS, none of which has been excavated.

GAGES LAKE PICNIC GROUNDS (*adm. 50c per car, including use of grounds and bathhouses; camp tents $7 a week, cabins $10; restaurant*), 10.3 *m.*, is a privately owned 12-acre tract adjoining Gages Lake (L). In summer the grounds are managed by students from the University of Illinois.

At 11.7 *m.* is a junction with State 20.

Right on State 20 to GRAYS LAKE, 1.8 *m.* (799 alt., 1,120 pop.), named for the lake at its western edge (*free swimming and fishing; boats, cabins, and cottages at moderate rates*). Local industries include cement plants, planing mills, a gelatin factory, a condensery, and a corn and pea cannery.

At 16.5 *m.* is a junction with State 63.

Left on State 63 to the SERBIAN ORTHODOX ST. SAVA MONASTERY (*grounds open*), 0.8 *m.*, diocesan headquarters of the Serbian Orthodox Church in Canada and the United States. The monastery was established in 1923 by Bishop Mardary (1890-1935), a Montenegrin cleric. The CHAPEL (*open to public*), a cement stucco structure of Russian and Byzantine styles, is topped by a central dome surrounded by 12 spires, symbolic of Christ and His disciples. Behind the chapel are outdoor STATIONS OF THE CROSS. Bordering a nearby stream are grounds where the congregation picnics. Clad in peasant garb, they sing native songs and perform old-world dances to the accompaniment of odd musical instruments.

LIBERTYVILLE, 18 *m.* (698 alt., 3,791 pop.), originally known as Independence Grove, was given its present name in 1837 when the post office was established. Indians, attracted by the mineral springs that dot the area, encamped annually near the settlement. Much of the forest in which they hunted remains uncut. Among the early purchasers of land in this vicinity was Daniel Webster (1782-1852), American orator and statesman. Wealthy Chicagoans later developed many estates on the surrounding wooded hills and fertile farm lands. Except for the employment offered by several small industries, most important of which is the FOULDS SPAGHETTI PLANT on E. Church Street, Libertyville is supported by the trade of estate residents and summer vacationists. On the eastern border of the city is the BURTON R. HERRING LOG CABIN (*private*), built of cypress imported from the owner's native Sweden at a reputed cost of $100,000.

Right from Libertyville on State 176 is MUNDELEIN, 2.8 *m.* (676 alt., 1,011 pop.), formerly named Area, a word formed by the initial letters of the Sheldon School of Business Administration's motto: "Ability, Reliability, Endurance, and Action." When the school buildings were bought by the Catholic seminary, the town was renamed to honor George Cardinal Mundelein, Archbishop of Chicago. At the center of the community is the Cardinal's titular church, SANTA MARIA DEL POPULO, a small brick structure of severe Colonial lines. At the south of Mundelein is DIAMOND LAKE (*boating, $1 a day, fishing, amusement park, 5 hotels, summer cottages*), which attracts hundreds of Chicago vacationists, and rivals the town's one industry, a shoe factory, as a source of income.

On 1,200 wooded acres bordering LAKE ST. MARY in the northern quarter of the town is ST. MARY OF THE LAKE SEMINARY (*grounds and chapel open to public 8-4 daily*), one of the most elaborate and carefully planned Roman Catholic theological seminaries in the world. The average enrollment is 300. Ranged on the beautifully landscaped grounds, site of the final session of the International Eucharistic Congress in 1926, are 12 brick and stone Colonial structures, designed by Joseph McCarty of Chicago, and built between 1920-35. At the center of the group is the CHAPEL (*all services private*), its refined Colonial lines modeled after those of a frame Protestant meetinghouse at Lyme, Connecticut, that Cardinal Mundelein admired as a boy. The interior is decorated in Renaissance style. Above the altar is a picture of the Holy Family by Francisco Zurbaran (1598-1662). The chapel is the gift of the late Edward Hines, Chicago lumberman, whose son, Edward Hines, Jr., killed in the World War, is entombed in a small chapel nearby.

South of the chapel are a LOURDES GROTTO and STATIONS OF THE CROSS. Beyond, ST. AUGUSTINE'S BRIDGE affords a good view of vast flower beds, one of which depicts the Cardinal's coat-of-arms. The FEEHAN MEMORIAL LIBRARY, nearby, contains valuable incunabula. Among the seminary's collection of autographs are those of several saints, and those of the signers of the Constitution and the Declaration of Independence. Other important items are a numismatic collection and a series of medals struck by the popes. Adjoining the seminary grounds on the east is the BENEDICTINE CONVENT OF PERPETUAL ADORATION (*open to public 8-5 daily; services at 4:15*), in the chapel of which nuns kneel in constant prayer.

Large tracts in the vicinity of Libertyville were owned and developed by Samuel Insull, Chicago financier, until the collapse of his utilities empire. Immediately south of Libertyville is his former estate (R), HAWTHORNE FARM (*open; apply at caretaker's lodge*). The 4,445-acre estate, representing an investment of more than $3,000,000, was developed by Mr. Insull from a few acres purchased in 1903. On the farm, always operated at a loss, he pursued his hobby of raising pure-bred Swiss cattle and blooded Suffolk-Punch draft horses. The INSULL MANSION (*closed*), with its 101 acres of landscaped ground in the northeastern section of the tract, was erected in 1921. At its rear are sunken gardens, bird sanctuaries, and an immense swimming pool; to the north are the lodge and a greenhouse large enough to serve a good-sized town; to the south are three artificial lagoons, formerly graced by goldfish and swans. Emptied now of its regal furnishings, its doors and windows boarded up, the ornate French Riviera mansion, imposing relic of a fallen dynasty, broods over its deserted gardens. Following the collapse of Insull's empire, Hawthorne Farm, with the exception of the mansion and its immediate grounds, was partitioned into smaller estates and sold.

At 21 *m.* is a junction with State 59A.

Right on State 59A to the COUNTRYSIDE DEVELOPMENT, 4.5 *m.*, a community sponsored and promoted by Samuel Insull. On the beautifully landscaped 2,000-acre tract are the homes of former executives and high-ranking officials of the Insull interests. On an island in artificial 495-acre COUNTRYSIDE LAKE is the $500,000 RESIDENCE OF SAMUEL INSULL, JR. (*private*). Nearby is the COUNTRYSIDE GOLF COURSE (18 *holes, daily fee*).

HALFDAY, 23.8 *m.* (668 alt., 221 pop.), oldest settlement in Lake County (1836), is a quiet village with a cluster of stores and lunchrooms.

WHEELING, 28.4 *m.* (650 alt., 467 pop.), dates back to a country store established in 1830. Formerly a relay point on the Chicago-Milwaukee stage route, the village is now a center for metropolitan roadhouse entertainment.

Between Wheeling and Des Plaines, US 45—here known as the Des Plaines River Road—parallels the Des Plaines forestways (L), a strip of woodlands maintained as six COOK COUNTY FOREST PRESERVES (*marked hiking trails and bridle paths; picnic facilities at short intervals*). In these and nearby forest lands early explorers encountered the Potawatomi. Several Indian mounds are preserved in the woodlands along the river. It was here that Father Marquette, traveling up the Des Plaines from the Illinois to Lake Michigan, is presumed to have first entered what is now Cook County. In PORTAGE GROVE PRESERVE a huge rock imbedded in the river bank is designated as the SITE OF MARQUETTE'S LANDING.

DES PLAINES, 36 *m.* (643 alt., 8,798 pop.), founded in the 1830's, was long called Rand, in honor of Socrates Rand, the first settler. Its present name, that of the river flowing through the community, was adopted in 1869. A commuting and industrial suburb, Des Plaines is widely known as the site of a Methodist encampment, held annually since 1860 (*public welcome; summer hotel and cottages at nominal rates; reservations should be made in advance*).

Des Plaines is at the junction with US 12 (*see Tour* 9) and US 14 (*see Tour* 10). South of Des Plaines By-Pass US 12 unites with US 45 for 23.5 miles.

At 41.2 *m.* is a junction with Lawrence Avenue.

Left on this paved road to an old INDIAN CEMETERY, 1.5 *m.*, maintained by the Forest Preserve District of Cook County. About the size of a city lot, it contains five graves of the Robinson family, Potawatomi who befriended the whites during the 1820's and 1830's.

South of the junction with Lawrence Avenue, US 45 traverses the western edge of the lake plain that early settlers found to be a vast swamp, usually submerged during the spring months. Gravel dumps, fruit stands, market gardens, switch tracks, smokestacks, barbecue huts, and patches of farm land flank the highway. In close succession are boom-time subdivisions, with unused sidewalks trailing off in high weeds, rusty water plugs, ragged tree plantings, and empty apartment houses staring across the plain.

At 46.5 *m.* is the northern junction with US 20 and By-Pass US 20 (*see Tour* 11); southward, By-Pass US 20 unites with US 45 for 13 miles. At 49 *m.* is a junction with US 330 (*see Tour* 12A), and at 52 *m.* is a junction with US 34 (*see Tour* 13).

LA GRANGE, 52.5 *m.* (645 alt., 10,103 pop.), named for Marquis de Lafayette's homestead in France, was the first suburb to be developed along the Chicago, Burlington & Quincy Railroad. Cossitt Avenue, a principal east-west thoroughfare, commemorates W. D. Cossitt, who founded the village, and, following its incorporation in 1879, became its first president. The site was first settled, however, in the 1830's. The MASONIC ORPHANS HOME (*open to public*), on an 11-acre tract at 9th and Goodman Sts., cares for children between 3 and 18 years of age. They attend public schools, but receive special training in music and manual arts at the home.

At 54 *m.* is a junction with 55th Street.

Right on this paved road to a junction with Wolf Road, 1.6 *m.;* L. on Wolf Road to Plainfield Road, 2.2 *m.;* R. on Plainfield Road to the TIMBER TRAILS GOLF COURSE (18 *holes, daily fee*), 2.5 *m.* In the yard of the caretaker's house a boulder marks the LAST CAMPING PLACE OF THE POTAWATOMI IN COOK COUNTY.

At 55 *m.* is a junction with US 66 (*see Tour* 17).

US 45 crosses the DES PLAINES RIVER VALLEY, 57 *m.*, a gorge carved by the outpouring waters of Lake Michigan when glaciers dammed its northern outlet. Later, when the glaciers receded and the lake again emptied northward, the abandoned valley was appropriated by the Des Plaines River. This natural pass between the Great Lakes and the Mississippi River was used by Indians, explorers, and fur traders. The ILLINOIS AND MICHIGAN CANAL, an important factor in the development of the State, was built through the gorge in 1848; the same route serves the SANITARY AND SHIP CANAL, which in 1900 reversed the current of the Chicago River (*see Tour* 22). In addition to these waterways and the river, the valley contains three railways, the Santa Fe, the Alton, and the Chicago & Illinois Western.

Between the Des Plaines Valley and the Sag Valley, US 45 crosses the ARGONNE FOREST PRESERVE, another Cook County conservation and recreation area.

At 59.5 *m.* are junctions with By-Pass US 12 (*see Tour* 9) and By-Pass US 20 (*see Tour* 11).

US 45 crosses the CALUMET SAG CHANNEL, 61.5 *m.*, which enters the Sanitary and Ship Canal 5 miles west, carrying treated domestic and industrial wastes of the Calumet steel district.

At 62 *m.* the highway passes through the PALOS HILLS FOREST PRESERVE (*picnic facilities*), a favorite objective of Chicago hiking clubs. Its hills and valleys, carpeted in season with wild flowers, serve as a bird refuge; thousands of swallows nest in the high banks of SWALLOW CLIFF.

At 62.7 *m.* is a junction with 123rd Street.

Left on this paved road to CAMP A-DA-HI (Ind., in the oaks) 0.5 *m.,* sponsored by the American Indian Art Institute to instruct children in Indian crafts, such as pottery making, during the summer months. Occupying the site of the grand council ground of the Sauk and Potawatomi, the camp is on Waubansie's trail; blazes made by the chief are still visible. In the MUSEUM (*open daily during summer; free*), ancient and modern rugs and pottery are exhibited.

BOURBONNAIS, 100 *m.* (640 alt., 685 pop.), earliest settlement on the Kankakee River, is named for François Bourbonnais, an obscure *coureur de bois.* Noel La Vasseur (1799-1879), fur-trader and partner of Gurdon Hubbard (*see Tour* 1), is credited with founding the settlement. He established a trading post here in 1832, and was responsible for the immigration of French-Canadians to the region in the forties. "From Bourbonnais," wrote an early historian, "went people who established every other French town in Kankakee and Iroquois Counties. Kankakee in a large measure, St. Anne, L'Erable, St. Mary, Papineau all acknowledge Bourbonnais as the mother." Its early character is undiluted by industrialism and the inhabitants still speak French in their homes.

Local limestone buildings, some nearly a century old, are faintly reminiscent of a provincial French village. ST. VIATOR COLLEGE, on College Avenue, is a Roman Catholic institution, founded in 1865. Its six buildings are ranged on a 43-acre campus; the average enrollment is about 500. NOTRE DAME CONVENT, College Ave. and Convent St., was established by Roman Catholic Sisters of Mercy in 1852. The popularity of French courses in both institutions tends to maintain the purity of the French spoken locally. The impressive Roman Catholic TRINITY CHURCH, on College Avenue, was built in 1847 of limestone from nearby quarries.

Right from Bourbonnais on State 113 to ROCK CREEK PARK, 6.5 *m.* (*adm.* 50c *per car; boats* 50c *per day; fishing, swimming*), a privately owned tract of about 400 acres at the confluence of Rock Creek and the Kankakee River. The canyon of the creek, studded with ferns and columbines, cedar and basswood trees, contains a small fan-shaped waterfall. The site was once used as a camping ground by the Potawatomi.

BRADLEY, 101 *m.* (648 alt., 3,048 pop.), organized in 1892 as North Kankakee, was renamed three years later in honor of David Bradley, who established an agricultural implement factory in the village; other industrial enterprises include a Venetian blind factory and a furniture manufacturing plant.

KANKAKEE, 103 *m.* (631 alt., 20,620 pop.), seat of Kankakee County, is named for the river which flows through the city. Originating as an extension of Bourbonnais, Kankakee was incorporated as a separate community in 1855 around the depot of the newly constructed Illinois Central Railroad. Bourbonnais, without a railroad, was easily outstripped by the newer town which, by 1900, had 13,500 inhabitants.

In CENTRAL SCHOOL, 420 E. Merchant St., is a COLLECTION OF SCULPTURES by the late George Gray Barnard, internationally known American sculptor who once attended the school. Donated by Barnard in 1936, the 45 pieces became the subject of controversy when the president of the board of education objected to the displaying of nudes in public schools. A sculptor was accordingly hired to adorn the offending statues with draperies and fig leaves. Barnard conceded fig leaves for the males but balked at draperies. Metropolitan reporters made a field day of the incident. Finally, the collection was accepted in its original condition. It includes the heroic *Maidenhood, Prodigal Son, The Hewer, Crouching Venus,* and the models of the fountains erected on John D. Rockefeller's estate at Tarrytown. Also noteworthy is a death mask of Lincoln, from which Barnard's highly praised bust of Lincoln (included in the collection) was modeled.

The KANKAKEE STATE HOSPITAL (*grounds open daily, tours conducted at stated intervals*), Jeffery St. at the Kankakee River, was established in 1878, and ranks high for its treatment of the insane. It was one of the first institutions to adopt the cottage system of housing patients. The main building is surrounded by smaller units, the simplicity of which, with the spaciousness of the grounds, suggests a well-planned college campus. Organized recreation is an important factor in the treatment of the 3,800 patients.

Kankakee is at a junction with US 52 (*see Tour* 15).

Section b. Kankakee to Mattoon, 125 m.

Between Kankakee, 0 *m.*, and Mattoon is corn, in fields of green or yellow, waving in the breeze of early morning, shimmering in the heat of noonday sun, in long swells, in quiet planes, from the highway to the horizon. Hedgerows separate the fields, oak groves shade the farmsteads, but no hill breaks the prairie, and only a few tributaries of the Wabash cut their willow-marked courses across its surface. This is the great cash-grain region of the State, one of the richest and most completely cultivated farming areas of the world; this is the land of corn, the heart of the Illinois prairies.

Fertile, unleached black loams, developed from the thick, flat deposits of the Wisconsin ice sheet, a long, hot growing season, and properly distributed rainfall provide ideal conditions for the cultivation of corn. Proximity to Chicago, the corn market of the Nation, determines the unusual economy of the region—the cash sale of the grain, rather than its use on the farm in the feeding of livestock, which is the general practice elsewhere in the Corn Belt. Second in importance to corn is oats, which fits well in the crop rotation scheme. Since its plant-ing and harvesting seasons differ from those of corn, its cultivation enables the farmer to spread his work.

The farmstead of the prairie is strikingly unlike that of the dairy region. No giant barn, no silo overshadows the farmhouse. A small out-building shelters the few animals and stores their food, another pro-tects the machinery. For the produce of the prairie does not remain on the farm, but goes directly to the nearby town where it is stored in the huge elevators that tower over each village, to be sold eventually in Chicago.

CHEBANSE (Ind. little duck), 11 *m.* (667 alt., 523 pop.), a German community dependent chiefly on agriculture, is divided by the county line; 296 of its residents live in Iroquois County, 227 in Kanka-kee County.

DANFORTH, 24 *m.* (658 alt., 369 pop.), a village of trim white and green houses, is named for A. H. and George Danforth, who in the late 1850's purchased 27,000 acres of swampland in the vicinity and induced 30 families to emigrate from the Netherlands and settle here. The Dutch built windmills and dug ditches, drained the land, and estab-lished farms. Danforth was platted in 1872.

At 27 *m.* is the northern junction with US 24 (*see Tour* 16); for two miles US 24 and US 45 are united.

GILMAN, 28 *m.* (654 alt., 1,620 pop.), is the birthplace of James Robert Mann (1856-1922), Illinois Representative who sponsored the Mann Act.

On the northern limits of Onarga, 31.5 *m.*, is a junction with a graveled road.

Right on this road to LARCH FARM (*private, open on request*), 0.3 *m.*, the former home of the noted detective, Allan Pinkerton (*see Tour* 11). Completed in 1873, the one-story building with watch tower was once a show place of Iro-quois County.

ONARGA, 32 *m.* (657 alt., 1,469 pop.), was the home of Benjamin Hardy, composer of "Darling Nellie Gray." The 500-acre ONARGA NURSERY (*open to public*), at the northern city limits, grows vines, shrubs, rose bushes, and fruit, shade, and ornamental trees.

PAXTON, 50 *m.* (794 alt., 2,892 pop.), seat of Ford County, was settled in the 1850's by Swedish emigrants, who maintained Augustana College here between 1853 and 1875. A cannery and a woman's gar-ment factory are the principal local industries.

South of Paxton thousands of acres are planted in soy beans, of which Illinois produces more than any other State. An important ele-ment in the economy of the Illinois corn belt, soy beans rotate well with corn and serve to fix nitrogen in the soil.

RANTOUL, 61 *m.* (758 alt., 1,555 pop.), is named for Robert Rantoul, an early member of the board of directors of the Illinois

Central Railroad. A MUNICIPALLY OWNED POWER PLANT furnishes all revenue for city expenses, except a small tax for maintenance of a band and the public library.

CHANUTE FIELD (*visited only by special permission*), occupying a square mile at the southeastern city limits, is a United States Army Air Corps technical school. Established in 1917, the school trained men for service in the World War. In January 1939 the firehouse, warehouse, and guardhouse were destroyed by fire, together with valuable equipment. It is probable that these structures, which were of wood, will be replaced by sturdier buildings. Six hundred enlisted students, 600 regular Army troops, and 70 officers, 30 of whom are students in the radio school, are stationed at the field.

CHAMPAIGN (740 alt., 20,348 pop.), and URBANA (721 alt., 13,060 pop.), 78 *m.*, (*see Champaign and Urbana*).

Points of Interest: University of Illinois, Crystal Lake Park, Champaign County Courthouse, and others.

TOLONO, 87.3 *m.* (736 alt., 790 pop.), its name coined by J. B. Calhoun of the Illinois Central Railroad, is the town in which Lincoln last spoke to the people of Illinois when he left the State in February 1861 to assume his duties as President. A boulder in the village park marks the SITE WHERE LINCOLN SPOKE.

The pattern of PESOTUM, 92.5 *m.* (720 alt., 404 pop.), is as familiar and recurrent in this area as the John Deere tractor and the Harvester plow. Dominated by the grain elevator on the railroad, its life revolves around the storage and shipping of grain. The highway, paralleling the railway tracks, is the business street. Grocery, dry-goods, and farm-machinery stores; a tavern, pool room, and barber shop; bank, post office, and at least two churches care for the needs of the town and its nearby farms. Away from the highway on the half-dozen streets are the residences, usually frame. There are no curbs; the paved streets merge in an irregular line with the narrow parkway. Lawns, flower beds, and vegetable gardens surround the houses. At the edges of the village are the larger homes, the cemetery, and then the abrupt beginning of farm and field.

TUSCOLA (Ind. a level plain), 101.5 *m.* (653 alt., 2,569 pop.), like many a city on the Illinois prairie, was settled long after the towns on the Ohio and Mississippi Rivers. Not until the coming of the Illinois Central Railroad in 1855 was the prairie opened to extensive cultivation. The new railroad resulted in the platting of Tuscola in 1857, and its designation as seat of Douglas County two years later. In Tuscola Joseph G. "Uncle Joe" Cannon (*see Tour* 1), for many years Speaker of the House of Representatives, practiced law (1861-72). In Tuscola is RADIO STATION WDZ (1020 kc.), popular among farmers in this region for its daily grain and livestock market broadcasts. The main local industries are a broom factory and a woodworking plant that produces trellises and ironing-boards.

At 102 *m.* is a junction with US 36 (*see Tour* 18).

ARCOLA, 110 *m.* (681 alt., 1,686 pop.), named for a town in Italy, was platted in 1855. The community is at the northern border of the broom corn belt, which extends south to Neoga. Used in the manufacture of brooms, the plant differs from grain corn in its finer leaf and brushy tassel. The species most common to Illinois are white Italian and Black Jap (or Spanish), which grow from 8 to 15 feet tall. Bordering the railroad tracks in Arcola are large red sheds where the "broom" is graded and shipped. Some of the product is used in a local broom factory. The *Broom and Broom Corn News,* trade organ of the broom industry, is published here. West of Arcola is a large Amish colony (*see Tour* 18).

MATTOON, 125 *m.* (725 alt., 14,631 pop.), an industrial community, was established as a shipping center in the early 1850's when the Big Four Railroad laid its tracks through this section. The young community was named for William Mattoon, an official of the Illinois Central, who was instrumental in developing the town. Mattoon manufactures shoes, furniture, and Diesel engines, and does a considerable retail and wholesale business in grains, feed, and fertilizers.

In June 1861, Gen. Ulysses S. Grant mustered the Twenty-first Illinois Infantry into the State service at Mattoon. Grant's local military activities are narrated on a BRONZE TABLET at the east side of the Illinois Central depot, Broadway and 18th St. The U. S. GRANT HOTEL, Charleston Ave. and 17th St., honors the memory of the general. In the hotel is preserved an old flag that Grant gave to a resident of Mattoon.

Mattoon is at the junction with the Lincoln National Memorial Highway (*see Tour* 21).

Section c. Mattoon to Norris City, 118 m.

Between Mattoon, 0 *m.*, and Norris City US 45 crosses a region of mixed farming, a prairie land that differs sharply from that of the cash-grain area to the north. The two regions are separated by the Shelbyville Moraine, a long ridge immediately south of Mattoon that marks the maximum advance of recent glaciation. The country south of the moraine, though once glaciated, has been exposed to erosion perhaps 40 times as long as that to the north. Numerous streams cross its surface, and leaching has robbed its soils of much of their fertility. Corn, conspicuous in the landscape, shares the fields with hay and winter wheat. Rougher lands are in pasture, and peach and apple orchards are common.

In the northern half of the region numerous valleys, steep sided and wooded, break the level of the prairie. In the south, where the glacial drift is very thin and topography is controlled by underlying bedrock, the surface is one of gently rolling slopes, broad valleys and rounded divides.

At 2 *m.* is a junction with a paved road.

Right on this road to the MATTOON FISH HATCHERY (*open daily*), 4 *m.* PARADISE LAKE (*boating, fishing*), nearby, is annually stocked with about 750,000 fish from the hatchery.

The northern border of the SHELBYVILLE MORAINE is marked by a slight rise of land, 7 *m.*, and then a descent of nearly a hundred feet in the course of a few miles. This terminal moraine extends from east of the Indiana Line westward to the center of Illinois, then northward into Wisconsin. The long, irregular tree-topped ridge is most conspicuous from the south.

NEOGA, 14 *m.* (659 alt., 995 pop.), is on the southern border of the broom-corn belt. Neoga (Ind. place of the Deity) is becoming important as the center of an apple- and peach-growing section.

EFFINGHAM, 28 *m.* (591 alt., 4,978 pop.), incorporated as a village in 1861, had its formative years during the great German immigration to this region. Devoid of Teutonic stolidity, however, is Effingham's present slogan, "Heart of the U. S. A." Local economy is dependent upon trade with nearby farms and the employment offered by small industries that manufacture gloves, shoe heels, church furniture, and butcher blocks. At the western edge of Effingham is 34-acre LAKE KANAGA (*cottages and bathing beach*), its shore lined with virgin oak and hickory.

Effingham is at a junction with US 40 (*see Tour* 19).

At 61 *m.* is the western junction with US 50 (*see Tour* 20), with which US 45 is united for 4 miles through FLORA, 62.5 *m.* (490 alt., 4,393 pop.). The city, named for the daughter of one of its founders, is the chief industrial center of Clay County. Manufactured products include shoes, cheese, underwear, and furniture. Flora is the headquarters of the Egyptian Seed Growers' Exchange, a co-operative organization of the redtop grass seed growers of southern Illinois; the subsidiary Redtop Growers' Warehouse Association also has its main office here.

South of Flora are pear orchards and meadows of redtop-clover. Several OIL WELLS, 80 *m.*, are part of the new field centering about Clay City (*see Tour* 20), which boomed in 1937.

FAIRFIELD, 89 *m.* (451 alt., 3,280 pop.), seat of Wayne County, dates from 1819. Two factories produce clothing, a third manufactures automobile parts. Gen. Lew Wallace (1827-1905) spent several days here in the 1870's, defending his interests in land litigation. While a guest at the JACKSON HOTEL he is said to have worked on the manuscript of *Ben Hur*. William E. Borah, U. S. Senator from Idaho, was born about six miles northeast of Fairfield.

Left from Fairfield on State 15 to ALBION, 17 *m.* (447 alt., 1,666 pop.), founded in 1818 as the central settlement of the English colony organized by Morris Birkbeck and George Flower. Dissatisfied with economic conditions in England after the Napoleonic Wars, Flower and Birkbeck came to America to establish a colony that would provide better opportunities than those afforded the English working class. They traveled through Pennsylvania, Ohio, Indiana, and Illinois in search of a suitable site; they did not consider the region farther north because of the climate, and their hatred of slavery prevented them from settling any farther south. Their final selection was the prairie between Bon Pas Creek and the Little Wabash River in Illinois.

"Bruised by the brushwood and exhausted by the extreme heat we almost despaired," Flower wrote in describing his first glimpse of the prairie, "when a small cabin and a low fence greeted our eyes. A few steps more, and a beautiful prairie suddenly opened to our view. At first, we only received the impressions of its general beauty. With longer gaze, all its distinctive features were revealed, lying in profound repose under the warm light of an afternoon's summer sun. Its indented and irregular outline of wood, its varied surface interspersed with clumps of oaks of centuries' growth, its tall grass, with seed stalks from six to ten feet high, like tall and slender weeds waving in a gentle breeze, the whole presenting a magnificence of park-scenery, complete from the hand of Nature. . . . From beneath the broken shade of the wood, with our arms raised above our brows, we gazed long and steadily, drinking in the beauties of the scene which had been so long the object of our search."

Unlike many Americans, the Englishmen were charmed with the prairie. "I shrank from the idea of settling in the midst of a wood of heavy timber, to hack and hew my way to a little farm, ever bounded by a wall of gloomy forest. . . ." wrote Flower.

While Birkbeck completed the business of acquiring the land with their pooled funds, Flower returned to England where he sold his holdings. He organized and sent several parties of prospective colonists over from England and in March 1818 returned to America with about 51 persons, as well as agricultural implements, seeds, and animals for breeding. New colonists continued to flock in—on foot, horseback, and in wagons. The English colonists did not take to pioneer hardships as readily as did so many of the American frontiersmen, but their suffering was mitigated by an intense desire for land ownership. The colony prospered, and by October 1818, had grown to 200 persons, all English.

The need of a central village to accommodate incoming colonists and to furnish supplies and services became increasingly apparent. One evening a group of men met with Flower in his cabin to plan the new town; there were no candles in the house, so in the dark "each one took his couch and carried on the discussion." Late in the night the site of the village was finally decided upon. "Now for a name," wrote Flower. "We were long at fault. At last we did what almost all emigrants do, pitched on a name that had its association with the land of our birth. Albion was then and there located, built, and peopled in imagination. We dropped off, one by one, to sleep, to confirm in dreams the wanderings of our wakeful fancies."

The comparative wealth and intelligence of Albion's leaders subsequently influenced the culture and politics of the surrounding country. Birkbeck's *Notes on a Journey* and *Letters from Illinois*, which were widely read in America and abroad, attracted many travelers and called attention both to the English settlements of Illinois and to the West as a whole.

The simple log cabins that first sheltered the colonists have long since vanished. The oldest existing structure is the HARRIS HOUSE (R), one-half block west of the public square. Gibson Harris, a surveyor, bought the building from Francis Dixon in 1826; it has since been enlarged and remodeled. The PUBLIC LIBRARY, corner of State 15 and State 130, was built in 1842 as the home of Dr. Frank B. Thompson. Its sophisticated design, widely differing from the Greek copybook style current at that time, reflects the culture of the English immigrants who planned it. Architectural features typical of the Georgian style are evident in the hipped roof, the small pediment that interrupts the cornice line, the splayed stone lintels with projecting keystones, the stone band-courses at first and second floor sills, and the elliptical arched doorway with fanlight and side lights. North of the library is the GEORGE FRENCH HOUSE, built in 1841 from designs by the owner. This structure also has a fanlighted doorway and band-courses, but the roof is gabled, with a sturdy chimney at each end.

Left (N) from Albion 10 *m.* on State 130 to a junction with a graveled road; R. on this road to WEST SALEM, 12.5 *m.* (506 alt., 825 pop.), settled by German Moravians from North Carolina in 1838. At the grave of Emma Pfeil in the now abandoned MORAVIAN CEMETERY is a marker said to be the WORLD'S SMALLEST TOMBSTONE. It is 5⅞ by 10½ by 2 inches. The graves are in four groups, according to the choir system: married men, married women, boys and bachelors, and girls and maiden women. To indicate the equality of all before God, interments were made by death dates rather than by families.

Ahead (E) from Albion on State 15 is MOUNT CARMEL, 35 *m.* (465 alt., 7,132 pop.), Wabash County seat. As noted in Peck's *A Gazeteer of Illinois* (1834), "this town was laid off in 1818, by Rev. Thomas S. Hinde of Ohio, on the project of establishing a moral, temperate, and industrious village." The present city is the trade center of a prosperous farming area; its manufactories produce straw-board and electrical equipment. From 1900 until recent years Mount Carmel, by reason of its location on the Wabash River, had a lucrative mussel industry. During that period more than a million dollars worth of pearls were found. In the basement of the CARNEGIE LIBRARY (*weekdays only* 1:30-7:30), on 5th Street, is a collection of Indian artifacts excavated in the region by the late Dr. Jacob Schenk.

ENFIELD, 109 *m.* (422 alt., 744 pop.), was settled in 1813. Senator William E. Borah once attended school in the now abandoned brick SCHOOLHOUSE, crowning a hill (R) at the southern limits of the city. Main attraction of the annual Enfield Homecoming Day (*first Sat. in Oct.*) is a mule sale; the animals are paraded through the streets and then sold at auction.

At 110 *m.* is a junction with State 14.

Left on State 14 is CARMI, 9 *m.* (399 alt., 2,932 pop.), platted in 1816 as the seat of White County. The one local manufactory produces underwear. A Rooster Day, on which farmers and townsmen trade surplus fowls, is held here each spring. The JOHN CRAW HOUSE (*private*), a long story-and-half structure on the south side of the courthouse square, was built in the early 1820's, and served for a time as White County's first courthouse. The two rooms of logs covered with weather-boarding constitute the structure as it was first built; the other two rooms were added by Gen. John M. Robinson (1794-1843), senator from Illinois and justice of the State Supreme Court.

Rolling land in this area marks the transition from the level prairies of central Illinois to the hilly, rugged country prevalent in the southern part of the State.

NORRIS CITY, 118 *m.* (444 alt., 1,109 pop.), a trading center

for an agricultural and coal mining district, was named in honor of a
pioneer settler, William Norris. In Norris City is a junction with
State 1 (*see Tour* 3A).

Section d. Norris City to Kentucky Line, 84 m.

Between Norris City, 0 *m.*, and the Kentucky Line, US 45 is a
highway of transition. The landscape becomes increasingly rolling until the first unmistakable hills, the State's lone mountain range, the
Illinois Ozarks, appear on the horizon. As the landscape changes, so
do the people. Homesteaded by infiltration from the Ohio River, earliest avenue of entry, southern Illinois saw the first homogeneous settlement of any considerable size. Here, more than anywhere else in the
State, the people are aware of their historical background; here family
ties, often amounting to clannishness, give the region a solidarity
rarely encountered in the north. While a Chicagoan is commonly a
stranger to his apartment neighbor, most residents of southern Illinois
know several people in any town within a hundred miles.

The early history of Illinois is peppered with the names of the
southern towns: Kaskaskia, Cairo, Cahokia, Vandalia, Shawneetown.
But with the opening of the Erie Canal and the transfer of the State
capital to Springfield, the tide of commerce and politics swept northward until, as shown in the 1930 census, 80 per cent of the population
was massed in the northern half of the State.

ELDORADO, 13 *m.* (388 alt., 4,482 pop.), a mining town, has
for the past decade and a half seen a steady cross-State migration of
its young men to Alton, Wood River, and East St. Louis. When an
Eldoradon becomes entrenched in one of these industrial areas, he
commonly has his "buddy" visit him, offering to "put him up" until
he too can get a job. Among local factory workers it is lengendary
that Eldorado mothers frighten their unruly children, not with the
bogeyman, but with the threat that they can't go to Alton or East St.
Louis when they grow up.

HARRISBURG, 20 *m.* (400 alt., 11,625 pop.), built on a slight
elevation, at night is announced for miles by the scarlet neon spear of
the 230-foot TOWER OF RADIO STATION WEBQ (1210 kc.). Platted
in 1853, the town assumed industrial character almost at birth. Between 1860 and 1885, planing, flour, and woolen mills were established, the latter playing an important rôle during the Civil War when
Southern cotton was not available.

Two coal mines were opened south of Harrisburg about 1885, but
these and subsequent mines were not operated to any great extent until
the Big Four Railroad strengthened its tracks and roadbed to handle
heavy freight.

The coal boom began in earnest in 1905 when 13 mines were
opened locally. As these were worked out and abandoned, new shafts

were sunk. Today, with 21 mines, Saline County, of which Harrisburg is the seat, ranks fifth among the coal-producing counties of Illinois. Large sums have been spent on machines that remove coal dust and other dirt by washing. Piled near each mine is the refuse of the process, the gob pile, which, frequently set ablaze by spontaneous combustion, lights the near landscape with a weird flicker.

On Vine Street, south of the square, is WHISKEY CHUTE, formerly a segregated vice district and saloon row where miners had their jugs filled, and hard drinkers drowned their sorrow. Modern saloons have replaced the old, but the neighborhood is not so rowdy as formerly.

WILLIAMS HILL (1,065 alt.), highest elevation in southern Illinois, is visible (L) at 21.3 m. On clear days the 100-foot steel lookout tower at its summit is discernible against the blue sky. WOMBLE MOUNTAIN, north of Williams Hill, is smaller but clearly visible between two gaps in this ridge of the Illinois Ozarks.

CARRIER MILLS, 27 m. (392 alt., 2,140 pop.), is a mining town named for William H. Carrier, who established a sawmill here in 1870. Known locally as "Cat Skin" or "Cat Hide," the community faces the Ozarks, two ridges of which lie in the distant blue haze.

The highway passes under the Edgewood freight cut-off, 32.5 m., of the Illinois Central System. South of the subway the line tunnels through the Ozarks at three points, with a total tunnel length of 10,424 feet.

STONEFORT, 35.5 m., originally two miles southeast of its present site, moved in 1872, when the Big Four Railroad was built through this section. The name is derived from the RUINS OF AN OLD STONE FORT. In the Illinois Ozarks there are seven of these prehistoric structures, each consisting of an area on a cliff or bluff, barricaded on its accessible side by a loose stone wall. The walls here were originally 4 feet thick and 8 feet high, with one opening, but the stones now lie scattered about or have been carried away. The function of the structure is conjectural: a prehistoric fort, or a pound in which buffaloes were trapped and easily slain by being stampeded over the cliff.

The Johnson County line, 35.5 m., approximates the northern edge of the OZARK RIDGE. This uplifted and folded belt of sandstone and conglomerates, in places 700 feet above the surrounding country and more than 1,000 feet above sea level, is a continuation of the Ozarks of Missouri. From the Mississippi to the Ohio, the belt is 70 miles long and from 15 to 40 miles wide.

NEW BURNSIDE, 38 m. (560 alt., 299 pop.), founded in 1872 when the Big Four Railroad was built, was named for the railroad president, Maj. Gen. Ambrose E. Burnside. Fruit raising in the region is now so important that the U. S. Weather Bureau maintains a reporting station in the village.

South of Burnside the highway climbs into the fruit section of the

Ozark Ridge, which is blanketed from mid-April to mid-May with
pink and white blossoms.

At 41 *m.* is a junction with the Eddyville Road.

Left on this graveled road to TRIGG TOWER, 1 *m.*, a forest lookout named for
L. O. Trigg of Eldorado, who devoted years of voluntary service to the establishment of a National forest in the Illinois Ozarks.

At 8 *m.* a road (L) branches 0.4 *m.* downhill to BURDEN FALLS, a narrow
scarf of water tumbling into a jagged gorge.

Ahead on the Eddyville Road is the BELL SMITH SPRING RECREATION AREA
(*swimming, picnic facilities, hiking trails*), 10.6 *m.* Along Bay Creek and its
tributaries, within a mile of each other, are BELL SMITH SPRING, a deep SWIM-
MING HOLE, a semi-circular GROTTO carved in limestone by a stream, and a
NATURAL BRIDGE with a span of 150 feet and a center clearance of more than 20
feet. In gorges 25 to 75 feet deep are clear blue streams that flow through jungles
of fern. After heavy rains, torrents 15 feet deep roar down the rocky canyons.

The OLD FORT MASSAC-KASKASKIA TRAIL, 42 *m.*, as late as 1880
was plainly marked with mile signs carved or burned into tree trunks.
A short distance beyond the junction with the old trail, US 45 begins
the southward descent of the Ozark Ridge. COOPER'S BLUFF, a high
wooded cliff, is visible (L).

VIENNA, 53 *m.* (405 alt., 874 pop.), is built around a public
square in which stands the Johnson County Courthouse. The county
was organized in 1812, and Vienna was selected as the county seat
six years later.

South of Vienna, US 45 descends into a valley and winds through
wooded hills. On the first night of his march from Fort Massac to
Kaskaskia (June 29, 1778) George Rogers Clark camped at the
western base of INDIAN POINT, a forested bluff visible at 59 *m.* (R).

At 60 *m.* is a junction with an improved road.

Right on this road to KARNAK, 6.1 *m.* (340 alt., 771 pop.), largely a com-
pany-built logging and milling town. Oak, willow, black gum, sweet gum, and
cypress are cut in the surrounding forests and hauled to Karnak to be milled.

Ahead on the improved road to a junction with State 37, 9.3 *m.;* L on State
37 to NEW GRAND CHAIN, 12.2 *m.* (405 alt., 373 pop.), named for a chain of
rocks in the Ohio River, three miles distant. The town, once on the river banks
at that point, was moved to its present site in 1872, with the coming of the Big
Four Railroad. Immediately south of the village a marker commemorates VA
BACHE TANNERY AND FORT (1702-04) and CANTONMENT WILKINSON-VILLE
(1787-1804). Of these sites—a short distance upstream and inaccessible—that of
Cantonment Wilkinson-Ville has been definitely established, but many authorities
place the site of Va Bache several miles north of what is now Cairo.

Va Bache Tannery and Fort was built in 1702 by a party of French and
Indians led by Charles Juchereau de St. Denys, lieutenant general of the jurisdiction of Montreal. Outposts were established from which Juchereau's hunters
shipped buffalo skins downstream to be tanned. At the Belle Garde outpost Father
Jean Mermet, Jesuit chaplain of the expedition, founded the mission of Assumption. In the summer of 1703 an epidemic caused the death of half of those at Va
Bache, including Juchereau. The tannery was operated until the following year
and then abandoned.

Cantonment Wilkinson-Ville, an outpost of Fort Massac (*see below*), was estabished at the chain of rocks, downstream from the fort, at the time of the political intrigue known as the Spanish Conspiracy. Commanded by Lieut. Col. David Strong, the camp had accommodations for 1,000 men.

Southward from the junction with the improved road, US 45 follows an embankment across the flat land known as CYPRESS SWAMP, formerly a 100,000-acre tract of virgin forest in which bald cypress trees predominated, many towering 150 feet above the swampland. Between 1885 and 1890 this extensive forest was felled by lumbermen, who entered the swamp in boats, cut the trees, usually several feet above the ground, and floated them to a sawmill. Now only isolated cypress trees remain. A large part of the swamp has been drained, cleared of stumps, and converted into farm land.

METROPOLIS, 75 *m.* (329 alt., 5,573 pop.), seat of Massac County, developed from two pioneer towns, Massac and Metropolis City. About 1796 a small settlement was established immediately west of Fort Massac, and 40 years later it was platted as the City of Massac. In 1839 William A. McBane and James H. G. Wilcox, dreaming of a metropolis that would be the "City of the West," platted another town to the north of Massac and called it Metropolis City. McBane believed this to be the only feasible place, near the mouth of the Ohio River, to build a railroad bridge. In 1917, long after his death, the present bridge was completed. When Massac County was formed in 1843, Metropolis City was chosen as the seat, and two years later incorporated as a town. In 1892 the two communities united under the present name.

Metropolis stands on slightly rolling land. Its broad streets are shaded by great trees, an occasional magnolia lends Southern charm. The homes are generally surrounded by wide lawns. Contrast is afforded by the rickety shacks and grounded boathouses of BRICKBAT RIDGE, two blocks long, on the riverfront west of the railroad bridge. The income from the MUNICIPAL WATER AND POWER PLANTS provides funds for all city departments, eliminating the necessity for a general tax levy.

An OLD LOG BUILDING, northwest corner of 4th and Ferry Sts., sided and used as a flower shop, was formerly the schoolhouse where Robert G. Ingersoll (1833-1899), agnostic, orator, and writer, first taught school in 1852.

At the foot of Ferry Street is the FERRY LANDING. Two steamboats maintain constant service across the Ohio River (*rates: one way*, 10c; *cars, one way*, 50c; *round trip*, 75c).

FORT MASSAC STATE PARK (*picnic facilities*), 76 *m.*, stands on a promontory that commands a view of 24 miles of the Ohio River. The strategic site was fortified by the French in 1757, shortly after the outbreak of the French and Indian Wars. At first called Ascension, the fort was renamed Massiac in honor of the incumbent

French minister of Marine. As part of the territory ceded to the British by the Treaty of Paris (1763), the fort was abandoned by the French, and soon destroyed by the Cherokee.

During the English occupation (1765-1778) the ruins were left untouched until 1794 when, owing to trouble with Spain and the Indians, President Washington ordered "Mad Anthony" Wayne to refortify the site. Capt. Zebulon Pike was placed in command and here his son, Zebulon Montgomery Pike, subsequently the discoverer of Pike's Peak, served as a subaltern. The new fort was named Massac, a corruption of its previous name rather than, as persistent legends have it, a shortened form of "massacre."

Fort Massac figured obscurely in the Spanish Conspiracy. From it were dispatched the troops that garrisoned Cantonment Wilkinson-Ville (*see above*), ostensibly to protect Fort Massac from a downstream attack. Historians are agreed that Wilkinson, then in command of the United States Army, was implicated with Carondelet in the conspiracy to place Kentucky and possibly other contiguous parts of United States territory under the jurisdiction of Spain. The plan envisioned the capture of Fort Massac, but no attack was made. Wilkinson, it is said, revealed the conspiracy to his government.

After service in the War of 1812 the fort was abandoned. Although never important as a military post, it played a large part in the economic history of the region. At the end of the eighteenth century the Ohio River came into prominence as a trade medium, and Congress created several districts for the collection of duties on tonnage and merchandise. One of these was the district of Fort Massac, with the fort as port of entry. All boats carrying goods along the Ohio were compelled to stop at the fort where inventories of cargoes were made and taxes assessed. After 1807 the districts were rearranged; Illinois and the surrounding area were incorporated in the district of Mississippi.

As described by Gov. John Reynolds, who visited Fort Massac in 1855, the "outside walls were 135 feet square, and at each angle bastions were erected. The walls were palisaded with earth between the wood. A large well was sunk in the fortress, and the whole appeared to be strong and substantial in its day. . . . The site is one of the most beautiful on La Belle Riviere, and commands a view that is charming."

Dedicated as a State Park in 1908, the site retains only the scarcely discernible bastions and ditch. Four cannons mark its corners. At the center is a bronze STATUE OF GEORGE ROGERS CLARK, by Leon Hermant, which commemorates Clark's crossing of the Ohio at this point on his way to Kaskaskia in 1778.

BROOKPORT, 84 *m.* (335 alt., 1,336 pop.), is an agricultural trading center on the north bank of the Ohio River. A tie-treating plant and a mussel shell button factory are the principal industrial establishments. During the Ohio River flood of January, 1937, parts of Brookport were under 6 to 14 feet of water.

Right from Brookport on an improved road to DAM 52, 1.4 *m.*, built in 1926 as part of the Government system of dams to facilitate navigation on the Ohio River during low water. It is one of the largest movable wicket dams in the world. When the river rises toward flood-stage, the 487 wickets, each four feet wide, are laid down and the lock gates opened. Traffic then passes over the dam instead of through the lock.

US 45 crosses the Kentucky Line on a toll bridge (*car and passengers,* 50c) spanning the Ohio River to Paducah, Kentucky (*see Kentucky Guide*).

TOUR 3A

NORRIS CITY—SHAWNEETOWN—CAVE-IN-ROCK; 39 *m.*, STATE 1

Hard-surfaced roadbed throughout.
The Baltimore & Ohio R. R. roughly parallels the route between Norris City and the junction with State 13.
Accommodations limited.

BETWEEN Norris City and Cave-in-Rock this section of State 1 crosses the eastern tip of the Ilinois Ozarks, a narrow range of hills which runs east and west across the State. The southern half of the route roughly parallels and finally terminates at the Ohio River, here the boundary of Illinois. Encountering few villages, the highway traverses a region left in the backwash of history as the American frontier moved westward.

NORRIS CITY, 0 *m.* (444 alt., 1,109 pop.) (*see Tour 3*), is at the junction with US 45 (*see Tour 3*).

At 17.9 *m.* is a junction with State 13.

Left on State 13 to SHAWNEETOWN, 9 *m.* (350 alt., 1,440 pop.), an important port in early days. Easternmost Illinois city on the Ohio River, Shawneetown was the rough-hewn portal to the Middle Border. An endless stream of pioneers and goods from the East was brought to the wharves here in keelboats propelled by sturdy rivermen, who sang and cursed and sweated as they labored over the long sweeps.

Settled early in the nineteenth century, Shawneetown soon became the seat of Gallatin County and the land office for a vast territory; as such, it was one of the most important financial centers in the new country. Shawneetown's income was augmented materially by the nearby salines (*see below*), from which salt was carted into the town and there transferred to keelboats for shipment to the East and South. Local residents like to tell of the time when several men rode down more than 300 miles from the tiny settlement of Chicago to obtain financial assistance from this established commercial center; they painted a bright picture of the prospects of their village, and requested a loan of $1,000. Having sent investigators to evaluate Chicago's possibilities, the local bank refused the loan on the ground that the village was so far from Shawneetown that it could never amount to anything.

Shawneetown's early advantage lay in its strategic site on the banks of the Ohio. The low bottom land, periled by floods every year, had nothing but its wharves to recommend it. In 1817 Morris Birkbeck wrote in his *Notes on a Journey in America*, "This place I account as a phenomenon, evincing the pertinacious adhesion of the human animal to the spot where it has once fixed itself. As the lava of Mount Etna can not dislodge this strange being from the cities which have been repeatedly ravished by its eruptions, the Ohio, with its annual overflowings, is unable to wash away the inhabitants of Shawneetown."

The town bore the yearly invasions of the Ohio unprotected until the unusually severe flood of 1884, after which it constructed a comprehensive levee system. But in 1898, and again in 1913, Shawneetown was under water. In 1932 the levee was raised 5 feet above the 1913 high-water mark, a margin of safety that seemed to be ample for any emergency.

But Shawneetown had not envisioned anything like the 1937 flood. By January 24 of that year menacing yellow waters were slipping silently past the town only a few inches from the levee top. Meteorologists predicted a further rise. Small groups of people huddled on street corners, terrified, waiting; the telephone service ceased; hemmed in by the ever-swelling Ohio, Shawneetown flashed a desperate cry for help over an amateur's short-wave radio. Responding to the call, a river packet and several motorboats evacuated the townspeople just as the waters began to trickle over the levee. A roaring crashing avalanche soon inundated the cuplike townsite. At its height the flood topped the levee by 6 feet and covered three-fourths of Gallatin County. Between Shawneetown and Harrisburg, some 25 miles distant, State 13 was under 8 to 14 feet of water; motorboats navigated the entire distance to rescue marooned families.

The 1937 flood marked the end of Shawneetown's "pertinacious adhesion" to the riverbank, for there was no longer reason to remain. Gone were the packets and keelboats which induced her to hazard annual submersion. Gone was the steady traffic of settlers, goods, and singing rivermen. With the aid of the State, the RFC, and the WPA, a project is under way for transplanting the town to the hills 4 miles back from the river, which it is estimated will take 2 years. The State plans to establish a State park at the present site of Shawneetown. Some old landmarks will remain in the park; others will be removed to the new site.

The DOCKERS RIVERSIDE HOTEL, placidly surveying the broad Ohio, was built in 1870; its dormered mansard roof and cast iron porch railings are reminiscent of New Orleans. One block downstream from the hotel the levee bulwarks the OLDEST BANK BUILDING IN ILLINOIS (*private*), a modest little cottage built in 1812. Here the State's first bank was opened in 1816 and precociously carried on its business. In 1839 the institution was moved to the new FIRST NATIONAL BANK BUILDING, at Main and Washington Sts., where it is still housed. At the time it was built, public buildings and banks alike were designed to resemble Greek temples. This is a particularly well-proportioned example much admired by architects, with an imposing flight of steps leading to a fine Greek Doric portico of sandstone brought down the Ohio by flatboat from eastern quarries. The building cost $80,000, a huge sum for that period.

The balconied, two-storied, brick RAWLINGS HOTEL faces the river, one block north of the Riverside Hotel; it was constructed on the site of an old tavern bearing the same name. Here in 1825 a splendid fete honored the visiting La Fayette, who walked from the boat landing to the hotel on a gayly colored path of calico. At the height of the feasting and drinking, it is said, an old and tattered French soldier appeared at the door of the reception room. He made no effort to intrude but stood eying the celebration wistfully. Suddenly La Fayette recognized the man in the doorway as one of his bodyguard during the Revolution. The general rushed across the room, embraced the soldier, and led him to a place of honor at the table.

The POSEY BUILDING, at the southwest corner of State 13 and Main St., was built as a residence by a son of Gen. Thomas Posey, officer under Washington during the Revolution; it consists of two units. The three-storied building facing Main Street is of square, brick construction; the two-storied wing in the rear is also of brick, and has an outside stairway leading to the second floor. Robert G. Ingersoll's first law office was on the second floor of this wing, just at the top of the stairway. The crumbling remains of GENERAL POSEY'S REVOLUTIONARY WAR FLAG are framed and hang in Voyl's Drug Store, on Main Street one block north of the Posey Building.

The OLD SLAVE HOUSE (*adm.* 10c), 18.7 *m.*, topping a hill (R), sits back from the highway almost obscured by trees. The Southern Colonial house was built in 1834 by John Cranshaw, an Englishman, and has a sinister air heightened by its lonely site. Local opinion is divided as to the building's original use. Some believe that it was a station on the Underground Railroad; others that it was a prison for captured runaway slaves who were resold in the South. Available evidence favors the latter belief; Cranshaw it is said, gave elaborate parties on the lower floors with profits he gained from the terrified slaves he kept imprisoned in the upper part of the building. The first floor has spacious reception and drawing rooms; the second floor has five large bedrooms. But under the eaves on the third floor are tiny cells, each less than the height of a man, equipped with two narrow wooden bunks. Chain anchors are imbedded in the floors of these cells, and the door frames appear to have been cross-hatched with bars. A strange contraption of timbers on this floor, according to the present residents, was a torture instrument.

At the southern end of a bridge across the Saline River, 20.5 *m.*, is a plaque indicating the road to Nigger Spring.

Right on this road to NIGGER SPRING, 0.7 *m.*, encased below ground and flush with the surface in a lining of old timbers. This spring is almost the last vestige of what was once one of the most important industries in Illinois. Here brine slowly oozes to the surface in a slimy pool, giving off an unpleasant, pungent, sulphurous odor. Indians made salt here long before the coming of the white man; it was the discovery of their workings that led to the development of a great salt industry. Scattered in surrounding fields are shards of pottery used by the Indians in evaporating the brine. White men introduced iron kettles to facilitate this process. To aid in the development of the industry, the State legislature set aside more than 180,000 acres of woodland as a fuel supply, and the Constitution of 1818 exempted from the antislavery clause "the tract reserved by the salt works near Shawneetown." The salines reached their greatest productivity during the first half of the nineteenth century, when more than 500 bushels of salt were made a day. Production gradually declined when other sources of salt were discovered, and by 1875 the springs had been abandoned.

At 29.5 *m.* is a junction with a graveled road.

Right on this road to HIGH KNOB TOWER (*ladder type; not more than three persons are allowed to ascend at a time*), 10 *m.* This 60-foot tower, perched on the highest point of a knob of rock, affords a view of an area perhaps 50 miles in diameter.

At 30.5 *m.* is the junction with a graveled road.

Right on this road to POTTS HILL SPRING and the SITE OF POTTS TAVERN, 0.1 *m.* The tavern, razed in 1938, was a balconied, two-storied, frame structure. Numerous gruesome legends center around the nearby spring and the tavern; in one of its rooms 100-year-old bloodstains were still visible at the time of its demolition. Billy Potts operated this charnel house in collusion with a gang of renegades at Ford's Ferry, 15 miles to the east. The gang used to direct travelers to the tavern, where Potts murdered them for their money. Potts Tavern was the legendary scene of a story that occurs in the folk tales of many races. Potts' son, it is said, committed such a flagrant and brutal murder that he had to flee the country. Some 15 years later he returned, wealthy from crime, heavier and fully bearded. Young Potts was amused that his father did not recognize him; he made the mistake of displaying his wealth and was promptly killed by his father, who learned his identity the following day when the gang at Ford's Ferry, to whom the son had made himself known, came to the tavern.

CAVE-IN-ROCK, 39 *m.* (340 alt. 430 pop.), is a tiny Ohio River town, at the eastern edge of which is 60-acre CAVE-IN-ROCK STATE PARK (*picnic facilities, woodland trails*), named for a natural cave in the river bluff. The yawning cavern opening, midway between the summit of the bluff and the normal water line, was long a landmark for Ohio River boatmen, unmistakable even from the far side of the river. The graceful arch is 55 feet wide at the base and about 20 feet high; the cave tunnels about 200 feet into the bluff, with a small chamber branching right from the rear.

The front and interior of the cave are etched with a mosaic of names and initials of picnickers, but the most interesting words ever daubed on its smooth limestone walls were long ago effaced. In 1797 Samuel Mason, an officer of the Continental Army and the black sheep of a distinguished Virginia family, came to frontier Illinois. Converting the den into a wilderness caravansary, he fashioned a great sign above its entrance, announcing it as a "Liquor Vault and House of Entertainment." Snaring victims with these lures, Mason plundered travelers and flatboat crews. When Mason's notoriety reached such a height that even the frontier could not ignore it, he abandoned the cave and left the territory. His hide-away was soon appropriated by a long line of scoundrels, thieves, and counterfeiters. Among these were the notorious badmen, Duff, Sturdevant, Philip Alston, "Big"

Harpe, and "Little" Harpe. Vigilante bands finally routed the outlaws from Cave-in-Rock. Unused for more than a century, the cave and the surrounding tract were acquired by the State in 1929 and developed into the present park.

A ferry operates throughout the year across the Ohio River at Cave-in-Rock (*automobiles, $1; passengers, 25c each*).

TOUR 4

(BELOIT, WIS.) —ROCKFORD—LA SALLE—BLOOMINGTON—
DECATUR—VANDALIA—CENTRALIA—CARBONDALE—
CAIRO—(WICKLIFFE, KY.); US 51
Wisconsin Line to Kentucky Line, 430 *m.*

Hard-surfaced roadbed throughout.
The Chicago, Burlington & Quincy R. R. parallels highway between Rockford and Rochelle; the Chicago, Milwaukee, St. Paul and Pacific R. R. between Rochelle and Mendota; and the Illinois Central R. R. between Mendota and Cairo.
Good accommodations at short intervals.

US 51 closely follows the third principal meridian, established when the Northwest Territory was surveyed and divided into townships. Practically bisecting the State, the route connects the wooded dairy lands of the north with the bald cypress and orchard country that borders Cairo. Crossing the corn belt and mixed farming regions, traversing mining and industrial districts, passing through remnants of hard-wood forests and the Illinois Ozarks, US 51 offers a representative cross-section of the State.

Section a. Wisconsin Line to Bloomington, 156 m.

In its northern section US 51 follows the valley of the Rock River for a short distance, crosses the rolling prairies and woodlands of a diversified farming country, and enters the Illinois River gorge at La Salle, head of river navigation and terminus of the Illinois and Michigan Canal. Southward toward Bloomington are the rich corn fields and scattered coal beds of central Illinois.

US 51 crosses the Wisconsin Line, 0 *m.*, from Beloit, Wisconsin (*see Wisconsin Guide*), into SOUTH BELOIT, 1 *m.* (742 alt., 2,361 pop.), an Illinois adjunct of the larger city. Almost wholly industrial, the suburb contains a large foundry, a grinding machine shop, and an air-conditioning equipment plant.

Southward, the highway winds through the sand and gravel plains and terraces of the beautiful Rock River valley, at times commanding a full view of the river, at others losing it in a maze of trees. In the boulder-strewn bed of the broad and powerful Rock many waterpower sites have been developed; a chain of manufacturing cities extends along its banks from Wisconsin to Rock Island.

ROCKFORD, 17 *m.* (720 alt., 85,864 pop.) (*see Rockford*).

Points of Interest: Rockford College, Swiss Cottage, Harry and Della Burpee Art Gallery, Beattie Park, and others.

Rockford is at the junction with State 2 (*see Tour* 4A) and US 20 (*see Tour* 11).

CAMP GRANT, 21 *m.*, lies on the east bank of the Rock River. At one time the training camp for more than 50,000 men of the 86th Division, 4,000-acre Camp Grant is now maintained by the State for the use of the Illinois National Guard, but is subject to recall by the Federal Government in case of war. The annual encampment of 10,000 State militiamen usually takes place early in August. BELL BOWL, a vast natural amphitheater named for the late Maj. Gen. George Bell, Jr., the last regular army commander stationed here, is used for troop reviews.

At 38.7 *m.* is the junction with State 64.

Right on State 64 through the hamlet of KINGS to the junction with a graveled road, 2.5 *m.*; R. on this road to WHITE ROCK CENTER CEMETERY, 3.7 *m.* In the middle of the cemetery, marked by a large granite boulder, is the GRAVE OF JOHN CAMPBELL, captain of the Regulators, a pioneer vigilante group. The inscription on the grave recalls the violent and bloody frontier days less than a century ago. "John Campbell," it reads, "assassinated by prairie bandits in June 1841. His life was sacrificed for law and order." Campbell was killed by David and Taylor Driscoll, leaders of a bandit gang that for years made life and property insecure in DeKalb and Ogle Counties. The murder was the answer of the gang to a concerted action on the part of Campbell and other settlers to rid the region of the renegades. In retaliation, the Regulators rounded up all Driscolls. The two leaders escaped, but John Driscoll and his sons, William and Pierce, were caught. Pierce, aged 13, was spared because of his youth; the others were shot.

ROCHELLE, 44.2 *m.* (793 alt., 3,785 pop.), is one of those pleasant northern Illinois towns that seem to have grown out of the soil. Attesting the fertility of these prairies are the magnificent elms and maples that shade attractive houses and overhang colorful gardens. Extensive fields of peas, corn, pumpkins, and asparagus in the vicinity feed the local Del Monte cannery, and in the summer canning season Rochelle is crowded as additional hands are employed. Other industrial establishments include a spinning mill and a plant manufacturing small Diesel locomotives.

Two residents of Rochelle are remembered as composers of popular songs. One was Charles Butterfield, who wrote "When You and I Were Young, Maggie"; Francis Roe composed that sentimental theme song of the Civil War, "Just Before the Battle, Mother."

SPRING LAKE (*municipally owned bathhouse, small fee*), R. of US 51, is an unusual combination of landscaped pool and beach, framed by a beautiful waterfall and rock terraces.

Rochelle is at the junction with US 330 (*see Tour 12A*).

At 56 *m.* is the junction with US 30 (*see Tour 12*).

The highway ascends the northern slope of the BLOOMINGTON MORAINE, one of the longest and largest glacial ridges known to geologists. The Bloomington, here merged with the Shelbyville Moraine (*see below*), marks the farthest advance of the Wisconsin Glacier, last in the series of ice sheets that blanketed most of Illinois long ago. These irregular ridges, west of the highway between this point and Bloomington, were formed by the glacial debris that the huge ice sheet deposited as it melted at its outer edge.

MENDOTA, 74.1 *m.* (750 alt., 4,008 pop.), an attractive city with elm-shaded streets, serves the needs of the surrounding agricultural area, and processes and markets its products. An important canning center, Mendota annually ships some 4,000,000 cans of corn; some of the farms in the vicinity yielded more than 100 bushels of corn to the acre in 1938. A factory manufacturing corn cultivators, an engineering works, and a woodworking machinery plant supplement the canning industry in the economic life of the town.

Mendota is at the junction with US 34 (*see Tour 13*) and US 52 (*see Tour 15*); US 51 and US 52 are united for 6.5 miles.

South of Mendota the route enters the northern edge of the La Salle coal district. The first recorded discovery of coal in what is now the United States was made by Jolliet in 1673, when he and Father Marquette reached the Indian village, Kaskaskia, that lay on the Illinois River, a few miles east of La Salle. Below an east-west line across the State at this point, the whole of Illinois—with the exception of the Ozark region and strips along the Mississippi and Ohio Rivers—is underlaid with coal deposits of varying thicknesses. Little of the estimated 200 billion tons has been tapped.

At 79.7 *m.* is the southern junction with US 52 (*see Tour 15*).

At 86.9 *m.* US 51 divides, one branch (R) entering Peru, the other (L) skirting the city to La Salle (*see below*).

PERU, 90 *m.* (459 alt., 9,121 pop.), appears to be a continuous city with La Salle, which adjoins it on the east. Both owe their early growth to the Illinois River, and both lie on its northern bank. Founded in 1835, Peru (Ind., plenty of everything) was made the terminus of the Illinois and Michigan Canal because it was at the head of navigation on the river. It lost the canal-to-river transshipping business to La Salle, however, when that city built a steamboat and canal basin.

Nevertheless, both cities profited greatly from the flood of commerce that came down the river on barges and steamers. The twin communities began life on the river terraces, but their growth soon forced them up the slopes and out on the prairies. Peru, partly because of its steeper site, failed to keep pace with La Salle.

Water transportation was such an irresistible lure to industry in the early days that even when canal traffic declined most of the factories remained. In the case of Peru and La Salle this was particularly true, because for many years local concerns were favored by low rail rates; the railroads were well aware of the competitive potentialities of the canal.

The PERU WHEEL COMPANY PLANT (1851), 2 Brunner St., and the STAR UNION PRODUCTS COMPANY BREWERY (1845), Brewster and Jackson Sts., are operated by two of the oldest manufacturing concerns in the State. The WESTCLOX FACTORY of the General Time Instruments Corporation (*open, Mon.-Fri.,* 10 *a.m. and* 2 *p.m.*) covers seven blocks on US 6 at the eastern edge of town. The company employs 3,000 persons and has a maximum daily production of 30,000 watches, clocks, and alarm clocks; the Big Ben and Westclox are made here.

The ILLINOIS RIVER BRIDGE, 1700 Water St., a wooden swing-type span turned by hand, is one of the oldest major bridges in the State, having been constructed in 1869. At that time its middle girder, 310 feet long, was considered a remarkable engineering achievement. At the base of the bridge is the SOUTH SHORE BOAT CLUB (*rowboats at nominal fees*).

Peru is at the junction with US 6 (*see Tour* 14), which unites with US 51 for 2 miles.

LA SALLE, 92 *m.* (448 alt., 13,149 pop.), was named for the French explorer who came down the Illinois River in 1679. The town was born in 1827 when plans for the Illinois and Michigan Canal crystallized. The opening of the canal to navigation in 1848 was greeted with enthusiasm or apprehension by Midwestern cities, depending on their locations. As the locks swung open to pass the first freight-laden boat, the transportation system of the whole region was shattered and reassembled in a new picture. The rich central prairies of Illinois now poured their crops into Chicago rather than St. Louis; within four years Chicago was receiving almost four times as much corn as the Mississippi port. Far across Lake Michigan sawmills began to buzz in the wooded sections of Michigan, and lines of steamers puffed across the lake and into the canal with much needed lumber for the booming prairie towns.

The new waterway pumped money and prosperity into La Salle for a decade. The decline of steamboating began here somewhat earlier than on the Mississippi. The competitive advantage of the railroads was increased by the comparative shallowness of the Illinois River, the irregularity of steamboat service, and the lack of co-ordination between river and canal vessels. By the nineties canal traffic had greatly diminished. In this crisis La Salle turned to nearby coal deposits, and the railroads influenced many enterprises to remain in the town.

Principal revenue source for La Salle is the MATTHIESSEN & HEGELER ZINC COMPANY PLANT (*no visitors*), La Harpe St., between 11th St. and O'Connor Ave., established in 1858 by two German immigrants who were attracted by the town's coal, water facilities, and proximity to Galena zinc ore. Spelter and sheet zinc, zinc wire, and boiler plates for ships are the chief products, from which the most important by-product is sulphuric acid; goods are still transported by water down the Illinois to the river-to-rail terminal at Peoria.

The HEGELER HOME (*private*), 1307 7th St., built in 1874 by Edward C. Hegeler, co-founder of the zinc company, is a large stone and concrete structure, with mansard roof, small balcony porches, cupola and bays; it is modeled after a Rhine River castle.

The LA SALLE-PERU-OGLESBY JUNIOR COLLEGE (*visitors welcome*), 6th and Chartres Sts., established in 1924, offers liberal arts and pre-professional courses of the freshman and sophomore college years. Its main building, a handsome brick Tudor-Gothic structure, is in La Salle; its fine stadium, immediately west in Peru, sprawls at the base of a natural hollow.

La Salle is at the junction with US 6 (*see Tour* 14).

The highway crosses the old Illinois and Michigan Canal between Locks 14 and 15, only a short distance apart. In the basin at Peru (R) boats were lowered into the Illinois River. Along the canal front are old pilings and antiquated warehouses, reminiscent of steamboat days. The canal and towpath (L) are being improved by the WPA as a recreational spot.

The viaduct across the canal merges into the SHIPPINGSPORT BRIDGE over the Illinois River. At its southern end is the SITE OF FORT WILBOURN, where the 22nd Army of Illinois Volunteers was mustered into service for the Black Hawk War. Here on June 16, 1832, Abraham Lincoln enlisted as a private in Jacob N. Early's company.

Although coal mining was once of major importance in this area, production has fallen off materially. The more profitable strip mines around Wilmington to the east and the thicker seams exploited by the Southern Illinois collieries have reduced activities here.

OGLESBY, 95.5 m. (465 alt., 3,910 pop.), named for Gov. Richard J. Oglesby, is one of the largest cement-producing centers in the State, utilizing the vast deposits of limestone and slate which outcrop in the Vermilion Valley nearby. The city's long brightly-lighted main street is dotted with many taverns, but hotels and shops are markedly wanting. Oglesby does its shopping in La Salle or Peru, for it is almost wholly an industrial town.

At 97.8 *m.* is the junction with a graveled road.

Left on this road to the junction with another graveled road, 1.8 *m.;* L. on this road along the top of a bluff overlooking the deep Vermilion Valley to BAILEY FALLS, 2.6 *m.,* where Bailey Creek tumbles into the Vermilion. Immense limestone blocks, loosened by rains and weather, have crashed down the steep slopes and now lie in the stream bed below the falls like houses left stranded by a flood. Lumbering has recently revived in this wilderness area; long ago there was a sawmill at the falls.

At 108.3 *m.* is the junction with State 18.

Left on this paved road, past many barns with Gothic windows and steeple-like cupolas, to STREATOR, 12 *m.* (625 alt., 14,728 pop.), center of an important clay-producing area along the Vermilion River. Streator owes its highly indus-trial character to the great shale, clay, and sand deposits which crowd up to its southern limits, and to the veins of coal which underlie them. Coal mining began here in 1872, and the importance of the enterprise is reflected in the fact that the city soon changed its name from Unionville to Streator in honor of the coal company's president.

On the heels of coal came glass. A small bottle works was established in Streator in 1873. Beds of siliceous sand used in the manufacture of glass lay at the community's doorstep, and quantities of coal were available. Until the twentieth century the delicate and involved task of converting sand into glass bottles was performed by a colorful crew of glass-blowers. Many of these highly skilled craftsmen were itinerant workers, but they could command high wages. In time machines replaced these artisans, and the town's glass plants passed from local ownership into the hands of a nation-wide combine.

Streator's products are mainly mineral in origin, as tile, brick, pipe, and glass, or depend largely on coal in their making, as acetylene and foundry products.

In RIVERVIEW CEMETERY, at the western city limits, is the GRAVE OF GEORGE "HONEY BOY" EVANS, born in Streator in 1870. Evans first appeared in amateur theatricals, then clerked in a bookstore, and finally joined Haverly's Mastodon Minstrels at Chicago in 1892. Composer of songs and monologues, author of the immensely popular "The Good Old Summer Time," he was the outstanding black-face comedian of his day. In New York, Evans headed the Cohan and Harris minstrel show, eventually took over the company, and toured the road until his death in 1915.

WENONA, 113.7 *m.* (696 alt., 1,005 pop.), is a marketing and shipping point for soy beans and corn, for this area lies on the west-ern edge of the east-central Illinois grain region.

Soy beans are cultivated both for their seeds and for forage. Flour prepared from soy beans is a standard food for diabetes sufferers; soys are the basic ingredient of a popular sauce or liquid condiment used with fish and meat. Many fields of this cash crop border the highway south of Wenona; Illinois produces more soy beans than all other states together.

EL PASO, 137.2 *m.* (749 alt., 1,578 pop.), has a tile and concrete block factory, as well as three grain elevators and a cannery, common industrial features of small Illinois towns that act as funnels into which pour the products of nearby farms.

El Paso is the home of Lester Pfister, who, after 10 years of experimentation, perfected a remarkable hybrid corn. Pfister's experiments began in 1925 when Henry Wallace, then an Iowa farm editor, later Secretary of Agriculture, convinced him that a satisfactory hybrid could be developed. During the course of 10 years of trial and error, the corn breeder was the object of daily ridicule from neighbors because of his paper bags, which he carefully wrapped around tassels and ear-shoots. Pfister intermingled the various pollens until at last by inbreeding and crossbreeding he produced a high-yield corn. After years of mortgaging his farm, begging the bank for more loans, and striving to get enough food for his wife and children, Pfister's faith was rewarded in 1935, when he began marketing his corn seed. Pfister has now enlarged his farm to 580 acres, and rents an additional 800. Today his seed corn is planted on 2,000,000 acres in Iowa, Ohio, Illinois, and Indiana, crops on which were worth $10,000,000 in 1938.

El Paso is at the junction with US 24 (*see Tour* 16).

At 144.6 *m.* is the junction with a paved road.

Left on this road to LAKE BLOOMINGTON (*swimming, fishing, boating*), 3.6 *m.*, the source of Bloomington's water supply, and now a major recreational area; many attractive permanent and summer homes border its shores. Created by damming Money Creek, 500-acre Lake Bloomington, with a maximum depth of 35 feet, has a wooded margin of 1,400 acres. The Italian Renaissance brick PUMPING STATION (*open 7 a.m.-8 p.m. daily*), with red tile roof, is near the dam at the northern end of the lake. Just southwest of the station is a stone gateway in which is imbedded a PLATE IN MEMORY OF SILAS HUBBARD (1855-1900), a family doctor, whose kindness and philanthropy have almost become a legend in this region. Inside the gate is the STONE-HUBBARD MEMORIAL, a stone bench constituting a dual memorial to Melville E. Stone (1848-1929), co-founder of the Chicago *Daily News*, later general manager of the *Associated Press*, and Elbert Hubbard (1856-1915), author and humanist; the beautiful Money Creek valley was the boyhood playground of both Stone and Hubbard.

At 147.8 *m.* is the junction with a graveled road.

Left on this road is HUDSON, 0.7 *m.* (768 alt., 330 pop.), where a group from New York, known as the Hudson Colony, settled in 1836. The original town lots were apportioned by lottery, each buyer paying $235 for four lots and 160 acres of land. The first house of the Hudson Colony, built by James T. Gildersleeve, is called FIVE OAKS (*private*), and is the birthplace of Melville Elijah Stone (*see above*). The gray frame, two-story, Greek revival structure has a square wing at the north, and a small front porch. The formality of its fine walnut interior is relieved by numerous stone fireplaces. Five Oaks received its name from five oak trees on the grounds that appear to rise from a single root.

In Hudson is the site of the last village of the Potawatomi in this area. In 1831 mischievous white boys burned the wigwams to the ground while the Indians were away on a hunting trip. The peaceful Potawatomi made no attempt to avenge the act or rebuild their village, but moved on to Galesburg and thence westward across the Mississippi.

BLOOMINGTON, 156 *m*. (830 alt., 30,930 pop.) and NORMAL (790 alt., 6,768 pop.) (*see Bloomington and Normal*).

Points of Interest: Home of American Passion Play, McBarnes Memorial Building, Illinois Wesleyan University, Illinois State Normal University, and others.

Bloomington is at the junction with US 66 (*see Tour* 17).

Section b. Bloomington to Vandalia, 115 m.

Between Bloomington and Vandalia the highway winds among the great grain fields of east central Illinois, a region of rich black loam. The flat or gently rolling terrain, the result of glaciation, makes mechanized agriculture both possible and profitable.

South of Bloomington, 0 *m.*, US 51 again crosses the Bloomington Moraine (*see above*). At this point the formation, a chain of low hills, follows an east-west line. West of the city the Bloomington Moraine merges with the Shelbyville Moraine (*see below*), and swings northward.

At 7.7 *m*. is the junction with a graveled road.

Left on this road is RANDOLPH, 0.2 *m*. (781 alt., 49 pop.), which has clung to existence with little variation in population for more than a century. Among its first settlers was Gardner Randolph, who, with his family, moved here in 1822 from North Carolina. Their first shelter was made by driving four poles into the ground and covering three sides with brush and bark. This shelter gave scant protection from the bitter cold and merciless blizzards of Illinois winters, but the family managed to survive. The SITE OF THE FIRST RANDOLPH HOME is marked by a red granite boulder.

At 0.8 *m*. is the junction with a graveled road; R. here to the junction with another graveled road, 1.4 *m.*; L. on this road to the STEWART HOUSE (*open*), 1.7 *m.*, built in 1833, the oldest house in McLean County. The brick used in its construction was baked on the site, an early utilization of the excellent clay in the region. The two-story house of red brick adjoins a private residence and is now used as a storehouse. The old structure has a gabled roof, a one-story wing, and green shutters.

HEYWORTH, 12.3 *m*. (747 alt., 959 pop.), is an agricultural trading center; according to tradition, the village site, then heavily timbered, was for many years the camping ground of the Kickapoo tribe.

CLINTON, 24.4 *m*. (746 alt., 5,920 pop.), seat of De Witt County, reputedly was the first town to hear a Lincoln aphorism that has been endlessly re-echoed. Here, on July 27, 1858, Stephen A. Douglas falsely charged Lincoln during their campaign for the United States Senate with advocating political equality for Negroes. Lincoln was in the audience, and at the conclusion of Douglas's speech announced that he would speak that same evening at the courthouse. Today, on the courthouse lawn, a life-size LINCOLN STATUE, by the Belgian artist, Van den Bergen, marks the site of the speech and quotes Lincoln's remark that "you can fool all the people part of the time and part of the people all of the time, but you cannot fool all the people all the time."

Clinton was on the circuit of the Eighth Judicial District, and was frequently visited by Lincoln. Here, while opposing Douglas in a railroad case, he first met George B. McClellan, then an engineer for the Illinois Central, later appointed by Lincoln to the command of the Northern Armies.

The BARNETT HOTEL (*for admittance apply to owner*), 738 N. Grant St., an old buff frame building, Greek Revival in design, was a stopping place much favored by Lincoln and other notables of the time. The building, now a private residence, has been moved from its original site and has undergone numerous alterations; but the old bar rail, still a steadying influence, serves as the hand-rail on the stairway to the second floor.

The GRAY HOUSE (*private*), 121 N. Quincy St., built in 1836 by Postmaster Miles Gray, functioned for years as Gray's residence, the town post office, and a busy tailoring establishment. Now its rough-hewn logs are hidden under weather-boards, and the old building is used as a storehouse.

South of Clinton US 51 runs along the inner edge of the SHELBYVILLE MORAINE, which roughly divides Illinois into three agricultural sectors. To the north and east is the cash grain area, where corn is raised for the nearby Chicago market on soil formed by the most recent glacier, the Wisconsin. To the south and west are the older leached soils of the Illinois glacier. The western section, younger and heavily mantled with loess, also achieves a high yield of corn, which is fed to cattle and hogs or shipped to the more distant markets.

DECATUR, 46.9 *m.* (683 alt., 57,510 pop.) (*see Decatur*).

Points of Interest: Millikin University, Administration Building of A. B. Staley Manufacturing Company, Lake Decatur, M. L. Barry Memorial Fountain, and others.

Decatur is at the junction with US 36 (*see Tour* 18) and the Lincoln National Memorial Highway (*see Tour* 21).

South of Decatur the highway traverses the Shelbyville Moraine (*see above*). The large glacial ridge, which enters the State from Indiana along an east-west line, here swings abruptly northward to join the Bloomington Moraine (*see above*), west of that city.

MACON, 57 *m.* (721 alt., 800 pop.), is the home of the EASTERN STAR SANITARIUM (*visitors welcome*), an institution maintained by the Order of the Eastern Star of Illinois to care for its aged and infirm members.

MOWEAQUA, 63.2 *m.* (632 alt., 1,478 pop.), an agricultural and mining community, was the scene of a Christmas Eve mine disaster in 1932 that smothered the holiday spirits of the whole region under a pall of death. Fifty-four men working in a local mine were entombed and fatally burned by a terrific explosion of gas. Scores of rescuers rushed from family celebrations to the mine and dug frantically in the bitter cold in a desperate effort to save the victims, but their work was in vain. The ill-fated mine has been closed since 1935.

PANA, 82.1 m. (693 alt., 5,835 pop.), is announced from a distance by smokestacks rising from acres of tilted glass panes. Of the many enterprises that cluster around Illinois' coal mines, Pana's rose-growing is perhaps the strangest and certainly the simplest in operation. Because the chief requisite of hot-house floriculture is steam heat supplied by coal, rose culture is particularly suited to mining regions. Five flower firms, with 102 greenhouses, ship 15,000,000 cut roses annually from the Pana district. Local production of coal for domestic and industrial use is also important.

KITCHEL PARK, in the southern part of the city, has tennis courts, a swimming pool, picnic accommodations, and a tourist camp. In the park, visible from the highway, is a statue of Liberty, guarded on either side by a soldier and a sailor, erected by the citizens of Pana Township to their men who served in the World War.

At 110.9 m. the ILLINOIS STATE PENAL FARM (open daily, 8-5) is bisected by the highway. Convicts who work the 1,233-acre tract and the additional 2,000 acres that are leased by the State have nicknamed the institution the "Peanut Farm." The low buff-colored buildings, with their cloistered walks, are more suggestive of a quiet place of learning than of a penal colony. In 1937 a hospital and six dormitories were added to the institution, increasing the prisoner-capacity from 700 to 1,400. Only petty offenders, such as those guilty of misdemeanor, are kept here; their sentences range from sixty days to a year.

VANDALIA, 115 m. (503 alt., 4,342 pop.), basking in the fertile Kaskaskia River valley and banked by one of the Illinoisan moraines, was the second capital of Illinois (1819-1839). Created in virgin wilderness and growing rapidly in its first few years, Vandalia loomed large in the early history of the State.

The State legislature, meeting at Kaskaskia in 1819, decided to bolster its insignificant treasury by the currently popular method of town-lot speculation. Accordingly a land grant was procured from the Federal government and that same year a new State capital, 60 miles east of the Mississippi, was laid out. For the next 20 years Vandalia was the political center of Illinois, the forum for such frontier statesmen as John Reynolds, Ninian Edwards, Stephen A. Douglas, and Abraham Lincoln. But in 1837 the "Long Nine," a junta of 6-foot legislators under the leadership of Lincoln, organized a successful bloc that obtained legislation removing the capital to Springfield two years later. The story is persistent locally (although it has no basis in fact) that during the struggle over the removal of the capital Lincoln jumped out of one of the second-story windows in order to break a quorum that would have awarded the honor to Vandalia for another 20 years. After losing the capital to Springfield, Vandalia assumed the lesser rôle of seat of Fayette County.

The VANDALIA STATE HOUSE (*open daily* 8-5), erected in 1836, was the fourth Capitol of Illinois. The first was a rented building in Kaskaskia. The second, in Vandalia, was a two-story log structure, destroyed by fire in 1823. The third, of brick, was razed to make room for the one now standing. This two-story, white brick building, of simple Greek Revival design, has been restored to its original appearance and is preserved as a public museum. The main entrance is protected by a two-story galleried porch with slender arcaded posts instead of the usual heavy columns supporting the pediment; above the gabled roof is a cupola. The upper room at the western end has ten long benches, a semicircular railing, and a rostrum that are all original pieces. Present plans are to furnish the whole building with furniture of Lincoln's period. In this building was issued, March 4, 1837, the city charter of Chicago, then but a little-known village far in the unsettled north.

In front of the old building stands a MADONNA OF THE TRAIL MONUMENT, 18 feet high, erected by the D. A. R. in 1928 to mark the western terminus of the Cumberland Road (*see Tour* 19). One of twelve monuments in different states commemorating the Cumberland Road, this one is the figure of a pioneer woman who holds an infant in her arms, while a small boy clings to her skirts.

The frame MOREY BUILDING, 419 Gallatin St., during Vandalia's heyday was the most pretentious rooming-house in town. Lincoln roomed on the second floor while serving in the legislature and it was here, tradition has it, that he first met Stephen A. Douglas. Today the front of the building is occupied by shops.

Vandalia is at the junction with US 40 (*see Tour* 19).

Section c. Vandalia to Cairo, 159 m.

South of Vandalia, 0 *m.*, US 51 enters a country where coal becomes more and more important, reaching its culmination at Carbondale, which lies close to the most productive bituminous veins in the United States. South of Carbondale stretches the cross-State range of the Illinois Ozarks. Here the coal veins, so prevalent a few miles north, were stripped from the uplifted belt of hills by age-long processes of erosion. Fruit farms cover the hillsides for a 40-mile stretch and then the road drops abruptly from the hills into the lush delta region near Cairo, the lowest point in the State.

VERNON, 12.5 *m.* (505 alt., 245 pop.), in the Keiffer pear district of Marion County, is a shipping point for the peach and pear crop of the many orchards surrounding the village.

PATOKA, 15.6 *m.* (507 alt., 546 pop.), named for an Indian chief, drowsed for generations and then, in 1937, suddenly found itself the center of a feverish oil boom in which much of southern Illinois was leased by oil companies. The old oil fields to the south and east had been producing sluggishly for many years, but the new wells of Patoka gushed sufficiently to excite the landowners with prospects of developing one of the largest oil fields in the State.

SANDOVAL, 26 *m.* (509 alt., 1,264 pop.), a small mining and farming community, was a busy railroad terminal until the adoption of standard gauge tracks by the Baltimore & Ohio R. R. in 1871. At Sandoval it was necessary to transfer freight carried over the 6-foot tracks of the B. & O. to the narrower tracks of the Illinois Central. The transfer was made by an arrangement of parallel tracks along which freight cars were drawn by oxen, and the freight shifted from car to car by hand. Upon its decision to change to standard gauge tracks the B. & O. was faced with the problem of narrowing its entire line 15 inches between Cincinnati and St. Louis. To avoid interruption of schedules company officials determined to effect the change overnight. On July 21, 1871 an army of 1,000 track-layers was distributed at five-mile sections of the road and promptly, like soldiers advancing on an enemy, proceeded to sever the tracks and respike them closer together. At 8 A. M., July 22, 1871, the B. & O. became a standard gauge road and Sandoval ceased to be a freight terminal.

Sandoval is at a junction with US 50 (*see Tour* 20).

CENTRAL CITY, 30.8 *m.* (498 alt., 1,148 pop.), has grown but little since its incorporation in 1857, and retains its original German atmosphere.

CENTRALIA, 32.9 *m.* (495 alt., 12,583 pop.), and Central City were named for the Illinois Central System. With Wamac, a suburb to the south, they form a continuous urban area.

Self-advertised as the "Gateway to Egypt," Centralia pushes the claim by embellishing the façades of several of its business houses with a variety of Egyptian motifs. Egypt is the name popularly applied to the southern quarter of Illinois, partly because of the delta-like character of the region, and partly because of the frequency of Egyptian place-names.

Centralia, platted by the Illinois Central in 1853, was originally definitely German. Early business and banking institutions had German backing; both English and German were taught in the schools, and in three of the five early churches services were in German. The German influence is seen in several established commercial concerns, in the many *Saengerfeste,* and in the dominant architecture of homes and business structures.

The Illinois Central in 1855 established its Centralia shops in what is now the heart of the business district. At that time experiments were begun with coal as fuel for locomotives. The first locomotive to burn Illinois coal successfully was converted from a wood-burner in these shops, and by 1868 the use of coal in locomotives had become general. Centralia's location in the heart of the southern Illinois fruit belt resulted in early attempts to produce refrigerated cars, and in 1868 the "Thunderbolt Express," first temperature-controlled fruit train in America, began regular operation between Centralia and Chicago.

Fruit crops of the region are valued at more than $1,000,000 annually. Until some time after the Civil War, strawberries constituted the principal crop, but today peaches are cultivated extensively, as are apples and Keiffer pears.

WAMAC, 34.4 m. (497 alt., 1,232 pop.), is a name coined from the first letters of the counties in which the town lies—Washington, Marion and Clinton. Incorporated as a city in 1913, Wamac for awhile enjoyed a boom as an oasis for surrounding dry towns.

IRVINGTON, 39 m. (530 alt., 344 pop.), in the 1890's was the strawberry capital of "Egypt." Hundred-acre strawberry patches were common, and the Illinois Central ran special non-stop trains to Chicago with the fruit. As the picking season approached, a horde of transients from all parts of the country invaded Irvington to exchange their services as strawberry-pickers for food and drink. Gradual substitution of peach orchards for strawberry fields has deprived the village of its annual boom.

ASHLEY, 50 m. (559 alt., 772 pop.), was named for John Ashley, an early settler.

Left from Ashley on State 15 to MOUNT VERNON, 15 m. (463 alt., 12,375 pop.), seat of Jefferson County. Settled by Southerners and today peopled largely by descendants of Southern families, the city retains its Southern charm and emphasis on family ties and traditions, despite its industrial development. Although the site of Mount Vernon was chosen as seat of newly formed Jefferson County in 1819, it grew very slowly; new residents were mostly from Kentucky and Tennessee. With the coming of the railroads the community entered upon a period of industrial growth. A car manufacturing company was early established, and the five railroads that now serve the town brought other industries.

The APPELLATE COURT BUILDING, 1400 W. Main St., a gray brick and stone structure in the shape of a Maltese cross, was built in 1854. Of Greek Revival design, the entrance pavilion is adorned with fluted Ionic columns, and topped with a fine classic pediment. The arched portal is approached by a long double flight of cast-iron steps. The building originally housed the southern grand division of the Illinois Supreme Court. When the Supreme Court was centered in Springfield (1897), the Mount Vernon building became headquarters of the Fourth District Appellate Court.

Ahead on State 15 is FAIRFIELD, 47 m. (451 alt., 3,280 pop.) (see Tour 3c), at a junction with 45 (see Tour 3c).

TAMAROA, 66.2 m. (510 alt., 881 pop.), was named for the Tamaroa Indian tribe that inhabited this region. Failure of local coal mines to operate regularly has caused the town to decline in recent years.

At 66.5 *m.*, south of the village limits, is a junction with an improved road.

Left on this road three blocks is a 60-acre tract of narcissuses, daffodils, and peonies, known as MAPLE LAWN GARDENS (*visitors welcome*). During the blooming season, which is at its height about Easter, the flowers are sold and shipped in carload lots. A private road system enables visitors to penetrate to the heart of the gardens and enjoy their beauty and fragrance.

DU QUOIN, 76.2 *m.* (468 alt., 7,593 pop.), was named for Jean Baptiste Du Quoigne, an Indian of French extraction, chief of the Kaskaskia tribe. It is a vital link in the mining communities that make southern Illinois one of the most important coal areas in the United States. During 1935, 13 mines operated in this region, five of them shipping 1,732,000 tons of coal to outside markets. Although this is primarily a mining region, farms are important and agricultural well-being is reflected in the substantial homes of retired farmers.

Right from Du Quoin on State 152 is the UNITED ELECTRIC COAL COMPANY MINE (*inspected upon application to general manager*), 5 *m.*, one of the largest strip mines in the Nation. A giant electric dredge here scoops out 12 cubic yards of coal at each dip. During 1935 the mine produced more than 1,000,000 tons of coal.

DOWELL, 81.2 *m.* (400 alt., 832 pop.), is a brisk young mining town that sprang up in 1916 around the large KATHLEEN COAL COMPANY MINE. The town was named for George Dowell, legal advisor for the Progressive Miners of America.

ELKVILLE, 83.3 *m.* (400 alt., 1,133 pop.), narrowly escaped total destruction when a fire of undetermined origin swept through part of its business district, May 17, 1936. Much of the burned section has been rebuilt.

DE SOTO, 91.2 *m.* (386 alt., 673 pop.), still bears the marks of a devastating tornado that swept southern Illinois in 1925. Eighty persons were killed in De Soto, including 38 children who were trapped in the town school. Foundations of buildings flattened by the storm and never rebuilt are visible (R).

CARBONDALE, 97.5 *m.* (416 alt., 7,528 pop.), center of the southern Illinois coal fields, is a division point on the Illinois Central System. The railroad shops and the Southern Illinois State Normal University, the chief supports of the city, give it a composite atmosphere of industrialism and college activity.

The SOUTHERN ILLINOIS STATE NORMAL UNIVERSITY, in the southern section of Carbondale, founded in 1874, is the largest teachers' college in the State. It has a faculty of 124 members and an average enrollment of 1,500 students. The campus includes 11 buildings, mostly of red brick, which are designed in a modified Early American style of architecture. The zoology department maintains a MUSEUM on the third floor of its main building, which is being enlarged through Federal funds, and by August 1939 will be open to the public daily, except Sundays. Of particular note are a collection of venomous snakes native to southern Illinois, and the Irvin Pheitman exhibition of Indian relics.

Left from Carbondale on State 13, past the waters of CRAB ORCHARD LAKE, a Federal project completed in 1939, is a junction with State 148, 12 m.

Left 5 m. on State 148 is HERRIN (405 alt., 9,708 pop.), a principal center in the southern Illinois coal fields. The first shaft was sunk here in 1895; Herrin was incorporated as a village in 1898 and as a city two years later. As shaft after shaft went down during the first two decades of the twentieth century, Herrin's population rose from 1,500 to more than 10,000. An almost staid community of well-supported churches and substantial homes, Herrin today leads an orthodox existence. But in the summer of 1922, when the Nation's coal fields were closed by lockout and strike, occurred the "Herrin Massacre," a tragic incident in the long contest between the United Mine Workers of America and the coal operators.

The "Herrin Massacre" was occasioned by an attempt to operate a strip mine near Herrin with non-union labor while tension was at the breaking point in the community. On June 21 an armed clash occurred at the mine; two union men were killed and a third was mortally wounded. On June 22 the attack was resumed, but the strip mine workers soon surrendered and agreed to leave the county under a promise of safe conduct. On the way to Herrin the mine superintendent was taken aside and shot; the strikers' leader who had promised safe conduct was deposed; the captives were ordered to run for their lives under fire. Thirteen were killed immediately; later in the day seven others lost their lives. A special grand jury examined more than 300 witnesses and returned 214 indictments for murder and other charges. Local sentiment was such, however, that after several verdicts of acquittal, all remaining indictments were dismissed.

For months the press of the Nation editorialized on the incident, which was recognized as having more than local implications. William Allen White saw evidence of a "new doctrine" in the conflict. "Labor," he remarked, "is beginning to feel that skill has the same status as property. The right to apply their skill in the place where it will produce value, labor seems to regard as an essential human right. This is astonishing. But we can not ignore it—this belief of the laborer in his right to what he calls his job. He feels that so long as the place where he works is a 'going concern' his right to work is exactly upon the same footing as the owner's right to profit."

Ahead on State 13 is MARION, 17 m. (419 alt., 9,033 pop.), century-old city and seat of Williamson County. In the years preceding the Civil War, Marion was the home of Robert G. Ingersoll and John A. Logan. Here both young men were admitted to the bar. At the outbreak of the War, both men organized regiments of which they became colonels: Ingersol, the 11th Illinois Cavalry; Logan, the famed 31st Illinois Infantry. Logan's first recruits were two veterans of the Mexican War, who volunteered for service during a speech delivered by Logan on Marion's public square. Logan's oratory was highly instrumental in winning southern Illinois to the Northern cause.

State 13 continues eastward to HARRISBURG, 40 m. (400 alt., 11,625 pop.) (see Tour 3d), at a junction with US 45 (see Tour 3d).

South of Carbondale the highway enters the Illinois Ozarks, an uplifted and folded belt 15 to 40 miles wide and 70 miles long, extend-

ing from the Mississippi to the Ohio. A continuation of the Missouri
Ozarks, these hills in places rise as high as 700 feet above the surrounding country.

The CARBONDALE-COBDEN COUNTRY CLUB, 103.5 *m.*, is entered by
a graveled road (R) leading through the heavily-wooded hills. In the
center of the grounds is a sprawling, spring-fed lake, surrounded by
summer cottages, and a 9-hole golf course (*fee of $1 includes shower,
locker, and one day's play*).

At 106.8 *m.* is a junction with a graveled road.

Left on this road is the entrance, 2.4 *m.*, to GIANT CITY STATE PARK
(*cabins and picnic facilities*). Established as a State park in 1927, the 916 acres
of hills, forests, and fantastic rock formations have a historical background that
matches their scenery in interest. Here, during the Civil War, was a headquarters
of the Knights of the Golden Circle, a secret organization that favored the
Southern cause. Lying slightly south in the latitude of Richmond, Virginia, and
settled largely by immigrants from Southern or border states, this locale harbored
many Southern sympathizers. The Knights of the Golden Circle stimulated resistance to the draft, circulated treasonable publications in the Union ranks, and
carried on espionage for the South.

A short distance within the park is the OLD STONE FORT (L). It consists of
a sandstone knoll, with steep, unscalable walls on three sides. Across the fourth
side, the only approach to the top, is a 7-foot wall of rough, unquarried stone.
The crudity of the fort's conception indicates Indian or pre-Indian origin. The
fort is one of seven in the Illinois Ozarks.

Near the center of the park is the section that gives it its name. Passages
that are almost streetlike in their orderly arrangement run between sundered
blocks of sandstone. On each side the sandstone rises 30 or 40 feet, its weathered,
pockmarked surface resembling the walls of a medieval castle. High upon the face
of one rock a bodyguard of Jefferson Davis chiseled "Albert S. Thompson,
Freemont Bodyguard, Feb. 22, 1862, A. D." At the park's highest point is a large
STONE LODGE (*lounge and dining room*), built by the CCC from rock gathered
in the vicinity. Sturdily constructed and commanding an excellent view of the
Ozark hills, it is the park's recreational center. Twelve one-room frame cabins
(*for rates and reservations address Concessionaires, Giant City State Park,
Makanda, Illinois*), each with shower and other facilities, are nearby.

At 111.5 *m.* is a junction with a graveled road.

Right on this road to ALTO PASS, 3 *m.* (748 alt., 485 pop.), the highest
point in southern Illinois served by a railroad. BALD KNOB TOWER, 9 *m.*, a 60-
foot lookout station of the forestry service, perches on a mound 1,030 feet above
sea level. Commanding a view of more than 600 square miles, it is one of the
most impressive vantage points in the entire State.

COBDEN, 119.1 *m.* (594 alt., 1,036 pop.), an important fruit
shipping point on the Illinois Central, was named for an English director of the railroad. It has been claimed that the refrigerator car
was an outgrowth of a strawberry refrigerator-box invented by Parker
Earl of Cobden. Cobden is the birthplace of Agnes Ayres, motion picture actress, who starred with Rudolph Valentino in *The Sheik*.

ANNA, 119.8 *m.* (629 alt., 3,436 pop.), an important fruit shipping center, is the home of ANNA STATE HOSPITAL (*only relatives*

may visit patients) ; the institution provides psychiatric care for 3,000 patients. After the main building burned in 1895, many new structures were added, including the modern yellow brick receiving ward.

Right from Anna on State 146 to JONESBORO, 2 *m.* (429 alt., 1,241 pop.), seat of Union County. Laid out in 1816 and named for a physician who was an early settler, Jonesboro is the oldest town in the county. The fairgrounds, on N. Main Street, is the SITE OF THE THIRD LINCOLN-DOUGLAS DEBATE, September 15, 1858; a marker near the town square commemorates the event. Lincoln and Horace White sat on the porch of the old Union House in Jonesboro, which was razed by fire in October 1937, and watched Donati's comet on the night before the debate.

WETAUG, 132.4 *m.* (356 alt., 434 pop.), perpetuates the name of a tribe of Cherokee Indians who camped at a large spring in the vicinity while passing through the country on their historic march from Georgia to Oklahoma. The spring ceased to flow following an earthquake that shook southern Illinois in 1896. The grave of one of the chiefs of the tribe is on the grounds of a local residence.

At 150 *m.* is the southern junction with State 37. Within the fork of the junction is a U. S. NATIONAL MILITARY CEMETERY, with graves of 5,686 soldiers of the Civil, Spanish, and World Wars. It was established here in 1864 because of its proximity to the Marine Hospital at Mound City.

Left on State 37 to MOUND CITY, 1 *m.* (327 alt., 2,548 pop.), an Ohio River town. On the river bank at the southern end of town the MOUND CITY MARINE WAYS, used during the Civil War, are still in operation. Here were laid the keels of three of the famous Eads iron-clad gunboats, and here also the boats of the western fleet of the Union army were repaired. This fleet played an important part in the western campaign, giving valuable support to General Grant's troops on the Tennessee River and at Vicksburg. The ways consist of a series of inclines up which the boats are hoisted by huge chains attached to a steam winch.

In January 1937, the swollen waters of the Ohio rose over the Mound City levee and covered the town, from which all inhabitants had fled. Weeks later they returned to find that many of their houses had been floated off their foundations. Refusing to abandon their homes, the residents immediately set about the arduous task of putting the town in order.

At 153.5 *m.* is a junction with State 3 (*see Tour* 8) ; between this point and Cairo US 51 and State 3 are one route.

CAIRO, 159 *m.* (318 alt., 13,532 pop.) (*see Cairo*).

Points of Interest: Halliday Hotel, Ohio Building, Cairo Public Library, Missouri Cotton Oil Company Plant, and others.

At Cairo is a junction with State 3 (*see Tour* 8).

US 51 crosses the Kentucky Line by bridge (*passenger car,* 75c) over the Ohio River, 5 miles N. of Wickliffe, Kentucky (*see Kentucky Guide*).

TOUR 4A

Two-lane concrete roadbed.
Hotel accommodations, picnic grounds throughout.

STATE 2, the Black Hawk Trail, between Rockford and Dixon is a route of historical interest and scenic beauty. The road and the region, popularly known as the Black Hawk Country, are named for the proud war chief of the Sauk and Fox, who, upon his exile from the State in 1833, said of this valley: "Rock River was a beautiful country. I loved my towns, my cornfields, and the home of my people. I fought for it. It is now yours. Keep it as we did."

Rock River, sometimes called the Hudson of the West, flows across rich plains in a deep wooded valley. The highway winds with the river, and the hills sweep gradually from the banks and then converge again upon them. Where bluffs line both banks, river and road are narrowly pressed between sloping walls. Occasionally rock outcroppings jut above the river in bluff formation and innumerable islands, tree-covered and varying in length, stud the blue-gray water.

In several places where the hills open out to widen the valley floor are the old communities upon which is centered the history of the region. Byron, a village with a city form of government, is near Stillman Valley, where occurred the opening battle of the Black Hawk War; Oregon is today the center of a busy art colony; Grand Detour is a breath of the past century.

ROCKFORD, 0 m. (720 alt., 85,864 pop.) (*see Rockford*).

Points of Interest: Rockford College, Swiss Cottage, Harry and Della Burpee Art Gallery, Effigy Mounds, and others.

In Rockford are junctions with US 51 (*see Tour* 4) and US 20 (*see Tour* 11).

Southeast of Rockford, State 2 bends with the river, losing sight of it frequently. Several well-marked State picnic grounds (*tables and fireplaces*) are set in grassy places on the river bank.

At 4.6 m. is a junction with a paved road.

Left on this road, across the Rock River to CAMP GRANT, 0.5 m. (*see Tour* 4).

ROCK RIVER FARMS (*private*) entered at 12.3 *m.* (R), border the road for three miles. This 1,800-acre tract, containing an immense country home and some of the most modern farm buildings in Illinois, was formerly the estate of Medill McCormick, former owner of the Chicago *Tribune* and one-time U. S. Senator.

State 2 skirts the river side of BYRON, 15.4 *m.* (729 alt., 915 pop.). The town, despite its size, has a city form of government, with a mayor and six councilmen, who represent its three wards. The community, chiefly a market for surrounding farms, was founded in 1835 by New Englanders, and named for the poet, Lord Byron, then at the height of his popularity in America. Settled largely by New Englanders, the community was vehemently anti-slavery; many of its members were active in abolitionist societies, and offered their houses and farms as stations on the Underground Railroad. The SOLDIERS MONUMENT, Chestnut and 2nd Sts., erected in 1866, was the first memorial to Civil War soldiers in the State.

Left from Byron on State 72 to STILLMAN VALLEY, 4.7 *m.* (707 alt., 348 pop.), the SITE OF THE BATTLE OF STILLMAN'S RUN on May 14, 1832, the opening encounter in the Black Hawk War (*see The Land and the People*). In Stillman Valley (R) is a monument to the twelve soldiers killed in the Battle of Stillman's Run. Nine are buried on the site, their graves covered with turf and marked with simple headstones and small flags. The other graves are in the nearby woods where the soldiers fell. The 50-foot monument of dark granite is topped with a figure of a citizen-soldier. Three sides of the base bear inscriptions; on the fourth are the names of the dead.

South of Byron are many beautiful stretches of country; the road levels off and is comparatively straight, with the hills a short distance from the highway.

The crossing of the LEAF RIVER, 19.7 *m.*, marks another scenic variation in the highway, which curves through rolling hills before it returns to the river level. Briefly the valley widens, to narrow again as the road runs through sloping groves of trees.

A wide bend in the river at 21.7 *m.* reveals a sweeping view of the bluffs, crowned by the STRONGHOLD, an estate of the late Walter Strong, former publisher of the Chicago *Daily News*. The great stone building is a faithful replica of a medieval European castle and was built, it is said, to fulfill Strong's boyhood desire to own just such a fortress. Strong, unfortunately, did not live to enjoy it.

Downstream, at 23.7 *m.* and 24.8 *m.*, are two fine views of the Black Hawk Monument (*see below*). Rising majestically from the heavily wooded bluff across the river, the huge figure, with folded arms and a gaze fixed on the country beyond the placid river, is impressive even from a distance.

LEGION SHAFT (R), 25.1 *m.*, a concrete block about four feet high, was erected in honor of Ogle County soldiers and sailors of the World War.

OREGON, 26.4 *m.* (702 alt., 2,376 pop.), seat of Ogle County, trading center and small industrial community, is known for its artistic associations. In 1843 Margaret Fuller (1810-1850) found inspiration in the region, praising the loveliness of the country in her writings; more recently other artists, associated with the Eagle's Nest Art Colony (*see below*), have discovered the quiet beauty of the river and have given the region its distinctive atmosphere.

These artists have contributed examples of their work to the OREGON PUBLIC LIBRARY ART GALLERY (*open 2-6 and 7-9 daily, ex. Fri., Sun., holidays*), on Jefferson Street east of State 2; Mrs. Frank O. Lowden contributed the additional room that houses the gallery.

The SOLDIERS MONUMENT (1916), on the courthouse lawn, one of the finest groups of its kind, is by Lorado Taft. In MIX PARK, Webster St. and State 2, is a small FOUNTAIN, "In Memory of Ruel and Maria Peabody, Pioneers," flanked by replicas of the two boys on Taft's *Fountain of the Great Lakes,* at the Art Institute in Chicago.

In the N. 500 block on the highway, on a lawn (L), is a LINCOLN BOULDER, where Lincoln spoke, August 16, 1856. The date inscribed on the boulder, September 9, is incorrect.

1. Left from Oregon on State 64, across the Rock River, to the first road (L), 0.5 *m.*

Left on this graveled road to the EAGLE'S NEST ART COLONY (*private*), 1.6 *m.*, founded by Lorado Taft, Oliver Dennett Grover, Ralph Clarkson, and Nellie Walker in 1898 on a 13-acre tract belonging to Wallace Heckman, who asked only that members of the colony give two public lectures yearly in Oregon on art subjects. Many artists, sculptors, and writers have found inspiration and quiet for their work at the colony, among them Charles Francis Browne, Horace Spencer Fiske, Henry B. Fuller, Hamlin Garland, James Spencer Dickerson, Allen B. Pond, Irving K. Pond, Harriet Monroe, and Clarence Dickinson.

Speaking of the site, Margaret Fuller declared "that Florence and Rome are suburbs compared to this capital of Nature's art." The artists live in pleasant cottages of wood and stone, facing the river. In the river below is MARGARET FULLER ISLAND, and at the riverside is GANYMEDE'S SPRING, marked by a marble table on which is inscribed:

GANYMEDE'S SPRING
named by
MARGARET FULLER (COUNTESS D'OSSOLI).
who named this bluff
EAGLE'S NEST,
and, beneath the cedars on its crest, wrote
"GANYMEDE TO HIS EAGLE,"
July 4, 1843

On the edge of the bluff is the BLACK HAWK MONUMENT, a 48-foot statue executed by Lorado Taft and presented by him to the State in 1911. The statue was intended by Taft to depict an idealization of the Indians who lived in this region, but popular fancy named it Black Hawk and that name is now generally accepted. Taft and his assistants worked an entire summer erecting the frame for the mold, covering it with burlap, and coating it with 10 tons of plaster of

MISSISSIPPI PALISADES

NATURAL BRIDGE, BELL SMITH SPRING

STARVED ROCK

COVERED BRIDGE

IN THE OLD LEAD COUNTRY

DOWN THE BLUFFS

CAVE-IN-ROCK

CAHOKIA MOUNDS

DEER PARK CANYON

CHANNAHAN LOCKS, ILLINOIS-MICHIGAN CANAL

BLACKHAWK STATUE

Paris. Into this mold they poured 265 tons of concrete. The head, attached later, was cast separately in the studio. Because the statue must withstand wind pressure, its foundation runs 30 feet deep into the bluff.

Ahead on State 64 to the first paved road (R), 0.8 *m.;* R. on this road to the automobile entrance (*marked*) to 4,600-acre SINNISSIPPI FARMS (*open daily*), 4.2 *m.* The farms, the property of Col. Frank O. Lowden, former Governor of Illinois, are divided into eight units, each worked by tenant farmers. Dairying is the chief source of income, with hog production next. The mechanically equipped farms are noted for their Holstein cattle and soil conservation methods. Their checkered fields are dotted with small stands of white pine. The word Sinnissippi, found frequently in this region, is a corruption of Sin-Sepo (Ind., Rock River).

2. Right from Oregon on State 64 to MOUNT MORRIS, 6.5 *m.* (916 alt., 1,902 pop.), settled in 1838 by colonists from Maryland, whose first act was the establishment of a school. From this vigorous interest in education grew the Rock River Methodist Seminary, established in 1840. In 1879 the seminary buildings were purchased by the Church of the Brethern, a German Baptist sect, who founded Mount Morris College, an institution which functioned until 1931, when four of its five buildings were destroyed by fire. In 1932 the college merged with Manchester College, North Manchester, Indiana.

In 1855 the Illinois Central laid its rails through nearby Polo instead of Mount Morris, and the young community, which had enjoyed a boom as the principal industrial and commercial center of the vicinity, settled down to a more gradual development. Among the industries established in this later period is the Kable Brothers Company, a printing enterprise which has grown from a one-room print shop of 1898 to a modern two-and-a-half-acre plant in which 32 presses print some 300 of the country's periodicals. The company employs as many as 850 workers and has an annual payroll of almost $1,000,000. The KABLE BROTHERS PLANT (*apply at office*) is on Wesley Avenue three blocks north of State 64.

South of Oregon the route climbs into the wooded hills, and passes along the base of DEVIL'S BACKBONE (R), 28.6 *m.*, the first of a series of fantastic rock formations along the route.

CASTLE ROCK, 31.3 *m.*, rises between the highway and the river. An easy climb to the 150-foot summit offers a splendid view of the river and the surrounding hills and valley. BIG CUT, 31.7 *m.*, exposes the rock structure on both sides of the highway. South of the cut the hills open again, giving a rolling edge to the horizon.

GRAND DETOUR, 36.9 *m.* (306 pop.), the village at the "Great Bend," as the pioneers knew it, or *Grand De Tour,* as the French traders had named it, lies on a horseshoe bend of the Rock River, fronting the water on two sides. The unpaved village streets are lined with ancient elms; many of the buildings are almost a century old; shops are few; wells and cisterns supply water; and ancient street signs direct the way to nearby settlements on stagecoach routes no longer in existence.

Major Leonard Andrus of Vermont visited Grand Detour in 1834, returned in 1835 with other settlers, and in following years built a dam for water power and erected saw and flour mills. He surveyed and built the road from Dixon to Grand Detour, extending it through Oregon to Rockford, and established various stage lines. In 1837 Grand

Detour's most noted citizen, John Deere, also from Vermont, settled in the village and opened a blacksmith shop. That same year he made a steel plow to break the sticky Illinois prairie loam, which had so disheartened other pioneers using wooden and cast-iron plows. For his plow blade Deere used an abandoned Sheffield steel saw from Major Andrus' mill; in 1841 Deere and Andrus became partners in Illinois' first successful plow manufactory. Grand Detour's industries began to decline after 1855 when a railroad was refused a right-of-way through the village. John Deere had withdrawn from the partnership with Andrus in 1847 to open a plow factory in Moline. In 1869, two years after Andrus' death, the Grand Detour factory was removed to Dixon.

Between the highway and the river is the MAJOR LEONARD ANDRUS MEMORIAL, designed by Avard Fairbanks of the Fine Arts Institute of the University of Michigan. The memorial bears a bronze plaque picturing Major Andrus in front of his plough factory as it appeared almost 100 years ago. A brief inscription on the monument, which marks the site of the factory, records the history of the enterprise.

Among several old buildings in Grand Detour is ST. PETER'S EPISCOPAL CHURCH, completed in 1850, the second oldest church of that denomination in Illinois. Built of local limestone with a charming pinnacled belfry of wood, its most unusual feature is a series of triangular-headed windows lighting the nave. Although the entrance door and window above have pointed Gothic arches, the cornice and all the mouldings are based on Greek originals.

South of Grand Detour the highway crosses the Rock River and the lowland that lies within the Great Bend, and then swings away from the river, which is encountered again on the outskirts of Dixon, partly screened by factories along its bank. From the lowland the highway climbs abruptly to the higher ground of Dixon's business district.

DIXON, 42 *m.* (659 alt., 9,908 pop.) (*see Tour* 12), is at the junction with US 30 (*see Tour* 12), US 330 (*see Tour* 12A), and US 52 (*see Tour* 15).

TOUR 5

Hard-surfaced roadbed throughout.
Usual accommodations throughout.

STATE 78 crosses a section of western Illinois from the sweeping
hills and valleys of Jo Daviess County to the pleasant level prairies that
border the Illinois River Valley. Industrial development is slight, and
the region is given over largely to diversified farming. The raising of
livestock, including blooded horses, and the cultivation of corn and
small grains are the primary activities of farmers.

Section a. Wisconsin Line to Kewanee, 96 m.

Along this northern section of the highway there are no large
cities, and traffic is usually light. Wild life is more plentiful than on
heavily traveled roads. Hawks, soaring from their fence posts, circle
into the air, screaming defiance; cottontail rabbits, suddenly alarmed,
scurry across the road to safety; quail feed nervously by the roadside,
emitting their plaintive calls; and groundhogs, less easily disturbed,
munch clover a few feet from the road.

State 78, a continuation of Wisconsin 78, crosses the Wisconsin
Line, 0 m., 6 miles south of Gratiot, Wisconsin (*see Wisconsin Guide*).

WARREN, 1.7 m. (1,005 alt., 1,179 pop.), settled by Alexander
Burnett in 1843, developed at the junction of the Chicago-Galena
Stagecoach Road and the Old Sucker Trail, which ran from St. Louis
to Wiota, Wisconsin. Organized as the town of Courtland in 1850, the
community changed its name three years later to honor both its founder's son Warren, and the Pennsylvania city from which he came. In
that year it became a station on the new railroad from Chicago to
Galena. It was a rough and ready pioneer community, and an early
writer noted that "being situated within a mile of the state line of
Wisconsin, Warren is a great resort for criminals who wish to get
out of that state." The weather-worn stone TISDEL HOTEL (L), built
in 1851, is a relic of those days.

Warren was the birthplace of William Langson Lathrop (1859-
1938), who as an unknown artist gained fame overnight when a
painting he had entered in a New York exhibit won the highest
awards. Lathrop moved East after this success, and spent the latter

part of his life in Pennsylvania. Other well-known residents of the
town were the lawyer, Paul Myron Minebarger, who became legal
adviser to the Chinese Nationalist Government, and Abner Dalrymple,
star of the old Chicago White Stockings, who was among the highest
salaried baseball players of his day.

At the fairgrounds on the eastern outskirts of Warren an annual
tri-county fair is held the early part of September, participated in by
Jo Daviess and Stephenson Counties, Ill., and LaFayette County, Wis.
At 5.3 *m.* is a junction with a graveled road.

Right on this road to APPLE RIVER CANYON STATE PARK (*picnic
and camping facilities; six-day limit, subject to renewal*), 3.5 *m.*, established in
1932. Limestone cliffs, wooded bluffs, the clear stream, its wildflowers, songbirds,
and small animals recommend it both to the casual visitor and the overnight
camper. Striking rock formations, small caves, and gulches are indicated by
arrows painted on a flat-topped rock that rests against a small knoll between
two shade trees near the river. The rock, at the far end of the playing field,
marks the SITE OF MILLVILLE, the sole reminder of a once prosperous milling
and mining community. Its two mills, built in 1836 and 1838, were the heart of
a hustling village, frequently harassed by Indians. After 1854, when the Frink
and Walker stageline through Millville was replaced by the railroad through
Warren, most of Millville's families moved to the more promising community
8 miles away. A few pioneers remained until the disastrous floods of 1892 forced
complete abandonment of the village.

At 11.1 *m.* is the eastern junction with US 20 (*see Tour* 11),
which is united with State 78 as far as STOCKTON, 13.1 *m.* (1,000
alt., 1,505 pop.) (*see Tour* 11).

South of Stockton the country becomes more rolling. The highway
winds through valleys banked by some of the highest hills in the State,
or follows ridgetops, which bring into view far-flung stretches of
countryside.

MOUNT CARROLL, 33 *m.* (817 alt., 1,775 pop.) (*see Tour*
15), is at a junction with US 52 (*see Tour* 15).

At 51.1 *m.* is a junction with US 30 (*see Tour* 12), which unites
with State 78 as far as MORRISON, 63.1 *m.* (670 alt., 3,067 pop.)
(*see Tour* 12).

South of the Rock River, 64.6 *m.*, is the heart of the Black Hawk
country, a region rich in historical interest, a land that knew Lincoln
and Jefferson Davis in the days of the Black Hawk War.

PROPHETSTOWN, 65.6 *m.* (627 alt., 1,353 pop.), on the banks
of Rock River, occupies the SITE OF THE VILLAGE OF WHITE CLOUD,
the Indian prophet, and presumably takes its name from that stern-
browed prophet, who cried out against the encroachments of the white
man. His village was destroyed May 10, 1832, at the outbreak of the
Black Hawk War.

Prophetstown is the market center for an extensive area. So rich
is the soil in the vicinity that an observer remarked in 1908 that
Prophetstown was perhaps the only rural section in Illinois "where

the tillers of the soil have automobiles. . . . It is said," he continued, "that in town and country around there are nearly twenty of these destructive machines."

Automobiles are no longer remarkable in the Prophetstown area, but Booster Rooster Day is a novel annual event, observed on an appointed day each spring, when merchants of the town pay 3c a pound above the current market price for roosters and pile crates of the crowing scolding birds along the sidewalks to attract business. Not infrequently, adding to the noise and confusion, some of the roosters escape from their coops, and are immediately pursued along and across the main thoroughfares by crowds of small boys.

RIVERSIDE PARK (*free*) is the front yard and civic playground of the town. Here are picnic facilities, a supply of fresh water, and good fishing in the Rock River.

HOOPPOLE, 76 *m.* (618 alt., 266 pop.), derives its name from the fact that in a nearby grove coopers formerly cut hickory bands for their barrels. An agricultural village of white cottages, Hooppole shows no evidence of the bitter quarrel that in early days pitted neighbor against neighbor. In 1880 A. A. Haff de-horned his herd of Texas long-horns to keep them from injuring each other in the feeding pens. He was promptly arrested and charged with cruelty to animals. Proving that the practice was neither cruel nor harmful, he was freed. Today, so widely has the practice been adopted, a herd of cattle with horns is seldom seen.

Each year, shortly after the harvest, Hooppole holds a plowing match that attracts large crowds. Started in 1930 by the Rev. Harry J. Stelling, the plowing contests—in which tractors are now used—bring farmers from many miles away, and agricultural implement manufacturers, seed merchants, and others arrange exhibits to advertise their products.

State 78 crosses the GREEN RIVER, 79 *m.;* settlers found this district extremely swampy, filled with grass and high weeds, which afforded refuge for thousands of game birds. Many hunters made a living by shooting these birds, and a cold-storage company was established in Kewanee to pack them for shipment to New York, Philadelphia, and Boston. Flocks of passenger pigeons were so huge that sometimes they darkened the light of the sun. Pioneers killed them in countless numbers, believing the flocks would never be reduced. But by the seventies the birds were fast dying out, and are now extinct.

The ILLINOIS AND MISSISSIPPI CANAL, 84.1 *m.* (*see Tour 22*), commonly known as the Hennepin Canal, is today utilized solely for fishing and drainage purposes.

ANNAWAN, 85.1 *m.* (626 alt., 489 pop.) (*see Tour 14*), is at the junction with US 6 (*see Tour 14*).

In the portion of Henry County near Annawan, Atkinson, and Kewanee, Belgian settlers play a game called *rolle bolle*. The game, which is played with heavy discs of wood, combines certain features of bowling and horseshoe pitching. So popular is the game in the region that the Henry County Fair, held annually at Cambridge, features a Rolle Bolle Day.

KEWANEE, 96 m. (853 alt., 17,093 pop.) (see Tour 13), is at the junction with US 34 (see Tour 13).

Section b. Kewanee to Virginia, 100 m.

In its southern section State 78 passes through some of the most productive farmland in the State, and roughly parallels Spoon River, which has its origin near Kewanee and empties into the Illinois River opposite Havana.

Between Kewanee, 0 m., and 5.4 m. State 78 and US 34 (see Tour 13) are united.

At 9.4 m. is the junction with State 17.

Right on this road to LAKE CALHOUN (private; admission by invitation only), 4.7 m., an attractive artificial lake set among thickly wooded hills. The highway is built across the dam, and the lake and grounds are visible from it. Many summer cottages encircle the lake, which is well stocked with fish; large picnic grounds with brick fireplaces are set in sylvan surroundings. Swimming and boating are particularly popular here, since there are no natural lakes in this part of the State.

The highway crosses SPOON RIVER, 19.2 m., made famous by Edgar Lee Masters, Illinois poet, in his Spoon River Anthology (see Tour 24). The composer and concert pianist, Percy Grainger, has written a piano solo, "Spoon River," based on an old folk tune played by fiddlers in 1857 at dances in Stark County.

This region is highly productive; the soil, a rich black prairie loam, produces large crops of corn and small grains. Livestock breeding, including blooded horses, is a major source of income. Veins of coal lie near the surface at various points, and are mined by gigantic mechanical shovels.

ELMWOOD, 33.4 m. (626 alt., 1,166 pop.), a coal town, was the birthplace of Lorado Taft (1860-1936). The sculptor's bronze statue, PIONEERS OF THE PRAIRIES, a memorial to his parents, is in CENTRAL PARK (L). The heroic figures represent a young settler, with wife and child, dog and gun; the statue stands on a large square base of polished granite. Speakers at the dedication ceremony in 1928 included Taft and Hamlin Garland, the novelist.

Between Elmwood and Canton is much mining activity; coal trucks going to and from the shafts hurry back and forth in the passing traffic. Many of the mines are visible from the road.

FARMINGTON, 41.3 *m.* (742 alt., 2,269 pop.), a mining town, was laid out in 1834. In March 1856 a "whiskey war" was fought here, when a group of crusading women, after numerous unsuccessful attempts to stop the sale of liquor, adopted the drastic methods later employed by Carrie Nation. The women marched upon the saloons, broke the windows, smashed the barrels and bottles with axes, and poured the contents in the streets.

Numerous wolves in this district, which killed young stock and poultry, were a serious problem to the pioneers, who organized wolf-hunts on a large scale. Hunters formed a circle several miles in diameter, and gradually closed in toward the center, driving the wolves before them. In the hunt of 1842 almost 5,000 men and boys participated.

CANTON, 51.7 *m.* (655 alt., 11,718 pop.), largest city in Fulton County, was founded in 1825 by Isaac Swan, who came to Illinois from New York in 1818 and to Fulton County in 1824. Swan staked claims at this spot, and after his lots were surveyed he offered one free to anyone who would build on it. He erected the first building, a log cabin, which was used as a temporary home for new arrivals, who gave it the characteristic Western name of "Swan's Catch-all." The proprietor later named his town in the belief that it was antipodal to Canton, China.

Although seriously damaged in 1835 by a tornado which took several lives, Canton has prospered from mining, manufacturing, and an advantageous position in the heart of the Illinois corn belt. The coal mines in and near Canton employ 1,000 men, supply the local market, and provide the second greatest source of income for the citizens.

The INTERNATIONAL HARVESTER COMPANY PLANT (*guide service, 8 a.m.-4 p.m.*), E. Elm St. and 2nd Ave., employs from 1,500 to 2,000 men in the manufacture of more than 1,400 types of plows, harrows, discs, and other agricultural implements. Sprawling over an area of 19 acres, the plant has a production capacity of two implements a minute. Under the name of Maple and Parlin, the local enterprise began the production of steel mold board plows in 1846. In 1852 William J. Orendorff supplanted Maple, and the P. & O. Plow Works, now one of the largest in the world, was created; in 1919 it became a part of the International Harvester Company.

Extreme primitiveness characterized the early operations of the plant. The first plows were made to order at a blacksmith's forge; farmers called in person to take away the finished product; in 1849 steam power was introduced in the plant. Among other farm implements and machinery developed here are the corn stalk cutter, the disc harrow with concave discs, and the lister.

The P. & O. Band, organized in 1847, gives 20 Saturday night concerts each summer in NATHAN JONES PARK in the center of the business district. An additional feature in Canton's musical life is the Civic Concert, held the first Tuesday in June.

At 56.5 *m.* is a junction with State 100.

Right on this road to a CENTRAL STATES COLLIERIES STRIP MINE, 2.1 *m.*, one of four large strip mines in the Canton area. A gigantic 1,000-ton dipper, with a mouth of 48 feet, scoops out great loads of earth to a depth of 40 feet, carving valleys and canyons, and building miniature mountains.

The hamlet of MAPLES MILL, 60.7 *m.*, was originally the saw-mill village of Slabtown, established in 1851 when timber was being cut for the Canton and Liverpool plank road. These plank roads played a picturesque rôle in the settlement of the Middle West.

At 62.2 *m.* is a junction with US 24 (*see Tour* 16), which unites with State 78 for 3 miles.

HAVANA, 73.1 *m.* (451 alt., 3,451 pop.), seat of Mason County, is at the confluence of the Spoon and Illinois Rivers. Long before Edgar Lee Masters wove the story of Spoon River and its people into his *Spoon River Anthology,* this water route was a busy artery of commerce. John Eveland's *pirogue* transported wheat and immigrants until 1824, when Maj. Ossian M. Ross (*see Tour* 16) initiated ferry service on the river. Two years later Ross rented his ferry and trading rights to Samuel Mallory, another settler, and thereby inadvertently precipitated the only clash between pioneers and Indians in Mason County. Unaccustomed to dealing with the Indians, Mallory was forced by a group of them to exchange whiskey for furs. Only the timely intervention of settlers saved Mallory in the excitement that ensued; 15 mounted men from Lewistown routed the Indians, who had consumed sufficient whiskey to contemplate the destruction of the entire settlement.

Major Ross was the father of Havana. His home, known for years as "Ross's Hotel," was used as a stopping place by settlers moving into the new country; the first session of the circuit court was held in this building. Ross also kept the first store in the little settlement, and later built himself a second home and six other houses, which he rented to settlers.

The arrival of the steamboat on the Illinois in 1828 marked the beginning of an era of prosperity for many river towns, in which Havana shared generously, becoming the shipping point for the grain and produce of a large area. By 1836 some 35 steamboats were operating on the river; in that year Havana had 445 "sailings." Then came the railroad, bringing with it a decline in river traffic, but water commerce is being revived to some extent by barge lines carrying grain, coal, and other heavy freight.

At the time when Havana was an important river community, fishing was a major industry. Daily catches of 100,000 pounds were common, and when the seines were hauled in at the end of the day the entire population assembled at the river front. From 1906 to 1908 the Illinois River was the second most important freshwater commercial fishing stream in the United States, being surpassed only by the swift Columbia, with its salmon. For a number of years the fishery has languished, owing to the reduction of spawning grounds, the pollution of the water by sewage, and the draining of many lakes near Havana.

Contemporary Havana is a quiet river town, filled with the memories of yesterday, yet not unmindful of the present. Its wide shady streets are flanked with modern bungalows and century-old brick mansions. Many of the broader streets are landscaped boulevards. The city is an important grain center, has several factories, and is a large turkey and melon market. An annual watermelon festival is held here, usually in the latter part of August. From 3,000 to 4,000 large watermelons, iced for two days, are served free of charge.

Lincoln appears in the background of Havana history in various rôles for a period of 26 years: as a returning soldier, as a surveyor, lawyer, and senatorial candidate. He usually stayed at the Walker House, known after 1866 as the TAYLOR HOUSE, one of the oldest hotels in the State, a three-story brick building, painted white, with old-fashioned wooden awnings in front. Lincoln's most memorable visit occurred in August 1858, during the course of his senatorial campaign against Stephen A. Douglas. Arriving early in the afternoon of the 13th, while Douglas was still speaking, Lincoln did not reply until the following day. A marker in ROCKWELL PARK commemorates the speech.

The MASON COUNTY COURTHOUSE, a small brick structure of simple lines, with a single cornice, is a replica of the original structure, built in 1851, in which Lincoln practiced law; in 1882 the old building was destroyed by fire.

1. Left (north) from Havana on the river road to the CHAUTAUQUA MIGRATORY WATER FOWL REFUGE, 2 m., which is being developed by the United States Biological Survey. This refuge for wild game and water fowl includes 4,600 fenced acres; its shore line of 11 miles is constantly patrolled to prevent illegal hunting. A 100-foot steel lookout tower at the general headquarters commands a view for several miles in every direction. Most of the refuge is as wild and primitive as when the Indians hunted here, and is filled in season with mallards, blue bills, blue wing teal, snow geese, red heads, wood ducks, and other migratory fowl. Members of the nearby CCC camp have constructed 500 nests for wood ducks, which are hung high in the trees and resemble sections of large branches. Nearly 100 feeding and storm shelters, 8 by 12 feet and 3 feet high, closed on three sides and open to the south, are scattered throughout the area. A function of the refuge is the care of wounded birds, which are nursed back to health, then banded and released. QUIVER LAKE (bathing, boating, fishing), immediately north of the refuge, has summer homes and tourist cabins along its shores.

2. Left (east) from Havana on State 10 to a junction with a graveled road, 9.5 m.; L. on this road to the HENRY HORNER TREE NURSERY (R), 10.5 m., operated by the Illinois Department of Conservation. Established in 1934 and

named for Governor Horner, the 80-acre nursery is the larger of two maintained by the State. Twenty million trees—pine, oak, hickory, walnut, maple, and other species—have been shipped by the nursery. Trees grown here are used in the various State parks, picnic areas, about memorials and monuments, and, more recently. along the highways. State-owned land along the highways approximates 100,000 acres and is gradually being landscaped. Much of the nursery is devoted to growing black locust trees, which are in great demand for checking soil erosion because of their rapid growth and extensive root system.

MATANZA BEACH (R), 77.5 m., is in the heart of the summer colony district along the Illinois River.

BATH, 81.7 m. (462 alt., 346 pop.), was surveyed November 1, 1836 by Abraham Lincoln, then Deputy Surveyor of Sangamon County. A white pole in MARKET SQUARE marks the starting point of his survey. A post office was established at Bath in 1842; B. H. Gatton, the first postmaster, received 43½c as his first three months salary. In 1843 Bath became the county seat but was supplanted by Havana in 1851.

The OLD RUGGLES HOUSE, one block left of State 78, two blocks beyond the square, was built by Gen. James M. Ruggles, friend and political ally of Lincoln. It is a large square building, unpainted for many years, with a cupola on the roof. From its porch Lincoln delivered a political speech on August 16, 1858, during his campaign for the senate. His friend Ruggles, a member of the Illinois General Assembly, although sick at the time, was so desirous of voting for Lincoln that he had himself carried to the Capitol on a stretcher.

The highway crosses the SANGAMON RIVER, 90.4 m., well known to all students of Lincoln. The region is marshy, and its numerous lakes and sloughs afford excellent fishing and hunting, and attract sportsmen from all parts of the State.

CHANDLERVILLE, 91.1 m. (464 alt., 824 pop.), was named for its founder, Dr. Charles Chandler, who is associated with an early Lincoln story. By an unwritten agreement early settlers left 80 acres on each side of a man's land free, so that the settler, as soon as he was able, could enter this additional land at $1.25 an acre. Violation of this rule was considered as reprehensible as stealing. A man whom Dr. Chandler had befriended insisted upon violating the code, at the expense of Chandler, with the remark: "To hell with the customs; I'm going to Springfield and enter the whole tract!" Chandler, short of money, borrowed funds, and started on horseback for the land office. Ten miles from Springfield he overtook two young men, one of whom became so indignant on hearing Chandler's story that he offered the doctor the use of his horse. Chandler accepted and beat his rival to Springfield. A short time later he decided to have his land surveyed and a neighbor recommended Abraham Lincoln, a young surveyor of Salem. Chandler was pleased when, on sending for Lincoln, he recognized the young man who had lent him his horse.

VIRGINIA, 100 m. (593 alt., 1,494 pop.) (see Tour 7), is at a junction with US 67 (see Tour 7).

TOUR 6

Hard-surfaced road throughout.
Chicago, Burlington & Quincy R. R. parallels route north of Fulton; Chicago, Milwaukee, St. Paul and Pacific R. R. south of Fulton.
Accommodations limited to larger towns.

IN ITS northern section State 80, following the valley of the Apple River, drops from the rugged unglaciated upland of Jo Daviess County to the steep-walled gorge of the Mississippi, near the Mississippi Palisades State Park. South of this point it crosses the sandy terraces of the great river, now hugging the low bluffs of the valley's side, now swinging close to the slow-moving water. Across arid farm lands, past old river ports, State 80 follows the Father of Waters down to the Quad Cities.

State 80 branches south from its junction with US 20 (*see Tour 11*), 0 *m.*, 12 miles east of Galena. To the north lies a country of sweeping grandeur—graceful rolling woodlands, blue hills, broad deep valleys, and rushing streams. Winding through the valley of the beautiful Apple River toward the distant Mississippi bluffs, the highway skirts numerous rocky cliffs quarried for their road-building material.

HANOVER, 5 *m.* (632 alt., 806 pop.), deep in the Apple River valley, was in early days a lively mining town, avidly exploiting the mineral wealth at its back door. But with the decline of the lead industry and the development of agriculture in Jo Daviess County, Hanover was forced to make an economic adjustment. The town took this problem in stride; it turned to the river, threw a dam across it, and erected a grist mill. For years this mill was the mecca of farmers of the surrounding territory, who carted their wheat and corn here to be ground. In 1864 a woolen mill was established, and soon this new industry labeled the village as a textile center. The modern four-story PLANT OF THE HANOVER MILLS (R) indicates the continued industrial growth of the little town in the valley.

At 11.8 *m.* is the junction with a concrete road.

Right on this road to the SAVANNA ORDNANCE DEPOT (*open 6:15 a.m.-5 p.m.*), 1.8 *m.*, in the SAVANNA NATIONAL FOREST, a 12,000-acre game and forest preserve along the Mississippi. Adjoining the depot is a proving ground where guns from the Rock Island Arsenal are tested.

Low bluffs (L) are seamed with shallow valleys and miniature ravines. The flood plain (R)—damp, cool, green—presents a quiet picture of pastoral loveliness. Herds of dairy and beef cattle dot the low-lying meadows; the better drained fields are in corn, hay, or small grains. Dense forests mass up along the water's edge to obscure the broad river.

Highway and railroad are narrowly squeezed between bluff and river at the NORTHERN ENTRANCE (L), 14.6 m., to MISSISSIPPI PALISADES STATE PARK (*picnic, camping facilities*), a beautiful 592-acre park on the towering cliffs (L). Its sheer bluffs, fern-clad slopes, weather-worn crags and densely wooded areas bring to mind the Palisades of the Hudson, for which the park is named. In summer the valleys and slopes are brightened with a mosaic of violets, bluebells, lobelias, bellworts, and wild geraniums. In this northern section, a recently acquired 110-acre tract separated from the main body of the park by privately owned lands, is a magnificent stand of white birch.

The MAIN ENTRANCE (L), 17.2 m., leads to the custodian's lodge, a shelter house, picnic grounds, and a refreshment stand. Foot and bridle trails—some 15 miles in length—radiate from the valley and wind through the park. SUNSET TRAIL, near the entrance, SENTINEL TRAIL, and FERN VALLEY TRAIL are among the most popular. Below the summit of the bluffs the river sweeps far to the north and south, the force of its current opposed only by bayous and side-channels, islands and wooded marshlands. In the background above the river rise the imposing hills in Iowa.

ANOTHER ENTRANCE (L), 17.4 m., leads to a Lilliputian valley in which camp sites border a broad expanse of lawn and trees; tables, a fountain, and fireplaces have been built here in shady nooks. INDIAN HEAD, a rocky promontory, rises from the shaded depth of the woodland and surveys the river. According to an old legend, the rock face, with aquiline features and high cheekbones, was carved by an Indian. Another natural formation, a pair of tall columns, spring from a huge rock base. Their general outlines are those of human figures, though the faces are not clearly defined. Numerous Indian mounds scattered throughout the park have yielded interesting relics; old Indian trails and stagecoach roads can still be traced.

The SOUTHERN ENTRANCE (L), 18.4 m., opens into a tiny parking and picnic ground, backed by high bluffs. The trail to the south winds up a wooded, mossy ravine to a shelter on the cliff top, from which is a fine view downstream of Savanna's waterfront. The northern trail to the shelter is longer and rougher. The view upstream from the cliff reveals an impressive profile of the bluffs, cutoff channels, wooded islands, meandering inlets, and a vast forested expanse of bottomland.

At the southern edge of the park, 18.9 m., is the junction with US 52 (*see Tour* 15), which unites with State 80 for 2.2 miles through SAVANNA, 20 m. (592 alt., 5,086 pop.) (*see Tour* 15).

Proceeding southward, State 80 swings back several miles from the river and traverses a broad sandy terrace near the base of valley bluffs.

The country with its short sear prairie grass suggests the arid High Plains ; the impression is heightened by the herds of white-faced Herefords that graze by the roadside, seemingly as much at home as on the Staked Plains of Texas, from which many of them were brought to be fattened before being shipped to market. Near occasional cultivated fields stand fine white farmsteads, with huge corncribs, clean barns, and tile or concrete silos. Many farms along the railroad have their own chutes and pens for handling the large herds of yearlings and 2-year-olds, which are each year imported from the western range, fattened on pasture, grain, and silage, and finally sold in the Chicago stockyards.

Labor Day is Melon Day in THOMSON, 31 m. (606 alt., 508 pop.) ; a carnival is held, and melons are served the 10,000 guests who flock into the little village. The region is a popular rendezvous for duck hunters ; the marshy backwaters, bayous, and sluggish tributaries of the Mississippi are feeding grounds for the flocks of ducks and geese that twice annually follow the Mississippi Flyway between the Gulf of Mexico and northern Canada.

On the lawn of York Community High School (L) Two MILLSTONES, inscribed "Pettit Mill, 1860," exemplify the early industry that created many an Illinois village.

Between Thomson and Fulton the landscape assumes an even more arid appearance, intensified by large areas of low sand dunes. The dry bluffs and terrace are not the result of a deficiency in rainfall, but are due to the sandy nature of the soil. Melons prosper in this soil and are the principal crop of the region.

At 35 m. is the junction with a graveled road.

Right on this road is LOCK AND DAM No. 13, 1.8 m., built by the Federal Government as a link in the 9-foot improvement project of the Upper Mississippi. The impressive streamlined locks and dam are navy-trim in their bright coat of aluminum paint.

FULTON, 38 m. (598 alt., 2,656 pop.) (see Tour 12), is at the junction with US 30 (see Tour 12).

ALBANY, 45 m. (596 alt., 450 pop.), formerly a bustling river port, was all but wiped out in 1860 by a disastrous tornado. The sloughs to the south and east of the village attract large numbers of ducks and geese every fall (hunting permitted).

A cottage and camp development extends south along the river to the Quad Cities, some 20 miles distant. The grassy woodlands on the higher land are popular camp sites ; much of the lower land is marshy and infested with mosquitoes. The current here keeps the river banks clear for boating and swimming, and has built up occasional clean sandy beaches.

At 64.5 m. is the junction with a graveled road.

Right on this road to LOCK AND DAM No. 14, 0.5 *m*. This dam, like all others on the Mississippi from Alton to the Twin Cities, is designed to maintain a 9-foot channel throughout, to prevent floods on the upper reaches, and to regulate the volume of water in the great river below its confluence with the Missouri and the Ohio. The locks are opened to any craft, day or night, summer or winter, principally to long tows of barges carrying heavy cargoes of limestone, sand, potash, and petroleum products. Many of the boats are now powered by twin-screw Diesel engines, but a few are of the old-fashioned type with rear paddle-wheels, the glory and pride of the river in early steamboat days.

The highway skirts HAMPTON (581 alt., 485 pop.), 65.5 *m.,* a relic of Mark Twain days on the Mississippi; an unpaved main street leads (R) across the railroad tracks to the center of the village. Ramshackle warehouses, deserted stores with broken windows clumsily patched with paper, bleak abandoned hostelries along the riverfront, a few weathered century-old houses along the old Galena Stage Road, and a tumble-down decayed landing stage at the water's edge, link the quiet life of the present community with its more vigorous days in the riverboat and stagecoach era. One of the better preserved structures in Hampton, the large brick building on the northwest corner of the main intersection, today bears the sign, YE OLD CURIOSITY SHOPPE.

EAST MOLINE, 69.3 *m.* (576 alt., 10,107 pop.) (*see Tour* 14), is at the junction with City US 6 (*see Tour* 14).

Southward, State 80 climbs the bluffs to the upland level, turns abruptly westward, and ends at the junction with US 6 (*see Tour* 14) in MOLINE, 75 *m.* (566 alt., 32,236 pop.) (*see Rock Island and Moline*).

T O U R   7

(DAVENPORT, IOWA) —ROCK ISLAND—MONMOUTH—VIRGINIA —JACKSONVILLE—ALTON—EAST ST. LOUIS— (ST. LOUIS, MO.) ;
US 67
Iowa Line to Missouri Line, 248.5 *m.*

Hard-surfaced roadbed throughout.
The Jacksonville & Havana R. R. parallels US 67 between Virginia and Jacksonville, the Alton R. R. between Jacksonville and Jerseyville.
Usual accommodations throughout.

SOUTH of the Mississippi and the industrial Quad Cities, US 67 crosses a prosperous agricultural region, passes through the college town of Macomb, and winds southeastward across rolling country to the Illinois River at Beardstown. Southward, the tour touches Jacksonville, another college center, and enters the Mississippi lowlands in the steel, brass, and chemical districts of Alton and East St. Louis.

Section a. Iowa Line to Virginia, 135 m.

This section of western Illinois is a fertile upland, crossed at regular intervals by forested valleys, which drain east or west into the great rivers that bound the region. In the small towns and old cities there is a subtle charm of architecture and grace of living, suggestive of New England, from which, indeed, western Illinois derives much of its cultural heritage.

US 67 crosses the Iowa Line, 0 *m.*, on the Government Bridge (*free*), which spans the Mississippi River from Davenport, Iowa (*see Iowa Guide*).

ROCK ISLAND, 0.5 *m.* (566 alt., 37,953 pop.), and MOLINE (575 alt., 32,236 pop.) (*see Rock Island and Moline*).

Points of Interest: Rock Island Arsenal, Black Hawk State Park, Vandruff's Island, Rock Island Dam, Plants of Deere & Company, Scottish Rite Cathedral, and others.

Rock Island and Moline are at a junction with US 6 (*see Tour* 14).

US 67 crosses the Rock River, 5 *m.*, and enters MILAN, 5.7 *m.* (571 alt., 888 pop.), a suburb of the Quad Cities. The Mississippi bluffs, soaring high above the water level, recede a mile or two from the river at Moline and Rock Island, but converge upon the Rock River at Milan. Their summits afford an excellent view of the low alluvial bottom land that borders both streams.

A marker (R), 6.4 *m.*, indicates that Lincoln, on May 8, 1832, while encamped approximately one mile west of this point, was mustered into the military service of the United States. A few days earlier he had been elected captain of a militia company from Sangamon County.

At the marker is a junction with an improved road.

Right on this road, part of which is paved, to ANDALUSIA, 7.8 *m.*, a small village. Clark's Ferry, from Andalusia to Buffalo, Iowa, was the most noted river crossing above St. Louis in the 1830's, and carried thousands of settlers to the Iowa territory. Early land speculators conceived a wondrous paper town at this site. Their elaborate maps, plats, and designs showing a beautiful city with thriving steamboat wharves, were so convincing that the schemers sold thousands of dollars worth of town lots in the East. When the bubble burst, the city that was destined to be the "metropolis of the Middle West" became the peaceful village of Andalusia.

Today the community's sole industry is the manufacture of pearl buttons from clam shells found in the shallow sloughs and lagoons of the Mississippi.

The clams are gathered in flatboats that drag behind them chains with dozens of four-pronged hooks. Open mussels close their shells instantly upon the hooks and are hauled into the boat; in shallow water the clams are gathered with rakes and forks. Button-making is a slow and tedious hand operation; each button is shaped singly by a rapidly revolving, water-cooled, cylindrical cutter, against which the shell is held. The size of the buttons is determined by the shape and thickness of the shell, which vary widely in different kinds of mussels.

South of Milan the highway climbs the Mississippi Bluffs to the upland level, a pleasantly varied region of broken prairie and woodland and deeply incised valleys. Numerous birds, among them the colorful cardinal and bluejay, hawks, owls, and an occasional eagle, inhabit this area. On the prairies are fine farms, with large corn cribs and silos, that specialize in hogs and dairy cattle. Sheep are pastured on the rougher lands.

VIOLA, 23.3 m. (797 alt., 566 pop.), is the center of local coal mining activities. Several mine shafts are visible from the highway in the vicinity of the village.

Right from Viola on State 83 to ALEDO, 7.9 m. (738 alt., 2,203 pop.), seat of Mercer County. Because of the extensive trading area it serves, the business district of Aledo is unusually large and modern in appearance. Although the land here ranks among the most productive in the State, the first settlers bought it so cheaply that a single crop sometimes paid for an entire farm. In spring and fall, however, the rich soil made roads and streets a quagmire. A story is told that before sidewalks were built in Aledo a prominent attorney, who afterwards became a member of the United States Congress, ventured too near the center of a main street, and became bogged in the thick oozing mass. After various rescue attempts had failed, a wagon was finally backed as near the victim as possible, and he was dragged ignominiously from the mud at the end of a long rope. The ROOSEVELT MILITARY ACADEMY, an accredited school with an enrollment of 100 boys, occupies five buildings on 22 acres of land on the northwestern edge of the city.

Between Viola and Monmouth, US 67 crosses numerous tributaries of the Mississippi that have carved their wooded valleys deep in the fertile upland. The first settlers came up these streams and homesteaded in the valleys. One man, it is said, housed his family in a hillside cave, dug a vertical passageway for a chimney. One evening, while the settler's daughter was entertaining a suitor before the fireplace, a venturesome calf that had been grazing on the hill above lost its footing, tumbled down the chimney, and landed bawling at the feet of the startled lovers.

MONMOUTH, 47 m. (762 alt., 8,666 pop.), commemorates the Revolutionary War battle of Monmouth, New Jersey. Established in 1831 as the seat of Warren County, which honors the memory of Joseph Warren, major general of militia at Bunker Hill, Monmouth, in common with other prairie towns, was long handicapped by bad roads. Early roads were wagon ruts at best; at worst, an endless succession of mud holes. In wet weather flatboats on wheels, drawn by horses, were used to transport people and merchandise. Their use avoided the cumbersome task of unloading and reloading at every stream that had to be crossed; bridges were rare. Wheelbarrows were also much in demand. When conditions became too bad, fences were taken down and new routes traced across open fields.

In Monmouth the streets were impassable for many weeks each year. Such signs as "No Bottom Here" warned travelers to keep off the beaten path. When Lincoln visited Monmouth in 1858 the streets were in such condition from recent rains that he was obliged to walk through the town. Plans for the welcoming committee to meet him on the Oquawka road had to be cancelled. Not until 1891, when Dr. William Taylor was elected mayor on a platform of paving the streets, were conditions bettered. Two years later Monmouth Township set to work surfacing its roads, and Warren County shortly after led the way in hard road construction.

The ILLINOIS BANKERS LIFE ASSURANCE BUILDING, on 1st Avenue one-half block R. of US 67, houses Monmouth's principal business firm, the third largest insurance company in Illinois. Organized in 1897 by a group of local businessmen, the concern has had a rapid growth.

Setting the cultural pace of the community is MONMOUTH COLLEGE, on E. Broadway between 7th and 9th Sts., a coeducational institution opened in 1856 under the auspices of the United Presbyterian Church. The 15 red brick college buildings on the tree-shaded, 30-acre campus lend a pleasant quiet beauty that helps offset the drabness of the business streets and square.

Monmouth is at a junction with US 34 (see Tour 13).

South of Monmouth the country is flat and largely cropped. This is a region of beef cattle finishing. The white-faced Herefords shipped in from the western range and the Aberdeen-Angus raised locally are fattened on corn for the Chicago stockyards. Attractive houses and corn cribs are conspicuous features of most farmsteads.

ROSEVILLE, 60 m. (736 alt., 975 pop.), a rural trading center and shipping point on the Burlington Railroad was originally called Hat Grove, because a nearby clump of trees resembled a man's hat. In early days farm products of the region were hauled by wagon from Roseville to Oquawka (see Tour 13) and shipped by Mississippi River boats to southern markets. Today the community is the center of an important clover, oats, and soy bean producing area.

GOOD HOPE, 71.6 m. (714 alt., 369 pop.), is spotted from afar by its grain elevator, which rises along the tracks of the Toledo, Peoria & Western Railroad. Many communities in this district have had two or three names in succession, but Good Hope had three, and possibly four, at once. In 1866 J. E. Morris platted the village of Sheridan here on the proposed line of the railroad. The following year W. F. Blandin laid out a rival town bordering it on the west, and called his future metropolis Milan. In the meantime the local post office was already known as Good Hope. Confusion reigned: the railroad issued its tickets to Sheridan; conductors called out Milan; all mail was addressed to Good Hope. And, progressing one more step toward hysteria, it is said that some residents called the village Clarkesville, in memory of its first settler.

Just before reaching Macomb US 67, which is relatively level south of Monmouth, suddenly toboggans over several hills and ravines. SPRING LAKE PARK (R) and GLENWOOD PARK (L), on the outskirts of Macomb, are public parks with swimming pools, picnic grounds, and other recreational facilities (free).

MACOMB, 79.5 m. (702 alt., 8,509 pop.), called Washington in 1830, later changed its name to honor Alexander Macomb, Commander-in-Chief of the United States Army (1828-1841), who, according to a tablet in Chandler Park, "served his country during a period of more than forty years without stain or blemish upon his escutcheon." It was incorporated as a village in 1841, and as a city in 1856. That the settlers of western Illinois, many of whom came from New England, honored their early military leaders is further evidenced in the name of McDonough County, which commemorates Commodore Thomas Macdonough, hero of the battle of Lake Champlain (1814).

Most villages and small cities in the region center about a public square, but Macomb has two—Chandler Park and Courthouse Square, separated by a short block. When the railroad that connects Macomb with the outside world was first proposed, many residents were against it. One prominent merchant, in arguing the negative side of the question, declared that a single train could carry away all the surplus yearly crops raised in McDonough County. Since that day Macomb has become an important manufacturing city. Its products include porcelain insulations, electric fencing, pottery, sheet metal, stokers, and soft drink dispensers; the 1938 and 1939 Illinois automobile license plates were made here.

The MCDONOUGH COUNTY COURTHOUSE, of red brick painted a cream color with foundation and trim of Sagetown limestone, was completed in 1872, and is fireproof throughout. An inscription on the cornerstone states that it was laid by the "Grand Lodge A. F. & A. M., A D. 1869, Aug. 14—A. L. 5869." Although in former years the cornerstones of numerous buildings in Illinois were laid by the Masonic Lodge, few remain that bear the date according to the Masonic calendar. The present courthouse is the third to occupy its site. The first, built in 1831 of logs, is said to have cost $69.50. The second, a splendid structure in the eyes of the pioneers, was a two-story, square brick building erected 1833-34, and used until 1869.

WESTERN ILLINOIS STATE TEACHERS COLLEGE, housed in seven buildings on a hilly, handsomely landscaped, 70-acre campus on W. Adams St. between Charles and Normal Aves., has an average resident enrollment of 900 to 1,000 students and an extension enrollment throughout western Illinois of 700 more. The college opened in September 1902 as Western Illinois State Normal School; 370 students were enrolled in the Normal and 180 in the Training divisions. Its first building, of Berean stone and brick, is still is use; most of the newer structures are of brick; the School of Arts is an adaptation of Egyptian architecture. Two- and four-year courses are offered at Western State, the latter leading to a Bachelor's Degree in Education. Additional courses of varying lengths are included in the curriculum, one a summer course for teachers who are employed during the winter.

The FOREST OF ARDEN (*private*), 216 N. Normal Ave., is the name that students of Western State have given the Shakespearean garden of their English professor, Dr. Irving Garwood. Such old-fashioned flowers as wild thyme, marigolds, and love-lies-bleeding are grown here from seeds imported from Stratford-on-Avon. The flowers border a natural amphitheater from which the garden has been developed. Fronting the amphitheater is a terraced stage where, each Midsummer Eve, Dr. Garwood and his students present *As You Like It* or *A Midsummer Night's Dream* in the manner of Shakespeare's day. Following the play, popular early ballads are sung, and traditional Old English dances are executed on the lawn. Closely set trees border the garden on three sides; a row of Lombardy poplars is the backdrop for the stage.

Right from Macomb on State 10 is CARTHAGE, 25 m. (676 alt., 2,240 pop.), seat of Hancock County. Incorporated in 1837, the community subsequently became an anti-Mormon stronghold. In the old jail Joseph Smith, founder of the Mormon Church (*see Nauvoo*), and his brother Hyrum were killed by a mob on the afternoon of June 27, 1844. Awaiting trial on charges of destroying an opposition press in Nauvoo, Joseph and Hyrum Smith had been lodged in jail to protect them from attack. To insure Smith's safety, Governor Ford had previously disbanded several companies of militia, gathered, against his orders, at Carthage with the avowed purpose of going to Nauvoo to search for alleged apparatus for making counterfeit money, but in reality "to strike a terror into the Mormon people by an exhibition of the force of the State." The governor assigned the Carthage Grays to guard the jail while he went to Nauvoo to acquaint the Mormons with the "excitement and hatred prevailing against them" and to warn against their use of "open or secret violence."

During his absence more than a hundred members of the disbanded militia companies, faces blackened to hide their identity, returned to Carthage, overpowered the non-resisting Carthage Grays, and stormed the jail. The Mormon leaders, accompanied by their friends, Willard Richards and John Taylor, later head of the Mormon Church (1877-1887), were lodged in an upper room that bore no lock. A volley fired from the stairway killed Hyrum Smith. For a brief moment the Prophet, armed with a small "pepper box" gun, was able to hold the mob at bay. When his gun missed fire, he ran to the window to leap out, but as he was silhouetted there three musket balls struck him. With an agonized "Oh Lord, my God," he toppled from the window. The mob rushed out, ascertained that he was dead, and then hastily dispersed. Richards had not been harmed, but Taylor received several wounds.

The OLD CARTHAGE JAIL, a sturdy two-story building of gray stone, has undergone several changes since that distant afternoon. The building was sold to a private family in 1870 and enlarged with a wing and a conservatory at the front. Later the Mormon Church acquired the property. The bullet holes and bloodstains in the upstairs room remain undisturbed. The building is regarded as a shrine by the many Mormons who annually visit it, and plans have recently been made for restoring it to its original state.

Following the departure of the Mormons from Illinois, Carthage went its prosaic way as a farm trade center. Abraham Lincoln in his senatorial campaign against Stephen A. Douglas visited the city on October 22, 1858, and addressed a crowd of 6,000. "Mr. Lincoln," noted the Chicago *Tribune*, "was in admirable spirits and voice and gave us the best speech ever made in Hancock County." A stone marker south of the entrance to the courthouse on the public square indicates the SITE WHERE LINCOLN SPOKE.

CARTHAGE COLLEGE, near the eastern city limits, a co-educational institution established in 1870 as the first Lutheran college in the Middle West, occupies low brick and stone buildings about an elm-shaded campus. At Carthage is RADIO STATION WCAZ (100 w.).

Ahead on State 10 is HAMILTON, 38 *m.* (515 alt., 1,687 pop.), a shipping point and community center for the adjacent fruit and farming area. Though somewhat dwarfed by its rival across the Mississippi, Hamilton has shared with Keokuk the advantages of river transportation and power development. LOCK AND DAM NO. 19, commonly known as Keokuk Dam, are clearly visible from the bridge (*toll,* 25c), 1.5 miles west of Hamilton, over which State 10 crosses the Mississippi, here the Iowa Line, to Keokuk, Iowa (*see Iowa Guide*).

One of the 26 locks and dams designed to improve navigation on the Upper Mississippi, the Keokuk development is at the foot of the Des Moines Rapids at a point where the river drops sharply over a limestone ledge. Completed in 1913 at a cost of $23,000,000, it is the largest hydro-electric development in the Mid-West. The power-house is on the Iowa shore, flanked by the lock and a seawall that protects nearby railroad tracks. Nearby are the only dry docks on the Upper Mississippi; the lock and dam are among the largest in the world. The dam develops 200,000 horsepower, which is transmitted to municipalities in Iowa, Illinois, and Missouri by cables supported on tall steel towers. St. Louis, Missouri, 144 miles south, is supplied with 60,000 horsepower under a 99-year contract. Dam and power plant are owned and operated by private enterprise; lock and dry dock are controlled by the Federal government.

Right (north) from Hamilton State 96 follows the Mississippi 12 miles to Nauvoo, along the shore of beautiful LAKE COOPER, formed by Keokuk Dam and named for Hugh L. Cooper, chief engineer of the dam's construction. The Mississippi, subdued by the downstream dam, provides a placid surface for boating, bathing, fishing, and duck-hunting. Infrequent colonies of summer cottages are on the wooded bluffs of the Iowa shore (L) and among the hills bordering the roadside (R). The Illinois shore throughout the 12-mile drive is a succession of hills where dense wood shade patches of ferns and wildflowers.

NAUVOO, 50 *m.* (620 alt. 966 pop.) (*see Nauvoo*).

Points of Interest: Oriental Hotel, Home of Joseph Smith, Site of Mormon Temple, and several others relating to the Mormons and the Icarians.

State 96 continues 9 miles east and north of Nauvoo, through a region of vineyards that have long supported the local production of wine, to NIOTA, 59 *m.,* a tiny cluster of dwellings at the Illinois end of the bridge (*toll,* 25c; *passengers* 5c *each*) over which State 96 crosses the Mississippi, here the Iowa Line, to Fort Madison Iowa (*see Iowa Guide*).

INDUSTRY, 92 *m.* (669 alt., 568 pop.), was first settled by William Carter, who built a log cabin here in 1826. The village, organized two decades later, reflects in its name the condition on which Johnson Dowin gave John M. Price an acre of ground—that he open a blacksmith shop on the plot.

South of Industry the highway rolls over fertile uplands or dips and winds through forested valleys as the route crosses tributaries of the Illinois River.

RUSHVILLE, 107.5 *m.* (683 alt., 2,368 pop.), founded in 1825 as Rushton in honor of the Philadelphia physician, Dr. William Rush, is the seat of Schuyler County, and the trading center of an extensive coal mining and grain and fruit growing district. During the Black Hawk War, Abraham Lincoln and his troops camped near Rushville. While they waited to move on a wrestling match was arranged between Lincoln and one Dow Thompson. When Thompson threw Lincoln twice, the latter's friends claimed a foul, but Lincoln declared that the two falls were fair, and added admiringly that Thompson "was as strong as a grizzly bear."

A tablet in the center of the public square recalls that here "Abraham Lincoln addressed the people of Rushville October 20th, 1858. He also practiced law in the courthouse which formerly stood on this spot." When Stephen A. Douglas arrived in Rushville to speak in the same senatorial campaign of 1858, his supporters decided to arrange a welcome that would be memorable in the history of the town. They borrowed a cannon from Beardstown, hauled it to the public square, and loaded it with a heavy charge of powder and wet scraps of leather. When the salute to Douglas was fired, the cannon was blown into a hundred pieces, but miraculously no one was hurt.

Another story involving cannon is told of early Rushville. In 1844, it is said, Governor Ford, at the time of the uprising against the Mormons at Nauvoo (*see Nauvoo*), left Springfield with a company of militia, and camped overnight in the village square. Possibly suffering from insomnia, Ford decided to amuse himself with pistol practice, and set up a target near the home of James Little. Little, furious at having his sleep so disturbed, invoked the local ordinance against shooting firearms in the village, swore out a warrant, and had Governor Ford arrested. Ford, nearly bursting with rage, paid a fine and left for Nauvoo, plotting a suitable revenge. On his return to Springfield, he passed through Rushville in the middle of the night, and ordered his men to set up their brass howitzers in the village square. When the cannons had been loaded and pointed skyward, Ford gave the command to fire. While the countryside echoed and trembled at the terrific cannonading, the frightened residents tumbled out of their beds and peered from windows. By the time they had summoned the temerity to approach the scene of the shooting the gleeful governor and his troops were leaving the village.

The present SCHUYLER COUNTY COURTHOUSE, dating from 1881, is a two-story building of faded brick, topped with a square clock tower. The cornerstone is dated according to the Masonic calendar, "June 24, A. L. 5881." The first county building was a log cabin on the north side of the square; in 1829 it was replaced by a plain unorna-

mented brick building which served until the present courthouse was
built.

On the western border of Rushville is SCRIPPS PARK, formerly the
80-acre farm of Edward Wyllis Scripps (1854-1926), founder of the
Scripps-Howard chain of newspapers. The park was given to the city
in 1922 by Mr. Scripps and his sisters, Virginia and Ellen Browning
Scripps. The latter contributed the $100,000 COMMUNITY HOUSE that
marks the site of the Scripps' farmstead, the birthplace of E. W.
Scripps. Also provided by Miss Scripps are the golf course, tennis
courts, athletic field, and caretaker's house.

South of Rushville are several abandoned coal mines, visible from
the highway. The size of the shafts and slag heaps indicates the small
scale of mining operations common in the vicinity, which supply local
markets with a cheap, low-grade bituminous coal. Only the better deposits in Illinois are worked by large scale methods. The highway, in
its descent to the Illinois River, follows closely the route of the old
turnpike road laid out in 1843.

From the crest of the bluffs, 116 m., is an excellent view of the
Illinois Valley. The historic old river swings lazily through its gorge,
now cutting close to the high bluffs that confine it, again following a
middle course through the heavy woods of the bottom lands. Numerous
lakes and sloughs, formed at flood stage, dot the valley floor. Between
the hamlet of FREDERICK, 116.9 m., and the toll bridge (25c per
car), 120.5 m., the highway parallels the river across the floodplain.
From the bridge the sea wall and natural levee that protect Beardstown are clearly visible.

BEARDSTOWN, 121 m. (444 alt., 6,344 pop.), lies on the floor
of the Illinois Valley. At its front door is the river, at its back door
the slough. Bordering it on three sides are the sandy soils of the
terrace. Originally called Beard's Ferry, the town's first white inhabitant was Thomas Beard, who came here in 1819 to live in the Indian
village that then occupied the spot. Beard operated a ferry across the
river for the convenience of the increasing numbers of pioneers who
were finding their way to this part of Illinois. He built himself a sturdy
log cabin, but unfortunately the site he had chosen was directly above
a den of rattlesnakes, which persisted in crawling through the cracks
in the puncheon floor, and it was some time before he got rid of these
unwelcome visitors.

Having outgrown its modest position as a small ferry crossing and
river port dependent mainly upon commercial fishing and clams,
Beardstown is important today as a farming and rail center. It is a
railhead of the B. & O., and the point at which the Burlington crosses
the Illinois River. Commercial fishing and clam fishing are still an
appreciable source of income; tons of watermelons and canteloupes
are exported from the region every year; among its most important

industries are the production of flour and feed and the manufacture of gloves.

Beardstown has been the scene of several serious floods, the worst of which (1922) submerged practically the entire town. On this occasion the Illinois River reached a record high of 23 feet, pounded through the levees, and spread out to form a lake 18 miles wide. After that disaster a huge cement sea wall, 29 feet high, was constructed, and the community once more composed itself in a feeling of security. Beardstown enjoys seasonal popularity as the center of one of the best duck-hunting regions in the Upper Mississippi Valley. Many hunting lodges maintained in the vicinity are open to the public (*for rates and reservations, address Chamber of Commerce*). Beside the river is a municipal park, with picnic facilities and playgrounds.

Outstanding among the town's old buildings is the CITY HALL (R), facing the park, a severe, two-story, red brick structure, distinguished by a single classical cornice, a gable pediment, and striking but somewhat modified classic lintels above the windows. Built as the courthouse in 1845 (Beardstown was the original seat of Cass County), it was the scene of the "Duff" Armstrong trial (1858) in which Lincoln defended the son of "Aunt Hanna" Armstrong, who had befriended him when he lived in New Salem. During the course of the trial Lincoln proved, by referring to an almanac, that the moon was not shining brightly at the time of the murder with which young Armstrong was charged, a refutation of the principal witness' testimony that weighed heavily in the defendant's subsequent acquittal. But even more important to Lincoln's case than this dramatic incident was his sincere powerful appeal to the emotions of the jury. Tears rolled down his cheeks as he pleaded for the boy, picturing the great sorrow of the mother, and the gruff, hardened, pioneer jurymen wept with him.

East of Beardstown US 67 and the B. & O. climb the valley of Lost Creek to the upland level. The hamlet of BLUFF SPRINGS, 126.5 *m.*, at the base of the bald, sandy bluffs, straggles with the highway up the fantastically eroded valley.

VIRGINIA, 135 *m.* (619 alt., 1,494 pop.), was platted in 1836 by Dr. Henry A. Hall, a former surgeon in the British Navy, who came to the region by way of the Ohio, Mississippi, and Illinois Rivers. The seat of Cass County, which commemorates Gen. Lewis Cass (1782-1866), Secretary of War under President Jackson and Secretary of State in President Buchanan's cabinet, Virginia was incorporated as a village in 1842. In early days the county seat moved back and forth several times between Beardstown and Virginia, but finally found a permanent home here in 1872, the year Virginia was incorporated as a city.

Virginia is at a junction with State 78 (*see Tour 5*).

Section b. Virginia to Alton, 85 m.

South of Virginia, 0 *m.*, US 67 crosses one of the oldest settled regions of Illinois. The only variations in the essentially agricultural landscape are the city of Jacksonville, the small farmers' towns strung along the railroad, 'occasional rolling woodlands, and, at Alton, the bluff-lined valley of the Mississippi.

JACKSONVILLE, 16 *m.* (613 alt., 17,747 pop.), early contender for the State Capital and State University, home of statesmen and site of schools and colleges, was founded in 1825, named in honor of Andrew Jackson, and made the seat of Morgan County. So impressed with the community was William Cullen Bryant in 1832 that in fancy he heard "the sound of that advancing multitude which soon shall fill these deserts." Three years later Shirreff remarked in his *Tour Through North America* that "Jacksonville contains about the same number of souls as Springfield, but is superior in buildings, arrangement, and situation."

Among early civic leaders, Jonathan B. Turner was most active. For years he labored among farmers, educators, and politicians, forwarding his ideals of industrial and agricultural education. The establishment of the State University was due in large part to his efforts, for his enterprise contributed to the passage in 1862 of the Morrill Act, which provided for the establishment of the land grant colleges. As editor of the *Illinois Statesman,* he showed little interest in sensational news items. Under the head of "Crimes and Casualties" he wrote: "Our paper is small, and if our readers will for the present just have the goodness to imagine a certain due proportion of fires, tornadoes, murders, thefts, robberies, and bully fights, from week to week, it will serve just as well, for we can assure them they actually took place."

First settled by Southerners, Jacksonville attracted so many Yankees during its early years that by the 1830's it was more New England in character than any other community in the State. Abolitionist sentiment was strong long before the Civil War, and the city was an important station on the Underground Railroad. Lincoln was well known in Jacksonville, and much in demand as a speaker. His lecture on "Discoveries and Inventions," February 11, 1859, was received with "repeated and hearty bursts of applause." The lecture was sponsored by Phi Alpha Society of Illinois College, which had a few days earlier elected Lincoln an honorary member.

Jacksonville was early distinguished as a center of education, culture, and statesmanship. ILLINOIS COLLEGE, 1101 W. College Ave., founded in 1829, was one of the first three institutions of higher learning to be chartered in the State. The "Yale Band," a group of seven young Yale graduates interested in the promotion of Christian education in Illinois, was largely responsible for the founding of the college. The Rev. Edward Beecher, brother of Henry Ward Beecher, was the first president. The first graduating class (1835), the first in Illinois, consisted of Richard Yates, Governor (1861-1865) and United States Senator (1865-1871), and the Rev. James E. Spilman, composer of "Sweet Afton." On January 1, 1903, the Jacksonville Female Academy, first school for women to be formally incorporated by act of the legislature (1835), merged with Illinois College. The two schools had been closely associated since their founding and had comprised, in effect, the first coeducational institution in the State. Today the combined colleges, with an enrollment of 385 occupy 16 red brick buildings on a 50-acre campus.

MACMURRAY COLLEGE, on E. State Street, was established in 1846 as a Methodist Episcopal school for women and was known as the Illinois Conference Female Academy. Its present name was adopted in 1930 to honor Sen. James H. MacMurray, who has contributed $2,500,-000 to the institution. The college, which is no longer denominational, is housed in 14 red brick buildings trimmed with stone, predominantly Georgian in design. Outstanding courses are those in the Conservatory of Music, the School of Fine Arts, and the Kindergarten Instruction and Vocational Home Economics divisions. MacMurray's resident enrollment comprises 500 students from 30 States, all of whom live in the college dormitories.

The ILLINOIS STATE SCHOOL FOR THE DEAF, opened in 1843 with four pupils, now one of the largest of its kind in the country, with an enrollment of 600 students, occupies an extensive group of red brick buildings at the west end of College Avenue. The STATE SCHOOL FOR THE BLIND, 658 E. State St., founded in 1847, is noted for its development of musical talent, particularly its performance of serious opera. The JACKSONVILLE STATE HOSPITAL for mental cases, 1201 S. Main St., has an average of 3,500 patients. Its numerous large buildings are set in beautiful tree-shaded, park-like grounds.

In Jacksonville two national figures began their practice of law—Stephen A. Douglas in 1834, and William Jennings Bryan in 1883. An impressive speech made by Douglas in Jacksonville, when the other members of his party were despondent, incurred his famous title, "The Little Giant." The SITE OF THE BRYAN HOME, College and Webster Aves., is marked by a granite boulder. Bryan was a graduate of Illinois College. Jacksonville was also the home of three Illinois Governors: Joseph Duncan (1834-38), Richard Yates the elder (1861-65), and Richard Yates the younger (1901-05). In DUNCAN PARK (*open upon request*), 4 Duncan Place, the stately Georgian house built in 1835 by Governor Duncan, such notables as Daniel Webster, Martin Van Buren, and Abraham Lincoln were entertained; it is now a chapter house of the Daughters of the American Revolution. Oldest woman's club in the United States is the Ladies Education Society of Jacksonville, organized in 1833 and still active.

South of Jacksonville to Jerseyville US 67 closely parallels the tracks of the Alton, as highway and railroad trace their course across farm lands, linking the cities and towns that serve this fertile region. Small crossroads communities are often identified from afar by towering grain elevators.

ROODHOUSE, 37.5 m. (650 alt., 2,622 pop.), a railroad center, was laid out by John Roodhouse, a pioneer farmer, at the junction of two branch lines of the Alton. The yards and roundhouse of the railroad are west of the highway. Coal yards along the tracks are supplied by nearby mines.

WHITE HALL, 41.5 m. (585 alt., 2,928 pop.), founded in 1820, is the center of an important clay field, in use since 1824, when William Heath began the manufacture of redware. The field supplies a large pottery which manufactures sewer pipe, stoneware, and drain tile; a narrow-gauge railroad connects the pottery with the clay pits. In the center of town (L) is Lorado Taft's MEMORIAL TO ANNIE LOUISE KELLER, a teacher who lost her life saving her pupils during a tornado that destroyed the Centerville School in 1927.

CARROLLTON, 50.5 m. (625 alt., 2,075 pop.), settled in 1818, the seat of Green County, honors the memory of her two statesmen: Thomas Carlin (1789-1852), founder of Carrollton and seventh governor of Illinois, and Henry T. Rainey (1860-1934), Speaker of the House in the Seventy-third Congress. A monument to Thomas Carlin is on the courthouse lawn. On the north edge of Carrollton, in Rainey Memorial Park (R), a bronze life-size STATUE OF HENRY T. RAINEY commemorates Carrollton's Representative, who served in Congress, except for one term, from 1903 to the time of his death. Executed by Frederick C. Hibbard, Chicago sculptor, the statue depicts the big bushy-haired Democrat, gavel in hand, as he presided over the House of Representatives.

Left from Carrollton on State 108 to WALNUT HALL (*by courtesy of Mrs. Rainey, house and grounds are open to visitors upon application*), 1 m., the estate of the late Henry T. Rainey. The spreading, three-story brick house with imposing columns and solid black walnut woodwork throughout marks the entrance to a 485-acre model farm. Mr. Rainey was an enthusiastic farmer; during the years he practiced law in Carrollton and later as time would permit, he took an active part in the management of the farm. Many pieces of historic or artistic value adorn the estate. Cannon and statuary of early days are about the lawn; the house is a museum of ancient firearms, swords, engravings, rare editions of books, and early American furniture. A Seth Thomas clock once the property of Thomas Jefferson is part of the collection. North of the house a camp grounds borders an artificial lake (*boats and bath houses; for permission to camp, apply in person to Mrs. Rainey or to foreman*). In a small park nearby is a herd of sacred Japanese deer.

JERSEYVILLE, 65 m. (652 alt., 4,309 pop.), is Jersey County seat and the home of many retired farmers. The town ships, in addition to local produce, much of the apple crop of Calhoun County, which is trucked in from Hardin (*see below*). The business district presents a pleasant though faintly archaic appearance with its wooden awnings over the sidewalks. The main street is quite wide, with parking places in the center, but even these ample facilities are taxed on Saturdays, when the farmers come into town for their weekly shopping.

Right from Jerseyville on State 38 to HARDIN, 19 *m.* (440 alt., 733 pop.), seat of Calhoun County and distributing center of a prosperous apple-growing region. The only county in Illinois not served by a railroad, Calhoun is a rolling, sparsely settled strip of upland squeezed between the Mississippi and Illinois Rivers. The village, inset among the cliffs bordering the Illinois, retains a faint though unmistakable backwoods flavor. The county buildings erected in 1848 and 1850 still serve their original purposes. Under the trees before the sagging brick courthouse, villagers gather daily to lounge on wooden benches and discuss the latest events. The main topics of conversation are apples and politics.

Calhoun County produced more than a million bushels of apples in 1937. A blossom festival is held here each spring, when the countryside is festooned with these fragrant white flowers; participants in the festival travel a 15-mile route that pierces the region's finest orchards. In October an apple harvest celebration consists of a parade and a ball climaxed by the crowning of an Apple Queen.

Hardin history contains several colorful anecdotes. Formed from a section of Pike County in 1825, Calhoun was so heavily wooded and its lumberjack population so unstable that a bill entitled "An Act to Abolish Calhoun County" narrowly escaped ratification by the State Assembly of 1836-37. John Shaw, otherwise known throughout the region as the Black Prince, controlled the political affairs of the county during its first decade of existence. Of heroic physique and compelling personality, the Black Prince, according to tradition, operated a country store, raised cattle, speculated in land, and rigged county elections. Shaw became county commissioner following a turbulent election marked by charges of poll-book tampering, deed-forging, and other flagrant irregularities. Deposed in a subsequent political encounter, the Black Prince finally fled the county.

South of Jerseyville the landscape becomes more rolling as the highway nears the Mississippi River.

At 73.7 *m.* is a junction with State 109.

Right on State 109 is a junction with an improved road, 3.1 *m.*
Left 3 *m.* on this road to ELSAH (429 alt., 137 pop.), a village isolated from the world in a valley on the river. Here in 1847 came Addison Greene, to build a cabin and live by selling cord-wood to steamboats. Other wood-choppers followed Greene, and eventually the settlement of Jersey Landing came into being. Attracted by the prospect of river commerce, Gen. James Semple, one-time United States chargé d'affaires at Bogotá, Colombia, and senator from Illinois, acquired Jersey Landing in 1853, changed its name to Elsah, and developed the community by giving a lot to any settler who would build a stone house thereon. A distillery and two grist mills were established, and the village enjoyed brief prosperity as a shipping port for farm produce. When the locomotive superseded the steamboat Elsah as a port ceased to be.

In 1888 the isolated village was almost reconnected with the outer world. In that year the owners of Eads Bridge, the only bridge then to span the Mississippi at St. Louis, thwarted the entry of Jay Gould's railroad into that city. Gould's engineers thereupon mapped their route to Elsah, where a bridge was to carry the rails to Missouri. Elsah, aroused by the possibility of a new lease on life, was disappointed at the last minute, when, after grades and culverts had been completed, Gould made an eleventh-hour deal with the proprietors of Eads Bridge, and abandoned his Elsah enterprise.

Elsah, at the mouth of its little valley, appears to have sprouted from the shady glen. Askew Creek, straddled by a stone bridge, trickles through the center of the village. Songbirds call across the tree-choked hollow. Iris, tulips, and hollyhocks border walks and roadway; rambler roses strew their color over fences and gates. Stone cottages front narrow streets. Above the doorway of the village filling-station in faded letters is a sign: "Buggies Made and Repaired."

East 1 *m.* from Elsah on a graveled road to PRINCIPIA COLLEGE (*grounds open* 8-4 *Mon.-Fri.*), for the sons and daughters of Christian Scientists. The college was moved to this site from St. Louis, Missouri, in 1935. Dormitories and classrooms of neo-Gothic and Tudor-Gothic architecture are grouped to suggest the compactness of an English village. The CHAPEL, designed in the manner of the Georgian churches of Sir Christopher Wren, has a lofty spire, a white paneled interior, and box pews lined with red damask. The college confers a Bachelor of Arts degree in foreign languages, history and social science, English and aesthetics, and mathematics and natural science.

Ahead on State 109 is GRAFTON, 7.5 *m.* (446 alt., 1,026 pop.), at the confluence of the Illinois and the Mississippi. Peck, in his *Gazetteer of Illinois*, summed up Grafton in 1834 as a "postoffice, one store, one tavern, and a number of families." The town was at that time owned by James Mason, who predicted that his village would become chief river port of Illinois. An incorporation was granted to Mason "for the purpose of converting into manufactured products, any article of the growth and production of this state, whether animal, vegetable, or fossil, and for the digging and exporting of stone." Peck optimistically observed, "It is expected that some of these branches of business will go forward." Forward they went, but tediously. In the post-Civil War years Grafton reached a fixed economic level which, though including a comfortable share of river commerce, was far below that hoped for by its founder. By the turn of the century the decline of the steamboat had forced Grafton to revert to fishing, boat-building, and "the digging and exporting of stone." Today, however, the community is optimistic about the revival of river commerce. Barge lines are carrying freight in increasing amounts, and Grafton hopes to get its share of the water trade.

West of Grafton State 100 follows the bluff-bordered shore of the Illinois River. A STONE CROSS (R), 9.7 *m.*, man-high and rough-hewn, marks the place where Marquette, Jolliet, and their companions entered Illinois in 1673, "dawn-heralds of religion, civil government, and consecrated labor."

PERE MARQUETTE STATE PARK, 14.1 *m.*, commemorates the explorer, who described the bluffs as "frightful for their height and length." Sixteen hundred and seventy acres of rugged hills tower above the Illinois. From their summits the Illinois and Mississippi look like tiny streams threading their way across a meadow of uninterrupted green. At the entrance (R) is the PARK LODGE (*hotel accommodations*), its broad terrace commanding a sweeping view of the great valley. The main park road winds upward over successive hills to McADAMS PEAK. Other roads, bridle paths, and hiking trails wind for miles through the park, connecting picnic grounds and hill-top look-out stations.

At 79.7 *m.* on US 67 is a junction with a graveled road.

Right on this road to CLIFTON TERRACE (*season June* 1 *to late fall*), 1 *m.*, a small summer resort at the base of the Mississippi bluffs. Patronized by residents of Alton and St. Louis the community consists entirely of summer cottages and one summer hotel. The steep, heavily wooded bluffs are popular with hikers; a public beach (*free*) affords swimming. Downstream are numerous river-view estates.

At 83 *m.*, on the northern limits of Alton, is a junction with State 111.

Left on State 111 to GODFREY, 2 *m.*, a small hamlet, the site of MONTI-CELLO COLLEGE AND PREPARATORY SCHOOL FOR GIRLS, whose soft gray limestone buildings are set in a beautifully wooded tract of 300 acres. Founded in 1835, Monticello was one of the first institutions west of the Alleghenies to offer advanced education for women. The school was established by a retired Cape Cod sea captain, Benjamin Godfrey, who believed that women should be educated in the same manner as men. When he erected a stone building at a cost of $45,000 and opened his school, the enterprise was considered sheer madness by most of the settlers of the State. Today Monticello, with an average enrollment of 180, offers a four-year preparatory course and two years of accredited junior college training.

Ahead on State 111 to a junction with Delhi Road, 3.3 *m.*; straight ahead on Delhi Road to the GODFREY MANSION (*open*) 3.4 *m.* (L). The two-story, gray limestone building houses a large private collection of Indian relics; among the 12,000 pieces are axes, peace pipes, farming implements, and religious and cere-monial objects.

ALTON, 85 *m.* (438 alt., 30,151 pop.) (*see Alton*).

Points of Interest: Lovejoy State Monument, Shurtleff College, Painting of the Piasa Bird, Owens-Illinois Glass Company, and others.

At Alton US 67 divides; one branch (R) crosses the Missouri Line on the Lewis and Clark Bridge (*car and driver,* 30c; *passengers,* 5c *each*), which spans the Mississippi River 22 miles N. of St. Louis, Missouri (*see Missouri Guide*); the other branch (L) continues southward through Illinois to East St. Louis (*see below*).

Section c. Alton to Missouri Line, 28.5 m.

Between Alton, 0 *m.*, and East St. Louis US 67 crosses the great flood plain of the river, the American Bottom. In the north are brass and leather factories and oil refineries, a concentrated manufacturing district. For 10 miles thereafter are farm lands, then suddenly begins the East St. Louis industrial area, a land of heavy industries, of steel and other metals.

In EAST ALTON, 4 *m.* (430 alt., 4,502 pop.), is the WESTERN CARTRIDGE COMPANY PLANT (*tours arranged upon application*), one of the world's largest manufactories of small arms ammunition. Since 1893, when the company established a powder mill, plant and city have grown apace. During the World War, a brass mill was built to meet the requirements of 23 contracts given the company by the U. S. Government and its allies. After the war the mill was adapted to industrial production of brass and other alloys. The company employs practically all of the workers of the town and many from Wood River —a total of approximately 2,500 people. Frequently the chatter of machine-gun fire from the testing grounds rises above the varied noises of the factory.

Continuous with East Alton is WOOD RIVER, 5.7 m. (430 alt., 8,136 pop.), site (L) of a major STANDARD OIL REFINERY (*no visitors*). The sandy wasteland that is now the city was selected in 1907 by the company because of the excellent transportation facilities of railroad and river. During the months when Wood River was taking form, it assumed the aspects of a turbulent mining town of the early West. It was in these days that another community, Benbowe City, sprang up on the edge of the new town. It was an old-time construction camp, where fist fights, drunken brawls, and shooting affairs were frequent. Residents of Wood River resented this riotous element so close to their more orderly town, and a bitter feeling developed. It is related that this antagonism found expression in a duel fought by two policemen of the rival towns, each standing within his own boundary, in which the Benbowe officer was killed. The Standard Oil Company later bought the site of Benbowe City, tore down the buildings, and fenced the grounds.

The establishment in 1917 of the SHELL REFINERY in the suburb of ROXANA, southeast of the Standard Oil plant, gave further impetus to the growth of Wood River. In the past two decades the city has completely outgrown its jerry-built aspect, and its general appearance has been improved by the development of a large COMMUNITY PARK (*pool and bathhouse*), L. of the highway. Frequently noticed by visitors, but imperceptible to residents, is the acrid odor of oil that pervades the town on summer days. More unforgetable is the piercing moan, as of some great beast in pain, that often comes at night when the stills are shut down for cleaning—the sound of whirling brushes sweeping through the vast network of pipes.

HARTFORD, 7.6 m. (425 alt., 1,566 pop.), exists solely because of the INTERNATIONAL SHOE COMPANY TANNERY (*apply at office*), L. of the highway. Established in 1915, the plant employs about 900 persons, and as many as 27,500 hides have been tanned here in a single week. Each hide goes through 110 separate processes of trimming, washing, kneading, scraping, shaving, and soaking before it is ready for use. Thirty-seven days are required to transform a hide from a raw, green skin to a finished piece of soft, pliable leather.

South of Hartford the scene changes abruptly. Industry gives way to agriculture, and, except for the dank luxuriance of the vegetation, the low-lying bluffs far to the east, and the dense growth of willows that mark the river's bank on the west, the landscape might be that of the most fertile of eastern Illinois prairies, with its rich black soil and its verdant farm lands.

But the American Bottom was not always so. Prior to the construction of levees and drainage canals in recent years, the Bottom was regularly flooded by the seasonal rise of the Mississippi and Missouri Rivers. Charles Dickens made a wearisome journey across these lands in 1843, of which he later observed in his *American Notes*:

"We had a pair of very strong horses, but travelled at the rate of little more than a couple of miles an hour, through one unbroken slough of black mud and water. It had no variety but in depth. Now it was only half over the wheels, now it hid the axle-tree, and now the coach sank down in it almost to the windows. The air resounded in all directions with the loud chirping of frogs, who, with the pigs (a coarse, ugly breed as unwholesome looking as though they were the spontaneous growth of the country), had the whole scene to themselves."

At 13.5 m. is a junction with US 66 (see Tour 17) and US 40 (see Tour 19).

For a short distance southward the corn fields continue on the rich alluvium of the valley, and then abruptly give place to the steel lands of the East St. Louis industrial area. Here the great plants of heavy industry spread over acres of prairie, and fill the air with their dirt and din and pungent smells. Tall stacks rise darkly against the sky and pour their smoke across the sun. The smoke pall is heavy on the land, and on the faces of the people is written the strife and strain of the factories. It is a rough, alien land of many races, a melting pot of steel and bone. Granite City, Madison, and Venice, known locally as the Tri-Cities, are principal units of this industrial area. At their best they are communities in which steel workers have built stout churches, good schools, and substantial bungalows; at their worst they are cindery wastelands broken by mill buildings and rows of grimy frame cottages.

GRANITE CITY, 18.5 m. (431 alt., 25,130 pop.), is named for its first product, granite ware. Although settled by pioneers from Virginia, Kentucky, and Tennessee as early as 1815, the site of Granite, as the city is colloquially known, remained in corn and wheat until well near the present century. William F. Niedringhaus, a St. Louis industrialist, bought 3,000 acres of the area in 1891. On a sultry August afternoon, Niedringhaus, accompanied by his son, George, ferried across the Mississippi to his property and from the eminence of a buggy selected a plant site for his National Enameling and Stamping Company. The plant, along with scores of two-family flats, was constructed in 1892. Shortly afterwards the Niedringhaus interests built a rolling-mill; in 1893 the American Steel Foundry was established; and, in 1896, Granite City was incorporated. Workers, merchants, and real-estate dealers gravitated to Granite overnight. The booming city, as though welling from the bottom-lands, spread from mill walls, and within two decades impinged upon older communities to the north and south.

The steel mills of Granite are mainly south of the business district; the residential area lies north. LINCOLN PLACE, extending north and south from Pacific Avenue, is the melting pot of the foreign-born population—approximately 10 per cent. The section was first called Hungary Hollow, after the dominant nationality there represented.

During a steel slump in 1907 the name was corrupted to Hungry Hollow. The present name was adopted at a mass meeting when the mills reopened. Festivals are held by the various nationality groups in LINCOLN PLACE COMMUNITY HOUSE.

The VOCATIONAL TRAINING SCHOOL (*open 9-3, Mon.-Fri., apply at principal's office*), Madison Ave. and 30th St., a unit of the Granite City High School, is housed in a group of modern brick buildings set back from the highway amid broad lawns. The school offers apprentice courses in chemistry, drafting, electrical and mechanical engineering, and pattern making under approximate shop conditions. Students design, pattern, and finish lathes, drill-presses, and other industrial equipment. Advanced students sometimes do machine work for local industries; in return, manufacturers supply the school with scrap metals. Near the center of town the highway passes the GRANITE CITY STEEL WORKS (L), and, shortly beyond, the COMMONWEALTH STEEL MILLS (R). Because of inherent occupational dangers none of the plants of the East St. Louis area is open to visitors.

MADISON, 20 *m.* (425 alt., 7,661 pop.), second largest of the Tri-Cities, is, like Granite, a product of the steel industry. A group of St. Louis industrialists, spurred mainly by the high cost of bringing coal into St. Louis over Eads Bridge, formed the Madison Land Syndicate in 1887 and promoted the construction of the Merchants Bridge (1890). The new bridge diverted St. Louis capital to the embryo Tri-Cities. The American Car and Foundry Company built a plant on the site of Madison in 1891. Two rows of flimsy, box-like houses erected near the foundry were incorporated in that same year as the village of Madison by the Land Syndicate. Home of mill workers, the community rises or falls with the fortunes of the steel industry.

Right from Madison on Broadway to VENICE, 1 *m.* (410 alt., 5,362 pop.), so named because its streets were often flooded by the river before the construction of the levees. Oldest and smallest of the Tri-Cities, Venice dates from a ferry landing established in 1804. It was platted in 1841, and, despite regular inundation, developed as a settlement and was incorporated in 1873. A flour mill and a sawmill gave promise that the village would further develop, but in 1882 the sawmill was dismantled and the flour mill destroyed by fire. However, in 1891 a switch-yard was built near the approach to the Merchants Bridge and Venice enjoyed a considerable growth in population. Least prepossessing of the Tri-Cities, Venice lies amid industrial sites and mazes of railroad tracks. Most of its inhabitants are employed in nearby steel mills, or in the varied industries of metropolitan St. Louis. Under the McKinley Bridge (*car and driver*, 20c; *passengers*, 5c *each*), which connects Venice with St. Louis, is KERR ISLAND. Inhabited in times past by fishermen, it has become attached to the mainland and been taken over as the dwelling place of more than a thousand Negro squatters. The settlement has evolved without restraint or direction. Crazy streets thread their way among hundreds of huts that are built of scraps of lumber, tin, and a variety of materials salvaged from river and alley.

Left from Broadway on 4th Street 1 *m.* to BROOKLYN (415 alt., 2,063 pop.), oldest and largest all-Negro community in Illinois. Although platted as a "paper town" in 1837 by five white men, the city was not incorporated until 1874, when it was named Lovejoy, in honor of the martyred Abolitionist editor, Elijah

P. Lovejoy. Government was then in the hands of white people, although Negroes comprised the larger part of the population. The development of the steel industry in the Tri-Cities, and the influx of Negro workers, so increased the proportion that by 1910 the community was wholly Negro. The town is largely dependent upon the industries of nearby cities.

At 25 *m.* is a junction with City US 40 (*see Tour* 19A), which unites with US 67 to the Missouri Line.

EAST ST. LOUIS, 26.5 *m.* (414 alt., 74,347 pop.) (*see East St. Louis*).

Points of Interest: National Stock Yards, Site of Bloody Island, Lake Park, and others.

East St. Louis is at the junction with State 3 (*see Tour* 8), City US 40 (*see Tour* 19A), and US 50 (*see Tour* 20).

US 67 crosses the Missouri Line, 28.5 *m.*, on the Municipal Bridge (10c), spanning the Mississippi to St. Louis, Mo. (*see Missouri Guide*).

TOUR 8

EAST ST. LOUIS—CHESTER—CAIRO; 149 m.; STATE 3

Hard-surfaced roadbed throughout.

The Mobile and Ohio R. R. parallels State 3 between East St. Louis and Red Bud; Missouri Pacific R. R. between Chester and Cairo.

Accommodations limited to principal cities.

THROUGHOUT its entire length State 3 roughly parallels the Mississippi River. Traversing the southern portion of the East St. Louis industrial area, the route crosses a region of rolling prairies and woodlands which saw the first extensive settlement in the State—the heart of the American Bottom, center of French colonization in the Mississippi Valley during the eighteenth century. Between Chester and Cairo the highway follows the Mississippi bottom lands, sometimes at the water's edge, generally inland at the base of the bluffs. In its southern half the route crosses the Illinois Ozarks, most rugged section of Illinois, and then drops to the lowest point in the State, the delta on which stands Cairo, once a busy port at the confluence of the Ohio and Mississippi Rivers.

EAST ST. LOUIS, 0 *m.* (414 alt., 74,347 pop.) (*see East St. Louis*).

Points of Interest: National Stock Yards, Eads Bridge, Site of Bloody Island, Lake Park, and others.

In East St. Louis are junctions with US 67 (*see Tour 7*), City US 40 (*see Tour 19A*), and US 50 (*see Tour 20*).

The CAHOKIA POWER PLANT, *3.4 m.* (*apply room 702, Union Electric Light and Power Co. Bldg., St. Louis, Mo., for visiting permit*), one of the largest in the Mississippi Valley, was the first designed expressly for the use of low-grade Illinois coal in pulverized form. Large mills reduce the coal to a powder that is blown by compressed air into the fireboxes beneath the 14 immense boilers. Each of the six smokestacks is 265 feet high and 21 feet in diameter at the top. The plant devours coal at the rate of one ton every 30 seconds.

CAHOKIA, *3.9 m.* (407 alt., 286 pop.), the oldest town in Illinois, has almost been swallowed by the encroaching industrial area of East St. Louis. Now little more than a cross-roads hamlet, Cahokia possesses but few reminders of the era when it exercised jurisdiction over a vast territory which included the present site of Chicago, more than 250 miles to the northeast.

Originally a summer camp of the Tamaroa Indians, it was visited in 1698 by Fathers Jolliet de Montigny, Antoine Davion, and Jean François Buisson de St. Cosme. The missionaries were guided by Tonti, the explorer, called "Iron Hand" by the Indians, who marveled at his artificial hand. By May, 1699 St. Cosme had completed a house and chapel here, the first church in Illinois. These founders of Cahokia were of the Seminary of Foreign Missions, and shortly they found themselves embroiled with the Jesuits, who previously had conducted all the missionary work in the Mississippi Valley. To Cahokia came the Jesuit Fathers, Julien Binneteau, Pierre Pinet, and Joseph Limoges, who began erecting another building as evidence of the rights of their order. When relations between the two orders became strained, Father Montigny went to France to obtain a settlement at court. On June 7, 1701, it was decreed that the Seminary of Foreign Missions "shall dwell alone in . . . Tamaroa and that they shall receive in a friendly manner the Jesuit fathers when they shall pass there in going to attend the Illinois and Tamaroa at their fishing and hunting grounds, where the said Jesuit fathers may establish themselves . . . ." The Jesuits retained jurisdiction over all the Mississippi Valley save Cahokia.

Around the little mission grew a sizable trading post. For some time there was considerable trouble with the Indians, occasioned by the crudities of the French *coureurs de bois.* Father Mercier reflected the spirit of the isolated community when he wrote, "All is confusion; we are always on the *qui vive.*" Trade flourished, however, and great cargoes of flour, lumber, pork, lead, and pelts were shipped by keelboat down the Mississippi to New Orleans.

Although Cahokia passed into British hands in 1765 and into

American in 1778, it remained almost wholly French in character until the end of the century. George Rogers Clark's troops came in 1778, but were removed in 1780 and for 10 years the settlements in the American Bottom functioned largely as autonomous city-states. Cahokia, having a strong religious element, governed itself with admirable discipline, in sharp contrast to nearby settlements. In 1786 Cahokians requested Congress to refrain from placing them under the jurisdiction of Kaskaskia (*see below*), on the grounds that Kaskaskia citizens were guilty of "incapacity, spite, and partiality." When the county of St. Clair was set up, in 1790, Cahokia, Kaskaskia, and Prairie du Rocher were made joint county seats.

But hard feelings persisted, and in 1795 Gov. Arthur St. Clair carved the county in two and created St. Clair and Randolph Counties, and named Cahokia and Kaskaskia as their respective seats. In 1809 the boundaries of these two counties were redrawn so that they included all of what is now the State of Illinois. Cahokia was county seat for a territory that is now included in the 80 northern counties of Illinois.

But Cahokia's decline was already under way. British jurisdiction had broken the influence of the Catholic Church, and in 1809 Father Urbain Guillet found the church buildings so dilapidated and the Cahokians so indifferent that he announced he would refuse to read the mass to them until they repaired the roof and windows of their church. Political decline followed; in 1814 the county seat was moved to Belleville for political and geographic reasons. The economic rise of St. Louis and East St. Louis, and the annual floods of the Mississippi, hastened Cahokia's decline.

Today the old French town bespeaks its former importance largely through the impressive CHURCH OF THE HOLY FAMILY, at the intersection with State 157 (L) in the center of the village. Almost in the shadow of the new church stands its immediate predecessor, the OLD CHURCH OF THE HOLY FAMILY, now a parish meeting hall. Completed in 1799, it was blessed in September of that year by Father Rivet, pastor of Vincennes. The original walnut logs, hand-hewn and set upright, in the Canadian palisade type of construction, have been covered with clapboard. The flaring eves are also suggestive of old Quebec. Behind the church is the old CAHOKIA CEMETERY, where for more than a century Indians, French colonists, and Negro slaves were interred in haphazard fashion; most of the headstones and markers have been removed. Fifty yards west of the old church stands the old PARISH HOUSE (*private dwelling*), a one-story brick structure erected by Father Loisel in 1833.

The old CAHOKIA COURTHOUSE (*open*), a small log cabin, also of the palisade type of construction, was moved to Chicago in 1904, where it was placed on exhibit in Jackson Park. Not until 1939 was it returned to its original site at Cahokia.

The JARROT MANSION (*for visiting permit apply to nun in charge*), a large two-story brick house, Colonial in design, lies just to the east of the new church. Built between 1799 and 1806 for Maj. Nicholas Jarrot, a judge of the Cahokia court, it is the oldest brick house in Illinois. Staunchly constructed, with walls a foot and a half thick, it withstood the terrific earthquake that rocked Cahokia in 1811, suffering only a few cracks in the rear wall. The use of black headers (bricks from the inside of the kiln laid to expose their ends) in every sixth row of bricks results in a horizontal banding of red and black in the south and east walls. The building is now used as a Roman Catholic school. Of Major Jarrot's hospitality, a visitor once wrote that so many balls were held here that he "often wondered how the ladies are enabled to support themselves under this violent exercise. . . ." In 1807 another guest commented on the gambling at the Jarrot Mansion: "Never did I see people embark with so much spirit and perseverance to win each other's money—I have frequently known them to sit thirty hours at the same table without any other refreshment than a dish of coffee or a glass of claret."

Immediately across the road from the mansion, in sharp contrast of past and present, is PARKS AVIATION COLLEGE (8-4:30 *daily*).

DUPO, 8.4 *m*. (422 alt., 2,082 pop.), bears a name contracted from Prairie du Pont (Fr., meadow of the bridge), so called because of a small bridge constructed across a creek in this region by Cahokians more than a century ago. Near the outskirts of Dupo, oil was discovered in 1928 and the town enjoyed the excitement of a boom. Wells were sunk in front lawns; the population grew rapidly, and land speculation ran high. But it soon became evident that the resources of the field were limited, and the boom subsided. Today, the total output of the field is a scant 200 barrels a day. The RAILROAD YARDS (R) provide employment for a majority of the town's working population.

South of Dupo the highway gradually ascends from the bottom lands to reveal (R) the Missouri bluffs.

The prim whitewashed brick cottages of COLUMBIA, 15 *m*. (490 alt., 1,791 pop.), hug the highway and evidence in their freshly scrubbed appearance the predominantly German ancestry of the inhabitants. Numerous unpretentious doorways of Greek revival influence similar to those of old St. Louis contribute to the charm of quiet streets. Columbia was one of the major stops on the old Kaskaskia-Cahokia trail. Quarrying of Keokuk limestone has been carried on here since 1840.

Between Columbia and Waterloo State 3 dips and rises through gently rolling farmlands.

WATERLOO, 22 *m*. (717 alt., 2,239 pop.), is the seat of Monroe County. On the old trail from Fort Chartres to Cahokia, it has grown up adjacent to the original settlement of Bellefontaine (Fr., beautiful spring), which long ago lost its identity in spite of the fact that it was the first American community in the old Northwest. Until the passage of the stricter marriage laws in 1937, Waterloo had a wide reputation as the Gretna Green of the St. Louis area. Signs advertising the marriage parlors of justices of peace lined the highway for several miles outside the city limits, and competition among the justices was spirited.

In the hamlet of LEMENS, 25 m., is a junction with a graveled road.

Right on this road to RENAULT, 11 m. (684 alt., 188 pop.), named for Phillipe François Renault, director-general of mining operations for John Law's Western Company, known to history as the "Mississippi Bubble" (see below). Renault left France in 1719 with 200 miners to search for precious stones and metals in the Louisiana Territory. En route, he stopped at Santo Domingo and bought 500 slaves, a number of which were brought to Illinois. After an unsuccessful treasure hunt Renault returned to France in 1742, and his slaves were sold to French colonists in this region. Until the present century there were Negroes in the vicinity of Renault and Prairie du Rocher who clung to French customs and spoke a mixture of French and English.

RED BUD, 36 m. (444 alt., 1,208 pop.) was named for the redbud trees that once grew in profusion near the village site. The tableland south of the village is known as HORSE PRAIRIE. Ponies that escaped from the French strayed to this region, became wild, and roamed the prairie until captured by incoming American settlers.

In the village of RUMA, 42 m., is a junction with State 155.

Right on State 155 to PRAIRIE DU ROCHER, 7 m. (396 alt., 510 pop.), a somnolent little town at the base of the bluffs. Prairie du Rocher was founded about 1722 as a result of John Law's "Mississippi Bubble." Law, a Scotch promoter, organized a company to exploit the resources of the New World and obtained a charter that granted complete jurisdiction over Louisiana Territory. The charter provided that 6,000 whites and 3,000 Negroes should be brought to the territory within 25 years. Law promised fabulous profits, and for several years the French indulged in mad speculation. The "Bubble" burst in 1720, resulting in financial ruin to thousands and severely wrenching the French financial system. The colonists that Law sent into the Mississippi Valley, however, encouraged the settlement of this area. As late as 1900 French was still spoken extensively in Prairie du Rocher.

In FORT CHARTRES STATE PARK (shelter house, picnic facilities), 11 m., stood, almost two centuries ago, the most formidable of all French fortresses in the Mississippi Valley. In 1718 France sent Pierre Duque, Sieur de Boisbriant, to erect a fortress in the Illinois Country. Two years later the work was completed and named for the Duc de Chartres, son of the French regent. Warehouses soon sprang up about the fort, large tracts of land were cultivated; and a town grew up in the shadow of the fort. "All roads lead to Fort de Chartres" was a favorite saying of the day.

The first fort was built of timber and soon fell into disrepair. A dozen years after its completion it was abandoned for a new fort at a nearby site, but this too was soon dilapidated. In 1751 the French decided to erect a fortification that would be both permanent and impregnable. The foundation was laid in 1753; three years later the new Fort de Chartres was finished.

Its massive walls were 18 feet in height and enclosed four acres of ground.

Each of the four bastions of masonry contained eight embrasures, forty-eight loop-holes, and a sentry box. Within the walls were a storehouse, a guardhouse with a chapel and priests' rooms on the second floor, a government house, a coach house and pigeon loft, and two great rows of barracks. Set apart from the other buildings, to avoid the danger of an explosion, was the magazine. Fort de Chartres' soldiers fought on many battlefields of the French and Indian War. Washington surrendered to them at Fort Necessity, and later they aided in the defeat of General Braddock.

The Treaty of Paris of 1763 ceded this area to the British, but it was not until 1765 that Louis St. Ange de Bellerive, commander of the fort, tearfully surrendered it to Capt. Thomas Stirling. Even the stolid Indians wept when the cross of St. George replaced the lilies of France. Many of the French left; those that remained were probably elated when the Mississippi steadily encroached on the fort. Finally, in 1772, its situation became so serious that the British withdrew their garrison and destroyed what remained of the proudest military structure in the West.

In 1915 the State of Illinois acquired the site of Fort de Chartres for use as a park. Underbrush was cleared away and the work of restoration begun. Today the FOUNDATIONS OF FORT DE CHARTRES, cleared of underbrush and repaired, sharply delineate the plan of the old fort. A park building, constructed on the foundation of the original supply house, contains a MUSEUM (*open* 8-5 *daily*) in which are preserved numerous relics unearthed on the site. The POWDER MAGAZINE has been restored; a GUARD HOUSE AND CHAPEL, an exact reproduction of the original structure, has been built. The WELL inside the fort wall, dug in 1754, is still in use.

At 55.5 *m.* is a junction with a hard-surfaced road.

Right on this road 1.5 *m.* to the entrance to FORT KASKASKIA STATE PARK (*shelter house, picnic facilities*), a 57-acre tract at the crest of the bluffs. The first fort was built here in 1733, more than thirty years after the first settlement. Rebuilt in 1736 with the aid of a special grant from the French crown, it was occupied until 1755, when the garrison was moved to Fort de Chartres. When the British took over after the Treaty of Paris, Kaskaskians destroyed the fort to prevent British occupation.

A turbulent period followed the removal of George Rogers Clark's troops in 1780, when this territory was theoretically in the hands of the Americans but no local government had yet been set up. The ruins of the fort were seized in 1784 by a renegade named John Dodge, who once had enjoyed the confidence of George Washington. For two years he ruled Kaskaskia like a tyrant, bullying the people, murdering the messengers they sent to bring aid. Describing Dodge's reign, Father Gibault wrote, "Breaking of limbs, murder by means of a dagger, sabre, or sword (for he who wills carries one) are common, and pistols and guns are but toys in these regions. . . . The most solemn feasts and Sundays are days given up to dances and drunkenness . . . with girls suborned and ravished in the woods, and a thousand other disorders which you are able to infer from these." After Clark restored order, the fort was never again used. Its site and plan can be traced by the EARTHWORKS, all that remain of the old fort.

A stone's throw north is GARRISON HILL CEMETERY. The founders and residents of old Kaskaskia were buried in the lowlands near the confluence of the Kaskaskia and Mississippi. After the Mississippi threatened to wash away the old graveyard, the State removed approximately 3,800 boxes, some containing whole families, to this new graveyard.

Facing the river at the base of the bluffs is the PIERRE MENARD HOUSE (*open*), a story-and-a-half structure, raised above a high basement on the river side, with a wide gallery porch, low hip roof, and dormer windows. The design of the house recalls the minor plantation houses of Louisiana. Menard was the presiding officer of the Illinois Territorial Legislature and the first Lieutenant Governor of Illinois. Born in Quebec in 1766, he entered the fur trade at Vincennes in 1787 and came to Kaskaskia in 1789 to establish a store. His enterprises prospered and he became a rich man, admired and respected by both pioneers and Indians. Old documents show that in 1820, while sub-agent of the Indian department, Menard spent $13 to have a Delaware chief and his party ferried across the Mississippi, $19.50 to furnish supper and breakfast for 13 Indians and to feed their horses, and $23 to purchase 400 pounds of beef and have a coffin made for an Indian who had been accidentally killed.

The Menard House was completed in 1802, and by pioneer standards was lavishly conceived and maintained. The foundation is of stone blocks, which support hand-hewn timbers, several of which are more than a foot square. The original furnishings were sold by Menard's descendants, and the present pieces were replaced by the State only after their authenticity had been established. The drawing room where Lafayette was entertained in 1824 contains a mantelpiece imported from France. Behind the house is a detached STONE KITCHEN, with a huge fireplace, a cavernous Dutch oven, and a sink carved from a solid block of stone. The SLAVE HOUSE nearby has been carefully restored.

Down the slope from the Menard House, and under the waters of the Mississippi, lies the SITE OF OLD KASKASKIA, the first capital of Illinois. Kaskaskia was founded as a Roman Catholic mission in 1703, four years after Cahokia (*see above*). For a hundred years their histories ran roughly parallel, for the broad movements of the struggle for the Mississippi Valley affected each simultaneously. The town was built around a large parklike square, on which stood the buildings of the Jesuits. On the narrow streets that branched from the square at right angles were log houses, usually a story and a half high, with pointed roofs of thatch or bark. The dwellings of wealthy residents were of stone quarried from the nearby bluffs, and contained such luxurious furnishings as gilt-framed mirrors, paintings, and even billiard tables.

Wearied of brutal British rule that followed the Treaty of Paris, Kaskaskia yielded peacefully to George Rogers Clark in 1778. It declined gradually until 1809, when it revived on becoming the capital of Illinois Territory, acquiring also the regional land office. In 1818 Illinois became a State, with Kaskaskia as the capital, but two years later the seat of government was transferred to Vandalia (*see Tour* 4). Occasional floods hastened Kaskaskia's decline, and near the end of the century the Mississippi broke through the low peninsula which separated it from the Kaskaskia River, changed its course, and eventually destroyed the town.

KASKASKIA ISLAND, between the new main channel and the old, is the only section of Illinois that lies west of the Mississippi River. The new community of Kaskaskia, in the center of the island, receives its mail by rural delivery from St. Marys, Missouri.

On the outskirts of Chester appear (R) the stacks and building of the MENARD BRANCH OF THE STATE PENITENTIARY (*only relatives may visit prisoners*); the grounds and farm lands cover 1,600 acres.

CHESTER, 62 *m.* (381 alt., 3,922 pop.), the seat of Randolph County, was founded by a land company formed in 1819, in Cincinnati, Ohio, to establish a settlement as a commercial rival of Kaskaskia. In GREENWOOD CEMETERY (R) a white granite monument erected by the State in 1883 marks the GRAVE OF SHADRACH BOND, first Governor of Illinois.

Left from Chester on State 150 is an old COVERED BRIDGE, 4 *m*. The bridge, which spans Marys River downstream from the highway bridge, was built in 1847 at a cost of $530. It was reputedly the scene of several stagecoach robberies and murders. The bridge has been recently repaired by the State, and a roadside park (*picnic facilities*) has been developed nearby.

ROCKWOOD, 71 *m*. (377 alt., 171 pop.), was known throughout southern Illinois as a timber market before the Mississippi changed its channel and receded from the town's backyard. In addition to supplying steamers with wood for fuel, the villagers manufactured flat-bottomed boats used in floating cargoes down the Mississippi.

On the southwest corner of the intersection with the Jacob Road, 81 *m*., an INDIAN MOUND is clearly visible from the highway. The mound, approximately 20 feet high and half an acre in extent, has not been excavated. Numerous mounds dot the valley throughout this section.

At 81.3 *m*. is the junction with a hard-surfaced road, marked by deep cuts on each side of it; that on the northeast corner has been cut through an INDIAN MOUND, clearly revealing a cross section of its structure.

Left on this road is FOOTPRINT ROCK (L), 0.5 *m*., encircled by a wooden railing. On the flat top of its huge bulk are impressions resembling those made by naked human feet; one resembles a very sharply outlined hand. Several of the clearest prints have been chiseled from the rock by vandals. The footprints are of adult size, with the exception of one set resembling those of a small child. These so-called prints were probably sculptured by Indians. Similar ones have been found in the vicinity under circumstances that render it highly improbable that they are of natural origin. One set of footprints, for instance, ascends a vertical wall; others have been found in various patterns, accompanied by circles and other geometric figures, indicating that the tracks had some symbolic significance.

At 85 *m*. is a junction with State 144.

Left on State 144 to SCENIC VIEW, 1.4 *m*., a graveled parking space at the top of the steep bluffs. On the horizon to the southeast the Illinois Ozarks rise abruptly, a great dark wall, thick-wooded to the summit. To the southwest the distant Missouri Ozarks loom faintly beyond the smooth Mississippi and the vast expanse of the bottom lands.

MURPHYSBORO, 8 *m*. (420 alt., 8,182 pop.), was virtually rebuilt after a destructive tornado in 1925. The SITE OF THE BIRTHPLACE OF JOHN A. LOGAN is marked on the railroad right-of-way opposite 310 S. 17th St. A more impressive memorial to the dashing soldier and politician is the Leon Hermant bronze EQUESTRIAN STATUE OF GENERAL LOGAN, 2123 Spruce St. Unexplained is the number, 1999, chiseled into the bronze base immediately below the sculptor's signature.

Ahead from Murphysboro on State 13 is CARBONDALE, 16 *m*. (416 alt., 7,528 pop.) (*See Tour* 4c), at a junction with US 51 (*see Tour* 4c).

Proceeding south, State 3 enters the Illinois Ozarks, which reach heights of more than 1,000 feet above sea level. Their heavily wooded slopes, slashed with deep dark ravines, change brilliantly with the seasons.

Illinois south of the Ozarks is an overlap between the North and South. Southern styles of architecture are common. The inhabitants speak with decidedly Southern accents. Such southern trees as the bald cypress and the tupelo gum grow in the swamplands, and the mistletoe is found on trees along the rivers. Azalea and southern short-leaf pine have been transplanted to these Ozark hills from the "piney woods" of the South and Southwest. Cotton is cultivated in occasional patches; orchards of peaches, apples, or pears are numerous. The southern black vulture is found here, as well as the turkey vulture of the North. In the lowlands the venomous water moccasin inhabits sluggish waters. The woods rattler is common. Numerous other plants and animals find either a northern or a southern limit to their range in this locality.

At 89 *m.* is a junction with a dirt road at the foot of FOUNTAIN BLUFF, a freak formation, 6 square miles in area, which juts from the level flood plain like a huge loaf on a table top. The bluff takes its name from the many springs that flow from its surface.

Right along this road the detailed features of the bluff are revealed. That the formation was once an island which weathered the rush of glacial waters through the Mississippi Gorge is evidenced by the sharp rise of the cliffs above the dead level of the flood plain. As the river has frequently changed its course, the formation may have remained an island until comparatively recent times. At present, however, the river washes only a single point on the west side. The rock towers in high solid walls; some sections are as smooth as polished ivory; others are rough and fissured. Large expanses are covered with lichens, moss, and small-leaved vines.

At 1.5 *m.* a foot bridge (L) spans a bog and leads up through a fissure. Here are a dam and a small swimming hole fed by springs. Above the dam are several paths leading to the upper levels. The geologic formations on all sides are of interest. Huge boulders of fused iron and sandstone line the way and shallow sandstone caves flank the paths at intervals. The summit can be reached from this point, but the climb is difficult.

At 91 *m.* is a junction with a graveled road.

Right on this road to the FOUNTAIN BLUFF FIRE TOWER, 2.2 *m.* (*Road is narrow and winding; down trip should be made in low gear.*) The 60-foot tower (*inside stairway type; visitors welcome, but not more than three at a time*) is topped with a lookout platform, where, during dry weather, a ranger of the State Forest Service is constantly on duty. Fires noted through field glasses are reported by telephone to district headquarters. The summit of Fountain Bluff commands a far-flung view of Illinois and Missouri, of the hills and the river, the fields, forests, and farms of the vast bottom lands.

At 94 *m.* is a junction with a graveled road.

Right on this road to GRAND TOWER, 1 *m.* (367 alt., 953 pop.). In the Mississippi River, between the Missouri shore and the town, is TOWER ROCK, for which the town was named. During President Grant's administration the river was dredged and cleared of rocks hazardous to navigation, but Tower Rock, because it might some day form a natural foundation for a bridge, was allowed to remain. Protected for this reason by the National government, the rock is called "the smallest national park in America." It is 60 feet high, of about an acre in extent. A popular picnic spot, Tower Rock can be reached from Grand Tower by motorboat (75c).

WOLF LAKE, (L) 103 *m.* borders the crossroads community of the same name, and offers the best fishing water along the route.

Left from Wolf Lake on a graveled road to the PINE HILL SKYLINE DRIVE, 0.6 *m.* The five-mile drive climbs steadily until it reaches the top of a range of the Ozarks and continues along the ridge (*caution, no guard rails*). At 4.4 *m.* and at 5.2 *m.* are two graveled OBSERVATION POINTS; the view from the first is the better; a jutting rock serves as the observation station. On the steep sides of the bluff below are numerous pines, rare in Illinois; it is for them that the drive is named.

In the hamlet of WARE, 107 *m.,* is a junction with State 146.

Left on State 146 to the SITE OF THE CHEROKEE ENCAMPMENT OF 1839 (L), 3.2 *m.,* designated by a marker. On this spot, during the winter of 1839, 13,000 Cherokee Indians, en route from Georgia to a new reservation in Oklahoma, and unable to cross the Mississippi because of ice floes, made their camp. Unaccustomed to the northern winter and unprepared for its rigors, nearly 2,000 of the tribe died of cold and privation.

At 5.5 *m.* is the entrance (L) to UNION COUNTY STATE FOREST (*shelter house, picnic facilities*). A 7-mile circular drive through the forest reaches many beautiful spots. South of the picnic grounds, in the center of the forest, is a WILD TURKEY FARM, where the State raises stock for its forest preserves.

At 125.4 *m.* is a junction with a paved road; in a wooded hollow at the intersection is a STATE ROADSIDE PARK (*picnic facilities*).

Right on this road is THEBES, 0.8 *m.* (335 alt., 751 pop.), once the seat of Alexander County. The old ALEXANDER COUNTY COURTHOUSE (*open*), built in 1846, is now in a half-ruined condition. Perched high on the river bluff, it is built of brick and stone in the general proportions of the Greek Revival, but in a starkly undecorated mode. The two-storied portico with its widely spaced but slender columns and dividing balustrade gives the façade the feeling of a very early and rather primitive Southern Colonial type. Thebes, first known as Sparhawk's Landing, was laid out in 1844. It figures briefly in Edna Ferber's novel, *Show Boat.*

HORSESHOE LAKE, (R.), 133 *m.,* is an extensive State game preserve and feeding ground for migratory fowl. (*Fishing permitted June 1-Sept. 30, from the lake shore only; no trot lines, set lines, or motorboats.*) The preserve consists of a 2,000-acre lake, shaped like a great horseshoe, in the middle of which is a 1,400-acre island, which can be reached by the custodian's motorboat (*no fees; arrangements made by telephone from Olive Branch*). The lake has been stocked with black bass and crappie. To protect fingerlings and fish eggs, the State annually traps turtles in the lake; in 1935 more than five tons of them were taken.

Between the middle of October and the end of March it is not uncommon to see 30,000 or 40,000 wild geese feeding at one time in the wheat fields of the preserve. Horseshoe Lake is at the approximate point of convergence of two of the three major flyways of the Canadian goose. Many ducks also feed at the preserve during the winter months, and the rare American egret and the great blue heron are frequently seen.

Although the principal function of the preserve is to supply a feeding ground for migratory fowl, many species of fur-bearing animals also inhabit the island: opposums, raccoons, mink, woodchucks, and skunks. Four deer, released in February 1935, have multiplied rapidly; they are seldom seen by visitors, except during the severe winter months, when they come to the edge of the wheat fields to feed.

Seven hundred acres of the island are planted in cereal crops, mainly wheat, to supply food for wild fowl, and 200 acres of virgin timber on the south end of the island afford sanctuary for the deer and small animals. The island, in the late spring especially, is brilliant with wild flowers.

At 145.5 *m.* is the northern junction with US 51 (*see Tour* 4), which unites with State 3 into Cairo.

CAIRO, 149 *m.* (318 alt., 13,532 pop.) (*see Cairo*).

Points of Interest: Halliday Hotel, Ohio Building, Cairo Public Library, Missouri Cotton Oil Company Plant, and others.

In Cairo is the southern junction with US 51 (*see Tour* 4), which crosses the Kentucky Line by bridge (*passenger car,* 75c) over the Ohio River 5 miles N. of Wickliffe, Kentucky, (*see Kentucky Guide*).

TOUR 9

(Hammond, Ind.) —Chicago—Des Plaines—Fox Lake—
(Lake Geneva, Wis.) ; US 12

Indiana Line to Wisconsin Line, 81.5 *m*.

Roadbed hard-surfaced throughout; four lanes for 58 miles in the Chicago area, two lanes northward.
Complete recreational facilities at lake resorts; accommodations otherwise limited.

In its southern section, US 12 skirts Chicago; its alternate, City US 12, passes through the Loop and rejoins the main route at Des Plaines, northwest of Chicago. Northward, the highway crosses the lake country that is one of the great city's summer playgrounds. The lakes, the only natural ones in Illinois except those along the rivers, lie in pockets in the rolling moraines of Lake and McHenry Counties. The hills, still largely forested, have all the beauty of spring and summer, the riotous colors of fall, and the bright white blanket of winter. Occasionally, a herd of dairy cows reveals the farming pursuits of the region, but little else varies the recreational aspect of the land.

US 12 crosses the Indiana Line, here the Chicago city limits, 0 *m.*, from Hammond, Indiana (*see Indiana Guide*), and proceeds northwest along Indianapolis Blvd. to Ewing Ave.; R. on Ewing Ave. to 95th St.; L. on 95th St.

At the intersection of 95th St. and Stony Island Ave., 4 *m.*, is the junction with US 330 (*see Tour* 12A). Here the route divides into City US 12 and By-Pass US 12.

Left (straight ahead) on By-Pass US 12 to a junction with US 45 (*see Tour* 3), 13.5 *m.;* R. on US 45, with which By-Pass US 12 is united for 23.5 miles, to Des Plaines (*see below*), at the western junction with City US 12, 37 *m.*

City US 12 proceeds north along Stony Island Ave. to the intersection of Michigan Blvd. with Jackson Blvd., the center of Chicago. CHICAGO, 16.5 *m.* (598 alt., 3,376,438 pop.) (*see Chicago*).

Points of Interest: Chicago Board of Trade Building, Union Stock Yards, Field Museum of Natural History, Art Institute of Chicago, Museum of Science and Industry, Adler Planetarium, Shedd Aquarium, University of Chicago and others.

In Chicago are junctions with State 1 (*see Tour* 1), State 42 (*see Tour* 2), US 41 (*see Tour* 2A), US 14 (*see Tour* 10), US 20 (*see*

Tour 11), US 330 (*see Tour* 12A), US 66 (*see Tour* 17), and the Illinois Waterway (*see Tour* 22).

North on Michigan Blvd. to Lake Shore Drive; R. (straight ahead) on Lake Shore Drive to Foster Ave.; L. (straight ahead) on Foster Ave. to Northwest Hwy.; R. on Northwest Hwy. to PARK RIDGE, 33.8 *m.* (658 alt., 10,417 pop.) (*see Tour* 10), which is at a junction with US 14 (*see Tour* 10).

DES PLAINES, 38 *m.* (643 alt., 8,798 pop.) (*see Tour* 3), is at the junction with By-Pass US 12 (*see below*) and US 45 (*see Tour* 3).

Between Des Plaines and Volo US 12 is known as Rand Road, named for Socrates Rand, pioneer land-holder along the Des Plaines River, who was largely responsible for the routing of the road. The path followed an Indian trail between what is now Chicago and Janesville, Wisconsin. The highway was the principal northwestern road in 1845, and was known as the United States Mail Route.

At 54 *m.*, on the southern shore of LAKE ZURICH, is a junction with State 63.

Right on State 63 to the village of LAKE ZURICH, 1 *m.* (873 alt., 368 pop.), which has been a summer resort for a hundred years. In 1836 Seth Paine, a Chicago merchant, purchased a lake-shore tract, erected a house, hired tenant farmers, and began a real estate development. His first step was to change the name from Cedar Lake to Lake Zurich, which he hoped would suggest the beauties of the famed Swiss resort. This change seems to have been warranted, for Lake Zurich has become a popular resort center.

WAUCONDA, 60 *m.* (800 alt., 554 pop.), began with the house of Justus Bangs, built in 1836 on the shore of the lake that now bears his name. Three years later a school was opened and a young man appointed teacher. He is said to have given the village its name— that of an Indian character in a story to which he had taken a fancy. An academy opened in 1856 functioned for a decade, and then rented its building to the district for use as a public school. The mainstay of economic life is the farm trade. Supplementary incomes are gleaned from summer colonists.

At 65 *m.* is the junction with State 20.

Left on State 20 to VOLO, 0.5 *m.*, a small hamlet known since 1877 as The Forks. The community is composed of the gray and yellow frame houses common in the lake country, but achieves a certain distinction by being set atop a low hill. Sharply contrasting with the rural hamlet aspect is ST. PETER'S CHURCH (Roman Catholic), of English Gothic design, which dominates the entire countryside. The handsome yellow brick building, modeled after Salisbury Cathedral in England, has a red slate roof and a bell tower. ST. PETER'S SCHOOL, also of yellow brick, abuts the church on the east.

McHENRY, 5 *m.* (758 alt., 1,354 pop.), on the Fox River, is the western gateway to the Chain-O'-Lakes. The first settler was Dr. Christy C. Wheeler, who erected a log cabin in 1836, and became McHenry's first storekeeper and postmaster. Early prosperity came to the settlement with the erection of several hotels on the Chicago Pike, a much-used route in the early days. In 1844 the town lost the county offices to Woodstock, but a decade later gained the Chicago & North Western Railway, which brought the development of such small industries as butter and cheese and pickle manufacture. The community today is largely supported by these activities, by trade with the farmers, and by incidental revenue from vacationists.

FOX LAKE, 70.5 m. (745 alt., 880 pop.), to the R. of US 12, is fittingly dominated by its railroad station, for it lives on resort and tourist trade. In summer and fall, cottagers come by the hundreds and week-end excursionists by the thousands to seek relaxation on Fox, Pistakee, Grass, and numerous smaller lakes in the vicinity. On the Fourth of July the whole of Chicago seems to crowd its beaches, bathhouses, barbecue palaces, dance halls, and picnic grounds. The overflow of visitors bridges the narrow straits that connect Nippersink and Pistakee Lakes and jams the newly developed facilities of CHAIN-O'-LAKES STATE PARK (*parking lots, bathing beaches, fishing, and picnic groves free; moderate rentals for canoes, rowboats, and bathhouses*), first unit of a group of parks that the CCC is developing on reclaimed land bordering the lakes. From Fox Lake motorboats take visitors through the Chain-O'-Lakes, past the Lotus Beds (*see below*) and down the Fox River as far as Fox River Grove. (*Rates vary with length of trip; departure is from N. end of bridge.*)

Right from Fox Lake village on Grand Avenue to the junction with State 59, 1.4 m.; L. here on a scenic drive along the south and east shores of Fox Lake. Except for the 3,200 acres in the newly-formed State parks, not a foot of lake shore is available to the public without charge. Numerous signs advertise fishing, boating, bathing, and camping facilities for rent; rates vary widely. Competition is intense. But the view is fine, and free.

At 4.5 m. on State 59 is the junction with a paved road; R. on this road 3.5 m. to LAKE VILLA (758 alt., 487 pop.), a railroad station and resort community whose boundaries encompass a lake of the same name. On the western shore of the lake and just within the western limits of the village is the entrance (*marked*) to the ALLENDALE FARM SCHOOL (*visitors by appointment*), an experiment in practical philanthropy. Founded in 1897 as a home for neglected or homeless boys, the community has grown to embrace a quarter-section of good farm land that stretches westward from the lake. The settlement consists of a group of large red-roofed gray wooden buildings, numerous cottages, and smaller farm buildings. The farm school, a non-profit organization, cares for, employs, and educates an average of 60 boys. Fishing, boating, swimming, and other sports are part of the recreational scheme. The community is organized as a junior municipality with a mayor and city council, a court, and a police department. A monetary system has been established, and each boy is paid for his labor and charged for his board and clothes in the legal tender of the farm.

At 6.5 m. on State 59 is the junction with a graveled road; L. on this road 0.5 m. to another unit of the CHAIN-O'-LAKES STATE PARK (*boating, fishing, picnicking, no bathing*). This park preserves the wild marshland along the eastern side of Grass Lake. Directly opposite the park are the lake's EGYPTIAN LOTUS BEDS, which attract thousands each fall to witness the bloom (*4 weeks beginning in early Aug.*). The waxy, pale yellow blossoms stand from 2 to 4 feet above the water, and perfume the air for miles around.

Ahead on State 54 is ANTIOCH, 9 *m.* (770 alt., 1,101 pop.), northern gateway and principal community of the Chain-O'-Lakes country. First settled in 1836, the village early established itself as a manufacturing center of service to the surrounding farmers. Today a large flour and feed mill and several dairy products plants are major factors in the town's economic life. For two-thirds of the year these and miscellaneous services support the community on a quiet, well-ordered plane. Then the Business Association swings into full stride, merchants restock their shelves, bunting is hung, bands play, and for four months the town reaps the golden harvest poured in from Chicago by bus, railroad, auto, and trailer.

SPRING GROVE FISH HATCHERY (*open*), 75.5 *m.*, is operated by the State. Here are spawned many of the thousands of fish taken annually in the well-stocked waters of the lake country. The hatchery forwards the work of the Natural History Survey by tagging specimens of the fish released. These, when caught and reported, aid in growth and migration studies carried on by the Survey.

RICHMOND, 80.5 *m.* (819 alt., 514 pop.), was first settled in 1837. The first GRIST MILL built in the community is still in use, grinding out flour and feed by the power of Nippersink Creek. Because of its location between Wisconsin and Illinois lakes, Richmond enjoys a bit of the summer resort trade. On many a summer's night its taverns, dance halls, and tourist camps are filled to overflowing.

US 12 crosses the Wisconsin Line, 81.5 *m.*, 10 miles southeast of Lake Geneva, Wisconsin (*see Wisconsin Guide*).

TOUR 10

CHICAGO—DES PLAINES—BARRINGTON—WOODSTOCK—
HARVARD—(JANESVILLE, WIS.); US 14
Chicago to Wisconsin Line, 68 *m.*

Roadbed hard-surfaced throughout; four lanes between Chicago and Barrington, two lanes westward.

The Chicago & North Western Ry. parallels the route.

Usual accommodations throughout.

FROM THE LAKE front in northern Chicago, US 14 runs westward to the suburb of Park Ridge and then angles obliquely to the Wisconsin Line, a through-traffic highway to the Northwest. Between

Chicago and Barrington the towns are largely commuting suburbs. Westward are the wooded hills that border the lake country.

CHICAGO, 0 *m.* (598 alt., 3,376,438 pop.) (*see Chicago*).

Points of Interest: Chicago Board of Trade Building, Union Stock Yards, Field Museum of Natural History, Art Institute of Chicago, Museum of Science and Industry, Adler Planetarium, Shedd Aquarium, University of Chicago, and others.

In Chicago are junctions with State 1 (*see Tour* 1), State 42 (*see Tour* 2), US 41 (*see Tour* 2A), US 12 (*see Tour* 9), US 20 (*see Tour* 11), US 330 (*see Tour* 12A), US 66 (*see Tour* 17), and the Illinois Waterway (*see Tour* 22).

US 41 follows Bryn Mawr Ave. in Chicago from its junction with Sheridan Rd., 0 *m.*, to Ridge Rd., 0.3 *m.*; R. on Ridge Rd. to Peterson Ave., 0.8 *m.*; L. on Peterson to Caldwell Ave., 5 *m.*; R. on Caldwell to Chicago city limits, 6 *m.*

PARK RIDGE, 10 *m.* (658 alt., 10,417 pop.), adjoining the north-western city limits of Chicago, stands on a wooded moraine that gives it its name. Here in 1853 came George Penny to verify reports of good red clay in the vicinity. He opened a brickyard and lumberyard; subsequently he produced five million bricks annually, sharply under-selling Philadelphia on the Chicago market. Admiring townspeople named their new community Pennyville. When Penny protested, they yielded only so far as to rename it Brickton. Gradually the clay deposits were exhausted and with the coming of the Chicago & North Western Railway, Brickton marked its transition from an industrial town to a commuting suburb by adopting the name of Park Ridge. The PARK RIDGE MASONIC TEMPLE, 115 N. Northwest Hwy., is the orig-inal George Penny house, built in 1854 of Penny's good red brick. The two-story rectangular building remodeled in 1928, contains some of the original furnishings. The PARK RIDGE SCHOOL FOR GIRLS (*open* 10-4 *Sundays and holidays*), N. Prospect Ave., was founded in 1876 when the Women's Committee had a $500 balance at the close of the Philadelphia Centennial. Its six cottages each house from 18 to 28 girls, and the school has its own greenhouse and 40 acres of farm land and orchard.

Park Ridge is at the junction with City US 12 (*see Tour* 9).

DES PLAINES, 13.5 *m.* (643 alt., 8,798 pop.) (*see Tour* 3), is at the junctions with US 45 (*see Tour* 3) and By-Pass US 12 (*see Tour* 9).

ARLINGTON HEIGHTS, 19 *m.* (704 alt., 4,997 pop.), was settled in the 1830's when pioneers followed an old Indian trail into the region. During June and July of each year, thousands of expectant Chicagoans follow the same trail on the early afternoon specials of the Chicago & North Western, and return, frequently somewhat subdued, on the early evening trains of the same line. Their goal is the ARLING-TON PARK RACE TRACK (*grandstand* $1, *clubhouse* $2; *pari-mutuel betting*), at the western edge of town. Largest of the four major tracks in the Chicago area, Arlington, opened in 1929, has an English turf track in addition to its main one of a mile and an eighth. Here on June 30, 1932, Equipoise set a world's record by running the mile in 1 :34 2/5.

Adjoining the intersection with Dundee Road, 26.5 m., is the DEER GROVE AND CAMP REINBERG FOREST PRESERVE (R). Two small lakes (*picnicking, camping, swimming*) and a herd of deer are features of this Cook County preserve.

The main street of BARRINGTON, 29.5 m. (824 alt., 3,213 pop.), is the dividing line of Cook and Lake counties. Founded in the 1850's, Barrington pursued an orderly development as an agricultural community until the post-World War boom. Then, attracted by the pleasant hilly country nearby, and aware of the country-squire tradition, Chicago millionaires began purchasing established farms and transforming them into country estates. Now, according to local residents, Barrington is "all shot with millionaires." The town's industrial character is inconspicuous, scarcely discernible behind landscaping and other camouflage. On the highway (R), at the northeastern edge of town, is the JEWEL TEA COMPANY PLANT (*2-hour tours conducted weekdays, 8-4:30*), a modern building of classic lines set in extensive landscaped grounds. The tour of the plant includes the coffee, tea, research, miscellaneous products, and packaging departments. Most novel of Barrington's industrial concerns is a corporation that manufactures tableware, vases, and similar products from a metal that simulates gold and has the strength of steel. The metal's formula, developed by Carl von Malmborg, is a carefully guarded secret.

West of Barrington the country becomes more heavily wooded, with pastures and wood lots predominating.

FOX RIVER GROVE, 34.5 m. (771 alt., 641 pop.), a summer home and resort town, stretches along the tree-bordered Fox River. A SKI HILL, at the eastern limits of the village, is the scene of an important one-day meet held in January ($1 *adm. includes parking space*) by the Norge Ski Club. Often viewed by as many as 20,000 spectators, the meet attracts the best skiers from the Northwest and other parts of the country. The property is owned by the club, which allows the public the free use of the hill except when meets are in progress.

The FOX RIVER, 35 m., is here the dividing line between Fox River Grove and CARY, 35.5 m. (811 alt., 731 pop.). Bordering the river (L) at the southern edge of the village is the CARY COUNTRY CLUB (18 *holes, daily fee*). Adjoining is the JOHN D. HERTZ FARM (*private*), home of a racing stable that includes Reigh Count, winner of the 1928 Kentucky Derby.

At 35 m. is the junction with State 31.

Left on State 31 to the junction with a graveled road, 2.3 m.; L. here to the junction with a second graveled road, 3.9 m.; R. here to CAMP ALGONQUIN (L), 4.7 m., on the banks of the Fox River, maintained by United Charities and the

Chicago *Tribune* as a summer camp for mothers and children from Chicago slums. The camp consists of a group of small houses and cottages clustered about a larger building, used as a dining hall and recreation center. Wholesome food, rest, and supervised exercise make up the daily schedule; swimming and boating are featured sports. Games, reading, and other amusements are planned for the children in the evening. Camp Algonquin cares for 380 persons at a time. Eighty undernourished youngsters spend the entire summer here; the balance of the quota are given two-week vacations.

CRYSTAL LAKE, 42 *m.* (875 alt., 3,732 pop.), deploys fan-wise from a central park. Like many other communities in this vicinity, Crystal Lake was first settled shortly after the opening of the Erie Canal (1825). When the Chicago & North Western laid its tracks two miles to the northeast, the village expanded, absorbing the new depot hamlet of Nunda that threatened its existence. The well-wooded shores of CRYSTAL LAKE (*fishing, boating, swimming*) at the south-western edge of town are dotted with numerous cottages and summer homes.

WOODSTOCK, 50 *m.* (943 alt., 5,471 pop.), was named for the Vermont town from which many of its first settlers came, in the 1830's and 1840's. Seat of McHenry County since 1844, the town is built around a square, on which are a number of Civil War monuments and a venerable spring house. The WOODSTOCK TYPEWRITER COMPANY PLANT (*apply at office*), 300 Seminary St., is that company's main plant. Largest factory in Woodstock, it manufactures typewriters that are sold extensively here and abroad. The tree-covered campus of the TODD SCHOOL FOR BOYS, 300 McHenry Ave., is surrounded by a high iron fence. The school was established by the Rev. Richard Todd, who came to the raw Middle Border in 1848 from Princeton University. Including the elementary grades and four years of advanced study, the course is based on the theory that every boy is a creator. Its dramatic branch is excellent; one alumnus is Orson Welles, a director-actor of stage and radio fame.

HARVARD, 62.5 *m.* (908 alt., 2,988 pop.), is entered from the south over the tracks of the Chicago & North Western, which brought a little boom to the town with its arrival in 1856. Harvard is now the junction point for two branches of the line. In recent years more and more Chicagoans have been taking advantage of the low rents in the nearby lake country and the rapid commuting service of the railroad, and Harvard, sixty miles out of the city, may eventually become a long-range suburb of the metropolis.

The STARLINE MODEL DAIRY FARM, at the town's northern limits, features an all-steel barn and a horizontal silo that has no post supports. The farm serves as a practical laboratory for the dairy equipment developed by the Harvard plant.

US 14 crosses the Wisconsin Line, 68 *m.*, 3 miles S. of Walworth, Wisconsin (*see Wisconsin Guide*).

TOUR 11

Concrete roadbed throughout; four lanes between Chicago and Elgin; two lanes between Elgin and Dubuque.

Chicago & North Western Ry. parallels US 20 between Chicago and Freeport.

Usual accommodations between Chicago and Freeport; good cabin camps between Freeport and East Dubuque.

US 20 crosses northern Illinois from Lake Michigan to the Mississippi River, traversing a region rich in historical associations closely linked with its topography. In its eastern half the highway crosses the most recently glaciated part of the State, a rolling country of fields and woodlands, low morainic ridges and frequently marshy depressions. The irregular, poorly drained land, with extensive areas suitable only for pasture or woodland, coupled with its nearness to large urban markets, makes this northeastern section the important dairy region of Illinois.

Elgin and Rockford, manufacturing centers of national consequence, lie in the broad valleys of the Fox and Rock Rivers—glacial outlet channels carved by the outpouring torrents of the Wisconsin ice sheet. Their industrial development stems from early utilization of local water power.

Section a. Indiana Line to Rockford, 105 m.

US 20 crosses the Indiana Line, here the Chicago city limits, 0 m., from Hammond, Indiana (see Indiana Guide), and proceeds northwest along Indianapolis Blvd. to Ewing Ave.; R. on Ewing Ave. to 95th St.; L. on 95th St.

At the intersection of 95th St. and Stony Island Ave., 4 m., is the junction with US 330 (see Tour 12A). Here the route divides into City US 20 and By-Pass US 20.

Left (straight ahead) on By-Pass US 20 to a junction with US 45 (see Tour 3), 13.5 m.; R. on US 45, with which By-Pass US 20 is united for 13 miles (see Tour 3), to the western junction with City US 20 (see below), 26.5 m.

City US 20 proceeds north along Stony Island Ave. to the inter-

section of Michigan Blvd. with Jackson Blvd., the center of Chicago.
CHICAGO, 16.5 *m.* (598 alt., 3,376,438 pop.) (*see Chicago*).

Points of Interest: Chicago Board of Trade Building, Union Stock Yards, Field
Museum of Natural History, Art Institute of Chicago, Museum of Science and
Industry, Adler Planetarium, Shedd Aquarium, University of Chicago, and
others.

In Chicago are junctions with State 1 (*see Tour* 1), State 42 (*see
Tour* 2), US 41 (*see Tour* 2A), US 12 (*see Tour* 9), US 14 (*see Tour*
10), US 330 (*see Tour* 12A), US 66 (*see Tour* 17), and the Illinois
Waterway (*see Tour* 22).

North on Michigan Blvd. to Washington Blvd., 16.8 *m.;* L. on
Washington Blvd. to the Chicago city limits, 25 *m.*

OAK PARK, 27 *m.* (630 alt., 63,982 pop.), is the largest community with village form of government in the United States. Appropriately named for its natural growth of oaks, Oak Park was first
settled in 1833 by Joseph Kettlestrings, who came with his wife in an
ox-drawn covered wagon from Baltimore, Maryland. Their descendants, and those of other early settlers, hold prominent positions in the
social and civic life of the community.

Almost since its inception Oak Park has been "bone dry" and well
governed. For 50 years the village fathers fought for local option so
that saloons might be legally barred. This the legislature was not empowered to grant until the passage of an enabling act in 1907. By that
time local option was scarcely needed, so "dry" was Oak Park in
sentiment and fact. Deeds to much of the land within the corporate
limits and beyond contained anti-saloon clauses inserted by the original
owners. During the fight tavern after tavern had been purchased and
their stock poured into the gutter.

The form of government has been simple and direct. Fathers of the
village are six trustees, who direct all municipal affairs. By a tacit
understanding among its citizens, the village is divided into six sections, and membership in the board is apportioned equally. All department heads (except the village clerk and village treasurer, who, with
the board, are elected by the people) are appointed by the trustees.
Authority is direct and responsibility is clear.

Known in the 1890's as Saints' Rest because of its many churches,
now even more numerous, Oak Park traditionally centers its social life
in its homes and churches, schools and charitable organizations.

Oak Park and adjacent River Forest were the early workshops of
Frank Lloyd Wright (b. 1869), and today constitute a gallery of his
distinguished architecture. He resided in the FRANK LLOYD WRIGHT
HOUSE (*private*), Forest and Chicago Aves., the nucleus of which was
built in 1891. Frame houses designed by Wright at the outset of his
career stand on the south side of Chicago Avenue in the 1000 block
and at 1030 Superior Ave. Though not illustrative of his mature style,

these structures foreshadow his break with the closed volume mode of building.

The evolution of Wright's philosophy of open planning and harmony of site and structure is documented by a series of Oak Park houses (*all private residences*), several of which are along Forest Avenue. The N. G. MOORE HOUSE (1894), 329 Forest Ave., is a compromise between Wright's ideas and Mr. Moore's taste for half-timbered English cottages. Next door is the more typical HILLS HOUSE (1906). Others include the ARTHUR HEURTLEY HOUSE (1902), 312 Forest Ave., at the rear of which is the finest and oldest of the magnificent oaks along Forest Avenue; the GALE HOUSE (1905), 6 Elizabeth Court; and the BEACHY HOUSE (1906), 238 Forest Ave.

The THOMAS HOUSE (1904), 210 Forest Ave., is typical of Wright's prairie style and his use of plaster over wood. All rooms are above the terrace level; there is no basement. The strong horizontal lines of the structure flow into the carefully graded, landscaped setting. The Thomas House is on the site of the Protestant Episcopal Church from which the Rev. Charles P. Anderson was called to the bishopric of Chicago.

The CELEBRITY ROOM of the Blue Parrot Patio, a tea house at 1120 Westgate Ave., is furnished and decorated by student-apprentices from Wright's summer home and colony, Taliesen, at Spring Green, Wisconsin. Silhouetted in black on lemon-yellow walls are the local houses that Mr. Wright includes in his canon of notable buildings. These include the Winslow House in River Forest, and Unity Temple and the Heurtley House in Oak Park. A mammoth scrapbook designed by a Taliesen apprentice contains biographical clippings concerning other Oak Park sons and daughters who have found their way into *Who's Who:* Ernest Hemingway and Janet Lewis, novelists; Doris Humphrey, the dancer; Dr. William E. Barton, clergyman and Lincoln scholar; his son, Bruce Barton, journalist and politician; Louis Caldwell, head of the bureau of radio law in Washington, D. C.; and various artists and musicians.

UNITY TEMPLE, Universalist Church at Lake and Grove Sts., is a notable interpretation of the cubic form. Designed by Wright and built in 1905, it has been termed the first concrete monolith in the world. Molded concrete gives the appearance and strength of stone blocks and columns. Such harmony is there of color, design, and form that the lack of a steeple is seldom noticed; Wright considers the spire a false symbol—the "lifting of a finger to a terrible God."

The FIRST CONGREGATIONAL CHURCH (1918), Lake St. and Kenilworth Ave., designed by Norman S. Patton, is of unusual architectural and historic interest. The square buttressed tower on the façade resembles those of English parish churches, while the main body of the church is patterned after the Gothic chapels of Oxford and Cambridge. Of rare beauty is the stained glass in the rose windows of the nave, in the clerestory windows, and in the lancet windows of the ambulatories. Throughout the church are numerous tablets and relics of significance. In the middle of the foyer is a column from the spire of Boston's celebrated Old North Church.

A fine Biblical museum, in the basement toward the rear of the church, houses the collection of Dr. William E. Barton, pastor 1899-1924, and part of the Jerusalem Exhibit of the St. Louis Exposition of 1904. The collections include domestic and agricultural implements of the Holy Land and relics of the early Christian Church. Such treasures as a Pentateuch, said to have been copied by a Samaritan priest from the oldest Biblical manuscript extant, and an undated painting of St. John the Divine, believed to have been done by a Russian before the days of oil paint, are in the pastor's study on the second floor.

In addition to public schools of high national rating, Oak Park has three Roman Catholic institutions directed by the Dominican Order: SAINT EDMUNDS, Oak Park Ave. and Pleasant St., built in 1910 and modeled after the Palais de Justice at Rouen; the BISHOP QUARTER BOARDING SCHOOL FOR BOYS, 605 Lake St., named for the Rt. Rev. William Quarter, a native of Ireland, who in 1844 became the first bishop of the diocese of Chicago; and FENWICK HIGH SCHOOL, Washington Blvd. and East Ave., of modified Gothic design.

Three local charitable institutions are of primary social value. HEPHZIBAH HOME, 946 North Blvd., equipped with library, infirmary, doll room, dining room, kindergarten, and four dormitories, has cared for orphans of nearby communities since 1897. OAK PARK AND RIVER FOREST DAY NURSERY, a brick and stone English cottage style building at Maple Ave. and Randolph St., cares for 30 children of employed mothers. The ECONOMY SHOP, South Blvd. and Grove Ave., a clearing house for used articles, was organized in 1919 to help support Oak Park charities. The shop earned $100,000 in its first decade.

OAK PARK CONSERVATORY, 621 Garfield Blvd., is celebrated for its annual Chrysanthemum Show (*Nov. 20-Dec. 20, 8 a.m.-9 p.m.; other shows each month through May; adm. free*). Summer exhibits are held in the city parks. The best known of these is the rose collection of 204 varieties, shown at a Century of Progress Exposition in Chicago (1933-4), exhibited annually in the small park at Marion and Greenfield Sts.

RIVER FOREST, 27.5 m. (631 alt., 8,829 pop.), is one of Chicago's finest residential suburbs. Distinctly younger and more open in appearance than Oak Park, River Forest enjoys on a more moderate scale the grace and ease of living of its larger neighbor.

In 1836 came the first settlers—Ashbel Steele, his wife, two sons, and seven daughters. In a clearing on what is now Thatcher Avenue, Steele and his sons erected their house. The pioneer home became the center of neighborhood hospitality, and the small square piano, brought overland with much labor, lent a note of grace to frontier life. Ashbel

Steele and his family established the pattern that River Forest was to follow—decorous home life, quiet hospitality, and a minimization of commerce. Into this quiet pattern the intrusion of industry has been neither long nor significant. In early days, previous even to the settlement of Steele, a sawmill and gristmill were built (1833) on the east side of the river, north of what is now Lake Street. This mill, the only one for 40 miles around, finished much of the lumber that went into the building of early Chicago. Today, rigorous zoning laws limit commerce and industry to a few small businesses along Lake Street, a few blocks east of the old mill site. Not even a movie house disturbs the residential calm of River Forest.

Early communication with Chicago was by means of the old Frink & Walker stagecoach. Drawn by four horses, it carried ten passengers —nine inside and one on top with the driver. The fare was fifty cents for adults, twenty-five cents for children. Lake Street had ruts hub deep, and there were no roads running north and south between River Forest and Chicago, nothing but trails leading to the several settlements. In 1849 the Galena & Chicago Union Railroad laid a single track of strap iron along the old stage route as far west as Elmhurst. The rails were wooden riders sheathed in iron; the ties were small and widely spaced. Wood was used for fuel and stored in long sheds along the right-of-way, and the small boilers of the engines necessitated the placing of water tanks every few miles. The first station was a freight car, heated with a small wood-burning stove.

Associated with the railroad, though he arrived more than a decade later, was Daniel Cunningham Thatcher, for whom one of the streets of River Forest is named. Formerly a Chicago business man, Thatcher retired to River Forest in 1854. Two years later he purchased a section of land near the Des Plaines River and built a house. The land is now known as Thatcher's Woods, and the Thatcher house (*see below*) is the oldest building in the village. In 1859 and 1860 Frances Willard (1839-1898), the temperance leader, boarded with the Thatcher family. At that time she was teaching in the lone River Forest school. In 1929 the village named one of its new schools for her.

In 1862 Thatcher persuaded the Chicago & North Western Railway to build a station on his property. The station was called Thatcher, and River Forest was known by that name until 1872, when the present name was adopted. On October 24, 1880, the community was organized as the Village of River Forest. The village seal, bearing the motto, *Silva in Flumine* (Lat., forest on the river), attests its attractive site.

The old THATCHER HOUSE (*open daily, free*), 511 Edgewood Place, houses the Trailside Museum of Natural History, which is under the supervision of the Chicago Academy of Science. The collections, planned to show the phylogenic relationships of the several life forms, are composed of invertebrates, fish, amphibians, reptiles, birds, and mammals. A geological exhibit comprises fossils from local quarries, cross-sections of underlying formations, and studies in rock structure. Assisting the curator and his two part-time assistants is a junior staff of 15 boys and girls, 12 to 18 years of age, who receive training in biology, geology, and museum methods. Facilities include a small reference library and a microscope with prepared slides.

ROSARY COLLEGE, Forest Ave. and Division St., a fully accredited Roman Catholic liberal arts institution for women, was opened in River Forest in 1922. The board of trustees consists of five sisters of the order of St. Dominic. The Gothic buildings, of Bedford stone, designed by Ralph Adams Cram, show to the best possible advantage against the natural beauty of the forest campus. CENTRAL HALL (1925) has a cloister walk extending its entire length; it contains the chapel, library, refectory, and social hall. LEWIS MEMORIAL HALL houses a little theater, exhibition gallery, and portrait studios. Collections include paintings, tapestries, and period furniture, contributed by Mrs. Edward Hines of Evanston. The MOTHER EMILY POWER MEMORIAL HALL, the students' dormitory, contains the gymnasium and a glass-roofed swimming pool.

In 1925 Rosary College inaugurated its Foreign Study Plan, whereby students, preferably in their junior year, can spend a year in Fribourg, Switzerland, at the Institut de Haute Etudes. In 1934 the Rosary College Program of Education for Leisure, without fees, was started. Since its inception more than 1,000 adults have taken advantage of the plan to further their education.

CONCORDIA TEACHERS COLLEGE, Bonnie Brae and Division Sts., is maintained by the Missouri Synod of the Evangelical Lutheran Church to train teachers for Lutheran elementary schools. The first group of buildings was dedicated in 1913. In these, as in all later buildings, yellow brick has been used, resulting in a pleasing harmony, heightened by a studied arrangement.

There is a library of 18,000 volumes, an art collection of 3,800 mounted prints, and a natural history museum. A teaching staff of 20 gives instruction to approximately 400 students.

The DOMINICAN HOUSE OF STUDIES (*reception rooms and daily Mass open to public; Christmas Eve Mass by invitation*), Division St. and Harlem Ave., is a preparatory college fitting students for the Dominican priesthood. The single college building, of stone, sharply etched against the well-kept lawn of the treeless 40-acre campus, is cruciform in plan.

Among the Frank Lloyd Wright houses in River Forest are the WINSLOW HOUSE (1893), or Auvergne Lodge, on Auvergne Place, one of his first buildings; and the ELIZABETH ROBERTS HOUSE (1906), on Edgewood Place (*both private*). Each house reveals Wright's desire to harmonize his buildings with the terrain, to recognize and accentuate the "natural beauty of the plain, its quiet level." The RIVER FOREST TENNIS CLUB (*private*), 615 Lathrop Ave., and the RICHARD

W. Bock Studio (*private*), 7820 Chicago Ave., both built in 1906, are other examples of Wright's work.

The River Forest Women's Clubhouse (1913), 526 N. Ashland Ave., was the first women's club building in the State. Harlem House, Lake and Williams Sts., now a bottling works, is a landmark from the turnpike days of Lake Street, when it served as a combination post office, drug store, and hotel. In the 1870's it was also a tavern and grocery.

MAYWOOD, 28.8 *m.* (628 alt., 25,829 pop.), a suburban community centering in a factory district along the railroad, developed in the 1880's, when industrial growth of the west Chicago area created demands for homesites. It now has various district neighborhood patterns, all harmonious but racially different.

MELROSE PARK, 29.9 *m.* (617 alt., 10,741 pop.), is essentially a residential city. Its factory population, almost half Italian, is employed in nearby manufacturing districts.

At 31.5 *m.* is the western junction with By-Pass US 20 (*see above*) and US 45 (*see Tour 3*).

Bordering the highway (L) for three miles are the Proviso Yards of the Chicago & North Western Railway. The best view is from the entrance to the yards, reached by a half-mile concrete drive (L) marked Blind Road, 33.2 *m.* The Proviso Yards, sometimes called the "Hump" because of the incline controlling switching operations, are the largest railroad yards in the world—three miles long and one-half mile wide, 960 acres in area. By means of an electrically operated system, aided by gravity, the old method of switching by engine crews is eliminated and in a single operation freight cars are distributed and classified on 59 tracks. Through-freight is saved 12 hours in shipping time, and cars for other destinations need no longer go into Chicago, but are delivered directly to the Outer Belt Line.

The operations of the yards appear chaotic, yet extreme precision and accuracy govern each maneuver. Puffing locomotives back long trains to the crest of the hump. Brakemen uncouple the cars, releasing them for their gravity run down an incline that drops 18 feet in 300 yards. From a tower nearby an operator presses a lever regulating the electric retarders. The same operator manipulates the electric switching apparatus, sending each car to its appointed track. The cars are then picked up by locomotives for assembly into out-going trains. Each of the 59 tracks has a capacity of 70 cars; the yard can classify and handle 4,000 cars daily. It is brilliantly lighted at night, permitting 24-hour operation. Refrigerator cars are served by a modern high-speed ice plant. The engine terminal roundhouse has stalls for 58 locomotives and a system of water tanks supplied by a 2,100-foot well.

Freight cars passing through the yards are checked for dry bearings, cracked wheels, and other defects. At the warehouse great motor caravans empty their loads into tractor truck trains, which dart along the tracks delivering merchandise to designated cars. High speed and accuracy prevent shipments from accumulating.

At 33.6 *m.*, is a junction with Mount Prospect Road.

Right on Mount Prospect Road to AHLERS MILL (*open*), 1.7 *m.*, in Mount Emblem Masonic Cemetery. Oldest and most notable of three Dutch-type mills in the vicinity, it was erected in 1850 as a gristmill. A venerable landmark, the mill is most impressive at night when its great wings are lighted. The base of the five-story tower is of massive stone; the superstructure is of hand-hewn timbers. The interior has been developed as an educational exhibit. All the working parts except the millstones are of wood. Two workmen brought from the Netherlands required six months to complete the great cogwheel, 12 feet in diameter. Visitors can climb to the deck by stairs and ladders, observing at the several levels the sails, drive-shaft, control levers, grain and meal chutes, storage bins, and millstones. The parts are almost wholly in their original form.

The highway skirts (L) ELMHURST, 34.5 *m.* (681 alt., 14,055 pop.), named for the majestic double row of elms that extends for nearly a mile along Cottage Hill Avenue. Elmhurst was first known as Cottage Hill, for its first home, HILL COTTAGE (*private*), 415 S. York St. Built in 1843 by J. L. Hovey, the house was conducted as a hotel for farmers driving to the Chicago market from Fox River and Rock River communities.

WILDER PARK, west side of Cottage Hill Ave., south of the Chicago & North Western tracks, was laid out in 1868 as the estate of Seth Wadham, a settler of ample means, whose massive house in the center of the park is now the ELMHURST PUBLIC LIBRARY. The estate eventually pased into the possession of Thomas E. Wilder, who ceded it to the city for a nominal sum, with the provision that the house be used as a public library and the grounds as a public park.

Across from Wilder Park is ELMHURST COLLEGE, coeducational institution founded in 1871 as Elmhurst Seminary. Later it became a junior college, and in 1934 an accredited four-year school. OLD MAIN HALL and OLD MUSIC HALL, the original buildings, are still in use, along with newer dormitories, a library, and gymnasium.

Elmhurst has been the home of Carl Sandburg, who for some time lived in the old TORODE HOUSE, 333 S. York St. Jens Christian Bay, author and head of the John Crerar Library in Chicago, and Rosamond du Sardin, novelist, reside in Elmhurst.

ADDISON, 37.5 *m.* (689 alt., 916 pop.), a quiet old village, has been a stronghold of the German Lutheran faith since the 1840's. Named for the eighteenth-century essayist, Joseph Addison, it is of interest for its religious institutions and its century-old houses. Several of the latter, still in use, are along the highway, as is the POST OFFICE, which dates from 1852.

At the junction of Addison and Army Trail Roads with US 20 is the KINDERHEIM (*open* 2-4 *daily*), a two-story brick building, to which children of Lutheran parentage are admitted on recommendation of the Chicago Juvenile Court. Founded in 1902 by the Rev. Augustus Schlechte, the Kinderheim functions as an industrial and domestic training school for some 240 boys and girls.

Adjoining the Kinderheim is the 41-acre tract of the EVANGELICAL LUTHERAN HOME, an orphanage. Those of school age attend St. Paul's Parochial School. After graduation and confirmation boys are given work on farms or in greenhouses, girls in supervised homes. More than 1,250 children have been provided for and launched upon self-supporting careers since the home's inception in 1873.

At 38.3 m. is the junction with Mill Road.

1. Right on Mill Road to the old HEIDEMAN MILL (*private*), 0.5 m. Now a notable landmark, it was built as a grist-mill in 1867, and was in use until 1929. Its 75-foot sailspread, reaching to within 20 feet of the ground, is visible for some distance. The mill tower is octagonal, 30 feet wide at the base and tapering to 15 feet at the top. Its revolving arms are closely latticed to hold the canvas.

2. Left on Mill Road to the WMBI TRANSMITTER (5,000 w.), 0.5 m., "the Voice of the Moody Bible Institute." Nearby is a cemetery of the 1830's. A large boulder near the roadside marks the GRAVES OF SOLDIERS OF GENERAL SCOTT'S ARMY who died during their march along this route in the Black Hawk War (1832).

West of Mill Road US 20 passes through a suburban region of golf and country clubs, farm lands and wooded marshes, local real estate developments, and the village of BLOOMINGDALE.

At 47 m. the highway skirts (L) the hamlet of ONTARIO-VILLE.

Left from Ontarioville, on the main graveled road running due south, to the ILLINOIS PET CEMETERY, 1.7 m. Here are buried canaries, dogs, cats, monkeys, and rabbits. Funerals follow a fixed routine. Birds and other small animals are buried in white plush boxes, larger animals in gray and silver-pine caskets. The hearse is a seven-passenger car, with a compartment for the dead pet. The tract of six acres, in charge of a caretaker, contains numerous granite monuments, appropriately engraved. Some have inlaid photographs of the pet. A cross marks the grave of a dog that saved its master's life.

Between Ontarioville and Elgin US 20 passes numerous dairy farms. At 50.8 m. the WGN TRANSMITTER (50 kw.) occupies a low Spanish-type building (R), flanked by tall towers, visible for some distance along the highway. Across the road, and slightly west, is the VILLA OLIVIA GOLF COURSE AND SWIMMING POOL (*open; greens fee 75c weekdays, $1 Saturdays, $1.50 Sundays and holidays*).

ELGIN, 54 m. (717 alt., 35,929 pop.) (*see Elgin*).
Points of Interest: Laura Davidson Sears Academy of Fine Arts, Elgin National Watch Factory, Elgin Watch Observatory, David C. Cook Publishing House, Northern Illinois State Hospital, and others.

Right from Elgin on State 31 to the YEOMEN CITY OF CHILDHOOD (*open*),

4 *m.*, a home and primary school for orphaned children of members of the Fraternal Order of Yeomen of America. Boys and girls between the ages of three and twelve are here admitted to a family-like environment. Later they attend high schools and trade schools in nearby communities. Three cottages accommodating 60 children comprise the main buildings. Recreational facilities on the 650-acre campus include a log cabin, swimming pool, and two artificial lakes stocked with fish.

WEST DUNDEE, 4.8 *m.* (739 alt., 1,697 pop.), was settled by Scots and English in the 1830's, and named for Dundee, Scotland. Allan Pinkerton (1819-84) immigrated to West Dundee from Glasgow in 1843, and established a cooper shop. While searching the country-side for wood to make barrel staves and hoops, Pinkerton found evidence of counterfeiting on an island in the Fox River. When transmitted to the sheriff, this information resulted in the capture of several counterfeiters. Pinkerton's talent for deduction was shortly afterwards rewarded by his appointment as deputy sheriff of Kane County. In 1850 he became Chicago's first detective.

Pinkerton's abolitionist activities in West Dundee are said to have brought about an early acquaintance with Abraham Lincoln. In 1861, as chief of the national detective agency that bears his name, Pinkerton prevented an attempt to assassinate Lincoln in Baltimore, Maryland. Lincoln subsequently commissioned Pinkerton to organize and direct the Secret Service Division of the Union Army, from which developed the U. S. Secret Service. The SITE OF PINKERTON'S COOPERAGE is at 3rd and Main Sts.

Right from West Dundee, across the Fox River, is EAST DUNDEE, 0.7 *m.* (739 alt., 1,341 pop.), a village settled largely by emigrants who left Germany because of the 1848 Revolution. Scottish and British antipathy against German neighbors prevented East and West Dundee from being organized as one community. Today, despite a homogeneous population, the two villages retain individual governments.

The HAEGER POTTERIES (*open* 8-4, *Mon.-Fri.*), 45 Maiden Lane, East Dundee, produce pottery and lamp bases. The clay is mixed by machine, shaped in plaster molds, and baked in gas and oil-fired kilns. A working unit of the Haeger Potteries was exhibited at the Century of Progress Exposition in Chicago (1933-34).

CARPENTERSVILLE, 5.5 *m.* (805 alt., 1,461 pop.), was settled in 1834 by young Angelo Carpenter of Uxbridge, Massachusetts, and his father and uncle. In the decades that followed, Carpenter all but built the settlement singlehanded. He established a sawmill, a grist-mill, a woolen mill, and a grocery store. In 1851 he platted Carpentersville. One of the enterprises with which he was associated, the Illinois Iron and Bolt Company, is the economic mainstay of the community.

In his later years Carpenter gave land and houses to less affluent townsmen, and engaged in philanthropies that were continued by his widow after his death in 1880. Among these are CARPENTER PARK, on the eastern edge of Carpentersville, and CARPENTER MEMORIAL HALL, a one-story brick building on Grove Street in which the public library is housed.

West of Elgin, which marks the northeastern border of the Chicago urban area, the landscape is essentially rural. Crossroad communities serve nearby farms. The only cities of consequence are Rockford, Freeport, and Galena. Between Elgin and Rockford US 20 crosses a rolling country of poorly drained fields, pastures, and woodlands, a region of intensive dairy farming.

HENPECK, 68 *m.*, identified by a church, tavern, and service station at a curve in the highway, was once an important stop on the old

Chicago-Galena stage road. The hamlet dates from a log cabin built in 1836 by Tenas Allen. During the Galena lead rush of the late 1830's and early 1840's as many as fifty men encamped here overnight. At the time of the Civil War, Henpeck had a post office, shops, and a population of more than a hundred. The country road that turns left from Henpeck follows the route of the old Galena Trail, also known as the Grant Trail.

The dominance of dairying throughout this region is everywhere apparent in herds of fine dairy cattle, large red barns, tall silos, and uniformly well-kept farmsteads. Croplands are largely in corn, with extensive areas in hay and pasture. In contrast with agricultural practices in central Illinois, where corn and other grains are harvested as cash crops, most of the corn in this region is cut before maturity for use as silage.

MARENGO, 77.4 *m.* (819 alt., 1,948 pop.), is noteworthy for its elm-arched roadway and the McGILL METAL PRODUCTS PLANT (*no visitors*), 127 E. Prairie St., one of the world's largest manufactories of mousetraps. Marengo is the birthplace of Egbert Van Alstyne, composer of "In the Shade of the Old Apple Tree," "Memories," "Little Church in the Valley," "My Pony Boy," and "Drifting and Dreaming."

The crossroads community of GARDEN PRAIRIE, 83.3 *m.* and the SITE OF AMESVILLE, two miles west, bear witness to an oft-repeated pioneer squabble between the beneficiaries of the old stagecoach lines and the early railroads. Garden Prairie came into being in 1849 when the Galena & Chicago Union Railroad built its station in the settlement rather than in Amesville, because of the refusal of one Ames, whose business came from the stagecoach trade, to allow its erection near his tavern. Part of the AMES TAVERN (1835) is incorporated in the frame residence, 84.9 *m.*

BELVIDERE, 89.5 *m.* (778 alt., 8,123 pop.), in the valley of the Kishawaukee River, was founded in 1836. Today a commercial and manufacturing city of diversified interests—the NATIONAL SEWING MACHINE PLANT, State St. and the river, dates from 1879—Belvidere was of early significance as a principal stop on the Chicago-Galena stage route. Among those who lent color to the young community was Big Thunder, a Potawatomi chief. So popular was he that after his death his body lay in state in a small stockade near the site of the present courthouse. Soon the chief's knife, tobacco, and most of his clothing disappeared. In course of time even his bones were filched by souvenir hunters, who, passing through the town by stagecoach, visited the stockade while the horses were being changed. But the young men of the village, wishing to keep the stockade attractive to tipping travelers, obtained a supply of sheep and hog bones and solemnly distributed them to curio collectors as part of the remains of Big Thunder. A memorial boulder on the grounds of the Boone County Courthouse, facing City Park, marks the GRAVE OF BIG THUNDER.

ROCKFORD, 105 *m.* (720 alt., 85,864 pop.) (*see Rockford*).

Points of Interest: Rockford College, Swiss College, Harry and Della Burpee Art Gallery, Effigy Mounds, and others.

In Rockford are junctions with US 51 (*see Tour* 4) and State 2 (*see Tour* 4A).

Section b. Rockford to Iowa Line, 93 m.

West of Rockford, 0 *m.,* US 20 crosses first the rolling hill lands of the Pecatonica Valley, a region of old glacial drift, then the sharply dissected driftless area of Jo Daviess County, part of the remarkably beautiful region unaffected by glaciation that lies in southwestern Wisconsin and adjacent parts of Illinois and Iowa. Sharp profiles of ridges, mounds, and valleys, clearly etched patterns of fields and woodlands varying in color and tone as the hour of the day or season of the year indicate, are revealed in panoramas as the highway follows a ridge crest, or are hidden from view as the road dips and winds through forested valleys.

This westernmost section is the old lead mining country, one of the earliest developed parts of Illinois. The mineral veins lie just below the upland level, exposed in the countless tributary valleys of the Galena and Mississippi rivers. The region abounds in landmarks of the frontier; the highway often approximates the old Galena stage route. Indeed, US 20 throughout much of its course follows closely this pioneer road, broken more than a century ago by the lumbering oxcarts that carried east-bound lead from the Nation's most productive mines to the young port of Chicago. Today richer fields have forced the mines from a competitive market, and little remains of the old days save the quiet little city of Galena and the enduring loveliness of the countryside.

An entrance (L), 14.3 *m.,* leads to the SEWARD FOREST PRESERVE (*open 7 a.m.-9 p.m.; picnic facilities; no camping*), attractively developed as a small park. The mile and a half graveled road, recently landscaped, leads through and across a forested valley in which flows a small brook. Stone bridges and embankments, fireplaces and shelter house are in keeping with the wilderness aspect of the park. A children's playground, on the grassy meadow of the valley, is well equipped.

FREEPORT, 28.6 *m.* (781 alt., 22,045 pop.), seat of Stephenson County, was first settled in 1835 by William "Tutty" Baker and his wife. Legend accounts for its maritime name in a land-locked community. The generosity of Baker, who freely shared his meals with all comers, was supposedly not shared by his wife, who objected, saying: "Look here, this place is getting to be a regular free port for everybody coming along the trail. You'd better call your new town 'Freeport,' for that is what it will be if you run it."

Freeport was settled in large part by unsuccessful miners returning east from the Galena lead region, among them many Pennsylvania Germans. Primarily an agricultural trading center, Freeport entered an industrial phase in 1853 when the Galena and Chicago Union Railroad reached the city from the east. Today a number of small plants produce or process a variety of manufactured goods.

On the courthouse lawn, at the junction of US 20 and State 75, is a CIVIL WAR MONUMENT, erected 1869. The tall stone shaft, surmounted with a bronze figure, stands upon a high base; on the four corners are life-size figures of a Civil War sailor, militiaman, cavalryman, and artilleryman. Engraved on each side of the base are the names of battles in which volunteers from Stephenson County fought; on a bronze plaque are recorded their names. Near the entrance of the courthouse is a tablet commemorating Col. Benjamin Stephenson, Illinois militiaman of 1812, who in 1816 negotiated a treaty that brought ten million acres into Illinois.

The National Iris Society has twice held its annual show in Freeport. The QUALITY GARDENS (*open upon application*), 871 W. Stephenson St., are among the city's most noteworthy. The blooming season is the latter part of May and early June.

A memorial boulder, N. State Ave. and E. Douglas St., marks the SITE OF THE SECOND LINCOLN-DOUGLAS DEBATE (August 27, 1858). Inscribed on a plaque are two quotations from the debate: Lincoln's, "This government cannot endure permanently half slave and half free," and Douglas', "I am not for the dissolution of the Union under any circumstance." Leonard Crunelle's statue, LINCOLN THE DEBATER, a fine bronze donated by W. T. Raleigh, stands just within the entrance to Taylor's Park, a mile east of the courthouse on State 75.

At Freeport is a junction with State 26.

Right on State 26 to CEDARVILLE, 5.2 *m.*; L. three blocks from the crest of the hill and R. to the end of the road to the BIRTHPLACE OF JANE ADDAMS (*private*) 5.9 *m.* The two-story, spacious, brick house, Greek revival in design, was built in 1850 by her parents, John and Sarah Addams. Here, with eight brothers and sisters, Jane Addams (1860-1935) grew to womanhood among surroundings far removed from those of Chicago's Hull House, where in later life she won international acclaim.

The homestead consists of 450 acres of meadow, woodland, and cultivated fields. Cedar Creek winds through the farm, passing close by the barn, built in 1848, where are three millstones and other relics of early days. Near the site of the mill operated by John Addams are two limestone caves in a vine-covered cliff. Towering old elms enhance the quiet beauty of fields and stream.

The homestead is now owned by Marcet Haldeman-Julius, niece of Jane Addams. Members of the Haldeman-Julius family spend their summers here and with the help of tenants operate the farm. In the family burial plot, some 1,200 feet west of the house, is the GRAVE OF JANE ADDAMS.

At 40.4 *m.* is a junction with State 73.

Right on State 73 to LENA, 1.7 *m.* (964 alt., 1,145 pop.), one of the few places in the United States where there are manufactured such foreign types of cheese as Camembert and Brie.

At 43.3 *m.* is a junction with a graveled road, identified by a marker.

Left on this road to the BATTLEFIELD OF KELLOGS GROVE (*picnic facilities*), 4.2 *m.* The grove, developed as a small park on the crest of a low hill, commands a magnificent view of the surrounding countryside. A granite shaft, surmounted with cannon balls, marks the site of the battle, fought on June 25, 1832, between Black Hawk's forces and those commanded by Col. John Dement. Within the iron fence that surrounds the monument are 25 small bronze plates, commemorating the volunteers killed in the encounter.

Immediately west of the junction the country becomes noticeably more rolling as the highway enters the deeply dissected, unglaciated region of Jo Daviess County, a land of far horizons, of ever-changing hills and valleys revealed in grand panoramas.

At 48.5 *m.* is the junction with State 78 (*see Tour* 5), which unites with US 20 for 2 miles.

STOCKTON, 50.5 *m.* (1,000 alt., 1,505 pop.), was named by Alanson Parker, an early settler, who envisaged the fertile prairie country as a stock raising center. In the latter decades of the nineteenth century this promise was realized. Then, with the development of cheap grazing land in the West and the centering of the stock yards in Chicago, it became more profitable for the farmers of this district to fatten cattle for market than to raise them.

Before this, however, Stockton had had its great days of another kind. Its lead smelters were running full blast. Money was plentiful, and soon spent. Today the mines of Jo Daviess County are closed and Stockton is content to look upon itself as an agricultural center.

Stockton is at the western junction with State 78 (*see Tour* 5).

The crest of TERRAPIN RIDGE, 60.8 *m.*, commands sweeping vistas to the north and east of the rolling farm lands and wooded hills, the deep, broad valleys and sharply silhouetted mounds of the Driftless Area.

On the eastern border of ELIZABETH, 62.8 *m.* (790 alt., 651 pop.), a historical marker defines the SITE OF APPLE RIVER FORT, established during the Black Hawk War. On June 24, 1832, the fort was attacked by 200 warriors, but successfully defended until relief arrived. Many such sites in this northwestern region mark skirmishes between the Indians and encroaching settlers.

At 65.5 *m.* is the junction with State 80 (*see Tour* 6).

From a ridge top a mile west is an excellent view (L) of the Apple River Valley, and (R) of the rolling hills of Illinois backed by

BITUMINOUS COAL MINER

COAL CARS

LARGE SHAFT MINE, SOUTHERN ILLINOIS

"GOPHER" MINE

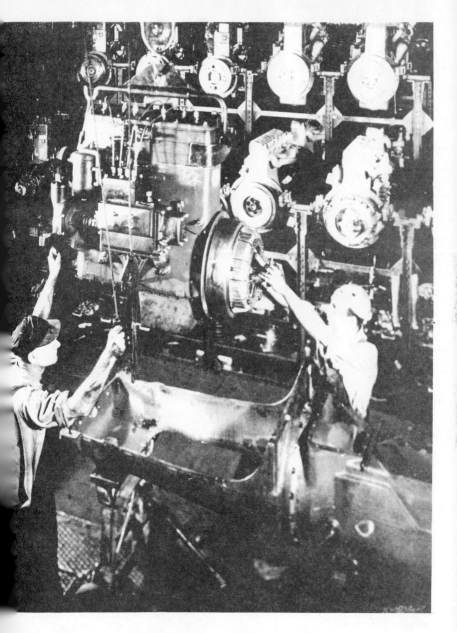

INTERNATIONAL HARVESTER PLANT

PACKING SLICED BEEF

AT ARMOUR'S

BUYING CATTLE

AT THE STOCKYARDS

NEW BOOM IN OIL

CEMENT FACTORY AT OGLESBY

HIRAM WALKER DISTILLERY, PEORIA

AMERICAN STEEL AND WIRE MILL, JOLIET

ILLINOIS RIVER LIFT BRIDGE, HARDIN

OLD AND NEW

CAHOKIA POWER PLANT

the Sinsinawa Mounds of Wisconsin. In this vicinity the highway enters what was once known as Rattlesnake Woods, now a ROADSIDE PARK (*picnicking*). The good second-growth of oak throughout this region has stimulated small-scale logging operations. Sawdust heaps, piles of seasoning lumber and cordwood, and occasional portable saw-mills and crew shacks are contemporary manifestations of the great industry that swept these hills and valleys of their virgin forests. The summit of HORSESHOE MOUND (1,070 alt.), 76 *m.*, is the highest point on the route.

GALENA, 78 *m.* (603 alt., 3,878 pop.) (*see Galena*).

Points of Interest: Grant Memorial Home, Grant Park, De Soto House, and others.

In the vicinity of Dubuque back-country roads (*inquire locally for seasonal conditions*) wind among the hills past log cabins, native stone huts, abandoned lead mines and furnaces, and Indian effigy mounds. In the fastness of the hills much corn whiskey—"Menominee dew"—was distilled during Prohibition.

Leaving the upland at 88 *m.*, the highway begins its long descent to the Mississippi bottoms, across which it winds its way along the base of the bluffs to EAST DUBUQUE, 92.5 *m.* (615 alt., 1,395 pop.), a bustling ferry landing before the construction of the highway bridge in 1887.

US 20 crosses the Iowa Line, 93 *m.*, midway on the toll bridge (*automobile and driver,* 25c; *passengers,* 5c *each*), spanning the Mississippi to Dubuque, Iowa (*see Iowa Guide*).

TOUR 12

(DYER, IND.) —JOLIET—AURORA—DIXON—FULTON—
(CLINTON, IOWA); US 30
Indiana Line to Iowa Line, 160 *m.*

Roadbed hard-surfaced throughout.
The Chicago, Burlington, & Quincy R.R. parallels US 30 between Aurora and Shabbona, the Chicago & Northwestern R.R. between Dixon and Fulton.
Usual accommodations throughout.

US 30, in its eastern section, skirts the Chicago area, avoiding the congestion of the metropolitan district. With the exception of Chicago Heights, Joliet, and Aurora, outlying industrial centers, the landscape along the route is essentially rural in character. A long-settled agricultural region, the farm lands of, northeastern Illinois are rich in legend and history, peaceful and prosperous in appearance.

Between the Fox and the Rock Rivers is the highly productive dairy and beef cattle country of northern Illinois. Corn, hay, wheat, and oats roll in long swells in the cool of spring breezes, ripen to waves of green and gold in the warmth of summer sun, or impart to the haze of early autumn their rich harvest colors. Fine beef and dairy cattle attest the wealth of the region. Sheep, hogs, and occasional flocks of goats feed in barnyards or woodland pastures.

Although much of the country crossed by US 30 was termed by Washington Irving "the Grand Prairie," this northern section of Illinois is frequently forested and generally more rolling than flat. From the lake plain of the east the highway rises and falls over the hilly, forested moraines of Will and Kane Counties, then rolls gently onward across the old drift-covered upland of western Illinois, past the valley of the Rock River, on to the gorge of the Mississippi, which it enters abruptly at Fulton.

Section a. Indiana Line to Aurora, 53 m.

US 30 crosses the Indiana Line, 0 *m.*, from Dyer, Indiana (*see Indiana Guide*). At 2.5 *m.* is a junction with US 330 (*see Tour* 12A).

The land locally is flat and wet, the bed of an old glacial lake. Drainage ditches are numerous, and fields are heavily tiled. Large areas are staked out for residential development; others are held for possible industrial expansion. Many acres are in truck.

CHICAGO HEIGHTS, 6.7 *m.* (694 alt., 22,321 pop.) (*see Tour* 1), is at a junction with State 1 (*see Tour* 1). West are more abortive suburban developments, extensive truck gardens, and wooded pasture lands.

Right of the highway at 10.5 *m.* is OLYMPIA FIELDS, a community developed in 1926 that consists exclusively of fine country homes adjacent to the 674-acre OLYMPIA FIELDS COUNTRY CLUB (*private*), distinguished for its four 18-hole golf courses. Of these, No. 4 is ranked among the five best in the United States. Here during the past eighteen years many of the championship tournaments of western and national associations have been played.

Among the million and a half dollar equipment of the club are facilities for polo, tennis, trap-shooting, and winter sports. Only life member is Charles Beach, founder of the club (1915) and promoter of Olympia Fields. His fondness for the classical Greeks explains the names of the community and of its roads, of which the principal one is Olympian Way.

The highway crosses HICKORY CREEK at 16.7 *m.*, which roughly parallels US 30 into Joliet. All communities on or north of the highway trace their origin to the old Hickory Creek settlement, which grew up in the 1820's along the winding miles of this tributary of the Des Plaines River. Indian occupancy of the section preceded the white man's coming by at least a hundred years. The Indians favored hickory wood for making bows and arrows, and stone arrowheads are yet found along the creek. Mounds and other Indian remains exist throughout the region.

At 18.2 *m.* is a junction with US 45 (*see Tour* 3). Open cultivated farm lands and heavily wooded hills alternate as the highway enters the morainic area of Will County.

The so-called LINCOLN HOTEL (*private*), 21.8 *m.,* is a red-brown brick structure (L), built in 1846 and reputedly visited by Lincoln when traveling the old Sauk Trail. The bricks, made locally, were molded by hand from mud and grass, and set in mortar made of clay from the creek. About 200 yards east of the building are excavations said to have been used as a hiding place for runaway slaves during the days of the Underground Railway.

NEW LENOX, 24.7 *m.,* is a Hickory Creek settlement of the 1820's. Its newer development, McINTOSH SUBDIVISION, on both sides of the highway, is a community of small farms, poultry yards, and kitchen gardens. The subdivision is the product of the "back to the land" movement recently popular in congested urban areas. Jessica Nelson North, in her novel of the 1930 depression, *Arden Acres,* refers to its income homes and chicken houses, equipped with latest improvements. Lots vary in size from a fraction of an acre to five acres.

At 26.9 *m.* is a junction with a graveled road, at the east end of the 18-hole CHERRY HILL GOLF COURSE (*daily greens fee*).

Right on this road, immediately over the steep railway embankment, is GOUGARS, 0.1 *m.,* site of the first post office in Will County (1832) and "downtown" for the entire Hickory Creek settlement. Today only the farm buildings of the fourth generation of the Gougar family remain.

The GOUGAR FARMHOUSE (L), immediately across the tracks, occupies the site of the original Gougar log cabin. The house was built about 1840. Here is preserved a COLLECTION OF INDIAN AND PIONEER RELICS worthy of museum protection, among them the skull of a chief with all his gear, found in an Indian mound on the south bank of the creek, and the account books (1836-40) of William Gougar's general store, with record of sales of such commodities as flour, corn, cloth, farm tools, and whiskey. According to family tradition Chief Shabbona frequently stopped here overnight. When alone he slept on the floor, rolled in his blanket. Once when his wife accompanied him she slept on the ground outside, while he stood guard all night. The BARN (1840) built by William Gougar with the help of pioneer neighbors is still in use. It is made of boards of walnut and oak, hewn into shape with axes, and held in place by wooden pegs.

Across Hickory Creek is the GOUGARS SCHOOLHOUSE (R), 0.3 *m.* The small frame building marks the site of the Hickory Creek log schoolhouse built in 1832. Nearby, in Higinbotham Woods (R), are earthworks traditionally known as the "Old French Fort."

North of the schoolhouse, at 0.4 *m.,* the graveled road separates two units of the Joliet park system (*see Joliet*). Left is the PUBLIC GREENHOUSE (*open daily* 9-4; *Sun. and Hol.,* 9-5; *adm. free*). The greenhouse, bordered by formal flower gardens and trimly kept lawns, lies on a slight rise of ground from which trails lead westward to other units of the park system. The conservatory, which houses a variety of the more common garden flowers, is distinguished by an unusually inclusive CACTUS COLLECTION. HIGINBOTHAM WOODS (R) is a wild-land preserve of 238 acres. An earth road, opposite the greenhouse, passes a FIRETOWER (R). An inside stairway leads to a platform at the top, which affords a sweeping view of the surrounding forest area, the city of Joliet, and the farm lands for miles around.

Immediately south of the greenhouse a hard-surfaced road follows Hickory Creek westward for 2 miles through several units of the park system to a junction with US 30 (*see below*) on the outskirts of Joliet. Enroute are 75-acre BIRD HAVEN, 327-acre PILCHER PARK AND ARBORETUM, 23-acre HOBBS PARK-WAY, and 60-acre HIGHLAND PARK.

At 28.7 *m.* on US 30 is the entrance (R) to the JOLIET PARK SYSTEM (*see above*), marked by Leonard Crunelle's STATUE OF ROBERT PILCHER.

JOLIET, 31 *m.* (545 alt., 42,993 pop.) (*see Joliet*).

Points of Interest: Joliet Wall Paper Mills, American Institute of Laundering Vocational Training School, Oakwood Mound, and others.

Joliet is at the junction with US 6 (*see Tour* 14) and US 66 (*see Tour* 17).

The vast form of STATEVILLE STATE PRISON (*see Tour* 17) is distinctly visible (R) at 33.5 *m.*, its light stone structure in sharp contrast with the green fields that surround it.

Between Joliet and Aurora lie the long-settled Plainfield farm lands, a prosperous agricultural region between the Des Plaines and Fox Rivers. Flat to gently rolling, the country is largely under cultivation; only occasional farm wood lots relieve the monotony of the unending cornfields.

An extensive water-filled gravel pit (R) forms small LAKE REN-WICK, 38.9 *m.*, which borders the roadside for a quarter-mile. The extent of the resource, one of the most important in Illinois, may be judged 'from the activities along the railroad on the far side of the lake, where whole trainloads of gravel are frequently made up.

PLAINFIELD, 40.3 *m.* (601 alt., 1,428 pop.), named for its prairie topography, originated as an Indian village, and was first known as a trading post, founded by the Frenchman Du Pazhe about 1790, later operated by Vetel Vermette for the American Fur Trading Company. It is next recorded as a stop on the rounds of Jesse Walker, "Daniel Boone of Methodism," missionary to the Indians, who preached here in 1826. The Rev. Mr. Walker's son-in-law, Captain James Walker, built a cabin near the Indian village in 1829; the settlement that grew up around it was for some time known as Walker's Grove.

On Old Main Street, State 126, R. of the highway along the river, are several examples of the Greek Revival style of architecture popular in the 1830's, among them the HALFWAY HOUSE, built in 1834 as a station on the Chicago-Ottawa State Road. The building served as post office on the first Chicago-St. Louis mail route. At that time the Joliet postmaster was obliged to come to Plainfield for the mail. Two decades later, however, following the completion of the Illinois and Michigan Canal (1848), Joliet quite eclipsed Plainfield.

The MILES V. HARTONG COLLECTION (*apply to owner*), in Mr. Hartong's home on the south side of the square, contains Indian relics, a variety of pioneer tools and furnishings, a collection of old county and State histories, and many early photographs and drawings of places of interest in Will and Cook Counties. The GRAVE OF THE REVEREND JESSE WALKER, who died in Des Plaines in 1835, is in Plainfield Cemetery. Fronting the highway is a FOUNDRY AND SHOPS, where small locomotives are manufactured for use in amusement parks and for other narrow-gauge purposes.

On the western edge of Plainfield the route crosses the DU PAGE RIVER, named for Du Pazhe, the trader. The stream, bordered by a magnificent growth of oak, elm, and maple, is dammed in the vicinity of the city. Downstream (L), just off the highway, is the WOOD HOMESTEAD, girlhood home of Mrs. Thomas Alva Edison.

At 49 *m.* is a junction with US 34 (*see Tour* 13).

AURORA, 53 *m.* (740 alt., 46,589 pop.) (*see Aurora*).

Points of Interest: Aurora Historical Society, Phillip's Park Museum and Zoo, Undstad Firearm Collection, Aurora College, and others.

Aurora is at a junction with State 31, which follows the Fox River northward (*see Tour* 12A) past Mooseheart and Batavia to Geneva, 9 *m.*, at a junction with US 330 (*see Tour* 12A).

Section b. Aurora to Iowa Line, 107 m.

West of Aurora, 0 *m.*, US 30 crosses a rolling, partly wooded region of fine dairy farms. Shortly beyond the city limits are several estates of prominent Chicagoans. FITCHOME FARMS (L), 3.6 *m.*, affords an opportunity to inspect modern dairying methods. Long plate glass windows open on the "milking parlor" where twice daily a herd of Holsteins is mechanically milked.

For 30 miles the highway parallels the tracks of the Chicago, Burlington & Quincy Railroad. At SUGAR GROVE (L), 7 *m.*, the Burlington's streamlined *Zephyr* saluted the Great Northern's 78-year-old *Billy Crooks* on the morning of March 17, 1939. The historic old wood-burning engine, the first steam locomotive in the Northwest, was on its way from St. Paul, Minnesota, to the New York World's Fair. With its two ancient coaches, it made the trip by stages, stopping at night because its kerosene lamps did not allow it to travel after dark.

Immediately west of the village of SHABBONA, 30.5 *m.*, is a junction with a graveled road.

Left on this road to a junction with another graveled road, 5.9 *m.;* L. here to the ROOKERY, 8.5 *m.*, on the farm of D. J. Shepardson, (*apply at house*), a grove of larches that serves as the summer home of a colony of black-crowned night herons. Known as "quawks" because of their bickering nature, they have migrated to the grove for at least forty years, usually coming about the first of April. The birds are more than two feet in height, with a green or black crown and back, pearly gray wings and tail, and yellow legs and feet. When frightened, the entire flock takes flight, executing an odd, running takeoff into the air. The colony of several hundred flies 20 to 25 miles daily to feed in the swamps bordering the Illinois and Fox Rivers.

At 40.5 *m.* is a junction with US 51 (*see Tour* 4).

At 54 *m.* is a junction with US 52 (*see Tour* 15), with which US 30 is united for 10 miles.

DIXON, 64 *m.* (659 alt., 9,908 pop.), seat of Lee County, honors the memory of John Dixon, first white settler, who opened a trading post and tavern here in 1830. Water power was a principal factor in attracting settlers and the several factories that later developed on the banks of the Rock River. Today, Dixon is an important center of the cement industry. In the law offices (*open*) of George Dixon, great-grandson of the pioneer, 108 E. 1st St., are many early documents pertaining to the history of Dixon and of this northwestern section of Illinois.

On the west bank of Rock River, one block L. of the highway, a little park (R) marks the SITE OF FORT DIXON. Here, facing the river, is LEONARD CRUNELLE'S LINCOLN, a large bronze statue depicting the youthful captain of volunteers in the Black Hawk War. A bronze plaque set in a nearby granite boulder summarizes Lincoln's military services in the summer of 1832. A bronze tablet on the base of the statue bears a bas-relief of John Dixon, "founder of the city of Dixon, April 11, 1830, proprietor of the Ferry and Tavern here during the Black Hawk War." Also shown in bas-relief are Fort Dixon and the ferry and tavern.

Dixon is at the junction with State 2 (*see Tour* 4A), US 330 (*see Tour* 12A), and US 52 (*see Tour* 15).

Right from Dixon on N. Brinton Avenue to DIXON STATE HOSPITAL (*open* 9-3, *Mon.-Fri., apply at office*), 2.8 *m.*, on a 1,057-acre wooded tract on the Rock River. Its 70 buildings of red brick with white stone trim, slate roofs, and state-house cupolas accommodate 4,000 inmates. The hospital was opened in 1918, and in 1931 was designated by the legislature as the State institution for the care of those afflicted with chronic encephalitis (sleeping sickness). Cases of epilepsy, feeble-mindedness, and post encephalitis also are treated here. Academic, occupational, and recreational instruction is given.

Left from the hospital grounds on a graveled road to the junction with a paved road, 3.2 *m.;* R. on the paved road to LOWELL PARK (R), 4.4 *m.*, a hilly, heavily wooded tract (*boating, swimming, picnicking*) overlooking the Rock River.

STERLING, 77 *m.* (645 alt., 10,012 pop.), separated from Rock Falls by the Rock River, is the outgrowth of two settlements, Chatham and Harrisburg; the latter, it is said, was named for Captain Daniel Harris of Galena, the first white man to navigate Rock River this far north. Captain Harris is reported to have arrived in 1836 with a load of provisions, which he sold to the settlers for a half interest in the town. Three years later, Chatham and Harrisburg united as the town of Sterling in order to be designated Whiteside County seat, a distinction which was won but later lost to more centrally located Morrison.

ROCK FALLS (646 alt., 3,893 pop.), platted in 1837, grew slowly until 1857, when a dam was built across the river connecting the town with its more prosperous neighbor. Later, when the Illinois and Mississippi Canal was built 30 miles to the south, a feeder was dug to connect it with the Rock River at this point. The twin cities today form an important unit in that long chain of industrial centers extending from the Mississippi up the Rock River far into Wisconsin.

Between the two cities, on an island in the river, reached by Avenue G from Sterling, is LAWRENCE PARK (*swimming pool, picnic facilities*), commanding a sweeping view of the river front on either side. The banks are lined with a variety of manufacturing plants. Many are builders' hardware factories; the district is said to be the center of that industry in the United States.

The STERLING MUNICIPAL COLISEUM, 3rd Ave. and 3rd St., L. of the highway, a two-and-a-half-story structure of light brick with stone trim, contains a theater and is topped by a roof garden. In Central Park, a block west of the Coliseum, is GRANDON CIVIC CENTER, an open air amphitheater equipped with a bandshell. At 6th Ave. and 7th St., on the grounds of the Central School, is a LINCOLN BOULDER, "in memory of Abraham Lincoln, who spoke here July 18, 1856."

Between Sterling and Morrison are several cabin camps in shaded groves along the roadside. Cropped fields and pasture-lands alternate with densely wooded valleys.

MORRISON, 94 *m.* (670 alt., 3,067 pop.), Whiteside County seat, is an old city on the Chicago & North Western Railway. The city and nearby Unionville were settlements before the railroad survey was begun. Because of prohibitive land prices in Unionville, the stage stop, the railroad was constructed through Morrison, which consequently progressed, while Unionville remained unincorporated.

In May 1874 James Sargent, inventor of the time lock, placed his invention in the door of the iron safe in the First National Bank of Morrison, where it gave satisfactory service for forty years. This was the first time lock installation in the United States.

On the western edge of the city, on Rock Creek (L), is the old
UNIONVILLE MILL (*visitors welcome*), erected 1858. The stone walls
are 2 feet thick, and the heavy beams in walls and ceilings are of hand-
hewn oak. The cement dam is 9 feet high and 84 feet long. The mill,
still water-powered, continues in operation, grinding flour and feed
for farmers of the community.

The densely wooded wild lands upstream from the highway on
the west bank of Rock Creek are the proposed site of a State park.
The abundance of wild life, the beauty of the valley, and the wealth
of historical associations recommend the site.

West of Morrison the highway winds through wooded hills cut
by deep ravines as it approaches the Mississippi.

The ABBOTT FARM (*private*) is R. of the highway at 99.8 *m.* The
region was early associated with the activities of a notorious band of
counterfeiters, who centered their operations in the basement of the
farm-house later purchased by the Abbotts and moved across the road
to its present location. In the process of moving the building several
bundles of bogus money and the plates used in their printing were
discovered. This led to the capture of Ben Boyd, master engraver of
the gang, in his workshop in Fulton. The evidence readily convicted
him, and he was sent to Joliet prison. The gang thereupon plotted to
steal the body of President Lincoln and to use it as a basis for negotiating the release of Boyd. (*See Lincoln's Tomb, Springfield.*)

At 105 *m.* is a junction with State 80 (*see Tour* 6) on the outskirts
of FULTON, 106.5 *m.* (597 alt., 2,656 pop.). The city, which commemorates the inventor of the steamboat, owes its early growth and
importance to river commerce, but is today largely a residential community, the center of a prosperous agricultural area. Local greenhouses,
conspicuous on the city's border, have more than 12 acres of rich prairie
soil under glass. Thousands of baskets of tomatoes and boxes of cu-
cumbers are shipped annually.

US 30 crosses the Iowa Line, 107 *m.*, on a toll bridge (*automobile
and driver*, 20c; *passengers*, 5c; *trailers*, 10c) spanning the Mississippi
to Clinton, Iowa (*see Iowa Guide*).

TOUR 12A

Roadbed hard-surfaced throughout; four lanes between Chicago and Geneva, two lanes westward.
The Chicago & North Western Ry. parallels US 330 between Chicago and Dixon.
Usual accommodations throughout.

US 330, an alternate route with US 30 (*see Tour* 12), crosses the Chicago metropolitan area, penetrating the very heart of the great city. In the course of its length, the route is variously a placid country road, a bustling suburban thoroughfare, or a feverish metropolitan boulevard. North of the junction with US 30 near the Indiana Line, the highway skirts the suburbs of steel-mill Hammond, Indiana, then crosses industrial wastelands that extend south from Chicago. Twenty-six miles of the route are in the city. West of Chicago US 330 passes suburbs that have scarcely a distinguishable break in contiguity. Between the Fox and the Rock Rivers the highway follows the gentle swell of prairie farm lands and passes through sedate little cities to its western junction with US 30 at Dixon.

North of the junction with US 30 (*see Tour* 12), 0 *m.*, 2.5 miles west of the Indiana Line, the route crosses fields of corn and onions, passes through a section of the GURDON S. HUBBARD FOREST PRESERVE, and enters the sparsely populated outskirts of LANSING, 4 *m.* (618 alt., 3,378 pop.). Lansing was organized in the 1860's by Dutch and German farmers. The village has since become an adjunct of the vast industrial area concentrated at the northwestern corner of Indiana.

At 7.2 *m.* is a junction with US 6 (*see Tour* 14). North of the junction the route skirts the SHABBONA WOODS FOREST PRESERVE (L).

CALUMET CITY, 8.7 *m.* (585 alt., 12,298 pop.), R. of the highway, is a residential outgrowth of Hammond, Indiana. Much of the city was built during a real estate boom of the 1920's. Calumet is the French name for the peace-pipe of the Indians. Part of the municipality was platted in 1833.

North of Calumet City the route traverses a stark industrial plain studded with grain elevators, steel mills, oil refineries, and freight car shops.

The CHICAGO CITY LIMITS are crossed at 10.5 *m.*, near the southeastern corner of the city. The route swings L. along the eastern edge

of the BEAUBIEN FOREST PRESERVE, and continues N. past
LAKE CALUMET to the intersection of Stony Island Ave. and 95th St.,
17.5 *m.*, which is also the junction with US 12 (*see Tour* 9) and US
20 (*see Tour* 11). US 330 continues ahead (N) on Stony Island
Ave. to the intersection of Michigan Blvd. with Roosevelt Road, in
downtown Chicago.

CHICAGO, 29.3 *m.* (598 alt., 3,376,438 pop.) (*see Chicago*).

Points of Interest: Chicago Board of Trade Building, Union Stock Yards, Field
Museum of Natural History, Art Institute of Chicago, Museum of Science and
Industry, Adler Planetarium, Shedd Aquarium, University of Chicago, and
others.

In Chicago are junctions with State 1 (*see Tour* 1), State 42
(*see Tour* 2), US 41 (*see Tour* 2A), US 12 (*see Tour* 9), US 14
(*see Tour* 10), US 20 (*see Tour* 11), US 66 (*see Tour* 17), and the
Illinois Waterway (*see Tour* 21).

The route continues L. from Michigan Ave. on Roosevelt Road
past CICERO (L), 36 *m.* (610 alt., 66,602 pop.) (*see Tour* 17),
BERWYN (L), 37 *m.* (612 alt., 47,027 pop.) (*see Tour* 17), and
OAK PARK (R), 37 *m.* (630 alt., 63,982 pop.) (*see Tour* 11), to
the intersection of Roosevelt Road and Harlem Avenue, 38 *m.*

Immediately west of Harlem Avenue is FOREST PARK, 39.8
m. (620 alt., 14,555 pop.), upon the Des Plaines River, a community
of the quick and the dead. In the many cemeteries that comprise nearly
one-half of the town's corporate area are approximately 250,000 graves.

A block south of the castelated entrance to WALDHEIM CEMETERY,
in the 900 block on S. Des Plaines Ave., R. of US 330, is a MONUMENT
TO THE MEN HANGED FOR THE HAYMARKET RIOT, November 11,
1887 (*see Labor*), a symbolic bronze by A. Weinert. Memorial services
for the four, Engel, Fischers, Parsons, and Spies, who are buried
here, are observed each year.

FOREST HOME CEMETERY, south of Waldheim and north of the
highway, is upon the site of a Potawatomi village and burial ground.
INDIAN RELICS, unearthed in the course of grave-digging, are displayed in the cemetery office. South of US 330 are several congregational tracts of the JEWISH WALDHEIM CEMETERY.

SHOWMEN'S REST in WOODLAWN CEMETERY, at the southern end
of the city, L. from Des Plaines Ave. on Cermak Road, is for deceased
members of the Showmen's League of America. Their first plot,
marked by a group of five granite elephants, was purchased to bury
63 circus performers who were killed in a train wreck at Gary,
Indiana, in July 1918.

The FOREST PARK BASEBALL MUSEUM (*Mon.-Fri., 7-6; Sat., 7-9*),
7212 W. Madison St., is probably the only one of its kind in the world.
Pictures from the time the game was called "Four Old Cat" through
the present; uniforms and bats of such famous players as Joe Tinker;
data and records since the beginning of baseball; and autographed

baseballs from all leagues form part of the extensive collection.

West of Forest Park the road emerges from the metropolitan area and enters prairie lands that are checkerboarded by farms, subdivisions, and country estates.

An entryway (L), 41 *m.*, leads through the 320-acre grounds of the EDWARD HINES, JR. MEMORIAL HOSPITAL (*visiting:* 2:30-4:30, *Tues., Thurs., Sun.*). The hospital established in 1920 for the care of World War veterans, commemorates the partial donor's son, killed in the War. The Federal government administers the institution.

The 29 buildings are on the site of an automobile race track, which accounts for the familiar designation of the hospital as the "Speedway." The extraordinary shape of the four-story main building, 2,640 feet by 50 feet, was dictated by the dimensions of the race track grandstand, upon the foundations of which the building rests. Here are housed the tuberculosis, medical, surgical, and neuropathological units, and the out-patient department. Most of the other buildings, which are of red brick, in a Colonial style, house the 1,200 employees of the institution. The cancer research unit of the hospital has issued important publications in that field.

Right of the highway, and opposite the hospital, is MAYWOOD (632 alt., 25,829 pop.) (*see Tour* 11).

BROADVIEW (L), 41.7 *m.* (625 alt., 2,334 pop.), an offshoot of Maywood, incorporated as a village in 1910, has no business district, for it is wholly residential. BROADVIEW ACADEMY, a Seventh Day Adventist coeducational school, Cermak Road just west of 19th Ave., has an average enrollment of 200 students, many of whom earn their tuition by working in the academy or on its 90-acre farm.

At 43.3 *m.* is a junction with US 45 (*see Tour* 3), By-Pass US 12 (*see Tour* 9), and By-Pass US 20 (*see Tour* 11).

Half a mile west of the junction, the road abruptly leaves the lake plain and enters the rolling moraines that spread throughout most of Du Page County. The route passes at some distance from the centers of several out-lying suburbs, their church steeples, smoke-stacks, and watertanks visible to the north. From the highway these communities seem lost in the dense green of trees that shade their quiet streets.

At 50.4 *m.* is a junction with Main Street, a paved road.

Right on Main Street is LOMBARD, 1.6 *m.* (708 alt., 6,197 pop.), named for Joseph Lombard, a Chicagoan, who platted the town in 1868. The first white settler in the area was Winslow Churchill, who in 1834, aided by friendly Indians, built a log cabin and established a claim to the region now the CHURCHILL FOREST PRESERVE on St. Charles Road. Sheldon Peck, journeying overland from Vermont, settled at Lombard in 1838 and built the PECK HOUSE (*private*), Grace Ave. and Parkside St., which functioned as a station on the Underground Railroad in pre-Civil War years. The neighborly aspect of contemporary Lombard has been depicted by Katherine Reynolds in two novels, *Green Valley* and *Willow Creek.*

LILACIA PARK, W. Maple St. and S. Park Ave., a 10-acre public garden, contains more than 300 varieties of lilacs. The park is the former estate of Col. William Plum, who, in pursuit of a life-long hobby, collected lilacs from throughout the world. Plum bequeathed the estate to the city of Lombard, and upon his death in 1927 the gift was accepted and the Lombard Park District was organized. The Plum home, in accord with the bequest, houses the HELEN W. PLUM MEMORIAL LIBRARY (*open*), which honors the memory of Colonel Plum's wife, Helen Williams, a descendant of Roger Williams. Jens Jensen, Chicago landscape architect, planned the beautiful arrangement of the park, which has since been developed by others.

Tulips border winding paths, with lilac bushes set slightly back from them. Especially notable are the President Lincoln lilac bush north of the library and the venerable white lilac on the north side of the lily pond. On the east terrace of the library is a magnificent silver aspen. In the southeast corner of the park the brilliant coloring of a Schwedler maple brightens the scene both in spring and fall. Southwest of the library ancient apple trees border the pathway; a large gingko tree is nearby.

The Lombard Lilac League presents a pageant in May of each year when the lilacs are in full bloom. Admission to the park is free, except during Festival Week, when there is usually a small charge.

GLEN ELLYN, 52.7 *m.* (766 alt., 7,680 pop.), is mainly north of the highway. In naming the community, Thomas E. Hill commemorated his wife Ellyn, and the picturesque glen at the foot of Cooper Hill. The founders of Glen Ellyn once dwelt at a stagecoach stop known as Stacy's Corners, one mile north of the present business district. In 1849 the Galena & Chicago Union Railroad was constructed south of Stacy's Corners, whereupon its citizens, anxious to be on the main line, transplanted church and houses to the present site. The new town was platted in 1851. LAKE ELLYN PARK borders a small lake in the northern part of the city.

WHEATON, 55.1 *m.* (753 alt., 7,258 pop.), seat of Du Page County, honors in its name Warren and Jesse Wheaton, godfathers of the town and of its three great assets: the railroad, the college, and the courthouse.

In 1838 the Wheatons laid claim to the land that is now the heart of the city. A decade later Warren Wheaton contributed a right-of-way to the pioneer Galena & Chicago Union Railroad. His generosity, in complete reversal of the price-boosting tactics then common among landowners, was amply rewarded by the subsequent growth of the town.

The college came in 1853, the year the town was platted. The Wesleyan Methodists, seeking a site for an orthodox school, selected Wheaton and founded Illinois Institute, "for Christ and His Kingdom." Warren Wheaton gave the original campus. Seven years later, when the school was reorganized under the auspices of the Congregationalists, he gave every other one of his town lots to assure the financial soundness of the institution. Renamed for its benefactor, WHEATON COLLEGE, Washington St. and Seminary Ave., undenominational but fervently fundamentalist, is today the largest liberal arts

college in Illinois, with 23 buildings and an enrollment of more than
1,100. BLANCHARD HALL, in the Victorian Gothic battlemented style,
is named for Jonathan Blanchard (*see Galesburg, Tour* 13), early
president of the college and one of the foremost abolitionists of
Illinois.

Securing the courthouse was not so simple. Since the formation of
Du Page County in 1839, Naperville (*see Tour* 13) had been the
county seat. Wheaton as early as 1857 attempted, without success, to
wrest that distinction from her neighbor on the strength of possessing
a railroad and a more central location. Ten years later, however, the
voters of the county determined in Wheaton's favor, and a courthouse
was built. Warren Wheaton gave the land, and he and his brother
each subscribed $2,000 for the construction of the building. But Naper-
ville, intent upon remaining the seat of justice, refused to recognize
the election as legal. Although the circuit court, after months of contention, upheld the vote, Naperville refused to give up the public
records. Injunctions were served and counter proceedings instituted.
Impatient of longer waiting, Wheaton resorted to direct action. One
night in July 1868 a body of men descended upon the Naperville
courthouse and made off with a wagonload of public records. Save
for several that were overlooked, and which subsequently have disappeared, they are now in the safe keeping of the county clerk in the
Wheaton COURTHOUSE, a large modern structure completed in 1938,
which stands on the site of three earlier ones.

Although the Wheatons were the "first family" of early days,
others were influential as the community developed, among them the
Garys. Erastus Gary had arrived in the vicinity in 1832. His son,
Elbert, the Judge Gary of steel fame, was born in Wheaton in 1846;
two terms as county judge gained him the title by which he was thereafter known. The GARY MEMORIAL METHODIST EPISCOPAL CHURCH,
Main St. and Seminary Ave., modern English Gothic in design, commemorates the family.

North of Wheaton on Main St. at Geneva Road is the THEOSOPHICAL
SOCIETY TEMPLE (*open* 9-5 *weekdays*), 1.5 *m.* The modern, three-story building,
of Cloister brick with Bedford stone trim, set in the midst of extensive landscaped grounds, was designed by Irving K. Pond, Chicago architect. MURALS
by Richard B. Farley in the reception room depict the evolutionary process as
interpreted by Theosophy. The LIBRARY of more than 15,000 volumes, primarily
on occult subjects, is one of the largest of its kind in the country. Various
speakers from many nations have addressed the open meetings held at four
o'clock on the fourth Sunday of each month. Addresses are followed by a tea
and musicale to which visitors are invited. Classes in theosophy (*Wed.,* 8 *p.m.*)
are open to the public without charge.

At 57.3 *m.* is a junction with a graveled road.

Left on this road is the CHICAGO TRIBUNE EXPERIMENTAL FARM, 1 *m.* (*open
in summer; free guide service*). A similar farm, under the direction of the

Tribune, is near Yorkville, (*see Tour* 13). The farms, established in 1934, are owned and operated by the Chicago *Tribune* in the interests of Mid-West agriculture. In co-operation with Federal and State agencies many improvements have been made in crops and livestock. Resistance to insects, drought, and frost has been developed in many strains of field corn. Many varieties or strains of rare and unusual crops are grown from seeds obtained from distant parts of the world. An annual event of the farm season is the horse and mule pulling contest held each summer at the Wheaton farms.

GENEVA, 66 *m.* (720 alt., 4,607 pop.), is on both sides of the Fox River. The antithesis of all that is martial, the peaceful riverside community indirectly owes its existence to the Black Hawk War. Soldiers returning from the frontier in 1832 extolled the Fox River country to footloose Easterners, some of whom ventured to the area within the following year. Following its founding, Geneva became an hospitable "jumping-off" place for pioneers bent on traveling farther west.

The elm-shaded sidestreets of Geneva contain frequent examples of mid-nineteenth century dwellings; notable among them is a GREEK REVIVAL HOUSE, 220 S. 3rd St. MILL RACE INN, southeast corner at the highway bridge, housed the first blacksmith shop in Geneva. Opposite, is an OLD MILL, still operated by water power, and using the original burrs to grind some of its products. The STATE TRAINING SCHOOL FOR GIRLS (*open* 9-4, *Mon.-Fri.*), S. Batavia St. on the east side of the river, provides academic, commercial, and vocational instruction for girls committed by juvenile courts.

1. Right (north) from Geneva on State 31 is ST. CHARLES, 2 *m.* (802 alt., 5,377 pop.), a century-old residential, industrial, and commuting center on the Fox River. The elaborate $600,000 HOTEL BAKER, which occupies the site of the old mill around which the pioneer community developed, is suggestive of the wealth that is concentrated in St. Charles' homes and nearby country estates. POTTAWATOMIE PARK, on the river at the north end of the city, preserves a fraction of the wildland beauty which has attracted many wealthy Chicagoans to the Fox River Valley.

2. Left from Geneva State 31 follows the Fox River 9 miles southward to a junction with US 30 (*see Tour* 12) at Aurora (*see Aurora*).

The RIVERBANK LABORATORIES (R), 1.3 *m.*, in a building of ultra-modern design, were established in 1919 by Colonel George Fabyn (1867-1936) for research in acoustics and to manufacture tuning forks, sound meters and other acoustical equipment. Colonel Fabyn's ability to solve codes and ciphers proved of great value to the Federal government during the World War. The vast FABYN ESTATE borders the river (L).

Right from State 31 at this point, 0.6 *m.* on a graveled road, to the PECK MERINO SHEEP FARM, where prize-winning American Merino sheep have been bred since 1860.

The two-and-a-half-story ultra-modern CAMPANA PLANT (*tours,* 9-4, *Mon.-Fri.,* 9-11 *Sat., on the hour*), 1.7 *m.,* is separated from the highway by a spacious lawn (R). The exterior of the building consists solely of glass blocks and pale green tiles in long horizontal rows.

BATAVIA, 3 *m.* (719 alt., 5,045 pop.), was named by early settlers for their home in New York. The business and residential sections are about equally divided by the river into an East Side and a West Side. As in Aurora, the post office, city hall, and other municipal service buildings are centrally located on an island. Factories that line both banks of the river manufacture windmills.

Among the earliest sites chosen for settlement following the Black Hawk War (1832), Batavia, because of its triple advantage of water power, fertile soil, and surface limestone, began its industrial career in 1837 with a flour mill. By 1850 it had developed an extensive commerce in limestone, which gave it the nickname of "Quarry City." Several fine old houses built of this local stone still stand along the highway. Among these are LOCKWOOD HALL (R), and the SNOW HOUSE (L), at the southern edge of town, both in the Greek Revival style. Right on Union Avenue is BELLEVUE REST HOME, built in 1856 for the Batavia Institute, a private academy soon superseded by public schools and taken over in 1867 by Dr. R. J. Patterson, a specialist in mental and nervous disorders. Mary Todd Lincoln was a patient here in 1875. The room she occupied retains the ornate dark walnut furniture fashionable in her time.

MOOSEHEART (R), 5 m., is a community founded by James J. Davis, the United States senator from Pennsylvania, and supported by the Loyal Order of Moose. The institution provides home, educational training through high school, and technical training in several trades for 1,000 children of deceased members of the order. The grounds are open from sunup to sundown daily (*guides available for each unit; cafeteria open to visitors at noon weekdays*).

Known to radio listeners as the City of Childhood, Mooseheart answers the description in almost a story-book sense. Here is a scientifically directed miniature society whose affairs are conducted by the child citizens themselves, aided by adult advisers. The children live in small groups in cottages, each headed by a housemother. Living conditions approximate home life as nearly as possible, and although all children, because of admission limitations, are fatherless, Mooseheart provides jobs for many mothers, thus saving a further break in the family.

Boys have a choice of training in one or more of eleven trades or professions; girls, in six. Each boy or girl receives full apprentice experience. When a new unit is to be built, the drafting class draws the plans and makes the blue prints, the concrete class produces structural materials, and the sheet metal class provides roofing and drain pipes. Other groups stand ready to paint, paper, or varnish; and the tin shop makes such utensils as dish pans and dust pans.

Apprentices in beauty culture and barbering gain experience with an average of 450 haircuts per week. Students in the power machine sewing class see the suits and dresses they make actually worn by the members of the community. Girls manage the cafeteria, under a trained supervisor. Student typists and bookkeepers assist in the business office. Journalism classes co-operate with the print shop in producing local reading matter. Children with musical or artistic gifts are trained to earn an income in orchestra, band, or designing studios. About 15 per cent out of each graduating class go to college. At the age of eight each child is taught to do his own shopping and to keep a check book. From junior high school his work is paid for in actual money, and he must budget his accounts so that by graduation he will have saved at least $50.

Near the landscaped entranceway, which is marked by a monumental shaft, is the CLOCK TOWER, commanding an inclusive view of the 1,200-acre grounds. East is the rolling, wooded valley of Fox River; north, 20-acre Moose Lake; and south, the school buildings, athletic field, and playgrounds. West are the city's 125 buildings. Outstanding are the RECEPTION COTTAGE, where children undergo preliminary observation; the PHILADELPHIA MEMORIAL HOSPITAL, with state-house cupola; the OHIO PLAZA RESEARCH LABORATORY, also with cupola; and the one-story units of the PENNSYLVANIA BABY VILLAGE. The ROOSEVELT MEMORIAL BUILDING contains an auditorium seating 1,000, which is used as church, theater, or dance or banquet hall; the school bank and the community department store are also here. More than 3,000 children have been admitted to Mooseheart.

West of the city is the 800-acre farm, its grain-fields, gardens, greenhouses, and dairy barns operated on the most modern of agricultural methods. Vegetables, meat, milk, and eggs are produced for the community. In the clock tower are the CAFETERIA and the DISPLAY ROOMS where pottery, cakes, and other products of the specific training given older children are exhibited.

West of Geneva US 330 winds through undulating farm lands, at intervals entering brief tunnels formed by parallel rows o'f overarching elms.

The STATE SCHOOL FOR BOYS (R), 70.7 *m.*, the companion institution of the State school in Geneva, cares for an average of 650 boys between the ages of ten and seventeen. In a village that consists of 6 farmhouses and 14 red brick, tile-roofed cottages arranged around a square, the boys are given academic and vocational training. The school is not a penal institution; "sentences" are worked out in terms of work units and scholastic credits.

At 75 *m.* is a junction with State 47.

Left on State 47 is ELBURN, 0.8 *m.* (848 alt., 548 pop.), a farming center that dates from 1854, when it was platted along the Galena & Chicago Union Railroad. Public sentiment in the vicinity, as in all of Kane County in the 1850's, was definitely abolitionist. Tradition has it that Lincoln, while visiting a cousin in Elburn in 1858, was greeted by a local organization calling itself the "Lincoln True Hearts," which pledged him its active support in the senatorial contest. Northern Illinois was as strongly pro-Lincoln as southern Illinois was pro-Douglas.

At 2 *m.* on State 47 is a junction with a graveled road.

Left on this road to JOHNSONS MOUND (*picnic facilities*), 4.9 *m.*, in a unit of the Kane County Forest Preserve. The mound, which rises noticeably above the low, rolling farm lands, is attractively developed as a county park. From the keeper's cottage at the entrance a road (*closed to automobiles*) circles the mound to its summit. Right of this road, a few hundred yards into the woods, is SHABBONA ELM, standing in solitary grandeur in an opening of the forest. The tree has been identified by experts as approximately 325 years old. Portia Gilpin, in *Memoirs of a Giant Tree*, tells the stories this lofty water-elm might tell, could it speak. A bronze tablet in front of the tree, placed by the Fox River Valley Woodcraft Council, states that the tree was named "in honor of the Pottawatomi chieftain of this region . . . on the 12th Sun of the Wild Rose Moon, 1922."

DE KALB, 91 *m.* (886 alt., 8,545 pop.), named for Baron Johann De Kalb, major general in the American Revolutionary Army, was known until 1938, when the industry was transferred elsewhere, as the "barbed wire capital of the world." In 1874 Joseph E. Glidden patented an improved barbed wire. About the same time Jacob Haish patented a barbed wire manufacturing process. The patents clashed, and the longest drawn-out litigation recorded in patent infringement jurisprudence resulted. GLIDDEN HOSPITAL, 1719 S. 1st St., is a memorial to Joseph Glidden. HAISH MEMORIAL LIBRARY, Oak and N. 3rd Sts., commemorates its donor, Jacob Haish. The building, designed by White & Weber of Chicago, is of Indiana limestone in soft shades of buff and brown. It is considered one o'f the most beautiful modern buildings in Illinois. Fred M. Torrey, of Chicago, carved the four interior panels depicting art, history, fiction, and science, and the two exterior ones depicting the author and the reader.

NORTHERN ILLINOIS STATE TEACHERS COLLEGE, founded 1895, occupies 67 acres of natural woodland on the Kishwaukee River. The five buildings of the college, R. of the highway at the western end of town, accommodate an average enrollment of 950 students quarterly.

HOPKINS PARK, on the northern edge of De Kalb, provides, in addition to picnic and camping facilities, a modern swimming pool and bath house (*nominal fee*), and an open-air auditorium.

Right from De Kalb on 1st St. is COLTONVILLE, 3.2 *m.*, identified by a rural schoolhouse at a junction with a graveled road. On the R. side of the road, immediately opposite the schoolhouse, is a monument that marks the SITE OF THE FIRST COURT HELD IN DE KALB COUNTY. Nearby, slightly to the north, was an old Potawatomi Indian village. A depression on the Adee farm, which now occupies the site, reveals the place where the exhumed body of Capas, chief of the Potawatomi, lay.

ROCHELLE, 108.5 *m.* (793 alt., 3,785 pop.) (*see Tour* 4), is at a junction with US 51 (*see Tour* 4). West of Rochelle extensive fields of asparagus line the highway for two miles. The 1,500 acres of intensively cultivated land are owned by the Rochelle Asparagus Company, which operates a local cannery.

ASHTON, 118 *m.* (817 alt., 868 pop.), a thrifty German-American village, centers upon the MILLS AND PETRIE MEMORIAL, a community building named for the partial donors. The modern structure of stone and yellow brick, erected in 1936, houses a library, a stage, and a gymnasium that may be converted into an assembly hall, play room, or roller skating rink.

DIXON, 135 *m.* (659 alt., 9,908 pop.) (*see Tour* 12), is at a junction with State 2 (*see Tour* 4A), US 30 (*see Tour* 12), and US 52 (*see Tour* 15).

TOUR 13

Junction with US 66 (Riverside) —Mendota—Princeton
—Galesburg— (Burlington, Iowa) ; US 34.

Riverside to Iowa Line, 221 m.

Four-lane concrete roadbed between Riverside and Naperville, two-lane westward.
Chicago, Burlington & Quincy R. R. parallels route.
Usual accommodations throughout.

US 34 traverses a region of rolling glacial drift on the northern boundary of the great prairies. Where the underlying bedrock is exposed, it is utilized locally as building stone, crushed rock, or raw material for the manufacture of cement. Elsewhere, glacial sands and gravels are quarried for use in construction industries. The landscape, often hilly and partly wooded, resembles both the dairy country to the north and the grain lands to the south. Some cities along the way are service centers for neighboring farmers; others are primarily residential, the seats of schools and colleges; industry generally is of secondary importance. The soil of the region is its great resource, supporting fine herds of dairy cattle and yielding rich harvests of corn and grain. ·

Section a. Riverside to Princeton, 108 m.

US 34 branches west (R) from a junction with US 66 (*see Tour 17*), 0 m., 10.3 miles southwest of the Chicago Loop, at the boundary between (L) LYONS (615 alt., 4,787 pop.) (*see Tour 17*), and (R) RIVERSIDE (630 alt., 6,770 pop.).

Occupying densely wooded park land, Riverside was one of the earliest residential communities in the United States to be laid out on a preconceived plan. The project originated in 1866 when the Riverside Improvement Company commissioned Olmsted and Vaux, New York landscape architects, who designed Central Park and later the Columbian Exposition grounds, to plan an ideal Chicago suburb. Noting the "low, flat, miry, and forlorn character" of what was then the Chicago suburban area, the architects selected the site of Riverside because of its forest, the Des Plaines River, and existing railroad facilities. Frederick Law Olmsted drew the plans, using the winding course of the river as a motif. The improvement company, estimating a net profit of $7,000,000, spent $1,500,000 to establish the village. Subsequent development has followed Olmsted's plan. The community resembles a park, its houses and shrubbery complementing the scenic beauty of the river. One third of Riverside is reserved as park land.

At 1.7 m. is (R) the junction with a paved road.

Right on this road to 31st St., 1.4 *m.*; L. on 31st St. is the CHICAGO ZOOLOGICAL PARK, 1.5 *m.* (10-5 *daily. Adm.: children free at all times; adults free Thurs., Sat., Sun., legal holidays; other days,* 25c. *Wheel chairs,* 50c *per hour; attendant,* 25c *extra. Free parking and rest rooms at N. and S. entrances. Children's playground, wooded picnic grounds,* 11-*acre artificial lake in NW. section. Restaurant at E. end of Mall. Children may feed animals, providing food is wholesome.*)

The park, better known as Brookfield Zoo, is managed by the Chicago Zoological Society, a non-profit organization of Cook County civic leaders. The 196-acre tract, a gift of the late Edith Rockefeller McCormick, has landscaped grounds divided into quadrants by an east-west mall and a north-south thoroughfare which connects the two entrances. The buildings, of provincial Italian style, were designed by Edward H. Clark.

Most of the lairs are of the natural habitat type, without bars. Against a background of artificial rocks and thickets of shrubbery, the animals appear to roam free in their native environment. Carnivorous mammals are in the northeast quarter of the park; bears and small animals in the southeast; herbivorous mammals in the northwest; and birds, insects, primates, and reptiles in the southwest. There are more than seven miles of exhibits, all labelled. Magnifying glasses attached to the cases housing ants, bees, and other insects allow close observation of their life.

Typical of the care given the animals are the cages for the penguins. Because they are apt to stand in direct sunlight until overcome by sunstroke, the penguins are quartered in a large refrigerator-like compartment into which no direct sunlight can enter. Of the nine species of antelope in the zoo, five are the only ones of their kind in captivity. Relatively rare specimens include Kodiak bears and a pair of African elephants.

Most popular of all specimens is the giant panda, Mei-Mei (Chinese, baby sister), acquired by the zoo in February 1938. Mei-Mei's predecessor was the famed Su-Lin (Chinese, a little bit of something precious), captured by Mrs. William Harvest Harkness in the mountainous wilds of western China in November 1936. Su-Lin died in 1938; mounted and glassy-eyed, he now stands in the Field Museum of Natural History.

The route passes through the southern part of BROOKFIELD, 1.9 *m.* (620 alt., 10,035 pop.), a suburban community of three separate population centers: Hollywood, Congress Park, and Brookfield. The development of this area in the 1890's followed extensive purchases of land by members of the Ogden, Armour, McCormick, and Rockefeller families. The principal residential sections occupy former Armour properties.

LA GRANGE, 3.7 *m.* (645 alt., 10,103 pop.) (*see Tour 3*), is at a junction with US 45 (*see Tour 3*).

US 34 skirts the northern limits of WESTERN SPRINGS, 5.1 *m.* (668 alt.; 3,894 pop.). Incorporated by Quakers in 1866, the village was named for local mineral springs which were believed to have medicinal qualities; the springs dried up some years ago. The largest of these, its site now planted with flowers and enclosed with trees, was in SPRING ROCK PARK (*playgrounds and wading pool*), Central Ave. and 47th St.

The offices and archives of the Western Springs village government are quartered in the lower stories of an unusual circular brick and stone structure, formerly used as a water tower. Also unusual in a community of Western Springs' size is its Little Theatre Group, which presents five plays each winter, and its Symphony Orchestra, which gives free Sunday afternoon concerts during the summer in SYMPHONY WOODS, Lawn and Chestnut Aves.

HINSDALE, 6.7 *m.* (691 alt., 6,923 pop.), which borders the route on the south, was named for H. W. Hinsdale, an early director of the C. B. & Q. Railroad. Built upon morainic hills, which here rise gently from the lake plain, Hinsdale provides the quiet and seclusion sought by its commuting population. On the north edge of Hinsdale is Fullersburg, settled in 1835 by Jacob Fuller, his six sons and six daughters, and annexed to Hinsdale in 1923.

FULLERSBURG INN, a two-story structure near the intersection, was built of handcut lumber shortly after the Fuller family arrived. Now used as an antique shop, the inn is said to have been visited by Lincoln, and to have served as a station on the Underground Railroad. It is the birthplace of Loie Fuller (1862-1928), author of *Fifteen Years of a Dancer's Life* (1913). The rear wing of the frame house (*private*), diagonally opposite the old inn, was formerly the TOLL HOUSE on the Southwestern Plank Road. The plank road was laid between Chicago and Hinsdale in 1850.

Right from Hinsdale on York Road is the GRAUE MILL (*open*), 0.3 *m.*, a three-story brick structure built in 1847-52. The mill was operated until the 1920's, and in 1934 was restored.

At 7.7 *m.* is a junction with State 54.

Right on State 54 to a junction with 31st St., 1 *m.*; L. on 31st St. is the ST. FRANCIS RETREAT HOUSE (Roman Catholic), 1.5 *m.*, where week-end retreats for laymen are offered by the Franciscan Fathers. The house and grounds, generally known as Mayslake, were the country estate of Francis Peabody, fuel magnate. In transmitting the property to the Franciscans, his widow and son marked the spot where he had died with PORTIUNCULA CHAPEL, a copy of the Portiuncula chapel at Assisi. ST. JOSEPH'S COLLEGE, reached by the entrance to the retreat house, was founded at Teutopolis, Illinois, in 1862 and removed to Mayslake in 1927. It is a preparatory seminary of the Franciscan Order for boys between the ages of 12 and 16.

At 9.2 *m.* is a junction with Cass Avenue.

Left on Cass Avenue through the village of WESTMONT (740 alt., 2,733 pop.) to 63rd St., 2.5 *m.*; L. on 63rd St. to ILLINOIS PET MEMORIAL PARK, 3.3 *m.*, more than two acres in extent. The park, platted in 1926, is divided into 42 blocks of 52 lots each. Dogs, cats, birds, rabbits, and turtles are interred under markers ranging from plain granite headstones to the iron statue of a dog that saved his master's life.

DOWNERS GROVE, 11.2 *m.* (717 alt., 8,977 pop.), incorporated in 1873, was named for its founder, Pierce Downer, who emigrated from Rutland, Vermont, in 1832. He settled at the intersection of two Potawatomi trails, between what are now Oakwood and Linscott Avenues, and Grant and Lincoln Streets. The exact site is marked by the DOWNER MONUMENT, which consists of a bronze tablet imbedded in a granite boulder from the foundation of Downer's barn.

Downers Grove, a commuting suburb, has quiet shaded streets; Maple Avenue (47th St.) is bordered with century-old maples planted by settlers in hope of obtaining a sugar supply. The necessity for the local production of sugar had been overcome by the time the trees matured, and they were never tapped.

Among the several old houses of the city is the BLOGETT HOMESTEAD (*private*), 812 Randall Street, a pioneer structure built of black walnut by Israel Blogett in 1836. It was Blogett who with Samuel Curtiss laid out Maple Avenue in 1838. The two men, having created the road by hitching their oxen to a huge log and dragging it back and forth across the prairie, set out the sapling maples that have become the street's majestic canopy.

On the east side of North Main Street, near Ogden Avenue, is a large two story frame house, the ROGERS PIONEER HOMESTEAD (*private*), built in 1845-1846 by Joseph Ives Rogers, who, with his sons, was an early settler in Downers Grove. The timbers of the old house are of oak, cut and hewn on the Rogers' farm.

On Main Street, adjoining the village hall, is DOWNERS GROVE CEMETERY, a source of recurring political contention. Its location in the center of the business district has caused agitation for its removal since the 1870's. But, as some residents maintain, if Boston keeps the Granary Burying Ground, Downers Grove need not apologize for this memorial to its pioneers. A low retaining wall along Main Street is a compromise effected by the Woman's Club in 1921.

The AVERY COONLEY EXPERIMENTAL SCHOOL (*visiting by appointment*), 1400 Maple St., is nationally known among educators. Opened in 1911 with two free kindergartens, it now includes the elementary grades. Teaching methods are based on the theory outlined in *Education Moves Ahead,* by Eugene Randolph Smith, president of the Progressive Education Association.

Right from Downers Grove on Highland Avenue is the THRASHER FAMILY BURIAL GROUND (*private*), 1.7 *m.* Enclosed with iron railings supported by heavy corner stones, it is an example of the family burial plots common in pioneer days. In contrast is the modern CHAPEL HILLS MEMORIAL PARK, 1.8 *m.* on Highland Avenue, where 80 acres of greensward are unbroken by mound, monument, or gravestone. All markers are of bronze, set flush with the turf. A children's section, known as the EUGENE FIELD MEMORIAL PLOT, was dedicated in 1928 by the Rev. Leland Hobart Danforth, rector of the church in Kenilworth where Eugene Field is buried (*see Tour 2*).

At 14.7 *m.* is a junction with State 53 (Joliet Road).

Right on State 53 is the MORTON ARBORETUM, 1.1 *m.* (*free; administration building open 9-12 and 1-5 weekdays; 10-12 and 2-5 Sun.; map of grounds upon request; picnicking limited to large groups applying in advance.*) The arboretum was established in 1921 by Joy Morton (1855-1934), whose father, Julius S. Morton, a pioneer in the reforestation movement, inaugurated Arbor Day. The Morton residence adjoins the aboretum. In the family burial ground, within the tract, is the GRAVE OF JOY MORTON.

The Georgian ADMINISTRATION BUILDING, a memorial to the founder, contains a horticultural information bureau and an excellent herbarium. The immediate lawns are landscaped with rare plants and shrubs. The arboretum proper, bisected by the highway and criss-crossed with supplementary roads, will eventually contain every tree and shrub that can adapt itself to this climate. Within the 700-acre tract are 20 miles of hiking trails, and 4,500 varieties of trees and plants, arranged in four general groups: systematic, by botanical relationships; geographic, by native habitat; ornamental, in landscape patterns; and economic, for timber-value tests. All are identified by tags. The favorite visiting seasons are crabapple-blossom time in early May; lilac season in late May; the June display of 1,100 varieties of iris; and early autumn, for the petunias.

At 15.4 *m.* is a junction with a graveled road.

Left on this road 1 *m.* to the ST. PROCOPIUS ABBEY, COLLEGE, and ACADEMY (*open, tours arranged*), conducted by the Benedictine Fathers (Roman Catholic) for Bohemians. Established at Chicago in 1890, the college and academy were removed here in 1900. The college has an average enrollment of 145; the academy, 30. Nearby is the ST. JOSEPH BOHEMIAN ORPHANAGE (*open 9-4*), which comprises the Lisle Manual Training School for Boys and the Lisle Industrial School for Girls, both maintained by the Sisters of St. Benedict. The Sisters also conduct the adjoining SACRED HEART ACADEMY, a boarding and day school for girls, with an average enrollment of 75.

At 16.2 *m.*, immediately west of a small tributary of the Du Page River, is a junction with a graveled road.

Left on this road 1 *m.* to NAPERVILLE PARK, the grounds of the Naperville Park Campmeeting Association, affiliated with the Illinois Conference of the Evangelical Church. The latter group holds annual camp-meetings here during July and August.

The highway skirts the northern limits of NAPERVILLE, 18.7 *m.* (693 alt., 5,118 pop.). Shortly after the first settlers immigrated here in 1831, the Black Hawk War forced them to flee to Fort Dearborn. Returning with a company of volunteers, they built a stockade known as Fort Payne in June 1832. The settlement profited from the caravans of covered wagons rolling west from Fort Dearborn, and by 1833 its population numbered 180.

The first settler in Du Page County was Bailey Hobson, who staked his claim in 1830, returned the following year, and established a grist mill. In 1832 came Joseph Naper, who built the first saw mill and platted the town site. Naperville became county seat in 1839, a distinction it retained until 1868 when Wheaton (*see Tour* 12A) ended a long legal dispute by forcibly removing the records.

The most famous of the old buildings in Naperville is the PRE-EMPTION HOUSE, northeast corner S. Main St. and Chicago Ave., a two-story frame structure of Greek Revival design built in 1834. For years it was the most renowned tavern in the region; it is now occupied by a saloon.

The richest historically of Naperville's old houses is the BAILEY HOBSON TOWN HOUSE (*private, except to teachers and students of history*), 506 S. Washington St. Built in the 1840's, the two-story frame structure, houses a large library and a wealth of early records and pioneer furnishings. Other buildings of Naperville's early years are the NEW YORK HOUSE, northeast corner Main and Jackson Sts., built as a hotel in 1849 and now occupied by a general store; the ROBERT N. MURRAY HOUSE (*private*), 215 S. Main St., a one-story frame structure with an excellent doorway of Greek Revival design; the OLD BAPTIST CHURCH, Washington and Jefferson Aves., a frame building of Greek Revival style built in 1843 and now used as a storehouse; and the MARTIN HOUSE (*private*), Ogden Ave. at the city limits, of the New England cottage type, built in 1933.

NORTH CENTRAL COLLEGE, School Ave. and Brainard St., a co-educational institution maintained by the Evangelical Church, was founded at Plainfield in 1861. In 1870 the college was moved to Naperville, occupying the north and central sections of OLD MAIN, a limestone structure of Italian Gothic design. The average enrollment of the college is 500. The elevation on the Fort Hill Campus, end of Ellsworth St., is the SITE OF FORT PAYNE. Affiliated with the college is the EVANGELICAL THEOLOGICAL SEMINARY, School Ave. and Loomis St., housed in three structures of Collegiate Gothic design.

The KROEHLER COMPANY MAIN PLANT (*tours arranged by application in advance*), between Ellsworth and Loomis Sts., was established here in 1887 as the Naperville Lounge Factory and is now one of the world's largest manufacturers of upholstered furniture.

1. Left from Naperville on S. Washington Street is PIONEER PARK (*picnic facilities*), 1.3 *m.*

The two millstones, near the junction of S. Washington Street and Goodrich Rd., are from Bailey Hobson's mill which stood at this site. Left from the mill site on Goodrich Road is the BAILEY HOBSON HOUSE (*private*), a two-story frame structure built in the 1830's.

2. Right from northwestern Naperville on Warrenville Road is WARREN-VILLE, 2.9 *m.*, a crossroads hamlet settled a few years after Naperville. Its tannery and gristmill drew trade from as far as Galena. One of the earlier institutions of learning in Illinois, the Warrenville Academy, was removed to Rockford in 1854 to become the nucleus of Rockford College.

One block northeast of the Warrenville bridge, which spans the west branch of the Du Page River, are the ALBRIGHT STUDIOS (*open Sun. afternoons only*), occupying two modern stone and stucco buildings and an 1854 structure that was once a Methodist church. The studios are used by Adam Emery Albright and his twin sons, Ivan Lorraine and Marvin Marr Albright (Zsissly). A distinguished collection of their paintings is housed here.

At 36.7 *m.* is a junction with State 47.

Left on State 47 to a junction with an unimproved road, 0.9 *m.*

Right here to a 21-acre STATE FISH HATCHERY (*open*), 1 *m.* About 1,000,-000 fish are bred here annually. North of the hatchery is a 75-acre STATE GAME

FARM (*open*), where silver, golden, mutant, Amherst, and ring-necked pheasants are bred.

At 1 *m.* on State 47 is YORKVILLE (584 alt., 492 pop.) on the south bank of the Fox River.

Right from Yorkville on Fox Road 3 *m.* to the CHICAGO TRIBUNE EXPERI-MENTAL FARM (*open in summer*, 8-5; *free guide service*). The 1,332-acre farm is conducted in the same manner and for the same reasons as the Tribune Farm at Wheaton (*see Tour* 12A). A HYDRAULIC RAM, which lifts spring water uphill to buildings and grounds, has been in operation for more than 40 years.

PLANO, 41.5 *m.* (649 alt., 1,785 pop.), its skyline dominated by a water tower and two grain elevators, is the trading center of a rich agricultural area. Kleng Peerson led a band of Norwegian Quakers to this region in 1835. Three years later one of the party, Ansten Natte-stad, visiting Norway, stimulated further immigration to the district by circulating Ole Rynning's *True Account of America for the Instruction and Use of the Peasants and Common People.*

Left from southwestern Plano on a graveled road is MARAMECH HILL, 1.5 *m.*, between the confluence of Big Rock and Little Rock creeks. The hill is believed by many to be the site of a dramatic siege during the wars between the French and the Fox Indians in the early part of the eighteenth century. In the late summer of 1730 a band of 300 Foxes with their families, bound for the Iroquois country, were surprised by a large force of French soldiers and their Indian allies. The Foxes entrenched their position and were besieged for more than three weeks. Under cover of a storm on the night of September 8, 1730, the Foxes slipped out of their "fort," but their departure was detected, and on the following day they were overtaken and ruthlessly slaughtered. The topography of Maramech Hill fits surviving descriptions fairly closely, but plausible claims have been made for other sites.

SANDWICH, 46.1 *m.* (657 alt., 2,611 pop.), named for Sand-wich, Massachusetts, is entered on a street flanked with trees and comfortable frame houses. Plows, reapers, windmills, and cornshellers are manufactured locally.

At 59.2 *m.* is (L) a junction with State 23.

Left on State 23 to a junction with a graveled road, 3.1 *m.;* R. to a junction with another graveled road, 4.8 *m.;* L. is SHABBONA STATE PARK (*camping and picnicking facilities*), 5.6 *m.* The 7-acre tract, bordering a tributary of the Fox River, commemorates the Potawatomi chief who befriended the settlers at the time of the Indian Creek Massacre. In 1832 Blackhawk urged Shabbona to unite his tribe with the Sauk in a war to drive all white inhabitants from the frontier. Shabbona refused and fled from the war council. In the night he mounted his pony and rode eastward to warn the settlers, although he knew few white men and did not speak or understand English. Sauk spies pursued him as he zigzagged his way over 200 miles of prairie and forest, spreading the alarm. His son, Pepys, traveled to the west on the same errand. Most of the settlers heeded the warning and escaped, but fifteen were caught and killed. The SITE OF THE INDIAN CREEK MASSACRE is marked by two monuments. One, a granite shaft, was erected by the State of Illinois in 1906; the other, of local stone, was erected by William Munson in 1877. At the north edge of the park is a museum which contains Indian and pioneer memorabilia.

MENDOTA, 77.2 *m.* (750 alt., 4,008 pop.) (*see Tour* 4), is at junctions with US 51 (*see Tour* 4) and US 52 (*see Tour* 15).

PRINCETON, 102 *m.* (719 alt., 4,762 pop.) (*see Tour* 14), is at a junction with US 6 (*see Tour* 14).

Section b. Princeton to Iowa Line, 115 m.

West of Princeton, 0 *m.,* US 34 and US 6 are united for 16 miles (*see Tour* 14).

At 27 *m.* is the junction with a graveled road.

Right on this road to FRANCIS PARK (*picnic grove, playgrounds*), 0.5 *m.,* named for Fred Francis (1856-1926), the eccentric inventor and brilliant mathematician who gave this 40-acre tract with its buildings and equipment to the people of Kewanee. Born of pioneer parents in the log cabin that stands in the park, Francis first achieved recognition at the University of Illinois, from which he was graduated with honors in mathematics. His talents were put to practical account during 11 years with the Elgin Watch Company, in the course of which he developed and patented several processes of watch manufacture.

In later years Francis retired to the family homestead and devoted his energies to mathematical experimentation, and the construction and constant improvement of Francis Park. He designed and built the FRANCIS HOUSE (*"The janitor will admit visitors to the building only when it is safe to do so without admitting flies or mice," reads Francis' will*), a one-story brick structure of eclectic design. It is equipped with an air conditioning system devised by Francis, and has doors that open automatically into rooms which wander from one level to another. A highly involved mathematical problem, conceived and solved by Francis, appears on the dining room wall as decoration. An artist of considerable accomplishment, Francis collected the statuary that adorns the interior of the house and landscaped the adjoining grounds.

KEWANEE (Ind., returning track), 30.5 *m.* (853 alt., 17,093 pop.), is industrial, both in warp and woof. Along the railroad that bisects the city are several large factories; one produces Kewanee boilers, familiar to almost every third janitor in the country; another manufactures Boss gloves, well known to legions of manual laborers.

The older part of Kewanee, south of Division Street, it still known as Wethersfield, although it has been part of the corporate city since 1924. In 1836 it was a new-born colony, the enterprise of the Connecticut Association, a group of influential Easterners "having in view the establishment of a colony for promoting the cause of education and piety in the State of Illinois." The Roman Catholics had already established a number of thriving communities in Illinois. The members of the Connecticut Association deemed it their duty to foster Protestantism in the rapidly growing State.

Wethersfield was accordingly founded and named for the parent community in Connecticut. Shares sold to New Englanders at $250 each gave title to 160 acres of prairie, 20 acres of woodland, and a town lot. In the summer of 1836 John Kilverton built the FIRST LOG CABIN, now preserved on the grounds of the high school, near the southern city limits. The first church, a plain structure of logs, was erected the same summer. Three years later the first school was opened; soon an academy was founded. The colony subsequently became a center of anti-slavery and Union settlement.

In 1854 the Military Tract Railroad, later the C. B. & Q., was built one mile north of Wethersfield. A settlement, destined to become Kewanee, took root near the depot, and many colonists removed to the new community; with the establishment of industrial plants along the railroad, scores of European immigrants arrived. By 1857 Kewanee, its population exceeding 2,000, had far outstripped the older Wethersfield.

A company here, one of the earliest of its kind in the country, began manufacturing steam and hot water equipment at Kewanee in the 1850's. From this enterprise evolved both the KEWANEE BOILER COMPANY PLANT (*open; conducted tours*), Franklin Street, and the WALWORTH MANUFACTURING PLANT, producing fitting and monkey wrenches, two of Kewanee's three major industrial concerns. Wethersfield, withdrawn from the railroad and conscious of her century-old traditions, shuns industry and remains strictly residential.

Kewanee is at the junction with State 78 (*see Tour* 5), which unites with US 34 for 5.4 miles.

At 35.2 *m.* is a junction with State 30-93.

Left on this road to the hamlet of ELMIRA, 5.2 *m.*, known in early days as the Scotch Settlement, which celebrated its centennial in 1938 with pageants and Scottish ceremonials. The immigrant founders were six weeks on the ocean, many more on the cross-country journey, and reached Stark County only after innumerable hardships. These pious settlers became strong Abolitionists, and made the village an important station on the Underground Railroad. Escaped slaves were hidden by day in attics, barn lofts, or in the timber, then escorted on moonless nights to the next station north.

GALVA, 43 *m.* (849 alt., 2,875 pop.), is the Anglicized form of Gefle, name of the seaport in Sweden whence the first settlers emigrated. The town was established in 1854 as an outgrowth of the communistic religious colony of Bishop Hill (*see below*), founded in 1846 by Erik Jansson. Galva's shops and railroad gave the more worldly minded Janssonists the opportunity to render unto Caesar the things that are Caesar's. At Bishop Hill it was one for all; at Galva it was every man for himself.

At 47 *m.* is a junction with a paved road, identified by a schoolhouse and a marker at the corner.

Right on this road to BISHOP HILL, 2.6 *m.* (786 alt., 208 pop.), named for Biskopskulla, Sweden, birthplace of Erik Jansson. (*All buildings, other than private residences, are open to visitors. If locked, inquire for key at garage S. of filling station on E. side of park. Residents are pleased to show buildings; no tipping, but contributions for maintenance of buildings are welcomed.*)

Bishop Hill was settled in 1846 by a group of Swedish emigrants led by Erik Jansson, a religious farmer who broke with the established church of Sweden and preached that the Bible alone could properly be used in religious services. Jansson conducted public burnings of hymnbooks and catechisms, and was frequently arrested by Swedish officials. He finally announced that "inasmuch as the inhabitants of my own country refuse to accept the truth," he and his followers would "turn to the heathen."

The small group crossed to America, came by way of canal and the Great Lakes to Illinois, and settled here in Henry County. They literally dug themselves in the first winter, hollowing out caves in a gorge near South Edwards Creek. In the following spring they began the establishment of a communistic colony. The basis of Jansson's communism was that of religion and necessity; he was unaware of the coeval political theory formulated by Karl Marx.

The colony prospered for a brief period. Families lived separately but labored together; having previously been higher, the maximum working period was set at 18 hours a day. They ate in a common dining hall and received their clothing from the community storehouse. These hardworking and progressive farmers readily adopted contemporary agricultural inventions. Flax, from which they made linen sold on a national market, and broomcorn, which they exported in large quantities, were the principal crops. In time Bishop Hill, with a population of 1,500, became the most important settlement between Peoria and Rock Island.

Internal squabbling disrupted Bishop Hill, as it disrupted almost every similar communal venture in Illinois. Jansson's dictatorship ended with his murder in 1850, and the administration of the colony passed to his wife. Wrested from her, it eventually became lodged with the colony's business representative, Olof Johnson, at Galva (see above). Financial mismanagement by the trustees split Bishop Hill into pro- and anti-trustee factions. Religious dissension hastened the colony's disorganization. One faction abandoned communism in 1861 and divided the property in equal portions; the other did likewise the next year. In the succeeding era, Bishop Hill, railroadless, rapidly declined. The colonists were converted to Methodism and Seventh-Day Adventism; not even the tenets of Jansson's creed survived. Today Bishop Hill is an atrophied village inhabited by descendants of the Swedish colonists. Elm, maple, and walnut trees planted in the early days shade quiet streets and old houses.

The STEEPLE BUILDING, northeast corner Main and Bishop Hill Sts., is a three-story brick and plaster structure, built in 1854 and now used as a dwelling. A classic portico dominates the façade. Pilastered pediments ornament the side walls and an octagonal cupola surmounts the hip roof. The bell, which still tolls the hour, and the clock in the cupola were made by the colony blacksmith. The clock, running since 1859, has no minute hand; as a villager explained: "In Bishop Hill we don't watch the minutes. Even the hours don't need watching here."

The OLD COLONY CHURCH, southwest corner Front and Bishop Hill Sts., a white two-story frame structure, was built in 1848 and is now used as the village meeting hall. Among the Janssonite memorabilia housed here are a spinning wheel, 93 oil paintings by Olof Krans, a lathe upon which the bedposts of the colony were fashioned, and a colorfully decorated bandwagon, designed for either wheels or runners. Krans, a blacksmith by trade, was a self-taught artist; most of his paintings are portraits of the founders, both men and women, but some depict early buildings, landscapes, and pioneer farming practices.

Just west of the Old Colony Church is the BAKERY AND BREWERY BUILDING, a three-story brick structure now used as an auditorium. The ball park west of this building is the SITE OF BIG BRICK, the four-story communal living quarters built in 1848-51. Men and women worked side by side in constructing the Big Brick. The basement was used as a kitchen and dining hall. In the 96 rooms of the upper stories families occupied suites, or single chambers, according to their needs. The building was destroyed by fire in 1928.

Among other old buildings that remain are the SCHOOL HOUSE (1860), west end of Main St.; the CHEESE FACTORY, a two-story structure of red brick and yellow plaster; the COLONY STOREHOUSE, a two-story brick building that now houses the post office; and the COLONY HOSPITAL, a two-story structure of red brick and yellow plaster, west of Park Street. Several old colony houses, now private residences, border the park on the south. In the park is the BISHOP HILL MEMORIAL, a granite boulder dedicated to the memory of the pioneers of the community "by surviving members and descendants, on the 50th anniversary of the founding of the colony, Sept. 23, 1896."

In the BISHOP HILL CEMETERY, E. Main Street, a white marble monument marks the GRAVE OF ERIK JANSSON. Below a shallow depression near the monument are the remains of 96 colonists who died during the winter of 1846-47. The SITE OF THE DUGOUTS in which the colonists lived during the winter of 1846-47 is along the upper edge of the ravine that extends northwest at the north end of Park Street.

GALESBURG, 70.5 m. (788 alt., 28,830 pop.), is one of the few Illinois cities that grew along a preconceived plan, rather than accumulating haphazardly around a group of pioneer cabins. The city was conceived in Oneida, New York, its site was chosen after a careful examination of land in Indiana and Illinois, and its plan was laid out before its proprietor-settlers came West.

In 1835, George Washington Gale, a thin Presbyterian minister, circulated among his parishioners in the Mohawk Valley a prospectus for a community he contemplated founding on the frontier. The paucity of religious and educational institutions there alarmed him, and he hoped that the proposed community would remedy the situation somewhat. Land was to be bought with money from a joint fund, and the nucleus of the village was to be a manual labor college whose chief function would be the training of ministers for the Middle Border. Gale believed that settlement of the land by a group of sober industrious farmers would raise land values, and from the sale of farms at an increased price he expected to obtain a fund to endow the college.

Into the Reverend Mr. Gale's plan some 50 families poured more than $20,000. A "spying-out" committee selected and purchased, for $1.25 an acre, 20 square miles of land here. In 1836-37 the families came west, some overland, some by way of the Erie Canal and the Great Lakes, a few of the more affluent along the Ohio and Mississippi Rivers. On arrival they built a temporary town, Log City, at the grove that bordered Henderson Creek. From here they went out on the prairie to the selected site and built permanent residences, because it had been decided that there were to be no crude log cabins in the new city. Many built their new houses at the grove, where lumber was plentiful, and then hauled them with oxen to the new town. Despite Galesburg's planned beginnings, it does not differ perceptibly from other prairie towns with no such orderly birth. Its streets follow the typical checkerboard pattern centered on the usual public square.

The strict morality of the early Galesburgers was combined with hard-headed practicality and versatility. Perhaps the most prolific of the pioneers were the Ferrises, one of whom, Olmsted Ferris, experimented with popcorn and later introduced it into England. The Prince Consort, Albert, became interested and the prairie New Englander gave a "command performance" of corn-popping before Queen Victoria. Another Ferris invented the ferris wheel, first exhibited at the Columbian Exposition in Chicago in 1893. Harvey Henry May, one of the original settlers, invented in 1837 a steel self-scouring plow, thus further complicating the historical problem of the invention of the first steel plow.

Archetype of all the moral New Englanders who settled here in the West was Jonathan Blanchard, early president of Knox College. In 1854 Galesburg obtained its first railroad by draining the resources of the town to raise a $250,000 subsidy. On the second Sunday of the railroad's operation Blanchard, magnificent in black frock coat, strode out to the tracks and curtly commanded the locomotive engineer to put the engine up and refrain from profaning the Sabbath. "You can go to hell and mind your own business," replied the engineer. "I'll take my train out as ordered."

The engineer's attitude was prophetic, for the railroad broke the grip of the New Englanders on Galesburg, and the population increased from 880 in 1850 to 4,000 in 1856. Galesburg was made a division point on the Burlington; the railroad's shops were established here; and the line is now the city's major employer. In 1857 a large number of Swedes from the Bishop Hill colony (*see above*) came to Galesburg, further diluting the authority of the founding fathers. Galesburg's increased distinction enabled her to wrest the county seat from Knoxville, occasioning the decline of that town. During the Civil War the deeply intrenched abolitionist sentiment of the New Englanders made Galesburg a strong anti-slavery town in the midst of communities which definitely favored the South. Galesburg was one of the most important stations on the Underground Railroad, and many of its Negroes are descended from slaves who were smuggled up from Cairo in farm wagons covered with hay.

Memorial to the New Englanders is KNOX COLLEGE, bounded by South, Cedar, Brooks, and Cherry Sts. Chartered in 1837, four years before Galesburg was incorporated, it began to function in 1838 in a crude frame building that also served as preparatory school, church, and town meeting hall. The college was a heartbreaking problem to the early settlers. Gale's prospectus had offered scholarships with each farm, and the school opened with the equivalent of 500 four-year scholarships outstanding. For a time the institution was named Knox Manual Labor College, and all boys worked several hours daily on the college farm to pay their board. Tuition for the few whose parents had no scholarship was $24 a year, exclusive of room rent. The boom in land prices that followed the coming of the railroad, however, aided Knox financially. The college was retarded for some time by a violent jurisdictional quarrel between the Presbyterians and the Congregationalists, who were about equally represented among the founding fathers. The quarrel was resolved by a decline of sectarianism, and although this broke the bond between town and gown, Knox's scholastic standing was greatly improved.

In 1870 women were admitted to the full college course, although previously a "female department" had been operated in close conjunction with the college. In 1909 Karl Baedeker laconically listed eight of the United States' 400 colleges as being "well-known," and included Knox with Amherst, Dartmouth, Williams, and Rutgers. Lombard College, founded by the Universalists in 1851, was absorbed by Knox in 1930. Knox students have included Carl Sandburg, Don Marquis, Eugene Field (by adoption from Lombard), and George Fitch, whose humorous "Old Siwash" stories in the *Saturday Evening Post,* based on Knox College, gave the American language a catchword for freshwater colleges. At OLD MAIN, oldest building on the campus, the fifth Lincoln-Douglas debate was held on the raw windy afternoon of October 7, 1858. The building is the only structure associated with the seven debates that is still standing.

With an enrollment (1938) of some 600, Knox is still careful to proclaim itself a "Christian college," but has long since abandoned the original purpose of its founders, the training of missionaries for the prairie country. The connection between town and campus is now more casual, and Galesburg, although rightfully proud of its school, no longer looks upon it as a family possession.

Southwest of Galesburg US 34 crosses the rich rolling farmlands of Knox County. Along the railroad, which here closely parallels the highway, are agricultural villages founded in the 1850's. Their chief economic and physical feature are lofty grain elevators, several of which are co-operatively owned.

MONMOUTH, 87 *m.* (762 alt., 8,666 pop.) (*see Tour 7*), is at a junction with US 67 (*see Tour 7*).

The highway enters BOGUS HOLLOW, 104 *m.*, a wild ravine leading to the bottom lands of the Mississippi. The hollow is said to have been the rendezvous of a band of counterfeiters once notorious throughout this region. On the upland level that flanks the ravine are several INDIAN MOUNDS of the Mississippi cultural group. Emerging from the ravine at the foot of the bluffs, the highway traverses a broad flood plain.

At 106 *m.* is a junction with State 164.

Right on State 164 is GLADSTONE, 1.3 *m.* (543 alt., 274 pop.), platted in 1856, its houses clustered about a grain elevator. Early settlers were largely Irish, Swedish, and German immigrants. Limestone quarries along nearby Henderson Creek have yielded much of the stone used in the piers of bridges on the Upper Mississippi.

Left from Gladstone 2.5 *m.* on a graveled road just north of the railroad tracks is LOCK AND DAM No. 18, one of 26 on the Upper Mississippi designed to assist in the control of floods on the lower river and to maintain a 9-foot channel between St. Louis and the Twin Cities.

Ahead on State 164, roughly parallel to the highway bridge over Henderson Creek, is (R) a COVERED BRIDGE (*picnicking*), 3.4 *m*. The bridge is more than a hundred years old, with massive oak beams held together with wooden pegs. The structure has been reconditioned by the State. Above the entrance is this warning: "Five dollars fine, for leading or driving any beast faster than a walk, or driving more than thirty head of cattle, mules, or horses at a time on or across the bridge."

OQUAWKA (548 alt., 777 pop.), 6.2 *m*. Henderson County seat, originated as a small trading post established in 1827 by the Phelps brothers. Its name is derived from Ozaukee (Ind., yellow banks), by which the site was known to Indians who crossed the Mississippi at this point on northward hunting expeditions. Oquawka's principal industry is the manufacture of pearl button blanks from mussel shells. Heaped shells litter the waterfront; crushed shells surface adjacent streets. Oquawka is also the base of small scale lumbering operations. Timber cut on nearby islands is floated downstream and sawed here by portable mills.

The HENDERSON COUNTY COURTHOUSE, one block north of State 164 on 3rd Street, is a two-story tetrastyle structure of Classic Revival design. Overshadowing the portico is an open cupola, topped with a weathervane. The building was given to Henderson County by the Phelps brothers in 1842. First circuit court judge to preside here was Stephen A. Douglas, whose handwriting appears in the records (1841-43).

North of Oquawka along the Mississippi are several beaches and camp sites (*with or without charge, according to accommodations and locations; a few cabins for rent*). Natural sand beaches afford good swimming; the adjoining woodlands support a variety of wild life.

East of Oquawka on State 164, at the east end of the bridge across Henderson Creek, 8 *m.*, a dirt road leads (R) to RADMACHER MILL (*open*), 0.2 *m.*, built in the 1830's. The mill, operated by the waterpower of Henderson Creek, grinds feed, flour, corn meal, and buckwheat. Its tightly fitted woodwork of bins, chutes, cleansers, and elevators is of California redwood; the huge mill stones are French burrs. The auxiliary steam plant at the rear of the mill has not been used for 19 years. The COVERED BRIDGE opposite the mill was built in 1846, and is still in use.

GULFPORT, 114.5 *m.*, consists of a scattering of cottages on the bottomland at the eastern approach to the Burlington Bridge. The village is all that remains of East Burlington, platted as a ferry port in 1855, but abandoned after completion of the bridge.

US 34 crosses the Iowa Line, 115 *m.*, midway on the toll bridge (20c), spanning the Mississippi to Burlington, Iowa (*see Iowa Guide*).

TOUR 14

Roadbed hard-surfaced throughout.
The Chicago, Rock Island & Pacific Ry. roughly parallels the route.
Accommodations at short intervals.

US 6 crosses the State almost due east and west, from the Indiana Line just south of Chicago to the Mississippi River at Davenport, Iowa. After skirting the heavy industrial area south of the metropolis, it parallels the Illinois River from its origin at the confluence of the Kankakee and Des Plaines, to the town of Depue, where the river swings sharply south. West of Depue the route traverses prairie land given over almost wholly to agriculture, and ends in the extensive industrial area centering on Rock Island and Moline.

Section a. Indiana Line to La Salle, 96 m.

US 6 crosses the Indiana Line, 0 *m.*, from Hammond, Indiana (*see Indiana Guide*).

GREEN LAKE SWIMMING POOL (25c) is in the SHABBONA WOODS FOREST PRESERVE (R), 1.5 *m.* Shortly west, at 1.9 *m.*, is a junction with US 330 (*see Tour* 12A).

The highway crosses the Little Calumet River into SOUTH HOLLAND, 4 *m.* (600 alt., 1,873 pop.), in the heart of the truck farming region described by Edna Ferber in *So Big*. Three out of four of the mail boxes before the neat houses bear typical Dutch names, for the community, settled in 1840 with a great influx of farmers from the Netherlands, has preserved its racial composition against the later influx of Poles and Italians to the industrial towns that adjoin South Holland.

The chief pursuit of the community is the raising of onion sets—onions less than an inch in diameter, raised from seed, stored until the following season, then planted by commercial growers to produce marketable vegetables of larger size and better quality than those raised directly from seed. On the rich black muck that was once lake bottom, flat as a calm lagoon, seed is sown thickly in late March and April. Throughout the early summer the young plants are carefully weeded, then, in August, are harvested. During the winter they are stored in long low warehouses; early the following year, they are sifted, cleansed, culled, and packed. The entire job, from planting to packing, is done by the Italian and Polish women and girls of the nearby industrial centers. The South Hollanders do the marketing and buying, largely on a co-operative plan. Twenty years ago, almost the entire onion set crop of America was produced in this vicinity. Other important centers have since entered the field, but South Holland still ships 400 to 500 carloads annually. The seed, about 75,000 pounds a year, is purchased from western states.

HARVEY, 6.1 *m.* (608 alt., 16,374 pop.) (*see Tour* 1), is at a junction with State 1 (*see Tour* 1).

Beyond MARKHAM, 7.9 *m.* (593 alt., 349 pop.), the road rises above the flat lake plain and winds over the rolling Valparaiso Moraine, which extends almost to Joliet.

OAK FOREST, 10.5 *m.*, does not include in its population figures, estimated at 800, the 3,000 aged men and women and 475 patients of the OAK FOREST INFIRMARY (*open* 10-4 *daily*) and TUBERCULOSIS HOSPITAL (*open* 3-4:30 *daily*), which are today the town's chief reason for being. The infirmary and hospital, established in 1911, are maintained by Cook County, as is the ST. MIHIEL RESERVATION FOREST PRESERVE, which flanks the wide grounds of the institutions.

At 17.7 *m.* is a junction with US 45 (*see Tour* 3).

JOLIET, 33 *m.* (545 alt., 42,993 pop.) (*see Joliet*).

Points of Interest: Joliet Wall Paper Mills, American Institute of Laundering Vocational Training School, Oakwood Mound, and others.

Joliet is at the junction with US 30 (*see Tour* 12) and US 66 (*see Tour* 17).

At the south limits of Joliet, on the west side of the river, the basin of the BRANDON ROAD DAM borders the road (L). The LOCKS, 35.7 *m.*, provide a 33-foot step for the traffic on the Lakes-to-Gulf Waterway. Nearby is a lock of the old Illinois and Michigan Canal, its 100-foot length and 20-foot width in sharp contrast to the 600 x 110 foot dimensions of the new installation. At this point, the canal channel has been absorbed by the Brandon Pool, which rises 15 feet above parts of Joliet. Over the spillways of the 1,569-foot dam, connecting with the lock, glides a thick sheet of water, an imposing cataract. Basic facilities for the possible utilization of the drop in developing hydro-electric power have been installed by the State.

CHANNAHON (Ind., meeting of the waters), 44 *m.*, is a village at the confluence of the Du Page and Des Plaines Rivers. Settled in 1832, Channahon shortly received impetus in its development from the Illinois and Michigan Canal. In its heyday, there were six grain elevators within four miles of the town. Several steamboats carried corn to Chicago, but most of the freight was carried in canal boats drawn by mules along the towpath. Industry once flourished here, notably quarrying and the manufacture of farm equipment, but now only a quiet rural community survives.

Left from Channahon, near its northern border, on a graveled road (*inquire locally*) are the BRISCOE MOUNDS, 0.5 *m.*, on the Briscoe farm. Two mounds— one 90 feet in diameter by 10 feet in height, the other half as large, both nearly round and sloping smoothly to the top—comprise this mound group, one of five in the Joliet area. These two mounds are unexcavated.

Bordering the highway bridge is one of the most attractive parts of the Illinois and Michigan Canal Parkways System, which extends the length of the canal, in a narrow belt; to date it has been improved only in spots. In this ROADSIDE PARK (*picnic facilities, shelters*) is a new system of spillways and wastegates, and two old canal locks. One lock drops water from the canal into the Du Page River, and the other drops it again into the canal channel on the other side of the river.

Left from the roadside park on the tree-arched towpath (*one-way graveled lane*) along the canal is McKINLEY WOODS, 3 *m.*, a Will County Forest Preserve (*picnic facilities, shelters*). Just before the entrance to the woods, in the canal, is the remains of the *City of Pekin,* an old canal boat.

Immediately across the river from the woods is the site of the FISHER MOUNDS. Comprising two large mounds, 60 feet and 50 feet in diameter, and 6 smaller ones, they were thoroughly excavated by a University of Chicago field party in 1929 and gave a rich yield. The Fisher Mounds revealed three successive civilizations and cultures, the last giving evidence of contact with white men. Several hundred fully articulated skeletons were discovered. These and the pottery, tools, and other artifacts are housed in the Museum of the Anthropology Department, University of Chicago.

Ahead on the towpath is a PARKING AREA, 4 *m.*, commanding a view of the confluence of the Des Plaines and Kankakee Rivers, which here form the Illinois. DRESDEN HEIGHTS LOCK AND DAM, 5.7 *m.*, on the towpath, is the next below the Brandon Lock on the Illinois deep waterway system. The towpath ends at the lock, but connects, on the same side of the canal, with a graveled road leading to the AUX SABLE CREEK AQUEDUCT AND LOCK of the Illinois and Michigan Canal, 8.7 *m.* An iron aqueduct carries the canal across the creek, and a few yards beyond, Lock No. 8 drops the canal to a lower channel. The road crosses the canal, 8.8 *m.*, turns R., and leads back to the highway, 10.5 *m.* (5.4 miles west of the roadside park).

West of Channahon, US 6 roughly parallels the Illinois River for 60 miles. In the early days of the Illinois country the river was of tremendous importance, an avenue of exploration and, later, of commerce. In 1673 Jolliet described the valley as "most beautiful and most easy to be settled. This river is wide and deep," he wrote; "it is stocked with brills and sturgeons. Game is there in abundance. There are prairies three, six, ten, and twenty leagues in length and three in width. . . . A settler would not be required to spend ten years cutting down and burning timber." Although the valley of the Illinois was not settled under the flag of France as he had hoped, its rapid development following the completion of the Illinois and Michigan Canal amply supported Jolliet's judgment.

At 56.1 *m.* is a junction with US 52 (*see Tour* 15), with which US 6 is united for 0.7 mile.

MARSEILLES, 73.5 *m.* (506 alt., 4,292 pop.), an industrial community since its beginning, lies athwart a stretch of rapids in the Illinois River. It is the only city in the region that uses water power almost exclusively. Coal is used only in time of ice jams or for special industrial tasks, such as the drying of paper, the manufacture of which is an important industry of the city.

Left from Marseilles on Main Street, across the Illinois River, is the 407-acre ILLINI STATE PARK (*picnic facilities, shelters*). The large island in the park, two and a half miles in length, was formed when a channel was cut for the deep waterway. Between Marseilles and the island is the MARSEILLES DAM, part of the system used for passing the Marseilles rapids. The MARSEILLES LOCK, at the west end of the island, drops traffic into the river below the rapids.

OTTAWA, 81 *m.* (486 alt., 15,094 pop.), at the junction of the Fox River with the Illinois, was laid out in 1830 by the Illinois and Michigan Canal commissioners. However, it was not until after the Black Hawk War (1832) that the influx of settlers became stabilized. New Englanders came first, bringing with them their political, religious, and educational beliefs. In the thirties and forties, Ottawa was an important center for travel between Chicago and the Illinois Valley. The completion of the canal and the development of waterpower established the city as an industrial and wheat center, and attracted the immigration of eastern and southeastern Europeans.

In 1858 the city of Ottawa counted a population of approximately 5,000, but on August 21 of that year her public square accommodated a crowd of twice that figure. It was the day of the first Lincoln-Douglas debate. The New York *Evening Post* of August 27 reported that "by wagon, by rail, by canal the people poured in, till Ottawa was one mass of active life. Men, women and children, old and young, the dwellers on the broad prairies, had turned their backs on the plough, and had come to listen to these champions of the two parties. Military companies were out; martial music sounded, and salutes of artillery thundered in the air. Eager marshals in partisan sashes rode furiously about the streets. Peddlers were crying their wares at the corners, and excited groups of politicians were canvassing and quarrelling everywhere."

The three-hour debate, on the extension of slavery into newly-formed states and territories, was marked by strong feeling on both sides. The crowd was vociferous in its loyalties, cheering its favorite, heckling its opponent. It was a grand parade of politics.

In Washington Park, at Columbus and La Fayette Sts., a huge boulder marks the SITE OF THE FIRST LINCOLN-DOUGLAS DEBATE. At the northwest corner of Columbus and La Fayette Sts. stands the REDDICK HOUSE, now the public library, a three-story red brick limestone trimmed building with a high front stoop. It was built in 1859 for

William Reddick, an Illinois State senator. The APPELLATE COURT-HOUSE, opposite the Library, is an example of the Greek Revival style of architecture. The LINCOLN SUN DIAL, on the lawn of the Ottawa Boat Club, at the bridge, designates the spot where Lincoln was mustered out of service at the close of his first enlistment of the Black Hawk War.

The major part of Ottawa covers the terraces formed by the Illinois River. To the north rise the river bluffs, on which stand many imposing old homes. Overlooking the valley is the CATON HOUSE, a large, faded red brick structure with bays and dormered windows, built by John Dean Caton, former chief justice of the Illinois Supreme Court. Mrs. Arthur Caton, the judge's daughter-in-law, who later married Marshall Field, acquired the house and it became a great summer social center. From the Fields, the house passed into the hands of Mrs. Albert J. Beveridge, widow of the late senator from Indiana.

Nearby is THE OAKS completed in 1860 for the Civil War General W. H. L. Wallace, who was killed at the Battle of Shiloh. The grey stone house, with an overhanging gabled roof, and a Gothic window above the entrance, has a distinct individuality and contains many original furnishings and relics, including a Boston piano, and a 33-star blood-stained flag from the Battle of Shiloh. In a small burial plot in the surrounding grove of white oaks is the GRAVE OF GENERAL WALLACE and those of others of his family.

Immediately west of Ottawa, near the river, in an Italian settlement of small frame houses known as Lof-town, is the LIBBY-OWENS-FORD GLASS FACTORY, largest industrial plant of the Ottawa region. The company uses the surrounding extensive deposits of St. Peter sandstone, a superior glass sand, in the manufacture of safety glass. Clay products, agricultural implements, and playground equipment also are made in Ottawa. An indispensable item for the playgrounds and back yards of America, the colored "mibs" and "shooters" known to every boy, are turned out in a single plant, at the rate of more than a million and a half a day.

Left from Ottawa on State 71 to the EAST ENTRANCE to STARVED ROCK STATE PARK (*hiking, boating, swimming, and fishing; picknicking, camping, lodge facilities*) 7 m. This oldest of Illinois State parks, a narrow strip of bluff, woodland, and terrace fronting the south bank of the Illinois River for more than 4 miles between Ottawa and La Salle, contains in its more than 900 acres wildlands as varied as any in Illinois. Its principal natural and historical feature, Starved Rock, towers 140 feet above the river, commanding a scene of extraordinary beauty, the locale of French and Indian associations.

Within the park, which was opened in 1912, are almost 50 points of interest—canyons, caves, bluffs, and rocks—fancifully or historically named, all well marked and connected by 18 miles of trails. The two main trails parallel the river, one along the banks, the other on the bluffs. The many canyons are narrow gorges, carved deeply in the sandstone of the bluffs, of varying lengths, cool and shady, and overgrown with ferns, vines, and flowering plants. In wet seasons in some of the canyons water pours in tiny cascades over the rocky floors. Caves are shallow, high vaults carved in the base of the bluffs.

Within the eastern section of the park are a SULPHUR WELL and a SALT WELL, two of the numerous mineral springs along the river in La Salle County. Here also are SKELETON CAVE; ILLINOIS, KASKASKIA, OTTAWA, and HENNEPIN CANYONS; COUNCIL CAVE and CAVE OF THE WINDS; and DIMMICK HILL. In the central section natural features include HIDDEN, OWL, LA SALLE, HORSE-SHOE, TONTI, LONE TREE, and WILDCAT CANYONS, and the odd formations, PULPIT ROCK and WITCH'S KITCHEN. Rustic signs point the way to these several features.

The SOUTH ENTRANCE (R), 11 m., leads to the western third of the park. At the entrance is the CAMP GROUND (50c per car first night, 25c thereafter; all camping facilities). A LODGE and a dozen CABINS (for rates and reservations address Concessionaires, Starved Rock State Park, Utica, Ill.) have been built of logs by the CCC. In this western section the bluffs recede from the river; on the broad terrace are the main parking area and the refreshment and food concessions. Here also are a SWIMMING POOL (25c) and a PIER from which park boats make an hour-and-a-half excursion on the river (adults, 40c; children, 20c). The CCC has effected many improvements in the park; all buildings, shelters, and trails are designed to fit into the landscape of the bluff and woodland.

Starved Rock dominates the natural features of this section of the park, but associated with it are many lesser formations. LOVERS LEAP is a popular promontory overlooking the river; at its base is STARVED ROCK LOCK AND DAM and LAKE STARVED ROCK. Nearby is LOST LAKE and such fantastically eroded forms as JACOBS LADDER, the DEVILS BATHTUB, and the DEVILS NOSE.

STARVED ROCK rises from dense woodland that covers and obscures the Rock from the park side. Artificial and natural steps lead to the summit, which affords a commanding view of the river and of Buffalo Rock State Park (see below) across the Illinois. It was in September 1673 that Jolliet and Marquette, returning from their exploration of the Mississippi River, stopped at an encampment of Kaskaskia Indians across the river from Starved Rock. Marquette recorded in his journal that the village consisted of 74 cabins. Two years later, fulfilling his promise to the Indians, Marquette returned to establish a mission at the village.

After giving preliminary instructions to the chiefs and old men at the village, he called together a great council, which was held three days before Easter. Mats and bearskins covered the council ground, and four large pictures of the Virgin Mary were hung by pieces of taffeta from lines that had been stretched overhead. The father stood in the center and seated in a circle about him were the 500 chiefs and elders; in the background stood the young men, who numbered about 1,000 in all, and the women and children. Marquette gave the Indians ten presents, symbolic of the ten religious messages that he delivered, and concluded by saying mass. A second council was held two days later, after which the father made preparations for his return. The journey out to the village had been an exceedingly strenuous one, and Marquette's health was seriously impaired. Certain that he could not live much longer, he hastened on the return trip to Mackinac in order that he might die within its walls, but death overtook him on the way.

In 1679 La Salle and Tonti visited the same village, and were impressed with the strategic value of the Rock. Three years later they undertook the erection of a fort, Fort St. Louis du Rocher, on its summit. The fort was maintained by Tonti after La Salle's death in 1687, but was finally abandoned in 1702. French fur traders occupied the structure intermittently until 1721, when it was burned by the Indians. Today no relic of the fort remains. Only the strength of the Rock suggests the power that Louis XIV let slip through his hands when he turned a deaf ear to the plans of La Salle to colonize the Mississippi Valley.

On the summit of the Rock a MEMORIAL TABLET records the legendary incident from which Starved Rock derives its name. During the early French occupation of the region, Indians of the Illinois Valley settled in large numbers along the river banks under the protection of the fort. Allied with their protectors, they fought against the other Indian tribes. After the French withdrew from the region the tribal wars became more bitter, culminating in the annihilation of a band of Illinois Indians (1769) on the summit of Starved Rock. Pontiac, Chief of the Ottawa, fleeing from the British, who had broken his tribe, was murdered at Cahokia by one of the Illini among whom he had taken refuge. The remnants of the Ottawa, allied with the Potawatomi, thereupon waged war fiercely upon the Illinois, finally forcing one of the remnants of the tribe to seek shelter on the summit of the Rock. Here they were safe from attack, but not from hunger and thirst. Baskets lowered to the river to draw up water were seized by their enemies. In a desperate attempt to escape all but a few were slain. These lived to tell the tale that has given Starved Rock its name.

The episode is purely legendary, but it harmonizes so perfectly with the geography of the region that it has become an ineffaceable part of the folklore of Illinois.

At 11.6 m. on State 71 is a junction with State 178.

Left on State 178 is DEER PARK (open May-Oct.; adm. 25c; closed 1 hr. before sundown), 1 m., a 240-acre heavily wooded estate, with a deep gorge carved in the sandstone by a tributary of the Vermilion River. The canyon is one and a half miles in length. Under an arched bridge a waterfall drops 55 feet to a lower dell. Seepage of mineral waters has in places streaked the grotesquely carved walls with bright color. Tradition has it that the Indians used the park's canyons as enclosures for deer, which furnished the winter's meat supply. A HERD OF DEER and a REPRODUCTION OF A PIONEER STOCKADE AND BLOCKHOUSE attract visitors.

From the junction of State 71 and State 178 the route is continued north on State 178, past the WEST ENTRANCE to Starved Rock State Park, 12.6 m., to the SITE OF OLD UTICA, 13.2 m., on the north bank of the Illinois River. Old Utica, failing to gain the terminus of the Illinois and Michigan Canal, moved bag and baggage to its present site when the canal was opened (1848) a mile to the north.

UTICA, 14.2 m., today serves Starved Rock visitors with post office and tourist accommodations, and operates a cement mill and associated industries.

At 15.5 m. is the end of State 178 at a junction with US 6 (see below).

West of Ottawa US 6 leaves the valley to cross rolling farm lands. At 84.9 m. is a junction with a graveled road.

Left on this road is BUFFALO ROCK STATE PARK, 2.3 m. (shelters, picnic facilities), which takes its name from a huge, tree-topped rock rising 100 feet from the north bank of the Illinois River. Erosion detached the rock from the valley bluffs, forming a channel which is now used as a passage for the Illinois and Michigan Canal and the Chicago, Rock Island & Pacific Railroad. The rock served the French as an early military, trading, and missionary post, and later became a principal stronghold of the Illinois Indians in their losing fight against the encroachment of the northern tribes into the Illinois Valley. These, in turn, pressed by the white men, stayed on briefly. Today, picnic benches and shelters occupy the site of trading posts and forts, and shod feet tread the trails worn by mocassins and buffalo hoofs.

At 90.2 m. is a junction with State 178, the western entrance to Starved Rock State Park (see above).

LA SALLE, 96 m. (448 alt., 13,149 pop.) (see Tour 4), is at a junction with US 51 (see Tour 4).

Section b. La Salle to Iowa Line, 86 m.

Contiguous with La Salle, 0 *m.,* is PERU, 2 *m.* (459 alt., 9,121 pop.) (*see Tour* 4), at a junction with US 51 (*see Tour* 4).

St. Bede College and Academy (L), 3.9 *m.,* founded in 1889 by the Benedictine fathers, is the preparatory seminary of the Peoria Catholic diocese. The long red-brick, four-story building, half a mile from the highway, is surrounded by spacious grounds. A Natural History Museum on an upper floor (*apply at office*) contains a large collection of local and foreign specimens and a fine group of Indian relics.

The highway passes through the northern fringe of SPRING VALLEY, 5.6 *m.* (465 alt., 5,270 pop.), once the scene of extensive mining operations now succeeded by manufacturing.

At 7 *m.* is a junction with State 89.

Right on State 89 is CHERRY, 7.1 *m.* (682 alt., 636 pop.), scene of the State's worst industrial disaster, a mine fire of November 1909, in which gas and smoke took the lives of 270 men; only 20 were rescued after being entombed for eight days. In the cemetery at the south edge of the village stands a Memorial to the Victims of the Cherry Mine Disaster; on November 13 of each year, services are held in their memory. The site of the mine, at the north end of Cherry, is marked by a huge pyramid, a pink and gray mine dump.

At 10.7 *m.* is a junction with a paved road.

Left on this road is DEPUE, 1.5 *m.* (473 alt., 2,200 pop.), which functioned as a river port until the decline of the steamboat. A zinc smelter saved the town, but killed all vegetation in the vicinity. Recent plantings are returning the forest growth.

Lake Depue, a three-mile inlet of the river, served as a harbor in early river traffic days. The lake is the scene of the annual Labor Day water sports carnival of the Midwest Outboard Association. William Cullen Bryant, who visited his brother, John Howard, at nearby Princeton, is said to have received the inspiration for his poem "To a Water Fowl" from Lake Depue. An unusual change in the habits of wild life has taken place along the Illinois River. The advent of the mechanical corn picker has caused thousands of wild ducks of several varieties to winter in the valley. The corn picker leaves many kernels of grain on the fields, thus furnishing a winter food supply for the ducks.

At Depue the Illinois begins the "Great Bend" to the southwest, and the highway, continuing westward, no longer follows the river. Instead, the route roughly parallels the Illinois and Mississippi Canal, which is laid out in an abandoned valley of the Illinois. The glaciers blocked this ancient course with deep drift and forced the river to carve the Great Bend and swing far southward before joining the Mississippi. The canal, opened in 1907, was built at a cost of 7 million dollars and was expected to join the Quad Cities—Rock Island, Moline, East Moline, and Davenport, Iowa—with Chicago and the towns along the Illinois and Michigan Canal. But the Rock Island

Railroad, following the same course, accomplished the same purpose more successfully, and the canal was scarcely opened before it fell into disuse. Today it finds greater use as a fishing stream than as a commercial waterway.

The route is across the western upland of the State, a region of glacial drift, partly wooded, partly prairie—a gently rolling countryside of villages and small towns, of corn and hogs, of sober industry and quiet beauty.

PRINCETON, 22 m. (719 alt., 4,762 pop.), is the seat of Bureau County and a center of nursery, orchard, and farming activities. Laid out in 1833 by colonists from Northampton, Mass., Princeton's streets are arched by the great elms planted by its founders. Strongly abolitionist before the Civil War, it was the home of Owen Lovejoy, abolitionist preacher and brother of Elijah Lovejoy, the abolitionist editor who was killed by a pro-slavery mob at Alton. At the east edge of town is the white frame OWEN LOVEJOY HOMESTEAD (R). Red brick chimneys rise from the gabled roof of the newly painted house, and contrast with the bright green shutters.

The CYRUS BRYANT HOUSE, 1110 S. Main St., was built of brick in 1844. Its wide black walnut wainscoting and other original features are little changed. In the front yard, a boulder marks the site of the log cabin that Cyrus and his brother John built when they preempted the land. The JOHN BRYANT HOUSE, 1518 S. Main St., of the same period, is a brick structure, with a porch made of boulders. The Bryants were brothers of William Cullen Bryant. John was a poet in his own right, a representative in the State legislature, a founder of the Republican Party, and a friend of Abraham Lincoln.

At Princeton is a junction with US 34 (see Tour 13), with which US 6 is united for 16 miles.

WYANET, 28.5 m. (656 alt., 859 pop.), is on the Illinois and Mississippi Canal. At the western edge of the village is the WYANET FISH HATCHERY and LOCK No. 21 (L).

The highway crosses the ILLINOIS AND MISSISSIPPI CANAL, 30.5 m. The level terrain in this area facilitated the construction of the canal; little cutting or grading was necessary. Of this unbroken prairie a Scotch traveler wrote in 1835, "I recommend [it] to British sportsmen, as a country likely to afford them amusement and instruction. A person may cross the Atlantic with a brace of dogs in one of the best vessels, and travel to the prairies, and devote a year to the excursion, living in the best style the country affords, for the sum of £200 sterling. If he were economical in crossing the ocean, and living with settlers, and serving himself while in Illinois, the expense would be under £120."

At 38 m. is a junction with US 34 (see Tour 13).

ANNAWAN, 47 m. (626 alt., 489 pop.), center of an extensive

stock farming and coal mining region, is at a junction with State 78 (*see Tour* 5).

Between Annawan and ATKINSON, 52.8 *m.* (647 alt., 689 pop.), the landscape is torn by the pits and mounds of active and inactive strip mines. The State is currently planning to plant thousands of trees in this waste area and develop it for recreational uses. Settlement in the region is dominantly Belgian.

GENESEO, 60.8 *m.* (639 alt., 3,406 pop.), was settled in 1836 by colonists from Bergen and Geneseo, New York. The city is a farm trade center, and also has a corn and pea cannery and a bandage factory. The highway passes along the old business street. With the arrival of the railroad, the commercial section was moved three blocks northward.

Right from Geneseo on a paved road is the GENESEO STATE FISH HATCHERY and LOCK No. 24 of the Illinois and Mississippi Canal, 2.7 *m.*

At the hamlet of BRIAR BLUFF, 72 *m.*, US 6 divides: City US 6 proceeds north through the eastern suburbs of Rock Island and Moline; By-Pass US 6 continues west.

Left (straight ahead) on By-Pass US 6 to a junction with 27th St., 7 *m.;* R. on 27th St. to 23rd Ave., at a junction with State 80 (*see Tour* 6), 9.7 *m.;* L. on 23rd Ave. to 19th St., 10 *m.;* R. on 19th St. to MOLINE, 11.3 *m.* (*see below*), where By-Pass US 6 crosses the Iowa Line, 12 *m.*, on a toll bridge (15c) over the Mississippi River to Bettendorf, Iowa (*see Iowa Guide*).

North of Briar Bluff, City US 6 crosses the GREEN RIVER, 72.5 *m.;* the ILLINOS AND MISSISSIPPI CANAL, 73 *m.;* and the ROCK RIVER, 74 *m.*

CARBON CLIFF, 75.4 *m.* (570 alt., 494 pop.), and SILVIS, 76.7 *m.* (576 alt., 2,650 pop.), adjoining communities, are on the eastern limits of the Quad Cities, and contain mainly the dwellings of workers in those cities. The remainder of the route is over city streets.

At 77.3 *m.* is a junction with State 80 (*see Tour* 6), which is the corporate boundary between Silvis and East Moline.

EAST MOLINE, 78.3 *m.* (576 alt., 10,107 pop.), incorporated as a city in 1907, is an industrial extension of Moline and Rock Island, and with those cities shares the distinction of being one of the largest farm implement manufacturing centers in the world. The INTER-NATIONAL HARVESTER COMPANY PLANT (*guide service Mon.-Fri.*) on 3rd Street north of the highway, is the largest of East Moline's industrial plants. EAST MOLINE STATE HOSPITAL (*visiting* 9-11 *and* 2-4 *daily*), overlooking the Mississippi River, from the east side of State 80, cares for more than 2,000 patients. The main building is in the castellated Gothic style. Immediately west of the hospital grounds, separated from the shore by a narrow channel of the Mississippi, is CAMPBELL'S ISLAND STATE PARK (*picnic facilities*). An obelisk marks the SITE OF THE BATTLE OF CAMPBELL'S ISLAND, in which Major John Campbell defeated a large band of Indians under Chief Black Hawk during the War of 1812.

MOLINE, 82 *m.* (575 alt., 32,236 pop.), and ROCK ISLAND, 85 *m.* (566 alt., 37,953 pop.) (*see Rock Island & Moline*).

Points of Interest: Rock Island Arsenal, Black Hawk State Park, Vandruff's Island, Rock Island Dam, Plants of Deere & Co., Scottish Rite Cathedral, and others.

Rock Island and Moline are at a junction with US 67 (*see Tour 7*).

City US 6 crosses the Iowa Line, 86 *m.*, on the Government Bridge across the Mississippi River to Davenport, Iowa (*see Iowa Guide*).

TOUR 15

(KENTLAND, IND.) —KANKAKEE—MORRIS—MENDOTA— DIXON—SAVANNA— (DUBUQUE, IOWA); US 52
Indiana Line to Iowa Line, 218 *m.*

Roadbed hard-surfaced throughout.
Between Mendota and Polo the Illinois Central R. R. parallels the highway.
Usual accommodations throughout.

US 52, picking its erratic course across northern Illinois, passes several points of historic and economic interest. Rivers intimately associated with the development of the State—the Kankakee, the Illinois, and the Rock—are crossed at historic sites that have become cities of industrial importance. An extensive coal field and a variety of farming regions, as well as an everchanging topography, vary the scene. Three State parks and several monuments to pioneers recall the frontier rôle that this section of Illinois played in the development of the Middle West.

US 52 crosses the Indiana Line, 0 *m.*, 4.5 miles W. of Kentland, Indiana (*see Indiana Guide*). West of the Indiana Line US 52 and US 24 (*see Tour 18*) are united to SHELDON, 2.3 *m.* (685 alt., 1,121 pop.), which has grown from a switch established in 1860 by the Toledo, Peoria & Western Railroad and which was named for one of its directors. Later came the Big Four Railroad, and the town became an important shipping point for grain. A 1,200,000-bushel terminal grain elevator and a small local one rise from the railside above the little prairie town.

IROQUOIS, 6.5 *m.* (649 alt., 231 pop.), on the north bank of the river of that name, is the successor to the pioneer towns of Concord and Montgomery, on the south bank of the river, site of a Gurdon Hubbard trading post and first seat of Iroquois County; the two were long known as Bunkum. In 1871 the Big Four Railroad brought order to the confusion of names by calling its station Iroquois, and four years later Concord, which had survived Montgomery, incorporated under that name.

DONOVAN, 11 *m.* (667 alt., 375 pop.), was settled by Swedish immigrants after the coming of the railroad. Paradoxically, the settlement, which has been dry throughout its existence, bears the name of the keeper of the Buckhorn Tavern, an inn that stood on the nearby Hubbard Trail.

At 17.8 *m.* is a junction with State 1 (*see Tour 1*).

At 23.6 *m.* is a junction with a graveled road.

Right on this road is L'ERABLE, 1 *m.*, a tiny hamlet settled by French-Canadians and named for the maples that were once numerous on the site. The tall white spire of the 65-year-old CHURCH dominates the community, which before the advent of the automobile was a thriving farm center. Many descendants of the original settlers remain, and French is still spoken.

KANKAKEE, 42 *m.* (631 alt., 20,620 pop.) (*see Tour 3*), is at a junction with US 45 (*see Tour 3*).

For 20 miles the highway follows the wooded course of the Kankakee River, first navigated by La Salle in 1679. The river derives its name from that of the valley, Kyankeakee (Ind., beautiful land). Settlement has destroyed but little of its charm.

BRAIDWOOD, 65 *m.* (585 alt., 1,161 pop.) (*see Tour 17*), is at a junction with US 66 (*see Tour 17*).

At 67.6 *m.*, at a westward bend of the highway, is a junction with a graveled road.

Right (straight ahead) on this road to the NORTHERN ILLINOIS COAL COMPANY PLANT (*apply at office*), 1.5 *m.* This region, one of the major coal fields of the State, is the scene of extensive strip mining. Within an 8-mile radius, between the Mazon and Kankakee Rivers, are long ridges of shale, dumped by the great electrically operated strippers. The huge scoop shovels, which could easily pick up an automobile, remove the overburden to a depth of 60 feet, exposing the coal, which is washed and loaded at the rate of 6,000 tons daily. The vast "bad lands" created by the stripping may some day be forested and converted into a recreational area. The lagoons between the ridges have already been stocked with fish. The shaly concretions, found in abundance on the ridges, contain perfect fossils of early types of plants.

The SITE OF THE DIAMOND MINE (R), 68.8 *m.*, was the scene of a disastrous flood, February 16, 1883, in which at least 74 miners were

drowned. Only 28 bodies were recovered. When the search was abandoned the mine was sealed, and a monument was later erected to the
memory of the dead.

COAL CITY, 70.6 *m.* (562 alt., 1,637 pop.), dates from the opening of shaft mines here in 1875. When operations became unprofitable
under this method, strip mining was introduced. The tremendous machines that scrape away the earth and scoop up the coal are Diesel
powered and electrically operated, each capable of mining more than a
million tons of coal a year.

MORRIS, 84 *m.* (504 alt., 5,568 pop.), on the north bank of the
Illinois River, was platted in 1842 and named for Isaac N. Morris, one
of the Illinois and Michigan Canal commissioners, who was instrumental in having the village selected as the county seat. Completion of
the Illinois and Michigan Canal (1848) hastened the development of
the community. Its favorable location on the railroad and waterway
has made Morris an important shipping point 'for the surrounding
region and an important paper manufacturing center.

Excavations in the business district have unearthed archeological
material, indicating that the site was long occupied by Indian tribes.
La Salle records a large Indian village in the vicinity. A fine COLLEC-
TION OF FOSSILS gathered in the Mazon River fossil beds, and some
5,000 INDIAN RELICS are exhibited in the law offices (*open*) of George
Bedford, 302½ Liberty St.

On the western edge of Morris is GEBHARD WOODS STATE
PARK (*picnic facilities*), on the north bank of the Illinois and Michigan Canal. The 33-acre woodland was donated by Fred Gebhard in
1932 and improved by the CCC. The park adjoins the ILLINOIS AND
MICHIGAN CANAL STATE PARKWAY, a hundred-mile strip of land
along the historic waterway acquired by the State Division of Parks
in 1935. The old towpaths are being developed as pleasure drives, and
the entire 3,742-acre tract is being improved as a continuous parkway.

East from Morris, on a road along the canal, is EVERGREEN CEMETERY,
1.5 *m.*, where a rough boulder marks the GRAVE OF SHABBONA (1775-1859),
Chief of the Potawatomi, who, with his tribe, remained friendly to the settlers
during the Black Hawk War.

At 85 *m.* is a junction with US 6 (*see Tour* 14), with which US
52 is united for 0.7 miles.

At 108.5 *m.* is a junction with a graveled road.

Left is NORWAY, 1.6 *m.*, the first permanent Norwegian settlement in America. The site of the village, on the rolling prairies overlooking the valley of the
Fox River, was selected by Cleng Peerson, Norwegian colonizer who brought
the first boatload of settlers from his homeland to Orleans County, New York,
in 1825. Nine years later, having discovered better lands in the West, he led
them to the Fox River and founded the community of Norway.

For 30 years Cleng Peerson roamed the prairies and woodlands of the
Mississippi Valley. From upper Wisconsin to distant Texas he established Nor-

wegian settlements, 30 or more. Good humored and quiet, of a roving nature, he was welcomed wherever he went. Rarely did he work for pay, and whenever a few odd dollars came his way they were spent in founding new settlements. He died in Bosque County, Texas, December 16, 1865, in his eighty-third year, and is buried there.

In 1934, when the village of Norway celebrated the hundredth anniversary of its founding, the State of Illinois erected the CLENG PEERSON MEMORIAL, a bronze plaque mounted on a granite boulder commemorating Peerson's achievements.

TROY GROVE, 129.6 m. (654 alt., 259 pop.), is the birthplace and boyhood home of James Butler Hickok (1837-76), the "Wild Bill" of the West. At 18 he went to Leavenworth, Kansas, where he took part in frontier struggles. During the Civil War he served as a scout for the Union Army and later (1866-71) he was United States marshal at various places in the West. He toured the East with William F. Cody ("Buffalo Bill"), during 1872-73. The following year he went to Deadwood in the Black Hills of South Dakota, where, two years later, he was murdered by Jack McCall. The "WILD BILL" HICKOK STATE MONUMENT, L. one block from the highway, erected in 1929, commemorates the frontiersman.

At 132 m. is a junction with US 51 (see Tour 4), with which US 52 is united for 6.5 miles through MENDOTA, 137.5 m. (750 alt., 4,008 pop.) (see Tour 4), which is at a junction with US 34 (see Tour 13).

In AMBOY, 154 m. (752 alt., 1,972 pop.), the small-town grocery store out of which grew the mercantile firm of Carson Pirie Scott & Company was opened in 1854 by Samuel Carson and John T. Pirie, Scotch-Irish immigrants. Four years later their fellow-countryman, J. E. Scott, arrived at Amboy and the firm was established. By the close of the Civil War the company had branch stores in Mendota and Polo, and headquarters in Chicago. In 1934 the firm presented the city of Amboy with a drinking fountain, Main St. and the highway, to commemorate their first store.

The first newspaper in Lee County was published in Amboy in 1854 by Augustus Noel Dickens, brother of Charles Dickens. The enterprise was short-lived. A MEMORIAL BOULDER on a lawn at 109 Main St. marks the site where Lincoln spoke briefly, August 26, 1858, on the night before his Freeport debate with Douglas.

At 157 m. is a junction with US 30 (see Tour 12), with which US 52 is united for 10 miles through DIXON, 166 m. (659 alt., 9,908 pop.) (see Tour 12), which is at a junction with State 2 (see Tour 4A) and US 330 (see Tour 12A).

POLO, 179.7 m. (836 alt., 1,871 pop.), a trading center for an extensive stock raising community, was named for Marco Polo. U. S. Grant used to buy hides here for his leather shop (see Galena).

Right from Polo on a hard-surfaced road is WHITE PINES FOREST STATE PARK, 7 m., a 315-acre tract of white pine acquired by the State in

1927. The forest is the only one of its kind in Illinois and contains the southernmost stand of white pine in the Mid-West. Towering to heights of 90 to 100 feet above a thick carpet of needles, these most graceful of American evergreens provide an unchanging background for the red cedar and American yew with which they are associated, and for the varied deciduous trees of the forest that brighten with their ever-changing colors the constant green of the pines. Three principal trails, 10 miles in extent, wind throughout the forest and follow the banks of Pine Creek as it crosses the park on its way to Rock River. The CCC has built a log and stone LODGE and several CABINS (*for rates and reservations address Concessionaires, White Pines Forest State Park, Mt. Morris, Ill.*).

At 181.2 *m.* is a junction with State 26.

Right on this road is FORRESTON, 9.1 *m.* (931 alt., 908 pop.), scene of an annual sauerkraut festival. During the one-day celebration, (the last Thursday in September or the first Thursday in October), 20,000 visitors crowd Forreston's streets, eat a free lunch of sauerkraut, weiners, rye bread, and coffee, listen to German bands, and amuse themselves at tent-shows and other concessions. Although many acres of cabbage are raised in the vicinity the kraut is imported from Wisconsin. The celebration has been held since 1913, and was inspired by a native of Forreston who was so pleased with a kraut festival he attended in Iowa that he thought it would be nice for Forreston to have one, too.

LANARK, 198 *m.* (883 alt., 1,208 pop.), trades with the farmers, cans their vegetables and, seasonally, is the center of operations for extensive fox hunts. It is also known to lovers of American poetry as the home for many years of the Illinois poet, Glenn Ward Dresbach.

MOUNT CARROLL, 205.5 *m.* (817 alt., 1,775 pop.), is the seat of Carroll County and the home of FRANCES SHIMER JUNIOR COLLEGE, a school for girls founded in 1853, with an average enrollment of 165. The college is housed in a dozen red brick buildings, in the Georgian style, set in a trim quadrangle.

Mount Carroll is at a junction with State 78 (*see Tour* 5).

Right from Mount Carroll on a graveled road is SMITH'S PARK (*small adm. fee*), 2 *m.* In their wildland beauty the grounds are typical of much of Carroll County. Wooded ravines, steep-walled canyons, tall trees, winding streams, and the caves of an abandoned lead mine are features of the park.

Between Mount Carroll and Savanna US 52 crosses rough, rolling country as it approaches the Mississippi. The land forms are less rugged than are those of the Driftless Area to the north, but the sweeping panoramas afforded by the low hills are otherwise comparable.

At 215 *m.* is a junction with State 80 (*see Tour* 6), with which US 52 is united for 2.2 miles through SAVANNA, 216.1 *m.* (592 alt., 5,086 pop.), on the bank of the Mississippi north of the grassy plains for which the town was named. In 1828 the little community came into existence as an agricultural settlement and river port. The land was fertile and the Indians friendly, and the town prospered.

In 1838 John Smith came with his wife and eight children from Louis-ville, Kentucky, and started a brick kiln. Others followed and, with the coming of the railroad in 1850, Savanna gained the importance it enjoys today: a principal railroad center, the trading town of a wealthy 'farming region, and the shipping point of livestock and truck destined for the Chicago market. Savanna is the third largest terminal of the Chicago, Milwaukee, St. Paul & Pacific. On the 50 miles of track in its yards, 35,000 cars of perishable commodities are iced annually. The city is also the terminal point for three main line divi-sions of the Chicago, Burlington & Quincy. The OLDEST BRICK HOUSE in Savanna, 210 Main St., was built in 1838 of bricks from Smith's kiln.

US 52 skirts the southern border of MISSISSIPPI PALISADES STATE PARK (*see Tour* 6) and crosses the Iowa Line, 218 *m.*, on a toll bridge (*car and driver*, 25c; *passengers, 5c each*) spanning the Mississippi to Sabula, Iowa (*see Iowa Guide*).

TOUR 16

(KENTLAND, IND.) —PEORIA—LEWISTOWN—QUINCY— MISSOURI LINE; US 24

Indiana Line to Missouri Line, 249.8 *m.*

Hard-surfaced roadbed throughout.
The Toledo, Peoria & Western R. R. parallels the highway between Sheldon and Peoria; the Wabash Ry. between Mount Sterling and Quincy.
Usual accommodations throughout.

IN ITS eastern reaches US 24 crosses a hundred miles of prairie, relieved now and then by wooded moraines. This rich farming country has lured many settlements of various sects of the Mennonite faith, Germanic peoples whose simple tenets of religion and ways of life— strengthened by being transplanted from the Old to the New World— have contributed a distinctive element to American culture. Between Peoria and Quincy the route first follows the course of the Illinois River, one of the best hunting and fishing areas in the State. Then it swings westward to cross the valley of the Spoon River, the locale of Edgar Lee Masters' *Spoon River Anthology,* passing many of the scenes immortalized by this Illinois poet. At the western terminus of the route is Quincy, fronting the Mississippi, a one-time abolitionist center and today a major industrial city of the State.

Section a. Indiana Line to Peoria, 116 m.

US 24 crosses the Indiana Line, 0 *m.*, 5 miles west of Kentland, Indiana (*see Indiana Guide*). West of the Indiana Line US 24 and US 52 (*see Tour* 15) are united as far as SHELDON, 2 *m.* (685 alt., 1,121 pop.) (*see Tour* 15).

At 9.7 *m.* is a junction (L) with State 1 (*see Tour* 1), which unites with US 24 for 2.7 miles.

WATSEKA, 11.9 *m.* (634 alt., 3,144 pop.), Iroquois County seat, was platted in 1860 as South Middleport. It was renamed in 1865 in honor of Watch-e-kee (pretty woman), Potawatomi wife of Gurdon Hubbard. Assigned to Illinois in 1818 by the American Fur Company, Hubbard subsequently established trade relations with the Potawatomi in eastern Illinois; prompted by business acumen rather than love, he married Watch-e-kee, niece of Chief Tamin. Hubbard tired of her after two years and gave her to his partner, La Vasseur. "Our separation was by mutual agreement," Hubbard later said, ". . . because I was about to abandon the Indian trade." Watch-e-kee died at the Kansas reservation of the Potawatomi in 1878. The SITE OF HUBBARD'S CABIN (1821) is marked by a split boulder on which a bronze plaque commemorates Hubbard as the first white settler to enter Iroquois County.

Designated as the seat of Iroquois County in 1865 and built in a period of florid but not meritless architecture, Watseka has many buildings reflecting the affluence of the period. Large brick houses of Victorian design, occupied by retired farmers, line tree-shaded streets. The business district contains buildings the modern fronts of which are belied by elaborate cornices of the 1890's. Particularly interesting is the FIRST NATIONAL BANK, a three-story brick structure with a delicate Adam frieze. Watseka industrial plants include a grain elevator, a large chick hatchery, and a cheese factory that sends vat material to Chicago for the manufacture of golf balls.

The IROQUOIS COUNTY COURTHOUSE, one block west of the highway, a two-story brick building with a mansard roof and an ornate cupola, was designed by C. B. Leach and built in 1866 at a cost of $28,000. The COURTHOUSE MUSEUM (*open* 9-4 *weekdays*) contains World War memorabilia and artifacts removed from local Indian mounds.

At 19.2 *m.* is a junction with State 49.

Left is CISSNA PARK, 16 *m.* (684 alt., 588 pop.), the center of a community of some 1,500 members of the Apostolic Church, who are known in Illinois as New Amish. The founder of the church, Samuel Frolich, a deposed minister of the Reformed Church in Argau, Switzerland, enlisted converts for his new sect from among the Amish, and his followers continued proselyting among the Amish in America. Because of this close association in their early history, the customs and habits of the Apostolic Church members differ little from those of the Amish, and the error in calling them such is a technical one. Both men and women wear simple dark clothing. The men are bearded, but do not have mustaches. Simplicity of habit, dress, and home is practiced; and they keep themselves strictly aloof from non-member neighbors, avoid civil government, do not take oaths, and refuse to bear arms. This last prohibition caused them embarrassment at the time of the World War, but their appeal to President Wilson was successful. Farming is their chief occupation.

An expression of their religious severity, their large bare frame church is utterly devoid of ornament. The men and boys sit on one side of the hall, the women and girls on the other. The sermon is delivered by one of six men who sit on a raised platform; any of these who feels moved to speak may rise and deliver the sermon. Singing by the members is without accompaniment. Following the service, the congregation moves to a large dining hall in the building, where a simple lunch is served on plain tables; the families take turns in providing the Sunday communal meal. This custom is a survival of the time when meetings were held in the members' homes and the distances traveled were great.

At 25.2 *m.* is a junction with US 45 (*see Tour 3*), which unites with US 24 for 2 miles (*see Tour 3*).

CHATSWORTH, 43.5 *m.* (736 alt., 981 pop.), differs slightly from the usual farming communities along the route in that it has several small industrial plants; one manufactures tile and brick from clay found in the vicinity. The town was laid out in 1858, and the coming of the Toledo, Peoria & Western Railroad spurred its growth.

FORREST, 49.8 *m.* (688 alt., 915 pop.), was settled in 1836, but owes its development mainly to the railroads that opened up the area two decades later and to the arrival in the 1860's of German-Amish immigrants. Men of this faith, soberly dressed and bearded, but with clean-shaven upper lips, and women in equally sombre attire, are frequently seen along the streets and in the communities along the highway between Forrest and Peoria. They may be Mennonites, Amish-Mennonites, or members of the Apostolic Church.

The first Amish in Illinois settled along the Illinois River above and below Peoria, in what are now Woodford, Tazewell, and Bureau Counties. They had emigrated in 1831 from Alsace and Lorraine, and in the next 20 years others came from the same provinces, and from Bavaria and Hesse-Darmstadt. A few traveled westward from Ohio; and in the 1850's a number of Pennsylvania Amish joined the colony in Illinois. These pioneer settlements were all made in the timbered sections along the Illinois and its tributaries. In the late 1850's an eastward movement began to more fertile prairie lands, and the original congregations were gradually transplanted to these new communities, many of which are on or near US 24.

The first Mennonites reached Illinois in 1833 from Virginia, and many from Ohio, Pennsylvania, and Bavaria continued to settle here until the late 1840's. Their movement was similar to that of the Amish, except that some colonies were established along the northwestern border of the State.

Doctrinal differences soon split the Mennonite Church, for the Amish insisted on rigid adherence to early precepts. Gradually even the

Amish subdivided; the conservative group became known as the Old Order, or "hook and eye" Amish, because their clothing is fastened with hooks and eyes instead of buttons. Other Amish divisions, several named after leaders who broke from the parent body, are more elastic in their social and religious customs, and co-operate to some extent with the several Mennonite branches. The principal centers of the Old Order Amish in Illinois are in Douglas and Moultrie Counties (*see Tour* 3). The members of these different groups, estimated at 10,000 in Illinois, are a rural people; generally they form autonomous congregations and constitute themselves as individual farming communities.

FAIRBURY, 55.5 *m.* (686 alt., 2,310 pop.), essentially an agricultural trading center, has a local coal mine in operation. Of the city's eight churches, two are Apostolic; this sect has approximately 500 members in and about Fairbury.

CHENOA, 66.5 *m.* (722 alt., 1,325 pop.) (*see Tour* 17), is at a junction with US 66 (*see Tour* 17).

MEADOWS, 71 *m.*, was settled by Mennonites from Alsace and Lorraine; their church building is on the southern edge of the village. A large settlement of Amish occupy the farmlands north of the community.

GRIDLEY, 75.1 *m.* (752 alt., 709 pop.), has a congregation of "Egli" Amish, a group formed in the 1860's around Henry Egli, an Amish minister in Indiana. Today this division works in close co-operation with the old church. The town is named for Asahel Gridley (1810-81), a native of New York, who came to Illinois in 1831 and embarked on a career that included banking, law, politics, and service in the Civil War as a brigadier general.

EL PASO, 82.5 *m.* (749 alt., 1,578 pop.) (*see Tour* 4), is at a junction with US 51 (*see Tour* 4).

EUREKA, 96.3 *m.* (738 alt., 1,534 pop.), has developed around EUREKA COLLEGE, a coeducational school with a student body of 450; it occupies five red brick buildings on 20 wooded acres in the southeastern part of the city. The Disciples of Christ, followers of Alexander Campbell, founded a seminary here in 1848, which was expanded to an academy the following year and chartered as Eureka College in 1855; it was the first college in Illinois to admit men and women on an equal basis. In 1933 Eureka College inaugurated the Eureka Plan, which affords students part-time jobs to pay for their tuition and board.

An established community since the 1830's and seat of Woodford County since 1896, Eureka is the trading center of a prosperous farm area, and absorbs the local crops of peas, corn, pumpkins, and tomatoes in its canning factory.

On the northern outskirts of Eureka is the MENNONITE HOME FOR THE AGED (*not open*), a three-story building of brown brick, with generous porches, erected in 1922 and maintained by the Mennonite

Conference. Aged members of the sect are supported by their church; non-members pay their maintenance, but are usually cared for after their funds have become exhausted.

Right from Eureka on State 117 to a junction with State 116, 5 *m.;* L. on State 116 to METAMORA, 10 *m.* (813 alt., 707 pop.), site of the METAMORA COURTHOUSE, a State memorial. Here in the 1840's gathered lawyers and jurists who were soon to become renowned; among them, Abraham Lincoln, Stephen A. Douglas, Robert Ingersoll, and Adlai Stevenson. The courthouse, substantially the same today as when built in 1845, is a two-story brick and walnut timber structure of Greek Revival design; the bricks were burned in the village. Four fluted Doric columns support the pediment, and an octagonal cupola, encircled with an iron railing, overshadows the portico. A hall, with offices on either side, runs the full length of the first floor. On the second floor is the old courthouse, restored as nearly as possible to its original condition, in which are pioneer relics of the Woodford County Historical Society. Just south of Metamora, in a locust grove, a marker designates a SITE WHERE LINCOLN SPOKE in 1858.

WASHINGTON, 104 *m.* (766 alt., 1,741 pop.), is chiefly an agricultural center and the home of retired farmers. A canning factory is seasonally operated.

EAST PEORIA, 114 *m.* (478 alt., 5,027 pop.), at the base of the bluffs on the flood plain of the Illinois River, is an industrial and residential adjunct of Peoria. The CATERPILLAR TRACTOR COMPANY PLANT (*tours,* 9:45 *a.m.–2 p.m., apply at office*), 600 Washington St., is one of the largest of its kind in the world. These tractors are being used extensively the world over in industry and road building. FONDU-LAC PARK, Springfield St. and Stewart Ave., at the summit of a steep hill, affords an extensive view of Peoria and the Illinois River Valley.

EAST PEORIA is at a junction with State 29.

Left on State 29 to a junction with a graveled road, 2 *m.;* R. on this road to FORT CRÈVE COEUR STATE PARK, 2.5 *m.,* a 14-acre tract on hills bordering the Illinois River. A granite monument marks the probable SITE OF FORT CRÈVE COEUR (Fr. broken heart), built by La Salle in 1680 and named for a fort in the Netherlands. La Salle chose the site for a temporary fortress, January 15, and a small, makeshift structure was completed several weeks later. In March of the same year La Salle returned to Quebec, leaving Tonti in command. To him he sent word to explore Starved Rock (*see Tour* 14A) as a possible site for a permanent French fort. Upon Tonti's departure the dissatisfied troops destroyed Fort Crève Coeur and went off into the wilderness with its store of powder and provisions. The fort was never rebuilt. Fort Crève Coeur was the second French fort in the West.

PEORIA, 116 *m.* (608 alt., 104,969 pop.) (*see Peoria*).

Points of Interest: Hiram Walker & Sons Distillery, Peoria Municipal River and Rail Terminal, Bradley Polytechnic Institute, and others.

Peoria is at a junction with US 150.

Right on US 150 to a junction with a graveled road, 9 *m.;* R. on this road to JUBILEE COLLEGE STATE PARK, 11.5 *m.,* where stands the main building of a pioneer college founded by the Rt. Rev. Philander Chase (1775-1852), first Bishop of the American Protestant Episcopal Church in Illinois. The CHAPEL-DORMITORY-CLASSROOM is a sandstone structure with recessed portals and Gothic windows. The stone was quarried in a ravine near Kickapoo Creek and the lumber was shipped from St. Louis by way of the Illinois River. The cornerstone was laid April 3, 1839, "the day fine," as noted by Bishop Chase, "the sky serene, and just enough wind to remind us of the breath of God." The preparatory school of the college was opened in 1840.

Jubilee College was chartered by the State in 1847. At the first commencement exercises, held that year, five students were graduated. The freshman curriculum included "Livy and the Odes of Horace, Xenophon, Herodotus, Demosthenes, the Epistles of the New Testament, Algebra, Geometry, Logarithms and Trigonometry, Classical Antiquities, and Ecclesiastical History." The young ladies' school offered "all the usual English branches, with the addition of the classics, if desired." Fees for the scholastic year of 44 weeks, including board and lodging, were $100.

Jubilee College, the second school established by Bishop Chase (as first Bishop of the American Protestant Episcopal Church in Ohio he had founded Kenyon College in 1824), continued to prosper for several years after the Bishop's death in 1852, then fell into financial difficulties, and was finally closed during the Civil War. Attempts to reopen the college immediately after the war and again in 1883 failed. The site of the present park was acquired by the State in 1934. The one-time campus, shaded by spruce and oak, overlooks the peaceful valley of Kickapoo Creek. In Jubilee Churchyard, marked by a stone lectern, is the GRAVE OF BISHOP CHASE.

Section b. Peoria to Missouri Line, 133.8 m.

Southwest of Peoria the highway follows hilly terrain, offering beautiful views of the lowlands, and for about 35 miles the broad Illinois River (L) is visible. The villages and towns passed are scarcely more than crossroad communities, with a general store, a post office, and a name; many of the latter suggest the chief industry of the region, coal mining.

BARTONVILLE, 5.3 m. (694 alt., 1,886 pop.), a suburb of Peoria, is inhabited largely by miners, for the region is underlaid with coal; local factories manufacture steel wire and fence. At the southern edge of Bartonville is the gateway (R) to a road leading to the bluff on which are the 30 buildings of the PEORIA STATE HOSPITAL, an institution for the care of the feeble-minded and insane. Some 3,000 patients, both male and female, are treated here.

ORCHARD MINES, 8.7 m., is at a junction with State 9.

Left on State 9, across the Illinois River, is PEKIN, 2 m. (479 alt., 16,129 pop.), settled by pioneers of English descent from Virginia, Kentucky, and Tennessee. Later, many French and Germans followed. The first schoolhouse, known as the Snell School, was fortified during the Black Hawk War and called Fort Doolittle. As a young lawyer, Abraham Lincoln argued many cases in the old courthouse at Pekin.

The city, a rail center for the surrounding agricultural and mining region, lies on a rolling prairie, and is banked by hills and low bluffs to the north and east. The region has long been popular with sportsmen, for fishing is good in the Mackinaw River to the east and game is usually plentiful.

KINGSTON MINES, 13.9 *m.* (502 alt., 326 pop.), is on the site of an ancient Indian village; from local gravel pits have come innumerable Indian skeletons and relics. Slag piles of active and inactive mines line the highway.

At 31.8 *m.* is a junction with a graveled road.

Left on this road is LIVERPOOL, 2.5 *m.*, which reflects in its name the optimistic visions of its founders. Once a river town of considerable importance, many a pudgy steamer, whistle shrieking, smokestack coughing clouds of sparks, nosed up to its wharf. Liverpool served as a convenient depot at which to transfer goods bound for Canton, Lewistown, and other inland cities. Today it is a commercial fishing port, and the center of one of the State's finest hunting grounds, as evidenced by numerous private hunting lodges in the vicinity.

At 32.3 *m.* is a junction with State 78 (*see Tour 5*), which joins US 24 for 3 miles.

At 37.3 *m.* is the junction with a graveled road.

Left is the DICKSON MOUND (40c *per person, special group rates*), 3.5 *m.*, which has been owned by the Dickson family for three-quarters of a century. The father of the present owner unearthed Indian skeletons while grading the crescent-shaped mound to fill the basin between its arms. No anthropological significance was placed on the find until later years. Only a small portion of the mound has been laid open, but 230 skeletons have been exhumed and left lying in their original postures, together with some of their possessions—tools, pottery, weapons, and ornaments. The skeletal exhibits appear in all kinds of positions and apparently without pattern, in small groups, family groups, and singly. The excavated portion reveals at least five different burial tiers, each of which must have corresponded to the existing surface of the hill. Underlaid with earth, other burials were placed upon preceding ones, until the top of the mound reached a height of 50 feet. A building has been erected over the main excavation to protect the exhibits; other diggings are in progress. The nearby DICKSON MOUND MUSEUM houses artifacts and other material taken from the excavations, and also the Edward W. Payne Stone Age and Indian Collection, one of the largest of its kind.

LEWISTOWN, 39.3 *m.* (596 alt., 2,249 pop.), seat of Fulton County, was the boyhood home of the poet, Edgar Lee Masters, and many of its characters and incidents have been immortalized in his *Spoon River Anthology*.

Lewistown, the oldest town in the county, was one of the first laid out in the Military Tract, a huge section between the Illinois and Mississippi Rivers set aside by the government for soldiers of the War of 1812. Maj. Ossian M. Ross, a veteran, came here in 1821, accompanied by his wife, three children, a blacksmith, a carpenter, and several other workmen; this group founded the present city of Lewistown, naming it for Ross' son.

Ross had been preceded by at least two other settlers. John Eveland, his wife and 12 children, had arrived earlier from the East in a 40-foot, hand-hewn cottonwood *pirogue*. "Doc" Davison, the almost mythical recluse and misanthrope, also predated the Ross party in the region.

Davison is said to have left the East to escape civilization, and it is certain that he fled Lewistown as soon as white settlers began to arrive. Public appearances were so abhorrent to Davison that once, when he was summoned for grand jury service, he made a hasty get-away in a canoe. Ignoring the legal consequences of this defection, he somehow completed the perilous river journey to Starved Rock (*see Tour* 14A), where he died after several years of contented isolation.

By 1823 Ross had organized Fulton County, carving it from old Pike County, which then extended from the Illinois River to the Mississippi. In the same year he donated land for a frame courthouse and jail and built a small tavern. The tavern rates were two shillings for "victuals," three shillings per night for "horsekeeping," one shilling for lodging, and one shilling for a half pint of whiskey.

Until 1825 Fulton County embraced the entire northern part of Illinois, including Fort Dearborn (Chicago); residents of this large area journeyed to Lewistown to pay their taxes, and to secure marriage, tavern, and ferry licenses.

In addition to the "public squear," as an old document has it, the town founder donated a "burying yard," and sites for a meeting house, a schoolhouse, and a Masonic temple. Having thus dowered Lewistown, Ross, after a decade, established Havana (*see Tour* 5) on the Illinois River, where he spent his remaining days.

The old Ross MANSION (*not open*), 409 E. Milton Ave., was built by his son, Col. Lewis W. Ross. Modeled after a mansion on the Hudson River that Colonel Ross admired, it served as the inspiration for the "McNeely Mansion" of Masters' *Anthology*. The main body of the house is square, with a wide hall splitting the center. To the rear the structure extends at three different heights, in New England style, beginning with the servants' quarters, and terminating in the wood and carriage houses. The 17-room mansion was built of brick kilned in its own dooryard; the stone for its foundations came from the Spoon River Valley. The house has enameled in-folding shutters, curiously carved banisters on its great double staircase, and an imported white-tile fireplace that Marshall Field tried vainly to buy. Formerly, several tame deer roamed a 20-acre enclosure at the rear.

The architect of the mansion was a Democrat and reputedly a Southern sympathizer during the Civil War. When draft riots broke out in the southern part of Fulton County, a cannon was trained for several days on the structure. After being damaged by fire, the Ross House was restored in recent years, and now presents much the same appearance as in early Civil War days.

The MAJOR NEWTON WALKER HOUSE (*not open*), 1127 N. Main St., built in 1833, is a commodious white brick structure, in which Abraham Lincoln was several times a guest. In remarkably good condition, it today stands guard over the cluster of tourist cabins that surrounds it. In the opening poem of the *Anthology*, Masters introduces the builder as

> ... Major Walker who had talked
> With venerable men of the revolution . . .

Walker served with Lincoln in the State legislature at Vandalia and their friendship continued after the capital was removed to Springfield. During his declining years he was fond of relating many anecdotes about Lincoln, for whom he often played the fiddle, in exchange for some of the great man's stories. Walker died in 1899 at the age of 96.

Lewistown has had four courthouses. The courtroom of the most renown, built by Major Walker in 1838, echoed to the eloquence of Lincoln, Baker, and Ingersoll; Stephen A. Douglas presided as judge in the 1840's. On a memorable night in 1895, the Major's 90th birthday, the courthouse was razed by an incendiary as the last act in a bitter county seat "war" between Lewistown and Canton; the incident provided dramatic material for several of Masters' poems. A new edifice was soon built by popular subscription. The two central pillars of the destroyed courthouse, the LINCOLN PILLARS, between which Lincoln stood when speaking here in 1858, now serve as a memorial to the soldier dead in the Protestant Cemetery.

The PHELPS STORE, Main and Washington Sts., somewhat modernized, was built as an Indian trading post in 1825 by Judge Stephen Phelps, who had come from Sangamon County the previous year with his five sons. One of the boys, William, endeared himself to the Indians and was christened by them Che-che-pin-e-quah (powerful neck and shoulders). Later known as "Captain," William Phelps transported furs to St. Louis for his father, using first a canoe, then a raft with sails, and finally a sailboat. Although a friend of Black Hawk and Keokuk, his successor, William aided the Government materially in the Black Hawk War.

The architecture of the CHURCH OF ST. JAMES, Broadway and Illinois Sts., erected during the early days of the Civil War, is Victorian Gothic. The red brick structure, with a shingle roof and 10-foot buttresses on either side, is now dilapidated after 20 years of disuse. As originally planned by the New York architect, Edwin Tuckerman Potter, son of Bishop Alonzo Potter, this Episcopal Church was 66 feet long and 26 feet wide; a wing was added later.

In PROCTOR'S GROVE, southwestern Lewistown, Douglas spoke to 5,000 persons one day shortly before the famous Lincoln-Douglas debates began in 1858. Of Douglas' eloquence on that occasion, Masters exclaims:

> But Douglas!
> People out yonder in Proctor's Grove,
> A mile from the Court House steps,
> Could hear him roar . . . .

Over a grave in OAK HILL CEMETERY, on a gentle knoll **north of** town, stands a figure of a woman on a marble shaft. The inscription reads:

William Cullen Bryant
Died March 24, 1875,
Age 24 years

Not Bryant the poet, but a young namesake is buried here. He was accidentally killed while duck hunting on Thompson's Lake in the vicinity; he is the "Percy Bysshe Shelley" in Masters' *Anthology:*

> At Thompson's Lake the trigger of my gun
> Caught in the side of the boat
> And a great hole was shot through my heart.
> Over me a fond father erected this marble shaft,
> On which stands the figure of a woman
> Carved by an Italian artist.

DUNCAN'S MILLS, 43.9 *m.*, site of one of the first grist **mills in** the region, is today little more than a ghost town. Only one of its houses is now inhabited; a few tumble-down shacks squat on the hill (R) along the road.

Right from Duncan's Mills on State 10 to a junction with a graveled road, 7.5 *m.;* R. is BERNADOTTE, 10.5 *m.*, a pioneer village on the Spoon River, once an active community built around a flour mill but now practically abandoned. The old mill is in ruins. William Walters, first settler (1826), legend says, bought the town site from the Indians for 50 deerskins. Later, Walters and a band of whites drove the Indians across the Mississippi. Bernadotte had many thriving years; its one fishing and two packing plants prospered; it gained a substantial income from summer visitors; its future seemed assured until the railroads passed it by.

Surrounded by verdant hills, Bernadotte's chief assets today are its natural attractions. In his youth Masters spent some time on the peaceful, tree-lined shore of Spoon River, which he described in his poem on Isaiah Beethoven, who came to Bernadotte to finish his life:

> They told me I had three months to live,
> So I crept to Bernadotte,
> And sat by the mill for hours and hours
> Where the gathered waters deeply moving
> Seemed not to move.
>
> .   .   .   .   .
>
> But here by the mill the castled clouds
> Mocked themselves in the dizzy water;
> And over its agate floor at night
> The flame of the moon ran under my eyes
> Amid a forest stillness broken
> By a flute in a hut on the hill.

Beethoven remains unrecognized by Spoon River natives, but Dr. William Strode, whose home was the literary and scientific center of Bernadotte, was obviously the William Jones of whom Masters writes:

> Once in a while a curious weed unknown to me,
> Needing a name from my books;
> Once in a while a letter from Yeomans.
> Out of the mussel-shells gathered along the shore
> Sometimes a pearl with a glint like meadow rue:
> Then betimes a letter from Tyndall in England,
> Stamped with the stamp of Spoon River.
> I, lover of Nature, beloved for my love of her,
> Held such converse afar with the great
> Who knew her better than I.

Dr. Strode gathered a collection of over 500 mounted birds and almost 1,000 species of freshwater clams and univalves.

ASTORIA, 57.6 m. (662 alt., 1,189 pop.), is an amalgam of two earlier villages. The eastern part of the town was christened Washington when it was laid out in 1836; in 1837 Vienna was platted just to the west. Later, these twin villages were named for John Jacob Astor, who owned land in the vicinity. Astoria was a station on the old four-horse stagecoach line between Peoria and Quincy. The new town soon acquired stores, a mill, a tannery, and a post office. William H. Scripps, father of John L. Scripps, newspaper publisher, came in 1840 from Rushville and began a successful career as a merchant and pork packer. There are no manufactories in Astoria today; it is a retired farmers' town, and its principal economic activity is buying and selling farm products.

RUSHVILLE, 72.8 m. (683 alt., 2,388 pop.), (see Tour 7), is at a junction with US 67 (see Tour 7).

The highway crosses the La Moine River, 81.8 m., to RIPLEY (701 alt., 168 pop.), a village of small weathered farm houses clinging to hillsides between which US 24 sharply turns. In the 1830's and 1840's the community enjoyed a period of prosperity, when its 18 potteries employed over 200 workers; no trace of the kilns remains.

In MOUNT STERLING, 90.6 m. (711 alt., 1,724 pop.), is the seat and largest city of Brown County, and was settled in 1830 by Robert Curry, who built a house upon the highest elevation in the vicinity. He named the village that developed around him for the mound and the "sterling" quality of the soil. The community became the county seat in 1839.

The residents of CAMP POINT, 109.8 m. (738 alt., 1,000 pop.), are mostly of German descent. Several institutions—a church, a bank, and a newspaper—date from the beginnings of the settlement, about 1870. BAILEY PARK, a 50-acre wooded tract, formerly the meeting place of annual chautauquas, is now a picnic ground.

COATSBURG, 115 m. (761 alt., 199 pop.), a shipping center for grain and livestock, was surveyed by R. P. Coates in 1855. When the courthouse in Quincy burned in 1875, Coatsburg, more centrally located, became an unsuccessful rival for the seat of Adams County. In 1885 Coatsburg was incorporated as a village. One of the first German Lutheran churches in this section of Illinois was established here in 1862. In this village of neat frame and brick buildings facing broad streets lined by great trees a chrysanthemum show has been held every year since November 1898.

QUINCY, 132.8 *m.* (602 alt., 39,241 pop.), as well as Adams County of which it is the seat, were named for John Quincy Adams, President of the United States at the time of their founding. Quincy begins at the Mississippi, hurdles steep bluffs, levels out on the uplands, and trails off into woods and farmlands. The city occupies the site of a Sauk Indian village.

John Wood (1798-1880) and Willard Keyes, two young Easterners, established claims on the site of Quincy in 1822. Their cabins, along with those of several other pioneers, comprised a tiny settlement called The Bluffs. John Wood became the leading citizen of The Bluffs and of nineteenth century Quincy. He was a power in State politics and in 1860, as Lieutenant Governor, filled the unexpired term of Gov. William H. Bissell, who died in office. It was at Woods' petition that the State legislature created Adams County in 1825, and empowered commissioners to select a site for the county seat at the center of the area. Willard Keyes thereupon volunteered to lead the commissioners to this spot, and under his guidance the delegation scrambled through "bogs, quicksands, and quagmires," eventually arriving at Keyes' cabin. There, so the story goes, they were persuaded to designate The Bluffs as the site of the Adams County seat. Quincy was platted later in the same year.

Despite an epidemic of Asiatic cholera that decimated the population in 1832, Quincy rapidly became one of the most important settlements on the upper Mississippi. Across the river from the slave state of Missouri, the village was in the border region where early clashes between pro-slavery and anti-slavery groups foreshadowed the Civil War. Pioneer abolitionist of Quincy was the Rev. Asa B. Turner of Templeton, Massachusetts, brother of Jonathan Turner, then a teacher at Illinois College, Jacksonville. Under the Rev. Mr. Turner's direction, the first church in Quincy, a graceless structure called the Lord's Barn, was completed in 1831.

Dr. David Nelson, Presbyterian minister and author of the hymn "The Shining Shore," having narrowly escaped assassination by a Missouri slave owner, sought refuge in Quincy where he was sheltered in the Rev. Mr. Turner's home. An abolitionist society organized shortly after Dr. Nelson's arrival was generally believed to have been founded by the two ministers. An open meeting of the society, scheduled to be held in the Lord's Barn, prompted pro-slavery groups to issue circulars that called on the citizens of Quincy and northeastern Missouri to "help clean out the abolitionists." When a mob gathered before the Lord's Barn on the night of the meeting and pelted the structure with stones, the forewarned audience seized clubs, hatchets, and muskets hidden under the pulpit, and, led by deacons of the church, rushed forth brandishing their weapons. Startled by this swift counter-attack, the mob fled and the abolitionists concluded their meeting without further disturbance.

Dr. Nelson also founded the Mission Institute, the scene of disorders between pro-slavery and abolitionist groups in 1836. To maintain peace the Institute was closed, but Missouri bushwhackers later set fire to the building and destroyed it. The Madison School, 25th and Main Sts., occupies the approximate SITE OF THE MISSION INSTITUTE.

In 1835 residents of Columbia began to demand that their village be declared county seat because of its position at the true center of Adams County. An election to settle the question was held in 1841; Columbia won by 91 votes. Although Stephen A. Douglas, then circuit judge, issued a mandamus ordering immediate recognition of the voters' decision, the county commissioners dawdled at Quincy. Residents of Quincy, meanwhile, convinced that the supporters of Columbia had stuffed the ballot boxes, appealed to the Supreme Court of Illinois. While their case was pending, the State legislature looped off ten eastern townships from Adams County and created the new county of Marquette. When the Columbians learned that their village now occupied a borderline position in Marquette County identical to that of Quincy in Adams County, they were so furious that they refused to organize a local government. The legislature enlarged the new county in 1847 and changed its name to Highland, but the inhabitants persistently smothered all attempts to form a government. At last the embarrassed legislature reunited the territory with Adams County, which restored harmony, oddly enough.

In the middle of the nineteenth century Quincy became, and remained for 20 years, the second largest city in Illinois. Some 20,000 hogs—"long-legged, long-snouted, fleet as a deer"—were shipped by steamboat to St. Louis in 1847; in later years annual hog shipments rose to 70,000. Quincy factories produced plows, shoes, stoves, wagons, carriages, organs, corn-planters, and steam engines. These plants, together with tobacco works, flour mills, tanneries, saw mills, and breweries, employed 8,000 men. Goods exported during the 1850's annually averaged $15,000,000 in value. Steamboat landings for the 10 months that the Mississippi was open to navigation in 1853 averaged five a day. In addition to many of the above, the town's chief businesses today include the manufacture of drills and pumps, chemicals and dyes, chicken raisers' supplies, and almost every conceivable kind of electric wheel.

Quincy was displaced as second city of Illinois by industrial communities that boomed in the post-Civil War decades. Its commerce dwindled with the decline of the steamboat. During the last quarter of the nineteenth century the city entered a transitional stage in which industrial and agricultural products that had formerly found an outlet in the holds of 40 steamers shrank to the capacity of a single spur line railroad. The untimely contraction left an economic vacuum, later filled by industrialism and improved railroad transportation, which have shaped the contemporary city.

QUINCY BAY, an inlet of the Mississippi northeast of the city, was a winter harbor for steamboats. The bay is divided into lower and upper bays, connected by a stream called the Narrows. The upper bay affords boating, fishing, and swimming.

Along the QUINCY LEVEE (*steamboats for moonlight excursions; daily summer trips to Hannibal, Mo.*) are a scattering of ramshackle warehouses and venerable buildings that date from the steamboat era. The CLAT ADAMS GENERAL STORE, 200 N. Front St., a favorite haunt of rivermen, still offers customers, as Harold Speakman notes in *Mostly Mississippi,* "anything from an anchor or a pound of oakum to a bunch of carrots and a box of talcum powder."

WASHINGTON PARK, sprawling in the center of the business district, was used until 1835 as a camping place for pioneers who had business at the county courthouse. The park contains a STATUE OF JOHN WOOD, a founding father. A bronze bas-relief by Lorado Taft marks the SITE OF THE SIXTH LINCOLN-DOUGLAS DEBATE (October 13, 1858). In this debate Lincoln divested the slave question of political issues and trenchantly observed: "I suggest that the difference of opinion, reduced to its lowest terms, is no other than the difference between the men who think slavery a wrong and those who do not think it wrong."

Broadcasting station WTAD (900 kc.) has studios in the Western Catholic Union Building. The Newcomb Hotel, 4th St., stands on the SITE OF THE QUINCY HOUSE, an elaborate hotel, once the most luxurious on the Mississippi north of New Orleans. Stephen A. Douglas lodged at the Quincy House several times.

The more impressive mid-nineteenth century mansions in Quincy have outlasted their residential purpose. The St. Joseph Home for Girls, 1385 N. 8th St., includes among its buildings the O. H. BROWNING HOUSE; Browning was a U. S. Senator during Lincoln's Presidency and Secretary of the Interior under Andrew Johnson; Lincoln was escorted here by a large crowd on the morning of his debate with Douglas.

The QUINCY AND ADAMS COUNTY HISTORICAL SOCIETY MUSEUM (*free; visiting hours, Sun., Mon., Wed.* 9 *a.m.–noon; daily* 3 *p.m.–*5 *p.m.*), 425 S. 12th St., occupies a 17-room frame house built by John Wood in 1835. Some claim that it originally stood across the street and was moved to its present site about 1865. The museum contains many interesting exhibits of early Quincy rugs, books, pictures, ceramics, metalware, and manuscripts. On the lawn in front of the building is the only remaining capstone from the old Mormon Temple at Nauvoo (*see Nauvoo*).

The WOOD HOUSE, on the grounds of St. Peter's School, 11th and State Sts., is a massive octagonal structure built in 1865 of stone blocks set in lead. The LORENZO BULL HOUSE, Main and 16th Sts., built by a wealthy pioneer who was a cousin of the Reverend Mr. Turner's wife, is used by the Quincy Women's City Club and 20 affiliated organizations; the Quincy Art Club maintains studios in a remodeled barn on the estate.

The WHITE HOUSE INN, 12th and Elm Sts., was built in pre-Civil War years for Edward Everett, who had secret rooms constructed in it to hide fugitive slaves. The ST. BONIFACE CHURCH, Main and 7th Sts., was completed in 1847; William Lamprecht, American church artist, designed four of its stained-glass windows and painted the windows above the altar.

RIVERVIEW PARK, in northeastern Quincy, overlooks the Mississippi River; on its bluff is Charles Milligan's STATUE OF GEORGE ROGERS CLARK. INDIAN MOUNDS PARK (*municipal swimming pool*) has a number of mounds, and is the site of a Black Hawk War skirmish.

In WOODLAND CEMETERY, S. 5th St., is the GRAVE OF JOHN WOOD, marked by a monument. SOLDIERS MONUMENT, a white marble shaft dedicated to Adams County men killed in the Civil War, surmounts an Indian mound in the cemetery.

BALDWIN PARK, 30th and Main Sts., an amusement spot and site of the annual Adams County Fair, was the home of Maj. Thomas B. Baldwin, a pioneer balloonist and aeronautical experimenter for the government. Major Baldwin thrilled and astonished residents of Quincy in 1887 by making a parachute jump from an altitude of 4,000 feet.

The ILLINOIS SOLDIERS AND SAILORS HOME (*open*), at the north end of 12th St., was established in 1887 for veterans of American wars and their dependents. The 200-acre grounds along wooded bluffs above the Mississippi contain a deer enclosure, an artificial lake, and beautiful sunken gardens.

US 24 crosses the Missouri Line, 133.8 *m.*, midway on the QUINCY MEMORIAL BRIDGE (*toll* 50c) spanning the Mississippi, 7 miles east of Taylor, Missouri (*see Missouri Guide*).

T O U R   17

CHICAGO—JOLIET—BLOOMINGTON AND NORMAL—
SPRINGFIELD—(ST. LOUIS, MO.); US 66
Chicago to Missouri Line, 288 *m.*

Four-lane concrete roadbed between Chicago and Joliet, two-lane hard-surfaced southwest; heavy traffic, sharp corners, and narrow pavement necessitate cautious driving.

The Atchison, Topeka & Santa Fe Ry. parallels US 66 between Chicago and Joliet; the Alton R. R. between Joliet and Springfield; Illinois Central System between Springfield and Mount Olive; Litchfield & Madison Ry. between Mount Olive and Edwardsville.

Accommodations at short intervals.

US 66, the most heavily traveled major highway in the State, cuts diagonally across Illinois between the great population centers of Chicago and St. Louis. Along its course are the State Capital and half a dozen State institutions. Industrial cities and county seats in which Lincoln practiced law alternate with farm villages and mining towns that will be long remembered in the labor history of the State and Nation.

Section a. Chicago to Joliet, 40 m.

CHICAGO, 0 *m.* (598 alt., 3,376,438 pop.) (*see Chicago*).

Points of Interest: Chicago Board of Trade Building, Union Stock Yards, Field Museum of Natural History, Art Institute of Chicago, Museum of Science and Industry, Adler Planetarium, Shedd Aquarium, University of Chicago, and others.

Chicago is at the junction with State 1 (*see Tour 1*), State 42 (*see Tour 2*), US 41 (*see Tour 2A*), US 12 (*see Tour 9*), US 14 (*see Tour 10*), US 20 (*see Tour 11*), US 330 (*see Tour 12A*) and the Illinois Waterway (*See Tour 22*).

Angling southwestward from Chicago, US 66 crosses the southern portion of CICERO, 7 *m.* (610 alt. 66,602 pop.), largest of Chicago's suburbs. Although its northern and eastern limits touch Chicago, Cicero is economically independent of its huge neighbor; its Western Electric plant alone employs, at peak periods, more than the suburb's total working population.

In the middle of the last century only 10 families lived on the swampy lowlands where Cicero now stands. At the first township election in 1857, 9 of the 14 persons who voted were elected to office. The township grew slowly until Civil War days when its farmlands, enhanced in value by the needs of the embattled North, began to attract scores of homesteaders from the East. Cicero was incorporated as a town in 1867 and continued to progress. The dank lowlands were drained by some 50 miles of ditches; offshoots of the main community were bound together by a system of permanent roads; and in 1869 Cicero received a city charter.

Foresighted land speculators perceived that Chicago would advance irresistibly westward, and in the last quarter of the 19th century boulevards, delineated along cornfield furrows, were elegantly named. Hetty Green, the eccentric millionaire, and Portus Weare, shrewd wheat speculator, were prominent among the early dealers in Cicero real estate. With a flair for promotion, Weare built a 20-room frame house, designated "Ranch 47," which stood at the northeast corner of 52nd Avenue and 25th Street. Surrounding "Ranch 47" were rows of cabins copied from those in the Klondike. In the following decades Cicero was weakened by territorial losses and strengthened by industrial gains. Two sections of Cicero were annexed to Chicago in 1892, and in 1901 the contiguous communities of Berwyn and Oak Park seceded to establish separate municipalities.

Stimulated by the growth of Chicago and its own development as an industrial area, Cicero more than tripled its population between 1910 and 1920. Among those attracted to Cicero in the booming twenties was Al Capone, "Public Enemy Number One," who established headquarters in a hotel near the Western Electric Company plant and organized a chain of speak-easies, honkytonks, and gambling houses along the streets on the north and west sides of the plant. Attended by some 200 henchmen, Capone here directed the affairs of his brewing and related enterprises until his indictment by a Federal grand jury at Chicago in 1931. The inhabitants of Cicero, pained by the notoriety that Capone's operations had brought their city, immediately purged their government and made intensive efforts to efface evidence of his activities.

The city has slightly more than a hundred industrial plants. Saws, stoves, castings, forgings, building materials, and telephone equipment are the main products. Generally neat and closely knit, the residential sections consist in large part of compact blocks of detached, two-family brick houses, with double porches and miniature lawns.

The J. STERLING MORTON HIGH SCHOOL, 25th and Austin Sts., is known among educators for its curriculum and advanced methods of instruction. The broadcasting station WHFC (1420 kc.) is at 6138 Cermak Road.

The huge WESTERN ELECTRIC COMPANY PLANT (*closed to visitors*), Cermak Rd. and Cicero Ave., was established here in 1902. Prior to 1929 the company employed 40,000 workers in manufacturing telephone equipment, audiphones, broadcasting systems, and other electrical appliances.

Left from Ogden Ave. on Cicero Ave. 1.5 *m.* to SPORTSMAN'S PARK (*half-mile track*) and the HAWTHORNE RACE TRACK (*one-mile track*), which straddle the line between Cicero and Stickney. The two race tracks, of local importance only, conduct one-month meets during September and October on a non-conflicting schedule.

Cicero merges imperceptibly with BERWYN, 9.2 *m.* (612 alt., 47,027 pop.), named for a town in Pennsylvania. Berwyn, unlike the usual Illinois municipality that grew from a Black Hawk War village to a Civil War town and then to a World War city, was ready-made in 1890 by Charles E. Piper and Wilbur J. Andrews, two realtors who provided their subdivision with essential facilities and relied on the future growth of Chicago to supply a populace. Berwyn was incorporated as a village in 1891, and chartered as a city in 1908.

During the first two decades of the present century, Berwyn was a typical suburb in which harried commuters relaxed of an evening, weeded gardens, set hens, and mowed their lawns. Indicative of this period are the many flat-roofed one-story houses, sold on the supposition that the buyer would in time save sufficient money to add a second story and transform the structure into a two-family flat, which seldom happened. A large part of the commuting population then worked in the Western Electric Company plant at Cicero, by reason of which the city was plunged into mourning on July 24, 1915, when the *Eastland,* chartered for a company excursion, rolled over in the Chicago River and drowned 812 persons. The majority were from Berwyn.

The metropolitan population continued to expand until it reached the bursting point. World War prosperity released the pressure, and in 1921 Berwyn experienced a frenzied building boom. Blocks of bungalows, each the counterpart of the other, rose on the prairie as fast as hands could lay brick, spread mortar, and attach roofs. A bare rectangle of land frequently became an inhabited city section within three months. Municipal building codes were rigidly enforced throughout the boom, accounting for the trim substantial dwellings of present Berwyn.

Berwyn is wholly residential; its economy lags or races with the quantity of production in Cicero or Chicago plants. The inhabitants are predominantly Bohemian by birth or descent.

GAGE FARM, Harlem Ave. between Cermak Rd. and Riverside Dr., has been the subject of frequent litigation since 1881. In that year Chicago obtained judgment against David A. Gage for losses totaling $507,700 which had occurred in his term as city treasurer (1869-73), and acquired his 225-acre farm as part payment. By the expansion of the metropolitan area the value of the farm gradually increased until it exceeded by $1,000,000 the amount of the judgment. Mrs. Clara

UNIVERSITY OF CHICAGO

BAHAI HOUSE OF WORSHIP, WILMETTE

HAISH MEMORIAL LIBRARY, DE KAL

CENTENNIAL BUILDING, SPRINGFIELD

NEWBERRY LIBRARY

MUNDELEIN COLLEGE

MacMURRAY COLLEGE

MODERN GRADE
SCHOOL

HIGH SCHOOL
CHICAGO HEIGHTS

WESTERN ILLINOIS
TATE TEACHERS
COLLEGE, MACOMB

DEERING LIBRARY, NORTHWESTERN UNIVERSITY

BROAD WALK, UNIVERSITY OF ILLINOIS

ALMA MATER GROUP

UNIVERSITY OF ILLINOIS

Gage Clark, David Gage's daughter, brought suit to obtain the difference between the judgment and the enhanced value of the farm. A Federal District Court ruled that Chicago had a clear title to the property, and in 1934 the United States Court of Appeals upheld this decision. Until converted into a nursery, its present use, the idle property cost Chicago $99,500 in taxes paid to Berwyn.

At 10.3 *m*. is the junction with US 34 (*see Tour* 13).

On the left the highway borders STICKNEY, 10.8 *m*. (605 alt., 2,005 pop.). The town, although its limits touch Chicago, is incompletely developed, and offers few accommodations other than a considerable stretch of taverns. In the southwest corner of MOUNT AUBURN MEMORIAL PARK, 41st St. at Oak Park Ave., is a Chinese burial ground, where the traditional Chinese rites are observed. Mourners in the cortege are each given wrapped nickels; punk sticks are lighted; a bottle of rice whisky is passed around. Three portions of food—pork, rice, and chicken—are left at the grave, with three sets of chop sticks. Most of the graves are temporary; the remains are exhumed at intervals and shipped to China in small steel boxes.

LYONS, 11.1 *m*. (615 alt., 4,787 pop.), stands at the edge of one of the earliest known sites in the State—the portage between the Chicago and Des Plaines Rivers, used by Marquette and Jolliet and by the Indians before them. Today Lyons is largely residential, its working population finding employment in nearby manufacturing towns and in Chicago.

At 12.5 *m*. is a junction with State 213.

Left on State 213 to SUMMIT, 1.1 *m*. (602 alt., 6,548 pop.), situated at the imperceptible crest of the watershed between the Great Lakes and the Mississippi drainage systems. Rain falling on the east side of town drains into the Atlantic Ocean; that falling on the west side into the Gulf of Mexico. The gargantuan CORN PRODUCTS COMPANY PLANT (*visitors welcome*), in the southern part of the city, is the largest corn refinery in the world. It is highly mechanized; employs 1,700 persons when working at capacity; and grinds as much as 80,000 bushels of corn a day. Corn is here processed into syrup, starch, cooking oil, and scores of by-products used in the manufacture of candy, chewing tobacco, beer, mucilage, fireworks, ink, and stationery.

Bordering the highway (L) is a tremendous LIMESTONE QUARRY, 14 *m*. From a distance the narrow-guage trains seem like children's toys scooting about the quarry floor or crawling up the long incline of the crusher.

At 15.5 *m*. is a junction with US 45 (*see Tour* 3).

The LYONSVILLE CHURCH (L), 17.3 *m*., at the crossing of Wolf Road, is reputedly one of the oldest Congregational Churches in northern Illinois. It served as a recruiting station during the Civil War. Back of the church is the MAPLE CREST GOLF CLUB (18 *holes, daily fee*); across Wolf Road is the INDIAN HEAD GOLF CLUB (18 *holes, daily fee*).

Lyonsville marks the eastern limit of the flat lake plain of ancient Lake Chicago, the forerunner of Lake Michigan. Westward lies the faintly rolling, wooded Valparaiso Moraine, one of the long crescent ridges of debris left by the glaciers.

STATEVILLE (L), 36 *m.*, is Illinois' new modern prison for men (*visiting limited to friends and relatives of prisoners*). The prison, largest of the State's penal institutions, raises its light brick walls in the center of a 60-acre enclosure, near the middle of the 2,200-acre State Penitentiary Farm. Care of the 4,100 prisoners, all first offenders more than 26 years old, is as modern as the building.

JOLIET, 40 *m.* (545 alt., 42,993 pop.) (*see Joliet*).

Points of Interest: Joliet Wall Paper Mills, American Institute of Laundering Vocational Training School, Oakwood Mound, and others.

Joliet is at the junction with US 30 (*see Tour* 12), and US 6 (*see Tour* 14).

Section b. Joliet to Bloomington and Normal, 93.5 m.

South of Joliet, 0 *m.*, US 66 leaves the valley of the Des Plaines and cuts diagonally cross-country, bridging the Kankakee and the head waters of the Mazon, Vermilion, and Mackinaw Rivers.

ELWOOD, 10 *m.* (646 alt., 257 pop.), serves a countryside that has witnessed a notable experiment in farm rehabilitation. In 1924 Arthur States, manager of the Roger Wharton estate, introduced improved agricultural practices that enabled ten of the twelve tenants of the estate to purchase land of their own with their share of farm income.

WILMINGTON, 17.7 *m.* (549 alt., 1,741 pop.), manufactures roofing and serves as a shopping center for Kankakee River resorts. A century ago, Thomas Fox laid out the town of Winchester on this site. In 1854, when another town proved prior rights to the name, settlers incorporated the village as Wilmington. Fox improved his investment in land by building a grist, saw, and carding mill, around which the community developed. Coal diverted attention from agriculture for a short time during the 1860's, but the town has always been essentially a trading center.

ISLAND PARK, a 35-acre wooded island in the Kankakee River, is one of the popular picnicking spots of the vicinity (*restaurants, cabins for rent, facilities for picnicking, boating*).

BRAIDWOOD, 22 *m.* (585 alt., 1,161 pop.), is surrounded by heaps of eroded, vari-colored earth, thrown up in the process of strip mining. In 1865 settler William Henneberry, in sinking a well, struck a rich 3-foot vein of coal 70 feet down. The new field attracted many mining syndicates, some from as far as Boston. By 1873 the community had grown to 3,000 and was incorporated as a city; in 1880 the population numbered 9,000, and as many as six long coal trains pulled out of

Braidwood daily. Miners lined up for three blocks at the pay window on pay day; 117 saloons, a large race track, and a music hall flourished. In the following decade more pits were closed than opened; as new fields were discovered in the vicinity, residents jacked up their houses and wheeled them to the new bonanzas. Mining was resumed in 1928 with modern strip methods, but intense mechanization precluded a revival of the roaring days of old Braidwood.

During its boom days, with an influx of thousands of transient miners of every nationality, Braidwood served as a laboratory both for labor organization and for the establishment of safety practices in mining. Impetus was given the movement by such tragic disasters as the flooding of the Diamond Mine (*see Tour* 15), which in 1883 took the lives of 74 men. Racial strife complicated the problems of labor, especially in 1877, when Negroes were imported by the operators to break a 9-month strike. Out of the Braidwood field have come such figures as John Mitchell, national labor leader; W. D. Ryan, Illinois arbitrator of mining disputes; Dan McGlaughlin, union leader and mining executive; and John H. Walker, State representative. Anton J. Cermak, Bohemian youth who later became mayor of Chicago and was killed (1933) in an assassin's attempt on the life of President Franklin D. Roosevelt, worked in the mines here until he was seventeen.

Braidwood is at the junction with US 52 (*see Tour* 15).

GODLEY, 24.5 *m.*, now merely a highway stop with one school, a few taverns, and a score of scattered houses, was once a booming coal town peopled by a thousand Scotch, Irish, and Welsh, the overflow of Braidwood's mining population. During the 1880's, 21 mines were in operation within a mile and a half of Godley; by 1906 all were closed. Bohemians have since settled in the village. Their pursuits are largely agricultural, and Godley's boom mining era is recalled only in the great "gob-heaps" that almost encircle the town.

BRACEVILLE, 26.5 *m.* (583 alt., 219 pop.), repeats the story of Godley—the census of 1890 reported a population ten times today's. Slag heaps in the vicinity are monuments of past activity; sad little piles represent the sporadic efforts of unemployed miners to salvage a few tons of coal from the closed mines.

GARDNER, 29.5 *m.* (590 alt., 869 pop.), is surrounded by slag piles, but beyond lie the farmlands that support the town as the center of a grain and stock-raising region.

DWIGHT, 39 *m.* (641 alt., 2,534 pop.), is known to thousands as the home of the KEELEY INSTITUTE (*visitors welcome*), an institution for the treatment of alcoholism and drug addiction. Dr. Leslie Keeley, a Civil War surgeon, came to Dwight after the war and continued the study of alcoholics that he had begun among Union soldiers. In 1879, when he made his famous pronouncement, "Drunkenness is a disease and I can cure it," he was sharply challenged by Joseph Medill, editor of the Chicago *Tribune*. Medill selected six of the worst alcoholics he could find in Chicago and sent them to Dwight for Keeley's treatment. When they returned, Medill capitulated and admitted, "The change for the better was so great that I scarcely recognized them. They went away sots—and returned gentlemen." The Keeley Institute has treated more than 400,000 patients, including 17,000 physicians and many hundred women, and has branches in California, Arkansas, and North and South Carolina. The average cure takes four weeks, and is based on Dr. Keeley's original assumption that chronic drunkenness is a disease of the nerve cells, and must be treated as such.

Occupying the old buildings of the Keeley Institute and the Livingston Hotel is the DWIGHT VETERANS HOSPITAL (3-4:45 *Mon., Fri., Sun. and holidays*), W. Main St. and Mazon Ave. A unit of the Veterans' Administration Facility, the hospital accommodates 225 patients.

Right from Dwight on State 17 is the STATE REFORMATORY FOR WOMEN (*arrange for group tours in advance*), 2 *m.* Completed in 1930, it is a small community in itself, occupying 160 acres, a third of which are wooded. Eight limestone buildings of the Normandy cottage type are arranged informally around a burr oak grove. Other structures include the Medium Security Building, where sick inmates are treated; a recreation center named in honor of Jane Addams; administration offices; and a receiving cottage. The reformatory resulted from the concerted action of State clubwomen to secure an advanced penal institution for women in Illinois. The prison aims to rehabilitate as well as confine.

Between Dwight and Pontiac the highway proceeds through a region of rich cornfields; the grain fields and the small trim farmsteads are text-book illustrations of the Illinois farm.

PONTIAC, 57.5 *m.* (647 alt., 8,272 pop.), named for the great chief of the Ottawa Indians who opposed the British in the French and Indian War, serves this fertile countryside with shops, railroads, and small industrial plants. Founded in 1837, Pontiac was named by Jesse W. Fell, a leader in the development of central Illinois and a personal and political friend of Lincoln. Pontiac is the seat of Livingston County, and on the courthouse lawn are several memorials, newest of which is the PONTIAC MONUMENT, a cairn of glacial boulders with a bronze tablet telling the warrior's story. The nearby SOLDIERS AND SAILORS MONUMENT received one of the shortest presidential dedications on record. Erected in 1902, it was dedicated with a few hasty words by President Theodore Roosevelt, before an audience of less than a dozen people, who congregated briefly under a terrific downpour.

The chief community playground is RIVERVIEW PARK, bounded on three sides by the Vermilion River, and on the fourth by Park Street, containing a swimming pool, auditorium, and picnicking facilities.

At the southern edge of town is the PONTIAC BRANCH OF THE

STATE PENITENTIARY (L), an institution that has given the terse expression "out at Pontiac," a meaning understood throughout the State without further explanation. In 26 buildings some 2,200 young men between the ages of 16 and 21 are imprisoned. Social rehabilitation is undertaken by psychoanalysis and individually adjusted programs of education, shop work, and recreation.

CHENOA (Ind., white dove), 68 m. (722 alt., 1,325 pop.), grew up at the junction of the Peoria & Oquawka and Chicago & Mississippi Railroads during the 1850's. Matthew T. Scott laid out the town in 1856. Two fires years ago destroyed the old false front structures of the business district; they were replaced with the red brick buildings that today are the town's chief characteristic.

Chenoa is at the junction with US 24 (*see Tour* 16).

LEXINGTON, 76.3 m. (746 alt., 1,292 pop.), commemorates the Massachusetts battleground. When settlers came to the townsite in 1828, they found villages of the Kickapoo and Delaware tribes about 3 miles south. Although alarms during the Black Hawk War caused fortifications to be erected hastily along the streams, the little band of settlers weathered the uneasy period without losing a single scalp. With the coming of the Chicago & Mississippi Railroad in 1854, the town became an outlet for the produce of the region and this continues to be its chief economic function.

TOWANDA (Ind., where we bury our dead), 84.7 m. (787 alt., 453 pop.), is the center of one of the first settled regions in this part of the State. In 1826 one John Smith homesteaded at Smith's Grove, and a post office was established in W. D. Moore's house near the present village, long before Towanda was laid out in 1854 when the Chicago & Mississippi Railroad came through. Among the founders was Jesse W. Fell, leader of half a dozen similar pioneering efforts. Most of Towanda's inhabitants are retired farmers, and the surrounding area is noted for the quality of its grain and livestock.

BLOOMINGTON, 93.5 m. (830 alt., 30,930 pop.) and NORMAL (790 alt., 6,768 pop.) (*see Bloomington and Normal*).

Points of Interest: McBarnes Memorial Building, Illinois Wesleyan University, Illinois State Normal University, and others.

Bloomington is at the junction with US 51 (*see Tour* 4).

Section c. Bloomington to Missouri Line, 154.5 m.

Between Bloomington, 0 m., and Springfield is the Lincoln country. Here the young lawyer rode circuit, made friends, and gained the political support that helped him to win the Republican nomination and the Presidency. South of the Capital are prairies and coal fields, which give way near East St. Louis to a major industrial area.

At 11 *m.* is an intersection with a graveled road.

Left on this road to the FUNK BROTHERS SEED FARMS (*visitors welcome*), 3 *m.* On the company's 22,000 acres many improvements have been made in livestock breeding and seed development. A hybrid corn that is chinch-bug resistant is a notable achievement. Each year seed from 6,000 or 7,000 acres is shipped to corn-growing states and to many foreign nations. Since 1928 the farms have also grown soy bean seed.

ATLANTA, 21.5 *m.* (720 alt., 1,169 pop.), repeats the story of the town that moved to the railroad. In 1854 the 8-year-old village of Newcastle, over a mile from the newly laid tracks of the Chicago & Mississippi Railroad, moved bag and baggage to the site of Atlanta, then known simply as the station stop of Zenia. The railroad prospered, the town boomed, and in 1855 the present name was adopted. The Atlanta *Journal* records that at a Fourth of July rally four years later, the "Hon. A. Lincoln was present and made a few remarks in reply to Mr. Sylvester Strong, who then and there presented him with a walking cane."

LINCOLN, 32 *m.* (591 alt., 12,855 pop.), seat of Logan County, is the only town named for Lincoln with his knowledge and consent. The original settlement was Postville, a short distance to the west; the coming of the railroad brought the change of site and name. In 1839 speculators Isaac and Joseph Loose of Franklin County, Pennsylvania acquired title to a quarter section of land from the Federal government at a cost of $200. In 1853 promoter Colonel Latham purchased the tract from them, for $1,350. Meanwhile, his colleague, Assemblyman Colby Knapp, persuaded the legislature to call a special election in Logan County to determine whether the county seat should remain in Mount Pulaski or be removed to Latham's quarter section of prairie. Latham granted the Chicago & Mississippi Railroad, which was rapidly extending its line in the vicinity, a right-of-way through the townsite, and exchanged a two-thirds interest in his land for the financial backing of Virgil Hickox and John Gillett.

The three partners then engaged the Springfield lawyer, Abraham Lincoln, to prepare documents which established joint ownership of the land, gave power of attorney to Latham, and bestowed on the townsite the name of Lincoln—against the advice of their lawyer, who warned them that he "never knew anything named Lincoln that amounted to much." After the townsite had been surveyed, lots were announced for sale. Contracts drawn by Lincoln provided for the release of the purchasers in the event the county seat was not established on the site within one year. To be on the safe side, Latham deeded to the county the sites of the courthouse and the jail, and the tracts that are now North and South Parks, and in the election that followed the town of Lincoln was duly constituted the seat of Logan County; proceeds from the sale of lots totaled $6,000.

Lincoln attended this first sale of lots but made no purchase. Four years later, however, quite without intent, he acquired one as compensation for $400 that he, as endorser of a note given by James Primm to a New York bank, had been obliged to pay.

The LOGAN COUNTY COURTHOUSE, in the center of the city, stands on the site of two earlier buildings in which Lincoln practiced law in the years 1854-59. Previously, when Postville had been the county seat, Lincoln had included that court in his rounds of the Eighth Judicial Circuit. The SITE OF THE POSTVILLE COURTHOUSE, off US 66(R) on 5th St., is marked by a memorial plaque, but the building is in Henry Ford's museum at Dearborn, Michigan. On Broadway, adjoining the present depot, is the SITE OF THE OLD ALTON DEPOT, where the first Lincoln County volunteers entrained for the Civil War, April 19, 1861; where Stephen A. Douglas, enroute from Springfield to Chicago, spoke briefly for the Union cause, April 26, 1861; and where the Lincoln funeral train halted for a few minutes at sunrise, May 3, 1865.

LINCOLN COLLEGE, Ottawa and Keokuk Sts., founded in 1865, is a Presbyterian coeducational junior college enrolling about 100 students. At the southern edge of town, on a tract recommended by the Illinois Medical Society, stands the LINCOLN STATE SCHOOL AND COLONY. An institution for feeble-minded, it cares for some 4,000 patients, many of whom help farm the adjoining 1,800-acre tract.

In BRAINERD PARK, at the southwestern limits of Lincoln, are the buildings and grounds of the LINCOLN CHAUTAUQUA, one of the oldest and largest in the country. The chautauqua has been held annually since 1902, when it opened with such celebrities as William Jennings Bryan.

On the banks of Salt Creek adjoining the chautauqua grounds is the SITE OF A KICKAPOO INDIAN VILLAGE, to which Mrs. James Gillham and her three children were brought from Kentucky by Indians in 1790, thus becoming the first white persons to set foot in Logan County (*see below*).

1. South from Lincoln on Kickapoo Street are the LINCOLN LAKES, 3 *m.*, a 114-acre body of water in old gravel pits. Annually restocked, the lakes have long been locally popular among fishermen. A sand beach, bathhouse, and pure water afford good swimming.

2. Southeast from Lincoln on State 121 is MOUNT PULASKI, 10 *m.* (637 alt., 1,445 pop.), which in 1847 succeeded Postville (*see above*) as seat of Logan County. The MOUNT PULASKI COURT HOUSE, built in that year at a cost of $3,000, functioned as the seat of justice until 1853, when Lincoln (*see above*) persuaded the voters that it was more centrally located. The building served various public purposes in the following years, and in 1936 was acquired by the State as a historical monument. It is a small structure, about 30 by 40 feet, of two stories; originally, the lower floor was devoted to county offices, and the upper to the court chamber. The Greek Revival building is of brick, and the

unadorned walls support wooden pediments of free classical lines devoid of
ornamentation. The interior of the courthouse is being restored to look again as
it did in the days when Mount Pulaski was the principal town in Logan County.

US 66 crosses Salt Creek, 35 *m.*, in the vicinity of the LOGAN
COUNTY SCULLY LANDS, part of the vast properties of William Scully
(1821-1906), who at one time was one of the greatest landholders in
the United States. Scully, an Irish landowner, arrived at Philadelphia
in 1851 with much money and a passion for land. With a horse and a
spade the young Irishman rode through Pennsylvania, Ohio, Indiana,
Illinois, Missouri, Kansas, Nebraska, and Wisconsin, probing the soil,
What land he liked, he bought. In 1853 he settled in Logan County,
imported several Irish families, and engaged in farming on a vast scale.

After the Civil War, Scully inaugurated a system of tenantry and
returned to Europe. This aroused a storm of criticism, leading to the
passage of a State law in 1889 against alien ownership of land. Scully
circumvented this by taking up residence in Washington, D. C., and
becoming a citizen. His holdings assured, he returned to England
where he was known as "the great American farmer," and there he
resided until his death. Of the 200,000 acres he once owned, 50,000
acres were in Illinois. His 30,000-acre Logan County estate is still
owned by his heirs.

ELKHART, 43 *m.* (592 alt., 448 pop.), is the home town and
burial place of Richard J. Oglesby (1824-99), farmer, carpenter,
ropemaker, lawyer, forty-niner, Mexican and Civil War soldier, three
times governor of Illinois, and United States Senator.

Left from Elkhart on a hard-surfaced road to ELKHART HILL, 1 *m.* On the
crest of the sharply rising moraine, commanding a far-flung view of the level
prairies, stands OGLEHURST (*private*), a 30-room house built by Governor
Oglesby in 1891. Here too lived his son, the late John G. Oglesby, one-time
lieutenant-governor of Illinois. Nearby is the OGLESBY MAUSOLEUM, in Elkhart
Cemetery.

SPRINGFIELD, 61.9 *m.* (598 alt., 71,864 pop.) (*see Springfield*).

Points of Interest: State Capitol, Lincoln's Tomb, Lincoln's Home, Centennial
Building, Supreme Court Building, Sangamon County Courthouse, and others.

Springfield is at the junctions with US 36 (*see Tour* 18) and the
Lincoln National Memorial Highway (*see Tour* 21).

At 64.3 *m.* is a junction with Springfield's Belt Highway.

Left on this highway to SPAULDING DAM, 2 *m.*, which impounds the waters
of Sugar Creek to form LAKE SPRINGFIELD, water supply and chief recreational
area for the land-locked capital. Completed in 1935, the 4,270-acre lake and
marginal lands of almost the same extent are owned and have been developed by
the city. Income from the lease of residence and cottage sites is used to meet the
$2,500,000 obligation incurred in the improvement of the property. Private clubs,

public parks, year-round residences, and summer cottages border the winding shore line. At the dam is the MUNICIPAL WATER AND LIGHT PLANT (*open*). Above the entrance to the purification plant is inscribed, "Monument to the ability of the people to serve themselves and build for posterity."

LAKE PARK, 6.3 *m.*, on the east side of the lake, is a naturally wooded park with a good beach and beach house. The VACHEL LINDSAY MEMORIAL BRIDGE, a low graceful concrete span, connects the park with the west shore, across a narrows in the lake. At the far end of the bridge is a bust of the Springfield poet by Adrien Voisin.

The LINCOLN MEMORIAL GARDEN, 9 *m.*, was landscaped by Jens Jensen and is being gradually improved with the co-operation of garden clubs throughout the country. When completed, it will include a patch of flowered prairie, a common enough sight in Lincoln's day but now rare.

US 66 crosses an arm of Lake Springfield, 68.3 *m.;* at the southern end of the bridge is a junction (L) with the highway that encircles the lake. BRIDGE VIEW BEACH (R), a beach for Negroes, is patronized by thousands of that race from all over the State.

At 84.5 *m.* is a junction with a graveled road.

Right on this road is VIRDEN, 7.3 *m.* (674 alt., 3,011 pop.), a coal mining town, the scene of the Virden riot, October 12, 1898. Miners struck when the local company withdrew from the Illinois Coal Operators Association and refused to pay the rates established by that association and the miners' union. According to the Carlinville *Democrat,* the company imported 300 Southern Negroes and 75 armed guards. The miners opposed the efforts of the guards to bring Negroes into the mine. Ten miners and six guards were killed and about thirty wounded. To an outraged public, Governor Tanner, who had sought arbitration of the strike, declared: "These avaricious mine owners who have so far forgotten their duty to society as to bring this blot upon the fair name of our State have gone far enough . . . and I say now to all such and others that this is a thing of the past, that it shall not be tolerated in Illinois while I am governor." Warrants charging company officials with conspiracy to murder were drawn but never served. Virden Day is observed by the town and surrounding communities each year at Mount Olive (*see below*).

At 97 *m.* is a junction with State 108.

Right on State 108 is CARLINVILLE, 13 *m.* (627 alt., 4,144 pop.), widely known throughout the State for its million-dollar MACOUPIN COUNTY COURTHOUSE (*open* 8-5), which local wags have nicknamed "The White Elephant." In February 1867 the county commissioners ordered a $50,000 bond issue to erect new quarters for the county offices. The bonds bore 10 per cent interest and were to be repaid within 10 years, but this sum scarcely laid the foundation. More and more bonds were issued, and taxes rose higher and higher, until a "courthouse tax" of 50c on each $100 valuation in real, personal, and mixed property was levied. This the taxpayers bitterly fought, but without success. In January 1870 the building was completed, at a total cost of $1,380,500, but not until July 1910 was the last bond retired. Citizens of the county then staged a two-day celebration, which was attended by Governor Charles Deneen. Natural gas, recently discovered in the vicinity, was piped to the courthouse square, and as a climax to the celebration, the last bond was burned by the Governor. As the scrap of paper crumbled to ashes, 20,000 people shouted themselves hoarse, and the whistle of every factory and mine in the county was blown for ten minutes.

At the time the courthouse was built, no public building in the Middle West compared with it architecturally. Even today architects come to study its design. The limestone building consists of two rectangles, which cross at the center and are surmounted with a dome. The larger rectangle is 80 by 181 feet; the dome rises 191 feet above the street. The 40-foot columns that support the roof of the portico, the detail of the cornice, and the decoration of the interior are Corinthian. Every door in the building is of iron; each of the elaborate outer doors weighs more than a ton. All interior trim is of iron or stone. The most impressive chamber is the Circuit Court Room under the dome; facing the rows of polished walnut seats stands the $1,500 judge's chair, mounted on a track behind the vari-colored marble bench.

BLACKBURN COLLEGE, at the end of College Avenue, was opened in 1857 as a theological school, but since 1912 it has been known as the school where everybody works. In that year the Rev. William M. Hudson became president of Blackburn and inaugurated the self-help plan whereby all students perform two and a half hours of manual work daily. Academic requirements of this class A junior college are strict, but equally essential for admission are the need and willingness to work. Enrollment is limited to 300. So successful has been the plan that $225 is all the student pays for board, room, and tuition each school year. The rest of his expense is met by work, or is paid out of income from the college's $1,000,000 endowment. All the work of office and maintenance routine is done by the students. The farm is operated by the men, the kitchens by the men and women. The trim brick buildings of the college, of simple modern design, have been built by the men. The forwarding of Christian ideals through co-operative work and study, which is the intent of the college, was the goal of its founder, the Rev. Gideon Blackburn, formerly president of Center College, Kentucky, who initiated plans for the school in 1837 but died before his hopes could be realized.

In Carlinville, August 31, 1858, Lincoln addressed a scattered audience whose sympathies were largely with Douglas. "Black Republicanism" was not popular in southern Illinois. But 71 years later, during the celebration of the city's centennial, 1,500 people gathered at South Broad and 1st South Streets to unveil the LINCOLN MEMORIAL, a 7,000-pound boulder upon which is recorded in bronze the fact of Lincoln's address.

The OTWELL IRIS FIELDS (*visitors welcome*), North Road at the city limits, are a patchwork quilt of perfumed color every May, when the 25 acres of ordered beauty, bearing 300 varieties of irises, attract thousands of visitors. For years the Otwell Tree Planting Clubs, organized by Will Otwell, have conducted a private reforestation program, which annually plants more than 1,000,000 trees. Members are pledged to plant at least one tree a year, but every day is Arbor Day to Mr. Otwell. During 1934 he set out 3,000 black walnut trees, and planted seed for 250,000 more. Black walnuts are Mr. Otwell's favorite tree, but he does not try to influence club members. "The main thing," says Mr. Otwell, "is to plant trees and influence others to do the same."

The highway skirts the limits of LITCHFIELD, 105.4 *m.* (683 alt., 6,612 pop.), an old mining town, center of a coal field that underlies parts of six counties. Shaft mines in the immediate vicinity dot the landscape with their gob piles and tipples. Litchfield, incorporated in 1859, was the scene of the first commercial oil production in Illinois, in 1882; the small pocket then tapped has long since been exhausted. Today, Litchfield is a trim prosperous little city with an International Stove Company factory and other industries.

MOUNT OLIVE, 115.8 *m.* (681 alt., 3,079 pop.), in the heart of an old coal field, is an orderly and even-tempered small city. Mount

Olive was the home of English-born Alexander Bradley (1866-1918), a leading figure in the struggle for union organization and recognition here and throughout the State. He gained the title of "General" in 1897, when he led an army of organizers into the southern Illinois fields and welded together the then weak and timid miners' locals. At this time, according to his autobiography, he was wined and dined by the mine operators at the famed Tony Faust's in St. Louis and offered $600 to cease his activities. Instead, he bought a Prince Albert, a silk hat, and a silk umbrella, and returned to camp to scatter $5 bills among his men, saying, "Here's shoes for you."

More widely known was "Mother" Jones (1830-1930), born Mary Harris, in Cork, Ireland. Brought to America at the age of five, she enjoyed somewhat better schooling than usually fell to the lot of an immigrant's daughter. Until the death of her husband and four children in 1867 her activities were the more or less conventional ones of teaching, dressmaking, and caring for her family. But throughout the remainder of her long life of one hundred years, she worked wholeheartedly and untiringly for the cause of labor. In his introduction to her autobiography Clarence Darrow described her as one of the most forceful and picturesque friends of the American labor movement: "She was a born crusader, a woman of action, fired by a fine zeal, a mother especially devoted to the miners. Wherever fights were fiercest and danger greatest, Mother Jones was present to aid and cheer. She had a strong sense of drama. She staged every detail of a contest. . . . Her personal non-resistance was far more powerful than any appeal to force."

She worked throughout the Nation, "a little old woman in a black bonnet with a high falsetto voice and a handsome face framed in curly white hair and lighted by shrewd kindly gray eyes." She organized marches of wives of striking miners, armed with mops and brooms. She led a column of children into New York to protest child labor. In 1913 she was convicted by a military court of conspiracy to murder, but a Senate investigating committee set aside her conviction. Militant as she was, she was opposed to woman suffrage. On her death she expressed a wish to be buried in Mount Olive.

The UNION MINERS CEMETERY, on the northwestern limits of the city, has become a shrine of American labor. The GRAVE OF "MOTHER" JONES is marked with a simple headstone. A tablet on the GRAVE OF ALEXANDER BRADLEY memorializes the "General" and 20 of his followers, who gave "their lives to the cause of clean unionism in America." Nearby rises the granite shaft of a monument erected in 1936 "to the everlasting memory of Mary 'Mother' Jones, 'General' Alexander Bradley, and the martyrs of the Virden riot of 1898."

STAUNTON, 120.2 m. (622 alt., 4,618 pop.), lies in the midst of tipples and slag heaps that clutter the landscape up to its very door. Long before coal was mined here, the community was an important

trading point for settlers. In 1817 John Wood of Virginia built the
first log cabin. Other Easterners followed, and in 1835 the village was
laid out and named for one of its founders. Staunton is both a coal
mining and farming center.

EDWARDSVILLE, 140.2 m. (554 alt., 6,235 pop.), named in
honor of Ninian Edwards, governor of Illinois Territory (1809-18)
and one of the first landowners in the vicinity, was platted in 1813. In
the same year, an Indian agency and a government land office to record
deeds to lands given the militia of the War of 1812 were established
here. Soon after Illinois became a State in 1818, a board of trustees
was created by the legislature to supervise the affairs of the town;
not until 1837 did the inhabitants vote to incorporate. The community
developed slowly until the fear was laid that the seat of Madison
County was to be transferred to rapidly growing Alton. Eight governors of Illinois have made Edwardsville their home.

James Gillham was perhaps the earliest settler. He first visited the
locality in 1794 in search of his wife and children, who had been taken
captive from their Kentucky home by a band of Kickapoo. In the
region he learned from French traders that his family was being held
for ransom in the Kickapoo village on Salt Creek, near the present
site of Lincoln (see above). With two Frenchmen as interpreters and
an Irishman as intermediary, he effected their return. So impressed
was Gillham with the beauty and fertility of the Edwardsville region
that in 1800 he settled on the site. Several of his relatives from South
Carolina soon followed, and the Gillhams became the most numerous
family in the area.

Most of the pioneers were from the South; as the community developed, a clear-cut social structure evolved. Three classes in society
were recognized in the first half of the nineteenth century, according
to an early resident. The first was the "white man, born in a slave
state, who calls himself the real western settler. The second class of
society is the negro [the freed slave]. The third class consists of the
Yankee from across the mountains." This prejudice against the "Yankees" continued until they became influential business men.

Among the first enterprises was coal mining, an industry that still
flourishes. As early as 1850 strikes are recorded. On a single day in
that year miners "sat down" three times in the pit of Henry Ritter,
the pioneer operator. The first strike Ritter met by agreeing to pay a
higher percentage. The second he met in like fashion. When news
came of the third, he went to the shaft and announced that the hoist
would be removed in fifteen minutes; no more strikes were recorded
on that day.

The MADISON COUNTY HISTORICAL SOCIETY MUSEUM (open Wed.,
1-3; other times upon application), on the third floor of the courthouse, contains among other pioneer and Indian relics the square
piano of Elijah Lovejoy (1802-37), Alton editor and stormy abo-

litionist. Of a type common in the 1770's, it is small and low, without pedals, its keyboard but 28 inches from the floor. The date of manufacture is unknown, but it is presumed to have been made by the firm of Astor & Company, established in this country by the brother of John Jacob Astor in 1772.

Dominating VALLEY VIEW CEMETERY (R), 142.2 m., is the State-owned EDWARD COLES MONUMENT, a tall shaft with a bust by Leon Hermant of Illinois' second governor (1822-26). The son of a rich Virginia planter, Coles once served as secretary to President Madison. In 1819 he came to Illinois by wagon and flatboat; on reaching the State, he immediately freed his slaves and gave each 160 acres of land. This section of Illinois contained many slavery sympathizers, and the Virginian's surprising repudiation of slavery was frequently raised as a bitter issue in subsequent political campaigns.

At 145.5 m. is a junction with US 40 (see Tour 19); US 66 and US 40 are united (see Tour 19) between this point and the Missouri Line, 154.5 m., which is crossed midway on the CHAIN-OF-ROCKS BRIDGE (25c), spanning the Mississippi to the northern limits of St. Louis, Missouri (see Missouri Guide).

TOUR 18

(ROCKVILLE, IND.)—DECATUR—SPRINGFIELD—
JACKSONVILLE—(HANNIBAL, MO.); US 36
Indiana Line to Missouri Line, 225 m.

Hard-surfaced roadbed throughout.
Baltimore & Ohio R. R. parallels route between Indiana Line and Decatur; Wabash Ry. between Decatur and Jacksonville.
Usual accommodations.

US 36 extends almost directly east and west across central Illinois through one of the most fertile sections of the State. Between the Indiana Line and Decatur the land is level, except where notched by streams. Many of the prosperous farms along the route have been reclaimed from swamps. The money crop of much of this region is broom corn, cultivated locally since 1865. The forty miles west of Decatur, a segment of the Lincoln National Memorial Highway (see Tour 21), is rich in Lincolniana. In its western section the land becomes more rolling as the highway crosses the Illinois River and proceeds to the valley of the Mississippi.

US 36 crosses the Indiana Line, 0 *m.*, 8 miles west of Montezuma, Indiana (*see Indiana Guide*).

At 8 *m.* is a junction with State 1 (*see Tour* 1).

NEWMAN, 24.2 *m.* (651 alt., 1,054 pop.), was founded in 1857 and named for B. Newman, son-in-law of the Methodist circuit-rider, Peter Cartwright. The village was industrially active during the 1890's, with two tile factories which supplied materials for draining nearby swamps; the factories closed when drainage operations ceased. Newman has a sweet corn cannery and a dairy products plant that manufactures casein.

At 30.1 *m.* is a junction with paved road.

Right on this road is MURDOCK, 0.5 *m.*, platted in 1881 and named for John D. Murdock, who had built a grain elevator here three years earlier. Exploratory shafts sunk in 1929 revealed a 7-foot vein of coal under the community at a depth of 200 feet, but mining operations have not been undertaken (1939). The PENTECOST CHURCH served in Chicago as a dance hall at the Century of Progress Exposition; in 1936 the structure was moved to Murdock and dedicated as a religious tabernacle.

A LOG CABIN (R), 35.2 *m.*, was built in 1830 by John Richmond, the first settler in what is now Douglas County. He emigrated from West Virginia in 1829.

At 35.4 *m.* is a junction with an oiled road.

Right on this road is PATTERSON SPRINGS, 0.1 *m.* (*fishing, swimming, and picnicking*).

TUSCOLA, 41.3 *m.* (653 alt., 2,569 pop.) (*see Tour* 3), is at a junction with US 45 (*see Tour* 3).

A BOOSTER STATION (L), 45.2 *m.*, is one of a series of pumping stations along the pipe line that carries natural gas from Oklahoma to Indianapolis, Detroit, and other northern cities; the gas is here given a "boost" along its way.

The CARTWRIGHT CHURCH (R), 45.7 *m.*, a white frame structure, was named for Peter Cartwright, fighting Methodist preacher who came to Illinois from Kentucky in 1823. His reasons for moving were: "I had six children and felt that my holdings of 150 acres were insufficient. . . . In Kentucky, there was class discrimination shown in favor of the children reared without work as against those who were taught to work. There was the dangerous possibility that my four daughters might marry into slave families. Lastly, the new country needed preachers."

In the cemetery beside the church is the GRAVE OF DR. DAVID HANSON, an infantry captain killed in the World War while attempting to rescue a fellow officer. The Alumni Association of Northwestern University, from which Hanson was graduated, marked his grave with a 10-ton memorial boulder, on which the French government placed the Croix de Guerre.

At 49.8 *m.* is a junction with a graveled road.

Left on this road is ARTHUR, 7.5 *m.* (675 alt., 1,361 pop.), the trading center of an Amish colony. The village was platted in 1873 by surveyors of the Paris & Decatur Railroad. The town has two broom factories and a plant that makes caskets, burial vaults, and oil storage tanks.

The Amish, a branch of the Mennonites (*see Tour* 16), settled near the site of Arthur in 1864. The colony now approximates 3,000. Modernism and mechanization have made no impression on it; native customs and manners have been rigidly preserved. Traditional crafts are handed down from father to son, mother to daughter. The men wear black, broad-brimmed felt hats and home-made suits, fastened with hooks and eyes. The women wear aprons, bonnets, tight-waisted blouses, and voluminous skirts. A horse and buggy, as evidenced by rows of hitching racks in Arthur, is the usual mode of conveyance. "Pennsylvania German" is spoken in the Amish homes.

Amish children attend public elementary schools, but receive the equivalent of high school training in private schools supported by the colony. Church services are held in members' houses, the wall partitions of which are generally constructed so that they can be hooked to the ceiling, thus providing space for the congregation. Frugal, industrious, and skilled in agriculture, the Amish are the most prosperous farmers in the region. When an aged couple is no longer capable of arduous work, they give their farm to their eldest son and retire to the "Grandpa House," a small cottage near the main dwelling. Clannish in the best sense of the word, the Amish, as has been said by one of them, "have no fatherland; God is supreme with us. The laws of the colony are our religious faith."

At 74 *m.* is a junction with the Lincoln National Memorial Highway (*see Tour* 21), which unites with US 36 for 44 miles (*see Tour* 21).

SPRINGFIELD, 118 *m.* (598 alt., 71,864 pop.) (*see Springfield*).

Points of Interest: State Capitol, Lincoln's Tomb, Lincoln's Home, Centennial Building, Supreme Court Building, Sangamon County Courthouse, and others.

Springfield is at the junction with US 66 (*see Tour* 17) and the Lincoln National Memorial Highway (*see Tour* 21).

BATES, 133 *m.,* a hamlet clustered about a white church and two grain elevators, is at the west end of the Bates Experimental Road, built by the State Highway Department in 1921. The 2-mile stretch of highway contains 63 kinds of paving material, periodically examined for comparative wear.

Between Bates and Jacksonville, US 36 passes through four agricultural centers, each clumped at the base of grain elevators. The fertile countryside is a checkerboard of corn and wheat fields. A comfortable standard of living is evidenced by large and well-maintained farmhouses. The barns, an infallible barometer of agrarian economy, are frequently topped with cupolas and decorated with lightning rods and weathervanes.

JACKSONVILLE, 154 *m.* (613 alt., 17,747 pop.) (*see Tour 7*),
is at a junction with US 67 (*see Tour 7*).

WINCHESTER, 171.7 *m.* (546 alt., 1,532 pop.), seat of Scott
County, had a grist mill as early as 1824, but was not platted until
1830 when, according to tradition, surveyors permitted a Kentuckian
to name the townsite in exchange for a jug of whiskey.

The business district fronting the minute public square consists of
shops built in the late nineteenth century, with several frame structures dating from the 1850's. In the square is the STEPHEN A.
DOUGLAS MONUMENT, a life-sized bronze of the Little Giant, who
"taught his first school and began his legal career here in 1833-34." A
nearby boulder marks the spot where Lincoln made his first speech on
the Kansas-Nebraska issue. The building now occupied by the Walker
Implement Company, on Main Street just north of the public square,
occupies the site of the schoolhouse in which Stephen A. Douglas
taught.

The SCOTT COUNTY COURTHOUSE, northeast corner of the square,
a two-story brick and stone structure of Romanesque style, designed
by James Stuart, was built in 1885. A stone tablet on the courthouse
lawn marks the SITE OF THE AIKEN TAVERN, in which Lincoln lodged
in 1854.

West of Winchester the route traverses rolling hills along the valley of the Illinois River. The highway crosses the river on a lift bridge,
ascends a winding road through outcrops of limestone, and emerges on
agricultural uplands.

PITTSFIELD, 191 *m.* (725 alt., 2,356 pop.), seat of Pike County,
was founded by settlers from Pittsfield, Massachusetts. The site was
purchased from the Government for $200. On May 5, 1833, eleven
lots were sold and several others were reserved for public purposes.
A courthouse and a Congregational church were subsequently built
on the town square. Pork-packing became the chief local industry, the
meat being packed in barrels made of white oak from the forests that
flourished nearby.

Early Pittsfield was a genuine transplantation of New England
culture. John Hay (1838-1905), private secretary to President Lincoln, ambassador to Great Britain (1897-98), Secretary of State under
Presidents McKinley and Theodore Roosevelt, and formulator of the
Open Door policy in China, spent two years here as a student and
spoke of the community as a center of "light and learning," especially
during the circuit court season. In a single case involving $50, it is
recorded, six of the eight participating lawyers later became United
States Senators. Life as he saw it during his student days at Pittsfield,
Hay portrayed in his *Pike County Ballads*. With John G. Nicolay, Hay
collaborated in the ten-volume *Abraham Lincoln: A History*.

Dominating the Pittsfield skyline is the spire of the PIKE COUNTY
COURTHOUSE, a three-story structure of Indiana limestone, designed

by Henry Elliot and built in 1894. The WORTHINGTON HOUSE (*private*), 626 W. Washington St., a tetrastyle frame structure of Classic Revival design, was built in the late 1830's to house a "female academy," which never opened. In 1847 the building was acquired and occupied by Dr. Thomas Worthington, who entertained here Abraham Lincoln, John Hay, and John G. Nicolay.

A boulder in CENTRAL PARK marks the spot where Lincoln spoke on October 1, 1858. This speech, as others delivered that year, is sometimes erroneously recorded as a debate with Douglas. There were only seven joint debates, as authenticated by the Abraham Lincoln Association of Springfield, which has published a day-by-day record of Lincoln's activities in the significant years 1854-61. Nevertheless, plaques in several Illinois towns commemorate "lost" or "forgotten" debates.

At 195 *m.* is a junction with US 54.

Left on US 54 through rolling hill country is the CHAMP CLARK TOLL BRIDGE (*car and driver,* 50c; *passengers,* 5c *each*), 15 *m.,* which crosses the Mississippi to Louisiana, Mo. (*see Missouri Guide*).

BARRY, 206 *m.* (683 alt., 1,506 pop.), entered on a tree-arched street, is the trading center of a dairying, agricultural, and horticultural area, noted for its large shipments of fine apples.

West of Barry the highway traverses wooded hill country and then descends to the wide valley of Hadley Creek.

Old-fashioned tin awnings project from the façades of several shops in KINDERHOOK, 212 *m.* (471 alt., 318 pop.), a village built on a hillside. Once ubiquitous in Illinois towns, over-walk awnings of wood or tin have in recent years gone the way of cigar store Indians.

US 36 crosses the Missouri Line, 225 *m.,* on the MARK TWAIN MEMORIAL BRIDGE (*toll* 35c), spanning the Mississippi to Hannibal, Mo. (*see Missouri Guide*).

TOUR 19

(TERRE HAUTE, IND.) —MARSHALL—EFFINGHAM—VANDALIA
—TROY— (ST. LOUIS, MO.) ; US 40.
Indiana Line to Missouri Line, 158 m.

Hard-surfaced roadbed throughout.
The Pennsylvania R. R. parallels the route between the Indiana Line and Troy.
Usual accommodations throughout.

US 40, a major transcontinental highway, follows the route of the old Cumberland Road, constructed by the Federal government more than a century ago at a cost of 7 million dollars. At that time it was the longest continuous highway ever built in this country ; the Illinois section was completed in 1837.

The most traveled thoroughfare in the Nation, the Cumberland or National Road, as it came to be called, bore a never-ending load of traffic. Great freight wagons lumbered over its length, crammed to overflowing with manufactured goods for the frontier, and returned laden with raw materials for the Eastern seaboard. Travelers of every description ate, drank, sang, and cursed in its roadside taverns and stage houses. Andrew Jackson, William Henry Harrison, James Polk, Henry Clay, and John Marshall rubbed elbows and exchanged a passing word with teamsters, actors, settlers, and soldiers of fortune. The east-west mail was carried on the Cumberland Road; in 1837 it took about 94 hours to travel from Washington to St. Louis.

In Illinois, as elsewhere along the route, stagecoach stations often bloomed into villages, almost overnight. Later, as the railroads inched their way westward and the State maintained a steady growth, these mushroom communities either dissolved into ghost towns or expanded into thriving cities. Today, as deserted sites or as prosperous county seats, they appear at short intervals along the cross-country chain that is US 40.

US 40 crosses the Indiana Line, 0 *m.*, 8 miles west of Terre Haute, Indiana (*see Indiana Guide*).

Entering Illinois, the route dips into four or five deep wide valleys which form a natural trench-work draining this productive region.

MARSHALL, 9.5 *m.* (606 alt., 2,368 pop.), seat of Clark County, was founded by William B. Archer, and named by him for his idol, Chief Justice John Marshall of the U. S. Supreme Court. Its broad shady streets bordered with fine old houses, the town has a contemplative air, as though recalling pleasant memories of the past. Its 103-year-old business district has kept pace with the time, however, by modernizing its buildings and illuminating its windows with neon lights.

Marshall is at the junction with the Lincoln National Memorial Highway (*see Tour* 21).

West of Marshall, US 40 crosses a STONE ARCH BRIDGE built by Army engineers more than a century ago as part of the Cumberland Road. Each stone in this bondless type of bridge was shaped to exact proportions by hand, and clamped together with keys to prevent slipping. When this section of US 40 was realigned and resurfaced in 1931, the bridge structure was also repaired. Today, traffic races across the same span that heard the creak and rumble of prairie schooners and stagecoaches many years ago.

CLARK CENTER, 14.4 *m.*, a tiny hamlet, dates from 1835. Its prospects were bright at its founding, but they were blighted in 1837, when Marshall snatched the honor of being designated the county seat. Originally, Clark Center was a stagecoach stop on the Cumberland Road.

MARTINSVILLE, 20.3 *m.* (562 alt., 1,206 pop.), platted in 1833 by Joseph Martin, was a lively trading post, stagecoach station, and tavern center. Many famous men and infamous rogues shared the tavern's food, drink, and roof for the night. Here stories and toasts were freely exchanged as travelers awaited the next stage westward. But Martinsville did not measureably develop until 1904, when oil and gas were discovered and a boom enveloped the region. By 1916 most of the wells had been drained, and the town lapsed into the slow and quiet existence of a country town. In recent years apple orchards have been planted in the neighborhood, and some apples are shipped from this point. A bronze plaque imbedded in a boulder on the high school grounds at the western edge of Martinsville commemorates the centennial of the town's founding.

The ILLINOIS PIPE LINE TANK FARM (*power plant and control room open*), 21.5 *m.*, stores oil piped here from Texas, Oklahoma, and the new Illinois Basin, its 200 tanks having a capacity of 7,500,000 barrels. The nucleus of this large tank farm was built to store oil from the first well in the vicinity.

Many of the retired farmers in CASEY, 26.4 *m.* (648 alt., 2,200 pop.), owe their incomes to the oil that underlay the homesteads of their grandfathers. An attractive town of fine wide streets and trim white houses, Casey was once a booming oil center, but now its chief industrial plant is a shoe factory.

GREENUP, 36.5 *m.* (554 alt., 1,062 pop.), was named for William C. Greenup, first clerk of the Illinois Territorial Legislature, who donated the townsite and obtained the incorporation of the village in 1836. Formerly the seat of Cumberland County, named for the famous road, Greenup has a more venerable appearance than other communities of equal age. The weather-worn building in the public square, all but hidden from the highway by great trees, is the town hall. Age is also apparent in many of the business buildings that flank the town hall. Some of these have porches—heavily encrusted with iron grill-work and supported by pillars that rise from the curb line—which jut out over the sidewalk, forming an arcade for pedestrians.

The tan frame CONZET HOTEL, one block west of the square on US 40, one of the oldest structures in Greenup, was a regular stopover for merchants, who displayed their wares and transacted business in a special room reserved for that purpose. Buyers gathered here and made their purchases in a leisurely manner, often spending the whole day in renewing their acquaintance with the men from whom they bought. One section of the sample room in the Conzet was part of the Barbour Inn, a frame hostelry erected by William Greenup in 1831.

West of Greenup, US 40 slips down to the Embarras River bottoms and passes (L) the CUMBERLAND COUNTY FAIRGROUNDS 37.2 *m.*, bordering the river, where are held (usually in mid-August) an annual agricultural show, horse races, and a homecoming celebration.

JEWETT, 41.6 *m.* (587 alt., 230 pop.), developed from the former town of Pleasantville, a stagecoach stop of a century ago. A tiny community with tiny frame houses, Jewett looks almost like a miniature village. On LAKE WOODBURY (*fishing, boating, camping facilities*), 44.2 *m.*, is a hamlet of the same name.

TEUTOPOLIS, 55.2 *m.* (602 alt., 710 pop.), is a German Catholic community established in 1839 by a group from Cincinnati, Ohio. ST. JOSEPH'S SEMINARY, across the railroad tracks and just south of US 40, has (1939) an enrollment of 70 students.

EFFINGHAM, 59.5 *m.* (591 alt., 4,978 pop.) (*see Tour* 3), is at junction with US 45 (*see Tour* 3).

A marker (L), 62.2 *m.*, at a dirt road immediately south of the Pennsylvania Railroad bridge, indicates the SITE OF EWINGTON. While Vandalia was still the capital of Illinois, Ewington was chosen as the seat of Effingham County and named for W. L. D. Ewing, Vandalia statesman, whose bill was responsible for inducing the legislature to create the county.

A few hundred feet south of the marker are the last remains of this once important village. Here, in the age-worn EWINGTON CEMETERY, are well-preserved headstones over the graves of early settlers, some of whom were soldiers in the Revolutionary War.

About 300 yards west of the cemetery, visible from the highway, is a two-story brick residence (*private*), rebuilt in 1912 from the original Ewington courthouse. Now a few hundred feet south of its former site, the building was constructed largely of the materials from the old structure, including the staircase and stair railing. One interesting feature is the diamond-shaped window over the small front porch.

Ewington's prosperity and importance were checked in 1852 when the Illinois Central tracks passed it by and continued into Effingham.

Seven years later this younger town plucked the county seat plum from under her rival's nose, and Ewington's decline was accelerated. For a time, the old courthouse at Ewington was transformed into the county poorhouse, but in 1880 even that humble institution was removed elsewhere.

ALTAMONT, 71.4 m. (623 alt., 1,225 pop.), named for a rise of ground about a mile to the west, was organized into a village in 1872. Hugging the junction of the Pennsylvania and Baltimore & Ohio railroads, Altamont manufactures clothing and egg cases; it also is a wheat-shipping center.

ST. ELMO, 76.8 m. (618 alt., 1,329 pop.), settled in 1830 by a group of Kentucky Catholics, lies in the center of the newly discovered Illinois oil field, and today is experiencing a boom. Formerly known chiefly for its Chicago & Eastern Illinois Railroad shops and the manufacture of bricks, St. Elmo has shaken off its leisurely ways, and its streets are now lively with lumbering oil trucks, leather-booted oil men, and optimistic predictions concerning oil. The people have taken on the carefree confidence of a community whose future is assured. Back-slappings and hearty laughs are the order of the day; oil is the magic word—the touchstone of good times. An oil refinery has raced into existence to accommodate the ever-increasing wells, and numerous shops for building and servicing drilling machinery have secured conspicuous spots along the town's streets. Several of the wells responsible for this striking metamorphosis border US 40 west of St. Elmo.

Before reaching Vandalia, the highway drops into the broad valley of the Kaskaskia River, lined with trees and wild flowers.

VANDALIA, 90 m. (503 alt., 4,342 pop.) (see Tour 4), is at the junction with US 51 (see Tour 4).

MULBERRY GROVE, 101 m. (559 alt., 596 pop.), ships molding sand from large deposits in nearby Hurricane Creek.

GREENVILLE, 110 m. (563 alt., 3,233 pop.), settled first in 1815 and today the seat of Bond County, is a hilly prosperous looking town with fine large houses. It has attracted an evaporated milk plant, a glove factory, and a concern that manufactures steel balls for crushing concrete. The DE MOULIN BROTHERS & COMPANY PLANT (open Mon.-Fri., afternoons preferred), 1000 S. 4th St., manufactures such unusual articles as costumes and paraphernalia for lodge ceremonies, banners, practically all of the circus uniforms used in the United States, and similar furnishings.

Greenville was the boyhood home of Robert G. Ingersoll (1833-99), Attorney-General of Illinois (1867-1869), famous orator and agnostic. In 1851 the Congregational Church called his father to its pulpit. Young Bob, then a devout studious youth of 18, accompanied his father and remained here studying law for two years.

GREENVILLE COLLEGE, 315 E. College Ave., on the site of an earlier school, was sponsored by the Free Methodist Church in 1892. In 1855

Stephen Morse of New Hampshire founded Almira College in Greenville, and dedicated the institution to the higher education of women. The building which housed all of Almira College is now the WILSON T. HOGUE HALL of the present school. Other buildings on the campus are the auditorium, the E. G. BURRITT GYMNASIUM, and CARRIE T. BURRITT HALL, a dormitory for women. Greenville, with an average enrollment of 300, offers a liberal arts course designed to develop that "breadth of culture and universality of interest combined with Christian character, which constitute in the highest sense a liberal education."

Right from Greenville on State 140 to attractive 106-acre GREENVILLE CITY PARK (*camping, picnicking*), 2 *m.*, constructed largely by WPA labor. The park, which includes 25 acres of woods and a lake (*swimming, boating, fishing*), is the result of 40 years of campaigning and fund-collecting by the clubwomen of Greenville. The women planned either an opera house in Greenville or a pleasant recreational spot in the vicinity; they chose the latter when WPA assistance was offered for such a project.

Settled in 1838, POCAHONTAS, 119.3 *m.* (515 alt., 976 pop.), was another of the numerous stagecoach stops on the Cumberland Road. Today it is a typical village, deriving part of its income from coal mines in the region.

The story of HIGHLAND, 129 *m.* (545 alt., 3,319 pop.), begins about 1804 when this region was settled by families from Kentucky and North Carolina. In this group came Joseph Duncan, his wife, and their baby, born during the hard journey northward. In 1817 Duncan was made Justice of the Peace, a very important office in those days, in which capacity he served for 40 years. The Duncan home became the hub of social life in the neighborhood, and was an enlivening influence in the otherwise drab, hard, homespun existence of these pioneers.

In the spring of 1831 Dr. Caspar Koepfli of Sursee, Switzerland, induced a small group of his countrymen to settle in the Midwest. Inspired by a recently published book in which a German traveler extolled the advantages of Missouri, Dr. Koepfli had long felt a keen desire to lead a pilgrimage to the new land. At that time Switzerland was threatened with over-settlement, and the doctor was shrewd enough to realize that certain qualities of the Swiss would make them excellent colonists.

After inspecting farmland near St. Louis, Dr. Koepfli's party of 15 adventurers moved on to Vandalia, then the capital of Illinois, to inquire about land titles in this State. Their return route led them through Looking Glass Prairie, which now cradles the town of Highland. Here they saw exactly the El Dorado they had been seeking, and here they eventually bought land and built homes. Pioneer life presented many obstacles to the Swiss group, but their letters home were so enthusiastic that before long the colony was increased.

Perhaps the most noted of these early Swiss was the poet, Heinrich Bosshard, who lived in Highland from 1851 until his death in 1877. Here Bosshard composed *Sempacher Lied,* part of which was incorporated in the Swiss national anthem. In LINDENTHAL PARK, east end of Lindenthal Avenue, is the BOSSHARD MONUMENT, a granite memorial to the poet.

Highland today is as trim as the cultivated prairies that surge up to the doorsteps of its outlying farms. Every city street is paved with concrete. The brick houses, with dormer windows, double chimneys, and blue or green shutters, have achieved an appealing mellowness. Green lawns and gay flower gardens bank the tree-shaded sidewalks.

As a Swiss community, Highland early acquired a reputation for its dairy products. In 1884 John Mayenard brought from Switzerland a new process for preserving milk and established a factory here, which developed until the enterprise had eight branches, with total assets of many millions. After a strike here in 1920, the original factory was closed and the headquarters of the company were moved to St. Louis.

Among the varied industrial establishments of Highland is the WICKS ORGAN COMPANY PLANT, 5th and Zschokke Sts. In 1914 this firm gained international attention in the musical world by developing a direct electric action which greatly simplified the operation and maintenance of its organs. The Wicks Company is one of the few organ makers in the world that manufactures the parts used in the construction of its instruments.

West of Highland, US 40 enters the major dairy region of the St. Louis area. Cows dot the hillsides black, white, and brown. Small modern farms, each with a gleaming white barn, appear along the highway.

In the vicinity of ST. JACOB, 134.8 *m.* (508 alt., 451 pop.), a dairy village, a fort was built during the Indian scares of 1812 to protect the pioneer families. Fort Chilton, as it was called, was never attacked and was abandoned soon after the Indians had been overcome. No trace of the early stockade remains, but numerous stories about it have survived. One relates that Abraham Howard, commander of the fort, became so enraged at the audacity of a troublesome Indian in the neighborhood that he set out alone and chased him 90 miles through the wilderness. Howard was gone for several days, and on his return proudly exhibited a scalp of straight black hair.

TROY, 141 *m.* (549 alt., 1,122 pop.), is an outgrowth of three villages—Columbia, Mechanicsburg, and Brookside. The first, Columbia, was a tiny community huddled around a tavern and a grist mill built by John G. Jarvis about 1814. Five years later land speculators bought the property and renamed it Troy for the New York town. Mechanicsburg was platted in 1836, and merged with Troy in 1857. The union proved a happy one. Nearby coal fields continued their productivity; in 1888 a railroad connected the town with East St.

Louis; in 1891 Brookside joined the fold, and in the following year Troy was incorporated as a city. Although dependent largely on local coal mines and a pump factory, Troy has the placid aspect of a farming community.

Troy is at the junction with City US 40 (*see Tour* 19A).

At 149 *m.* is the junction with US 66 (*see Tour* 17), which unites with US 40 for 9 miles.

The junction, at the base of the bluffs along the Mississippi, marks the eastern edge of the fertile AMERICAN BOTTOM, flat as a table top, extending along the river from Alton on the north to Chester on the south, a distance of almost 100 miles.

MITCHELL, 150.3 *m.*, is a little crossroads community on the northwestern border of the CAHOKIA MOUNDS (*see Tour* 19A). Several small mounds dot the plain on the outskirts of the village.

US 40 crosses the Missouri Line, 158 *m.*, on the CHAIN-OF-ROCKS BRIDGE (25c), spanning the Mississippi River to the northern limits of St. Louis, Missouri (*see Missouri Guide*).

T O U R   19A

TROY—COLLINSVILLE—CAHOKIA MOUNDS STATE PARK-- EAST ST. LOUIS—(ST. LOUIS, MO.); CITY US 40
Troy to Missouri Line, 21 *m.*

Four-lane concrete roadbed except for 5 miles west of Troy.
Pennsylvania R. R. roughly parallels the route.
Usual accommodations.

CITY US 40, an alternate of US 40 from Troy westward, bisects Cahokia Mounds State Park, one of the most important groups of prehistoric earthworks in America, and pierces the metropolitan area of East St. Louis.

TROY, 0 *m.*, (549 alt., 1,122 pop.) (*see Tour* 19).

COLLINSVILLE, 7.9 *m.* (473 alt., 9,235 pop.), was named for William Collins, one of five brothers from Litchfield, Connecticut, who established a settlement here in 1817. Pooling their interests, the Collins brothers, models of Yankee industry and jacks-of-all-trades, built a store, a blacksmith shop, a shoe shop, a wagon shop, a sawmill, a tannery, a distillery, and a small church, in which they took turns reading the services. The oldest brother, William, suffering a dearth of ideas for suitable sermons, wrote to the Rev. Lyman Beecher, his former paster in Litchfield, asking for suggestions. The Rev. Mr. Beecher quickly forwarded six temperance tracts, the substance of which William passed on to his congregation.

After one of these sermons on abstemiousness, so it is said, his wife asked, "Doesn't it look peculiar to be preaching against strong drink on Sunday and then be making and selling whiskey on Monday?" William wrestled with his conscience and the following day wrecked the distillery, which caused his brothers to move away from the village. When William died a decade later, his widow had a townsite platted and sold lots, stipulating in each deed that whiskey was not to be made or sold on them; the courts later nullified this restriction.

Collinsville was incorporated as a village in 1856 and welcomed its first train in 1869; the railroad made possible the exploitation of the region's thick coal seam; a furnace to smelt Missouri zinc ore was established, offering additional employment; three years later the village was incorporated as a city. Today it manufactures chemicals, canned foods, and women's apparel, in addition to being an important coal center. For several years Collinsville was the home of Tom Tippett, author of *Horse Shoe Bottoms* (1935), the first novel to deal with Illinois coal miners.

The BLUM MANUFACTURING PLANT (*open*), 232 Goethe St., one of the few cow bell factories in the United States, still makes the bells by hand, employing practically the same process used since its establishment in 1880.

The COLLINS' HOMESTEAD (*private*), 408 E. Church St., was built in 1821 by the Collins brothers in preparation for the arrival of their father, mother, and three sisters from Connecticut. The sprawling frame structure remains virtually as it came from their saws and hammers, with the exception of a portico at the front, which replaced the original two-story porch that ran the length of the house.

The MINERS' INSTITUTE, southwest corner of Main and Clinton Sts., providing the only theater with a stage in the city, was built as a labor center by five Collinsville locals of the United Mine Workers of America. In the spring of 1916 their committee was assured by the Springfield district officers that a loan would be granted if 10 per cent of the funds required could be raised locally and properly insured. To carry out the project, members voted to assess themselves one per cent of their earnings. In May 1917 work began on the building, which was completed at a cost of $140,000. By April 1, 1925 the entire indebtedness had been cleared by the five locals.

West of Collinsville, City US 40 slips down through the bluffs to the lowlands of the American Bottom, a narrow strip of the Mississippi Valley between Alton and Chester.

At 11.5 *m.* is (R) the FAIRMOUNT PARK JOCKEY CLUB (*racing meets in spring and autumn*).

The highway enters CAHOKIA MOUNDS STATE PARK, 12.7 *m.* The MUSEUM (*open 9-4 daily, 8-5 Sun.*), a low brick building (R), exhibits axes, pipes, pottery, arrowheads, skulls, and miscellaneous artifacts unearthed in nearby mounds. North of the parking lot looms the tremendous bulk of MONKS MOUND, the largest in the United States, named for the Trappists who built a monastery at its base in 1809; in 1813 the monks, decimated by fever, returned to France. A truncated pyramid with four terraces, Monks Mound is 104 feet wide and 1,000 feet long. Using primitive methods, more than 2,000 men would have to work two years to match it. A modern pathway buttressed by logs winds up to picnic grounds at the summit.

From the time of the early French settlers, the origin of the bulbous hills in this region has prompted speculation (*see Before the White Man*). Superstitious pioneers believed the area accursed and refused to tempt the wrath of forgotten gods by cultivating the land. Skeptics who boldly plowed the rich level fields were sometimes somewhat unnerved by upturning a cache of human bones. After five intensive surveys of the mounds, the first in 1921, Professor W. K. Moorehead of the University of Illinois concluded that the mounds were built between 1200 and 1500 A. D. by a people whose culture showed distinct Southern influences—a culture much more advanced than that of other early American Indians. He found quantities of flints, beads, shards, and other artifacts.

Professor Moorehead's explorations revealed that the tumuli were the hub of a village that extended 7 or 8 miles along Cahokia and Canteen Creeks. At one time more than 300 lesser rises spread out fan-like from Monks Mound, but the cultivation of farms and the super-imposition of contemporary communities have obliterated all but 85. The best of these are now in the 144-acre Cahokia Mounds State Park.

South of the museum are TEMPLE MOUND and RED MOUND, the latter named for the red earthenware it contained. Nearby is a mound made of dark pliable soil; the others in the Cahokia group are of clay and gumbo. Many fragments taken from ROUND TOP MOUND, south of the museum, suggest that it was a site for the manufacture of pottery. Opposite Round Top is another mound of similar shape in which were found flint tools used to decorate pottery. Farther south is a broad shallow pit, occasionally filled by rains and known as LAKE CAHOKIA. The mound builders probably dug much of the earth used in construction from this pit.

City US 40 skirts FAIRMONT CITY, 15 *m.* (420 alt., 1,827 pop.), an industrial suburb of East St. Louis. Fairmont City began life in 1910, fathered by a roundhouse of the Pennsylvania Railroad. It was first christened Willow Town; its present name was adopted in 1914 when it was incorporated as a village. During a prolonged strike in 1918 at the local zinc works Mexican workers were imported. Today this group numbers one-quarter of the population, being employed in the town's zinc, fertilizer, and chemical plants.

At 17.5 *m.* is the junction with US 67 (*see Tour 7*), which unites with City US 40 to the Missouri Line.

EAST ST. LOUIS, 19 *m.* (414 alt., 74,347 pop.) (*see East St. Louis*).

Points of Interest: National Stock Yards, Site of Bloody Island, Lake Park, and others.

East St. Louis is at the junction with US 67 (*see Tour 7*), State 3 (*see Tour 8*), and US 50 (*see Tour 21*).

City US 40 crosses the Missouri Line, 21 *m.,* on the Municipal Bridge (10c), spanning the Mississippi to St. Louis, Mo. (*see Missouri Guide*).

TOUR 20

(Vincennes, Ind.) —Lawrenceville—Flora—Sandoval— East St. Louis—(St. Louis, Mo.) ; US 50

Indiana Line to Missouri Line, 151 *m.*

Hard-surfaced roadbed throughout.
The Baltimore & Ohio R. R. parallels the entire route.
Usual accommodations throughout.

Following the old Trace Road, marked out by Indians and buffalo, US 50 runs through rolling broken prairie west of Lawrenceville, across the lowlands of the Embarras and Little Wabash Rivers, and descends into the American Bottom to reach the Mississippi at East St. Louis.

The Trace Road connected Bear Grass, now Louisville, Kentucky, with Cahokia on the Mississippi, a few miles below East St. Louis. From 1805 to 1824 post riders on horseback carried the mail over the road. In 1824 a four-horse stage and mail route was established; in 1837, under an ambitious State improvement program, the road was graded. Bridges and culverts were hewn from white oak felled along the road, and between Vincennes and Lawrenceville miles of trestle-work were constructed. But too many expensive improvement schemes soon plunged the young State into bankruptcy, and the Trace Road was turned over to a private company, which completed the work, planking the treacherous swamp sections. Toll gates were set up and all travelers paid tribute to the company. Eventually the plank road decayed and the State first graveled the highway and then, with the advent of the automobile, paved it with concrete and eliminated many dangerous curves.

US 50 crosses the Indiana Line, 0 *m.*, on the LINCOLN MEMO-RIAL BRIDGE, spanning the Wabash River from Vincennes, Indiana (*see Indiana Guide*). The bridge, erected jointly by Illinois and Indiana in 1931, marks the place where the Lincoln family crossed to Illinois in 1830. It commands an excellent view of the Wabash and of the George Rogers Clark Memorial on the Indiana bank.

At 0.5 *m.*, at the Illinois end of the bridge approach, is the junction with the Lincoln National Memorial Highway (*see Tour* 21).

LAWRENCEVILLE, 8.8 *m.* (472 alt., 6,303 pop.), lies on the west bank of the Embarras River, so named by French explorers because of the difficulty of crossing the stream at flood time, when the river, joined with the Wabash, spread over lowlands to form a lake 7 or 8 miles wide. Lawrenceville, the seat of Lawrence County since 1821 when both were organized, was named for Capt. James Lawrence, commander of the *Chesapeake* in the War of 1812, remembered for his dying exclamation: "Don't give up the ship."

Lawrenceville is in the heart of the Lawrence County oil fields, and oil refining is its principal industry. The first paraffin-free oil was produced here in 1924. Pipe lines convey oil to local refineries from fields in Illinois, Kentucky, and Oklahoma. In 1906 the first oil well in Lawrence County was brought in. Gushers were frequent, and the county enjoyed a boom. Lawrence quickly became first among oil-producing counties of Illinois; production in the field enabled Illinois to rank third among the States in the output of crude oil in 1907 and for many years thereafter, but has now declined to a negligible amount.

The French were the first settlers in the Wabash River region, many entering Illinois from Vincennes, an old French settlement and the capital of Indiana Territory. Captain Toussaint Dubois, veteran of the American Revolution, settled about 1780 in this vicinity, where he built a house and planted the first orchard in the region. His holdings included 1,000 acres within the present city of Lawrenceville. Jessie K. Dubois, the captain's youngest son, was a friend of Abraham Lincoln, with whom he served in the legislature. He accompanied the President-elect to Washington for his first inauguration, and four years later was one of those who brought Lincoln's body home to Springfield and served as a pall bearer at his funeral.

A large granite boulder, in the yard of the Elks Club, 12th and Walnut Sts., marks the site of the first circuit court held in the county on June 4, 1821.

The LAWRENCE COUNTY COURTHOUSE, of red brick and stone trim, was built in 1889. A bronze tablet on the wall of the north entrance honors 21 Revolutionary War soldiers buried in the county. Three German field guns, captured during the World War, stand on the lawn.

The first woman executed in Illinois was tried, convicted, and hanged at Lawrenceville in 1845. Convicted of poisoning her husband so that she might marry another, Elizabeth Reed was hanged in sight of a large crowd.

Twin millstones, on the high school lawn, 8th and Walnut Sts., relics from the old Brown Mill on the Embarras River several miles downstream from Lawrenceville, show plainly the wear of many years.

LINCO TANK FARM (L), 12.3 m., contains 43 oil storage tanks. A deep moat to prevent the spread of fire surrounds each of the 35,000-barrel tanks; steel pumps mark many oil wells (R). Local pipe lines connect with a nation-wide trunk system of pipe lines at Martinsville, some 40 miles to the north.

BRIDGEPORT, 13.1 m. (449 alt., 2,315 pop.), was the center of the early oil boom; the first producing sand was named "Bridgeport." A large oil company maintains a pumping station and large supply yards here. Otherwise, Bridgeport is a typical prairie town—a trading center, the home of a few retired farmers, a well-ordered little community of schools, churches, and modest homes.

OLNEY, 31.5 m. (484 alt., 6,140 pop.), seat of Richland County, was named for John Olney, lawyer and lieutenant in the Civil War, the lifelong friend of Judge Aaron Shaw, who successfully campaigned to have the site chosen as county seat and named for Olney. A shipping and trading center, Olney has a few minor industrial interests; a shoe factory employs 700 persons, and in 1936 a large oil company leased rights on 250,000 acres in Richland, Clay, and Wayne Counties, and established an office in Olney.

Olney is a city of fine old mansions, surrounded by lawns and large trees. During the early summer season the houses are covered with crimson ramblers. The Olney *Times* claims the distinction of having been the first newspaper to support Lincoln for the Presidency. The issue of November 1, 1858, bore a streamer reading: "For President in 1860, Abraham Lincoln of Illinois." William Beck, the owner, lived to see the Illinoisan elected, but died before the inauguration.

The RICHLAND COUNTY COURTHOUSE, a three-story, white stone building of Colonial design, with four fluted columns across the front, is surmounted with a clock steeple.

LARCHMOND, on the east side of Morgan St., south of Baird St., is a white, brick house of Colonial design, the former residence of Dr. Robert Ridgway, naturalist and one-time curator of the U.S. National Museum in Washington. The attractive grounds are open to the public, and contain many shrubs planted by Dr. Ridgway, an outstanding ornithologist and founder of the Ornithologists Union, who died in 1929 and was buried in Bird Haven (*see below*).

For many years Olney has been known as "the home of white squirrels." In 1902 some naturalist, possibly Dr. Ridgway, brought a pair of albino squirrels to Olney and liberated them; results were startling, even to a naturalist. Thousands of the little animals now scamper about the parks and courthouse square, and frisk over lawns, trees, and rooftops.

Right from the east side of the courthouse on Walnut Street to a junction with a graveled road, 1 *m.;* R. to BIRD HAVEN (*apply to caretaker*), 2 *m.* Bird Haven was purchased by Dr. Ridgway in 1906 as an arboretum. Within it grow 73 varieties of trees, of which 70 are native to the area. A graveled walk leads past the simple granite boulder that marks the GRAVE OF DR. RIDGWAY. Control of the arboretum is vested in the University of Chicago.

CLAY CITY, 47 *m.* (429 alt., 707 pop.), a shipping point and trading center for a prosperous agricultural region, came into existence with the building of the Ohio & Mississippi Railroad, now part of the Baltimore & Ohio.

Clay City includes within its corporate limits the SITE OF MAYSVILLE, first seat of Clay County. The Shawneetown-Vandalia Road crossed the Trace Road here. Two old mansions, with winding drives leading to their massive porticoes, and a number of shapeless and decrepit dwellings more than a century old, are all that remain of the Maysville of the early 1830's.

A few miles southeast of Clay City the first oil well in Clay County was brought in on February 26, 1937—the third new field opened in Illinois since May 1936. In the mild boom that followed, 10 leading oil companies and many independent operators obtained leases to more than 2,000,000 acres in southern Illinois.

West of Clay City are extensive fruit orchards. During the picking season numerous fruit stands appear along US 50, selling apples, pears, and peaches from nearby orchards.

A STATE PICNIC GROUND (*tables and ovens*), 52 *m.,* is one of many wayside parks being developed along major Illinois highways.

At 52 *m.* is a junction (L) with US 45 (*see Tour 3*), which unites with US 50 for 4 miles (*see Tour 3*).

SALEM, 80 *m.* (544 alt., 4,420 pop.), seat of Marion County, is a center of the latest (1939) Illinois oil boom. Along US 50 in the western part of town are scenes of feverish activity as galvanized iron buildings are thrown up in wild confusion; oil is the sole topic of conversation.

Along the thoroughfares in the older parts of town, architecture varies in style from the simple Colonial in brick, through ornate Victorian, to modern "five-room efficiency." Laid out in 1813, on the

St. Louis-Vincennes stagecoach route, Salem was not incorporated until 1837. Salem was the birthplace and boyhood home of William Jennings Bryan (1860-1925).

The BRYAN MUSEUM (*open* 8-5 *daily*, 1-5 *Sun. and holidays*), 408 S. Broadway, was originally his residence. The museum contains many personal effects of the Commoner, including letters to his mother and the table on which he stood as a lad, delivering declamations to his playmates.

The JAMES S. MARTIN HOUSE (*private*), 709 Main St., built by the Civil War general who later became a U. S. Senator, is an excellent example of the architecture of the Gilded Age. Hexagonal columns in clusters of three support the two-story porch, which extends the length of the house; the second-story railing is so ingeniously jointed that it appears to have been woven in wood. The rooms on the upper floor, finished in black walnut, are on different floor levels. In the parlor on the first floor are a massive red glass chandelier and a large porcelain tiled fireplace, before which the general used to sit and burn brazilwood.

ODIN, 86.3 *m.* (527 alt., 1,204 pop.), a peaceful mining and farming center, was known in the 1860's as "the hell-hole of the Illinois Central" because of a form of piracy practiced by young hoodlums of the community. Concealing themselves along the railroad embankment until the train stopped, they would scramble on board and scuttle off with the passengers' luggage.

SANDOVAL, 90.2 *m.* (509 alt., 1,264 pop.) (*see Tour* 4), is at a junction with US 51 (*see Tour* 4).

West of Sandoval the highway traverses prairie lands underlain by seams of coal and small oil pools.

The CARLYLE STATE FISH HATCHERY (*open* 8-5), 102.8 *m.*, distributes fingerlings throughout the State every year; graveled drives permit approach to the three large ponds, in which bass, bluegill, and catfish are hatched.

An old SUSPENSION BRIDGE (R), 102.8 *m.*, built in 1860, was the principal means of crossing the Kaskaskia River on the St. Louis-Vincennes Trail. The 35-foot towers support a span 280 feet long. The cables have rusted away and the bricks in the towers are crumbling, but small boys and romanticists still use the bridge with delight, even though the structure sways perilously.

CARLYLE, 103.7 *m.* (461 alt., 2,078 pop.), seat of Clinton County, is the SITE OF JOHN HILL'S FORT, which in 1812 stood on an elevation six blocks south of the present courthouse. The Indians were hostile here, and among the settlers slain was a man named Young, whose body was buried about 50 rods south of the fort. The mother of the slain man declared that she had sewed $5,000 in his clothing, and as late as 1833 unsuccessful excavations were made to find the body.

In 1836, when Indian forays had ceased, a notice posted throughout the area proclaimed: "Whereas, the town of Carlyle has been troubled with divers nuisances such as hogs, dogs, etc., notice is hereby given that on Tuesday, the 10th of January next, there will be a meeting of the town of Carlyle at the schoolhouse for the purpose of incorporating the said town; all persons interested will please to attend."

The TRUESDALE HOTEL, 8th and Fairfax Sts., built in 1858, is a typical example of an old-fashioned Midwest hotel, with its cubbyhole lobby and tin porch extending over the sidewalk. The interior remains practically as it was in Civil War days, and the establishment is conducted by descendants of the first proprietor.

BREESE, 112.3 m. (458 alt., 1,957 pop.), a mining and agricultural community, was named in honor of Judge Sidney Breese (1800-1876), eminent Illinois jurist and one-time resident of the city. Although Breese has no grouse, nor do its inhabitants ride to hounds, King Edward VII, then Prince of Wales, spent two days hunting near the village in 1860. While lost in the Santa Fe Bottoms south of Breese, the prince somewhat testily ordered a settler to lead him back to the village, so it is said. The man refused, and when the prince offered him money, declared vehemently that he was "not for hire."

TRENTON, 121 m. (498 alt., 1,271 pop.), incorporated in 1865, boomed with the development of the Illinois coal fields in 1876. Since 1915 it has declined steadily, and today is a farming center bordering fertile Looking Glass Prairie, which Charles Dickens described in his *American Notes* as a "typical American prairie."

LEBANON, 128 m. (457 alt., 1,828 pop.), platted in the first quarter of the nineteenth century, basks in the leisurely atmosphere of MCKENDREE COLLEGE, one block north of the highway on Alton St. Organized by pioneers in 1828 and named for William McKendree, bishop of the Methodist Church, the school is the oldest Methodist college in the Middle West, one of the three oldest colleges in Illinois. Originally a theological seminary, McKendree is today an accredited liberal arts college with an average enrollment of 250. The mellow brick buildings, dominated by the stately chapel spire, resemble those in a Currier and Ives lithograph. Forty-six varieties of trees, many of them a part of the original forest, add to the beauty of the 20-acre campus.

The MERMAID INN (*private*), 112 East St. Louis St., built in 1830 on the old St. Louis-Vincennes route by a retired sea captain, had as guests Abraham Lincoln and Charles Dickens. It is related, perhaps apocryphally, that one morning Lincoln had not finished his breakfast when the stagecoach was ready to depart. He remarked that if the coach left without him, it would soon come racing back. The coach left and Lincoln leisurely finished his breakfast. Soon the proprietor and his helpers were observed scurrying about in great excitement. The silver spoons had disappeared from the inn and it was reasoned that someone on the stage had stolen them. Officers were hastily summoned and pursued the coach on horseback. When they had forced the driver to return to the hotel, Lincoln calmly drew the silver from beneath the table, and "leisurely took his seat in the stage and the journey was resumed." In his *American Notes* Dickens declared that the Mermaid Inn "compared favorably with any village ale house of a homely kind in England."

US 50 skirts the central part of Lebanon, then ascends a knoll and passes a flour mill established in 1889, the principal industrial plant in the town.

Immediately west (R) of a STATE PICNIC GROUND (*benches, tables, outdoor fireplaces*), 130.8 *m.*, is the SITE OF ROCK SPRING SEMINARY, founded in 1827 by John Mason Peck, religious author and educator. The seminary was removed in 1831 to Alton (*see Alton*), where it later became Shurtleff College.

At 131.8 *m.* is a junction with a concrete road.

Left on this road is SCOTT FIELD (*open 9-6*), 3.4 *m.*, a United States Army aviation base established in 1917 to train World War fliers; it was named in memory of Corporal Scott, killed at the first aviation school at College Point, Md. Today (1939), because of its central location, Scott Field is being altered to accommodate squadrons of pursuit and bombing planes.

US 50 skirts the edge of O'FALLON, 134 *m.* (550 alt., 2,373 pop.), named for the town site owner, developed in 1854 along what is now the Baltimore & Ohio Railroad. Farming, mining, and manufacturing have sustained the town at various periods. It is now essentially a residential community, many of its workers finding employment in the nearby coal mines.

At 138 *m.* is a junction with State 159.

Left on State 159 is BELLEVILLE, 5.5 *m.* (529 alt., 28,425 pop.), whose fine houses and shady streets justify its name (Fr., beautiful city). Belleville is perched on top of the steep bluffs that form the eastern rim of the American Bottom. Although there were settlers in the Belleville region at the beginning of the nineteenth century, it was not until 1814 that the settlement was chosen as the seat of St. Clair County, succeeding Cahokia. A town was laid out, and immigration increased in 1818 when Territorial Governor Ninian Edwards, a large landowner, advertised the settlement in newspapers throughout the country and offered inducements to settlers. At that time Belleville was a place for hardy people; fighting was the principal pastime; one Zachariah Stephenson gained local fame for his willingness to fight anyone, anywhere, any time. In one of the bouts Zachariah's opponent bit off part of his ear, and Zachariah retaliated by biting off his adversary's nose. In 1819 the town was incorporated. Nine years later the discovery of coal underlying the area attracted a host of German immigrants.

Belleville is still known as a "Dutch town," and German is the only language spoken by many of the older inhabitants. Singing societies, such as the locally renowned *Liederkrantz*, founded in 1873, and such neighborhood customs as the *kaffe klatsch,* further indicate dominant Teutonic influence. The old brick houses on the side streets radiating from the public square are built against the property line in accordance with Old World custom.

No town in Illinois manifests such a bewildering combination of old and new in architecture; 1930 bungalows rub elbows with dwellings built in 1830. Nowhere else in Illinois can be found block after block of century-old, one-story brick cottages. The universality of brick construction, even for the humblest dwellings, is due to the fact that Belleville, a hundred years ago, abounded in brick manufacturing plants, making home-kilned brick the cheapest construction material available.

Of massive proportions, and of sturdy and enduring construction, the two-story brick GOVERNOR JOHN REYNOLDS MANSION, 110 N. Illinois St., has defied time and looks much the same as it did at the time of its construction in 1820; it is now used as a funeral home. The twin spires of the Gothic CATHEDRAL OF ST. PETER (Roman Catholic) tower above the corner at 3rd and Harrison Sts.

At 5 o'clock on the afternoon of March 5, 1938, a tornado, which caused wide-spread damage throughout the East St. Louis area, struck Belleville, killing eight persons and injuring many others. In the West Main Street residential district some 50 houses were leveled. A grade school, deserted at that hour, was demolished, but Belleville's large high school, 200 yards distant, was untouched.

The highway rounds a sharp curve, 141 *m.,* and descends gradually to the vast plain of the Mississippi known as the American Bottom.

FRENCH VILLAGE, 143 *m.,* consists of a few old houses scattered along the base of the bluffs; it was settled by French families from Cahokia in 1800.

EAST ST. LOUIS, 149 *m.* (414 alt., 74,347 pop.) (*see East St. Louis*).

Points of Interest: National Stockyards, Site of Bloody Island, Lake Park, and others.

East St. Louis is at the junction with US 67 (*see Tour 7*), State 3 (*see Tour 8*), and City US 40 (*see Tour 19A*).

US 50 crosses the Missouri Line, 151 *m.,* on the Municipal Bridge (10c), spanning the Mississippi to St. Louis, Missouri (*see Missouri Guide*).

TOUR 21

THE LINCOLN NATIONAL MEMORIAL HIGHWAY

(VINCENNES, IND.) —MARSHALL—CHARLESTON—DECATUR—
SPRINGFIELD—NEW SALEM STATE PARK—PETERSBURG

Indiana Line to Petersburg, 224 *m.*

Hard-surfaced except for graveled stretch between Marshall and Mattoon.

Between the junction with State 33 and Marshall the highway is paralleled by the Cleveland, Cincinnati, Chicago & St. Louis Ry.; between Mattoon and Decatur by the Illinois Central R. R.; between Decatur and Springfield by the Wabash Ry.

Accommodations limited except in larger cities.

NOTE: The Lincoln National Memorial Highway, not to be confused with the transcontinental Lincoln Highway, is designated by a special marker. Eventually it will be paved throughout and will probably be given a single highway number. At present (1939) it follows sections of US 36 and State highways 181, 33, 1, 125, and 97.

THE LINCOLN NATIONAL MEMORIAL HIGHWAY was routed by a commission appointed to determine the much disputed path of the Lincoln family in moving from Indiana to Illinois in 1830. From the Indiana Line to Decatur it closely follows the route of their migration. From Decatur it extends west to Springfield and thence northwest to New Salem State Park and Petersburg, both rich in Lincoln associations. Eventually the route will be continued from Petersburg to Beardstown, on the Illinois River, along a road surveyed and frequently traveled by Lincoln. The course of the Memorial Highway is winding; its function solely that of tracing a historic route.

The Lincoln National Memorial Highway crosses the Indiana Line, 0 *m.*, on the LINCOLN MEMORIAL BRIDGE, a low graceful span erected in 1931, over the Wabash River from Vincennes, Indiana. (*see Indiana Guide*). At the bridge approach on the Illinois side, in a small roadside park (*camp sites, picnic facilities*), is the LINCOLN TRAIL MONUMENT. The work of Nellie Walker, Chicago sculptor, the monument depicts the Lincoln family entering Illinois.

At 0.5 *m.* is the junction (R) with State 181, along which the Memorial Highway turns abruptly northward, following the route of the Lincoln family in its trek up the Wabash to Palestine. For fifty years it had been the main traveled route between Vincennes and Canada.

The Lincoln family, a closely-knit family group of thirteen, crossed the Indiana line into the new country of Illinois in March of 1830. Spring was on its way, but the long dead prairie grasses were still half frozen in the loam. The stout lumbering wagons were piled high with household goods, iron pots and feather beds, sturdy chests, rough-hewn tables and stools, a plow for the new fields and axes for the new homes. It is probable that Sarah Lincoln, a calm and imperturbable woman, with deep set eyes, rode in one wagon; her two daughters, their husbands and children rode in the others. Thomas Lincoln, past fifty, probably led the caravan on horseback. Abraham Lincoln, just 21 but a grown man in labor and experience, guided one of the ox teams over the dismal plain.

Years later when someone asked Lincoln about his early life, he replied briefly that "it was the short and simple annals of the poor." He was seven years old when Thomas Lincoln moved the family from Hardin County, Kentucky to Spencer County, Indiana. The family came in the late fall, a difficult time to enter a new country, and had only a short season in which to cut logs for shelter before winter closed in on them. The winter was spent in a "half-faced camp," a rude three-sided shelter of logs open to the south, heated with an open fireplace. They lived on game, which was plentiful, drank melted snow, and slept on leaves and skins of wild animals. In the spring they built a cabin, cleared a plot of land, and planted a crop. During the summer, relatives from Kentucky joined them and life was less lonely. But in the second year "the milk-sick," a dread disease of the pioneers, struck the small community and in a few days Nancy Lincoln died. Her aunt and uncle died soon thereafter, and Dennis Hanks, a cousin, moved in with the Lincolns.

For a year the household struggled forlornly, and then Thomas Lincoln left for Kentucky and returned after a few weeks with a new wife, Sarah Johnston Lincoln, her three children, and a load of household goods. Sarah Lincoln, energetic, kindly, with a passion for cleanliness, swept out the corn husk beds, ordered a wooden floor for the cabin, and washed up her husband's children. Soon she won their confidence and affection.

Abraham Lincoln at an early age was strong and tall. He performed with ease the many tasks of a settler's life. He chopped wood, tended crops, fed the animals, threshed the grain, carried water, and even assisted his father in occasional jobs of carpentry and cabinet-making. School was a luxury; he attended only "by littles" — not more than a year throughout his life. But he learned to read, and before he left Indiana, he had read every book within reach. He read at meal times, before the fire at night, on fence rails during the noontime rest, on his way to the mill. Sarah Lincoln kept the other children from disturbing him, and smoothed over the impatient disapproval of his father. She inquired earnestly about the things he read, and he told her about them, explaining carefully and simply when she did not understand. Knowing always that a book was his for only a limited period, he committed long passages to memory or made notes on whatever paper was available. He made calculations on the hearth shovel, on the walls around the fireplace, on the hearth stone. He acquired extraordinary powers of concentration, and a habit of contemplation that distinguished him throughout his life.

Lonely as he was in his groping for knowledge, he was also deeply social. He frankly disliked isolated labor and found most satisfying work performed with other people. He enjoyed going to the mill, the conversations around the stove in the store, house-raisings, the life along the river. He talked with strangers and discussed politics, religion, law, and the slavery question with the men about Gentryville. He attended spelling-bees in the school house until — so the legend goes — he was ruled out because his side always won. He learned the bluff roistering ballads of the frontier and roared them tunelessly around the log-burning with his cousin, the "irrepressible" Dennis Hanks. His insatiable curiosity was ever concerned with people, events, problems, in the scene about him, and in the past. He knew the lore of his day and was a popular story teller, droll, witty, and Rabelaisian. At nineteen he made a trip to New Orleans in a flat boat.

On February 12, 1830, he was twenty-one years old and stood six feet four inches in his raw-hide moccasins. His legs were so long that his buckskin breeches scarcely covered half of them. He was sincerely loved and admired by most of the inhabitants of Spencer County, but he was restive. His sister, Sarah, had died in childbirth. His foster sisters were married, one of them to Dennis Hanks. Life in Spencer County was becoming constricted. The community was static; the land poor. In that year the "milk-sick" returned. The Lincolns, remembering Nancy Lincoln, and watching their cattle drop in their sheds, sold their farm and set out for the limitless plains and virgin soil of central Illinois.

RUSSELVILLE, 9.6 *m.*, a tiny river town with a ferry that has been in operation for more than a century, was the first community encountered by the Lincoln family in Illinois. Residents maintain that it was here, rather than at Vincennes, that the party crossed the Wabash.

Settlements in eastern and central Illinois in 1830 were few and scattered. The party often traveled for hours without seeing a person, a house, or an animal. The half-thawed ground softened to the great iron-bound wheels of the wagons, and the oxen strained at the yoke, the long whips of the drivers lashing over their backs. Young Lincoln had a small stock of peddler's goods—needles, thread, knives, and buttons, which he had bought from a storekeeper in Gentryville. These he sold to occasional settlers along the trail, observing the ways of the new people, eager with questions. There were no bridges over the streams, and often the men and beasts painfully broke a layer of ice formed on chilly nights. The March winds, unobstructed by hills, swept across the open prairies, harsh and biting. Fifteen miles was a "good piece" to make in a day.

PALESTINE, 25.5 m. (450 alt., 1,670 pop.), was a town of some importance in 1830, although it consisted merely of five stores, two taverns, a steam saw and grist mill, and thirty families. Here was one of the six land offices in the State, to which settlers came from as far as Chicago to register their claims. Here at the time William H. Byford, later a distinguished surgeon and professor of gynecology at Rush Medical College, was learning the tailor's trade to support his widowed mother with whom he had that year migrated from Indiana.

The Lincoln family, it appears, was impressed with the town. One of the children always remembered it because it had a "holy name"— the first town she'd ever heard of with a holy name. A traveling juggler passed through on the same day as the Lincolns, and Abraham, his coonskin cap pushed back from his seamed face, watched with amusement and some wonder the performance of sleight-of-hand.

The Memorial Highway proceeds west from Palestine on State 33 to a junction with State 1, 29.8 m., over which it continues (R) to MARSHALL, 57 m. (606 alt., 2,368 pop.) (see Tour 19). Marshall is at the junction with State 1 (see Tour 1), and US 40 (see Tour 19).

Northwest from Marshall the Memorial Highway follows a graveled road (indicated by trail marker) through back-country where goats and pigs are often the only signs of habitation. The cross-roads settlements of DOLSON, 65 m., and WESTFIELD, 76 m., are the only communities encountered.

CHARLESTON, 85 m. (686 alt., 8,012 pop.), the seat of Coles County, was probably deep in mud the day the Lincolns passed through with nothing to distinguish them from other westward moving settlers. Twenty-eight years later Abraham Lincoln was to ride into Charleston again, a candidate for the United States Senate and a political adversary for whom Stephen A. Douglas had a shrewd respect. In 1858, in the full still heat of an early fall day, Lincoln drove into Charleston in a carriage. The roads were thickly laid with dust; the day was fair; the town bulged with visitors. Farmers and townspeople came from miles around in wagons, carriages, on horseback, on mules, on foot. There was a special train of seven cars from Indiana. An 80-foot banner overhanging the main street pictured the young pioneer driving a team of oxen on his first entry into Charleston. A parade was held to honor the occasion. In a wagon decorated with blue and white cloth, and festooned with leaves and flowers, clustered 31 girls wearing blue velvet caps, representing the states of the Union. Back of them a young woman rode a spirited horse and bore a banner, "Kansas—I will be free." The correspondent of the New York Post was shocked; "an unfortunate decoration for a young lady," he wired his editor.

The Site of the Fourth Lincoln-Douglas Debate (September 8, 1858) is at the western edge of town near the eastern end of the county fairgrounds on State 16. A crowd of 12,000 packed closely around the stands heard Lincoln express himself clearly on the question of Negro equality, answer the vexing charges of Douglas that he advocated intermarriage, his shrill voice picking carefully over a sentence until it came to the word or phrase he wished to emphasize. As in other debates Douglas referred to Lincoln's position in the Mexican War, charging that he had voted against supplies for the army in Mexico. Lincoln with sudden drama whirled to the back of the platform and seizing Orlando B. Ficklin, a former fellow-representative and a staunch Douglas man, dragged him to the front of the platform before the aroused mass of listeners, and forced a denial. Impatient with personal bickerings, Lincoln sought always to lay the issues before the people, plainly and simply, as if he were talking in a country store or explaining an idea to Sarah Lincoln. "I don't keer fur them great orators," Sandburg reports a farmer to have said. "I want to hear just a plain common feller like the rest on us, that I kin foller an' know where he's drivin'. Abe Linkern fills the bill."

Near the western end of the county fairgrounds is the GRAVE OF DENNIS HANKS, marked by a tombstone which bears his proud but doubtful claim that he taught Abraham Lincoln to read and write. Ten years older than Lincoln, he was his daily companion and ever-faithful friend through all the years in Indiana. Gay, boisterous, kindly, a skillful hunter, a picturesque talker, he shared to some extent his cousin's restless curiosity. Years later Herndon, Lincoln's law partner and biographer, asked him, "How did Lincoln and yourself learn so much in Indiana under such disadvantages?" Dennis replied, "We learned by sight, scent, and hearing. We heard all that was said and talked over and over the questions heard, wore them slick, greasy, and threadbare."

In Morton Park, Lincoln Ave. and 2nd St., is the SALLY LINCOLN CHAPTER HOUSE of the Daughters of the American Revolution, named in honor of Lincoln's stepmother, Sarah Lincoln. The two-story log cabin, erected in 1832, five miles south of town, was moved here in 1926 and furnished with pioneer pieces. As the home of Joel T. Rennels and his father, it was sometimes visited by Lincoln as he traveled between his parents' home and Charleston in the years he rode the circuit. The COLES COUNTY COURTHOUSE, in the public square, replaced the building in which Lincoln practiced law. Its files contain valuable documents on the title to the Lincoln Homestead at the State Park south of the city.

EASTERN ILLINOIS STATE TEACHERS COLLEGE, Lincoln Ave. between 4th and 7th Sts., housed in seven buildings of unfinished Bedford stone, Norman in design, has an average enrollment of 800 students. The college was authorized by the legislature in 1895 and opened in 1899. For eight years it granted only a teaching certificate, but now gives a four-year course leading to a B. Ed. degree, and a two-year course that qualifies teachers for elementary school work. A high school and grade school conducted in conjunction with the college serve as laboratories for student teachers.

South (L) from Charleston the Memorial Highway proceeds over graveled roads (*marked*) past the sites of three of the four Thomas Lincoln homes in Illinois.

In the cross-roads community of CAMPBELL, 92.5 *m.*, is the SARAH LINCOLN HOUSE, preserved by the State as a Lincoln family memorial. Here Sarah Lincoln lived from the death of her husband in 1851 until her own death in 1869. It was here that Lincoln visited her just before his first inauguration. Simple-hearted and intelligent, Sarah Lincoln often understood her husband's son better than did his father. She recognized his needs to be more complex than those of her own children. Close to the end of her life she said of him: "His mind and mine — what little I had — seemed to run together. He was here after he was elected president. He was a dutiful son to me always. I think he loved me truly. I had a son, John, who was raised with Abe. Both were good boys; but I may say, both now being dead, that Abe was the best boy I ever saw or ever expect to see."

The LINCOLN LOG CABIN STATE PARK, 94.5 *m.*, comprising 86 acres of the last Lincoln farm, is a memorial to Thomas Lincoln rather than to his son. The old pioneer never realized the hopes that impelled him toward Illinois. He was past fifty when he came—a thick-set man with a round face, dark eyes, and coarse black hair. Easy in his fellowship with other men, he failed to understand his son, particularly in his early years. Nevertheless, Lincoln often visited him at his several homes.

In 1841 Abraham Lincoln purchased from his father the 120-acre farm on which his parents were living. After Thomas Lincoln's death ten years later, Lincoln sold 80 acres to his stepbrother, John D. Johnston, from whom his father had bought the land. A later owner cultivated the 40 acres that Lincoln had retained, and in 1888 obtained title to them by virtue of his undisputed occupation of the property for 20 years.

The reconstructed THOMAS LINCOLN CABIN stands in the park. The original cabin was shown at the Columbian Exposition in Chicago in 1893, and then mysteriously disappeared. The reconstructed cabin, built by the State, stands on the old stone foundation. Like the original, it has two sections; the west room of the original was built by Thomas Lincoln in 1837 when he acquired the farm; the east half was a cabin purchased by him, moved to the site, and joined to the first section with clapboards. The root cellar to the east has been rebuilt on the brick floor of the original, and a grindstone and other crude implements have been replaced. Beside the kitchen door is a duplicate of the ox yoke that Thomas Lincoln always hung there.

The 32-foot well dug by Thomas Lincoln was restored in 1936; all of the original stonework was retained with the exception of the top four feet.

The Memorial Highway continues on the graveled road northwest from the State Park. In SHILOH CEMETERY (R), 97.5 *m.*, a small plot along the road, are the GRAVES OF THOMAS AND SARAH LINCOLN. The original sandstone shaft has been all but chipped away by souvenir hunters; a remnant still stands a few yards from the graves, which are marked by a new monument erected in 1924. Here, on January 31, 1861, shortly before he assumed the Presidency, Lincoln and his step-mother visited his father's grave.

The SITE OF THE THIRD LINCOLN FAMILY HOME IN ILLINOIS (R), 101 *m.*, is marked by a plaque. Here from 1834 to 1837 Sarah and Thomas Lincoln cultivated a small farm.

The SITE OF THE SECOND LINCOLN FAMILY HOME IN ILLINOIS (R), 104 *m.*, is identified by a memorial marker. Here Sarah and Thomas Lincoln moved in 1831 from the vicinity of Decatur in Macon County. Young Lincoln, feeling that he had fulfilled his responsibility to his father, left home and henceforth was on his own.

At 107 *m.* is a junction with State 121, over which the Memorial Highway proceeds northward (R) to MATTOON, 110 *m.* (725 alt., 14,631 pop.) (*see Tour 3*), at a junction with US 45 (*see Tour 3*). From Mattoon the Memorial Highway continues northwest on State 121 to a junction, 150 *m.*, with US 36 (*see Tour 18*), which the Memorial Highway follows for 44 miles.

DECATUR, 154 *m.* (683 alt., 57,510 pop.) (*see Decatur*).

Points of Interest: Millikin University, Administration Building of A. B. Staley Manufacturing Company, Lake Decatur, M. L. Harry Memorial Fountain, and others.

Decatur is at a junction with US 51 (*see Tour 4*).

Decatur marked the end of the Lincolns' long journey from Indiana. They inquired here for the whereabouts of John Hanks, their kinsman, who had already selected for them a site high on the bluffs above the Sangamon River a short distance downstream. Seasoned logs lay ready for their use and they built a cabin, cleared ten acres of land, sowed it with corn, and split rails to fence it. Fall was mild and beautiful, but in December a two-day blizzard covered the ground with three feet of snow. On the open prairies it piled up in 15-foot drifts; in the fields it all but topped the corn shocks. Game was scarce, communication impossible. Immured in their lonely cabin, with no reserves of food but the corn from their first small crop, the Lincolns suffered acutely. In the spring the snow melted away in a flood, and the slowly receding waters stagnated in pools far beyond the river banks. When the floods receded, Sarah and Thomas Lincoln moved to Coles County, while Abraham struck out for himself.

West of Decatur the Memorial Highway (US 36) passes a marker (R), 163 *m.*, calling attention to the SITE OF THE FIRST LINCOLN FAMILY HOME IN ILLINOIS, 3 miles to the south and at present inaccessible. The State plans to create a park on the site, erect a reproduction of the cabin, and eventually build a road to it from the Memorial Highway.

CAMP BUTLER NATIONAL CEMETERY, 187.3 *m.*, opened in 1862, contains the bodies of many Union and Confederate soldiers. Still used, the cemetery accepts for burial the body of any honorably discharged U. S. soldier. During the Civil War the site, with adjacent lands, comprised a huge training camp and military prison. Here approximately one-third of the Illinois regiments that served in the Civil War were mustered into the Federal service and given preliminary training.

SPRINGFIELD, 194 *m.* (598 alt., 71,864 pop.) (*see Springfield*).

Points of Interest: State Capitol, Lincoln's Tomb, Lincoln's Home, Centennial Building, Supreme Court Building, Sangamon County Courthouse, and others.

Springfield is at a junction with US 66 (*see Tour 17*) and US 36 (*see Tour 18*).

From Springfield the Memorial Highway follows State 125 westward to a junction with State 97, the Lincoln Trail, 202 *m.*, which it follows northward to NEW SALEM STATE PARK (*free parking, picnic sites, and fireplaces; restaurant, overnight accommodations in immediate vicinity*), 222 *m.*, an authentic reproduction of the village in which Abraham Lincoln spent six of his early Illinois years.

In the spring of 1831 Lincoln met Denton Offut, a swaggering, boastful, frontier entrepreneur with a genius for conceiving all types of undertakings and indifferent success in performing them. He was attracted to Abe, admiring his strength, his drollery, and his popularity, and hired him, and two others, to help him take a flatboat to New Orleans. Upon their return he engaged Lincoln to run a grocery store and a mill in New Salem. The village had been settled in 1828, but possessed fewer than 100 inhabitants when Lincoln arrived. He strolled into town on election day and presently found himself on the edge of the voters. Voting was by acclamation, and the clerk, pressed for assistance, asked Lincoln to help him. Thus on his first afternoon in New Salem Lincoln came to know the names and faces of all the men in the district.

He quickly endeared himself to the community. Established in Offut's grocery, he measured off calico, weighed out tea and sugar, wrote letters, and arbitrated disputes. He became acutely aware of his educational shortcomings and remedied them by long hours of pouring over such books as *Kirkham's Grammar*. On warm days customers found him outside the store reading under a tree in the dooryard, lying flat on his back, his feet high on the trunk, circling the tree as he followed the shade. As in other frontier towns, sports in New Salem were crude—cock-fighting, horse racing, wrestling, and rough horse-play. Offut's loose tongue had spread stories of Lincoln's tremendous strength throughout the district, and one day the Clary Grove Boys roistered into town with Jack Armstrong, their champion, and challenged Lincoln to a wrestling match. He accepted cheerfully. A ring formed and for a time the match was even. Then Armstrong began to falter, and his friends rushed in. Lincoln, stung to anger, challenged any man in the crowd to single combat. None dared accept, and the match was called off. Finally tempers cooled, and Lincoln and Armstrong shook hands. Thereafter they were firm friends.

In the spring of 1832 Offut closed his store, and Lincoln, out of a job, volunteered for the Black Hawk War. He was elected captain of his company, and—or at least so goes the legend—was obliged to carry a wooden sword for two days because his men broke into the officers' supplies and pilfered a quantity of whiskey. Following the war he returned to New Salem, and became partner in a store that failed, leaving him burdened with debt. He was appointed postmaster, but the fees from the office were too small to provide a living. It was as a deputy surveyor of Sangamon County that he spent the balance of his residence in New Salem. Before the Black Hawk War Lincoln had announced himself candidate for the legislature. He was defeated at the time, but in 1834 he was elected, and in 1836 he was re-elected. Meanwhile, encouraged by his friend, John T. Stuart of Springfield, and aided by the loan of Stuart's books he was studying law.

In New Salem, perhaps for the first time, Lincoln fell in love. He met Ann Rutledge shortly after he came and lived with her family for a while. She was a quiet girl, gently bred, with yellow hair and blue eyes. At the time, she was engaged to John McNeill, but McNeill left New Salem for a prolonged period, and the friendship between Ann and Lincoln grew into love. Then suddenly, in the summer of 1835, she died. The following months were in many ways the most critical period of Lincoln's life. He suffered the deepest melancholy, impervious to sympathy, apathetic, lonely. His friends feared for his sanity. But in time the friendly consideration of his neighbors restored him to normality. He continued his study of law, and in the spring of 1837 he was admitted to the bar. In nearby Springfield, which had just been designated the future State capital, his old friend Stuart was eager to take him into partnership. Thus it happened that one April day in 1837, Lincoln packed his few belongings in his saddle bags and rode out of the frontier village in which he had spent six eventful years.

New Salem, already declining, sank rapidly. Two years later, when Petersburg was made the seat of Menard County, it received the final blow. In a few years only the slowly crumbling ruins of a few cabins marked its site. So it remained until 1906, when William Randolph Hearst purchased the land and conveyed it to the Old Salem Lincoln League, which subsequently deeded it to the State. Much research preceded the restoration. In the Sangamon County archives the original New Salem plat was found, giving the numbers and dimensions of the lots. Descendants of the original settlers were consulted, and preliminary work in clearing the ground uncovered some of the original foundations.

Only the ONSTOT COOPER SHOP was still in existence when the restoration was begun. Of the score of buildings that stood here during Lincoln's day, 15 have been reconstructed. Houses, shops, and sheds were built of black walnut and red and white oak, as were those of Lincoln's day, and furnished with authentic period pieces, many from the original cabins. Not only have chairs, tables, spinning wheels, and clocks of the period been found and placed in proper setting, but boot-jacks, potato mashers, butter bowls, and candle molds add to the reality of home and store and tavern. Old wells are complete with their windlass ropes and buckets, and rail-and-rider fences surround garden spots.

The center of interest is the LINCOLN-BERRY STORE, with its meagre stock, its barrel of brooms, its wide friendly fireplace. Other buildings include the RUTLEDGE TAVERN, home of Ann Rutledge; the HILL-MCNEILL STORE, owned by Lincoln's rival for Ann's affections; and DENTON OFFUT'S STORE, where Lincoln first worked upon arriving at New Salem. In addition, there is a stone MUSEUM, which contains the burrs from the Rutledge mill, an old covered wagon, and many other objects.

PETERSBURG, 224 m. (524 alt., 2,319 pop.), the seat of Menard County, is at present (1939) the western end of the Lincoln National Memorial Highway. In time, the route will be extended westward to Beardstown, on the Illinois River, along a road surveyed and frequently traveled by Lincoln.

In OAKWOOD CEMETERY, at the southwestern edge of Petersburg, is the GRAVE OF ANN RUTLEDGE, marked by a headstone that bears Edgar Lee Masters' lines:

> "Out of me unworthy and unknown
> The vibrations of deathless music;
> 'With malice toward none, with charity for all.' "

TOUR 22

THE ILLINOIS WATERWAY

CHICAGO — JOLIET — STARVED ROCK STATE PARK — PEORIA —
PERE MARQUETTE STATE PARK — GRAFTON; CHICAGO RIVER,
SANITARY AND SHIP CANAL, AND DES PLAINES
AND ILLINOIS RIVERS

Lake Michigan to the Mississippi River, 327 *m*.

Draught on Sanitary and Ship Canal, 20 ft.; on Des Plaines and Illinois Rivers, at least 9 ft. Minimum vertical clearance on the waterway, 16.5 ft. (over Sanitary and Ship Canal). Channel markings: (L) black and white (nun) buoys; (R) red can buoys. Where unmarked, the channel is in the middle of the river. In other than the channel, and particularly in lakes and sloughs, the water is commonly shallow, and sand bars and other obstructions to navigation are numerous. Only craft of very light draught should leave the main channel.

Strip maps and two Government publications pertaining in part to the Illinois Waterway are available, without charge, to pilots of pleasure craft: *Pilot Rules for the Rivers Whose Waters Flow into the Gulf of Mexico,* and *Regulations to Govern the Use, Administration, and Navigation of the Ohio River, the Mississippi River above Cairo, and their Tributaries* (apply U. S. Engineer's Office, 433 W. Van Buren St., Chicago). The raising of the waterway bridges and the locking of boats over the dams are services rendered all craft without charge; there are, however, certain restrictions, which are set forth in the above mentioned publications.

Mooring, fueling, and repair facilities and overnight accommodations are available at the larger cities. Camping and lodge facilities are offered at Starved Rock and Pere Marquette State Parks; for rates and reservations address Concessionaires.

THE ILLINOIS WATERWAY, although essentially a commercial highway, is growing increasingly popular as an avenue of pleasure travel. Its historical associations are the richest of any of the traveled routes in the State. In beauty and variety its scenery rivals that of any part of Illinois; the opportunities it affords for hunting and fishing are exceeded only by the Mississippi in the southern part of the State. Along its course are some of the wildest and least populated sections of Illinois. The waterway has been, perhaps, the most significant single factor in the history of Illinois, and upon that factor emphasis is here laid. For this reason the larger cities and State parks along the route are treated briefly and only insofar as they pertain to the story of the river; their full descriptions are cross-referenced to other parts of the book.

CHICAGO (598 alt., 3,376,438 pop.) (*see Chicago*).

Points of Interest: Chicago Board of Trade Building, Union Stock Yards, Field Museum of Natural History, Art Institute of Chicago, Museum of Science and Industry, Adler Planetarium, Shedd Aquarium, University of Chicago, and others.

Chicago is at the northern end of the Illinois Waterway. The CONTROL LOCKS, 0 *m.*, at the entrance to the harbor, mark the beginning of the Chicago River, which formerly emptied into Lake Michigan approximately a mile to the southwest. During the hundred years of engineering since the Illinois and Michigan Canal was begun, the flow has been reversed—the river has been made to drain out of the lake, rather than into it. The locks, opened in 1938, prevent the pollution of lake water, which sometimes resulted during storm periods when the river backed up into the lake.

Right of the locks is NAVY PIER, built by the City of Chicago in 1916, used for amusements, expositions, and the docking of lake steamers. Here are the offices of the harbor master, sales and storage rooms for small boats, and service facilities for pleasure craft. West is NORTH PIER TERMINAL, on Ogden Slip, where lake freighters and an occasional European tramp tie up at the great warehouses.

Left of the locks is the U. S. COAST GUARD STATION, and in the southwest corner of the harbor, the ILLINOIS NAVAL RESERVE ARMORY. South of the breakwater is a YACHT BASIN, jammed in summer with every variety of pleasure craft, from saucy cat-boats to long sleek yachts. Farther south ADLER PLANETARIUM dominates the tip of Northerly Island, its red granite walls and bronze dome in sharp contrast with the Grecian white of SHEDD AQUARIUM and the classic mass of FIELD MUSEUM, a short distance west. Ahead and L. the imposing façade of the Loop rises along the west side of Michigan Ave.

The OUTER DRIVE BRIDGE, 0.4 *m.*, opened October 5, 1937 by President Roosevelt, links the north and south lake shore drives. When the full sweep of this lake boulevard is completed, motorists will be able to travel a continuous parkway the entire length of the city, from the Indiana Line to Evanston.

The MICHIGAN AVENUE BRIDGE, 0.8 *m.*, marks the point at which the Chicago River formerly turned sharply to the south, to enter the lake at what is now the foot of Madison St. It was established in its present course in the 1830's. Left at the bridge is the SITE OF FORT DEARBORN, the military post established in 1803 around which developed embryonic Chicago. Right is the white tiled WRIGLEY BUILDING and, opposite, the graceful Gothic lines of the TRIBUNE TOWER.

The MERCHANDISE MART, 1.4 *m.*, wherein hundreds of American manufacturers maintain offices and showrooms, rears its great mass on the R. Twenty-five thousand people spend a third of their lives in this building, which has a total floor space two-thirds the area of the Loop.

At a sharp southerly bend of the river, 1.6 *m.*, the NORTH BRANCH OF THE CHICAGO RIVER enters the main stream. Below this point the route follows the South Branch; the reversal of flow, accomplished when the South Branch was linked with the Des Plaines River by canal has made it the main stream.

At 1.9 *m.* the river passes two of Chicago's finest office buildings: the CIVIC OPERA BUILDING (L), built by Samuel Insull in 1929, and the DAILY NEWS BUILDING (R), fronted by an extensive plaza along the waterway.

Along the river, for the greater part of its length, sometimes clearly in view, again hidden beneath tall buildings, is the network of rails over which moves the volume of freight that makes this city the busiest rail center in the world. Right, at 2.1 *m.*, is Chicago's UNION STATION, into which many of the rails are diverted. The NEW POST OFFICE BUILDING, 2.3 *m.* (R), is the largest structure in the world devoted to the handling of mail.

Downstream, the river flows between parallel networks of rails, bordered by warehouses and manufacturing plants. For a mile or so it follows a course that was straightened in the 1920's to facilitate the extension of streets south of the Loop. It then curves slowly westward, and for nearly two miles is bordered (R) by a dozen slips along which are the docks where lake freighters and Mississippi River barges load and unload. On 21 acres of State-owned land at this point, the State proposes to build a modern river-and-rail terminal.

At the SOUTH FORK (L), 5.5 *m.*, is the junction with the abandoned ILLINOIS AND MICHIGAN CANAL, which the modern waterway parallels to La Salle. Opened in 1848, the canal was for 30 years a vital influence in the development of the State, and by linking Chicago with the Mississippi River enabled the lake port to outstrip St. Louis as the dominant commercial center of the Midwest. Railroad competition in the latter half of the century reduced its traffic, but the canal continued to operate into the early 1900's. Today its hundred-mile right-of-way is being developed by the State for recreational purposes, and the old towpaths are being converted into pleasure drives.

At 6.1 *m.* the waterway leaves the river and enters the SANITARY AND SHIP CANAL, which it follows for 30 miles to Lockport.

The canal, opened in 1900 as the Chicago Drainage Canal, serves the dual purpose implied in its new name: to remove the treated industrial and domestic waste of Chicago and some of its suburbs, and to replace the outmoded Illinois and Michigan Canal as a highway of commerce. Principal users of the canal are a few large independent companies and the Federal Barge Line, a Government owned and operated fleet of barges and towboats that carries freight between Chicago, Minneapolis, St. Louis, Kansas City, and New Orleans.

The channel, 20 feet deep and 160 to 300 feet wide, is cut through solid rock in its first seven miles. On calm days this stretch is easily navigated, but in stormy weather the passage is difficult, for a heavy wind can wreck a small boat upon the rocks. However, such winds are rarely experienced, since the canal lies in a deep valley and on either side is a high spoils bank, formed of the excavated rock through which the channel is cut. These high embankments screen the adjoining lands, which are utilized by railroads and varied manufacturing plants.

At 13.2 *m.* is the OLD CHICAGO PORTAGE FOREST PRESERVE (R), a section of the once heavily traveled portage between the Chicago and Des Plaines Rivers; the route of Indians, explorers, missionaries, traders, trappers, and soldiers; the crossing between the waters that flowed eastward past Quebec and Montreal and those that found their way southward to New Orleans and the Gulf.

Jolliet crossed this low divide in 1673 and envisioned a canal that would link these two waterways. La Salle followed him, and a decade later, in reporting the geography of the region, noted the possibility of a canal through the portage. His enthusiasm for the project, however, was tempered by his experiences in traversing the portage. At times of high water, he noted, the floods of the Des Plaines so completely inundated the region that a canoe could pass from one river to another in water at least two feet deep. But during the low water stage the Des Plaines was often completely dry, and the Kankakee, with which it joined to form the Illinois, carried so small a volume of water that a canoe could not be floated above Starved Rock. In short, La Salle pointed out, a canal that would effectively link the Chicago and Illinois Rivers would have to be, not half a league in length, as Jolliet had optimistically reported, but the maximum length of the portage, nearly 100 miles. The Illinois and Michigan Canal, opened 165 years later, measured 96 miles, from Chicago to La Salle. The length of the modern Sanitary and Ship Canal, less than a third of this, is made possible only by the diversion of a considerably greater volume of water from Lake Michigan, and by the use of modern engineering in damming and dredging the channels of the Des Plaines and Illinois Rivers.

Immediately west of the portage the DES PLAINES RIVER enters the valley (R), and parallels the waterway for 23 miles to Lockport. Left is the old Illinois and Michigan Canal. On either side of the mile-wide valley the wooded bluffs rise sharply to the rolling upland. Between approximately 18 *m.* and 23 *m.* the ARGONNE FOREST PRESERVE (L) borders the valley—an extensive Cook County recreational area largely in its original wildland state. West of the preserve is the mouth of the CALUMET SAG CHANNEL (L), 23.5 *m.*, a tributary of the Sanitary and Ship Canal. This channel, which leads southeast to Calumet and Indiana Harbor on Lake Michigan, is being improved to accommodate barge traffic.

LEMONT (L), 26.9 *m.* (605 alt., 2,582 pop.), an old towpath town, raises its hill-crowned head among the trees. Downstream is the village of RCMEOVILLE (L), 31.3 *m.* (590 alt., 133 pop.), which developed along the Illinois and Michigan Canal. The industrial plant visible from the waterway is a GLOBE OIL REFINERY. Petroleum and petroleum products are among the principal goods transported on the waterway; they are second only to coal in tonnage.

A BUTTERFLY DAM occupies the center of the channel at 34 *m.* Its function is to serve as an emergency dam should the one at Lockport fail to function. Inasmuch as it remains open at all other times, it is not equipped with locks.

At LOCKPORT (L) 34.5 *m.* (582 alt., 3,383 pop.), once an important shipping and transfer point on the Illinois and Michigan Canal, is the lock that controls the volume of water withdrawn from Lake Michigan. Here were the offices of the canal company, among whose records are preserved many documents pertaining to the days of the canal's construction and operation. These include maps, field notebooks, correspondence, newspapers of a century ago in which bids for canal contracts are advertised, and such miscellaneous records of the disbursing office as the pork and flour contracts for 1838-39. Among the items is a prospectus of the Illinois Central Company offering for sale, in 1855, 2,400,000 acres of "selected proven farm and woodlands in tracts of any size to suit purchasers, on long credit at low rates of interest, situated on each side of the railroad, extending all the way from the extreme North to the South of the State of Illinois."

Right, at 35.5 *m.,* are the buff limestone buildings of STATEVILLE STATE PRISON (*see Tour* 17), set squarely among the varied greens and yellows of cultivated fields.

LOCKPORT LOCK AND DAM, 36.1 *m.,* marks the end of the Sanitary and Ship Canal. The lock chamber is 110 feet wide, 600 feet long, has a lift of 41 feet, and can be filled or emptied in 12 minutes. The upper gates are of the vertical lift type, each 20 feet high and weighing 190 tons. The lower gates are 60 feet high, are of the mitering type, and weigh 315 tons apiece. Two emergency dams, of 50 and 75 tons, are part of the lock's equipment. They are for use in the event of damage to the lock gates. A feature of the Lockport development is a small chamber for locking pleasure craft. None of the other locks on the waterway is so equipped.

Adjoining the locks is the HYDROELECTRIC POWER PLANT (R) of the Chicago Sanitary District, the only property retained by that authority when it surrendered title to the Chicago Drainage Canal, as the Sanitary and Ship Canal was known before it was acquired and improved by the Federal government. By measuring the amount of water passed through the turbines, and by computing the volume used for lockage purposes, Army engineers in charge of the waterway control the total amount of water diverted from Lake Michigan. This diversion, as established by the United States Supreme Court in 1930, averaged 5,000 cubic feet per second until December 31, 1938. At that time it was reduced to a maximum of 1,500 cubic feet per second, a volume of water that some shippers and canal authorities believe to be inadequate to maintain sufficient flow for sanitary purposes and adequate channel depths for navigation.

Downstream from the Lockport Dam the waterway follows the improved channel of the Des Plaines River for 18 miles to its junction with the Kankakee. JOLIET, 38.5 m. (545 alt., 42,993 pop.) (see Joliet), long an important shipping point on the river and waterway, is bisected by the canalized stream, which flows at street level in the northern part of town, but near the southern border of the city is actually at a higher elevation than the valley floor, so that boats sail along above the general level of the city. Only the residential districts on the wooded bluffs are high above the canal.

BRANDON ROAD LOCK AND DAM, 41.2 m., is the second of the series on the Illinois Waterway. The lock, 110 by 600 feet, has a lift of 31 feet. The dam, which has a retaining wall 2,000 feet in length, not only maintains the upstream level, but also confines the waters of BRANDON ROAD POOL, a turning basin considerably above the level of the valley bottom. Headgate structures for a possible power house have been built into the dam, but no power development has as yet been undertaken.

At the southwest corner of the pool is one of the locks of the Illinois and Michigan Canal, now permanently closed and used as part of the retaining wall. Downstream, the old canal (R) parallels the modern waterway, and seems by comparison a tiny ditch, with its trickle of water that seeps through the lock gates. Gone is the pageant of barge and packet, the holiday crowds on canal excursions, the drivers and horses along the towpaths. In its place is the modern waterway, sleek and efficient in its long graceful dams, its electrically operated locks, navy-trim in their bright coat of aluminum paint. Its modern steel barges, four, six, eight, ten at a time, locked in tow, pushed up or down the waterway by twin-screw, Diesel-powered boats, move in one tow more freight than the entire fleet operating on the old canal could have carried in a week. The old canal was done to death by the railroads; the new waterway competes with them on an equal footing.

At 50 m. the Du PAGE RIVER enters the Des Plaines at the little town of CHANNAHON (R), an important shipping center in the days of the old canal. Three packets, the *China*, the *Whale*, and the *King Brothers*, carried flour to Chicago and Kankakee. The development of rail transportation put an end to Channahon's commercial activities.

At 54 m. (L) the KANKAKEE RIVER joins the Des Plaines to form the ILLINOIS RIVER, which the waterway follows for 273 miles to Grafton and the Mississippi. For 63 miles, between the junction of the Des Plaines with the Kankakee and the Great Bend, west of

La Salle, the Illinois River flows in a westerly direction through a broad, deep valley carved thousands of years ago by the outpouring waters of a melting ice sheet. Even the improved river of today, which carries many times its normal volume of water, seems strikingly undersized as it flows through a gorge 100 to 200 feet deep and a mile and a half to two miles wide. It was at this point that La Salle, having descended the Kankakee, first entered the valley of the Illinois in the winter of 1679-80.

DRESDEN ISLAND LOCK AND DAM, 55.6 m., third of the series on the Illinois Waterway, has a lift of 17 feet and a standard lock chamber, 110 by 600 feet. In this preliminary stretch of the river the valley sides are less steep than they are shortly downstream, and fields of corn often spill over the crest of the upland and descend to the river's bank, bringing to the waterway an agricultural scene that is generally out of view.

MORRIS (R), 63.7 m. (504 alt., 5,568 pop.) (see Tour 14), important once as a grain shipping center, is now building and operating new elevators to meet the new river conditions. Here grain is stored and loaded onto the carriers, which are made up into tows semi-weekly. One or more of the 300-foot barges is commonly tied up at Morris.

SENECA (R), 74 m. (521 alt., 1,185 pop.), lies well within the gorge. A little town at the base of hundred-foot bluffs, astraddle the Illinois and Michigan Canal, Seneca is scarcely visible from the river. The products of its sawmills built many a river town a century ago.

MARSEILLES, 80.1 m. (506 alt., 4,292 pop.) (see Tour 14), is at the head of a rapids that have contributed to its development as an important manufacturing city. MARSEILLES DAM, fourth on the waterway, is at the head of MARSEILLES CANAL, through which traffic passes the two-and-a-half-mile rapids. MARSEILLES LOCK, of standard size, with a lift of 21 feet, is at the western end of the canal. BELLS ISLAND (R) separates the waterway from the river; ILLINI STATE PARK, a game refuge and bird haven, occupies 407 acres on the mainland (L).

At 87 m. is the junction with the FOX RIVER (R), at the northern limits of OTTAWA, 87.5 m. (486 alt., 15,094 pop.) (see Tour 14). Although an industrial city, Ottawa, as seen from the waterway, is one of the loveliest of Illinois River towns. Beautifully situated, the residential districts mount from the river to the encircling bluffs on both sides of the stream. Boats of the Federal Barge Line usually change their tows at Ottawa; low bridges over the Sanitary and Ship Canal limit the use of the upper waterway to craft of low clearance.

In the 10 miles below Ottawa is the most rugged section of the valley. Here the sandstone bluffs rise precipitously 100 to 150 feet above the water. Tributary streams have carved deep canyons, and wind and water have eroded the soft rock into fantastic forms. At 92.5 m. (R) is BUFFALO ROCK STATE PARK (see Tour 14), dominated by a peculiarly shaped block of sandstone that rears its hump a hundred feet above the valley floor. Between the rock and the bluffs is a large turning basin of the Illinois and Michigan Canal.

On the left bank of the river throughout this section is STARVED ROCK STATE PARK (*see Tour* 14A), 900 acres of wildland as varied as any in Illinois. The body of water at this point is known as LAKE STARVED ROCK. Two channels are marked: the one close to the south bank is for pleasure craft; the other, the main channel, leads to the lock.

STARVED ROCK LOCK AND DAM, 96.2 *m.*, is the fifth of the modern installations on the Illinois Waterway. Immediately downstream (L) the historic old promontory, STARVED ROCK, rises 140 feet above the water's edge. Here in 1683 La Salle established a French fort, and here, according to legend, a band of Illinois Indians later met the tragic death from which the Rock derives its name. West of the Rock is the boat entrance to Starved Rock State Park, marked by two mooring piers and two black buoys.

OGLESBY (L), 100.8 *m.* (465 alt., 3,910 pop.), is at the mouth of the VERMILION RIVER. The Marquette Cement Company, a local industry, ships extensively by water, using its own boats and barges. A single tow often carries a load equivalent to that of 50 box-cars.

LA SALLE (R), 103.1 *m.* (448 alt., 13,149 pop.) (*see Tour* 4), bears only slight resemblance, as seen from the waterway, to the city of more than half a century ago that was the head of steamboat navigation on the river and southern terminus of the busy Illinois and Michigan Canal. Empty streets face the waterfront; many of the warehouses are deserted or gone; shipping has moved inland to the railroad. Only recently is there a slight about-face in the pattern of business activity. The docks and warehouses at which the new river barges tie up, and a few other structures, modern and business-like, indicate that La Salle is again depending upon the river that gave her birth for at least part of her economic life.

The TERMINUS OF THE ILLINOIS AND MICHIGAN CANAL (R), 104 *m.*, today scarcely noticed from the waterway, was once the hub of commercial activity on the Illinois River. Here cargoes were transferred between canal and river; here as many as 100 canal boats were anchored at one time; and here, on occasion, a dozen steamboats, with their black stacks, huge paddle wheels, and gingerbread trim, crowded the wharf.

Steamboating actively began on the Illinois in 1828, but it was not until several years later that the first organized steamboat line was put into operation. It ran only as far upstream as Naples, 65 miles from Grafton. However, by 1841, sixty boats were serving Peoria; and by 1851 a regular, dependable trade was being carried on between St. Louis and La Salle. Fastest service of the day was that of the Five Day Line, which made the 260 miles between the two cities within that period, rather than the customary week. In La Salle there still live river men who recall the days when the *Prairie Belle,* the *Garden City,* the *Amazon,* the *Messenger,* and the *Aunt Lettie* belched the black smoke from their tall stacks and churned the river white with their great paddles.

PERU (R), 104.5 *m.* (459 alt., 9,121 pop.) (*see Tour* 4), sister city of La Salle, shared in the glory of the old days, then turned her back on the river and entered into the industrial life that came with the development of the railroad. The revival of river traffic has affected the modern city only indirectly.

SPRING VALLEY (R), 108.6 *m.* (465 alt., 5,270 pop.), a manufacturing town, spreads over the bluffs and straggles out onto the valley floor. Until recent decades the region was the scene of extensive coal mining activity.

At the GREAT BEND OF THE ILLINOIS, 116 *m.*, where the river swings abruptly south, is the mouth of the ILLINOIS AND MISSISSIPPI CANAL, a 75-mile channel opened in 1907 between the Illinois River and the Mississippi at Rock Island. Although intended as a link between the two waterways, the canal has proved too small for modern purposes. The cost of improving it has been estimated to be $12,000,000, a greater sum than the potential use of the waterway would warrant. At present it has been abandoned, save for drainage purposes.

HENNEPIN (L), 119.7 *m.* (505 alt., 312 pop.), named in honor of Father Louis Hennepin, early missionary pilot who accompanied the explorers of the waterway, was intended as the eastern terminus of the canal. But the little town has shared the fate of the $7,000,000 project it was to serve, and is today of no more importance on the river than the score of other settlements passed by the Federal Barge Line.

Downstream from the Great Bend the character of the waterway differs sharply from that of the upper river. The narrow gorge of the Starved Rock section gives place to a broad valley, two to six miles in width. The bluffs remain equally steep, and rise to even greater heights, commonly 150 to 200 feet, occasionally 300 feet or more above the valley floor. The river winds lazily between its banks, for the drop in this lower 200 miles is so slight that there is scarcely a current. Oxbow lakes, sloughs, and marshes border the stream, and islands dot its channel. Sandbars alternate with marshlands, and extensive woodlands cover the valley floor and mount the gentler bluffs. These at times rise sharply from the water's edge, sheer cliffs of sandstone or limestone, or again are so far removed from the river as to be indistinct on the far horizon.

In early days the valley teemed with wild life, and today game fish and fowl, protected by conservation, abound in this lower region. Waterfowl inhabit the marshy bottom lands, upland birds are numerous on the prairies and in the woodlands back of the bluffs, and in the lakes, channel, and backwaters of the river are a variety of game fish.

Downstream from Hennepin the river passes SENACHWINE LAKE (R), which occupies a five-mile stretch of abandoned channel. The lake is named for the last of the Potawatomi chiefs in this region, who died about 1883. He is said to be buried in a mound overlooking the lake. Its mouth, at 128.5 m. (R), is all but hidden in the wooded marshlands that separate the lake from the river. Islands are numerous in this section of the valley. Boats should stay in the main channel; the chutes or sloughs, as river men call the passages behind the islands, are shallow and filled with sandbars and snags.

HENRY (R), 131.5 m. (491 alt., 1,658 pop.), is a small river town on the crest of an extensive terrace. This long platform, which rises sharply a hundred feet above the valley floor, represents a level at which the river formerly flowed, before cutting its way to its present bed. Backing the terrace are the main valley bluffs, which rise another hundred feet to the upland level. The terrace is largely given over to stock farming. The HENRY LOCK (R) is not in use.

At approximately 137 m. are the SPARLAND PUBLIC SHOOTING GROUNDS (R), one of several tracts along the river set aside for public hunting. Downstream are the river towns of LACON (L), 138.1 m. (501 alt., 1,548 pop.), and CHILLICOTHE (R), 146.7 m. (490 alt., 1,978 pop.). Opposite the latter are the WOODFORD COUNTY PUBLIC SHOOTING GROUNDS (L), 148 m., at the north end of PEORIA LAKE, largest body of water on the river, a mile or more in width and 18 miles in length, in reality a series of two lakes joined by a narrow strait. On the shores of the upper lake is the ILLINOIS VALLEY YACHT AND CANOE CLUBHOUSE (R). On the banks of the strait La Salle first encountered the Illinois Indians. Here his men camped for 11 days in January 1680.

PEORIA (R), 164.6 m. (608 alt., 104,969 pop.) (see Peoria), is a major industrial and commercial city of Illinois. On the west bank of the lake is the new, highly efficient RIVER AND RAIL TERMINAL, where cargoes are exchanged between freight cars, trucks, and river barges, mechanized and modern to the last detail, this vast municipal improvement vividly illustrates the significance of the river in the economic life of Illinois and specifically of this city, one of the ranking river ports of the State.

EAST PEORIA (478 alt., 5,027 pop.) (see Tour 16), situated for the most part on the valley floor, is built around the large CATERPILLAR TRACTOR COMPANY PLANT (L), visible from the waterway.

PEORIA LOCK AND DAM, 169.5 m., completed in 1938, is of the wicket type, a form of dam that can be laid down on the river bed during high water and raised and placed in operation during low water stage.

FORT CRÈVE COEUR STATE PARK (L), 172 m. (see Tour 16), marks the site of the ill-fated fort established by La Salle in 1680 as a base for proposed exploration and eventual colonization of the

Mississippi Valley. A granite marker commemorates the founding of the fort and tells the story of its desertion.

PEKIN (L), 174.4 *m.* (479 alt., 16,129 pop.) (*see Tour* 16), one of the earliest settlements in Tazewell County and its third county seat, was often visited by Lincoln and other members of the bench and bar who traveled the eighth judicial circuit. During the period of steamboat traffic Pekin was a major port on the Illinois. Eighteen hundred arrivals and departures were recorded in 1850.

COPPERAS CREEK LOCK (R), 190.2 *m.,* one of the old series of river improvements, is now used as a coal loading dock. The many lakes in this section of the valley afford excellent duck hunting during the season.

LIVERPOOL (R), 199.5 *m.,* is one of the early river towns. A port of some consequence in early years, it later declined, but is linked by rail with Dunfermline, has two coal docks, and to a degree is realizing the expectations of its founders, who named it with a purpose.

The SPOON RIVER flows into the Illinois at 206.7 *m.* (R). Along this stream, which drains a fertile, long settled region to the north, are the scenes of Edgar Lee Masters' *Spoon River Anthology* (*see Tour* 16).

HAVANA (L), 207.1 *m.* (451 alt., 3,471 pop.) (*see Tour* 5), one of the old river ports, is today one of the most popular centers of duck hunting on the lower river.

GRAND ISLAND, six miles long, divides the river at 214 *m.* Two miles down the east channel (*very shallow*) is the town of BATH (462 alt., 346 pop.) (*see Tour* 5), which was surveyed by Abraham Lincoln.

Below Grand Island lakes become even more numerous as the river meanders over a valley six to eight miles wide. At 229 *m.* (L) the SANGAMON RIVER enters the Illinois. It seems a small stream, yet it has been navigated. In 1832 a steamboat, the *Talisman,* loaded to the guards with miscellaneous freight, put out from Cincinnati, Ohio, destined for Springfield, Illinois. Down the Ohio she steamed to the Mississippi, up the Mississippi to the Illinois, up the Illinois to the Sangamon, and up the Sangamon to Springfield, there safely discharging her freight and passengers. But the trip up the Sangamon had been difficult, and on the return voyage the captain of the *Talisman* put a young man of the vicinity at the wheel. This youthful pilot, who brought his boat safely down the river, was Abraham Lincoln.

BEARDSTOWN (L), 238 *m.* (444 alt., 6,344 pop.) (*see Tour* 7), one of the early cities of Illinois, lies low on the valley floor, and has at times suffered disastrous floods. Today it functions primarily as a trading center for an extensive agricultural region, and as the focus of hunting activities on the lower river.

LA GRANGE LOCK AND DAM, 249.6 *m.,* is of standard size, 110 by 600 feet.

MEREDOSIA (L), 255.5 *m.* (446 alt., 820 pop.), lies at the mouth of MEREDOSIA LAKE, a five-mile body of water that provides good fishing and hunting. Lake and town take their name from a corruption of the French *marais d'osier,* or "swamp of the basket reeds."

It was at Meredosia that the first railroad in Illinois, a section of the Northern Cross (*see Transportation*), met the river. That was in 1838, when steamboating was just getting under way. It was not until 1878, however, when receipts on the Illinois and Michigan Canal fell below operating costs, that the locomotive seriously threatened the supremacy of the riverboat. For 40 years the two systems of transportation developed side by side in the young State.

NAPLES (L), 261 *m.* (448 alt., 252 pop.), now a minor grain shipping point, is important in river history as the one place where a steamboat was built on the Illinois River. She was the *Olitippa,* and ran long before there was any regular steamboat service on the river.

The building of this and other Mississippi-type steamboats required no extensive plant or machine equipment. A man who wanted to build a boat had only to erect a shed or shelter on the bank in the early spring. A crude sawmill did the original cutting of logs; the rest of the work consisted of hand hewing or cutting with flitch saws. Skilled workers with drawknife, gauge, axe and adze shaped the hull timbers, fashioned the kelson, and formed the stem. The long keel was laid down first. From this the ribs were extended out on either side. The hull was finished and floored over and sometimes the upper decks were added before the machinery, brought in by boat, was installed. So durable were the engines used in many of these boats that they were often used over and over again, outlasting the life of several hulls.

GRIGGSVILLE LANDING (R), 266 *m.,* was once a busy port. Today it is the landing for VALLEY CITY, a short distance inland and not visible from the river. A local cement plant, recently established, ships some of its product by water.

Downstream, in its southernmost 60 miles, the river spreads broadly over the valley floor. Past the Pike County towns (R) of FLORENCE, 271 *m.* (438 alt., 105 pop.), MONTEZUMA 277.1 *m.,* BEDFORD, 278.3 *m.,* and PEARL, 284 *m.* (451 alt., 492 pop.), the old stream winds its way among wooded islands, now swinging close to the valley sides, again sweeping in great bends down the center of the gorge. In this lower section are many small communities that have existed for a century or more, with the river as almost their sole contact with the outside world. Their names commonly carry the suffix of "landing," as Buckhorn Landing, Gravel Point Landing, Retzers Landing, and Lange Landing. They are quiet, colorful reminders of days now gone when the steamboat was the grandest thing afloat.

KAMPSVILLE (R), 295.7 *m.* (449 alt., 388 pop.), an old river town, is now a major recreational point in southwestern Illinois. BAR-

THOLOMEW BEACH, one of the finest on the river, attracts many vacationists from the St. Louis area.

Downstream lie HURRICANE ISLAND (*eastern channel is safer*), 299 *m.*, and DIAMOND ISLAND (*western channel is safer*), 301.5 *m.* These two islands, like many others in the river, are a riot of wild vegetation. Trees and undergrowth form a thick sunshade for woodland flowers and creeping vines. Colorful birds dart in and out among the shadows, and small water animals grub for food among the roots and bushes.

HARDIN (R), 305.5 *m.* (448 alt., 733 pop.), the seat of Calhoun County, is the last town on the river. Calhoun County, a long limestone ridge between the Mississippi and the Illinois, is all but divorced from the remainder of the State. The only county in Illinois without a railroad, it is in large part undeveloped. The ridge drops precipitously into the rivers that bound it; the area is wild, and for miles at a time appears to be uninhabited. Towns are few, and even small settlements are limited to the rivers or to the fertile ridge tops and gentler valley slopes that support the finest apple orchards of the State. Hardin is the principal shipping point for this important crop, part of which is still sent by water to St. Louis and other river ports. However, since the completion of the new bridge that here spans the river, most of the crop is trucked to railheads in the counties to the east.

Below Hardin the approaching confluence of the Illinois and Mississippi Rivers is foreshadowed by the ever increasing breadth of the valley, the constantly decreasing height of the headland to the west, and, often, the smoke of invisible steamers passing on the larger river. In this last stretch, high on the eastern bluffs that overlook the Illinois and command far-reaching vistas of the Mississippi and even of the Missouri, is PERE MARQUETTE STATE PARK, 321 *m.* (*see Tour 7*). The park commemorates in its name the French priest and explorer who with Jolliet and five other companions visited the region in 1673. A large STONE CROSS (L), 325.5 *m.*, marks the site where the party first entered Illinois.

GRAFTON, 327 *m.* (446 alt., 1,026 pop.) (*see Tour 7*), is on the Illinois shore just at the point where the two rivers meet. Save in extremely rainy weather, the Illinois retains its naturally clear beauty and refuses, for several miles, to mingle with the mud-stained waters of the Mississippi. Thus for a considerable distance there is presented the spectacle of two great rivers flowing side by side in the same channel, each retaining its identity.

FIFTY BOOKS ABOUT ILLINOIS

Abraham Lincoln, 1809-1858, by Albert J. Beveridge. Two volumes, Houghton, Mifflin, Boston, 1928. Political developments in Illinois preceding the Civil War.

Abraham Lincoln, the Prairie Years, by Carl Sandburg. Harcourt, Brace, New York, 1926. An excellent literary biography.

The American Livestock and Meat Industry, by R. A. Clemen. Ronald Press, New York, 1923. Contains a good account of a great Illinois industry.

As Others See Chicago, edited by Bessie Louise Pierce. University of Chicago Press, Chicago, 1933. The recorded impressions of visitors from 1673 to 1933.

Blue Book of the State of Illinois, edited by Secretary of State. Published by authority of the State of Illinois, 1903-1907 to date. A biennial synthesis of the administrative program and record of all the major departments of the State.

Checagou, From Indian Wigwam to Modern City, 1673-1833, by Milo M. Quaife. University of Chicago Press, Chicago, 1933. A short, popular account.

Chicago and its Makers, by Paul Gilbert and Charles Lee Bryson. Felix Mendelsohn, Chicago, 1929. Hundreds of photographs give distinction to this volume.

Chicago, A Portrait, by Henry Justin Smith. Century Co., New York, 1931. Picture of city against the background of its history.

Chicago: The History of its Reputation, by Lloyd Lewis and Henry Justin Smith. Harcourt, Brace, New York, 1929. The best of the one-volume histories.

The Conquest of Illinois, by George Rogers Clark. Milo Milton Quaife, Editor, Lakeside Press, Chicago, 1920. Memoirs of the campaign in Illinois, 1778-1779.

Early Narratives of the Northwest, 1634-1699, edited by Louise Phelps Kellogg. Scribners, New York, 1917. English translations of original narratives, including those of Marquette and Tonti.

The Era of the Civil War, 1848-1870, by Arthur C. Cole. Illinois Centennial Commission, Springfield, 1917-20. (Centennial History of Illinois, Vol. III.)

The Eve of Conflict, by George Fort Milton. Houghton, Mifflin, Boston, 1934. Stephen A. Douglas and his part in the history of Illinois and the Nation.

From Quebec to New Orleans, by J. H. Schlarman. Buechler Pub. Co., Belleville, Ill., 1929. General account of the French regime in North America, but with emphasis on Illinois.

The Frontier State, 1818-1848, by Theodore C. Pease. Illinois Centennial Commission, Springfield, 1917-1920. (Centennial History of Illinois, Vol. II.)

The Geography of Illinois, by Douglas C. Ridgley. University of Chicago Press, Chicago, 1921. Best general account.

"Here I Have Lived," by Paul M. Angle. Abraham Lincoln Association, Springfield, Illinois, 1935. Springfield of Lincoln's day.

Historical Encyclopedia of Illinois, with Commemorative Biographies, by Newton Bateman and Paul Selby. Munsell, Chicago, 1915. Valuable for reference.

History of Chicago, by A. T. Andreas. Published by author, Chicago, 1884-86. Three volumes. Deals with period from 1637-1884.

A History of Illinois, by Thomas Ford. S. C. Griggs Co., Chicago, 1854. Mainly of early statehood days.

A History of Illinois Labor Legislation, by Earl R. Beckner. University of Chicago Press, Chicago, 1929. A fair-minded study.

History of the Illinois State Federation of Labor, by Eugene Staley. University of Chicago Press, Chicago, 1930. The history of the State Federation from 1884 to 1930.

I Am a Man: the Indian Black Hawk, by Cyrenus Cole. State Historical Society of Iowa, Iowa City, 1938. A thoroughly documented and comprehensive account of Black Hawk and the Black Hawk War.

Illinois, by Allan Nevins. Oxford, New York, 1917. A history of the University of Illinois.

The Illinois and Michigan Canal, by James William Putnam. University of Chicago Press, Chicago, 1918. Detailed study of its economic history.

The Illinois Country, 1673-1818, by Clarence W. Alvord. Illinois Centennial Commission, Springfield, 1917-1920. (Centennial History of Illinois, Vol. I.)

Illinois in 1818, by Solon J. Buck. Illinois Centennial Commission, Springfield, 1917-1920. (Centennial History of Illinois, Introductory volume.)

Illinois: Resources—Development—Possibilities. Illinois Chamber of Commerce, 1930. A condensation covering agriculture, mining, transportation, manufacturing and related subjects.

The Industrial State, 1870-1893, by Ernest L. Bogart and Charles M. Thompson. Illinois Centennial Commission, Springfield, 1917-1920. (Centennial History of Illinois, Vol. IV.)

Joseph Smith and his Mormon Empire, by Harry M. Beardsley. Houghton, Mifflin, Boston, 1931. A readable biography of the Mormon leader during the Illinois period.

The Life of George Rogers Clark, by James Alton James. University of Chicago Press, Chicago, 1928. One of the best of the many biographies of Clark.

The Lincoln-Douglas Debates of 1858, edited by Edwin Erle Sparks. Illinois Historical Collections, III. The text of the debates, and examples of contemporary comment.

Lincoln's New Salem, by Benjamin P. Thomas. Abraham Lincoln Association, Springfield, Ill., 1934. An account of the Illinois village, now rebuilt, in which Lincoln spent six eventful years.

Mary McDowell, Neighbor, by Howard E. Wilson. University of Chicago Press, Chicago, 1928. A biography throwing light on labor and social conditions in the Chicago stockyards district.

Memoirs of Gustave Koerner, 1809-1896. Two volumes, Torch Press, Cedar Rapids, 1908. Nearly all the prominent Illinoisans of the nineteenth century figure in the pages of this autobiography.

Midwest Portraits, by Harry Hansen. Harcourt, Brace, New York, 1923. Essays on Midwest writers.

The Modern Commonwealth, 1893-1918, by Ernest L. Bogart and John M. Mathews. Illinois Centennial Commission, Springfield, 1917-1920. (Centennial History of Illinois, Vol. V.)

The Mound Builders, by Henry Clyde Shetrone. Appleton, New York, 1931. An important section deals with Illinois.

My Own Times; Embracing Also a History of My Life, by John Reynolds. Chicago Historical Society, Chicago, 1879. An Illinois classic by the fourth governor of the State.

The Pioneer History of Illinois, by John Reynolds. Fergus Printing Co., Chicago, 1887. Another Illinois classic by Governor Reynolds.

Re-Discovering Illinois, by Fay-Cooper Cole and Thorne Duel. University of Chicago Press, Chicago, 1937. Summary of what is known of the first inhabitants of the State.

The Romance of the Reaper, by Herbert N. Casson. Doubleday, Page, New York, 1908. An account of invention, perfection and manufacture of agricultural implements, one of Illinois' important industries.

The Story of Illinois, by Theodore Calvin Pease. McClurg, Chicago, 1925. Concise and authoritative.

The Story of Northwestern University, by Estelle Francis Ward. Dodd, Mead, New York, 1924. Traces the founding and development of the university.

The Story of the University of Chicago, 1890-1925, by Thomas Wakefield Goodspeed. University of Chicago Press, Chicago, 1925. Brief but authoritative.

Suggested Readings in Illinois History, compiled by Paul M. Angle. The Illinois State Historical Society, Springfield, Illinois. Excellent bibliography compiled by the Illinois State Historian.

The Tale of Chicago, by Edgar Lee Masters. Putnam, New York, 1933. A vivid narrative, though colored by the author's own opinions.

They Broke the Prairie, by Ernest Elmo Calkins. Scribners, New York, 1937. Galesburg's early history.

Twenty Years at Hull House and *The Second Twenty Years at Hull House,* by Jane Addams. Macmillan, New York, 1910, 1930. Two volumes of autobiography which give a history of Chicago's famous settlement.

Wau-Bun, the "Early Day" in the Northwest, by Mrs. Juliette A. Kinzie. Edited by Milo M. Quaife. Lakeside Press, Chicago, 1933. Autobiographical account of frontier days in Wisconsin and Northern Illinois.

CHRONOLOGY

1673   Jolliet and Marquette pass down the Mississippi from the Wisconsin to the Arkansas, and return up the Illinois River.

1675   Marquette founds mission at Indian town of Kaskaskia, near present Utica, Illinois.

1680   Robert Cavelier, Sieur de La Salle, builds Fort Crevecoeur on the Illinois River near the present city of Peoria.

1682-   Fort St. Louis built by La Salle on Starved Rock.
1683

1699   Priests of the Seminary of Foreign Missions at Quebec establish Mission of the Holy Family at Cahokia.

1703   Jesuits establish Mission of the Immaculate Conception at Kaskaskia.

1712   Succession of battles and campaigns begins between the Fox and the French and their Indian allies.

1717   By decree of French Royal Council, Illinois passes under government established for Louisiana.

1718   (Approximate) Construction of Fort de Chartres begun.

1731   Illinois becomes royal province, governed directly by King of France.

1763   Treaty of Paris signed, whereby France cedes to Great Britain her North American possessions east of the Mississippi.

1765   British occupy Fort de Chartres.

1772   British abandon and destroy Fort de Chartres, but keep small garrison at Fort Gage in Kaskaskia, seat of government.

1774   By Quebec Act boundaries of Quebec are extended southward to the Ohio and westward to the Mississippi.

1778   George Rogers Clark captures Cahokia and Kaskaskia. Legislature of Virginia sets up territory conquered by Clark as county of Virginia.

1779   John Todd, commissioned county lieutenant by Gov. Patrick Henry of Virginia, arrives in Illinois Country and establishes civil government.

1783   By the treaty which concludes the War of Independence, the boundary of the United States is extended to the Mississippi, except for East and West Florida.

1784   Virginia cedes Illinois Country to National government.

1787   Northwest Territory, including Illinois, organized by ordinance of Congress.

1790   Arthur St. Clair, governor of Northwest Territory, visits Illinois settlements for first time.

1795   By Treaty of Greenville Indians cede large area to the whites, including several tracts in Illinois. Among these is future site of Fort Dearborn.

1800   Illinois included in newly organized Territory of Indiana.

1803   Fort Dearborn built on south side of Chicago River. Indians cede vast tracts of land by treaties of Fort Wayne and Vincennes.

1804   Chiefs of Sauk and Fox tribes, sign away all their lands east of the Mississippi. Land offices established at Kaskaskia and Vincennes.

1809   Western part of Indiana from Vincennes north to Canada organized as Territory of Illinois with Kaskaskia as capital.

1810   POPULATION: 12,282. Mail route Vincennes to St. Louis, via Kaskaskia, Prairie du Rocher, and Cahokia established.

1812   Illinois becomes territory of the second grade.

1812   American garrison evacuating Fort Dearborn massacred by Indians.

1816   Fort Dearborn rebuilt.

1818   Enabling act fixes northern boundary of Illinois at 42 degrees 30 minutes. First Constitutional Convention elected and writes state constitution, which is submitted to Congress without popular vote. Illinois admitted as state, with seat of government at Kaskaskia.

1820   POPULATION: 55,211. State capital moved to Vandalia.

1821   General Assembly charters State Bank of Illinois.

1823   Rush to lead mines at Galena commences.

1824   People vote against calling convention to amend constitution to permit slavery.

1825   First canal charter granted.

1827   Congress gives 224,322 acres to State to aid in building a canal.

1830   POPULATION: 157,445. Lincoln family moves to Illinois. Canal commissioners survey and plot two towns, Chicago and Ottawa.

1831   Governor John Reynolds calls out the militia against the Sauk and Foxes, but uprising is settled peaceably.

1832   Black Hawk invades Illinois. His braves are driven into southern Wisconsin and defeated by United States army and Illinois and Wisconsin militia.

1833   Chicago incorporated as town.

1834   Abraham Lincoln elected to State Legislature.

1836   Construction of Illinois and Michigan Canal begins.

1837   Elijah P. Lovejoy, editor of Alton *Observer*, murdered by a pro-slavery mob. State appropriates $10,000,000 for the building of railroads and other improvements. Legislature votes to move capital to Springfield. Chicago receives city charter.

1839   State capital moved to Springfield. Mormons come to Nauvoo.

1840   POPULATION: 476,183. Liberty Party organized.

1844   Civil War in Hancock County results in murder of Mormon leaders, Joseph and Hyrum Smith.

1845   Free school law enacted.

1846   General exodus of Mormons begins: 2,000 cross the frozen Mississippi. Abraham Lincoln elected to Congress.

1847   Cyrus McCormick, reaper manufacturer, comes to Chicago and opens plant.

1848   Second State Constitution adopted. Illinois and Michigan Canal opened.

1850   POPULATION: 851,470.

1851   Illinois Central Railroad granted charter.

1853   Illinois State Agricultural Society chartered and first state fair held. Illinois Wesleyan University (Bloomington) opens.

1855   Northwestern University opens. Legislature authorizes system of free schools.

1856   Various elements opposed to Kansas-Nebraska bill organized as Republican Party. Illinois Central Railroad completed.

1857   Illinois State Normal University opens.

1858   Lincoln and Douglas engage in series of debates.

1859   Douglas re-elected to United States Senate.

1860   POPULATION: 1,711,951. Republican National Convention (Chicago) nominates Abraham Lincoln for Presidency.

1861–1865   Civil War: Illinois furnishes 256,297 soldiers.

1865   Lincoln buried at Springfield.

1866   First post of Grand Army of the Republic mustered in at Decatur.

1867   University of Illinois founded (Urbana).

1868   Republican National Convention (Chicago) nominates U. S. Grant for president. Construction of new state capitol begins. First river tunnel in U. S. completed under Chicago River.

1870   POPULATION: 2,539,891. Third state constitution adopted. St. Ignatius College, later Loyola University, founded.

1871   Fire burns large section of Chicago, causing a loss of $192,-000,000. Completion of deepening of Illinois and Michigan Canal.

1876   The right of the State to regulate business "clothed with a public interest" upheld by U. S. Supreme Court in case of Munn v. Illinois. Lake Forest University opened.

1878   State Board of Health organized.

1880   POPULATION: 3,077,871.

1881   Aurora, first city to light streets electrically.

1884   Knights of Labor meeting (Chicago) demand eight hour day.

1886   Haymarket riot.

1888   State capitol completed.

1889   Illinois State Historical Library founded.

1890   POPULATION: 3,826,351. Panic in Chicago Board of Trade.

1891   Australian ballot act passed.

1892   University of Chicago opens. John P. Altgeld elected governor.

1893   World Columbian Exposition held (Chicago).

1894   Workers in Pullman Car Company plant strike. American Railway Union calls general railroad strike in sympathy. President Cleveland sends Federal troops to Chicago in defiance of Governor Altgeld.

1896   William Jennings Bryan, addressing Democratic National Convention at Chicago, begins free-silver movement.

1898   Spanish-American War: Illinois raises nine regiments of infantry, one of cavalry, and battalion of artillery. St. Vincent College, later De Paul University, founded.

1900   POPULATION: 4,821,550. Chicago Drainage Canal opened.

1901   Body of Abraham Lincoln removed from temporary vault to reconstructed monument (Springfield).

1902   People of Illinois vote for adoption of direct and popular election of United States Senators.

1903   Fire in Iroquois Theatre (Chicago) causes 596 deaths. Centennial of Fort Dearborn celebrated in Chicago.

1904   Theodore Roosevelt nominated by Republican National Convention (Chicago).

1906   State Highway Commission organized.

1907   Law permitting local option for consumption of alcoholic liquors passed. Hennepin Canal connecting the Illinois and Mississippi opened. Act passed providing for new charter for city of Chicago.

1908   Republican National Convention nominates Taft at Coliseum (Chicago).

1909   Ten hour law for women passed.

1910   POPULATION: 5,638,591. Primary act passed.

1912   Republican National Convention (Chicago) nominates Taft. Revolting Roosevelt forces launch progressive movement at Orchestra Hall. United States Senator William Lorimer ousted from Senate.

1915   Steamer *Eastland* capsizes in Chicago River, 812 drown.

1917   Executive branch of State government reorganized. Race riots in East St. Louis.

1917-   World War: Illinois contributes 16,000 enlistments and 193-
1918   338 drafted men.

1918   Illinois celebrates centennial. Law of 1917 for construction of State-wide system of hard roads approved by voters.

1919   Race riots in Chicago. State act requires private banks to take out charters or go out of business.

1920   POPULATION: 6,485,280. Harding nominated at Chicago.

1922   Twenty-two are killed at Herrin in coal strikes. People overwhelmingly defeat proposed new constitution.

1923   Road bond issue of $100,000,000 authorized by general assembly. Governor approves anti-Ku Klux Klan bill.

1926   Eucharistic Congress of Roman Catholic Church held in Chicago.

1929   Children required to have completed elementary grades before they can go to work. Obligatory school year raised from six to eight months.

1930   POPULATION: 7,630,654.

1932   Franklin Delano Roosevelt nominated by Democratic National Convention (Chicago).

1933   General Assembly enacts general sales tax of 2 per cent. Mayor Cermak of Chicago dies of wound inflicted by Zangara in attempt to kill President-elect Roosevelt. Century of Progress opens in Chicago. Closes November 1, 1934.

1935   General Assembly increases retailers' occupation tax from 2 to 3 per cent.

1936   General Assembly enacts old age security law, occupational disease compensation law, and law providing for permanent registration.

1937   Eight hour law for women passed. General Assembly passes bill requiring medical examination for venereal disease before marriage. Ten men killed and many wounded during strike at Republic Steel Company plant. Ohio River rises in disastrous flood that renders thousands homeless in Southern Illinois.

INDEX

Abraham Lincoln Center (Chicago), 297

Adams County, 580, 581

Addams, Jane, 40, 86, 127, 202, 221, 222, 295, 372, 521, 590; Birthplace of, 521; Grave of, 521; Study of (Hull House), 221

Addison, 516

Ade, George, 120

Adler, Dankmar, 103, 211

Adler, Max, 229

Adler and Sullivan (architects), 101, 103, 213

Adler Planetarium and Astronomical Museum (Chicago), 229, 230, 632

Albany, 471

Albion, 27, 100, 109, 428-429; George French House, 429

Albright, Adam Emery, 545

Albright, Ivan Lorraine, 545

Albright, Marvin Marr, 545

Aledo, 474

Alexander County, 169, 500; Courthouse, old (Thebes), 500

Algren, Nelson, 127

All-Illinois Society of the Fine Arts, 115, 212

Allen, Tenas, 519

Allendale Farm School (Lake Villa), 504

Allin, James, 163

Allouez, Father, 17, 19

Almira College (Greenville, 608; Wilson T. Hogue Hall, 608; E. G. Burritt Gymnasium, 608; Carrie T. Burritt Hall, 608

Alschlager, Walter W., 239

Alschuler, Alfred S., 105, 208, 299

Altamont, 607

Altgeld, Gov. John Peter, 6, 40, 42, 83, 84, 85, 86, 119, 125, 181, 201, 254, 256; Monument (Chicago), 256; *Pardon Message,* 83

Alton, 22, 29, 32, 33, 34, 35, 51, 65, 99, 149-155, 487, 598; College, 155; Dam, 152; *Evening Telegraph,* 154; Lovers' Leap, 154; *Observer,* 34, 387; Seminary, 155

Alton Railroad, *see Chicago & Alton Railroad*

Alto Pass, 454

Alvin, 402

Amalgamated Clothing Workers of America, 86, 88

Amboy, 10, 567

American Bottom, 3, 15, 24, 56-57, 149, 309, 312, 488, 493, 610, 611, 613, 620

American Bridge Company (Chicago), 66

American Can Company, 66

American Farm Bureau Federation, 76

American Federation of Labor, 81, 85

American Fur Company, 58, 194

American Miners' Association, 78

American Railway Union, 84, 85

American Steel and Wire Company, 66

American Tin Plate Company (Joliet), 66

Amesville, Site of, 519

Amish Sect, 601

Amish—Mennonites, 571

Andalusia, 473

Andersen, Captain Magnus, 255

Anderson, Rt. Rev. Charles P., 511

Anderson, Margaret, 126, 299

Anderson, Pierce, 105

Anderson, Sherwood, 122, 125, 299

Andover, 33

Andrews, Wilbur J., 586

Andrus, Maj. Leonard, 460

Angle, Paul, 127

Anisfeld, Boris, 112

Anna, 109, 454, 455; State Hospital, 454

Annawan, 463, 562

Anson, Adrian "Pop," 370

Anti-Slavery societies, 34

Antioch, 505

Antrobus, Jacob, 110

Apostolic Church, 570, 571

Apple River, 469; Canyon State Park, 462; Fort, Site of, 522; Valley, 522

Archer, William B., 604